MARKETING FOR NONPROFIT ORGANIZATIONS

MARKETING FOR NONPROFIT ORGANIZATIONS

Second Edition

David L. Rados

AUBURN HOUSE
Westport, Connecticut • London

Library of Congress Cataloging-in-Publication Data

Rados, David L., 1933–
    Marketing for nonprofit organizations / David L. Rados.—2nd ed.
        p.   cm.
    Includes bibliographical references and index.
    ISBN 0–86569–254–8
        1. Nonprofit organizations—Marketing.   I. Title.
    HF5415.R237   1996
    658.8—dc20   95–13609

British Library Cataloguing in Publication Data is available.

Library of Congress Catalog Card Number: 95–13609
ISBN: 0–86569–254–8

First published in 1996

Auburn House, 88 Post Road West, Westport, CT 06881
An imprint of Greenwood Publishing Group, Inc.

Printed in the United States of America

The paper used in this book complies with the
Permanent Paper Standard issued by the National
Information Standards Organization (Z39.48–1984).

10 9 8 7 6 5 4 3 2

the Susan B. Anthony Coin,'' in ''Final Report—Phase One: Research Study into Market Acceptance of the New One Dollar Coin,'' Project Director, Claude R. Martin (Ann Arbor: Division of Research, Graduate School of Business Administration, University of Michigan, 1979), pp. 5, 6.

William Butler Yeats, ''To a Wealthy Man Who Promised a Second Subscription to the Dublin Municipal Gallery if It Were Proved the People Wanted Pictures,'' *The Poems of W.B. Yeats: A New Edition*, ed. Richard J. Finneran (New York: Macmillan, 1983), reprinted with permission of Simon & Schuster, Inc. and A. P. Watt Ltd. on behalf of Michael Yeats.

Every reasonable effort has been made to trace the owners of copyright materials in this book, but in some instances this has proven impossible. The author and publisher will be glad to receive information leading to more complete acknowledgments in subsequent printings of this book and in the meantime extend their apologies for any omissions.

To Peg

Contents

Preface   xi

I. Introduction

1. Introduction   3
2. What Is Marketing?   24

II. Tools for the Marketer

3. The Financial Side of Marketing Decisions   45
4. Behavior of Clients and Backers   62
5. How Price and Other Costs Influence Behavior   83
6. Marketing Research   104

III. Marketing Strategy

7. Focus: Competition, Segmentation, Targeting, and Positioning   129
8. Marketing Strategy—The Preliminaries   160
9. Developing a Marketing Strategy   177

IV. The Elements of the Marketing Program

10. Product and Service Strategy   195
11. Delivering the Goods (and Services) by Means of Channels of
    Distribution   226
12. Prices and Other Costs Borne by Clients   252

13. Communications　　　　　　　　　　　282
14. Advertising　　　　　　　　　　　　　312
15. Personal Selling　　　　　　　　　　　333
16. Public Relations and Sales Promotion　　355
17. Control and Organization　　　　　　　377

V. Obtaining Resources

18. Giving and Raising Funds　　　　　　　399
19. The Cost of Raising Funds　　　　　　420
20. Volunteers and Board Members　　　　433

Selected Bibliography　　　　　　　　　451
Index　　　　　　　　　　　　　　　　453

Preface

This is a book about the marketing problems that arise in nonprofit organizations. Its aim is to help the reader analyze such problems more effectively and devise better solutions to them. I devote a good deal of attention to the financial consequences of marketing actions, because marketing programs consume cash and they are usually expected to generate it, and any good marketer must worry about the balance of the two.

This book has been written with two readers in mind. One is a student, typically one who is studying administration or management: business administration, public administration, arts administration, or what-have-you. Supplemented by readings and other assignments, the book is suitable as a text in a course dealing with nonprofit marketing.

The other reader is a manager (or would-be manager, or other interested party) working for (or with) a nonprofit organization. Managers want not so much to learn about marketing as to learn to *do* marketing, to analyze problems as marketers do, and to put into effect marketing programs that offer some modest hope of success. For them the book will require more, for the analysis of marketing problems is demanding and hard to learn without others around who are dealing with the same issues. Without ever going near the piano a student can learn a great deal about the history of the piano, its musical literature, and its great artists; and he can develop a discriminating ear. But he cannot learn to play. In the same way, without doing any marketing, managers can learn a great deal about marketing (perhaps even from this book), but they cannot become marketers. Still, they can read with care and try to work out answers to the many questions that appear. They should try to put into practice the methods described in the book.

Marketers, like judges, never solve problems in the abstract. Instead they deal with specific problems whose solutions are hemmed in by fact and by the imperatives of finances, competition, the resources available to the organization, and the environment. This means that although this book is about marketing in general and contains many generalizations, the reader must not be taken in. "There is nothing so useless as a general maxim," Macaulay tells us. There are no maxims in this book; but there are many recommendations and exhortations, which, because they are general, always need qualification (or should I say "almost always"?). That is, the specific demands of the situation the marketer finds himself in can override a generalization. Marketing calls for judgment, then, which makes it harder to learn, harder to do, and harder to write about; and the successful marketer is one who discriminates between generalizations, much as a judge decides which legal principle applies to the specific facts of the case.

I have deliberately drawn examples and cited research from many areas of the nonprofit world. In doing so I hope to show the broad applicability of marketing concepts and methods of analysis. In addition, I have included a fair amount of the kind of analysis I would hope that readers will master as they work through the book. As with all such analysis, based inevitably as it is on incomplete knowledge, there is room for dispute, and readers may well reach different conclusions from mine. Therefore, the analysis I put forward is best seen as food for thought, or as a model, rather than as the last word on the issue in question.

I first got interested in nonprofit marketing while I was at Columbia University. I remember sitting in my office wondering how grown-ups could possibly get so concerned over selling another four hundred carloads of mascara or dog food before the end of the quarter. It just didn't seem worthy of anything serious in life. This was the moment that New York State began its lottery. It didn't take me long to realize that the lottery faced every classical marketing problem.

Product. It had to design a prize structure. Should it have one big prize and lots of little prizes, or one big prize and no little prizes? Should it give mostly medium-sized prizes? Should some of its prizes be noncash prizes, like tickets to play the lottery again?

Price. What should the tickets cost?

Distribution. What should ticket agents receive as compensation for selling tickets? Were banks the right place to sell tickets? (That one was easy. No one in New York City ever goes into a bank by choice.) If not banks, then where? How could the lottery stimulate its agents to display posters and remind shoppers to pick up lottery tickets instead of change, say?

Advertising. In which media should the lottery advertise? With what message? Should it emphasize winnings or helping education? How often should the lottery repeat its message?

Selling. How many salesmen should the lottery employ to call on ticket agents? How should they be compensated and motivated? What should their job be?

Target markets. Who were the best targets for lottery marketing efforts? What if the most likely buyers were "wrong" in some social or political sense?

This last question was my first introduction to the complexities of nonprofit marketing. No commercial marketer would ever ask if his proposed market were wrong politically. It just doesn't happen. (Well, it almost never happens.) No commercial marketer would worry about whether the people most likely to buy his product would be better off not buying it at all. But a nonprofit marketer must worry about such issues, because he has more at stake than merely making as much money as possible.

The result of my musings sent me up to Albany where I wrote my first nonprofit case study, and a fascinating case it was, widely reprinted over the next decade. Before long I was offering a course in nonprofit marketing, a humbling experience, particularly the year I had three students, one of whom signed up for the course thinking it was another course. (I'm sorry to say that it took him several weeks to figure things out. Doesn't say too much for the quality of my students.) It was an arduous experience, too, because there were no textbooks, no teaching materials, few articles, and few reports on nonprofit marketing issues. My students and I muddled on, both learning, both enjoying the challenge of applying marketing analysis in such a different setting. Finally, several years later came the first edition of this book, and now the second edition.

I should say a few words about sexist language and political correctness. I try to write well, I love words and the English language, and I labor to be clear and avoid ambiguity. I have read a great deal of poetry in my life, which has given me an appreciation of the sound and rhythm of my mother tongue. Enter now a passage like this: "Through charitable remainder trusts a donor gives a charity a donation to hold in trust: he/she claims a charitable deduction on her or his income-tax return, and he or she enjoys income for a fixed period of time or until he dies."

What does "he/she" mean? It can't mean "he and/or she" because "he and she" makes no sense, even granting how enlightened we are concerning sexual disorders. So it must mean "he or she," which, although clumsy if overused, is simpler and more natural. If there is a simpler, more natural expression, my rule is to use it. The reversal, "her or his," presumably to show that the woman need not be subordinated by her male oppressors, calls attention to itself, which good writing doesn't do. Notice as well how it causes you to stumble as you read the sentence. By the end of the sentence the writer, dismayed at how rank the sentence has become, balks at putting yet another "he or she." Even the writer dislikes her own prose.

It is a grotesque sentence. No one with any feeling for English could write it nor would any competent editor pass it. I not only could not write such a sentence, I will not write it. In plain words, I find such prose insensitive and deeply offensive.

My solution to sexist language is not to worry much about it, write my way around it sometimes, but always, always write plain, clear English. That comes first. The reader can expect to find a hint here or there throughout the book that I have not bought the party line; but it will be only a hint.

For anyone who loves English as I do, political correctness causes both dismay and hilarity. PC euphemisms are bad writing: They corrupt language and because they do, they corrupt thinking. I hate writing that makes it harder to think clearly, and therefore I consider PC writing insensitive and deeply offensive; but at a time when political civility has perhaps reached new lows—I say "perhaps" because stinging invective has always marked American political discourse—PC does have one benefit. It's funny. At least it used to be funny before it reached the point where the latest euphemisms—well, are they real? Calling looters "nontraditional shoppers" and sadomasochists "differently pleasured"—that's funny. Then I read that *alcoholics* is out. The new term is *people of stupor*. That's funny too. It's a joke, right?

It must be a joke.

But is it?

I can't tell, at least not for sure. When a movement reaches a point where its methods and spoofs of its methods cannot be told apart, it loses me and, I suspect, the fashion will soon move on. The point of all this is that I am not a PC writer. I write with my ear and my mind on a far more important matter, clear, simple, robust English. Whether I have pulled it off is for you, the reader, to decide.

Many friends and associates have read parts of the manuscript, as have my long-suffering students. Friends and associates have made suggestions, sometimes tactfully; students, of course, would not dare. I am indebted as well to the staff of the Walker Management Library who never flagged in answering my many questions and helping me locate many items.

During the many years that I have been thinking and writing about nonprofit marketing, I have learned a great deal; but it is dispiriting to realize how much more there is to learn. I would welcome reactions from my readers, even criticism, at least, temperate criticism. It is also disheartening to contemplate the finished manuscript, haunted as I am by Karl Kraus's aphorism, "A writer is someone who can make a riddle of an answer."

Part I

INTRODUCTION

Chapter 1

Introduction

This book is about nonprofit marketing.

It is a term that puzzles most people who are not in business, and it brings a smile to the businessman's face as he thinks of the old quip, "We're not supposed to be nonprofit but we are." Still, one need have only the most casual exposure to nonprofit organizations before encountering a variety of marketing problems that are the same as those businesses face, and a variety of other problems, unlike those seen in business, that resemble marketing problems.

This book treats this second class of problems: marketing problems that are not seen in businesses. I shall refer, in passing, to traditional marketing problems but give them no emphasis because they are not unique to nonprofit organizations. Take an advertising agency that devotes most of its energies to commercial clients—airlines, liquor, industrial fasteners, dog food, cosmetics. When it is asked to make a proposal for, say, a U.S. Navy enlistment campaign or a travel campaign for the Irish Tourist Board, or to work for the reelection of the governor of California, it applies the same skills, knowledge, contacts, and habits of mind that it brings to its commercial accounts. The client is nonprofit, but the problem is treated as any commercial account is treated.

I imagine that readers of this book already understand something of marketing and how businesses operate.[1] This background is necessary to get the most from this book. For one thing, nonprofit marketing is best seen and understood as part of the larger topic of marketing. When this book was first written, nonprofit marketing was little more than a shoot. There were no professional associations, no journals, no conventions, and no campaign to dignify the trade with an exalted denomination. Today nonprofit marketing is in leaf, though it is still young. There are many books in the field, both textbooks and trade books; there are several academic journals devoted to nonprofit issues and two academic periodicals that deal only with marketing issues.[2] Today, then, there are marketers who bring their training and cast of mind to the marketing problems of nonprofit organizations. These men and women speak a marketing cant and, even more, they *think* in marketing definitions and abstractions. (Readers who are frightened by this should seek other entertainment. This book is not for them.) This means that nonprofit marketers must bring to the problems they face considerable knowledge and experience in commercial product planning, distribution, pricing, promotion, and marketing research. Knowledge of the quirks and special problems that arise only in nonprofit organizations will not be enough.

Another reason why knowledge of business marketing is necessary is that many nonprofit organizations deal with situations in which business firms are important factors. To propose realistic solutions in such situations, and to implement them, a nonprofit marketer must know how businesses operate and how their managers think. Before it can propose a workable program, a nonprofit organization working for safer car seats for children must understand why some manufacturers choose to make cheap, relatively unsafe seats and why retail sales clerks find it easier to sell the cheap seats instead of more expensive ones. And an organization cannot hope to propose a realistic scheme for recycling empty soda bottles without understanding the economics of grocery retailing.

The need for general marketing knowledge also arises in judging the marketing solutions of third parties. A social problem of some type arises, let us say, and a nonprofit organization, public or private, given the task of correcting the problem, proposes or puts into effect a marketing program. Now the question arises whether the organization is really trying or whether the program is merely window dressing. It is not unknown for organizations to embrace programs that they hope will fail, or that they know will fail, or that they intend will fail. How do we judge whether a medical school that says it recruits minority students but cannot find any good ones is really trying? How do we judge whether posters that warn against the dangers of excessive gambling and are displayed in the betting parlors of New York City's Offtrack Betting Corporation are just an empty gesture? How do we judge whether a private commuter railroad is really trying to attract riders and make a profit or merely building a stronger case for a takeover by the state? In each case, a sound marketing analysis, based on general experience in marketing, will provide partial answers.

Although a background in business marketing is important to the nonprofit marketer, it is no longer enough for the problems that are unique to the nonprofit sector. It is these unique problems that are treated in this book.

NONPROFIT ORGANIZATIONS

It is possible, but not practical, to fill most of life's needs by relying solely on nonprofit organizations. You can be born in a hospital that is part of a nonprofit hospital chain, receive medical care from a nonprofit health maintenance organization, bear all of your education in nonprofit private schools or at the hands of the state, and be buried by a nonprofit burial association in a nonprofit cemetery. It is possible to eat at nonprofit restaurants; buy food, clothing, furniture, auto repairs, and appliances from consumer cooperatives or thrift shops; buy gas, water, and electricity from municipal utilities; talk over a cooperative telephone system; ride on city-owned buses and subways; live in apartments owned and operated by housing associations or in a commune that has organized itself as a nonprofit corporation; swim at public beaches and picnic in public parks, visit historic sites, borrow books from a library, and attend concerts, plays, operas, ballets, and lectures given by or sponsored by nonprofit organizations. Should you run afoul of the law, you may be represented in court by a legal aid society; and should you serve time, other nonprofit organizations stand by to help you return to society. If you are interested in correcting a social wrong through the courts, nonprofit organizations may provide lawyers and money. You cannot buy stock in a nonprofit organization, but you can have a buy or sell order executed on a nonprofit stock exchange, buy insurance from mutual insurance companies, and place your savings in mutual savings banks. Your credit may be rated by a nonprofit credit bureau, and if you go too deeply into debt, nonprofit credit counseling agencies stand ready to help. You can borrow money from a credit union. You can watch noncommercial television and listen to noncommercial radio, read news from the wires of a nonprofit news service, subscribe to nonprofit magazines and newspapers, watch sports provided by the schools, play golf at a nonprofit country club or on a city course, and fly to an overseas vacation on state-built airplanes owned by government-run airlines. You can drink at social and fraternal clubs and gamble at church bazaars. No matter how eccentric, uncommon, or depraved your passions, there is probably a nonprofit organization whose members share them. And, of course, you can work for nonprofit organizations, which, taken all together, are diverse enough to find room for almost every skill and inclination. If you choose to work in the profit sector, you will also certainly join a nonprofit trade or professional association, and you may contribute money or time as a volunteer to charity.

Their variety is bewildering. The Society for the Preservation and Encouragement of Barber Shop Quartet Singing in America, the Council on Abandoned Military Posts, the American Concrete Institute, the National Association of Music Executives in State Universities, the International Association of Near-Death Studies, the Society of Jewish Bibliophiles, the Association for Women in Mathematics, the Association of Gay Psychologists, the American Cleft Palate Association, the Christian Movement for Peace, the I Have Lived Before Club, the Sons of Spanish-American War Veterans, the Antique Outboard Motor Club, the Sport Balloon Society of the United States, the Lovers of the Stinking Rose, the American Federation of State, County, and Municipal Employees, the National Association of Membership Directors of Chambers of Commerce, the American Association of Sheriff Posse and Riding Clubs, and the Ancient Mystic Order of Bagmen of Baghdad Imperial Guild are all nonprofit organizations;

as are (at least technically) the New York Stock Exchange, the American Medical Association, the Power Saw Manufacturers Association, and the Metropolitan Life Insurance Company, which alerts us to the fact that some non-profits are largely or exclusively concerned with the weight of their members' pocketbooks. There are nonprofit organizations that devote their efforts solely to the nonprofit sector, like the Philanthropic Advisory Service and the National Information Bureau, both of whom keep watch on the operations of NPOs, as well as the Graduate Management Admission Council. There are even nonprofit organizations of nonprofit organizations like the Independent Sector, the Foundation Center, the Philanthropic Roundtable, the National Association of Community Action Agencies, the Society for Nonprofit Organizations, the National Coalition of Hispanic Health and Human Services Organizations, and the Conference of Consumer Organizations.

The Associated Press is nonprofit, as are the 14,000 credit unions in the country and some 300 credit consulting services (for those with too much debt). In 1986, there were 6,800 hospitals in the United States, all but 800 of them organized and operated as nonprofit organizations. Local governments run 84,000 elementary and secondary schools, and the Roman Catholics run another 11,000. There are some 6,700 museums, 850 opera companies, 400 opera workshops—virtually all of them nonprofit; and there are about 26,000 foundations, all in the business of giving away money.[3] There are roughly 1,600 orchestras, but taking out youth orchestras, college and university orchestras, and those with annual budgets of less than $100,000 leaves only about 400.[4] Only four magazines published in America have circulations over ten million but two of them are published by nonprofit organizations.[5]

Their sizes vary enormously.[6] The American Association of Retired Persons has 28 million members, the Teamsters Union has 2 million members, the American Legion 2.8 million, the Boy Scouts 4.7 million, the Girl Scouts 3.1 million, and the Church of Scientology has, or claims, 8 million (but perhaps only 50,000 active adherents). The National Woman's Christian Temperance Union has 200,000 members, the American Civil Liberties Union 250,000, and the Camp Fire Girls 450,000. The American Philatelic Society has 54,000 members, and the American Philatelic Congress 800; the Daughters of the American Revolution has 204,000, but the Sons of the American Revolution has only 24,000. Although the large ones are conspicuous, most nonprofit organizations are in fact small, like the North American Transvestite/Transsexual Society with 22,000 members, the American Medical Writers Association with 2,600 members, the Fire Marshalls Association of North America with 1,200, the American Association of Stratigraphic Polynologists with 1,034, the Klingon Language Institute with 750, Pilots for Christ International with 700, the Friends of Terra Cotta with 625, the National Fox Hunters Association with 400, the Finnish-American Historical Society of the West with 400, the American Society for Personnel Administration with 200, the Elvis, This One's For You Fan Club with 200, the American Bralers Association with 182, the American Blind Skiing Association with 175, the Panel of American Women with 150, the Permanent Charities Committee of the Entertainment Industries with 133, the Russian Nobility Association in America with 132, the Association of U.S. Members of the International Institute of Space Law with 110, the North American Tiddlywinks Association with 100, the Council of Chief State School Officers with 56, and the International Association of Siderographers with 11.[7]

No one knows how many nonprofit organizations there are. Merely to list the *national* organizations in the United States takes 2,300 pages in the *Encyclopedia of Associations,* and the Internal Revenue Service needs a fat, telephone-sized directory to list in fine print the names of the one million plus tax-exempt organizations on its books.[8] But many organizations like churches, religious bodies, and groups with receipts of less than $25,000 a year are not required to file a return with the IRS, and many others that should file do not.

Local organizations presumably outnumber national organizations several times over. Oleck has estimated that Ohio had 100,000 charters for business corporations in 1971 and 30,000 charters for nonprofit corporations. But such estimates can hardly be taken as definitive. Oleck himself cites another study that estimated that in 1969 Ohio had 150,000 business corporate charters and 70,000 nonprofit charters. "The proportion of one nonprofit to every two or three profit corporations (seems) to be average in most states."[9]

But the corporation is only one of five legal forms a nonprofit organization can take. When Oleck adds in the figures for these other forms, a process that involves a good deal of guessing, he concludes that there are probably almost as many nonprofit organizations as profit organizations. And, since Ohio is a typical industrialized, urban state, it is likely this conclusion holds for much of the country as a whole.

But mere numbers do not count for much. A more important question is: How important are nonprofit organizations, taken as a whole, in the national economy? Governments dominate, of course. In the early 1990s, federal, state, and local governments employed about 18.8 million workers, or about 16 percent of the total labor force, and their purchases from the private sector sustain perhaps another 10 million workers. All told, then, direct and indirect activities by governments create jobs for 28.8 million workers, roughly one-quarter of the labor force.[10]

Private nonprofit organizations also employ workers and through their purchases sustain still more, about 6.7 million direct and perhaps another 2 million indirect, for a total of 8.5 million workers. Both private and public nonprofit organizations, then, employ, directly and indirectly, 37.5 million workers, nearly one-third of the labor force.

Similar figures for output of goods and services show that the nonprofit sector accounts for some 26 percent of the gross national product. These figures, then, show the nonprofit sector employing one worker in three and producing one-quarter of the nation's output.

Overall, the nonprofit sector showed robust health during the 1980s, which some have called the "Decade of Greed." Between 1980 and 1990, total charitable giving rose from $49 billion to $104 billion and individual contributions from $134 to $281, both well ahead of the rate of inflation; the average number of hours a week contributed by volunteers rose from 2.6 to 4.7; and the proportion of Americans who said they were involved in charitable activities increased from 29 to 41 percent.[11] By one estimate, the nonprofit sector's share of gross national product increased from 5.5 to 6.4 percent; by another, total gross receipts of charities and private foundations increased from 4.2 percent of the U.S. gross domestic product in 1975 to 10.6 percent in 1990.[12] Not all the news was wholesome. The number of pieces of third-class or junk mail increased from eight to nearly twelve billion, roughly one mailing a week to every man, woman, and child in the United States. Nonprofits were responsible for a healthy chunk of that total. In the late 1980s, for example, Greenpeace, an environmental agency, was mailing sixty million pieces a year.

WHAT DOES "NONPROFIT" MEAN?

Readers coming for the first time to nonprofit marketing problems face a new setting. Whatever knowledge they have of tax and corporate law does not embrace nonprofit organizations. This section provides some background on this question.

The most conspicuous characteristic that sets the nonprofit organization apart is its nonprofit status. But what does this mean? It does not mean that the organization can't be a business. It does not mean that the organization can't run at a profit, although "surplus" is a more customary and seemly term. New York University's law school, for example, used to own a spaghetti factory; the Mormon Church owns a newspaper in Salt Lake City, eleven television stations, two radio stations, a department store chain, an insurance company, and a controlling interest in the Utah-Idaho Sugar Company; and to judge from its annual reports, the Chesapeake Bay Trust, an environmental group, barely knows what to do with the money it raises each year (see Table 1.1).

Nonprofit organizations may themselves be business entities of a type, trying to or expected to produce a surplus of revenues over costs. In 1990, the Daughters of Charity National Health System, with some fifty-five hospitals under its care, the nation's largest nonprofit hospital system, had a surplus of $190 million. Trade associations seek to improve the profitability of the industry they represent, and labor unions seek to raise wages and improve working conditions. Labor unions often control enormous pension funds, supposedly for the benefit of their members; but in managing them they behave little better than elected public officials. Nonprofit hospitals earn most of their keep by providing medical care to paying customers, not to charity cases. Intermountain Health Care, which runs twenty-four nonprofit hospitals, was threatened with the loss of its tax exemption; so it "sharply increased" the amount of charity care it provided. After the sharp increase its yearly spending on charity cases (as a percentage of

Table 1.1

Income and Expenses of the Chesapeake Bay Trust, 1986–1989

	1986	1987	1988	1989
Donations	$96,000	$196,000	$161,000	$879,000
All Other Revenue	7,000	102,000	75,000	137,000
Total Revenue	103,000	298,000	236,000	1,016,000
Total Expenses and Grants	91,000	230,000	125,000	363,000
Surplus	$ 12,000	$ 68,000	$110,000	$654,000
Surplus as Percent of Total Revenue	12%	23%	47%	64%

Source: Annual Reports for 1986 to 1989.

its gross revenues) had risen to one percent.[13] The U.S. Postal Service, created in 1970, is expected to run at a profit; it is not too strong to say it is required by law to run at a profit, although it does not. The Passport Office is required to generate surpluses and it does, collecting $26 million in fees in 1975 and spending $16 million for operations. As part of their operations, nonprofit organizations may sell goods and services at prices greater than their cost. The Trappists bake bread and make jam, and universities run dormitories, cafeterias, sports arenas, and consulting firms. A nonprofit organization, in fact, may merely front for a business. We can imagine, say, a nonprofit society for retired persons whose executives own a profit-making drugstore, an insurance company, a gift shop, and perhaps a resort hotel or two, all of which draw much of their business from the society's members. (The IRS does not smile on such self-dealing.)

What does "nonprofit" mean then? A business operates to enrich its owners and managers. A nonprofit organization permits no enrichment. None of its surplus, if indeed there is any, is passed on to individuals. There are (usually) no owners or shareholders, and there are never dividends or other monetary disbursements of the surplus to individuals.[14] Clarkson has put this more formally. The two differences between profit and nonprofit organizations are that:

(1) certain rights or claims to benefits in [nonprofit] organizations are not transferable by sale as they are in [for-profit] organizations, and (2) managers or workers in nonprofit organizations do not have the exclusive claim on residual products (the current flows of money and nonmoney benefits) that is characteristic of for-profit enterprises.[15]

Financial gain says nothing about an organization's status. The key to being a nonprofit is motive.

Historically, legislatures (and courts) have considered two approaches in answering the question of what is a nonprofit organization. One is to list the things a nonprofit does, and then say any organization whose principal activities are on the list is nonprofit. This is the functional approach, and the list typically includes these purposes: charitable, scientific, or educational; recreational, social, or cultural; political, civic, or governmental; trade or professional; and religious. The functional approach, however, offers spongy ground when the difficult cases arise. Just what is the religious purpose of a bingo game, or the educational purpose of trying to build a nationally ranked football team?

The second approach we have already discussed. This is the economic approach, which sees a nonprofit organization as one formed for any (lawful) purpose other than passing monetary profits on to members, officers, or managers. Reasonable compensation to employees or members is, of course, permitted. But there are difficulties here as well. "Profit" is taken by some to mean only direct, tangible, monetary returns on investment or payments from income. Others argue that profits should also include indirect monetary benefits as, for example, the savings in food expenditures earned by members of a consumers' cooperative, the appreciation in value of works of art owned by museums, or the benefits gained for firms in the toy industry by the exertions of its trade association.[16]

As this discussion suggests, the line dividing for-profit from nonprofit organizations can be thin. There are some nonprofit organizations whose aim is the enrichment of private individuals or businesses. Take, for example, the nonprofit hospital established by Dr. T. A. Lowry in Sweetwater, Tennessee. The hospital first leased and later bought its premises from Dr. Lowry. His clinic shared the same building. The hospital and clinic bought supplies together, paid each other's utility bills, and sent joint statements to patients. Nurses and technicians who worked for one also worked for the other, and the hospital lent more than $200,000 at easy terms to a nursing home owned by the doctor. In this case, the U.S. Tax Court was not amused and the hospital lost its tax exemption.[17] Self-dealing, which is what Dr. Lowry was accused of, can even arise between two nonprofit organizations. A nonprofit medical society owned and occupied a building registered as historic for its architecture. It set up a charity for the preservation of historic buildings which was controlled by the society's officers. It then gave its own building to the new charity in return for a rent-free, fifty-year lease on the first floor. The charity renovated the rest of the building and rented rooms on the second floor to both charitable and noncharitable groups, rooms the medical society could use free. The IRS frowned. It found the terms were far more favorable to the medical society than to the charity and that the charity was operated for the private benefit of the medical society and its members. The charity lost its tax exemption and had to pay back taxes on most of the income it had received.[18]

Table 1.2 sums up the major differences between profit and nonprofit organizations.

Table 1.2
Principal Differences between Profit and Nonprofit Organizations[19]

	Profit	Nonprofit
Who owns it?	Investors	Another nonprofit, or no one
Can it distribute profits?	Yes	No
To whom is management ultimately accountable?	Shareholders	Board
Sources of revenue?	Sales	Donations, grants, perhaps sales
What taxes are paid?	Property, sales, income, and so on	None--generally exempt
Organization's purpose?	Profit for owners	Mission for which the nonprofit exists
Sources of capital	Equity, debt, and retained earnings	Donations, debt, government grants, and fund balances
Measures of success	Profit, return on investment	Performance of mission, success in fundraising
Who determines success?	Customers	Clients and contributors

Nonprofit Corporations

Nonprofit organizations are creatures of economic forces and the needs of society. Nonprofit corporations are creatures of the law. Any U.S. citizen has a constitutional right to assembly and to petition the government, and therefore, within broad limits, has a right to establish any association he wishes. But to establish a nonprofit corporation and to qualify for a tax exemption he must receive permission from the state.

As the corporation is the most important form used by the nonprofits, it is worthwhile to discuss it for a moment. The corporate form offers the same general advantages to profit and nonprofit organizations:

1. Ownership can be freely transferred.

2. Individual owners are not responsible for the debts and liabilities of the corporation, and the corporation is not responsible for claims against its owners.

3. The corporation can enter into contracts; it can sue and be sued; it can buy, hold, or sell property.

4. It has a perpetual existence. It continues, despite the withdrawal of its owners, until its owners dissolve it.

Table 1.3
Classification of Nonprofit Corporations under New York State's Not-for-Profit Corporation Law*

	Typical Activities	*Examples*
Type A	Civic, political, fraternal, social, trade, and the like	Mostly common benefit organizations
Type B	Charitable, educational, cultural, and prevention of cruelty	May be either service organizations or commonwealth organizations. Foundations are also here
Type C	Production, finance, marketing, and other business purposes	Mostly nonprofit businesses
Type D	Anything not covered under Types A, B, and C	A housing authority or a bridge and tunnel authority

Source: "New York's Not-For-Profit Corporation Law." *New York University Law Review* 47 (1972): 761-791.

* Several of the terms here will be defined later in the chapter.

5. Resources can be assembled and applied, allowing the corporation great range and scope in its activities.

Perhaps these advantages do not mean as much to a nonprofit organization as to a business, but they are substantial nonetheless, and Oleck predicts the corporate form will continue to dominate for some time to come. Nonprofit corporations themselves come in two forms: those controlled by private bodies and those controlled by governmental bodies. New York State goes further and classifies nonprofit corporations into four subgroups (see Table 1.3).

The corporation, incidentally, has an ancient heritage. An invention of the Renaissance, it was already mature by the American colonial period. In colonial times, in fact, business was carried on not by corporations but mostly by partnerships, incorporated associations, societies, and groups of undertakers (or entrepreneurs). It was the corporate form that was devoted to nonprofit activities. First towns, then boroughs and cities incorporated, and private corporations established. As Joseph Davis has written, in a phrase astonishing to one brought up to think of corporations as the preeminent form of business organization, these private corporations were established "for ecclesiastical, educational, charitable and even business purposes."[20]

Nonprofit corporations, indeed all nonprofit organizations, enjoy a number of privileges. They may be granted the power of eminent domain; in some jurisdictions they are free of the obligation to contribute to unemployment compensation funds; they pay no customs on art imports; they are exempt from several provisions of the Robinson-Patman Act; and they pay lower postage when mailing in bulk. The postage subsidy is substantial (see Table 1.4). Under common

Table 1.4

Estimated Postage Subsidy to a Nonprofit Association that Publishes a Quarterly Magazine

Commercial second-class rate for a nine-ounce magazine	$.35		
Nonprofit second-class rate	.21		
Savings per issue	.14		
Circulation	100,000		
Postage savings per issue		$14,000	
Postage savings per year			$56,000
Commercial third-class rate for 600,000 subscription mailings a year	$.167		
Nonprofit third-class rates	.084		
Savings per mailing	.083		
Size of mailing	600,000		
Postage savings			$ 49,800
Total annual savings to nonprofit organization			$105,800

law, nonprofit organizations are free of tort liability, so that, if someone is cut (say) by glass in the dessert at a church supper or gets food poisoning from improperly handled produce at a food bank, he has little hope of bringing suit and winning. In setting user fees, the federal government is permitted, but not required, to grant exemptions to nonprofit organizations, and Public Law 480 enables them to obtain surplus farm commodities free if they are sent overseas, with the government even paying shipping costs. Traditionally, state agencies have been exempt from federal security laws, and there are exemptions as well for most other nonprofit organizations. Until recently, nonprofit organizations were only lightly bound by copyright law, and nonprofit hospitals in forty states enjoy as the most valuable benefit of their nonprofit status the right to issue tax-exempt bonds to finance construction. Nonprofit corporations are also permitted a looser corporate form.[21]

All these are mere pleasantries compared with their two major privileges. One is the right to receive donations, gifts, and bequests that provide tax deductions to the giver. The other privilege is their exemption from federal income tax under Section 501(c) of the Internal Revenue Code and, in cities and states, from most local taxes as well.[22] Nonprofit organizations rarely pay local property taxes, for example, and they often pay no state ad valorem taxes or franchise taxes. New York City, for one, grants tax exemptions to cemeteries, fallout shelters, naval bases, private colleges, art institutions, the World Trade Center, nursing homes and hospitals, publicly owned and publicly assisted housing, synagogues, parsonages, charitable and fraternal organizations, commuter railways, all state or federal buildings, and, of course, all city-owned property.[23]

These two privileges—the right to receive donations and the exemption from taxes—can be combined. Take a commune, for instance, that receives tax-exempt status from the IRS and whose members work at outside jobs for which they are paid. Suppose the members now donate all of their pay to the commune. The members would get a charitable deduction and pay no individual tax, and the commune would not pay any tax either.[24]

The organizations most free of government regulation are the churches and religious bodies. This immediately raises the question: What is a religion? It has a system of belief, worship services at regular intervals, clergy, and the like. The Salvation Army, for example, is a Christian sect whose members attend Salvationist worship centers. Officials of Volunteers of America can be members of many Christian denominations and attend church where they may. Of its 6,000 employees, 400 are VOA ministers who have completed a course of religious study, program training, and nonprofit management. The VOA does operate a few worship centers, most commonly a room in a VOA building. In any event, both the Salvation Army and the Volunteers of America are churches.

Now consider the case of Habitat for Humanity International. It raises funds in most states, nearly $40 million in 1993. All NPOs that raise funds, except religious charities, are required to register with state authorities in almost forty states and many cities and towns. All but religious charities are required to file Form 990 with the IRS to report income, expenses, and other items. Habitat does file a form 990, but its bylaws describe it as a "Christian housing ministry." It claims it should be free of state registration requirements because it is a religious charity. All this raises two questions: Is Habitat indeed a religious charity, and even if it is, is it a good idea for Habitat to give the appearance of wanting to hide something? Neither question is difficult to answer.

The general explanation for these privileges is not charity on the part of the government, but the belief that the activities of these organizations in promoting the general welfare relieve the government of the need to spend for these ends. The privileges, therefore, can be seen as a form of financial back-scratching.

Note as well that there are some things nonprofit organizations cannot do. They cannot pay out their surpluses, as we have seen. Upon being dissolved, they cannot merely liquidate their assets and pay them to current owners; the assets must be given to another tax-exempt organization. They cannot devote any substantial part of their activities to propaganda, lobbying, or influencing legislation and still receive tax-deductible donations. The no-lobbying rule seems clear at first glance. But nothing in law or in government regulations is clear after that first glance. Consider this:

- Just after Thurgood Marshall resigned from the U.S. Supreme Court and well before President Bush nominated Clarence Thomas, the National Organization for Women leapt into action. It added an urgent message to a fundraising appeal about to be mailed. "I need you to join us," wrote the president of NOW, "more than ever. NOW is about to embark on what will be a titanic struggle to protect a woman's right to abortion and our fight for equal rights."[25]

There is no doubt that a target like a Supreme Court nominee is good for business, nonprofit business, I mean. One estimate is that groups opposing the nomination of Robert Bork raised over six million dollars before the Senate confirmation hearings, and another six million after they started. There were sharp increases in the number of members and volunteers too. The question here is this: When a nonprofit tries to influence the appointment of a judge, any judge, is it lobbying?

Finally, nonprofit organizations cannot avoid taxes on all income but only on income generated by the organization in pursuit of its specific charitable or nonprofit activities. Income from regularly operated trades or businesses not substantially related to the organization's exempt income is subject to UBIT, the unrelated business income tax. The intent of UBIT is to keep nonprofits honest. Which immediately raises a new question: What does "unrelated" mean? Here are two examples:

- A nonprofit organization wanted to provide its members with a membership benefit, a subscription to a magazine published by a commercial publisher. Magazine publishers like to increase the circulations of their magazines because the higher the circulation, the higher the advertising rates they can charge. For these purposes, the best circulation is paid circulation. So the NPO and the publisher struck a deal to make it appear as if the circulation was paid. The NPO offered its members subscriptions and paid the publisher eight dollars for each one. The publisher in turn paid the NPO eight dollars per name to add the members' names to its mailing list. In other words, the deal was a wash.[26]

Did this deal generate unrelated business income to the NPO? The IRS decided it did not.

- The Lincoln Park Zoo Shop at the Lincoln Park Zoo in Chicago sells souvenirs and gifts. Which of them are related to the zoo's function and hence not subject to the unrelated business tax, and which are not related and hence taxable? The IRS decided that it would exempt items that tried to teach something about animals. So it decided that items in the *shape* of an animal were exempt but items with *pictures* of animals on them were not.[27]

Now the reader knows what "unrelated" means.

In the last few years, as a result of the Tax Reform Act of 1986, unrelated business taxes have risen sharply:

Year	millions
1985	$30
1986	53
1987	120
1988	138

| 1989 | 116 |
| 1990 | 128 |

Source: Internal Revenue Service.

There continues to be an enormous amount of oratory devoted to this tax. Small businesses competing with nonprofit businesses say they suffer a competitive disadvantage because they pay taxes and the nonprofit businesses don't. It is a tempest in a thimble. The revenues that UBIT has generated have atomic dimensions because the tax is paid not on gross income but net income, and most nonprofits don't have any net income, much less a lot. In addition, $128 million in tax versus some $300 billion in operating expenditures for all tax exempts means that the tax runs 46 thousandths of one percent of expenditures.

A Second Classification of Nonprofit Organizations

Although legal forms are important, there is another way of classifying nonprofit organizations that is more useful for our purposes, and that is on the basis of their relationships to two groups: those who back the organization, *backers,* and those who are in contact with it and who consume its goods and services, *clients.*[28]

A *business* is set up by private backers who own it and expect returns for their investment. Customers pay to receive goods and services from the business.

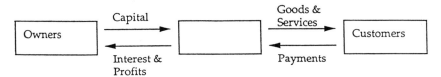

A. Business Firm

A *nonprofit business* is much the same. Those legally responsible for it provide the initial capital required, but thereafter the nonprofit business is expected to support itself. Organizations like these, which are expected to support themselves selling goods and services, I call nonprofit businesses.

Like a business firm, it looks to customers as the sole source of revenues. Government-run businesses like the Tennessee Valley Authority, the Cleveland Municipal Lighting Company, and Amtrak are expected to produce revenues large enough to pay operating costs (and sometimes capital costs); and others, like the various state lotteries, must produce profits. Privately owned, nonprofit businesses are likewise charged with paying their own way. Examples would range from the Rand Corporation and the University of Chicago Press to sheltered workshops for the mentally retarded.

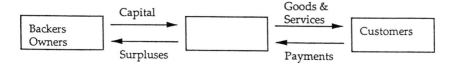

B. Nonprofit Business

Common benefit organizations, like nonprofit businesses, are principally concerned with those who consume its services; however, these consumers are not outsiders. They are members of the organization, and the organization exists for the common benefit of the members.[29] Because the members also back the organization with fees and donated services, we can represent a common benefit organization like this:

C. Common Benefit Organization

Most small nonprofit organizations are common benefit organizations: bridge groups, neighborhood sewing groups (Stitch and Bitch), burial associations, self-help groups, consumer cooperatives. (There is nothing necessarily nonprofit about cooperatives, however. Consumer cooperatives tend to be nonprofit, but wholesale cooperatives owned by retailers and cooperatives that market agricultural produce are not.[30]) But many giants also exist primarily for the benefit of members: churches, credit unions, political parties, trade unions, professional and trade associations, SPEBSQSA, the PTA, the American Legion, health maintenance organizations, and all types of clubs, fraternities, and veterans' groups.

Service organizations are sometimes supported partly by fees paid by clients and partly by backers who contribute time and money; sometimes the clients of a service organization pay no fees at all, in which case all its support comes from backers. In either case, the service organization is unable, or unwilling, to finance its operations solely from client fees. When finding backers who will provide continuous financial support becomes essential to the survival of the organization, the organization is a service organization; and to survive, service organizations must raise funds. They look like this:

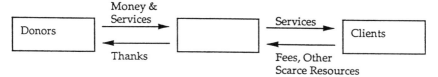

D. Service Organization

Readers need only attend to their daily mail to learn the names of dozens of service organizations, all soliciting funds: the American Cancer Society, Boys' Town, the college alumni association, the local hospital, the National Multiple Sclerosis Society, the Sloan-Kettering Foundation, the local foundation for the blind, and so on.

Commonwealth organizations aim to benefit society as a whole, the public at large.[31] They are created by the public and (often) paid for by taxes; and typically, though not always, they are government bodies going by such names as agency, board, commission, office, administration, department, authority, and the like. Commonwealth organizations look like this:

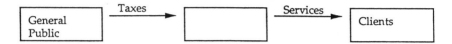

E. Commonwealth Organization

As with any such classification scheme, these five categories will not fit every situation. An organization may run a perpetual deficit and need constant infusions of cash. Yet, if its energies are devoted to finding and serving customers, if its subsidy is more or less assured, it is a nonprofit business. Commonwealth organizations benefit the public at large, but many of them are also service organizations, treating clients with individual attention and care. Moreover, an organization of one type may run one of another type; a museum runs a museum shop; a university operates a conference center; a port and harbor authority runs a commuter line. But it is important to see nonprofit organizations as dealing with both backers and clients, and to learn that the relations between organization, backers, and clients can take many forms.

A Note on Terms

Throughout this book, I shall use the term ''nonprofit organization'' and the abbreviation NPO as a general term that refers to any nonprofit institution: charities, nonprofit businesses, labor unions, common benefit organizations, foundations, research institutions, government agencies, and so on. ''Backers'' will be my general term used for supporters of an organization, those who provide it with money or time or other valuable assets; and ''clients'' will be the term for those the organization aims to serve. Wherever possible I will use more specific words, but, otherwise, for want of better, I will use these three.

We have considered several aspects of the nonprofit world. Two brief questions dealing with terminology remain. The first is: How is it spelled—non profit, non-profit, or nonprofit? I don't know. The first edition used ''nonprofit,'' this edition ''nonprofit.'' I have no idea which is better. The second question is: Is there a difference between ''nonprofit'' and ''not-for-profit?''

No.

Table 1.5
Prevalence of the Four Types of Foundations, 1988

Type	Percent
Independent	81.4
Community	2.6
Operating	2.3
Corporate	13.7
	100.0
(Base)	6,615

Source: The Foundation Directory (New York: Foundation Center, 1989), p. v.

APPENDIX

As lawyers and economists see them, nonprofits come in five flavors.[32] *Individual enterprise* is usually seen in the form of charitable contributions and public benefit work, both of which can give rise to tax deductions for the individual. Setting oneself up as a charity to *receive* gifts and bequests is quite another thing, however, normally allowed only to organizations. A *partnership* is defined by statute as an association of two persons or more who come together as co-owners to carry on business for profit. Take away the profit motive and you would have a nonprofit partnership. But this, admittedly, is a rare bird.

In fact, the nonprofit partnership would probably be called an *association* (or society), a group that does not have a formal charter but is united in purpose and acts together. Because associations usually adopt the methods and forms used by corporations, and because governmental and tax authorities often treat them like near corporations, most associations find it disadvantageous to operate without written articles or a charter. Thus, they tend to become nonprofit *corporations.*

The last important form taken by nonprofit organizations, and the most recent historically, is the *foundation.* An endowment is set up to receive contributions and endowments from a single person (or a small group of persons) and a corporation or association is set up to carry out the plan of the founder, which for the most part is to give away money.[33]

Foundations come in four varieties: (1) independent foundations get their funds (usually) from families or individuals. They spend their funds on specific subjects or programs and often restrict their giving to local areas; (2) community foundations get their funds from other foundations and from individuals. They spend their funds in local communities, as the name implies; (3) operating foundations do not make grants to others. Instead, they spend their funds on programs they themselves manage; (4) corporate foundations are set up and managed by private businesses to carry out their giving policies. Corporate foundations tend to favor specific program areas. (See Table 1.5.)

The rich have so abused foundations that many tax authorities see them as nothing more than tax-exempt personal holding companies. In the 1930s there

Table 1.6
A Classification of Private Nonprofit Organizations

I. Arts, Culture, Humanities
    A. Arts, culture, humanities

II. Education
    B. Education and related—
       formal and nonformal

III. Environment and Animals
    C. Environmental quality,
       protection, and beautification
       (including Environmental
       Health and Safety)
    D. Animal related

IV. Health
    E. Health—general and
       rehabilitation
    F. Health—mental health, crisis
       intervention
    G. Health—mental retardation/
       developmentally disabled

V. Human services
    H. Consumer protection, legal aid
    I. Crime and delinquency
       prevention—public protection
    J. Employment
    K. Food, nutrition, agriculture
    L. Housing
    M. Public safety, emergency
       preparedness, and relief

    N. Recreation, leisure, sports,
       athletics
    O. Youth development
    P. Human service, other,
       including multipurpose (also,
       social services—individual and
       family)

VI. International
    Q. International

VII. Public Health—General
    R. Civil rights, social action,
       advocacy
    S. Community improvement,
       community capacity building
    T. Foundations
    U. Research, planning, science,
       technology, technical
       assistance
    V. Voluntarism, philanthropy,
       charity

VIII. Religion
    W. Religion and spiritual
       development

IX. Other, Including Nonclassifiable
    X. Reserved
    Y. Mutual membership benefit
    Z. Nonclassifiable

Source: National Taxonomy of Exempt Entities, developed by the National Center for
Charitable Statistics (Washington, D.C.: Independent Sector, 1987).

were 240 foundations in the country; but such has been the zeal of the rich for
charity that by 1969 there were over 30,000, perhaps as many as 50,000, and
in 1969 the New York State Attorney General reported that foundations in New
York State alone were increasing at the rate of one hundred a month.[34]

A Formal Taxonomy of NPOs

Frustrated by its inability to collect useful statistics, the nonprofit sector set
about in the 1980s to develop a classification that would apply to all NPOs.
Table 1.6 summarizes the results. But it is only a summary. Each of the letters
has a more detailed set of subcategories.

QUESTIONS

1. The U.S. Postal Service is expected to run at a profit. Is "profit" the right word? Why or why not?

2. Most nonprofit organizations have trouble breaking even, much less producing a surplus. At breakeven, a nonprofit would not pay any income tax. So why is there so much concern over the tax exemption on the part of nonprofits?

3. An NPO cannot pass on any of its surpluses to (say) its board members or senior managers. What's to prevent these people from sopping up the surplus by paying themselves well, enjoying generous expense accounts, and furnishing their offices with expensive art?

NOTES

1. Readers without previous experience or training in marketing will, I trust, learn a good deal from this book. They will learn even more if they read one or two standard marketing textbooks as they work their way through this book.

2. The one is *Journal of Nonprofit & Public Sector Marketing* (Binghamton, N.Y.: Haworth Press). I am sorry to say that it is not a good journal. The other is *Advances in Nonprofit Marketing* (Greenwich, Conn.: JAI Press), published from time to time.

3. Figures in the paragraph are all from the *Statistical Abstract of the U.S. 1989* (Washington, D.C., 1989). The figure for museums is from *The Official Museum Directory, 1990, United States and Canada* (Washington, D.C.: American Association of Museums, 1990), pp. A-8.

4. Wolf Organization, *The Financial Condition of Symphony Orchestras, Part I— The Orchestra Industry* (Washington, D.C.: American Symphony Orchestra League, 1992), p. 1.

5. The two are *Modern Maturity,* published by the American Association of Retired Persons with a circulation over 21 million, and *National Geographic Magazine,* published by the National Geographic Society with a circulation around 11 million. (The other two are *Reader's Digest* and *TV Guide,* both around 16 million.)

6. All these figures are from the *Encyclopedia of Associations,* passim; *Encyclopedia of Associations,* vol. 1, 27th ed. (Detroit: Gale, 1993).

7. The figures in this paragraph all come from the *Encyclopedia of Associations* (Detroit: Gale, 1989). But how good are the figures? The Encyclopedia gives the number of Boy Scouts as 4.7 million, and the number of Girl Scouts as 3.1 million. *The Statistical Abstracts of the United States* gives the figures for 1987 as 5.3 million and 2.9 million. For a short article on fan clubs, see "Fan Clubs Thrive on Old TV Series, Minor Celebrities." *Wall Street Journal,* July 19, 1990, p. 1+.

8. Department of the Treasury, Internal Revenue Service, *Cumulative List of Organizations,* Publication 78 (Rev. 1–90), revised to September 30, 1989. The IRS squeezes about 200 nonprofit organizations to a page.

9. Howard L. Oleck, "Nature of American Non-Profit Organizations." *New York Law Forum* XVII (Spring 1972): 1066.

10. All the figures quoted on employment and output are found in Eli Ginzberg's "The Pluralistic Economy of the U.S." *Scientific American* (December 1976): 25–29. Figures for 1963 are found in a readable study by Eli Ginzberg, Dale Hiestand, and Beatrice G. Reubens, *The Pluralistic Economy* (New York: McGraw-Hill, 1965).

11. Don't put much faith in these estimates of how many hours volunteers put in or what proportion of the adult population volunteers. We shall see in Chapter 20 that all such estimates are iffy.

12. For the first estimate of the size of the nonprofit sector, see *The Chronicle of Philanthropy,* January 9, 1990, p. 12. Note that the dates for the individual contributions are 1977 and 1987, not 1980 and 1990. For the second, see "Sources of Statistics of Income Data on Nonprofits and Charitable Giving" (Washington, D.C.: Internal Revenue Service, 1992).

13. *Chronicle of Philanthropy,* November 28, 1989, p. 20+. One percent devoted to charitable care is quite low. A report on the percentage of nonprofit hospital expenses devoted to charitable care and bad debts (as a proportion of hospital expenses) ran: North Carolina 6.7 percent, Florida 7.6 percent, California 3.1 percent, Tennessee 10.5 percent, and Virginia 7.0 percent. See *Nonprofit Times,* vol. 2, no. 5 (August 1988), p. 1.

14. Although cooperatives try to return dividends to their owners each year.

15. Kenneth W. Clarkson, "Some Implications of Property Rights in Hospital Management." *Journal of Law and Economics* 15 (1973): 363.

16. See Norman A. Sugerman and Harlan Pomeroy, "Business Income of Exempt Organizations." *Virginia Law Review* 16 (1960): 424.

17. *Wall Street Journal,* August 25, 1976, p. 1.

18. *Wall Street Journal,* May 23, 1990, p. A1.

19. See Robert K. Mantz, *Financial Reporting for Nonprofit Organizations* (New York: Garland, 1994), p. 41 for an alternate, rather spongy treatment of the differences.

20. Joseph S. Davis, *Essays in the Earlier History of American Corporations,* vol. 1 (Cambridge, Mass.: Harvard University Press, 1917), p. 49.

21. See Howard L. Oleck, *Non-Profit Corporations, Organizations, and Associations.* 3d ed. (Englewood Cliffs, N.J.: Prentice-Hall, 1974), pp. 223–229.

22. Exemptions for religious or apostolic organizations are granted under Section 501(d); and exemptions for "social welfare" organizations, together with civic leagues and local associations of employees, are granted under Section 501(c)(4). Both 501(c)(3) and 501(c)(4) organizations are exempt from federal income tax. But there are two differences between them: (1) contributions to 501(c)(3) organizations are deductible, but those to a 501(c)(4) are not. (2) 501(c)(3) organizations cannot engage in "substantial lobbying activities," but 501(c)(4) organizations can. Both Consumers Union and the Sierra Club are examples of 501(c)(4) organizations. See The Commission on Private Philanthropy and Public Needs, *Research Papers, vol. 4, Taxes* (Washington, D.C.: Department of the Treasury, 1977), pp. 2045–2047. Finally, note that foundations are treated differently from all others.

23. *New York Times,* March 28, 1976. Not all of these organizations were nonprofit.

24. See the discussion in Lee Goldstein, *Communes, Law and Commonsense* (Boston: New Community Projects, 1974), p. 72. Also see Kate Wenner, "How They Keep Them Down On the Farm." *New York Times Magazine,* May 8, 1977, p. 74.

25. Leslie Lenkowsky, "Judge Thomas and Truth in Fund Raising." *Chronicle of Philanthropy,* September 10, 1991, p. 45.

26. Gail Harmon, "IRS Spells Out Rules for Mailing Lists and UBIT." *Nonprofit Times* (May 1993), p. 18.

27. "When Should the Profits of Nonprofits Be Taxed?" *Business Week* (December 5, 1983), p. 191.

28. The organization typology presented here was originally put forward in Peter M. Blau and W. Richard Scott, *Formal Organizations* (San Francisco: Chandler, 1962), pp. 40–45. It was applied with a few changes to nonprofit organizations by Philip Kotler in *Marketing for Non-Profit Organizations* (Englewood Cliffs, N.J.: Prentice-Hall, 1975), pp. 29–34.

29. Blau and Scott call these mutual benefit organizations, but "mutual" here is not the best usage, although its misuse is widespread. See N. W. Fowler, *Modern English Usage* (Oxford: Oxford University Press, 1965), p. 377.

30. See E. P. Roy, *Cooperatives: Today and Tomorrow* (Danville, Ill.: Interstate, 1969). These agricultural co-ops had revenues of $57 billion in 1975, which gave them one-third of all U.S. agribusiness. See "The Billion-Dollar Farm Co-ops Nobody Knows." *Business Week* (February 7, 1977), pp. 54–63.

31. On its face, the word is "common" plus "wealth." Wealth, in turn, comes from a Middle English word meaning weal or state of well-being.

32. Oleck, "Nature of American Non-Profit Organizations," pp. 1083–1086.

33. *Foundations, Private Giving, and Public Policy.* Report and Recommendations of the Commission on Foundations and Private Philanthropy (Chicago: University of Chicago Press, 1970), p. 39.

34. *New York Times,* January 18, 1969, p. 1.

Chapter 2

What Is Marketing?

In the late 1960s it first dawned on teachers of marketing that nonprofit organizations engaged in marketing-like activities, and since then the question of just what marketing is has engaged the curiosity of a handful of them. A sensible way to continue, then, is with a discussion of what marketing means and how it relates to education. This chapter concludes by looking at the limitations of marketing and how marketers think.

WHAT IS IT?

Marketing aims to influence mass behavior. A business firm has customers to whom it wishes to sell and competitors over whom it wishes a modicum of influence. In addition, it often distributes its products through middlemen, retailers, wholesalers, jobbers, and the like, all of whom it wishes to influence.

Customers transcend all others, however, because they buy and thus provide the firm with revenues and, when things go well, with profits. A business firm normally finds its customers can choose among products and among suppliers. The firm, that is, cannot prescribe to its customers. Absence of control over persons to be influenced is, in fact, one characteristic of marketing.

One would certainly never *choose* to design a system in which individuals have choices, for choice leads to uncertainty, and uncertainty leads to waste and a life of stress for administrators. Theodore White, for example, has written on professional politicians' zest for primary elections as a means of picking candidates: "In primaries, ambitions spurt from nowhere; unknown men carve their mark; old men are sent relentlessly to their political graves; bosses and leaders may be humiliated or unseated. . . . Bosses and established leaders hate primaries."[1] In days of yore when students studied Latin, teachers of Latin were needed, their jobs secure, and school principals knew how many books to order and how many classrooms they would need. Today, schools no longer know for sure how many students will study any foreign language, let alone Latin; Latin teachers may be sent packing on little notice or, what is the same thing, asked to teach physical education; and because of fads, what students studied last year is a poor guide to what they will want to study next year. Teachers and principals hate elective courses.

Ways of Dealing with Choice

Choice and the uncertainty that accompanies it exist, however, and they force any organization that seeks to influence mass behavior to make choices itself, to find ways of dealing with choice. One is to ignore the world and its changes, hoping somehow that simpler days will return. Among nonprofit organizations this is a common reaction; often unable to use standard measures of performance, like sales or market share, they are prone to sanctify policies that have worked well in the past. A journalist would say that they had become prisoners of their own success. But in a society like America's, the natural itch is to try to do something—either to adapt to the new conditions or to change the world.

Violence is so effective in influencing behavior that governments have always tried to reserve it to themselves. How does a man impress on electoral officials his eligibility to vote? By seizing the right to vote. In the days before voters registered to vote, "it was not unusual for armed men to appear at the polls and demand the right to vote," after which they vanished.[2] It is a mark of our moral progress that elections today are stolen with much more circumspection. Violence has a long history in America. John Brown's murderous rampage in Kansas and his armed attack at Harper's Ferry before the Civil War served to sharpen antagonisms and whet the enthusiasms of those on both sides. Today a similar moral fury of those opposed to abortions or to nuclear power plants or to cutting of the redwoods leads some of them to threaten violence and from time to time to commit it. As the Irish patriot William O'Brian once wrote, "Violence is the only way of ensuring a hearing for moderation."

The government grants the right to threaten violence only infrequently and grudgingly to private parties, but it is done, the most common example being the right granted to labor unions to strike in support of their claims. Most labor disputes, however, are settled peacefully by arbitration and negotiation, a third way of influencing behavior.

The fourth way to deal with the problem of choice is to restrict it by limiting the alternatives from which clients may choose. Colleges control students' choices by requiring courses and prerequisites of them, and by limiting the elective courses they can take outside of their majors. Some methods of limiting choice have passed into proverbs: Hobson's choice is an all-or-nothing choice, the brainchild of Thomas Hobson, an English hostler who offered his customers only one horse, the one nearest the stable door; in this century Henry Ford offered a modern version of Hobson's choice for the Model T, "Any color as long as it's black."

In some situations, the most effective way to deny choice is to require behavior through legal means. In America barely half the eligible voters trouble to vote, even in presidential elections. This in spite of school lessons and editorial homilies on civic responsibility, as well as energetic drives to get out the vote by the League of Women Voters, the Advertising Council, and, most important of all, the political parties themselves. It is, by common consent, a Social Problem. How much simpler it is in Australia, where every citizen must vote or be fined.

One can influence behavior in a fifth way, by designing a program that adapts or conforms to existing patterns of behavior, so that people behave in the desired way because they find it easier. For this very reason a prepaid envelope gives a higher response in a fundraising campaign than an envelope without a stamp, and an envelope without a stamp gives a higher response than no envelope at all; people do not always have stamps or envelopes available, and an intention to give money, once postponed, may be forgotten. In fact it often is forgotten, as the results show.

An example currently in the news is the debate over air bags in cars. Only about one in four or five drivers uses a seat belt; the rest presumably forgetting them or exercising some Constitutional Right. A seat belt interlock that would not allow the car to start until the seat belts had been fastened did not suit the American public, and, as it was controversial, it was killed by Congress in 1974. Air bags offer more grounds for hope in that they promise to save about 9,000 lives a year because they require no action on the part of the driver or passenger. The air bag adapts itself to how drivers behave, not how they should behave.

These first five methods—forbidding choices, violence, negotiation, limiting choices, and adapting to existing behavior—all take individuals as they are. A sixth way of dealing with choice, the hardest way of all, is to try to change people so that they will behave correctly on their own. At one extreme, psychoanalysis and brainwashing and perhaps nagging aim at permanent, fundamental change; therapy and counseling lie in some middle range; and persuasion, which seeks shallow, short-lived changes, lies at the other extreme. (We leave to the reader to reflect on where education fits in all this.)

Persuasion

Persuasion of the sort employed by marketers seeks superficial changes in behavior. The individual must *already* be favorably predisposed to the general idea the marketer is trying to put across. If not, the marketing effort is sure to fail. The Women's Christian Temperance Union is still battling demon rum and other spirituous liquors; but even the most skillful and well-financed WCTU program could not be expected to save more than a handful, and this is so in spite of the incidence of alcoholism and other costs associated with drink and in spite of the general recognition that spirituous liquors are not healthy. The reason? The cultural and social forces that make us a hard-drinking country are simply too powerful for mere persuasion to overcome.[3] In fact, they were too powerful for even the law to overcome, as the failure of Prohibition makes clear. There is a lesson here in understanding the limitations of marketing. The law itself is limited. To earn respect it must reflect its society; law that is too weak generates vigilantes and law that is too draconian leads to widespread disobedience. Marketing, of course, has nothing approaching the power or majesty of the law, and whereas the law can afford, within broad limits, to ignore the desires of groups within society and still accomplish its ends, a marketer has to adapt to existing attitudes, opinions, and prejudices. Because it is easier to preach to the converted than to the heathens, one of the most important tasks for marketers is divining the predispositions of those whom they wish to influence.

Marketers use two of these methods of drawing out correct behavior: (1) they use persuasive communications, notably advertising, personal selling, and sales promotion, to communicate information, explain things, and bring about superficial changes in opinions and behavior; and (2) they adapt to existing patterns of behavior by designing products and services that are easy to use and by distributing them so that they are easy to find. Because prices affect behavior, marketers also set prices (within limits, at least); and because much of the success of a marketing program depends on predicting how clients will behave, they study and research clients. Thus, in this roundabout fashion, we have arrived at the marketing areas traditional in business firms and the world of textbooks: advertising, selling and sales promotion, product, price, distribution, and marketing research.

Marketing, then, deals with two of the many methods—persuasion and adaptation—by which A tries to get B to do his will, where B has freedom to act as he chooses. And as we shall use it in this book, marketing seeks to influence mass behavior. In most cases, mass means hundreds or thousands or even millions. But borderline cases arise when the number is small. Thirty-eight state legislators who are not on record for or against some constitutional amendment will be the focus of intense lobbying by the amendment's supporters and its opponents; and an organization that helps convicts return to society may call on no more than three or four agencies before getting the funds it seeks. Both are engaged in marketing. And marketing, as we shall use it here, is an activity of an organization. Marketing carried on by individuals is of interest only when they represent an organization.

Marketers are what are known as boundary spanners. They straddle the line, as it were, that separates the NPO from its world. They are part of their NPO, they know its strengths and weaknesses and its potentials. They also know about its clients and its backers. In fact, that is a major part of their job. They should know more about clients and backers than anyone else in the NPO, and they should represent their views and interests to the NPO.

I must frankly tell the reader that I am not satisfied with the definition of marketing in the paragraphs above. There are too many activities that, to my mind, have little to do with marketing but that might be called marketing on the basis of this definition. Propaganda uses some marketing techniques but it is not what I call marketing. What about nonviolent political protest? When Thoreau spent his night in jail for refusing to pay taxes, when he wrote *Civil Disobedience* to justify his action, surely he was not engaged in marketing. When half a million citizens congregate on the Mall in Washington to protest some new exaction of the government, or some familiar inaction, surely they are not marketing. "Freedom to act" is also vague, because there are many pressures and constraints on one's behavior. But at the least, the definition given above does rule out a great deal—violence, legislative activities, therapy, and the like—that to me have absolutely nothing to do with marketing.

IS MARKETING EXCHANGE?

Kotler sees the quiddity of marketing as bringing about "voluntary exchanges" to achieve any objective of an organization, but he stresses only one objective: command over resources, by which he means sales, share of market, and profits for a business firm, and funds and gifts for a nonprofit organization. Command over resources can be acquired in five ways, Kotler tells us. An organization can produce them itself, or it can beg, rob, or steal them. Kotler prudently does not recognize marketing in any of these four; instead marketing deals with acquiring command over resources by exchange.[4]

The idea of exchange penetrates economics. As economic creatures, people are assumed to want a variety of goods and services. For everyone, some of these goods and services are scarce; but everyone is willing to substitute some of any good to get more of another.[5] In this abstract view, exchange reflects nothing more than the different values placed on goods by different persons. Before an exchange a person has one set of goods, after it he has another; and in the process of the exchange he has given up goods to his trading partner and gained new goods from him. Both are better off after the exchange, the logic goes, for otherwise the exchange would not have taken place.

The idea of voluntary exchange is easily seen in commercial transactions where, say, I exchange my time and plenteous talents for goods and services through the medium of money. Kotler sees exchange as the essence of marketing: "The core concept of marketing is . . . the exchange of values between two parties"; and he tells us that exchange requires two conditions: that there be two parties and that each has something of value for the other.[6] He omits the third necessary condition—that the parties actually exchange something—presumably because it is self-evident.

This definition works well in commercial transactions, but Kotler goes further and sees exchange as pervading much of what goes on in society—taxpayers voluntarily exchange taxes and their cooperation for government goods and services; churchgoers contribute money and services and receive religious services in return; donors give to a charity and receive in exchange "feelings of well-being." Bagozzi carries this approach to its inevitable extreme and sees marketing as a "general function of universal applicability," the universe being All There Is.[7]

It is here that the notion of marketing as voluntary exchange begins to go off the track. To say that taxpayers volunteer their taxes is to misuse the word, and the feelings of well-being people get after giving to a charity are generated by the donors themselves, not something stocked by the charity to be sent off upon receipt of a donation. It is possible to have feelings of well-being without donating at all, simply by contemplating the good works of charity.[8] In fact, economists usually define philanthropy as a voluntary, *one-way* transfer of resources for purposes traditionally judged philanthropic. Here, "one way" means the donor receives nothing in exchange. (He may claim a tax deduction, but it comes from the government, not from charity.) Parents sometimes face the death of a child. Under certain conditions it may be possible to harvest the child's organs and transplant them into other children who otherwise would die. In general, about 40 percent of those parents who are asked to donate their child's organs say no; but those who say yes find the decision gives them solace in the face of their lacerating loss. They see donating organs as a way to have their child's too-brief life matter and somehow endure.[9] This gift is clearly a one-way transfer, yet there are nationwide marketing and education programs designed to increase the number of organs donated.

Another way to consider this issue of exchange is to ask: What is it that is being exchanged? In the affairs of daily life, when we buy a ticket to a concert, we are not exchanging money for a ticket. What is being exchanged is rights, property rights, specifically the exclusive right to occupy a seat and the right to transfer that right to someone else. In a nonprofit setting, however, it seems to make little sense to say that a welfare client has an exchange relationship with the welfare department, or that the Save the Whales Foundation is exchanging property rights with its backers or members.

Many activities that can unquestionably be classified as marketing fit this situation.

- A family planning agency works hard to persuade pharmacists to display condoms rather than keep them in a drawer and sell them only on request. What is the family planning agency exchanging with the pharmacists?

- To control communicable diseases like measles or listeria or AIDS, public health officials must know when an outbreak occurs. For example, prompt reports have provided the epidemiological clues to recognize such new diseases as toxic shock syndrome, Legionnaire's disease, and AIDS. In the 1950s, when a batch of Salk vaccine contaminated with live virus led to a national epidemic of polio, prompt reporting led to the realization that only one brand was contaminated. Without a surveillance program, many and perhaps all drug manufacturers would have stopped making the vaccine.

For such programs to work public health officials must rely on doctors to report the diseases. In fact, it is so important that doctors must report diseases classified as reportable to their state public health authority. Reporting is required by law. New York City, for example, requires every doctor to report promptly, by telephone in some cases, all cases of some seventy-three communicable diseases and clusters of three or more cases of unusual diseases.

But doctors are haphazard about reporting. Studies have shown various levels of compliance. In one, reporting rates were 35 percent overall, from 11 percent for viral hepatitis to 63 percent for tuberculosis.[10] This has led to programs of education to get doctors to report. In such programs what is being exchanged for what?

- The National Safety Council urges drivers to use their seat belts and to drive safely, and to do this it employs many standard public relations and advertising techniques— press releases, posters, advertising. Yet here nothing is exchanged: The driver gives nothing to the council, and the council gives nothing to the driver. Nor does the council seek command over resources as a result of its efforts.

- Some environmental group urges us to boycott a fish or a vegetable or a company, even another nonprofit organization that has raised its ire. The boycott campaign has many of the trappings of a marketing campaign—press releases, marches, appearances on television and radio, and advertising. Yet nothing is exchanged between the group and the general public. Nor for that matter is anything exchanged between the group and the fisherman (or the farmers or the company or the nonprofit).

Blair takes issue with Bagozzi's definition of marketing as lacking any limit.[11]

Marketing theory now lacks delimitation . . . [Bagozzi's definition] means that marketing deals with the creation and resolution of any exchange between human actors. Marketing, in other words, has become indistinguishable from social psychology, [which is] the science of social exchange and . . . embraces all aspects of exchange, including the creation and resolution of exchange.

Anthropologists reading this discussion of exchange would smile politely but fault it as being insular. Many more things can be exchanged than are dreamt of by the economist: men, women, children, their labor, the labor of animals, money, consumer goods, capital goods, ritual objects of no intrinsic value, status, prestige, territorial rights, political rights, and intangibles like a song or a name.[12] Are all of these exchanges marketing? When the Trobriand Islanders exchange gifts are they marketing? In Homer's *Iliad,* in the midst of the swirling battle before Troy, when Diomedes and Glaucus exchange threats, then recognize each other and exchange gifts, are we witnessing the first appearance of marketing in Western literature?

Let us sum up the discussion by saying that some marketing is exchange, but not all of it; that some exchange is marketing, but not all of it; and that readers are welcome to their own opinions.[13]

IS MARKETING A FORM OF EDUCATION?

Certainly not, as most people use the words. But educators do use marketing-like tools to pursue their objectives; and some marketing, at least some of the time and particularly in the nonprofit sector, has a distinct educational component.

Let us look a bit more carefully at just what education can do and what it can't.

Why bother to educate? Education lays a foundation for permanent behavioral change, for one. If clients change, they don't change for superficial reasons like a temporary price cut or a catchy jingle. Second, many professionals in nonprofit organizations find education appealing because they feel it is the way their organization's mission should be promoted. That is, they approve of slow and steady, they disapprove of hype, glitz, and marketing. Third, educational efforts tend to stress rational argument based on facts. It is well suited to audiences comfortable with such arguments, typically educated audiences. (It is poorly suited for those who are not well educated.) Fourth, education can be tailored to the target audience. For example, an AIDS education group might use cartoons to communicate safe sex messages to teenagers, and one-on-one sessions with peer educators to reach gay males in public sex environments with the same message. Finally, education is often cheaper, as it relies on low-key efforts over a long time period.

There are disadvantages to education, of course. Education takes a long time, a long, long time. Think about smoking. It took some four decades first, for the link between cigarettes and cancer to be widely accepted and second, for society to bring about massive changes in smoking behavior; and *still* in the 1990s some 29 percent of all adults smoke (in the United States). Think about AIDS and safe sex, where we face another decades-long battle. The sex drive is strong. It is stronger than that. It is a life force. Against such a powerful drive, education won't ever be able to do much, even in the long run. Second, some audiences need emotional or hyped pitches because they lack the ability to process rational arguments. This seems to many the antithesis of what education should be. Third, education cannot be single-shot or use only one medium. It must be sustained, and it must be pushed on many fronts and in many ways. But much government spending is on-again, off-again, the poorest budgeting pattern for educational efforts. Fourth, an educational campaign usually involves many partners, each acting without much coordination with others. This is true of much of the effort to disseminate the safe sex message. Finally, what must be obvious on its face, education can only do so much. How could anyone start smoking in the 1990s, given all that we know about smoking, have known for fifty years? (When I was a boy we called cigarettes coffin nails.) Slow and steady has worked a sea change on the face of American society concerning smoking, and everyone old enough to tie his own shoe laces knows that cigarettes are bad news; but by no means has everyone, still, after four decades, changed his behavior.

What then can one reasonably expect of an education effort? In the short run, one can't expect much. There simply isn't time. Thus, in the short run education is mostly a symbolic step. In the long run, though, in spite of all the difficulties of funding, loss of enthusiasm, burnout, continual emergence of new members of at-risk groups—education at its best can bring about permanent change. Note the striking success of the homosexual community in bringing about changes in its sexual practices. Between about 1980 and 1986 or so, there was a radical shift in homosexual sexual behavior, and the incidence of new AIDS cases dropped sharply. Alas, the changes weren't all that permanent, and once again we read reports of young gay men, new to the scene, engaging in unsafe sex.

The Differences between Marketing and Education

	Marketing	Education
Appeals	Any that work, including fear, hype, oversell, humor	Rational appeals preferred
Media	Media suitable to the audience	Person-to-person preferred
Time horizon	Generally short run	Generally long run
Marketing style	Can be hyper	Low-key

WHY NONPROFIT MARKETING PROGRAMS SO OFTEN FAIL

This chapter aims to develop a good sense of what marketing is. Part of understanding what something is is understanding what it isn't. We continue on our quest, then, by examining why marketing so often fails.

Nonprofit Marketers Get the Hardest Jobs

Nonprofit marketers often find themselves working on problems that commercial marketers would despair of handling. For one, the benefits of behaving correctly are often of little substance and because of this are hard to communicate. No one in his right mind would try to persuade a junkie in need of a fix to change his behavior (say) by planning ahead and getting a clean needle, or carrying clean needles around so he'll never be out. Nor would anyone have much hope of persuading most teenagers that condoms are something they should always use in having sex. Some will but many, perhaps most, won't. In both cases the imperatives of the moment overwhelm marketing messages.

They Often Must Market Services That No One Wants

Nonprofit marketers often market products and services for which there is little demand, which is like answering questions that no one wants answered. Some years ago, in response to pleas from the vending machine operators, the United States minted a new coin, the Susan B. Anthony dollar. The size of a quarter, it was never accepted by retailers, who found it far too easy to give a dollar in change instead of twenty-five cents. Now your mission, if you choose to accept it, is to persuade a retailer in New York City that he should accept the Susan B. Anthony. Why should he accept it, he asks. Patriotism? (Hardly.) It's good business? (Never try to tell a New Yorker his business.) Everyone else is accepting them? (Not true.) Because it is legal tender? (Not in New York; New York City is not part of the United States. Few Americans understand this.) It is hard even to contrive a reason that counts for much. Businesses try to avoid this problem by estimating the size of a market before they introduce a product. If there is no market, they abandon the idea. Nonprofit marketers must soldier on, expecting to fail, embracing the occasional success.

Nonprofit Services Often Lie at Extremes in Terms of Involvement

Clients are often little engaged by the issue that is so important to the non-profit marketer. Marketers have, in recent years, begun to distinguish among buying situations on the basis of how involved the consumer is in the buying decision. And typical of the way marketers think, they divide all products into two broad categories, low involvement and high involvement. Low-involvement products are simply not important to grown-ups; consumers buy them without much thought and will substitute one brand for another. Think about peas, envelopes, blank cassette tapes, and children's books. High-involvement products, such as automobiles, fine wines, and foreign travel, on the other hand, are more important to consumers, important emotionally.

There are degrees of involvement, then. But the run from commercial low involvement to commercial high involvement spans only the range of commercial products. (The idea, after all, was thought up by the commercial marketers.) Rothschild has argued that the nonprofit marketer faces more extreme situations, in which the client's involvement is lower than the usual commercial low-involvement situation encountered by the commercial marketer, or higher than commercial high involvement.[14] Thus, the Susan B. Anthony coin presents a situation where the client is much less involved than a commercial marketer is likely ever to encounter, and with it a more difficult marketing chore; and the campaign to encourage U.S. drivers to observe the 55 mph speed limit ran into situations in which the client was deeply involved, much more deeply than in a mere commercial transaction.

The 55 mph campaign had practically nothing going for it. The benefits—

lower speed meant less fuel, which meant a reduced dependence on imported oil, and a sizeable cut in highway deaths—were not to the driver but to society, and thus they were both remote and tenuous. Slower speed was not free. Matched against these distant, weak benefits were immediate costs. In a ten-hour day drivers averaging 65 mph will be one hundred miles closer to their destination than drivers going 55 mph, which explains why, on most super highways, a common sight in the rearview mirror is a truck grill. Finally, speeding is what has been called a folk crime—illegal without question, but, like cheating on one's taxes or parking illegally, a pursuit enjoyed by most law-abiding citizens. We might say that speeding is neither fattening, immoral, nor illegal; rather, it is an innocent pastime between consenting adults, that is, the driver and the police, to wile away the long hours on the road.

Marketing Is Inherently Inefficient

Marketing is inherently inefficient in bringing about changes in behavior. For one thing, the theory on which marketing is based is poor. There is no agreement on the meaning of central concepts and little on units of measure; research findings are rarely based on more than a single study and hence cannot be generalized; and the predictions based on marketing theory are vague. This means that much of the craft of marketing rests on trial and error, with an emphasis on error.

Many marketing programs simply do not work at all, or they fail in some way to meet their objectives (which often, of course, arise from poor objectives rather than poor marketing). For over two decades, marketing texts have commented on the high failure rate in the development of new products, usually saying that about 80 percent fail. Although this observation rests on unexamined definitions of "failure" and "new," it does illustrate what is encountered all too often in practice: Energy, planning, money, and time go into a marketing program and not much comes out. As an example, consider a political campaign. Much of what goes on in a campaign is marketing—opinion polling, fundraising, advertising, canvassing, PR. Do campaigns count? Yes, but not very much: "the campaign itself accounts for a very small percentage of voter choices, . . . between two and five percent."[15] In fact, it can be argued that most marketing programs most of the time neutralize competing marketing programs and that, as a result, none of the competing parties go anywhere. This concept has been put most convincingly by Andrew Ehrenberg, who has developed a powerful mathematical model of consumer repeat buying that *ignores* such irrelevancies as:

current or past marketing activities (such as advertising, consumer promotions, distribution, pricing, etc.), the nature of the brand and the product-field in question, the brand's sales level or share of the market, the brand's penetration level, the average rate of buying per buyer, the length of the time-period analyzed, the purchasing pattern for competitive brands, the general degree of brand-switching in the product-class, consumer attitudes toward the brand, usage habits, and indeed specific factors such as the particular time and country or region to which the data refer.[16]

That is, Ehrenberg's model ignores marketing as we know it without any harm to its ability to predict how clients will behave.

Marketing Programs Never Reach Everyone

Marketing programs never reach everyone they aim to reach. (We shall see, in fact, that they do not even try to reach everyone.) Not every young woman will see the advertisements to volunteer for the army, and most of those who do see them will not enlist. The draft, on the other hand—a program as far from marketing as it is possible to get—was not so limited. For over thirty years, everyone registered and draft evaders were counted in terms of parts per million.[17]

Marketing Works Poorly When Clients Don't Know Enough to Make Up Their Own Minds

A sixth limitation on marketing solutions arises when clients are unable to make the necessary choices. Schoolchildren do not know what is good for them, and therefore school curriculums give them little opportunity to exercise choice. Adults, at least, can be presumed to know their own minds, but they may not have the information or training to choose as well as they might. A common criticism of American politics turns on just this point, that many voters are too stupid to understand the issues and to see through the specious promises candidates make. (The counter argument is that they understand well the one or two issues that bear directly on them and that is all they need to understand.)

Those Who Work in Nonprofit Organizations Mistrust Marketing

A seventh limitation: many persons who work in nonprofit organizations cannot stomach marketing. At its best, for them it shades the truth or overstates its case; and at its worst it stoops and palters and double-talks. (Needless to say, I feel that such views are incorrect.)

Marketing Can Be Costly

Finally, marketing is often costly. It does not always require large amounts of money, but it often does; and when it does, the costs of the error in trial and error go up. It is also costly when one compares the cost of achieving a certain result with the returns. How wasteful, some argue, for states to raise money by running games of chance, lotteries, numbers games, and the like. In the early 1970s, New Jersey sold a fifty-cent lottery ticket, whose price was split as follows:

Revenues				
Price (at retail)		$.500		100%
Variable Expenses				
Prizes	$.240		48%	
Sales commission	.025	.265	5	53
Gross marketing earnings		.235		47
Programmed and non-variable expenses		.045		9
Net marketing earnings		$.190		38%

Source: Ronald D. Watson, "Lotteries: Can the Public and State Both Win?" *Business Review* (published by the Federal Reserve Bank of Philadelphia) (July 1973): 11. The terms in this earnings statement are explained in Chapter 2.

Here we see New Jersey paying 2.5 cents to sales agents and 4.5 cents for expenses, 7 cents in all to clear 19 cents. Now think of the obvious alternative, raising taxes. New Jersey is a state that already has a tax department, which is staffed and already collecting taxes. Raising the tax rate a small amount will cost only a pittance; in fact, except for printing up new forms and instructions, it may be that its marginal cost will be zero. Thus, the author of the article from which the figures above were taken says the same amount of revenue raised by New Jersey, at a cost of seven cents for each nineteen cents, could be raised in Pennsylvania by increasing its income tax .3 of one percent or its sales tax .5 of one percent. Such are the efficiencies of forbidding choice, or the inefficiencies of persuasion and adaptation.

IF MARKETING IS SO INEFFICIENT, WHY BOTHER WITH IT?

The Nonprofit May Have No Choice

No one who lacks the authority to tax has figured out how to compel backers to give. Even the trial lawyers are stymied. Since backers give only if it suits them, organizations must reach them by means of marketing.

Marketing Solutions Make for Happier Clients

Even those organizations that do not have to engage in marketing may choose to mix in some marketing, because when clients volunteer their response, the nonprofit organization usually enjoys a higher degree of client support than it would otherwise. Even the IRS uses some marketing tools, although I do not know that they produce happier taxpayers.

Marketing Solutions Serve Clients Better

Marketing solutions adapt to the short-run needs of clients—at least, they should adapt to these needs—and as a result, in the short run, the clients will see themselves as being served better than by other, more downright methods. Marketing, that is, is user friendly.

Marketing Provides a Focus for the Organization

Marketers ask searching questions of any organization—who are your clients? Who do you want your clients to be in three or five years? How well are you serving your clients? Are you delivering the right products and the right services? Answers to questions like these that are well thought out will affect the overall direction of an NPO, its aims, and the means it employs. None of this is insignificant stuff.

HOW TO THINK LIKE A MARKETER

You think like a marketer when your first order of business is satisfying your clients. The remaining pages of this chapter amplify and hedge this sentence.

First of all, just what is satisfaction? If you think about it for a short while, you will quickly decide it is more than some level of quality or performance by the NPO. Satisfaction does depend on performance but it also depends on expectations. I once dragged my children off, unwilling, to see Mozart's *Marriage of Figaro*. The scenery was dowdy, the singers competent but no more, and the orchestra underrehearsed. That is, the quality was poor. The opera was in English, however; it's funny and has some great tunes, and we had front row seats where we could understand almost everything the singers were singing. The children loved it. Low expectations and high performance yield satisfaction. The moral is that satisfaction depends on both what clients and backers expect and how the NPO performs.

You think like a marketer when your first order of business is satisfying your clients and your backers. A foundation wants its grantees to do well, it wants its grants to succeed, it wants to give support over several years. It doesn't call this marketing—but it certainly looks like what a marketer does. It thinks like a marketer. Yet client satisfaction rings a sour tone to many NPOs. ''We're here to educate,'' they say, ''or heal or aid or entertain or enlighten or support or discover or protect.'' And they are right. The NPO's mission is why it exists, and clearly the mission comes first.

Customer satisfaction in nonprofit organizations is not the be-all and end-all of a marketing program, as some believe about for-profit businesses. Nevertheless, having satisfied clients is a valuable asset: they

- are more likely to behave correctly on their own, without continued marketing reinforcement,
- generate favorable word of mouth, which spreads the word among others who might benefit from the organization,
- are more likely to come again or send someone else to experience what they have experienced.

Freshman orientation at colleges and universities used to mean a barbeque, some lectures, a Greetings, perhaps a big dance, certainly a campus tour led by a bored sophomore. It is now much more likely to expose students to fashionable topics like drugs, date rape, race relations, counseling, and the Help Center. The aim is to give freshmen a good start in their first year, under the assumption that what happens in this year is crucial to a student's chances for success over the entire four years. Colleges also don't want to lose freshmen. Roughly one in three freshmen does not return to the same school for the sophomore year. Why should the dean worry about that? After all, the bodies that leave will be replaced by other bodies, who will pay tuition. Not much will change. Except for ugly old economics. It is far cheaper to keep an existing student than to find a new one to replace one who is lost.

We are talking about satisfaction, again. Students' satisfaction is based partly on accidentals like how bad the food is and how awful their instructors are, but it is based mostly on substantials, friends, quality of education, whether they feel they are learning anything, and academic success. The evidence is that satisfied students cost less to educate, do better in their studies, and are more likely to stay the course.[18]

Satisfaction is particularly important when one thinks of backers. Backers have lots of choices, ways they can volunteer their time, causes they can give money to. Satisfied backers give again, they turn over less slowly, they give more or more often, they give in other forms (time), and, like satisfied clients, they generate good word of mouth.

Satisfied volunteers are more likely to stay the course, help in recruiting others, give money, talk up the NPOs, and turn less slowly. In a business, client satisfaction is an intermediate goal. The ultimate goal is financial—return on investment, profits, cash flow. The ultimate goal for an NPO is doing good—accomplishing its mission. We would never think that the goal of a corporation is to edify or beautify or house or spread truth and beauty.

So here is another qualification on the importance of client satisfaction. No NPO should put client satisfaction above everything. A business certainly doesn't. Yet the success of a business rests on customer satisfaction. If it doesn't satisfy its customers, and if they can go elsewhere, it will lose business. But it won't satisfy them without stint or let. It must learn to say no. Its aim is not satisfaction *per se* but satisfaction at a profit, which is its true mission.

An NPO must do the same: It must satisfy its clients and its backers while accomplishing its mission, the true purpose for which the NPO exists.

Once having decided that satisfaction counts, it is easy to find the first objects of a satisfaction survey, clients and backers. Then the nonprofit can begin to think whether it would be useful to measure the satisfaction of its volunteers, say volunteers who work off site, or its board members. One can look even farther afield. The American Red Cross measures the satisfaction of those who seek its help after a major disaster. After the severe earthquake in the San Francisco Bay Area, 68 percent of those helped said they were satisfied or very satisfied with the Red Cross. After Hurricane Hugo hit Puerto Rico, 60 percent said they were satisfied (or very satisfied) and after it hit the Carolinas, 80 percent were satisfied. The Red Cross even measured satisfaction levels of its own volunteers and asked them whether they would work again with it on another major disaster. (Most said yes.)[19] United Way needs ways to measure the effectiveness of the agencies to which it gives money. There are several ways of doing this, of course, including measures of costs and productivity. It also measures the satisfaction of its agencies' clients, under the reasonable assumption that if the clients are satisfied, the agency must be doing some things right.

The idea is sound, not just for the generals but the troops down in the trenches. However, it is not so simple. For one thing, the idea of satisfying clients rarely sits well with professionals and other staffers. Imagine trying to persuade a pastor that her aim in life should be satisfying her parishioners. For another, one will encounter situations in which one cannot please any one group without displeasing others. For example, water released from a dam during a drought on the Missouri River by the Army Corps of Engineers has competing uses— drinking water; farm irrigation; grain terminal; coal-fired power-generating plants that use water for cooling; barges; and recreation.

Let us return to the complaints of staff members about emphasizing client satisfaction; and let us consider the most unfavorable organization for such an argument, a hospital. Surely, what counts in a hospital is whether the patient recovers, not whether he is satisfied. Who cares if he is satisfied as long as he is better? Particularly when it is easy to fool patients, say, by giving them a prescription they don't need or ordering tests that are not needed; or by providing convenient access to ambulatory services through store-front clinics that may deliver poorer care.

Even here we argue on general principles that patients' views count for a lot. If patients are not to be the judge, who is? The doctors have their say, but they are not on the receiving end. All this is arguing from general principles. But general principles do not address the specifics of U.S. medical care in the 1990s. There is an oversupply of physicians in many medical specialties, patients are harder to fool, and competition from for-profit suppliers and health maintenance organizations has increased. In addition, patients are not stuck with the current doctor. One survey showed that some 85 percent of patients either had changed their physicians in the past five years or were thinking of doing so.[20] (There is quite a difference between changing and thinking about changing. The researcher here had a point to make.) It should be obvious, at least to someone reading a book on marketing, or to someone who has spent time in the doctor's office, that there is more to quality of care than mere technical proficiency. Patients quite reasonably expect to be treated like human beings, and, let us say, expect to have their questions answered and some attention paid to the amenities of their care.[21]

So, how does one think like a marketer? By (1) giving the interests of clients and backers prominence in making decisions, (2) making their satisfaction an important goal of the NPO, (3) organizing the NPO around these ideas, and (4) by rewarding those who do the best job of satisfying clients and backers.

QUESTIONS

1. In the book by Thomas Jones, *Lloyd George* (Cambridge, Mass.: Harvard University Press, 1951), Lloyd George, Prime Minister of England during World War I, was described as having an ability to frame "the argument or appeal best suited to the vanity, weakness or self-interest" of his audience (page 76). What, if anything, does this have to do with nonprofit marketing?

Questions on Exchange and Marketing

2. Exchange of gifts—say, in commemoration of the birth of a god—has been practiced throughout history. Clearly this is exchange. Is it marketing, too?

3. A visitor to a science museum stops to look at an exhibit and read the sign and labels. What if anything is being exchanged? Curators like to describe what goes on when a visitor stops at an exhibit as "education." Is exchange a part of education? If so, what is exchanged? Is education marketing?

4. In Homer, the Greeks burned thighbones of animals wrapped in fat as an offering to the gods. These sacrifices were done to appease the gods when they were angry, to ask for favors, to call down revenge for injuries, and sometimes merely to get on the god's good side. Is there an "exchange process" going on? What is being exchanged for what? Is this exchange marketing?

5. A little girl wiles her grandfather into buying her an ice cream cone. Is this marketing?

NOTES

1. Theodore H. White, *The Making of the President 1960* (New York: Pocket Books, 1961), p. 93.

2. Joseph P. Harris, *Registration of Voters in the United States* (Washington, D.C.: Brookings Institute, 1928), p. 6.

3. See Joseph R. Gusfield, "Social Structure and Moral Reform: A Study of the Woman's Christian Temperance Union." *American Journal of Sociology* 61 (1955): 221–232.

4. Philip Kotler, *Marketing for Non-Profit Organizations* (Englewood Cliffs, N.J.: Prentice-Hall, 1975), pp. 22–23.

5. Economists do not think of money as a good, because it is not valued for itself but merely for what it will buy. Money is seen as a means, not an end. The measure of substitutability, by the way, is called the indifference rate of substitution and is discussed in most economics texts. One of the best is Armen A. Alchian and William R. Allen, *University Economics* (Belmont, Calif.: Wadsworth, 1969).

6. Kotler, *Marketing for Non-Profit Organizations,* pp. 22–23.

7. Richard P. Bagozzi, "Marketing as Exchange." *Journal of Marketing* 39 (October 1975): 32–39.

8. Still, some donors—about 13 percent in one study—say they give because they expect benefits. See Commission on Private Philanthropy and Public Needs, *Research Papers Sponsored by the Commission on Private Philanthropy and Public Needs,* vol. 1, *History, Trends, and Current Magnitudes* (Washington, D.C.: Department of the Treasury), p. 205.

9. Elisabeth Rosenthal, "Parents Find Solace in Donating Organs." *New York Times,* May 11, 1993, p. B7.

10. Lawrence K. Altman, "Communicable Diseases Masked Behind Doctors' Erratic Reporting." *New York Times,* July 10, 1990, p. B5.

11. Ed Blair, Letter to the Editor. *Journal of Marketing* 41 (January 1977): 134.

12. Andrew P. Vayda, "On the Anthropological Study of Economics." *Journal of Economic Issues* 1 (1967): 88.

13. What difference does it make what marketing is? Not much. A book like this one seeks some common ground with its readers, and, to this end, a definition may be of some help. And in itself pursuing such a question is a harmless pastime. But practitioners dismiss such questions as trivial, and often novices fail to appreciate such definitions until their own experience and understanding have long since put the need for appreciation behind them. Besides, even a satisfying definition cannot hope to stand for long, as our conception of marketing alters.

14. Michael L. Rothschild, "Marketing Communications in Nonbusiness Situations, or Why It's So Hard to Sell Brotherhood Like Soap." *Journal of Marketing* 43 (Spring 1979): 11–20.

15. Xandra Kayden, "The Political Campaign as an Organization." *Public Policy* XXI (Spring 1973): 289.

16. Andrew S. C. Ehrenberg, *Repeat-Buying* (Amsterdam: North-Holland, 1972), pp. 21–22.

17. The only possible exception to this statement, in the three decades of conscription following passage of the Burke-Wadsworth Act in 1940, was the few years when the Vietnam protest was at its height. And even then, when called, most young men went.

18. Anthony De Palma, "New Greetings for Freshmen As Life and Campus Change." *New York Times,* August 28, 1991, p. A8.

19. Kristen A. Goss, "Red Cross Plans Major Changes in Its Disaster-Relief Operations." *Chronicle of Philanthropy,* August 13, 1977, p. 7.

20. N. Cousins, "How Patients Appraise Physicians." *New England Journal of Medicine* 313 (1985): 1422–1424.

21. On this three-part scheme of quality of care—technical, interpersonal, and amenities—see A. Donabedian, *Explorations in Quality Assessment and Monitoring,* vol 1: *The Definition of Quality and Approaches to Its Assessment* (Ann Arbor: Health Administration Press, 1980).

Part II

TOOLS FOR THE MARKETER

Chapter 3

The Financial Side of Marketing Decisions

Businesses have one objective, a financial objective, making money or, more formally, maximizing profit. They have other objectives, to be sure, and in public they often stress these others before the one; but when they make important decisions, profit is usually paramount.

Nonprofit organizations have two objectives, a financial objective and a mission. The financial objective typically is to generate a small surplus, or to break even, or to hold losses to a minimum. All try to run a surplus, but few do, and if they do, they will soon spend it on improving or expanding the mission. But the mission usually comes before the financial objective. Why does a business exist? To make a profit. How they make it isn't all that important. Why does a nonprofit organization exist? To carry out its purpose, its mission, and at the same time contrive to pay its bills.

Putting a financial objective second means just that. It is next most important after the mission. Putting it second does not mean a marketer can ignore it. Indeed, the nonprofit marketer must understand the numbers—to work out the implications of proposed programs, to make better decisions, to evaluate past programs. But the subject is far from simple, and this chapter can do little more than serve as an introduction. It is well to remember, in addition, the difference between businesses and nonprofits. Once a businessman has estimated costs and revenues, he is almost done with his analysis, because businesses exist to produce profits. They rarely undertake major expenditures unless those expenditures promise a satisfactory return. Nonprofit organizations do not exist to produce profits, and they often undertake major expenditures that have no hope of breaking even. So estimating costs and revenues does not decide the issue, as it usually does in business. Let Oscar Wilde's quip serve as a reminder: "What is a cynic? A man who knows the price of everything and the value of nothing."

Why should a nonprofit manager concerned with marketing bother with financial issues? For one thing, marketing is often charged with producing revenues—selling things or fundraising—or with bringing in other valuable resources like collections, donations in kind, volunteers, or members. It is common sense, as well as a high principle of economics, that no more should be spent on such activities than they are worth, which implies knowledge of both costs and benefits. The other side of this coin is that marketing consumes resources. And again it is common sense to measure how much is consumed. Just because benefits or costs are hard to reduce to numbers does not mean one should not do the job.

A second consideration is that all nonprofit organizations operate under financial constraints, budgets, and objectives. Marketing, as part of the whole, comes under these constraints.

Third, within the organization a nonprofit marketer must compete with other parts of the organization for money and resources. Financial analysis may well help the marketing unit compete by providing stronger justification for a proposed course.

Finally, for nonprofit organizations in general, and for marketing programs in particular, it is all too easy to spend too little or too much. Much of the difficulty, as we shall see, lies with the difficulty of linking inputs with outputs, spending with results. Financial analysis disciplines managers and their plans, and thus can help keep marketing on the track. It can be summed up simply—attention to the numbers means better marketing decisions.

INITIAL IDEAS

You, the reader, probably think you know what I mean by cost. But almost surely you do not. Cost is a subtle, complex idea, and there are, in fact, many kinds of costs. You cannot hope to apply cost concepts correctly without recognizing that there are many kinds. Moreover, different parties of interest to the nonprofit marketer bear different costs. Some costs are borne by the nonprofit organization itself, others by clients, and still others by groups like middlemen, the public at large, or backers.

Underlying the idea of cost is sacrifice. The cost of an activity is what must be sacrificed to attain or accomplish it. Economists think of cost in just these terms. To them, an activity uses resources like labor and capital. Because the resources are being used for one activity they cannot be used for another; the cost of the activity is the alternative use of the resources. This alternative use is what must be sacrificed to accomplish some end. It leads to our first point: If nothing is sacrificed, there is no cost. It looks like a feckless truism; but in application appearances can deceive, and a manager can easily be fooled into thinking there are costs when in fact there are none.

It is enormously convenient to measure costs in monetary units; but it is not necessary to do so, and in fact one might say that cost has nothing to do with money. To a small boy with fifty cents to spend, the cost of a candy bar is not fifty cents but the package of chocolate covered raisins he cannot have. What he sacrifices is the raisins. The idea of sacrifice enables us to identify costs even where no money is involved. What is the cost of watching a program on the tube? It depends; but it is certainly not a monetary cost. Assuming you plan to watch for an hour, just to relax, there are two possibilities: Either there is more than one show you would like to watch, or there is only one. If there is only one, you are not sacrificing anything to watch that one show, and the cost of watching it is zero. If there is more than one show you would like to watch, the cost of watching the show you do watch is missing the other show you would like to watch.[1]

The final point of this introductory section deals with the kinds of costs to be treated in this book. They are the costs needed to choose among alternative solutions to a problem, that is, to make a decision. Such costs might be called decision costs, but here they will be called relevant costs, the term used by managerial economists.

Relevant costs have the following characteristics:

1. Relevant costs must reflect *sacrifices,* or they are not costs at all.
2. Relevant costs are estimates of *future* costs. No manager should trouble about past costs, except insofar as they help in estimating future costs.
3. Relevant costs are *incremental* costs. A manager can ignore all costs except the costs that differ between alternatives.

With few exceptions, relevant costs are the only costs to be considered in this book. Let us look at what this idea of relevant costs means. One way of putting it: If there is no decision to be made, there are no costs. A second way of putting it: There is no way of deciding what something costs without knowing what decision is under consideration. Thus the question, ''What does it cost?'' has no answer. The only proper reply is, ''What decision are you considering?'' A third way of putting it: Costs are *defined* by decisions.

As our final example of economic cost concepts that bear on decisions in nonprofit organizations, let us discuss opportunity costs. Actions or decisions use resources—labor, cash, time, and the like. (Actions that use none of these resources are of little import.) The resources used in one action can usually be used somewhere else, to accomplish something else. Thus, in performing an action, in producing one outcome, you use resources that could have produced another outcome. Just as the small boy pays for his sweet by foregoing chocolate covered raisins, you pay for the one by foregoing the other.

This is the thinking that underlies opportunity cost. The opportunity cost of any resource used to produce one outcome is the maximum that resource could produce elsewhere. It is, therefore, the value of an opportunity passed up or foregone. In nonprofit businesses it is convenient to measure values in cash, and the opportunity cost of one alternative is the net cash flow of the next best alternative.

What is the opportunity cost of a unit of blood to a blood donor? To answer this question, you must know what his alternatives are. If he can sell his blood to a commercial, for-profit blood bank, the opportunity cost of giving his blood away is the foregone payment from the commercial blood bank (less any expenses). Suppose, instead, that the donor feels selling his blood is unthinkable. Then the opportunity cost of the donation is the value of the next best thing he might do with his time. It may be to earn a couple of hours' pay, or to read, or to play.

What is the cost of a charitable contribution? Again, it depends. If a taxpayer takes a standard deduction, his charitable contributions will not be listed separately, and the cost is the full dollar amount of the contribution. If deductions are itemized, the after-tax cost is smaller than the before-tax cost, and the cost of an additional dollar's contribution is one minus the taxpayer's marginal tax rate. (That is, if your combined federal, state, and city marginal tax rate is 43 percent, each dollar you give reduces your after-tax income by fifty-seven cents.) In either case, the cost of the contribution is the amount of consumption foregone by making the contribution, which is an opportunity cost.

COSTS BORNE BY THE NONPROFIT ORGANIZATION

The Organization's Costs as Seen by an Economist[2]

Marginal costs are the extra costs that result from the production of one extra unit. Marginal here means at the edge, or at the border. Why are these important? Because most decisions involve small changes. Perhaps the clearest way of thinking about marginal costs is in terms of total costs, the sum of all the explicit costs borne by an organization, as well as implicit costs (those costs that reflect the sacrifices entailed in using resources the organization owns, like equipment or curatorial time). Marginal cost can then be defined as the change in total costs associated with a small change in the quantity of output (in a given period of time). A medical school, for example, is considering increasing the number of students it accepts each year by one. What is the marginal cost of the extra student? In principle, the process is straightforward. Estimate all costs, both explicit and implicit, of running the school without the extra student; then estimate all costs, both explicit and implicit, of running the school with the student. The difference between the two total cost figures is the marginal cost of adding the one student.[3]

Sunk costs are costs that are irrevocable in a given situation, which can mean one of two things. Either the cost has already been incurred and is a historical cost, or the cost involved is to be incurred some time in the future but will be the same regardless of which course is chosen. If the latter situation exists, sunk costs present no problem. They may be included in the estimated costs of the alternatives being considered, or they may be omitted. In either case, because they do not change, they will not affect the relative attractiveness of one course over another. If the former situation exists, they are costs that arose because of a decision already made at some time in the past, costs that *cannot be changed* by *any* decision that might be made now or in the *future.* (Note that a cost may become sunk without any cash changing hands. As soon as a cost can no longer be recalled or undone, it is sunk.)

The classic examples of sunk costs are capital expenditures in a turnpike or a bridge. Once these costs have been spent, they cannot be unspent or called back. As such, they have nothing whatever to do with decisions involving, say, tolls. In fact, this rule can be dignified as the *sunk cost principle:* When making any decision, ignore sunk costs.

But here again we see that decisions define costs. If a decision is needed about whether a mobile blood bank will make evening calls as well as day calls, the operating costs of the van will (probably) be the same in either case, and as sunk costs they can be ignored. But if the issue involves replacing the mobile unit with another mobile unit, or with a stationary blood bank, the costs of operating the van will no longer be the same and should be included in the analysis.

The admonition to ignore sunk costs is familiar to every student of economics, and is found in a number of folk sayings:

Don't cry over spilt milk.

That's water over the dam.

Don't throw good money after bad.

This last is a most practical rule for poker, ignored only by losers. Even Lady Macbeth understood, as when she tells Macbeth.

> Things without all remedy should be without regard;
> What's done is done.[4]

>   (Macbeth, III, ii)

There is also support for the sunk cost principle in elementary marketing analysis. No client (or purchasing agent) cares much what something has cost its producer. A motorist is indifferent to whether the bridge over the Humber estuary in England, the longest bridge in the world, has cost £11 million or £67 million; indifferent to the financial condition of the bridge authority; indifferent to the plight of the toll collectors and their union; indifferent to the embarrassment of the planners or the losses of the government. He asks himself only whether the toll is worth the extra convenience of the bridge, and if it is not, he takes another route, perhaps the old, crowded, cheap bridge. How unpersuasive would be an argument that ignores the sunk cost principle:

Well yes, it's true that we had some major cost overruns, and that the bridge finally cost £67 million. But you can see that we must get that money back. The government lent the money to pay 75 percent of the capital costs, and we must repay them. Also, we are required to pay our maintenance from toll revenues. I'm sure you understand. That is why cars will pay 80 pence, instead of 12 pence, as they do to cross the Severn Bridge.

As long as the motorist has any choice, this argument will not persuade him. So one way of seeing the sunk cost principle is as a reminder that demand is a powerful determinant of prices, and that cost is not. (We will return to this point in Chapter 12.)

Yet for all its powerful logic, the sunk cost principle is not congenial to the human soul. It did not console Macbeth. Folk wisdom notwithstanding, few people discover it on their own, and those who supposedly understand it often ignore it or misapply it. One takes to heart the advice not to cry over spilt milk for only the most trivial losses. The reader, then, can expect vigorous argument in government and public life on the question of including sunk costs with other costs relevant to a decision.

The final example of economic costs relevant to marketing decisions is that of opportunity costs. Imagine a souvenir shop in a city-run museum that sells books, postcards, posters, and so on. It considers adding a line of historical reproductions, "genuine, authentic reproductions," as they would be called. What is the cost? There are two costs: (1) a cash cost equal to landed store cost (which is the invoice price of the merchandise plus inbound freight less cash discounts), and (2) an opportunity cost equal to the reduction in net profits that results when shelf space, whose amount is fixed, is withdrawn from some item already being sold by the museum shop and used for the new merchandise. If the souvenir shop has space it is not using, however, there will be no loss of profits, and the cash costs will be the only relevant costs.

The Organization's Costs as Seen by Managers

Managers use different terms to talk about their costs. *Variable costs* are costs that vary in proportion to small changes in activity. They may vary with the physical output of an organization, a handling fee per unit, for example. They may vary with revenues, such as book royalties and commissions granted to state lottery sales agents, and some firms that specialize in fundraising charge a percentage of the amount raised. They may vary with volume of production, such as shipping, labor, materials, or packaging. Although variable costs differ in principle from marginal costs, most managers can use variable cost as a rough approximation for marginal cost.

The second important type of cost is *nonvariable costs*. These are costs whose total does not change over a given period of time or over a normal range of operation. These qualifications are important because few costs can be changed in the very short run, say a day, and all costs can be changed in the long run, say a period of years. In addition, nonvariable costs may well not change as an activity is increased (or decreased) a little, within normal operating ranges; but they may well increase if activity is increased sharply above normal levels.

Traditional examples of nonvariable costs would include capital costs for equipment and buildings, most of the cost of a maintenance crew, and most of the cost of supervisors and administrators. In fact, however, these traditional examples of nonvariable costs beg the question. Like variable costs, nonvariable costs do not exist in the absolute. They are defined by the decision that is under consideration. Costs that appear to be given, to be ineluctably set for one period of time, may turn out to be at least partially controllable under a different cost control system. Imagine the legal staff of a public housing authority whose budget is not charged for the office space it uses. Under this control system, the legal staff will need more space than under a system in which its budget is charged with the rent.

And what is nonvariable in one decision may be variable in another. As we have said before, costs are defined by the decision. The costs of running a welfare branch office will be nonvariable for most day-to-day operating decisions; but when consideration is being given to closing the branch office, or consolidating its functions with others, these costs are no longer nonvariable. (However, as they do not vary with the output of the office, they are not variable, either.)

It should be pointed out that nonvariable costs go by other names. Perhaps the most common is fixed costs. They are also sometimes called capacity costs, because regardless of how much, or how little, a nonprofit organization is turning out, there are certain expenses that it must incur simply to stay open. These are the costs of providing ''capacity.'' But this is a definition that is not made with a decision in mind, and hence it is not as useful as it might be.

It would seem the world of costs is neatly divided in two, variable or nonvariable costs. But it is not the case. There are in-between costs, costs that change as an activity changes, although not in direct proportion. These are called semivariable costs (or, by some, semifixed costs). They mix two costs; they are part variable and part nonvariable, and they usually increase in steps: For every ten welfare workers, an additional supervisor is needed; for every additional million in lottery sales, three more clerks, and so on.

There is still one more cost that is neither variable nor nonvariable, but it is very important to nonprofit marketers. It is the cost associated with programs undertaken by an organization. Because such costs arise from administrative decisions, because they are associated with programs, they are called *programmed costs*. Instead of taking a percentage of the funds raised, many fundraisers charge a flat fee. To the organization that is raising the funds, it is a programmed cost. It does not vary with anything, and therefore it is not a variable, or semivariable, cost. It is not a cost that is set for one period, more or less out of the control of the manager, and thus it is not a nonvariable cost.

Instead, it is a cost that is caused by a decision to undertake a fundraising campaign, and it can be avoided if the organization drops the idea.

Programmed costs are neither variable, nor semivariable, nor nonvariable. They do not depend on volume, nor are they set and unalterable, as nonvariable costs often appear to be. Programmed costs arise because management wills them. There is no necessity about such costs. They can change each year, and the changes can be large.

- To fill an 1,800-seat hall for a series of concerts of contemporary music requires a certain amount of promotional expenses—newspaper advertising, posters, radio spots, perhaps some direct mail. But if the concerts are put into a 400-seat hall in the following year, presumably the promotional expenses needed to fill the hall will drop sharply. These promotional expenses are programmed costs. They are certainly not variable costs, nor in any sense are they fixed. They are associated with the contemporary music program, and hence are "programmed."

- A union planning an organizing campaign faces sizeable costs that are associated with the campaign and that happen not to rise in proportion to the company's size. They are programmed costs without question. And the fact that costs don't go up in proportion to size but member dues do makes organizing a big firm more attractive than organizing a small one.

These examples also illustrate another important characteristic of programmed costs, namely, that the relationship between input and output, between expenditure and result, is hard to call. In such situations, there is no practical way of deciding the lowest cost for a given output, or even the direction of change of costs that represents an improvement. There are no practical ways, for example, of deciding the lowest advertising budget needed to support a "Get Out the Vote" campaign, or how much should be spent on a safe sex campaign aimed at teenagers. If he said it, John Wanamaker said it better: "I know half of my advertising is wasted, but I don't know which half."

With production costs there is at least a clear link between inputs and outputs, and for a given output and level of quality we can safely say that less cost is better. With programmed costs there are situations in which more is better, and others in which less is better. It is often hard to tell one from the other. In addition, the relationship is inverted. Production costs are *caused by* sales and production. Programmed costs, particularly in marketing, aim to *cause* sales and production.

Moreover, programmed costs often come in indivisible lumps. A state development agency can send a display to a trade show, but it cannot send half a display. Advertising must be inserted a minimum number of times in media to maintain continuity. There is a similar type of threshold with a salesman calling on an account. He must call a minimum number of times each year or chance losing the business altogether. There is no necessary linear relationship on the other hand. Sending two displays to the trade show will not double sales. Two ads or two salesmen do not necessarily sell more than one.[5]

Two other types of costs are often encountered—avoidable costs and traceable costs. *Avoidable costs* are costs that can be avoided by ceasing to do something, and by not doing anything else in its place. Such costs come to mind naturally when thinking about closing down, or doing away with, some operation, like closing a naval depot or a state park for the winter. But when an operation starts up there will be costs that arise because of the new operation and that would not have been incurred if the new operation had not started up. These costs, too, are avoidable costs. As J. M. Clark wrote, "whenever a policy is being considered which will involve overhead expenditures that could otherwise be avoided, they are part of the cost of that policy."[6] In common usage, avoidable cost is what many mean when they simply say "cost." Note that avoidable costs can be variable, nonvariable, or even programmed, depending on the decision.

Traceable costs are costs that can be assigned or traced to a source responsible for it—a person, a service, a class of client, a middleman, a function, a department, or a region. They can be any of the costs already discussed. Traceable costs are sometimes called direct costs, in that there is a direct link visible between the cause of the cost and the cost itself. The opposite of traceable cost is common cost, a cost that cannot be traced to a single source.

The four costs that have been discussed—variable, semivariable, nonvariable, and programmed—are the most useful to a nonprofit manager. For many decisions in nonprofit organizations, it is possible to reclassify costs recorded in the accounting system to get a better idea of the cost changes a decision is likely to bring about. In fact, merely roughly dividing all costs into programmed, variable, and nonvariable costs would probably substantially improve the manager's understanding of the implications of his decisions. In the rest of this book, I shall use variable, nonvariable, and programmed costs frequently.

The first step in making use of these cost concepts is simply using them. It involves estimating variable, nonvariable, and programmed costs and putting them in a useful format. Suppose we are a university press considering a new edition of one of our better sellers, a book on the deserts of North America. The plates are expensive to prepare, but the setting of the text is no more complicated than for most books. Let us say we are to compose 200 pages of text at $34 a page and 120 pages of four-color photographs at $63 a page, for a total composition cost of $200 \times \$34 + 120 \times \$63 = \$14,360$. The cost for paper, ink, binding, and jacketing varies almost directly with the print order; say, it works out at about $21.00 a copy. The suggested list price is to be $64.95, and the price to the bookseller will be the list price less approximately 41 percent, or $\$64.95 \times (1 - .41) = \$38.32$. Royalties will be 12 percent of the list price or $7.79. (A good deal. Usually we pay 15 percent.) We hope to sell 4,000 copies, and we plan to spend $27,000 for advertising.

Table 3.1
Pro Forma Marketing Control Statement

	(000)	Per Copy
Revenue	$153.3	$38.32
Variable costs		
Royalties	31.2	7.79
Production	84.0	21.00
	$116.0	$28.79
Gross marketing contribution	$38.1	$9.53
Programmed costs		
Composition	14.4	
Advertising	27.0	
Net marketing contribution	$(3.3)	

The Marketing Control Statement

From these figures we can prepare a *marketing control statement* (MCS) that contains the important variable and programmed costs (see Table 3.1).

Note that the cash an NPO receives serves three ends: Part goes to pay for the cost of producing the product or service, part goes to pay for the cost of marketing the product, and what is left over contributes toward meeting all other costs.

The MCS summarizes the financial consequences of bringing out the new edition. Gross marketing contribution results when variable costs are subtracted from variable revenues, and this figure is itself variable. Each time the press sells another copy of the book, it increases its cash by $9.53. (In standard marketing parlance, gross marketing contribution is called simply "contribution.")

Programmed costs are not variable, and there is no point in even pretending they are, which is why they have not been shown on a per-copy basis. If we can sell 4,000 books, as we hope, we will not cover our planned programmed costs and leave negative net marketing earnings of $3,300. This figure, too, is cash; it is cash still left to be paid after paying both variable costs and all programmed costs. Were it positive, it would be cash available to pay any other expenses the press has. Note that it is not a profit. The correct term is "contribution."

Figures cast in this form also make it easy to answer "what if" questions:

- *What if* the press thinks it may be able to sell more than 4,000 copies? What is the minimum it must sell in order to cover the programmed costs of the book? Answer: ($14.4 + $27.0)/$9.53 = 4,340. As long as the book sells 4,340 copies, the press will cover the book's programmed costs, and thus it will break even.

- *What if* the press spends not $27,000 for advertising but $43,000? To just cover the extra $16,000 advertising, the press must sell an extra $16,000/$9.53 = 1,680 copies.

The marketing control statement brings together all the major items that marketing is responsible for: revenue, which comes from sales; and net marketing earnings, which are directly related to sales and programmed costs. (In the case of the university press, only advertising is a marketing controllable. Marketing should not be given responsibility for the costs of composition.)

A WORD ABOUT FUND ACCOUNTING

Businesses keep one set of books in which they record all their financial transactions, in and out. Nonprofit organizations do not do this. Their financial accounts are broken into pieces called "funds," each of which records transactions, in and out.[7]

Imagine your home as a financial entity. If your household were a business, it would use a single checking account. Receipts would go into the checking account, and as bills were paid money would be withdrawn from the checking account. At any time one could look at the check stubs and get a current balance to see where the household stood. Add to this an accounting of assets and outstanding debts, and one could draw up the household's balance sheet. If the household kept track of receipts and expenditures over time, at the end of the year it could work up a statement of the household receipts, expenses, and the balance of the two. Thus, it would get the standard financial summaries called balance sheets and income statements.

Now imagine your household is an NPO. It would not use one checking account. It would use several. It might devote one to household expenses (say), another to medical, a third to debt repayment, a fourth to savings, and a fifth to everyday expenses. Each checking account would receive deposits from time to time; and checks would be drawn on each to pay bills, but only bills that belonged to that account. One would never use the household account to buy food, for example. From time to time the husband and wife, acting as trustees of the five accounts, would sit down and decide to move funds from one account to another. They might withdraw some money from savings and deposit it in the everyday account to meet some extra everyday expenses; or surplus might arise in the medical account that could be moved partly into savings and partly used to pay debts.

The business household would draw up one balance sheet and one income statement. The nonprofit household would draw up five balance sheets and five income statements, one for each of its five accounts; and in addition it would record in its books transfers from one account to another. These might be called interaccount transfers; but as the accounts are called funds in nonprofit accounting, it is best to use the correct term, interfund transfers.

Fund accounting does not just seem complicated at first glance. It is still complicated after considerable exposure to it. It arose to meet the legal obligations of the nonprofit organization and moral expectations of backers. Let us say that a woman promises to give her prep school $25,000 a year for the rest of her life, the money to be used to build an endowment, the earnings of which will provide scholarships for minority students. She insists that only earnings on the endowment be used and not the endowment itself. How can she be reassured that the money will be used only for that one purpose? The prep school will set up a fund, a separate accounting entity. Her gifts and earnings on the endowment will be paid into the fund, and cash will be withdrawn to fund the scholarships. Her reassurance that the money will be used as she directs comes from the existence of this separate fund and her confidence in the capacities of the headmaster and the school's board of trustees who are legally and morally bound to follow her wishes.

Every nonprofit has a fund for everyday expenses. Usually it is called the Operating Fund or Current Fund. Most have other funds as well, typically like a Plant Fund, an Endowment Fund, and a Special Purpose Fund. An old non-profit or a large one may have hundreds of funds, each reflecting a specific gift or donation or purpose. As with the five checking accounts kept by the nonprofit household, each fund is an independent, self-balancing account with its own balance sheet and an income statement, and there will be an end-of-year set of interfund transfers. NPOs often publish abbreviated financial statements that show only the condition of the Operating Fund before interfund transfers. These can be misleading.

It is the transfers that complicate things to the outsider. Here is College A that gets all of its income from tuition. It has no endowment. Its operating fund statement looks like this:

		Operating Fund (millions)
Tuition		$70
Interest on endowment		0
Expenses		
Faculty	$40	
Administration	15	
Library	10	
Scholarships	10	75
Surplus		$(5)

Like any business facing a deficit, it faces a cold winter unless the administration can raise tuition or cut faculty costs, library costs, or the costs of its scholarships.

College B is just like College A except that it has a $200 million endowment that earns 7 percent a year or $14 million. Its books look like this:

		Operating Fund (millions)	Endowment Fund (millions)
Tuition		$70	
Interest on Endowment			$14
Expenses			
Faculty	$40		
Administration	15		
Library	10		
Scholarships	10	75	—
Surplus		$(5)	$14

At the end of the year College B transfers $5 million from the Endowment Fund to the Operating Fund to meet the operating deficit. Its final statements look like this:

		Operating Fund (millions)	Endowment Fund (millions)
Tuition		$70	
Interest on Endowment			$14
Expenses			
Faculty	$40		
Administration	15		
Library	10		
Scholarships	10	75	—
Surplus Before Interfund Transfers		$(5)	$14
Interfund Transfers		5	(5)
Surplus After Interfund Transfers		0	9

	(millions)
Endowment at Beginning of Year Amount	$200
Earnings on Endowment	14
Interfund Transfers	(5)
Endowments at End of Year	$209

That, in its essence, is how fund accounting works. To understand the financial condition of a business one must analyze its balance sheets and income statements; to understand the financial condition of a nonprofit one must analyze balance sheets and income statements for all of its principal funds, and scrutinize interfund transfers as well. With only the statement for the Operating Fund, one cannot draw any sensible conclusions as to the financial health of an NPO. In fact, one might well draw erroneous conclusions.

In spite of this, nonprofit organizations often publicize a summary of the condition of their Operating Fund, leaving the average person to assume that the Operating Fund is all there is. Why would they do this? For two reasons. The first is that few clients or backers want to read financial statements. They do not have the training. Even more important, they do not have the interest.

When clients do want full information, they need only ask and most NPOs will give. So an abbreviated statement does no harm, and in fact it will be read more broadly than the full financial statements. The second reason, by far the more important reason, is that it helps them raise money. Which college has the stronger fundraising appeal, College B as represented by its Operating Fund or College B as represented by both its funds plus interfund transfers?

	College B's Operating Fund	College B Both Funds
Tuition	$70	$70
Interest	—	14
Total	70	84
Expenses		
Faculty	$40	$40
Administration	15	15
Library	10	10
Scholarships	10 75	10 75
Surplus	(5)	9

WHAT BREAKEVEN MEANS

Now we consider what breakeven means. "Breakeven," "breaking even," "just covering costs" are often heard in both public and private nonprofit organizations. They not only highlight the difference between profit and nonprofit financial objectives. They provide reassurance that the social contract between society and the NPO—that it does not gouge, it does not charge what the traffic will bear—is intact. Nonprofit managers must realize, however, that just covering costs doesn't mean anything until they know which costs. A convenient way to look at this issue of which costs are covered is in terms of the marketing control statement.

Breakeven #1: Revenues cover variable costs and thus produce a zero gross marketing contribution. Since variable costs are mostly production costs, a service that breaks even on this level can be seen as just paying for the costs of its own production but no more. Marketing expenditures must come from other pockets.

Breakeven #2: Revenues cover variable costs and programmed costs and thus produce a zero net marketing contribution. At this level a service that breaks even covers both its production costs and marketing costs. It does not burden the rest of the NPO. It certainly does not generate any cash to help it.

Breakeven #3: Revenues do not cover variable and programmed costs but do cover costs after an interfund transfer. This is how College B broke even. It ran a deficit in its Operating Fund but arranged to transfer just enough from its Endowment Fund to cover the deficit. Many nonprofits and nonprofit programs break even on this definition. That is, the program runs at a cash deficit, as indicated by a negative Net Marketing Contribution; but by a bookkeeping entry, an interfund transfer, the program is made to break even.

Breakeven #3 is much beloved by the public sector. A government agency finds a program running at a deficit—that is, a negative net marketing contribution—but it wants to claim that the program breaks even and thus perhaps is no drain on the taxpayer. Nothing could be simpler. Either (a) have some other government body pick up some of the expenses in its budget, thus removing them from the agency's program, or (b) do not count all of the costs. A standard cost for government agencies to skip is depreciation, but it may decide that maintenance or pensions or what-have-you is not a "proper" charge to the program and simply leave them out.

How can one know which breakeven a nonprofit organization is using? By asking and by reading financial statements carefully. Occasionally, the financial statements contain a giveaway: Revenues equal costs to the penny. This can only happen when an interfund transfer has been made at the end of the fiscal year, after the marketing control statement (or other financial statement) has been prepared.

The moral should be plain: Don't accept "breakeven" on its face. Find out what it means and how it is calculated.

Estimating Costs

We have looked in great detail at the general nature of costs in nonprofit organizations. Now we turn briefly to the question of measuring these costs instead of merely talking about them.

For costs borne by the organization, nonprofit managers, like businessmen, look to their accounting system. It should serve four functions: determining income and preparing financial statements, motivating employees and managers, controlling costs, and aiding decision making.

Accountants cannot classify costs as relevant to a decision, for reasons that should be familiar: The way the problem is defined determines which costs are relevant. Therefore, nonprofit managers must view the costs provided by their accounting system only as a starting place. They must add some costs not provided by the accounting system (opportunity costs); they must take away others (those not involving any sacrifice, like sunk costs); and in all cases they must work with estimates of future costs, not the historic costs captured by the accountant.

They must be particularly alert to pare away allocated nonvariable costs from variable cost estimates. Regardless of what accountants call a cost, managers must find out how the cost behaves—whether it is in fact comprised only of costs that vary with the activity in which they are interested or whether it is smudged and loaded with cost allocations. Cost allocations are necessary in preparing financial statements, but they are useless in working out the implications of a proposed course of action. Suppose, for example, you know that the average cost of collecting a unit of blood is $59.50.[8] This average cost would typically include (1) variable costs that vary with the number of donors, like the plastic bags for catching the blood; (2) semivariable costs that vary with the number of medical personnel on site; (3) semivariable costs that vary with the location of the blood collection site and its hours of operation; and (4) nonvariable costs that (within broad limits) do not vary with any of the above. With such a jumble of costs, it is impossible to answer reasonable questions such as how much it will cost if the donor load goes up 3 percent next month or how much will be saved if it goes down by 18 percent.

Let us return to the medical school that is considering increasing its enrollment, let us say, by twenty. The cost of the increase is the increment in total costs caused by the extra students. It is hardly surprising that the associate dean of the medical school cannot go to the accounting system for an estimate of this cost: The system was not set up to aid in making such decisions. Such decisions come along once in a great while, and setting up an accounting system to furnish cost estimates for such infrequent decisions would be foolish. Instead, the proposal calls for a separate study, much as capital budgeting and investment decisions that arise in businesses do.

At heart, this special study is nothing more than an examination of the various expenditures made by the medical school to determine which ones will change. Will we have to increase library expenditures? No. Then ignore the library. Will the school's liability insurance increase? Yes. Find out by how much. Will the school need more deans? No. A sunk cost for this decision. Ignore it. And so on. The manager simply keeps asking: Will this change? Does that differ between options? Will this vary? This is a chore, but it is a manageable chore, and it will provide the answer (or an approximation that is good enough).

QUESTION

1. Managers call some of their costs fixed costs. If costs really are fixed, if they cannot be changed, does that mean they are sunk? Does that mean that fixed costs are irrelevant to some business decisions? Which ones?

NOTES

1. The cost of operating the set—electricity and the like—is irrelevant, as will be shown later. Note that there is a tiny proportion of the television audience that finds the cost of missing the second show too high. They watch one and tape the second, or try to watch both at the same time on two sets.

2. For a more detailed discussion of costs, see "What Every Marketer Needs to Know About Costs," pp. 17–38, in David L. Rados, *Pushing the Numbers in Marketing* (Westport, Quorum: 1992).

3. Of course, no one would proceed this way in practice. You would simply skip over

the costs you knew would not change and concentrate only on those costs you felt would change. The answer, however, should be the same.

4. Pronouncing on Shakespeare is only slightly easier than explaining the Federal Tax Code. It turns out that although Lady Macbeth says that what's done is done, what happens in *Macbeth* shows that she is wrong. The evil deeds of Macbeth and his Lady do indeed come back to torment them and finally destroy them. For this explanation I am indebted to Thomas Hambury, private conversation, October 26, 1992.

5. Some would deem the usage of "cost" in this chapter as loose. Let us see why. When you spend (say) eight dollars for two six-packs, you have sacrificed nothing. You have merely swapped eight dollars for some beer, and presumably you are as well off as you were before. Before you had eight dollars and no beer, now you have beer but no eight dollars; but your stock of economic goods retains its overall value. Now you drink the beer and your stock of economic goods falls. It is this *decrease* that is the cost of the beer, because it is the decrease that is the sacrifice. Thus, some careful writers on economic topics call the eight dollars an outlay or expenditure, not a cost. With a six-pack the distinction is hardly worth making. But with a durable good, like an automobile, the distinction is much more useful. When you buy a $16,000 car, you swap money for car, with the $16,000 being merely an outlay. The cost of owning the car is its loss of value over time, or depreciation. See the discussion in Armen A. Alchian and William R. Allen, *University Economics* (Belmont, Calif.: Wadsworth, 1967), pp. 221–246.

6. J.M. Clark, *Studies in the Economics of Overhead Costs* (Chicago: University of Chicago Press, 1923), p. 21.

7. Whether fund accounting is a good thing is a matter of some dispute. Start with these three articles, if you wish to pursue the matter: Regina E. Herzlinger and H. David Sherman, "Advantages of Fund Accounting in 'Nonprofits.' " *Harvard Business Review* (May-June 1980): 94–105; Robert N. Anthony, "Making Sense of Non-business Accounting." Ibid.: 83–93; and Richard Yeagar, "Is Fund Accounting Necessary?" *Fund Raising Management* (September 1987): 74–80.

8. For a discussion of the costs of collecting blood, containing dated figures, see P. Jacobs and W.S. Rawson, "Donor Recruitment and Blood Collection Costs for Red Cross Blood Centers." *Transfusion* 18, no. 3 (May-June 1978): 291–297.

Chapter 4

Behavior of Clients and Backers

It is impossible to influence human behavior without a theory. It may be simple; it need not be formal, it need not be explicit; but there will be a theory, a collection of general statements about motives, attitudes, personality, background, about who responds to what and how much they respond. We smile when we learn from Plutarch how the elders of Miletus solved a public health problem, an epidemic of suicide among young women, by decreeing that the bodies be displayed naked in the agora. Their unstated theory was sound—or wise—the epidemic ended, and the style passed to some new usage.[1]

THE NEED FOR A THEORY OF BEHAVIOR

Like the elders, most marketing executives must make do with notions and convictions about human behavior that they refine over time on the basis of experience and, perhaps, study. Although they are crude, these notions do serve in practice, although they are rarely clearly formulated and, in fact, often only exist on the subconscious level and are implied by the executive's actions. This lack of definition is to be expected. Few marketers have the training or inclination to think deeply or rigorously, and the phenomenon itself—the behavior of clients in settings where they have many choices—is complex. Simple rules of thumb survive only because they receive no scrutiny or, dare one suggest, because they work as well as the elaborate confections of marketing scholars.

There is an analogy between what marketers do and what professors do in professional schools—law, divinity, medicine, public health, perhaps business. Professors want to contribute to the advancement of knowledge and they want to influence their students, not merely by teaching them something but by changing their behavior. An important part of what goes on in professional schools is socialization, training the student to act like a professional, one of the initiates. Where do the professors get the theory of human behavior on which they base their choice of assignments, teaching style, and grades?

Certainly, not as part of their graduate studies; such subjects are demeaning. They simply pick it up as most of us do. They have been on the receiving end of a great deal of education themselves, which gives them a number of ideas; they talk with their colleagues about problems they have and how they solve them; they experiment, first trying one thing, then another, and finally, most useful of all, they grade papers and exams, where things not learned become uncomfortably obvious. They probably do not give much thought to their theories of education, formally or informally. Their failure to study does not arise from a lack of anything to study. Philosophers have been writing on education for thousands of years, and from time to time their theories have been put to test, most often in the twentieth century; and the life of the mind at most American colleges is quickened by the presence of schools of education on their campuses. For professors, then, there is both theory and opportunity to use theory.

Now consider, as an anticlimax, the plight of the marketers. They deal with four groups whose behavior and attitudes they wish to influence: competitors, middlemen, customers, and, more and more, government regulators. Marketing per se has nothing to say about the last, and it has only recently begun to theorize about competitors and middlemen. In the area of consumer behavior, there has been a great deal of research in the past thirty years, and some progress. Still, practicing marketers should not expect to find much specific in academic theories. They must do as teachers of marketing do: Take what seems to be useful from wherever, experiment, study if they wish, refine their beliefs, and go forward in dark uncertainty.

Marketing is not unique in its ignorance. One would expect other nonprofit managers to focus much of their energies on the behavior of others who are important to their organizations. But this is not the case. How much do union organizers know about what makes employees vote Yay or Nay in a representation election?

One group of authors writes.

Despite the universal interest in what has influenced our elections, interpretation has scarcely risen above the simplest impressionism. The explanations offered for an electoral result are astonishingly varied; they depend typically on the slenderest evidence, and disagreements are commonplace even among knowledgeable observers.[2]

But another author says it better: "No one knows why employees vote as they do in representation elections."[3]

Marketing lays claim, rather pretentiously perhaps, to being applied social science. That it is social there can be no doubt, but it is far more applied than science. Theories of human behavior—of competitors, middlemen, and consumers—should underlie and enlighten all of its activities, but what theories there are, with a few exceptions, are unsatisfactory intellectually, empirically, and aesthetically. Why is this? For one thing, some of what the theorists serve up is trivial. Dorwin Cartwright, in analyzing bond drives in World War II, enunciated as his first principle that "The 'message' (i.e., information, facts, etc.) must reach the sense organs of the persons who are to be influenced."[4] Which says nothing more than out of sight, out of mind. Marketing theorists have had a great deal of trouble with concepts and definitions: At least fifty-five definitions of the important notion of brand loyalty have appeared in the marketing journals.[5] Measurement poses vexatious problems, too. Many marketing theorists believe that involvement is an important concept in understanding the client, that the client with little involvement in an action or an issue differs from one who is highly involved. But how should involvement be defined? How should it be measured? Marketers have also been prone to publishing a piece of evidence on a phenomenon and then never returning to it. As Jacoby says, "Fewer than a dozen individuals . . . have conducted five or more separate investigations in systematic and sequentially integrated fashion designed to provide incremental knowledge regarding a single issue."[6] Ehrenberg identifies yet another source of weak theory when he correctly lays the blame on the failure of academics to study how consumers actually behave before they begin to theorize about them.[7]

THINKING ABOUT SMOKING

The result of this unhappy state of affairs is that practicing marketers must take their theories where they can find them. And they may come from many sources. As an example, let us suppose we want to discourage teenagers from smoking. There is no general cure for cancer nor is there any sign that one is about to be found. But lung cancer is clearly caused by smoking.

If you smoke cigarettes, you increase your risk of dying from lung cancer tenfold to fifty fold, the exact value depending on how much you smoke, the country you live in and various other factors. . . . There is every reason to believe that the abolition of cigarette smoking would largely eliminate lung cancer, the commonest of all forms of death from cancer.[8]

It is hard, however, to imagine a government in a developed nation having the wisdom, or courage, to eradicate smoking. So the effort to discourage teenagers from smoking must be partly based on persuasion, which means we need a theory. We need two theories in fact, one that deals with the decision to begin smoking, the other with the decision to continue smoking.

Starting to smoke. As is so often the case with significant social problems, there has been much research and there are many theoretical points of view. For instance:

- *Anthropological Influences:* Smoking is associated with the transition from childhood to adulthood. In this sense it belongs with other activities that make up the *rites de passage*—sexual experimentation, increasing freedom in making personal decisions, driving, and drinking.

- *Role Theory:* To a social psychologist a role is a pattern of expected behavior associated with a particular social status. And what is expected of an adult? Smoking, for one. It is grown-up, daring. It symbolizes the freedom and attractiveness of adulthood.

- *Family Influences:* One would expect these to have an influence, but the studies contradict each other, some linking parents' smoking with their child's, others showing no such link.

- *Ethnic Influences:* To the adolescent member of an ethnic minority, smoking may reflect assimilation in the American culture, or emancipation from his ethnic culture.

- *Peer Pressures:* Smokers are aroused to smoke by seeing others smoke, by smelling the acrid smoke, and by the added emotional support they get by smoking in the presence of others. There are also strong pressures to conform in groups of friends, so the nonsmoker is under pressure to smoke if most of his friends do.

- *Emotional Factors:* The first cigarette is always unpleasant, but young smokers quickly find smoking pleasurable and soothing. There are tactile and oral pleasures from the contact of the cigarette with the fingers and the mouth, and there are the pleasures arising from the irritation of the mucosa by the hot smoke and from the stimulation of nicotine.

From such a recitation, one could easily conclude that everyone tries smoking. But this is not the case. Many never try even one cigarette. Still more try one or two and then stop. Any theory that explains why one youngster begins to smoke must be able to explain why another does not.

Continuing to smoke. If it proves impossible to reach the adolescent experimenting with smoking, it may be possible to reach him after he has become a smoker and persuade him to stop. To do this, we must ask why smokers continue to smoke, despite all the information available to them.

- *Environmental Factors:* Ashtrays, vending machines, stores selling cigarettes are everywhere (well, almost everywhere), but legislation, regulation, and a growing hostility to smoking makes smokers pariahs. It is still easy to smoke in the 1990s, and it is hard to avoid smokers. In addition, there is cigarette advertising, which even nonsmokers cannot avoid.

- *Self-Concept:* For many smokers, smoking is not an activity outside themselves. Instead, it is an integral part of the smoker's self-concept. Not just the fact of smoking either, but how one smokes becomes part of the "real me."

- *Affective Influences:* Almost all smokers say they like smoking, that it tastes good. Cigarettes also serve to reduce tension.

- *Addictive Consequences:* Most smokers appear to be psychologically addicted to cigarettes. There probably is a physical addition to the drug nicotine. Mark Twain's quip covers both, ''To cease smoking is the easiest thing I ever did; I ought to know because I've done it a thousand times.''

This is a sample of what one could encounter in beginning to work on the problem of smoking. The marketer scorns the boundaries of academic disciplines and takes his ideas where he finds them. Like the magpie, he is:

> . . . a deft
> committer of theft,
> collector of things, of coins, pins, and any dazzling bit
> he can light on—junk or gem.[9]

''Junk or gem''—just so long as it appears to be useful in solving the problem.

Note how general this theoretical discussion has been. It is of little use to marketers to learn that smoking is related to the ''real me'' or that peers exert powerful pressures. It is of little use because to develop marketing programs marketers need answers to a much more specific set of questions.

Proposal	Some Key Questions
Increase the tax on cigarettes.	How much will consumption fall as price rises? How will smokers adapt to higher prices—smoke the cigarettes farther down? *Which* smokers are most sensitive to price? How much will smuggling increase?
Do away with advertising.	What influence does advertising have on the decision to start smoking? To continue smoking? What changes in marketing programs would be expected from the tobacco companies—lower prices? More sales promotion? Which smokers are most likely to be influenced by the advertising?
Encourage counteradvertising.	Which smokers are likely to be affected by counteradvertising? How many of them are there? Is counteradvertising cost effective? Would it be worth *buying* time for counteradvertising?
Limit the number of outlets and times of day when cigarettes can be sold.	How would smokers adjust to less convenient purchase? How would beginners adjust? Would they smoke less or simply buy more at any one time? Which smokers are most sensitive to such a program?
Encourage sale of very low tar and nicotine cigarettes, or of ''substitute'' cigarettes.	Will smokers smoke more cigarettes to get the same amount of tar and nicotine, or will they cut back? Will they smoke them farther down? If regular cigarettes are still available, will they smoke them? Are beginning smokers likely to think of the fake fags as sissy cigarettes?

We cannot expect to find the answers to any of these questions in the theoretical discussion above, or to the dozens of others that would arise in the course of formulating specific action plans.

ANALYZING BEHAVIOR

A General Approach

The steps involved in analyzing client behavior are easy to describe, but each step can be complicated.

Learn from others. The first step is a reminder not to go it alone. There are others in the organization who have ideas as to why clients (and backers) behave as they do. There are others outside the organization with similar ideas. There are other organizations facing the same problems from whom one can extract some useful ideas. There will often be others who have studied the problem and published. It may be possible to find others who have studied the problem and not published.

List the important factors. The second step calls for a list of factors likely to influence the client (or backer). It is here that one must begin to exercise judgment, which means first that I cannot explain very well what has to be done, and second that it is quite possible to make a hash of this step.

What is wanted is a list of important influences over which the marketer has some control. But in the process, important influences that cannot be controlled will also be uncovered or identified. These latter are helpful in that they lead to better understanding of how clients (and backers) behave, and to better predictions as to the outcome of the programs. The weather cannot be controlled, but in trying to understand voters, weather should be on the list. At the very least, predictions can be hedged: "Unless it rains. . . ." It is my belief that explicit models of client behavior (or backer behavior) rest on only a small number of independent influences. This means that practical marketing programs can typically be built on two or three, or four, or five interests, with all the rest—the myriad of other factors that in some way affect clients' behavior—being ignored.[10] The second step, therefore, calls for first listing many factors, and then separating out a few relevant interests from the many.

Model the decision process. In the third step, a model is built. This means, in most cases, that the small number of relevant interests are drawn together into some sort of order. A natural way of doing this that has also proved useful in analyzing many marketing issues is to model the behavior of clients in terms of the decisions they make. In this approach, the client is seen as going through a decision-making process. This all-purpose model will be explained shortly.

A second useful way to model the behavior of clients is in terms of the stages they typically pass through. Suppose we wish to get a better understanding of how a subscription audience develops for a company specializing in modern dance. Make a start by assuming, say, that a subscriber moves through three

Figure 4.1
A Simple Model of Audience Development

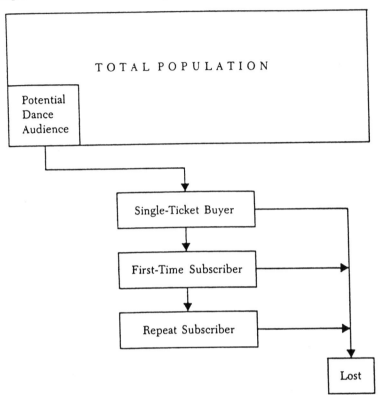

stages: first buying single tickets, then becoming a subscriber, and finally deciding to subscribe again. This process is illustrated in Figure 4.1.

Note first that there are no client interests in Figure 4.1. It is a picture of behavior only, of effects not causes. (Actually the picture shows only the resting points. The behavior occurs *between* the boxes in the picture.) But it suggests a great deal:

1. There is a possible segmentation scheme, namely, single-ticket buyers, first-time subscribers, and repeat subscribers. The last two would be a cinch to identify and treat differently. The first would be a bit harder, but not much harder.

2. The picture calls for measurement. What else besides ticket-buying behavior characterizes these three segments?

3. What are the dynamics involved? What proportion of first-time subscribers convert to repeat subscribers? What proportion of repeat subscribers repeat? What proportion of single-ticket buyers stop buying, and why? What is the half-life of a single-ticket buyer, or a repeat subscriber?

4. How much of the potential dance audience is the company reaching?

5. The picture is simple, showing an orderly movement from top to bottom. What proportion of our repeat subscribers progress this way? Are there paths missing on the diagram that we should know about? For example, how many subscribers skip the single-ticket box or how much of the "lost" audience returns at some point in the future?

Answers to these questions would go a long way toward helping the dance company improve its subscription efforts.[11]

Research. The fourth and final step is research. The picture of the dance audience discussed above suggests many questions. Providing answers is, in simple terms, the job of marketing research. Chapter 6 will treat marketing research.

Outside Influences on Behavior

The behavior of clients and backers is influenced by many factors that are beyond the marketer's art. Behavior is influenced by people around us, for example. Clients are members of *social classes,* which imprint some commonality on their behavior. *Family influences* can be strong in certain settings, as can such *cultural influences* as religion. It goes without saying that we would not try to teach effective means of birth control to devout Roman Catholics. But it took family planning agencies in the poor countries many years to become aware of the peasants' deep desire for children as economic wealth and as protection against an uncertain old age. People are influenced by the *roles* they play—I am a professor and am expected to be wooly-headed, pompous, warm, and engaging; you are a student, say, and are expected to take notes, pass exams, complain about your workload, and mispell common English words. It was once taken for a certainty that a senior business executive was a Republican, and when the chairman of the board came around he said, simply, "Make your checks payable to the Republican National Committee and send them to me." Outside influences like these influence behavior, but they cannot themselves be influenced, and as a practical matter, marketers take them as given. They influence them in that they must adapt to them.

The same is true of many inside influences that we know, or believe, influence behavior. Certainly, personality traits affect the choices clients make, as do their motives and their confidence in their ability to choose well. These factors, too, marketers must expect not to influence very much, if at all; instead they will adapt their programs to what they know about such traits of their clients (and backers).

But there are inside influences that can, without question, be touched by a marketing effort. A client's beliefs can sometimes be changed, his awareness heightened, his attitudes shifted, his opinions corrected, and his perceptions altered. In fact, although such shifts are rarely the sole objective of a marketing program or even the first objective, they are often important secondary objectives. A candidate for the school board must build awareness of his name among the voters and some knowledge of what he stands for. Winning comes first, and were it possible to win without the voters' being aware or knowledgeable, that would be fine. It is not, and therefore building awareness and knowledge is an important objective, but only because they contribute to an even more important objective.

CLIENT BEHAVIOR AS DECISIONS

In analyzing client behavior as a decision, the marketer imagines that the client's decision is broken into five parts: first, the recognition that a decision is needed; second, collecting information; third, evaluating and analyzing the information and making a decision; fourth, putting the decision into effect; and fifth, bearing, perhaps enjoying, the consequences.

Recognizing That a Decision Is Needed

Before an alcoholic can begin treatment, he must recognize that he is an alcoholic; but this proves far from easy for most alcoholics, alcoholism meaning what it does in our society, and the alcoholic's being able to hide behind his belief that he can always stop when he wants to.

Without a problem to be resolved, there is no need for the client to reach a decision. Therefore, the decision-making process only starts when the client realizes there is a difference between what is and what should be, that is, between the situation at hand and what the client would like the situation to be.

Since the client will not trouble to make a decision unless he recognizes a need to do so, marketers must find out how their clients arrive at this first stage. For many decisions, problem recognition is trivial. How does a subscriber to *Ms Magazine* know it is time to renew her subscription? The issues stop. And before that, she has received several notices reminding her to renew. But how does a smoker come to decide that he wants to stop smoking? This presumably takes a long time and is affected by a variety of influences and environmental factors. Knowing how a smoker comes to this resolve would clearly contribute a good deal to any marketing program designed to help people stop.

Collecting Information

The client now recognizes he has a problem and begins to search for solutions. This means collecting information on what options are available, what their consequences are, where more information can be found, and the like.

Let us look at something the reader may not be familiar with: carpooling, or ridesharing. Although carpooling will not cure baldness, it seems to cure most everything else, according to its advocates: "[It] . . . helps pollution, and energy use; requires relatively little capital; . . . is readily available, . . . increases the efficiency of existing equipment and facilities and reduces the demand for additional vehicles and road.'' What information does a potential carpooler need before he can decide?

- How do I find others interested in carpooling?
- Does carpooling work in terms of my own individual schedule?
- How do I avoid getting stuck with a blabbermouth or people who don't smoke?
- Does carpooling take longer than regular commuting?
- What does it cost?
- What happens when the carpool arrangement breaks down, say, because the driver is on vacation, or because one of the group wants to stay late?
- What about things like insurance? When there is an accident, are all members of the carpool covered by the driver's insurance, or will the insurance company wriggle out on some pretext?

These are examples of the kind of information that potential carpoolers will need. But an agency that wants to encourage carpooling also needs information. Perhaps the most important thing it needs to know is which commuter segments are most likely to convert to carpooling? Once this is known, the agency can develop communications messages that appeal to the specific needs of its segments. The agency can begin developing a way to deliver the messages. It can see clearly which groups it should *not* try to reach, and thus it is a fair way toward setting realistic goals for the carpooling project.

Most decisions made by clients (and backers) of nonprofit organizations, like most consumer decisions, involve little search for information. After all, if we had to stop to collect information every time a decision was called for, we would never get anything done. When a fund-raising appeal comes from Amnesty International, most potential backers make their decision on the spot, perhaps without even bothering to read the appeal for funds, perhaps without even bothering to open the envelope. When your membership in the National Audubon Society expires, you already have the information you need: Because you have been a member, you know a good deal about the society and what it does; you know whether you are able to take advantage of its offerings and whether you wish to continue supporting its work; you also know whether you have gotten your money's worth—and as a result you can make your decision with dispatch. In cases like these, habit and past experience serve in lieu of collecting data; nor can we expect clients or backers to devote much time to choices that aren't worth much time.

Other decisions require a good deal of spadework. If you are so perverse as to want to travel from San Diego to Nashville on Amtrak, you will need the patience of a mule merely to get a copy of the current timetable (from which you will learn that there is no such service). Collecting information about whether to go to college or where to go to college can take months and involve reading catalogs, visiting colleges, and talking to alumni, recruiters, advisors, current students, and friends; and the decision to take the veil may involve several years of thought, discussion, and prayer.

Perceived Risk

Another type of information that clients seek might be called reassurance. Clients often want to be reassured that they are making the correct decision. Decisions, after all, may turn out to be incorrect, or clients may feel they are not fully competent to make the decision with confidence. This awareness of the fact that a decision may turn out wrong is called perceived risk. More formally perceived risk arises when (1) there are significant uncertainties in the client's mind as to whether the decision will work out, and (2) the costs of a bad outcome are high. Picking a college generates a good deal of perceived risk because it is not easy for the prospective student to tell which college is the best for him, and if he chooses badly, the costs both monetary and emotional will be high.

The costs of a bad outcome fall roughly into three areas. One is a *functional risk,* the risk that the product or service being bought will not perform the function for which it is bought. A person considering enrolling in a health maintenance organization (HMO) may be fearful that the doctoring is not as good as it is, say, at the nearby hospital. He is concerned that the function for which he joins the HMO may not be fulfilled. The carpooler may worry that the scheme will not work, causing him to lose pay or scramble to get home. The second is a *financial risk,* the risk that if the decision turns sour the client will lose a lot of money. Sometimes one hears the argument that donors do not like to give money to performing arts groups that are near bankruptcy because they fear the group will fail and their money will go for naught.[12] Should a member of a nonprofit organization sign up for the group's $4,000 tour to South America? Such tours do not always work out, and if it does not, all that money will be gone. The third is *social risk,* the risk that the decision will have untoward consequences among one's friends, neighbors, and acquaintances. Buying a ticket to the opera may be thought uppity by one's friends and confessing to a love of ballet may be thought even worse.

What do clients do in the face of perceived risk? They may simply avoid it, if they can; but one cannot avoid deciding which college to go to. In these cases clients seek reassurance that they are doing the right thing, that their decision is correct. New computer software usually contains bugs, sometimes subtle, sometimes not. Note that this meets the two defining conditions for perceived risk—no one can tell whether the software is bug free, and if there are bugs the costs in the form of lost or incorrect work could be high. How might buyers reassure themselves in the fact of such perceived risk? Some have a simple rule: Never buy a software package whose number ends in zero. That is, don't buy

Version 3.0. Wait until Version 3.1 or 3.2 when most of the bugs in Version 3.0 will have been caught and removed.

We have seen that clients and backers want information to help them make better decisions and reassurance to help them face perceived risks. Where do they find this information and reassurance? There are two principal sources. The first includes actions under the marketer's control, the second actions and outcomes that the marketer does not control. The simplest example is communications with which the reader is familiar—advertising, personal selling, sales promotion, and public relations (to all of which later chapters are devoted).

There are other sources of information and reassurance that marketers control that may not be so obvious, such as instructions on a package or in it, a free sample, or a display.

- Where clients have difficulty judging quality, they may use price as a source of information; and reputation embodied (say) in a brand name or the name of the nonprofit organization also serves.

- Many Roman Catholic orders take in seminarians and postulants who are only fifteen or sixteen. A fifteen-year-old cannot be expected to have any reasonable grasp of the life led, say, by an oblate, yet he is powerfully interested in finding out. In our terms, he needs information on "what it is really like." How can a religious recruiter provide this information? One way is by providing a sample—bringing prospects to the seminary or convent and letting them live and work as a seminarian or postulant for a weekend, or a week. As long as the program reflects the true life of the order, the prospect will learn some of what he wants to know. Such a program benefits the religious order as well. Those who sample and then decide are more likely to stay the course than those who come without any prior exposure to the rigors of religious life.[13]

- How does one get through to teenage boys already in trouble with the law that prison is not cool or smart? Provide a sample, a sort of theme-park-from-hell, a few hours or a full day walking with inmates, eating food with them, talking with them, and looking at photos of inmates who have been beaten, slashed, or raped while serving time.[14] A longer transition program, which might last as long as a year, would also deal with the perceived risk faced by a young man.[15]

The second source of information and reassurance is one that marketers cannot touch: the client's own experiences with the nonprofit organization, his own past use of its services and products; what he is able to learn from talking to others, which marketers call word-of-mouth; and what is publicly available, say, in government reports, the pages of consumer magazines, or the news.

Convenience

Marketers put convenience high on the list of client benefits. They do this for the most fundamental of reasons: Clients are more likely to do what the NPO wants them to do if doing it is convenient. Thus, making things easy for clients serves the needs of both client and NPO. Certainly, some of the best examples of the benefits of making things easy for the clients and backers arise in fundraising. Ask prospective donors to find a stamp and the return goes down, measurably, over providing a stamped envelope. And many fundraisers have found that allowing donors to use credit cards increases the number of donors. Not only are the cards more convenient, but many donors want to use their cards to earn credits in frequent flier or other programs. (Donors are less likely to change their minds about giving as well, because changing their minds means they have to reverse the credit card charge and that is rather, well, inconvenient.)

Evaluating and Analyzing the Information

Information in hand, the client or backer turns to an evaluation of what he has learned and moves to a decision. Marketers imagine evaluation as being broken into four stages.

In the first stage the client decides which characteristics of the product (or service) are relevant to his needs and interests. The relevant characteristics are called attributes. Of course, the client has already been doing this, because collecting information certainly means collecting information about things that count in the decision. For example, below are listed some attributes that are associated with certain common nonprofit activities:

- Museum visit—nature of the collection, quality of the exhibits, parking, admission fee, travel time.
- Giving to a hospital—reputation of hospital, previous experience with the hospital.
- Magazine—interest in subject, price, sponsoring group, quality of articles.
- Birth control technique—cost, perceived safety, ease of use, effectiveness.
- Enrolling in a health maintenance organization—cost, travel time, quality of medicine, waiting time, quality of facilities.
- Public housing—neighbors, appearance, management, maintenance, rent.

In the second stage, the client weighs these attributes in terms of their importance (or salience). Here a distinction must be drawn between important attributes that differ between alternatives and important attributes that do not differ. A potential blood donor certainly wants good medical facilities and good treatment when donating blood. But if the donor believes that all the blood banks are pretty much the same in regard to this attribute, then, even though it is important, this attribute will not affect the decision.

In the third stage, the client decides how each alternative measures up against each of the attributes considered relevant. Table 4.1 contains what might go through the carpooler's mind in weighing carpooling against driving his own car or against taking mass transit. On each of the four attributes that are important—time spent en route, costs, flexibility, and time available to read and relax—the carpooler scores the three available alternatives. The table also

Table 4.1
Evaluation of a Commuting Decision

Attributes	Importance Weights	Carpooling	Drive My Own Car	Mass Transit
Time spent door-to-door	.4	45 min.	35 min.	80 min.
Costs	.2	$5.60	$4.40	$8.80
Flexibility of schedule	.2	Low	High	Low
Time available to do other things	.2	30 min. (on average)	None	80 min.
	1.0			

contains the carpooler's importance weights. Were he talking to us he would say, "Keeping down the commuting time is pretty important to me, certainly more important than the other three. The other three are all about the same as far as I'm concerned. I mean I don't think flexibility is really any more important to me than having time to read."

Finally, the client combines his judgments in the first four stages into some overall preference. Just how this is done has been the subject of much theorizing over the past ten years or so; and the details need not concern us here, largely because marketing researchers are far from agreement.

Putting the Decision into Effect

Choice means first that the decision maker commits himself to a course and second that he acts. In Stage 3 the client has evaluated the alternatives facing him and decided which he preferred. Normally, it would be expected that this preference would become an intention-to-act (in business an "intention-to-buy"), and the intention-to-act would lead to an act (a purchase, a gift, a pledge, and so on). Unfortunately, intentions, even good intentions, often remain merely intentions.

Even trivial situational factors can spoil intentions-to-act. Just above I mentioned the importance of providing backers reached by mail with business reply envelopes, because an intention to give without a stamp is worth a good deal less than an intention to give with a stamp. But situational factors need not be trivial. A major donor to a capital drive may forego his pledge if the stock market drops and reduces the values of the securities he plans to give. And his other financial commitments, as well as tax considerations, will affect the relationship between his intentions and his gift.

Nonprofit marketers, however, do not sit on their hands waiting to see what will happen. If they can identify those clients or backers who intend to act, they may be able to get them to act by nudging them in one way or another. One example of this is the political canvass, which is undertaken to identify which voters are for "our" candidate, which are for the other candidate, and which have not decided. Whether the canvass is done by telephone or on foot, the canvasser goes from door to door asking people how they plan to vote. Since canvassers work from precinct lists, they should know how many voters live at each address and who they are; and while they are at the door they confirm, or correct, this information.

Now comes election day. For each precinct canvassed there is a list of voters who intend to vote for our candidate. Poll watchers record who votes and if, say, voters for our candidate have not voted by 4 P.M., campaign workers can be sent out to round them up and drive them to the polls. Politicians see elections as too important merely to hope that intentions to vote become votes.

Bearing the Consequences of the Decision

The final stage involves evaluation of the consequences of the decision. After making the decision, the client or backer will experience some satisfaction, or some dissatisfaction, or most commonly both. The client's satisfaction is thought to be a function of the difference between what was expected and what was experienced. Expectations are based in part on the preceding decision process and in part on what the marketer has promised in advertising and other communications. Expectations are also based on the client's general knowledge about how organizations and products should work. For example, few voters with an IQ over 70 expect politicians to keep their promises.

The astute marketer does not stop once the sale has been made. This is because the best marketer is not so much interested in the sale as in generating client satisfaction. Why would anyone care whether patients are satisfied with the medical care they receive? For a good medical reason, namely, that satisfied patients are more likely to follow the doctor's orders than those who are dissatisfied.[16] The businessman is interested in generating consumer satisfaction and making a profit at the same time. The nonprofit marketer is interested in generating client satisfaction and not going broke while doing it. So while the sale—the act—is the fundamental particle of mercantile physics, it is not what this physics is about.

Marketers, in addition, have more practical aims in looking at what happens after the sale. For example:

• A satisfied client will want to do it again. This is of particular importance because it is (usually) much cheaper to land a repeat client (or repeat backer) than to land a new client (or new backer). Magazines often pay three to six times more to sign up a new subscriber than a repeat subscriber, and charities often pay more on average to bring in a new donor than the amount donated, while the repeat donor costs much less.

- A satisfied client will talk about the experience and thus may bring in still more clients (but only if word-of-mouth is an important information source).

- Research on how people use a nonprofit service will suggest a variety of possible improvements in its product and service offerings. It cannot help but be informative for a credit union to find out how its depositors like banking with the credit union and how those who borrow from it feel about the entire loan process.

We have discussed all this before, in Chapter 2.

It is sometimes a good idea to study dissatisfaction as well. People who adopt a pet at animal shelters often bring the animal back. Some of the returns cannot be avoided, as when the adopted pet does not get along with other animals in the family. But it may be that adopters were oversold, that they expected care of an animal to be too easy, or that they think the animal is sick when in fact it is not. All such information will help.

One useful measure of clients' dissatisfaction is their refusal to buy again. Becke, for example, found that 60 percent of the lower-class clients of family service agencies did not return for a second interview.[17] To a marketer, it is clear evidence that something is seriously wrong.

This long section has explained only one model of client behavior (and there is a great deal more that can be said about it). It might seem that the choice of a model is unimportant, something fit to command the attention only of a professor. But such models are not merely the playthings of the Academy. In public life, for example, there is much debate over *which* model should form the basis for public action. Wilkie and Gardner have argued that the model used by the Federal Trade Commission posits that shoppers are economic men, which means that consumers' psychological needs are often ignored; that price, brand, store reputation, and advertising are often seen as independent of each other, and that shoppers have unlimited amounts of time to shop, or what is the same thing, that time is free. Marketers naturally believe that they have better theories, for business applications to be sure, but for applications by nonprofit marketers as well. The point of this paragraph, however, is to underline the very first line of this chapter on behavior, namely, that the nonprofit marketer must have a theory.[18]

HOW CAN ONE LEARN CLIENT ANALYSIS?

Readers with time available may find it possible to take a course in analysis of consumer behavior, perhaps as part of a program of adult education, or perhaps as part of an academic program leading to a degree. Most schools offering graduate work in business administration have a course in consumer behavior. Although such courses naturally neglect nonprofit issues, the diligent student can still learn methods of analysis, questions to ask, and the tentative generalizations that pass for consumer theory. But at best an academic course is only a start, and many readers presumably will be unable, or unwilling, to subject themselves to such a such a distasteful chore. For them there are two general approaches that they can use to teach themselves client analysis.

The first involves working out the behavior that is needed to make the program work. It is called the normative approach, in which conjectures about client behavior contain the word "must." In the normative approach the analyst is basically constructing sentences that start: "In order for this program to work, clients must _____."

The second approach is the descriptive, or positive, approach. Here the analyst attempts to describe how clients behave, who they are, where they are, what they believe, and so on. A program that succeeds does so because it has met the interests of some target audience well. A successful program tells us something about certain people and their interests. Much as an archaeologist seeks clues to a past civilization by scrutinizing its leavings and artifacts, so should the marketer train himself to decipher the success (or failure) of a marketing program.

The two approaches obviously play against each other, but the normative approach is most useful before designing the program, because it forces into public what would otherwise be implicit assumptions about client behavior. The descriptive approach is better used when observing a program in operation that the marketer wishes to understand. "The program seems to be working," the marketer says. "This tells me something about how clients behave, because the program obviously suits their interests in some way."

Let us look at two simple examples. Before recycled soft drink cans can be used, the steel cans must be separated from the aluminum cans. The straightforward way to do this is to ask people to change their behavior—learn to tell steel from aluminum, keep three garbage cans instead of one, and change the way they organize garbage. It has the advantage of being inconvenient as well. The prediction is child's play—as only a few will bother, and most of them will not stay on the course, the program will fail. The marketer's approach? He would predict only a few highly motivated consumers would go to the trouble, and he would despair—until he learned about magnetic separators that can be installed in garbage depots and that will draw off the steel cans while leaving the aluminum behind. Here is a program that does not rely on behavior changes by the many but only by the few, the "garbos," who are easy to find and to influence. It has now become a manageable task, one much more likely to work.

As an example of the descriptive approach, let us puzzle out the meaning of the TKTS scheme to sell discount tickets to Broadway theaters. Note first the cost structure of a theatrical performance: Large programmed costs are incurred before the production starts. Once under way, variable costs of a given performance are relatively low, and unsold seats remain forever unsold. Therefore, the phenomenon that the reader has often observed—some type of discount scheme to sell the unsold seats. It is better to sell a seat than let it stand empty, but only so long as the discount scheme does not cut into that segment of the theater-going audience willing to pay full price. To accomplish this the discounts must be restricted—say, to students, the aged, for only certain performances, or for certain seats.[19]

In the TKTS scheme, tickets are sold at half price (plus a service charge), at a special TKTS box office in Times Square. The tickets are sold only on the day of the performance, and to buy a ticket the buyer must show up in person. The box office offers no amenities, which means that when it rains buyers get wet. Usually, two-thirds of the productions running on Broadway send some tickets over to the TKTS box office, but ticket buyers do not know which shows are available until they reach the window. While they cannot know which show they will see, ticket buyers are quite certain that they can get a ticket to something.[20]

This half-price ticket scheme has been enormously successful. Sales started at 7,000 tickets a week and doubled in the second year, at which point it was generating $4 million of extra revenue a year for the participating theaters, which was nearly 10 percent of the total Broadway gross.

Clearly, the scheme attracts buyers. But whom? In this case, there was an audience survey, in which ticket buyers at the box office filled out a questionnaire. Except for a few differences—the TKTS audiences were considerably younger than the overall Broadway theatergoers, somewhat better educated, and a bit less well paid—the audience was like every other arts audience, well paid, well educated, somewhat older than the overall population, and largely professionals.

TKTS ticket buyers clearly differ from regular Broadway audiences in at least two ways—they are price sensitive and they do not plan their trips to the theater. Regular theatergoers buy their tickets weeks, sometimes even months, in advance, and they pay full price. TKTS buyers are closer to what marketers call impulse buyers. TKTS buyers do little planning—the survey showed that over 60 percent of them decided to buy tickets no more than two days before they came to the box office.

The fact that buyers do not know which show they will be seeing tells us even more. TKTS buyers want to see a show, not a particular show; they are looking for an evening of theater rather than a given performance. In this way, they are buying the product of an industry rather than the product of a firm, and the TKTS pricing scheme has tapped a latent primary demand for theater rather than the secondary demand filled by traditional arts marketing programs.[21]

The next step is to wonder exactly who are these impulse buyers seeking theatrical entertainment. We know they are younger, on average. Many of them presumably suddenly find themselves in town with little to do, and hence a sizeable chunk of them may be tourists. Whether they are tourists depends largely on whether TKTS advertises in tourist media. If it does not, the only tourists will be those who happen on the box office, and most of the buyers will be local residents. Since 60 percent plan their trips to the theater with only one or two days' forethought, perhaps the other 40 percent, who plan farther ahead, are locals, or at least mostly locals.

The reader is invited to take up the analysis at this point, and to try to pursue the descriptive approach one or two more steps by characterizing the likely segments into which the TKTS buyers fall.

How can one learn consumer analysis? By study and by application, which are surely answers that are not new. Study can mean academic study for a few; but for most it means reading and also research. Consumer analysis is not a sterile game; it is about something, and the more the analyst knows the more likely his analysis will contain some morsels of truth. Application means trying one's tools in new situations and trying to puzzle meaning out of what has occurred. Application means either the normative approach, trying tools and concepts out in new situations, or the descriptive approach, which tries to winkle meaning out of observed behavior. The reader will surely make many mistakes. But with diligence, his analysis will improve.

QUESTIONS

1. In *The Empty Polling Booth*, on page 80, Hadley tells the tale of Don Bonkers, chief registrar of his county in the state of Washington, who sent college students into every home and apartment in his area to register voters. In about 15 percent of the dwellings, the student registrars were chucked out after they announced their business.

    (a) Which segment, or segments, of the nonvoting public is most likely to be doing the chucking?

    (b) Would you expect the 15 percent who chuck would have changed in the past two decades (say)? Why and in which direction?

2. A cancer screening program (CSP) aims, through early detection of cancer, to reduce cancer deaths, reduce the costs of cancer care, and catch people before it is too late for effective therapy. An important step in the development of an effective marketing of a CSP is the development of a theory of how consumers decide to be screened. As best you can, propose such a theory.

3. Some advocate laws that require public utilities to allow each consumer to pay an extra dollar beyond the amount due to the utility and to designate that the dollar be sent to a public interest group of his choice. Predict the (likely) consequences.

4. Commuter Connection, Inc., a nonprofit corporation, has developed an idea that it hopes will help ease the energy crisis, which is encouraging commuters to hitchhike to work and encouraging drivers to pick them up. The scheme is that commuters, both drivers and hitchhikers, register by submitting two photos and a detailed application including both home and work addresses, which are to be verified by Commuter Connection. Commuters are then given a yellow reflector sign slightly larger than a checkbook indicating the commuter's destination and a routing map. Both motorists and hitchhikers display the appropriate letters of their destination and then join up on streets leading to the freeways going to (and from) San Francisco. Predict the likely consequences of this program.

5. There is widespread evidence that patients taking medication on a doctor's orders frequently misuse the drugs. Published studies indicate that percentage of misuse runs

from 20 to 59 percent. In a study of diabetics, for example, 21 percent took either half or double the prescribed dose of insulin (because they could not read the syringe properly). In another study 34 percent of the patients treated for streptococcal pharyngitis (which is a king-sized sore throat) stopped taking the prescribed penicillin against the doctor's orders. What hypotheses would you put forward for such behavior, and how might a marketer contribute to better compliance from patients?

6. Most people do not get dental checkups twice a year. Instead they go to the dentist only when they are in pain. Why are "people" so reluctant to go to the dentist? Do they "know" what is best for them? Which "people"?

7. From time to time groups interested in symphony orchestras issue reports that express concern about the orchestra's chances of survival. The reports usually take the line that symphonies are out of touch with most Americans and that orchestras must make major changes or face at some indefinite time in the future smaller, white audiences and financial ruin. The reports also point out the growth in the number of blacks, Asians, Hispanics, and Indians, and urge orchestras to attract different ethnic groups and cultural groups to the symphony.

   Based on whatever you know or can surmise about those who attend symphony programs and those who don't, evaluate the likely consequences of programs to attract minorities.

NOTES

1. Cited in L. I. Dublin, *Suicide: A Sociological and Statistical Study* (New York: Ronald Press, 1963), p. 136.

2. Angus Campbell, P. E. Converse, W. E. Miller, and D. E. Stokes, *The American Voter* (New York: Wiley, 1960), p. 523.

3. T. Kennedy Helm III, "Union Waiver of Initiation Fees During the Organization Campaign." *University of Kentucky Law Journal* 63, no. 4 (1974–1975): 857.

4. Dorwin Cartwright, "Some Principles of Mass Persuasion: Selected Findings of Research on the Sales of United States War Bonds." *Human Relations* 2 (1949): 253–267.

5. Jacob Jacoby and Robert W. Chestnut, *Brand Loyalty: Measurement and Management* (New York: Wiley, 1978).

6. Jacob Jacoby, "Consumer Research: A State of the Art Review." *Journal of Marketing* 42 (Spring 1978): 89.

7. Andrew Ehrenberg, *Repeat-Buying* (Amsterdam: North Holland, 1972), pp. 218–231.

8. John Cairns, "The Cancer Problems." *Scientific American* (November 1975), p. 69.

9. From "The Magpie" by Jon Swan, 1959. *The New Yorker Magazine, Inc.* (1960). By permission.

10. The same general observation applies to segmentation. By all means segment, but unless special circumstances prevail, do not try more than a handful of segments. In fact, most marketing programs would probably do well simply by moving from one segment to two segments.

11. For more on this topic, see Adrian B. Ryans and Charles B. Weinberg, "Consumer

Dynamics in Nonprofit Organizations." *Journal of Consumer Behavior* 5, no. 2, (September 1978): 89–95.

12. One also hears the argument that donors do not like to give money to groups that are too well off: "Give to Yale? It already has more than enough." In fact, few donors are interested in information bearing on the financial conditions of nonprofit organizations.

13. See Godfrey R. Poage, *Secrets of Successful Recruiting* (Westminster, Md.: Newman, 1961), pp. 111–115. Poage calls this "A Program that Never Fails," but he does not say just what it is that it never fails to do.

14. Michael Marriott, "Youths in Trouble Get a Taste of Life Behind Bars." *New York Times,* July 5, 1992, p. A17.

15. For such a transition program, see the *Bridgeport Post,* June 2, 1990, p. D1.

16. V. Francis, B. H. Korsch, and Marie J. Morris, "Gaps in Doctor Patient Communication, Patients' Response to Medical Advice." *New England Journal of Medicine* 280, no. 10 (March 1969): 535–540. It also turns out, happily, that patients' appraisals of their doctor's performance correlate highly with professional criteria for assessing the same performance. On this, see for instance, A. I. Kisch and L. G. Reeder, "Client Evaluation of Physician Performance." *Journal of Health and Social Behavior* 10, no. 1 (March 1969): 51–58.

17. Dorothy F. Beck, *Patterns in the Use of Family Agency Service* (New York: Family Service Association, 1962), p. 18.

18. William L. Wilkie and David M. Gardner, "The Role of Marketing Research in Public Policy Decision Making." *Journal of Marketing* 38 (January 1974): 38–47.

19. Such a scheme, which extracts different prices from different customers, is called price discrimination by the economists.

20. William J. Baumol, "On Two Experiments in the Pricing of Theater Tickets," in *Economics and Human Welfare,* edited by Michael J. Boskin (New York: Academic Press, 1979), pp. 41–57.

21. Some marketing jargon: "Primary" demand is the demand for the products of an industry; "secondary" demand is the demand for the products of a firm. Economists use more straightforward terms, calling the first "industry" demand and the second "firm" demand.

Chapter 5

How Price and Other Costs Influence Behavior

The success of any marketing program rests on projections about how other parties outside the organization will behave. As the most important of these parties is the client, understanding client behavior bottoms the entire field of marketing. It is not too strong, in fact, to say that the special competence of a marketing manager is his understanding of how clients will respond to the organization's programs. In this section, therefore, we shall pursue one thread of this subject, the influence of costs borne by clients on their behavior.

Note, the influence of costs, not price. The distinctions between them apply to the world of commerce and politics, a world in which microeconomists divide all influences on behavior into two broad classes: price and everything else. This alone tells us that price fascinates the microeconomists, and, in fact, they devote most of their capacities to its analysis. The marketer, on the other hand, must be concerned with both influences; and when his price is zero, as it often is in nonprofit marketing, "everything else" becomes paramount.

The nonprofit marketer, then, cannot work solely with price. Nonprofit organizations often set prices below what the market will bear to encourage their clients by reducing the barriers (that is, the costs) that inhibit their behavior. Sometimes they give away goods and services by setting prices at zero. But, as we shall see, no price does not mean that there is no cost. As one observer of the human scene has put it, "Free means included in the price."

T COSTS

In this chapter we are not concerned with price at all but with the total cost of a course of action that must be borne by a client. We can think of this total cost as being made up of three separate costs: out-of-pocket costs, opportunity costs, and "all other" costs.[1]

Out-of-pocket costs, or OOP costs, are monetary costs, as the term suggests. Thus, although a subscription to a nonprofit journal charged to your credit card is not money out-of-pocket at the time of the purchase, the cost is a monetary cost and sooner or later (actually sooner) will have to be paid. Clients can bear OOP costs even when the NPO charges nothing. Parking, transit fares, postage, tolls, perhaps phone calls, or babysitting fees, and lost wages all are OOP costs incurred in taking a child to a clinic for a free vaccination.

OOP costs need not be nickel-dime items. Many nonprofit organizations testify at congressional hearings or before regulatory commissions. To prepare for such outings, a nonprofit organization may spend months collecting information, doing research, and hiring experts, as well as additional time preparing its testimony. Appearing at licensing hearings of the Nuclear Regulatory Commission cost, at one time, $50,000 to $75,000, according to one expert. As a result, the Federal Trade Commission, among others, pays nonprofit groups to participate in its hearings. Its payments have run from a couple of hundred dollars to $129,000 for the National Consumer Law Center's participation in rule making on credit practices. Recognition of the cost of such participation, in fact, has led the federal government to begin to pay for public participation at many of its proceedings.[2]

Opportunity costs, as we saw in Chapter 3, is the value of an opportunity passed up or foregone. With organizational decisions, what is usually passed up is cash. Clients' opportunity costs often take the form of cash too. "If I weren't here at the IRS getting free tax advice, I could be earning $36 overtime." Here the opportunity cost of the tax advice is the measurable advantage, $36 pre-tax, of the next best alternative. It is clearly cash foregone.[3]

Yet opportunity costs need not take the form of cash. At a government agency I have to make three visits and wait a total of three and one-half hours before I am permitted to transact my business. Although it is not time I can put to earning overtime, I do value my time at something, say $50. It is also an opportunity cost. The valuable thing foregone is time, not cash, but it can be *measured* in dollars nevertheless. (Merely as a reminder, we see from these examples that like all relevant costs, opportunity costs are defined by the nature of the decision. The same free tax advice might cost a gynecologist $500, a keypunch operator $18, and someone without anything better to do, a professor say, nothing. See the discussion in Chapter 3 again.)

The most important opportunity cost borne by clients of nonprofit organizations is time. Does it cost anything to vote? Of course it does. There are some modest OOP costs, but "time is the principal cost of voting: time to register, to discover what parties are running, to deliberate, to go to the polls, and to mark the ballot. Since time is a scarce resource, voting is inherently costly."[4] Much of this chapter will be devoted to time costs.

The third component of costs is a catchall, which might as well be called *all other costs*, or AO costs. These costs are not what one normally means by cost. They reflect all the other sacrifices and disutilities associated with a course of action. They are psychological or physical drains; they are intangible; and they cannot usually be measured in dollars. They are real costs, nevertheless, and they can substantially influence behavior.

There are many examples of AO costs. Sitting on an uncomfortable chair at a concert is such a cost, as are the frustrations of trying to get your name removed from a mailing list, not being able to take a course you want in college because it is not being offered, having to stand in an unheated bus rather than sit in one that has heat, not being able to smoke on an airplane, being unable to get a reservations clerk at Amtrak on the phone without trying a dozen times, or having the tax advice given you by the IRS turn out to be wrong. (It goes without saying that you bear the consequences of a mistake made by the IRS.)

Even in the 1990s there continue to be Americans who are ashamed to be on welfare. In one small study, welfare applicants in San Francisco were reluctant to seek help because they said applying for welfare made them feel inadequate or embarrassed. In a second survey of over 2,000 mothers on the dole in New York City, 58 percent were "bothered by being on welfare," and 56 percent agreed that "getting money from the welfare makes a person feel ashamed."[5] Such feelings of shame or embarrassment are AO costs. More important, they clearly affect how (some) welfare clients behave.

These three types of costs—OOP, opportunity, and AO—taken together, comprise the total sacrifices and disutilities associated with a particular act, or choice. Note again that they are all costs borne by individual clients, and they all have the potential of influencing behavior. These costs, taken together, will be called T costs, for total costs. Note as well that assessing T costs and their likely influence on how people behave is not as arid as one might imagine. We are talking about real influences that affect real people.

T costs are easily seen in commercial affairs. A consumer buys a product and pays the price, an out-of-pocket cost. But it is not the total cost. Traveling to the retailer and back takes time, an opportunity cost, and there may be more out-of-pocket costs for transportation, tolls, and parking. It takes time (opportunity cost) and effort (AO cost) to locate acceptable products and to compare them. There may be further time costs waiting for the sales clerk to acknowledge the customer's presence, or for the product to be delivered. It takes time and effort, perhaps even money, to carry the product home, unpack it, decipher the instructions, assemble it, and finally discard the box and packing materials. In addition, there may be substantial AO costs: physical fatigue, frustration, anxiety, and annoyance. Think of the classic American vignette of the father assembling toys for his children late on Christmas Eve.

T costs can also be seen in the nonprofit context. To go to the New York State Ballet in Lincoln Center, a suburban couple buys, let us say, two tickets for $40. In addition, there will be other out-of-pocket costs:

Dinner	$60.00
Babysitter	20.00
Tolls	3.00
Parking	9.00
Transportation	7.00
Cost before tickets	$99.00
Tickets	40.00
Total out-of-pocket cost	$139.00

The cost of the tickets is about three-tenths of the total. If the same couple lives around the corner from Lincoln Center and has no children, their out-of-pocket cost for dinner and tickets will be about $100, with the tickets now about 40 percent of the total. Even if the tickets were free, the couple would still incur substantial OOP costs—$99 in the first case, $60 in the second—that would affect how often the couple went to the ballet. And New York City being what it is there would doubtless be at least some AO costs—psychological wear and tear and physical fatigue for the suburban couple and perhaps for the Manhattan couple as well. Zero price does not mean that there are no T costs.

In daily affairs, in your life and in mine, price is what counts. Why? Because it is usually the most important component of the T costs; in fact, it is so important that in most cases one can, as an approximation, ignore all the other costs. At least, that is the tack taken in most elementary economic analyses encountered in textbooks. The conclusion should be clear: When there is a price, one should look not at the price alone but at the T costs. When there is a zero price, T costs become the only costs and cannot be ignored, even as an approximation.

As another example, consider the following five costs of using an automotive seat belt:

1. OOP costs of purchase and installation—once the seat belt is installed, these costs become sunk.
2. Costs of risk assessment—the costs incurred in estimating or learning whether a seat belt will significantly reduce the risks of driving.
3. Attentiveness costs—the cost incurred to pay attention to your seat belt, to remember to buckle up.
4. Physical discomfort—from wearing the belts, from contorting to buckle up, or from reaching across the car to roll down a window.
5. Aesthetic costs—"a residual category of undefinable unpleasantness that some automobile occupants apparently associate with the use of seat belts."[6]

A Closer Look at Time Costs

The principal opportunity cost is time. When you do something, it takes time. During that time you could be doing something else, in fact, lots of other things.

One of those things is the best use you could make of your time, and compared to what you are doing it is the next best thing you could do with your time. This idea of "next best" is what opportunity costs are all about. When you do one thing, you forego doing the next best thing, and this is part of the cost of doing the one thing.

The principal opportunity cost to clients is time. To understand time costs we need to break them down to subcategories. One way of doing this is as follows.[7]

Performance time. This comes in two varieties. Objective performance time deals with how much time clients take to behave correctly. Subjective performance time deals with how much time clients think it takes to behave correctly. One measures the first by observing clients, the second by asking them what they do.

Degree of flexibility in behavior. To what extent can clients determine when to do it?

Frequency. How often must it be done to be effective? Women are supposed to examine their breasts once a month for lumps and other abnormalities, but breast disease usually comes on slowly, so a woman can miss a month from time to time without mortal harm. So frequency is important to women but not that important.

Regularity. How important is *regular* performance in achieving the desired outcome? When I was a boy, I figured out a way to avoid dreary piano practice every day. I'd simply practice extra hard just before the piano teacher came. Alas, regular practice was far more important than a spasm of practice once a week.

Duration. For how long must the performance continue? Can it be done just once, like a vaccination? Must it be done over the period of a lifetime?

Disruption. To what degree does the behavior require the client to rearrange the way he runs his life? Can clients perform while doing other things?

Monitoring effort. How much effort must clients devote to monitoring or remembering or keeping records?

Let us talk about flossing. It is easy to see the right directions here. Clients are more likely to behave correctly when T costs are lower. In terms of flossing they will be lower when

- objective performance time to floss is low
- subjective performance time to floss is low
- people have a great deal of flexibility when or where they floss
- they can floss on their own schedule, floss when they like, skip it when they like
- regularity is not critical. Flossing always pays. If one flosses once, that's better than none at all.
- how long one continues to floss is not critical.
- flossing can be done almost anywhere, driving to work, in church, at the dinner table. It doesn't disrupt things.
- it's easy to remember when to floss.

Not all of these are right. People don't have a lot of flexibility when or where they floss. Most do it when they brush their teeth. People can floss on their own schedule but flossing pays bigger dividends if it is done regularly, say every day. Regularity is critical. Flossing once every month doesn't do much for the gums. And flossing is good dental hygiene, not for any age but for a lifetime.

Queues

In this section, we look at time spent waiting in line, which is another type of time cost. According to one economist, even businessmen like to see queues in front of their doors—for security and for the pleasure of administering them.[8]

To see Shakespeare in Central Park during the summer, you pay nothing. The tickets are free, courtesy of New York City and the supporters of the New York Shakespeare Festival. How then do you get a good seat? Or any seat at all? The best thing to do is to pick a fine summer day, pack a dinner, take a book, and join the queue sometime late in the afternoon, say, about 4:00 P.M. Around 6:00 P.M. or so, the queue will rouse itself and start inching ahead, and a bit later you will receive your ticket. Now it is time for dinner, because the performance does not start until 8:00 P.M. Even then you may wish to join another queue to get a good seat, because your tickets give you access only to the theater, not to a specific seat.

Seats are free as long as you will stand a two-hour wait, and good seats are free if you can wait three or four hours. "Free" here refers to OOP costs, but there are obviously opportunity costs in the form of time spent in the queue. If the day you pick is not fine, it may rain and the performance may be canceled. In terms of T costs, the performance is not free.

Queues impose costs, then; and if there are waiting costs, a rational consumer will consider whether the pleasures of the play are worth the wait. Thus, the queue serves much the same function that prices do; it rations or allocates the existing supply of tickets to those willing to pay the price. Free goods and services handed out first-come-first-served simply impose costs on clients in another guise.

Let us follow Barzel, who has treated this question at some length.[9] Consider Figure 5.1, which shows a traditional demand curve, except that the vertical axis is labeled "Costs Borne by Clients," instead of "Price." We are to suppose that there are two types of costs, an OOP cost called price, and an opportunity cost that arises from time spent in the queue. Figure 5.1 shows a traditional demand curve, which means that there is no waiting time, and that the cost borne by clients is price alone. With this interpretation, the figure shows two things: (1) as prices go up, quantity demanded goes down, and vice versa (just as we would expect); and (2) if the price drops to zero, only a finite quantity, OQ, will be demanded.

Now consider Figure 5.2, in which both OOP costs and time costs are shown. The curve labeled DD is the traditional demand curve, the same as in Figure

Figure 5.1
The Microeconomist's Traditional Demand Curve

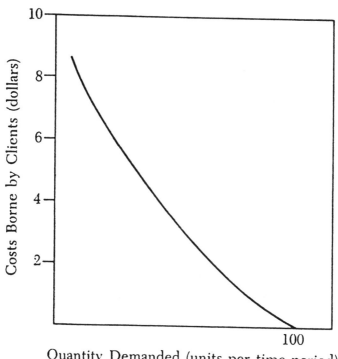

5.1. But the two curves to the left, *EE* and *FF*, represent the demand at different waiting times. *EE* might represent demand with a twenty-minute wait, and *FF* demand with a forty-minute wait. Any given OOP price, say *P,* the longer the wait, the lower the quantity demanded.

How long will a person wait? The longer the wait, the fewer persons will stand in the queue. For the market to clear, the marginal person must be at the point where the price he pays plus the cost of the wait equal his total valuation of the good (or service) for which he is waiting.

Now suppose the price of admission is done away with. What quantities will be demanded? These quantities are marked *OF, OE,* and *OD* on the horizontal axis of Figure 5.2. With no price and no wait, the quantity *OD* will be demanded; with a twenty-minute wait, they will demand *OF*. As before, the marginal person will weigh the time he must spend in line against the value of the goods or services for which he is waiting.

We can see a little more if we look at Figure 5.3, which deals with Shakespeare in the Park, where the rule is one ticket to a customer. The quantity now is all or nothing: Is it worth it to wait, say two hours, to get one ticket? For A it is. In fact, he would be willing to wait even longer than two hours to get his

Figure 5.2
Demand as a Function of Both Price and Waiting Time

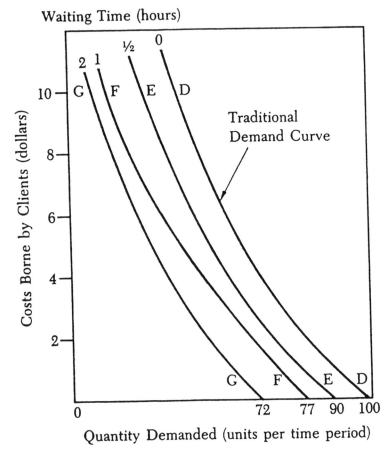

ticket (although this is not what the figure shows). C figures the wait is not worth it, and B is at the margin. His decision to join the line would be close, and if the line were slightly longer, he would toss it up.

Why the limit of one ticket per customer? Without a limit, the first person in line would take all the tickets and sell them. Would it not be possible for that person to take his ticket, go to the end of the line, and wait to get another? Yes, he could, but it probably would not be worth the bother for most. But for food stamps or housing subsidies, for example, going to the end of the line a second time could be worth a lot. It is this kind of thinking that leads to quotas and to rules about how often clients can join the queue and how much they can help themselves to when they reach the head of the queue.

Why are there no such rules and quotas for free goods like schools, roads, and parks? Because it is impossible to stash access to a park or road to be resold

Figure 5.3
Demand Curves for Three Persons (A, B, and C), All of Whom Must Wait Two Hours for a Ticket

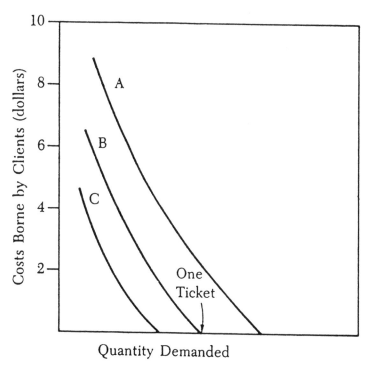

Quantity Demanded

at some later time, nor is a client constrained to one per unit of time (as with tickets to Shakespeare). To give away services without the tedium of rules, quotas, and procedures, the services must be such that they cannot be resold and that they can be consumed only one at a time.

OOP costs fall more heavily on some than others. It is a commonplace that the rich value an extra dollar less than the poor; hence a system with no waiting lines seems to favor the rich.[10] In much the same way, some writers presume that opportunity costs, in the form of time, fall more heavily on some rather than others. Here the commonplace is that the poor have more time or rather that the rich have less, and therefore in a system with no OOP costs, in which the total costs are time spent in line, the poor are favored over the rich. Some have even gone so far as to commend queues because time costs less for the poor and because they do away with the need for rules and quotas. "Whenever, in the interests of equity, the subsidy inherent in publicly provided goods needs to be varied by income class, queues can serve that function. They provide a test for rationing without requiring that resources be expended on an explicit means test."[11]

We have seen that queues serve to ration the available supply of goods and services by imposing costs on potential clients. But what causes queues to form? One reason is that demand for a good is not perfectly predictable. If demand could be predicted, an organization could trim its production to meet the demand; if it cannot predict demand, it will sometimes find that it is unable to produce fast enough to meet the demand and a queue will form. A second reason is a breakdown of the price mechanism. From the textbooks, it is possible to believe that a shortage should lead to an increase in price, which in turn will shorten, then eliminate the line. The price, therefore, will rise to clear the market. But with nonprofit organizations, things may not go like this. A city like Berkeley, California may control rents, and by forcing the price to remain below its market-clearing value, it contributes to what politicians who passed the law call a housing shortage, that is, a long wait for a low-rent apartment. Some private, nonprofit organizations may, as a matter of policy, not even consider charging for their services. A third factor leading to the formation of queues is the convenience of the client: Clients may well prefer to take delivery of goods and services when it suits them, not when it suits the organization. For many clients (and consumers) the most suitable of times is the Last Day, for example, with help in filling out income tax forms, buying antifreeze, buying Christmas presents, or making reservations at a national park.

Patients also have preferences about when they are admitted to hospitals for elective surgery. And since the effect of an American national health service (when it comes) will be to lower the price of medical care, which in turn will lead to queues, it is useful to look briefly at the experience of the National Health Service (NHS) in Britain.

The naive view of queues for admission to a hospital is to concentrate only on OOP costs. Since NHS is free, the patient pays nothing and long queues—years in length—form. How can these lines be shortened? Charging a price would work, but it is not acceptable for social or political reasons; increasing the supply of spells, then, should turn the trick. But here there is an unexpected problem, a "paradox," "despite considerable expansion in the supply of medical care, the excess demand remains as prominent as ever."[12] As the supply of medical services has increased, the demand has also increased, and the queues remain as long as ever.

An alternative approach is developed in this chapter, the view that there is no such thing as a free lunch. Culyer and Cullis adopt this approach too:

patients who wait for inpatient care actually do pay a price: they suffer pain or discomfort or inconvenience in waiting, are subject to uncertainty, may lose earnings, impose additional costs (both monetary and nonmonetary) on their families or households as well as having to tolerate the delay in delivery of what is presumably beneficial treatment or care. According to this view, waiting patients pay a time-price *for their admission.*[13]

Under the naive view of queues, the rational patient will join the queue as long as the value of the treatment is greater than zero (in monetary terms). But when we take the total cost approach by recognizing the costs of waiting, the rational patient will join the waiting list only if the anticipated benefits exceed the costs of waiting. (For the marginal patient, these two factors will be equal.) Now what would we predict would happen if (as was the case in Britain) the average length of a hospital stay decreases over time, in effect increasing the capacity of the hospital system? The prediction is straightforward. Shorter stays will at first shorten the wait, which in turn will lower the total cost of waiting. Since the benefits from medical care can be expected to remain about the same while the costs of waiting fall, we expect more people to join the waiting list, and the line will lengthen again. The total cost approach, therefore, predicts that increases in supply produce increases in demand, and the paradox disappears.[14]

ANALYZING BEHAVIOR USING T COSTS

Mass Transit

Let us make an example of mass transit, a long example that will make more clear the cost concepts discussed above and that will show how much insight can be gained from an analysis of T costs, even though it is only a partial insight. It is a point worth underlining. Understanding costs is only one of the steps that must be taken in trying to understand behavior, which is why this is the second chapter on analyzing behavior.

Above, we saw that

$$T \text{ costs} = OOP \text{ costs} + \text{opportunity costs} + AO \text{ costs}$$

though we smudged over the meaning of the plus sign. In talking about mass transit we can use more specific words, namely, "fares" for OOP costs, "time spent on the trip" for opportunity costs, and "comfort" for AO costs.

In any analysis of demand, it is always necessary to look at substitutes, which here means the automobile, a means of transportation to be sure, but one which, as Ambrose Bierce might have written, serves America in lieu of a state religion. Driving costs fall into two groups—trip costs, which are OOP costs for tolls and parking, and operating costs, which are costs for care and feeding and which do not change much with the number of trips made. These latter costs are certainly not variable and probably not semivariable. Instead, buying a car commits one to an annual expenditure for maintenance and depreciation that is not much affected by the number of trips taken or miles driven. Time costs also fall roughly into two groups—time spent getting to and from the mass transit station, and time traveling via mass transit. The comforts are privacy, flexibility in scheduling trips, speed, and air conditioning and heating that can be counted on to work. Given the dispersion of homes, shopping centers, and places of work, there is no feasible alternative to many automobile trips. And then there are the

Table 5.1
Elasticities of Demand for Travel via Auto and Mass Transit with Respect to Four Costs

A. Demand for Auto Trips with respect to:

Purpose of Trip	Auto Tolls, Parking	Auto Operating Costs	Transit Fares on Main Line	Transit Fares on Feeder Lines
	(own elasticity)		(cross elasticity)	
Work	-.1	-.5	-.1	0
Shop	-1.6	-.9	0	0

B. Demand for Mass Transit Trips with respect to:

	Transit Fares on Main Line	Transit Fares on Feeder Lines	Auto Tolls, Parking	Auto Operating Costs
	(own elasticity)		(cross elasticity)	
Work	-.1	-.1	0	0
Shop		-.3*	0	0

Source: Adapted from Gerald Kraft, "Free Transit Revisited." *Public Policy* 21, no. 1 (Winter 1973): 84.

* Information on separate costs not available.

intangible satisfactions such as status, feelings of power, and the sheer pleasure of driving.

OOP Costs: Fares

With mass transit, for some there will be tolls, parking fees, and the costs of driving to reach the station; but here we concentrate on fares. Marketers study the importance of OOP costs by examining what happens when fares change. The usual tool for doing this is elasticity. For our purposes, we will take elasticity to mean the percentage change in the number of trips people take in response to a one percent change in fares (or whatever it is we are interested in looking at), with all other factors held constant. Thus the

$$\text{elasticity of trips with respect to fares} = \frac{\text{Percentage change in number of trips}}{\text{Percentage change in fares}}$$

If fares are lowered 15 percent and trips increase 6 percent, the trip elasticity is $6\% \div -15\% = -.4$.[15]

Table 5.1 reports a number of elasticities (all rounded). Let us look first at trips to work, in part B of the table. We see very small elasticities. Commuters do not respond much to changes in fares. If, for example, fares went up 20 percent, the number of trips would go down only 2 percent. This low elasticity holds for both trips on the main line and for trips on lines that feed or provide access to the main line; it also enables us to predict the effect of sharp reductions in fares, such as are sometimes advocated by those who wish to stimulate the use of mass transit. Fare reductions cannot be expected to increase ridership very much.

The demand for automobile trips is likewise relatively insensitive to both parking and operating costs, although changes in automobile operating costs will draw a response five times larger than changes in tolls and parking.

What might explain these low elasticities? Mostly it is the absence of substitutes. Commuters need to get to work. Provided nothing else changes much, they will continue riding mass transit when the fares go up, and they will certainly not make more trips when fares fall. That would mean going to work more often to take advantage of lower fares. There are substitutes for many shopping trips, however. People can shop in a local community or by phone or mail, and shoppers can simply make fewer shopping trips on mass transit, buying more goods on each trip. So we would expect higher fare elasticities, for both mass transit and for automobile trips. It is what we observe in Table 5.1, and in fact, shopping trip elasticity with respect to tolls and parking is −1.6, a large figure.

Further insight into passengers' behavior comes from studying cross-elasticities, which are elasticities across categories; for example, percentage change in transit trips divided by percentage change in auto costs (tolls and parking); or percentage change in auto trips divided by percentage change in transit fares. By winking at the one cross-elasticity in Table 5.1 that is not zero, we can sum up what the cross-elasticities say in one sentence: Changes in auto costs have no effect on transit usage, and changes in transit fares have no effect on auto usage.

Time Costs: Time Spent En Route

With one exception (the influence of tolls and parking fees on shopping trips), OOP costs have little influence on choice of transit mode as long as everything else is held constant. (See Table 5.2)

Commuters are a good deal more sensitive to changes in travel times than to changes in fares. On main line routes, the fare elasticity is −.1 and the time elasticity is −.4; on feeder routes, the fare elasticity is −.1 but the time elasticity is −.7. It means that cutting an hour's ride on the main line by 10 percent will increase ridership by only 7 percent. Again, auto ridership is more sensitive than mass transit ridership to changes in travel time. And as with OOP costs, shoppers are more sensitive to changes in travel times than commuters. Note, particularly, "time spent out of auto," that is, time one spends hoofing it—from apartment

Table 5.2
Monetary and Time Costs of Five Modes of Transportation, by Income

Low Income ($.90/hr or $1,800/year)

Costs	Auto Expressways	Auto Arterial Routes	Commuter Railroad	Subway Only	Bus and Subway
Monetary	$1.13	$1.17	$.77	$.25	$.25
Traveling	.07	.12	.08	.10	.17
Waiting			.09	.02	.03
Walking	.02	.02	.18	.10	.12
Trip cost	$1.22	$1.31	$1.11	$.47	$.56
Trip cost/wage	1.4	1.5	1.2	.5	.6

High Income ($8.33/hr or $16,700/year)

Costs	Auto Expressways	Auto Arterial Routes	Commuter Railroad	Subway Only	Bus and Subway
Monetary	$1.13	$1.17	$.77	$.25	$.25
Traveling	.64	1.07	.78	.91	1.56
Waiting			.89	.20	.26
Walking	.21	.21	.88	.89	1.08
Trip cost	$1.98	$2.45	$3.52	$2.24	$3.15
Trip cost/wage	.2	.3	.4	.3	.4

Source: Donald N. Dewees, "Travel Cost, Transit, and Control of Urban Motoring." *Public Policy* 24, no. 1 (Winter 1976): 63. Adapted.

Note: Annual income is 2,000 times the hourly rate. The "trip" is door to door for each transportation mode.

to car or from parking lot to office or factory floor. Both shoppers and commuters are quite sensitive to changes in the amount they have to walk.

Why is time more important to the passenger than the fare? At the start, note that it is not true that time is more important to all passengers, only to some. To most, in fact, but not all. There are some who are willing to spend an extra ten, twenty, or forty minutes to save the inconvenience or expense of operating a car. But for the rest, apparently it is the old answer: Time is money, and the money value of time is a lot greater than the fare. There have, in fact, been a number of studies in transportation that have estimated what time is worth. Dewees, in summarizing a number of these studies, concluded that the value of travel time is roughly one-third the passenger's hourly wage rate, the value of waiting time roughly half the hourly wage rate, and the value of walking time roughly equal to the hourly wage rate.[16] The more passengers earn, the more costly time becomes, but as the fare is the same for all passengers, the *relative* price of time increases with income. (see Table 5.3). Thus, high-income pas-

Table 5.3
Time Costs as a Percentage of Total Trip Costs, by Mode of Transportation and by Income

Costs	Auto Expressways	Auto Arterial	Commuter Railroad	Subway Only	Bus and Subway
Low	8%	11%	31%	47%	55%
High	43%	52%	72%	89%	92%

sengers who commute on mass transit bear most of their costs in the form of time costs. Fare reductions, even free transit, will reduce their T costs, but not by much. Low-income passengers are likely to be much more sensitive to changes in the fare, but since the purpose of their trips is (primarily) to get to work, it is unlikely that a mere fare reduction will generate much extra business from commuters. Following this line of argument, the passengers most likely to be attracted by a reduced fare will have low incomes and will be considering discretionary trips, that is, low-income shoppers.

There are two lessons to be derived from this discussion, the first dealing with mass transit and the second with the general topic of costs. We have seen that fare (and OOP) elasticities are generally quite small and that time elasticities are somewhat larger, which is to say, travelers are relatively less sensitive to transit fares and relatively more sensitive to travel times. Cross-elasticities between auto and mass transit are mostly zero, which means there is very little hope of wooing many auto passengers away from their cars—even if mass transit were given away by setting fares at zero.

The second lesson is that such an analysis sheds a good deal of light on our understanding of the behavior of commuters and shoppers. Although it is not by any means the entire story, it does provide a great deal of insight. It lets us see, in particular, that even when fares are set at zero, there can still be substantial costs borne by clients, and these costs powerfully influence their behavior. The moral is that analysis of T costs is part of any competent marketing analysis in the nonprofit sector.

Jury Duty

Jury duty is a civic duty that often leaves the juror with a vivid sense of how our system of justice works, and thus by extension, how government works. (Others are bored, appalled, or sickened by what they see.) Only those who have participated, who perhaps have struggled with matters of guilt and innocence, the purpose of punishment, and the life of the victim versus the life of the defendant, know. Only they can know what serving on a jury can do to the juror. It has been called the closest one can come to true democracy in our society. The rest, who have never served or who have been called but avoided their duty, know nothing of the benefits of serving. They may be keenly aware of the costs, however. If they have read this chapter, they will be thinking in terms of T costs. Let us look at the T costs of jury duty in an effort to understand why so many try to avoid jury duty or ask for exemptions.

The OOP costs are typically small and many jurisdictions provide cheap parking for jurors. Most courts provide a mileage allowance for those who drive, and some allow for out-of-pocket expenses.[17]

The opportunity costs are more substantial. For one thing, many jurors who work for small companies will not be paid while they are on jury duty, nor will they be paid if they are self-employed. (I stress small and self-employed because almost all larger companies pay their full-time employees when they are called to jury duty, although there are often restrictions on the use of such paid leave. For example, part-time workers are much less likely to be covered, and some companies restrict the number of days of pay an employee can receive for jury duty.[18]) This loss of income is barely offset by juror's pay, which still runs on the order of ten or fifteen dollars a day, before federal, state, and local income taxes. (The federal courts spend with a more prodigal hand. Jurors get forty dollars a day.) This account is so small that it seems not to reach the level of what one might call compensation. It is almost derisory.

The other opportunity cost is time. A juror wastes a lot of time waiting for this and waiting for that. ''Waste'' suggests that the system could be efficient when it is not. It could indeed be more efficient, but some of the waste isn't waste at all. It is unavoidable given the unpredictability of courtroom proceedings.

Finally, there are the substantial AO costs of suffering endless, unexplained waits in hallways and dingy holding pens on uncomfortable benches suffering at the hands of those practiced in the insolence of office.

Courts are beginning to consider other ways. Many courts now ask jurors to come in on the first day to register, after which they are excused unless the court needs them, in which case the clerk telephones them and orders them back to the jury control room.[19] In other jurisdictions, jurors are required to serve only one day if they aren't selected for a trial. Still others are beginning to consider issuing fewer summonses to serve, and calling potential jurors less often. How could they do this? By increasing the list of prospective jurors and by reducing exemptions. New York, for example, automatically exempts twenty-three occupations like lawyers, doctors, police, firefighters, and clergy, as well as podiatrists, physical therapists, and embalmers.[20].

In sum, the T costs of jury duty look high and immediate for a substantial portion of the population, while the benefits are pale and distant. Add to this the widespread mistrust of our organs of government, and one has a situation in which a solution will be difficult to find. The one talked about most, which has in fact been adopted by some jurisdictions, is to eliminate all exemptions to serve. This solution is, of course, not a marketing solution. Instead, it is the standard governmental fix—requiring behavior of its citizens by law, or to put it another way, denying them any choices.

ESTIMATING COSTS

We have looked in great detail at the general nature of costs in nonprofit organizations. Now we turn briefly to the question of measuring these costs instead of merely talking about them.

Costs Borne by the Nonprofit Organization

For the costs borne by the NPO, nonprofit managers, like businessmen, look to their accounting system. It should serve four functions: determining income and preparing financial statements, motivating employees and managers, controlling costs, and aiding decision making.

Accountants cannot classify costs as relevant to a decision, for reasons that should be familiar: The way the problem is defined determines which costs are relevant. Therefore, nonprofit managers must view the costs provided by their accounting system only as a starting place. They must add some costs not provided by the accounting system (opportunity costs); they must take away others (those not involving any sacrifice, like sunk costs); and in all cases they must work with estimates of future costs, not the historic costs captured by the accountant.

To repeat an earlier point, managers must not be fooled by costs that contain allocated costs. Accountants may call this or that a cost, but managers must find out what drives the cost. The key question is: Does the cost vary with the thing they are interested in—say, the number of clients or the number of visits—or does it carry a burden of allocated costs? Costs that contain allocated costs do not help managers reach sound decisions (although they are indispensable for preparing financial statements and the like). We saw before that the so-called "cost" of a pint of blood is in fact made up of four costs, each with quite different properties. There are variable costs that vary with the number of donors, semivariable costs that vary with the number of personnel at the blood bank, semivariable costs that vary with the operations of the blood bank, and nonvariable (or fixed) costs that don't vary with any of these things.

Such cost figures make it impossible to answer simple but important questions, like how much will the cost of a unit of blood change if the blood bank increases its hours of operation, or if the number of donors drops off over the Christmas holidays. Variable costs are much more useful to answer such questions.

Costs Borne by the Client

Estimating costs borne by the nonprofit agency, then, can usually be done with dispatch. Coming up with costs borne by clients is another matter. They live outside the organization, and managers must look to marketing research to provide answers. They may well find that good studies already exist in the public domain. Sometimes these studies will give them the answers they need. I cannot, for instance, imagine a marketing manager in a mass transit system going to the trouble of buying research to be able to evaluate the time costs borne by the passengers. The manager would simply use Dewees's estimates or estimates from another study. Nor can I imagine a manager setting up a study to estimate fare elasticities. Almost certainly, the Simpson-Curtin formula would be used, which says (roughly) that the elasticity of trips with respect to fares is −.3.[22] But even if such studies do not give final answers, they may give insights, approaches, or first approximations to answers. It is worthwhile to point out that first approximations often settle issues, making more precise, but expensive, research unnecessary. It is foolish to spend more on research than it is worth.[23]

How can an NPO measure the costs borne by its clients? It can measure OOP costs by using a simple questionnaire. Such costs—bus fares, babysitters, meals, gas, parking, and lost income—are costs that clients are usually willing to talk about. At the same time, an estimate must be made of clients' incomes, because costs in the absolute mean much less than costs measured in proportion to income. Income can often be estimated by using published income figures for census blocks.

Second, the NPO must measure the amount of time clients spend in using the organization's services and how they value that time. Again, questionnaire research may be useful. We might want to know how much time is spent in traveling to and from the motor vehicle office, as well as the time spent, say, waiting for the office to open, waiting in a queue, waiting while the application is processed, and even time lost to clients who arrive too near closing time to be handled. Another aid to estimating time is the preparation of a flow chart depicting the clients' course through the maze.[24] Figure 5.4 shows one such chart for a New York City venereal disease clinic, and in fact one of the waiting times is marked on the chart, although whether or not the time is accurate is another matter.

How can a client's time be valued? It may, to repeat the point, be possible to locate a study already published that does most of the hard work. A second possibility is to find out, in one way or another, what typical clients earn and use their earnings as a rough approximation of the value of their time.

Figure 5.4
How Patients Are Supposed to Be Processed in a New York City Venereal Disease Clinic

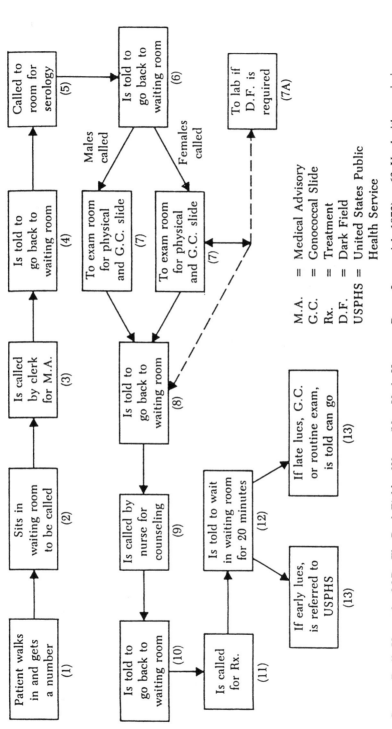

M.A. = Medical Advisory
G.C. = Gonococcal Slide
Rx. = Treatment
D.F. = Dark Field
USPHS = United States Public
Health Service

Source: Basile Yanovsky, M.D., *The Dark Fields of Venus* (New York: Harcourt, Brace, Jovanovich, 1973), p. 63. Used with permission.

NOTES

1. Remember that we are talking about clients here, not organizations. This "total cost" is the total cost borne by the client, which is not the same as total costs borne by the organization. Do not let the similarity of the words lead you to think the concepts are the same.

2. Ellen Berman et al., *Funding Public Participation in Department of Energy Proceedings* (Washington, D.C.: U.S. Department of Energy, Office of Consumer Affairs, September 1978), pp. 25–26.

3. It is interesting to note, however, that most do not have the option of varying their for-pay hours of work. "Of all employed male heads of households in 1971 less than 13 percent held jobs in which they were free to vary their work hours . . . and nearly half of those gained their flexibility . . . by taking a second job." S. J. Dickinson, *Five Thousand American Families—Patterns of Economic Progress,* vol. 1 (Ann Arbor: University of Michigan Survey Research Center, 1974), p. 190.

4. Anthony Downs, *An Economic Theory of Democracy* (New York: Harper and Brothers, 1957), p. 265.

5. John E. Mayer and Noel Timms, *The Client Speaks* (Chicago: Aldine, 1970), p. 99.

6. H. Preston Moore, Jr., "Self-Protective Safety Devices: An Economic Analysis." *University of Chicago Law Review* 40, no. 2 (1972–1973): 421–441. Quote at p. 429. I leave to the reader to judge how fanciful these costs are.

7. Karen F. A. Fox, "Time as a Component of Price in Social Marketing," in *Marketing in the 1980s,* edited by Richard P. Bagozzi et al. (Chicago: American Marketing Association, 1980), pp. 464–467.

8. P.J.D. Wiles, *Price, Cost, and Output,* rev. ed. (New York: Frederick A. Praeger, 1963), p. 61. A quirky but fascinating book.

9. Yoram Barzel, "A Theory of Rationing by Waiting." *Journal of Law and Economics* 17 (1974): 72–95. For another discussion, see Eugene Smolensky, T. Nicholas Tideman, and Donald Nichols, "Waiting Time as a Congestion Charge," in *Public Prices for Public Products,* edited by Selma Mushkin (Washington, D.C.: The Urban Institute, 1972), pp. 95–108.

10. Although it is a commonplace, I do not believe anyone knows if it is true.

11. Smolensky, Tideman, and Nichols, *Waiting Time,* p. 95.

12. A.J. Culyer and J. G. Cullis, "Some Economics of Hospital Waiting Lines." *Journal of Social Policy* 5, no. 3 (1976): 246.

13. Ibid., p. 247.

14. This exposition of the paper by Culyer and Cullis omits a great deal. For one thing, the total cost approach is too simple to predict very well. Part of the problem is that some of the costs of waiting in line—like pain from an untreated ailment or loss of productivity or earnings due to untreated illness—cannot be avoided by not joining the queue. Thus, they are sunk costs and are irrelevant to the decision made by the patient. Another difficulty is that the patient does not make the decision; his physician does. See the original paper for all this, and more.

15. An economically literate reader will recognize that (1) this is an arc elasticity, not a point elasticity, and (2) that price elasticities are often defined to have a positive sign. Negative signs are used here because we are also going to talk about cross-elasticities, which can be either positive or negative.

16. Donald N. Dewees, "Travel Cost, Transit, and Control of Urban Motoring." *Public Policy* 24, no. 1 (Winter 1976): 61.

17. Paula DiPerna, *Juries on Trial* (New York: Dembner Books, 1984), p. 86.

18. For details, see *Paid Leave for Illness and Personal Circumstances,* Personnel Policies Forum Survey No. 151 (Washington, D.C.: Bureau of National Affairs, December. 1993), pp. 22–24.

19. For an informative, fascinating view of the jury system, read Seymour Wishman, *Anatomy of a Jury* (New York: Times Books, 1986).

20. Jan Hoffman, "New York Casts for Solutions to Gaping Holes in Juror Net." *New York Times,* September 26, 1993, p. A9.

21. P. Jacobs and W. S. Rawson, "Donor Recruitment and Blood Collection Costs for Red Cross Blood Centers." *Transfusion* 18, no. 3 (May–June 1978): 291–297.

22. Thomas A. Domencich and Gerald Kraft, *Free Transit* (Lexington, Mass.: Lexington Books, 1970). The original work is J. F. Curtin, "The Effect of Fares on Transit Riding." *Highway Research Record,* no. 213 (1968).

23. It is foolish, but it is very often done. Part of the reason is that research serves other purposes than providing answers. Presidential study commissions should be useful, but their reports usually are forgotten. Consultants are often hired to bless preconceived conclusions. The problem of getting research used is much more difficult than doing the research itself, and much more important. As one might expect, most scholarly work is devoted to the less important question.

24. In fact, many welfare agencies already have such flow charts, requiring that all clients be treated as the chart dictates.

Chapter 6

Marketing Research

There appears to be a sharp distinction: Businesses try to increase their profits; and with such a simple, direct measure of how well they are succeeding, they can be expected to buy relatively little marketing research. They simply don't need it. Nonprofit organizations, on the other hand, having no single measure of their success, are forced into heavy use of marketing research.

THE NEED FOR RESEARCH

Well, no—of course not. It is businesses that are heavy buyers of research, and the nonprofit organizations that buy little. How can this be? For one thing, single measures of anything can mislead. Profits today cannot be understood isolated from profits yesterday, or from the capital necessary to produce those profits, or even from the profits earned by competitors. Growing sales do not warm a firm's managers if the market is growing even faster, and their product is losing share. For another, profits are an *ultimate* result, one that comes about because a series of other actions have been taken. It is only common sense to keep a close eye on things that lead up to the ultimate profit. In dealing with marketing, the sale itself says little beyond its mere existence, although mere existence is of surpassing importance. Managers need to know who is buying, how much they buy, whether they have bought before, and, if so, how often. They cannot afford to wait months before finding out if one of their television spots carries, or fails to carry, a double entendre, or to find out that most of the spot's intended audience did not understand it.

All this applies as well to nonprofit organizations, with the additional important consideration that there is no single, overall measure of performance. At least there is not a single measure for most. Some do have such a measure, however. In an election, there is only one vote per voter and only one winner. It should be clear what the vote means, and there should be little need for research to interpret the vote, but this is not the case. Of course, the winning politicians project onto the vote their fondest hopes; they praise the voice of the people and espy a mandate. Less excitable commentators often admit that they do not know what the vote means. And this is not surprising. In presidential elections, four years of political life are reduced in the end to one act, a vote for or a vote against. To what degree can a vote represent the voter? It is often the case that the American voter must choose between two unacceptable choices, and takes the less bad. With the increasing extremism of presidential candidates—Ross Perot and Jesse Jackson are examples—it is clear that many voters do not vote for one candidate, but against the other. Thus, we see that even so clear and straightforward an act as voting is filled with ambiguities and perplexities that obscure its meaning. Without additional research—based on a study of the opinion polls, and on the returns district by district and precinct by precinct—the vote carries little meaning. It can, in fact, be argued that not voting is as important an expression of political attitude as voting. And not voting must be studied using marketing research tools, for the nonvotes are not even counted.

There are two important points in all this. First, when an organization has a single measure of success—like winning market share or making the sales or raising the money—it needs marketing research to understand what the single measure means. Second, when an organization does not enjoy a single measure, it needs marketing research.

Someone Must Be Asking Questions

When do nonprofit organizations need information? They need it when they are failing and the failure is caused by inappropriate behavior of the organization's publics; in other words, when there is a marketing failure. They need it when the decisions being considered involve uncertainty and large stakes, in which case research may lessen the chance of error. They need it when internal pressures or external demands press the organization to become more responsive to its public. But since most nonprofit organizations make little use of marketing research, it may be more useful to look at the need for information from the other side, namely, the conditions under which organizations do not need information.

A nonprofit organization, or business firm for that matter, will not typically want information if it feels it is succeeding. It is possible to argue that research is still needed in such situations, but as a practical matter such advice is rarely taken. Imagine trying to persuade a politician to pay for an opinion poll in a year when he is not running or if he holds a safe seat. Nonprofit organizations typically feel they are succeeding when there are no large imbalances between what the organization needs and what it receives or between what it is capable of producing and what is demanded of it. Nonprofit organizations succeed when they do not suffer from shortages or from unused capacity.

In England, the National Blood Transfusion Service has made no attempt to collect and analyze information about donors. "One of the reasons for this lack of inquiry is that the Service . . . has never consciously been aware of a shortage or an impending shortage of potential donors. There have, therefore, been no internal or external pressures for more systematic information about the characteristics of those who give and those who do not give blood." Characteristically, the author of this passage, Richard Titmuss, a Fabian Socialist, goes on, "But why collect such information? In the opinion of the writer, no public service should be required as a matter of routine administrative processes to pile up, Kafka-like, vast masses of statistics just to satisfy computers and those who feed computers. There must be then some reason or reasons; someone must be asking questions."[1]

Shortages, then, indicate failure. The shortage that most wonderfully concentrates a manager's mind is financial, not just any financial difficulties, which to some nonprofit organizations are common as rain, but ones beyond the pale. But any shortage, in number of students or visitors or backers or clients, generates pressure for change and for information on which to base change.

Shortages often show up as unused capacity: a Shakespeare summer festival sells only 60 percent of the house; a college has empty classrooms and (horrors) tenured faculty are let go; a foundling hospital is unable to reach the women who could use its services and its census falls. In all of these situations, the search for solutions can usefully involve marketing research.

In addition to success, there is another factor that leads a nonprofit organization to avoid marketing research. This is a sense of professionalism and superior knowledge on the part of managers and others in the organization. Part of being a professional is controlling the exchange with the client. A legal aid lawyer does not ask his client what he wants; rather the lawyer tells the client what his problem is and recommends a solution and the client is allowed merely to take it or leave it. Many of the great political leaders, perhaps most, would have found it demeaning to ask their subjects what they wanted. A leader's job, after all, is to lead, not to ask advice of the led. The Duke of Urbino, Yeats tells us, did not so degrade himself:

> And Guidobaldo, when he made
> That mirror-school of courtesies
> Where wit and beauty learned their trade
> Upon Urbino's windy hill,
> Had sent no runners to and fro
> That he might learn the shepherd's will.[2]

THE FOUR TYPES OF RESEARCH

Managers use marketing research, then, to answer questions. And one way of classifying research is on the basis of the question. There are four:

1. Is there a problem? What is it?

2. What are the facts?

3. What will happen if I adopt a certain course of action?

4. How did things work out?

The first deals with exploration of the problem. The second and third provide answers to specific questions. The last provides feedback, and thus helps keep score.

Exploratory Research

Managers who commission exploratory research know little. They know, or perhaps only suspect, that they have a problem, but exactly what it is they cannot say. Their questions are vague and poorly formulated. They know too little to ask good questions, and without good questions, there is little chance of getting good answers. From exploratory research, they get ideas, insights, and hunches that usually serve only as the basis for further research. "We've pretty much decided that (1) turnover among our members is too high, and (2) the highest turnover occurs among our oldest members. So the next question is: What is causing it?" Occasionally, the results of exploratory research are so clear that an immediate decision can be made and there is no need for further research.

Because the researcher will proceed without preconceptions as to what will be found, exploratory research is sometimes commissioned as the first step in a large, extensive study. Used as the first step in such a study, it provides management with additional insights into the problems being dealt with, and it may suggest issues and items that otherwise would have been overlooked. Exploratory research can also serve to improve the efficiency of a major research study by identifying the types of questions respondents can and cannot answer, by suggesting when the research should be conducted, and by indicating the types of barriers the interviewers may have to overcome.

The simplest type of exploratory research is merely chatting. If you wish to learn why so few consumers are interested in using the Susan B. Anthony one-dollar coin, you can start by talking to people: Have they seen the coin, have they used it, and what do they think about it. This would doubtless lead to a more general discussion about coins in general: how they are used, how much change people generally carry, for what purposes coins are used, and how people decide when they have too many coins, or too few. This would get you started.

The other form of exploratory research is the focus group, in which a trained interviewer guides a small group through a loosely structured discussion of money in general and the one-dollar coin in particular.[3] The type of information the interviewer is likely to explore is similar to the list in Table 6.1.

Table 6.1
List of Discussion Topics for Focus Group Interviews with Consumers on the Susan B. Anthony Coin

1. *General Discussion of Currency*
   a. Retail payment system--charge, check, cash
   b. Amount of cash generally carried
   c. Bill denominations--old versus new
   d. Coin denominations
   e. Satisfaction with our currency system

2. *Discussion of Coins*
   a. How coins are used as opposed to bills
      - Change
      - Vending machines
      - Phone
      - Bus fare
      - Parking
      - Other
   b. Role of fifty-cent piece
   c. Role of penny--currency versus collector's item
   d. Threshold of coins carried
   e. Exchanging behavior to retain this threshold

3. *Discussion of Two-dollar Bill*
   a. Attitude toward it
   b. Perception of why it's recirculated
   c. Believability of government cost savings
   d. Usage of the two-dollar bill
   e. Examination or reasons for its lack of circulation
      - Superstition
      - Confusion with other bills--one dollar, twenty dollar

4. *Initial Reaction to the One-dollar Coin*
   a. Perceived need
   b. Usage
   c. Role in the existing currency system--is it a bill replacement or loose change?

5. *Examination of the Coin*
   a. Confusion with quarter
   b. Inflation impact--shrinkage of size

6. *Replacement Factors*
   a. Replacement for one-dollar bill
   b. Attitude toward two dollars as smallest note
   c. Perception regarding price of consumer goods
   d. Influence on pocket money denomination

7. *Summation*

Source: "Final Report—Phase One: Research Study into Market Acceptance of the New One Dollar Coin," Project Director, Claude R. Martin (Ann Arbor: Division of Research, Graduate School of Business Administration, University of Michigan, 1979), pp. 5 and 6.

Descriptive Research

The second type of research is descriptive research. It aims at describing a problem, much as a thermometer describes a patient's temperature, although research is neither as quick, as cheap, nor as accurate.

Most marketing research aims primarily to describe and to measure. Managers use it to describe all sorts of things: to measure how voters perceive candidates, describe which students stay to the end of a literacy course, find out how frequent users of mass transit intend to vote on a bond issue, rate prospects in a capital fund drive, measure how satisfied members of an organization are with its services, find out to what extent audiences for the ballet and the symphony differ, and estimate T costs of patients at a mental health clinic. It is this type of research that employs instruments with which the reader is presumably familiar—questionnaires, surveys, observations of behavior, and analyses of records—and something about which the reader may know little, use of databases. In San Francisco, KQED, the public television station, wanted to raise more large gifts, defined as $1,000 or more. To which of its members and friends should it direct its appeal? Enter the database. With the help of a fundraising consultant the station matched the names of its own donors with names in other databases that showed household income, buying habits, and other financial information, all in an effort to decide which donors were rich enough to make a large gift.[4] The station finished with a solid list of potential large givers.

Predictive Research

Marketing research can also provide rough predictions as to what will happen when a marketing program is undertaken. Marketers, after all, deserve some foretoken, or warning, that their plans will not go awry. Such predictive research can be based on observations, surveys, or experiments. A museum that is considering changing its admission fee from a flat fee to a voluntary fee might observe what has happened at other museums that have made the change; or it might ask its visitors for their reactions (although in matters involving cash such intentions predict poorly); or it might experiment by trying the idea (with appropriate controls) and seeing what happens. When they can be relied upon, such studies also help in setting realistic goals for a marketing program as well as in uncovering potential barriers to its success.

Feedback Research

The fourth type of marketing research keeps score by providing feedback about the organization's efforts. Feedback research helps answer the straightforward question, how are we doing?

This immediately suggests the question, "What are we trying to do?" and a nonprofit organization that does not know will find feedback research of little value. If you have no destination, it does not matter where you are or in which direction you are going.

Feedback research can prove exceptionally difficult when the link between the marketing program and the objective is weak. We might pretend, for a moment, that the warning on cigarette packages was put there by a marketer in an effort to strike fear into the breasts of smokers, which in turn should reduce the amount of smoking. It might be possible to detect a slight influence of the warning on fear, although I doubt it; but given the great number of other influences that bear on the decision to continue smoking, the impact of fear on cutting down would probably be nil. We shall return to this point in more detail when we discuss setting objectives for communications programs.

Perhaps the most common of all objectives subjected to measurement by feedback research is client satisfaction. To a marketer, if the client is not satisfied, the marketing effort is defective. Perhaps the best measure of satisfaction is one involving behavior. For example, how long are clients willing to wait in the queue before being served? Willingness to bear time costs is one measure. Clients who have experienced the services provided by a nonprofit organization and come back for more are on the face satisfied. Thus, we ask, as we did earlier, about repeat behavior—what proportion of our clients repeat, why do they repeat, why do clients drop us, and so on. Suppose you make up plaques to thank your thousand-dollar donors to your group's recreational programs for Hispanic children; but when you visit the donors in their offices, you never see the plaques hanging on the walls. So you try something different. You stop using plaques, which cost twenty dollars, and start giving donors framed drawings by children in the programs, which only cost four dollars. Over the next several months you see several on office walls. A simple, clear behavioral measure of a modest idea.[5] But behavioral measures are impossible in many situations. Then satisfaction can be roughly judged by surveys and questionnaires.

You will not have read this far in this book without believing that clients' satisfactions are worth measuring and that they count. But not everyone agrees. Rabushka and Jacobs studied the housing in which America's elderly live from a perverse point of view, that of the elderly themselves.[6] (They studied the 70 percent of the elderly who own their own homes, not the other 30 percent who rent, live with their children, or are in institutions because they cannot care for themselves.) And they concluded, to be brief, that elderly homeowners see themselves as much better off than housing authorities or social workers say they are. Applying professional standards as to what is acceptable housing meant finding anywhere from two to ten times as many housing problems as the elderly themselves acknowledged. Part of the reason is that housing experts often designate entire houses inadequate when only one part of it is defective or missing; for example, when there is no wash basin in the bathroom, although the owner is accustomed to using the kitchen sink.

These differences, and with them a "social problem," arise largely because of what Rabushka and Jacobs call a "needs/preference mismatch," which is the difference between what professionals feel the elderly need and what the elderly themselves actually want.

This same unwillingness to take the client's view is found among professionals in many nonprofit organizations. The authors of a study of the satisfaction of residents in HUD-assisted housing mention three common objections to letting satisfaction count: that residents' perceptions of their housing are influenced by past experience and past expectations and thus cannot provide a stable criterion; that when asked for their opinion, people will respond with unreasonable demands; and that residents lack insight and experience and are ignorant.[7]

The principal function of research in an organization is to answer questions, as we have seen. But research has other uses as well. Organizational politics often encourage research, or at least the appearance of research. The director of an aquarium may use a study to propitiate an influential board member, to gain leverage in arguing with other members of his organization, or to impress on businessmen the efficiency with which his organization runs. Research is sometimes undertaken simply because it is there for the taking. A board member may volunteer to perform a study, or university students may show up looking for a project to fulfill course requirements, or it may be possible to piggyback a request for research funds on a larger request for funds. And research is sometimes undertaken as proof that something is being done about a problem when the intent is to do nothing, thus the presidential study commission.

THE TYPICAL RESEARCH PROJECT

The typical research project consists of five stages:

1. *Where the data will come from.* There are two principal sources, secondary and primary data. Secondary data is already published, which means it is cheap, out-of-date, and not exactly what the NPO needs. Primary data is data that you collect yourself. It should be just what you want but it is expensive and takes time to get.

2. *How you will collect the data.* Here there are four principal ways. Observation, which means either by watching what your clients do, or by examining the leavings of their behavior—what they leave behind, how often they have renewed in the past, and so on. A study of past sales of healthy food in a high school cafeteria is an example of the use of observation. Focus groups, which we have already discussed. They are useful for a quick and dirty study. Surveys, which we deal with later. Experiments or formal tests are so expensive and so cumbersome to use that even businesses don't make much use of them. There are two exceptions to this statement, to be dealt with shortly.

3. *What instrument you will use.* Questionnaires are the most common research instrument. But it is often a good idea, where it is possible, to use mechanical instruments. Why do a survey to see how popular a book is? Simply measure its sales or the number of times it has circulated.

4. *Sampling plan.* Virtually all research wishes to draw conclusions about some group based on a sample of that group. How should the sample be drawn?

The technical aspects of the sampling plan is work for experts. But not the selecting of the sampling unit. Only a manager can decide who is to be surveyed. The sampling plan involves three general areas:

• Sampling unit—who is to be surveyed.

• Sample size—how many people.

• Sampling procedure—how respondents (the technical term of the people contacted) are chosen.

5. *Contact methods.* These deal with the various ways the researcher will contact the respondents. Surveys are the most common form of research done in the field. Let us look briefly at the three ways of doing surveys.

Mail is a good way to reach respondents who will not give personal interviews, and to survey respondents whose answers interviewers might bias. But mail questionnaires require careful testing beforehand, because the questions must be simple and clear. Also, the response rate is usually low, below 10 percent, and the response can come in slowly, at least over weeks, sometimes over months.

Telephone is good for gathering information quickly. It can be used for same-day research, for example. It allows the interviewer to clarify questions if the respondent doesn't understand them. And the response rate is typically higher than the rate for mail. Of course, only respondents with phones can be interviewed, but it is a snap for researchers to reach people with unlisted phones. (Odd fact: over 20 percent of the residential phones in the United States are unlisted.) And the survey must be short and sweet or the respondents will simply hang up.

Personal interviews are the most versatile of the three. Not only can the interviewer ask more questions, he can record additional information about the respondent, such as dress and body language. Alas, a personal interview is the most expensive of the three. It also requires more administrative planning and supervision. (How do you know that the interviewer actually administered the survey?) And it can be subject to interviewer bias or distortion.

Experimentation. No one uses experiments, I said just above. That overstates the case. There are two common uses of experimentation or formal tests in the nonprofit sector. One is a pilot test of a proposed program. The federal government sometimes hires NPOs to design and conduct tests of ideas it is considering.

The other is direct mail testing. Direct mail is as close to perfect as we have in this imperfect world when it comes to testing appeals or anything else. It is easy to measure results because the NPO has responses or contributions to count. (Modern software makes the job easy as well.) It is easy to run two or three tests simultaneously. One might drop half a million pieces but hold out 60,000 so that one would have a control group of 440,000 and two test groups of 30,000 each. The costs of testing are typically low. The NPO has already planned to drop half a million pieces. It's cheap to piggyback two test mailings on top of the planned mailing. The responses come in fairly quickly; always within months, but sometimes one can see which test mailing is the better and how it compares to the control mailing within a few weeks. Experimenting with direct mail is so cheap and so informative that most large mailers do a great deal of testing.

Types of Measures Used in Marketing Research

These four types of research deal with different types of decisions and problems within an organization. It is also useful to consider the question: What is it that we measure? In general, the answer rests on previous analysis of client behavior. The researcher measures what appears important in the models of client behavior.

But we can look at measures in other ways. Marketing research can measure three characteristics of backers and clients: states of being, states of mind, and behavior. (For examples of these three measures, cross-classified by the four types of research questions, see Table 6.2.)

States of being are characteristics (and attributes) of clients and backers. These measures describe what is verifiable, at least potentially. We could, if we wanted to take the trouble, find out how old a person is, his sex, whether he is a church member, and exactly how long he held his last job. Along with such hard information we could also collect soft information on states of being, such as what percentage of the symphony audience has had musical training or to what other colleges applicants to our school have applied.

States of mind are not even in principle capable of being verified. They consist of attitudes, feelings, beliefs, perceptions, knowledge, and intentions. There are no direct measures of such phenomena, and as a result researchers have to use indirect measures.

In addition to standard pencil-and-paper measures of states of mind, there have been many ingenious measurement schemes. We cannot directly observe the popularity of museum exhibits, but from maintenance records that record the frequency with which floor tiles in front of each exhibit have been replaced, we may be able to infer popularity. We cannot directly observe people's attitudes toward a radical political group, but we can leave stamped envelopes in public places, as if forgotten, and see what proportion of the letters are mailed by those who find them. The presumption underlying the lost letter technique is that people are more likely to mail a letter addressed to a group of which they approve.

Behavior is capable of being verified because it consists of actions and the

Table 6.2
Types of Measures

Types of Research	States of Being	Behavior	States of Mind
Exploration	What can a local mental health facility learn about potential volunteers to recruit them more easily?	Is turnover of members in the American Contract Bridge too high?	What attitudes and beliefs can be expected to slow or block introduction of the metric system?
Description	How well off is a potential donor to a building fund?	How long does it take (door to door) for the theater audience to reach the theater?	What proportion of the electorate has heard of our candidate?
Prediction	Which groups of commuters are most likely to take to carpooling? How can they be described?	If a public television station increases its average audience by 10%, how much will its members increase?	If the army halves its advertising budget, how much will recognition of the ad themes fall among target audiences?
Feedback	How effective are foundation grants in helping preserve historic sites?	To what extent do health warnings reduce smoking?	Now that the "safe city" campaign is over, do more people in fact believe the city is safe?

records left by actions. Behavior can be thought of as what can be observed. We cannot observe a museum visitor's age, although we may be able to guess it; nor can we observe his interest in its exhibits, although we may be able to infer it from the amount of time he spends before each one, but we can observe how long he stays in the museum, what route he follows, whether he returns to any exhibit a second time, whether he buys anything at the museum shop or in the cafeteria, and whether he talks to any museum personnel.

Some of the most important research nonprofits do is assessing behavior based on their own internal records. Fundraising programs collect several key indicators of the behavior of their contributors—the acquisitions of new donors, second gifts by first-time donors, successive gifts by repeat donors, and lost donors, those who stop giving. Tracking these four indicators over time and by donor segment and how the donors were acquired is almost enough to manage an entire fundraising operation. (What have we left out that's important? Costs, revenues, and net marketing contribution.)

What is secret behavior in an individual may well be capable of being observed in the mass. We may not observe how a given voter votes; but we can find out how each precinct went, although finding the records, persuading the election officials to release the figures, and then digging them out and copying them can all be disheartening.

MANAGERIAL ISSUES IN MARKETING RESEARCH

Research findings present a number of traps for the unwary or inexperienced manager. This section treats problems that arise with questionnaire surveys.

Problems with Questions

It is difficult to write a good question, for to be good a question must be understood by all respondents alike; it must be precise but not technical, free of bias, unobjectionable, free of ambiguities, double negatives and double meanings, neither too brief nor too long, and accurate in its references to time. It must not demand too much of the respondent, and it must allow the respondent to answer as he wants to. It is not difficult to write a good question. It is impossible.[8]

Some years ago, at a performance of the Metropolitan Opera, I tried to fill out an audience survey. One question that bothered me was: How did you learn that this performance was being given? I had not really learned it was being given at all. I subscribed to the opera and the performance was on my subscription. I suppose the best answer would have been, "I learned when I received my tickets before the season began." But here were the choices on the questionnaire:

Newspaper ads

Articles in newspapers or magazines

Leaflets or posters

Word from friend or associates

Critics' reviews

Radio or television

Mail order notices

Nothing fit, and I left it blank. Questions that respondents give up on are poor questions.

Another example is a poorly thought out question that appeared in a questionnaire sent to residents of the Willamette Valley in Oregon:

What is your marital status?

a. ( ) Single

b. ( ) Married

c. ( ) Divorced

d. ( ) Widowed

e. ( ) Separated

f. ( ) Retired

g. ( ) Other

The difficulty of writing good questions means that it is impossible to tell in advance whether the question is right, which is why all researchers worth their fee test their questionnaires. Only by testing the questionnaire can the problems be identified and corrected. In surveying blood donors in England, Beddington asked two questions that he hoped would elicit donors' motives for going the first time, and then for repeat donations.[9]

Q. 4   Please check on the list below the *main* reason why you give blood:

(a) General desire to help people

(b) To repay in some way a transfusion given to someone I know

(c) In response to an appeal for blood

(d) Some of my friends/colleagues give blood and encouraged me to join them

(e) Another reason (please state)

Q. 5   Could you say why you *first* decided to become a blood donor?

Beddington did not test his questionnaire, and confusion followed. Many respondents checked more than one item in question 4, some checking all four; and others checked items in question 4 and wrote replies to the open-ended question 5. This meant that it was impossible to determine whether there was a main reason and how that reason related to the factors influencing the original decision to donate. He concluded that the responses were "largely uninterpretable." Without a test such an outcome is inescapable.

Until recently, contributors gave to their local United Way, which then decided which charities would receive what. Contributors could not say that they wanted their money to go to the local ASPCA chapter. They were denied "donor choice." Now your local United Way has written a question that mentions "donor choice." Nothing wrong with that phrase, is there? Not on the surface. But that is what the pretest of a questionnaire is for, identifying problems you don't know about. (If you do know about the problem, you don't need a pretest to tell you.) It turns out that "donor choice" makes many people think of organ donations, body parts, and sperm banks. So on that question it's back to the drawing board.

Finally, what, if anything, is wrong with this question, which appeared in a poll on sexual knowledge:

What do you think is the age at which the average or typical American first has sexual intercourse?

Few respondents could possibly know the answer, either from their own experience or that of others; yet that will not prevent them from answering the question. How are respondents likely to learn the answer? For many it will be what they remember from a newspaper story or the evening news, which are themselves based on polls. The question, that is, doesn't so much measure sexual knowledge as familiarity with previous polls of sexual knowledge. Almost certainly that is not what the researcher wanted to measure.

Nonsampling Errors

A survey is done not because of interest in the group surveyed, the sample, but for information on a larger group, the population, which is not surveyed because it costs too much, takes too long, or because information need not be all that accurate. It requires that the sample be drawn with care so that the sample will, in fact, represent the population.

The best size for a sample is not easily determined, depending as it does on how much money is available for the survey, how accurate the results must be, how many subgroups are to be analyzed, and how much the manager already knows about the situation. It is important for monthly estimates of unemployment to be accurate to within .1 of one percent, and therefore the Current Population Survey done each month by the Census Bureau draws a sample of 60,000 households. As the Gallup poll is sold to news media and is used not to make decisions but to generate news stories, high accuracy is not necessary. It uses samples of around 1,500.

To draw a simple random sample—one in which each member of the population has the same probability of being selected—one needs a list of all members of the population. If this list, called a frame, is out-of-date or inaccurate, the sample results will not project accurately to the true population, but only the population represented by the frame. Perhaps the most spectacular of all frame errors was the one perpetrated by the *Literary Digest* in its 1936 Presidential Straw Poll. The *Literary Digest* made the mistake of choosing for its frame lists of owners of automobiles and of telephone subscribers. There were few such citizens in the depths of the Great Depression, but they were staunchly Republican, and the Straw Poll predicted Alf Landon would win with 58 percent of the vote. But he only received 38 percent (of the two-candidate vote), and the *Literary Digest* went down with him.[10]

A piece of research may aim to study one segment, but because of frame errors, it may turn out that it actually studies another segment. It is the manager's responsibility to make sure the researcher knows beforehand which segments he is supposed to study, and it is the manager's responsibility to know himself which segments have actually been studied. It is an elementary but insidious error for a manager not to take pains to find out what population the sample represents.

Problems with Interviewers

Interviewers give rise to another set of errors. They may misunderstand their instructions; they may subconsciously suggest answers to the respondent; or they may simply cheat, either by helping the respondent put down the ''correct'' answers or by filling out the questionnaire themselves without even seeking out the respondent.[11]

Problems with Respondents

The respondent can also cause problems. He may think he knows the answer to a question, but because of faulty memory he may not remember correctly; he may know it very well but not wish to say; or, like a student, he may not know the answer, not want to admit it, and answer as if he did know it. Not wishing to say is common with touchy or embarrassing issues, where it is unwise to take answers to direct questions at face value. We expect alumni to overreport their income on the alumni questionnaire, as we expect respondents to overreport their charitable donations and giving of blood and underreport deviant behavior like masturbation, compulsive gambling, drunkenness, and a love of modern poetry.[12] It can be particularly serious in surveys trying to uncover the size of a social problem, and it should lead to skepticism when reading figures, say, for the number of alcoholics or homosexuals or people who play the numbers game.

Robert Agranoff tells of one credulous candidate for office who knocked on doors in his district and learned that 80 percent of the people he spoke to would vote for him. He gave up, went back to his law practice, and began to plan his acceptance speech. He got 40 percent and lost.[13]

What could have gone wrong? Unless the reader knows a great deal about marketing research, he will not guess all of the respondent errors that arose in this case:

- Some of the people he visited were not registered to vote.
- Some were registered but did not vote.
- Some went to the polls but did not cast a vote in his race.
- Some who said they would vote for him forgot his name.
- Some learned that he belonged to the wrong party and voted against him.
- Some lied, promising to vote for him but intending all along to vote for his opponent.

Sampling Errors

There are two types of errors that arise in survey research, sampling errors and nonsampling errors. All of the errors discussed above are nonsampling errors.

Sampling errors help describe the uncertainty of survey results, where the uncertainty has arisen solely from the luck of the draw. Normally, in conducting a survey, a researcher draws a sample (of 200, say) and reports the results: "Seventeen percent of homes with televisions reported watching Ken Burns' special on the Civil War on the local public broadcasting television channel." But we could take a second sample in precisely the same way at the same time that might report that 15 percent watched; a third might say 18 percent, and so on. Assume that we can never know that in reality, the true rating of the broadcast was 16.5 percent. The individual sample findings are all within the margin of error expected under the sampling plan, and any one of the figures, 15 percent, 17 percent, or 18 percent, is as good an estimate as any other.

This variation in results that would result from repeated samples is described as sampling error. It has nothing to do with respondent errors or frame errors or poorly worded questions. It deals with differences in results that arise solely from the luck of the draw.

It can be said another way. A fear that any manager must deal with in evaluating survey questions is that he will be misled by the results, as the credulous candidate was by the 80 percent intention to vote. He might say to himself, "If this research were repeated, how much would the result differ from the results already in hand?" It is a substantial problem. Take the political campaign manager who finds his candidate has a lead of four percentage points in a private poll? Can it be believed? What is the chance that the survey is wrong and that the candidate is actually behind by some margin, however small?

There is yet another way to put the difference between sampling and nonsampling errors. The size of a sampling error is determined by the size of the sample.

In the simplest situation the relationship is inverse-square-root; as the size of the sample goes up by a factor of four, the sampling error goes down by a factor of two. Nonsampling errors are unaffected by the size of the sample. Whether the sample is big or small, they remain. The *Literary Digest* poll is a good example of this. The sampling error is of the magnitude of .07 of one percent, and there is less than one chance in a billion that the sample result is off by .2 of one percent.[14] It is a sampling error smaller than men of affairs can usually hope to enjoy. But the small sampling error was not enough; it was nonsampling error that killed the *Digest*.

Every elementary text on statistics (and on marketing research) develops this point and gives simple formulas for the case of the simple random sample. What is particularly important for the manager is not to forget that there are two errors. It is relatively easy to compute a sampling error or to get at least an estimate of its size. But it is so difficult to estimate the size of the nonsampling error that it is almost never done, at least not on a routine basis. Yet it is often, perhaps most of the time, the more serious of the two errors. The real issue in a political poll is not what proportion of the voting-age population intends to vote for candidate X, but what proportion of those who will actually vote intend to vote for candidate X.[15]

The Unimportance of the Sampling Ratio

It is worth a few words to try to teach the reader another morsel of statistics. The size of the sampling error is determined by the size of the sample. It is not determined by the sampling ratio, which is the size of the sample divided by the size of the population. With a sample of 200 drawn from a population of 20,000, the sampling ratio is 200/20,000 = .01. If the same sample is drawn from a population of 200,000, the sampling ratio is 200/200,000 = .001. In either case the size of the sampling error is the same. If the sample is drawn according to a statistical sampling plan, both samples contain the same amount of information. Just because the first sample comes from a population of 20,000 while the second comes from a population of 200,000 does not mean that one learns more from the first sample. Both contain the same amount of information.

If you belong to the host of readers who have never studied statistics, or even if you have studied it, you probably do not believe me. You may even believe that a sample so small as to constitute only .1 of one percent of some population cannot possibly tell you much about that population. You are wrong. You gain information from the work you do, and the larger the sample, the more you do and the more you learn. You are not penalized because of the size of the population you did not sample. That is why, as you can see for yourself, by noting the sample sizes reported by the news media when they publish their polls, they usually work with samples of a thousand or so. The voting-age population in the 1976 presidential election was around 144 million, and therefore the sampling ratio for such a sample is .000007. But the sample is still useful and—to repeat—contains the same amount of information as would a sample of 1,000 from a population of 100,000 or one million or even ten million.[16]

All this does not mean that the sampling ratio is useless, however. If a researcher were given the task of studying 3,000 members of a local YMCA, he might choose a sample of 300 but artfully stress the sampling ratio of 10 percent in order to coax the members into believing that the study was worthwhile.

Summary: Protecting Yourself Against Misleading Research

Given all these possible errors, how do managers protect themselves against being misled by marketing research? By being hard to satisfy. It can mean several things. The first is that the results of your research should fit with the results of other research. If the samples aim to represent the population of a city, the average age (and income of the sample), for example, should agree with known figures for the entire city.

Even when one has large samples and small sampling errors, it still pays to be tough-minded and seek a second opinion or do a second survey. Amnesty International USA (AI) raises almost all of its annual revenues by direct mail. Direct mail makes it easy to test, because the responses to the mailing can be coded so that the mailer can determine how many responses and how much money each appeal raised. AI's chief fundraiser had a simple rule to protect herself against a misleading result. She would repeat the test at a later date. If the second test agreed with the first, then she could rely on the results. Otherwise she had to move with caution. This simple rule served her in lieu of statistical procedures. AI deals with intensely political issues, and what is hot one year, say, Turkey or Somalia, may generate little interest among donors in a second year. Her simple rule protected her (and AI) against shifts in public opinion. Finally, I have pointed out that statistical procedures deal only with sampling errors, not nonrandom sources of error; but her simple rule gave her some protection against both types of error.[17]

Every survey of arts audiences shows that they are well above average in income and education. If your survey of, say, a symphony audience shows that the average education of your audience is about average, you must pause. The result is probably wrong, but perhaps not. How can you tell? By comparing one answer with other results from the same research, that is, by examining the results for internal consistency, which is the second way of getting research. Suppose, for example, that this particular questionnaire was distributed by volunteer ushers who paid no particular attention to who received the questionnaires; and that in addition, the questionnaire shows that 70 percent of the respondents were one-half of a married couple. Now the hypothesis comes to mind that in many couples it may have been the wife who filled out the questionnaire, and that wives in general have less education than their husbands. We have a simple test: Reanalyze the results and compare the level of education by sex. If the women show much less education (and if most of the respondents were in fact women), we have explained the odd result; if not, we have to keep on digging. Much of the time this process enables the manager to understand or explain counterintuitive results.

The third way to scrutinize the research is to compare it with a model of client behavior. One of the reasons for constructing such a model is to aid a manager in knowing what questions to ask. Another reason is that the model serves as a basis for comparison once the results are in. Yet another reason to model clients' behavior: Suppose we have developed an index of propensity to enlist in one of the military services and we find that young men and women with a high propensity to enlist have less education than those with a low propensity, and also the fathers of high-propensity respondents have less education than the fathers of low-propensity respondents. How are we to evaluate this finding? Does it seem plausible? There is no way to answer these questions without a model.

It is perfectly possible to construct the model after the fact. If we observe that high-propensity respondents have less education, we try to build a model that explains it. This is all right as long as it is done with care and common sense. The danger is that it is all too easy to build a model that explains *any* fact. So in the absence of an explicit theory dealing with the relation between propensity and education, developed before the data are in, the manager will perforce have to make sense of the results after the fact.

LIMITATIONS ON RESEARCH

For one thing, research findings can prove unwelcome. It is a curiosity much commented on that the federal government does, by and large, so little research before it undertakes new regulatory or legislative activities. The rational course would seem to be to test a proposal and *then* decide what to do. But this method contains grave dangers: The results may not accord with the ambitions of the proposal's supporters, and if they cannot safely ignore the results, they will be put to the trouble of reprobating them. We can only wonder at the courage of Senator Daniel Patrick Moynihan who, on learning that a test of a guaranteed annual income for the poor, a program he had supported for over a decade, showed that a guaranteed income reduced hours worked and increased marital instability, said, "We must now be prepared to entertain the possibility that we were wrong."[18]

Another example of limitations of research arose when Nelson Rockefeller was campaigning for the Republican presidential nomination in 1968. His polls showed that the electorate was worried more about conservative problems than about liberal problems, that is, more about crime, prices, drugs, and the international Communist conspiracy than about education, pollution, and reducing poverty. Sound political strategy called for him to act like a leader, not merely to copy Nixon's campaign. But Rockefeller himself was a liberal, emotionally committed to the less important issues and too proud to stoop to win. The result was that Rockefeller ignored his own polls and stressed the liberal issues in his advertising. The authors of a fine book on the 1968 election wrote drily, "It is never going to be easy to find candidates who combine the required force of character and intellect with a willingness to accept policies shaped by polls and computers."[19]

It is not merely that the federal government does little research beforehand; it also undertakes little research to find out what happens after the new regulation or legislation. As put by a staff member at the Federal Trade Commission, "It's rare for an agency to look at a rule once it's in place. Kudos come for getting rules on the books, not in worrying whether they're doing what they were intended to do in the first place."[20]

There are other difficulties in evaluating social programs as well. The goals for such programs tend to be vague. One need only read the preamble to a piece of enabling legislation to see this.[21] Program goals also often promise the moon, which may help build support for the program but impair the effectiveness of the feedback research. Finally, many social programs bear meager fruit; the smaller the effects, the harder and more expensive it is to find them. Peter Rossi has described all three of these factors in a concise phrase: The main problems in evaluating social programs are "vague goals, strong promises and weak effects."[22]

Unwelcome results are only one form that hostility to research takes. Sometimes research is done by an outsider, a hired pen, which often leads to mistrust by people within the organization.

And, of course, not everyone welcomes the premise that the marketer takes without examination—that the public should be served, that its interests count. This attitude is particularly common among professionals whose training leads them to expect to dominate the exchange between client and professional. The music director of a symphony orchestra decides what music is to be played. That is his job, and he has the training to do it. It is natural that he doubts the force of audience tastes on his decisions. Of course, this disdain can reach extremes, as in the case of the museum curators who refused to put chairs or benches in their galleries after a visitor survey showed a need for them, because they felt that tacky modern furniture would distract from the beauty of their masterpieces."[23] We might as well expect such professionals to say, "The only good researcher is a dead researcher."

Research also goes unused when it is commissioned absentmindedly, without planning. For example, the research may be designed to answer questions that no one wants answered and, like the pen that wrote under water, it is ignored.

Finally, research is of little use unless the organization wants to use it. Feedback research, indeed any evaluation, implies a willingness to change. If your mind is made up, the facts only confuse. An organization that uses feedback or other marketing research regularly is an organization interested in change, perhaps even in doing better. Research is often done in secret, not by design but by accident. The effect, nevertheless, is the same—people in the organization are surprised, or hurt, to learn about the study, and questions they would like answered have not been dealt with. It is not a good idea to inform the music director of a survey of audience reactions to his programs after the fact. Research is often commissioned when there are no resources available to implement its findings. And of course, without the active interest of an organization's senior manager or managers, without their commitment to getting the research done, and to using it, the research will die on the shelf.

A WORD ABOUT THE COST OF RESEARCH

It is, of course, obvious to the reader that research usually costs something. Typically, there are OOP costs as well as the need for active involvement by managers. It is management, after all, that decides what it wants to know and what use to make of the research.

Research also takes time. A quickie survey can be pushed through in a few weeks, sometimes in a few days; but most surveys take two or three months at the least. A larger study that starts with exploratory research may take even longer. But when the research deals with behavior rather than states of mind or states of being the times involved can be much longer. A test of fund-raising appeals in the mails takes several weeks to be prepared. Once the material has been dropped, replies will come in rapidly for the first several weeks, although they will continue to trickle in for a year or so. Market tests must be several times longer than the client's purchase frequency; therefore, although a new subscription price will begin to depress subscriptions immediately, it may be many months before its impact on renewals is known. Mailing lists used to generate subscriptions to a magazine cannot be properly evaluated until the magazine has observed how many new subscriptions the list produces and how many of these new subscribers renew. (Keeping track of such figures would besot the sturdiest bookkeeper, but there are computer programs that do just this.) The quality of a list, therefore, cannot be judged by how well it draws the first time around.

The test must also be long enough to allow the consumer or client to adjust to the new conditions. Seasonal-time-of-day (STD) pricing has been put forward in recent years as a possible way of encouraging consumers to use electricity more frugally. In such a STD pricing scheme, prices vary by time of day and time of year in accordance with the marginal cost of generating electricity; thus, electricity at night costs, say, five times less than electricity in the morning peak. How long should consumers be given to adjust to the new prices? Answer: at least seven years.[24]

Few managers can, or should, wait this long before deciding. While returns from a mail campaign will trickle in for a year, half of the returns usually come in the first several weeks, after which a manager can decide which lists to buy in full. Similarly, most managers should be able to select which STD scheme is best in much less time than seven years.

NOTES

1. Richard M. Titmuss, *The Gift Relationship* (New York: Vintage, 1971), p. 120.

2. William Butler Yeats, "To a Wealthy Man Who Promised a Second Subscription to the Dublin Municipal Gallery if It Were Proved the People Wanted Pictures," *The Poems of W.B. Yeats: A New Edition*, ed. Richard J. Finneran (New York: Macmillan, 1983), reprinted with permission of Simon & Schuster, Inc. and A. P. Watt Ltd. on behalf of Michael Yeats.

3. One modest discussion is Richard A. Hamilton, "Focused Group Interviews to Determine the Feasibility and Nature of a Kansas City Based H.M.O." *Akron Business and Economic Review* 10, no. 1 (Spring 1979): 50–53.

4. Vince Stehle, "A Broadcast Call for Major Gifts." *Chronicle of Philanthropy,* October 19, 1993, p. 23.

5. Holly Hall, "In Thanking Donors, Plaques and Dinners Aren't the Only Way." *Chronicle of Philanthropy,* March 23, 1993, p. 31.

6. Alvin Rabushka and Bruce Jacobs, *Old Folks at Home* (New York: Free Press, 1979).

7. Guido Francescato, Sue Weidemann, James R. Anderson, and Richard Chenoweth, *Residents' Satisfaction in HUD-Assisted Housing: Design and Management Factors* (Washington, D.C.: Office of Policy Development and Research, HUD, 1979), pp. 1–5.

8. This has a practical implication. If you are ever confronted with research that has come to the wrong conclusion, simply go over each question deliberately and you will be able to destroy the research, at least to your own satisfaction. For an example of this, see Jeffrey O'Connell and Wallace Wilson, "Public Opinion on No-Fault Auto Insurance: A Survey of the Surveys." *Law Forum* (1970): 307–341.

9. John Beddington, "Analysis of Blood Donor Motives," which is Appendix 6 in Titmuss, *The Gift Relationship,* p. 307.

10. Maurice C. Bryson has argued that the problem with the *Literary Digest* poll was not so much a frame error as a voluntary response error. See his article, "The Literary Digest Poll: Making of a Statistical Myth." *American Statistician* 30 (November 1976): 184–185.

11. A book discussing interviewing as interviewers see it is by Jean M. Converse and Howard Schuman, *Conversations at Random: Survey Research as Interviewers See It* (New York: Wiley, 1974).

12. One solution to this problem is use of the randomized response technique. See, for example, Michael S. Goodhart and Valerie Gruson, "The Randomized Response Technique: A Test on Drug Use." *Journal of the American Statistical Association* 70 (December 1975): 815–818. Researchers can also use unobtrusive techniques to get around such social barriers. The latter is illustrated in E.J. Webb, Donald T. Campbell, Richard D. Schwartz, and Lee Sechrest, *Unobtrusive Measures: Non-reactive Research in the Social Sciences* (Chicago: Rand-McNally, 1966).

13. Robert Agranoff, *The Management of Election Campaigns* (Boston: Holbrook Press, 1974), p. 14.

14. The sampling error of a mean when the mean is a proportion and the sample size is large is

$$\sqrt{\frac{p(1 - p)}{n}}$$

where p is the proportion and n is the sample size. A 95 percent confidence interval is 1.96 times this amount.

15. Because of this factor, it is standard to ask respondents in political polls whether they intend to vote. Over time, a skilled researcher can adjust respondents' answers by the likelihood of their voting.

16. There is one slight qualification. When the sampling ratio is large, say, above .1, the formula for estimating the sampling error then includes as one of its terms the sampling ratio. In practice, very few samples are as large as 10 percent of the population.

17. David L. Rados, ''Amnesty International USA,'' revised November 1993, unpublished.

18. *New York Times,* November 11, 1978, p. A23. He also continued to support research, saying ''I don't know what our final judgment on the research . . . will be. But the first thing is to get all the information on the record and take a hard look at it.''

19. Lewis Chester, Godfrey Hodgson, and Bruce Page, *An American Melodrama* (New York: Viking, 1969), pp. 387–391.

20. Robert B. Reich, then assistant director for evaluation, quoted in *Business Week* (March 28, 1977), p. 92.

21. For an example, see the case, ''The Federal Crime Insurance Program,'' in the first edition of this book.

22. Peter H. Rossi, ''Testing for Success and Failure in Social Action,'' in *Evaluating Social Programs,* edited by Peter H. Rossi and Walter Williams (New York: Seminar Press, 1970), p. 16.

23. Paul DiMaggio, Michael Useem, and Paula Brown, *Audience Studies of the Performing Arts and Museums: A Critical Review.* Research Division Report #9 (Washington, D.C.: National Endowment for the Arts, November 1978), p. 67.

24. John T. Wenders and Lester D. Taylor, ''Experiments in Seasonal-Time-of-Day Pricing of Electricity to Residential User.'' *Bell Journal of Economics* 7, no. 1 (Autumn 1976), p. 536. In a footnote the authors criticized STD tests currently in progress because none of them is to run for more than four years. ''This is simply not enough time,'' they write.

Part III

MARKETING STRATEGY

Chapter 7

Focus: Competition, Segmentation, Targeting, and Positioning

This chapter deals with the techniques that marketers use to focus their programs on groups of clients. They do this (in brief) by (1) finding some basis for subdividing their clients into submarkets, (2) choosing a few of these submarkets as the focus of their efforts, and (3) taking steps to ensure that clients see their organization in a correct perspective vis-à-via competitors. In marketing jargon, they (1) segment their markets, (2) target certain segments, and (3) position their offerings against the competition. We start with the last, competition.

COMPETITION

What do we think of when we think of competition? We may think of Darwin or of amateur sports; or we may think of business, which immediately calls to mind big-time college sports; but we may not think of a library, a housing authority, or the United States Olympic Committee.

There is substance to such instinctive thinking. Competition as practiced by nonprofit organizations is often a good deal less aggressive than competition on the gridiron or on Wall Street. Nonprofit organizations often choose to cooperate with their rivals instead of competing with them. Many nonprofit organizations, in fact, face no competition at all, or face only emasculated competitors. Governments, for example, prefer to deliver social services by means of single suppliers, monopolies.[1] Even nonprofit businesses worry less about their competition than businesses do about theirs, because the rewards from winning come to the organization, not to the managers.

We see a lessened concern with competition, or perhaps less of it, in the absence of measures of competition. Businesses can buy standardized research services that report the activities of their competitors, and their perduring attention on their competition shows up in the importance given market share as a marketing objective. Where standardized research services do not exist, trade associations will often fill in, collecting information on sales from members of the association and publishing composite figures for the industry. The nonprofit sector has nothing like these, which presumably tells us that there is little competition to measure; or it tells us that nonprofit marketing objectives rarely deal with market share (which, in fact, is true). Perhaps, it merely tells us that most nonprofit organizations do not worry much about competition in drawing up marketing plans. Instead, they can more or less ignore competition, saying in effect that outdoing the competition will not make the organization all that much better off.

The Growth of Competition

For all this, it is still necessary to discuss competition, because while some nonprofit organizations can slight their competition, others cannot. As Allen has written,

Many a not-for-profit community blood bank has fought until exterminated to preserve its assumed geographical boundaries from invasion by the American National Red Cross which has "come in" where it was not needed, with disastrous results to the smaller volunteer community blood bank which . . . was driven out of business.[2]

Nonprofit organizations such as these blood banks can succeed only in the face of competitive pressures, and to do this they must analyze their competitors and go them one better. And the director of a performing arts group in Dallas who is looking for new board members would be dismayed to see the competition from fifty-five small, seven mid-sized, and twelve large arts groups.[3]

But there is more. An effective competitive posture, which marketers call *market positioning* or simply *positioning,* has become important to organizational effectiveness and to survival. This has happened for several reasons:

- The need for government funds, for gifts, and for volunteers has increased.
- More and more NPOs are entering markets where stiff competition already exists, such as health and fitness clubs.
- Many institutions have found themselves facing weak demand for their services. As a result they have had to fight hard for clients.
- Many NPOs have set up nonprofit businesses to increase their income, which put them in competition with other nonprofit businesses and even for-profit businesses.
- There has been increasing use of a segmentation scheme in which clients are segmented into those who can pay and those who can't. The competition is, naturally, for those who can.

We have been talking about competition and competitors as if organizations compete toe-to-toe with other organizations. But that is probably not how organizations compete, at least not the large ones. "[G]iant corporations may not compete with other giants *as single entities,* but rather they have a large variety of intercompany relations including competitive ones."[4] A New Yorker cartoon caught this some years ago when it showed one dejected rooter after the Yale–Harvard game saying to another, "At least we have a better physics department." Here is the treasurer of a large museum commenting, in a conversation, on competition as she saw it:

I doubt that museums ever compete head-to-head. They only compete in areas, say, French porcelains or eighteenth century English furniture. But there are also people involved as well. They are in this for the ego kicks, for their psyches. They compete as individuals. They don't so much think of competition between their museum and another, but as between them and their counterpart at the other museum. So a curator of Greek and Roman antiquities competes with the same curator at another museum; and the director of one will be striving to outdo the director of another.

Their competition—the competition of these individuals—will be reflected, of course, in how their institutions behave. But the driving force is not an institutional one. It is a personal one.

The Arguments for Competition

There is not much point, in a book on marketing, in belaboring the idea that competition is socially desirable. Give clients a choice, give them an opportunity to take their trade elsewhere, and the organization will try to respond to their interests. Choice prods the organization to find out what clients want and to provide it.

Under competition, organizations smile on innovation rather than seeing it as punishment for their sins; and as competing organizations usually differ in their aims and methods, they can be expected to develop products and services that differ and that better serve the needs of particular market segments. By punishing the slack, competition rewards efficiency and, so the theory goes, drives down costs and prices. Just imagine what would be sitting on your desk if there were only one big supplier in the computer industry and competition were forbidden. Or do not imagine anything. Contemplate the state of public education in America, where parents have little or no choice about where they send their children. Some go further. They argue that competition is unnecessary because nonprofits have an ethical obligation to make the best possible use of their resources, both financial and human. My theory of ethics does not stretch quite that far, however.

Finally, competition can spur competitors to produce their best. Surely, this is why there are tournaments in sports and contests of all kinds. Surely, this is the intent of challenge grants, where a donor promises to donate one dollar for every four raised by an NPO. The ancient Greeks went even further and combined with their athletic games public competitions in music, pottery, poetry, painting, choral singing, oratory, and drama, because they believed that competition stimulated both the skill of the artist and the taste of the public.[5]

The Arguments Against

Such a line does not persuade everyone, however. If competition can bring out the best in people, it can also bring out the worst, driving people to push the line of propriety. The United States Postal Service competes with TNT Express Worldwide, a delivery company and also a major postal service customer. TNT's Mailfast unit has become a big competitor for international mail. When the USPS held its annual National Postal Forum for people in the mail business, TNT wasn't invited. What's more, the postal service banned TNT from renting rooms in the conference hotel. (Ho-hum. It rented across the street.) This is no more than petty, but it hints at the dark side of competition.[6] At its worst competition takes on a life of its own as people worry more about winning than about feeding the hungry or healing the sick. Some even go so far as to argue that the public expects the nonprofit sector to be kinder and gentler, not squeezing every penny out of its clients and not cutting corners wherever it can.

Competition is sometimes seen as costly. Although one cannot imagine the impact of effective competition—say, through a voucher system—on public schooling in this country, we suspect the changes it would bring about would be radical and in the right direction. But is it a good idea for public schools to spend money advertising for students, as they have begun to do in California?[7] Is it desirable to have nonprofit blood banks run by hospitals or the Red Cross competing with for-profit blood banks for their donors? Or to have a for-profit hospital competing for the paying patients with a nonprofit hospital that looks to paying patients to cover the losses of providing for the poor? Many say that such competition is harmful, that it would increase medical costs, lower the quality of medical care, lead to duplicate facilities, and cause overutilization of hospitals.

Is it desirable to encourage competition among children? Many argue that while some competition is inevitable, too much can harm a child, particularly those children who lose. One attractive feature of the Boy Scouts from its very beginning was the refusal of its founder to make merit badges competitive. Each boy earns his badges by meeting requirements, not by competing with other boys.[8]

I argued above that having several nonprofits competing in the same arena was beneficial. What happens when several becomes dozens, as it did in Milwaukee? In 1984, the city had a dozen NPOs working to prevent teenage pregnancies. Six years later it had forty-one such groups. To the sensible suggestion that some of the groups merge, their leaders argued against for two reasons: that mergers would mar the quality of the services they provided and that mergers would make them more bureaucratic and less responsive. Perhaps. But forty-one does seem far too many.[9]

There are barriers to competition, moreover. One of the Big Ideas of the 1990s for streamlining government and cutting costs was privatization, which means contracting with private companies to supply public services (like picking up the garbage, paving the streets, guarding the art museum, and maintaining the golf course). This Big Idea hasn't quite worked as it was hoped. Unions hate the idea, and many private suppliers have done a poor job. One thing that cities and states have learned is that there should be a lot of competition for the contract to pick up the garbage, and that the competition should include public-sector departments. In many instances workers in these departments have proved that they can do a better job of delivering cost-effective services than outsiders can. Then why didn't these employees do this beforehand? The answer is competition, and with it the threat of losing one's job or earning less pay. Such eventualities powerfully focus the mind.

To work, competition must be fair and it must match competitors of equal skills and capacities, which is why in tennis women compete against women, not men, and juniors do not play against seniors; and in society we often favor the weak or the small. For competition to work, clients must be competent. They must want information and want to make informed choices among suppliers; they must be able to order their objectives with some modicum of rationality, and they must be able to recognize individual shams and bogus organizations. Achieving such competence means working at it, and most clients, like most consumers, prefer to take their ease; or rather, they apprehend that the returns from developing competence are not worth the game. For competition to work, clients also need to evaluate suppliers: How have they performed in the past, and which groups do they serve best? Such evaluations can be difficult to do, and often they will be out-of-date. In fact, the many problems of evaluating the performance of public schools is one of the substantial barriers to improving them.

Competition for What?

Businesses compete for profits today, and for positions of advantage that promise profits in the future. Nonprofit organizations compete for what can be called "prizes," anything that the organization values and that furnishes it with coin of some kind.

In general, prizes vary with the type of organization and its aims. As we would expect, nonprofit business prizes are much the same as in business—sales, customers, operating surpluses, perhaps even market share. For common benefit organizations, the most valuable prize is typically members. A hospital with empty beds needs patients, and since patients do not admit themselves, the hospital tries to persuade doctors to admit more patients, or it tries to increase the number of heavy admitters on its staff. A museum, or a library, might seek several types of competitive prizes. It needs collections, for one. It may wish to build its collections, or fill them out, or it may merely wish to have the right to display a traveling exhibition. It wants endowment funds, and operating funds. And it may need to attract volunteers, say, to give tours of the museum or read to children. For a historic site the prize might well be visitors, for a mime troupe a federal grant, for a charity money, and for an impresario the right to stage a first performance.

Nonprofit organizations, like businesses, seek other prizes too, like working capital, competent managers, and reliable suppliers. But these are not usually the responsibility of marketing, although sometimes marketing may be involved. What makes competition important to marketers is that competitive prizes are controlled by third parties, usually clients or donors; and winning their favor involves changing their behavior in a way that meets and supports the goals of the organization.

Identifying the Competition

Just who one's competitors are is a question on which businessmen waste little time. Ask a manufacturer of bras who his competition is and he will say, "Other bra makers." And after a little prodding he may add, "Other bra makers in my price line, selling through the same retailers that I use, aiming at the same target market."

This illustrates the most elementary solution to the problem of identifying competitors: Like competes with like. Many nonprofit organizations can take this approach, and as a result they have little trouble identifying their competition. In some settings like competition is defined in a mechanical manner. For example, in setting student tuition and fees, the University of Washington has a formal "comparison group": seven other universities like it, with whom it is allowed to compare its own tuition and fees. In essence, it has its competition pointed out to it.[10]

The numbers game. As an example of the type of analysis to be followed in situations where like competes with like, let us look briefly at the legalization of the numbers game, which some have argued the state should operate to make money and as part of its efforts to control, and perhaps reduce, serious crime. The question is, can the state compete? What we will do is straightforward, that is, compare the legal and illegal games on several product attributes and use the comparison to identify potential sources of marketing problems.

The numbers game, or policy as it is sometimes called, is a lottery. In the most common form of play, bettors bet on a three-digit number from 000 to 999. The winning number is determined by an arbitrary mechanism, in New York City by the pari-mutuel handle at a nearby racetrack.

The bettor plays in spite of the fact that the game is not fair. A player who bets one dollar a day on a number and plays six days a week will hit a winning number on average every 3.2 years.[11] During this time he will have bet $1,000.

If he wins, he wins $600, but he is expected to tip the numbers runner who took the bet 10 percent of his winnings, or $60. Because his original bet of $1 is not returned, his net winnings are $600 − $60 − $1 = $539, and his original $1,000 has shrunk by $461. The (expected monetary) value of the game to the bettor is negative, but the large variance offers excitement and the hope of sudden shifts in fortune.

Now let us consider the problems faced by the state if it tries to legalize the numbers game and run the game itself.[12] The numbers game offers a constellation of interests that a state-run operation must meet if it is to drive out the illegal game.

Distribution is intensive in low-income areas of the city. Players can bet in their homes, in elevators, at the doors of their apartment buildings, or at their work stations. If they must go out to bet, they usually can find a runner near their home or job. They can send their children to place a bet. To match this distribution system, the state would have to license a wide variety of agents, especially private individuals, to sell numbers part-time. Agents would have to be paid on a straight commission basis, which means their gross income would probably be below the legal minimum hourly wage. Unions would object to such a system. Moreover, use of itinerant agents would require strict, close regulation to discourage these agents from taking bets for illegal games as well as for the state's game. The conclusion is that the state would probably find it difficult to match the existing distribution system as cheaply.

Players can bet any amount they want. The state can match this, although writing nickel and dime bets, which are common in the illegal game, would be too costly. Players choose the numbers they play. The state would have to match this particular feature of the numbers game, as it appears to be of considerable importance to the players to play hunches and bet lucky numbers.

Results are known the same day or the next day. Payoffs to winners are made within a few hours of winning. There is no reason why the state could not match this. Action is available six days per week, and a variety of bets is available during the day. The state can match this.

Placing a bet is simple. There are no receipts. When a player wishes to bet the same number day after day, as some do, he sees his runner only from time to time, when he comes to settle accounts. A state-run system would require more paperwork, and therefore bets would be somewhat harder to make.

Winnings are private, and thus neither taxed nor the object of desire of importunate relatives or debtors. The state has shown little willingness to exempt such winnings from taxation, but as most players earn low incomes, they pay little income tax anyway. For the middle class, tax-free winnings would probably carry substantial appeal. The state will probably ultimately be forced to grant such an exemption, if it is to accomplish its goal of driving the illegal game out of business. Whether the state would be able to keep winners' names private, relying only on word-of-mouth publicity, is doubtful. In this area, then, the state would probably find it difficult to match existing arrangements.

Betting is a social occasion. Bets are almost always placed with neighbors, friends, or acquaintances, and in familiar places.[13] The state would have difficulty constructing a "friendly" distribution system of this type, although any system of licensing of private individuals will go part way toward meeting this interest of the bettors. It is probable that state-run and -owned shops would appeal not to low-income players, but chiefly to infrequent or small bettors.

The conclusion of all this is that it would be possible for a state-run game to match most of the features of the existing numbers game and to draw away some of its business. However, it would be difficult for the state to provide the intensive distribution system of the illegal game as cheaply, and it seems unlikely that the state would provide the privacy of the illegal game. The necessary conclusion is that the existing game would continue to operate. If, in fact, a state-run game did begin to draw off significant amounts of business, the likely reaction of the bankers would be to alter the game to make it more attractive. (In addition, of course, some marginal bankers would fail.) The result of this competition is impossible to predict. Moreover, if a state-run game made the illegal game unprofitable, the bankers would not be driven out of business, but merely out of numbers into other illegal activities. In fact, organized crime first entered the numbers game as a substitute for activities legalized by the repeal of Prohibition.

Identification based on research. Nonprofit organizations that cannot use these commonsense methods for identifying their competitors must resort to research; but the basic idea still remains that most marketing decisions deal with issues in which like competes with like. (We shall look briefly at competition between like and unlike in a few pages.)

The first step is to start inside the organization, by asking those in management whom they see as their competition and what competitive "prizes" they are competing for. But this is only a start, for many managers in nonprofit organizations first say that they have no competition and then go on to describe it. And their observations are only perceptions of competitive forces, rather than more direct measures.

The second step is to ask the clients who the competition is. This involves investigation of the alternatives that clients consider when they are making a decision. This is hardly a new idea among marketers. In his theory of buyer behavior, Howard sees the choice of consumer brands as taking place not from among all brands in a market, but from among only those brands that come to the consumer's mind as alternatives worth considering. These brands form the consumer's "evoked set."[14] Who competes with the American Automobile Association? In general, all we can say is other auto clubs, such as the Montgomery Ward Auto Club or Amoco Auto Club, and auto clubs run by Ford, INA, and Exxon. To be more specific, AAA must study how clients decide to become members of an auto club and from among which clubs they choose. On this view, then, the alternatives from which the client chooses compete with each other; that is, competition takes place in the mind of the client.

The most reliable competitive identifications rest not on answers to questions but on observed behavior, not on what clients say but on what they do. (Sometimes, though, the client may be asked to explain his behavior.) In most nonprofit situations, this observing is done by examining records and other leavings of the clients. A nonprofit research institute bidding for a defense contract finds out who its competitors are by attending bid openings. Once it has been through this process a number of times, it can make some good guesses as to who its competitors will be on future bids.

University admissions officers have four potential measures of their competition:

- When students take an exam—say, the Scholastic Aptitude Test administered by the Educational Testing Service at Princeton—they put down where they want their scores sent, and they thereby reveal their evoked set, the schools they are considering. This information can be bought by the admissions officer (provided the students approve).

- If students visit the campus, they can be asked where else they have applied, or been accepted.

- When students matriculate, they can be asked where else they applied.

- When accepted students do not matriculate, they too can be asked where they have gone, and why.

All of these factors, except the first, combine measures of behavior with questioning. Note, as well, that they measure different aspects of competition.

This view of competition as a behavioral phenomenon has three implications. First, organizations that compete with each other may not know it. A father goes to a college bookstore to buy a gift for his daughter. A university press that publishes a one-volume encyclopedia competes with other books and, depending on what else the bookstore stocks, perhaps with records, prints, typewriters, and what-have-you. It is only possible to know who competes with whom by researching customers and their buying habits. (Although, as always, one must exercise common sense.)

A second implication is that a common competitor in many nonprofit situations is doing nothing, or at least is procrastinating. A public health agency urges women to get a pap smear, and they either get it or they do not. This dilatory strategy is perhaps the most common form of medical and dental treatment.

A third implication is that when the evoked set is defective in some way, it may prove difficult (or impossible) to identify competition. This situation can arise in several ways:

- When decisions are made one at a time, and as a result no *group* of alternatives is ever considered. If I have already subscribed to too many magazines in the past, then I will not subscribe to a new one now.

- When the competition proceeds in secret, it becomes impossible to determine the contents of the evoked set; as when a librarian knows that there are other libraries seeking a rich man's collection of incunabula but cannot find out who they are. (In which case, a shrewd guess must do.)

- When the client or backer is not competent to choose, the evoked set may be empty; as when a poor mother of eight says she has never heard that there are ways of preventing conception. For her there is no alternative to having still more children.

- When deliberation is not worth the candle, as with the woman who tosses all fundraising appeals in the wastebasket.

Once the competitors have been identified, the next problem is collecting information on them.

Sources of information on the competition. Where does one look for information? There are four broad areas from which the nonprofit can collect information on its competitors: the competitors themselves, the competitor's clients, those in the NPO, and all others. For information on competitors one can look to such sources as annual reports; newsletters; fundraising materials; reports to regulatory agencies like Form 990, which are open to public scrutiny; speeches; marketing brochures; and want ads. Information on the competitors' clients comes through normal marketing research like focus groups and surveys. People in one's own nonprofit like fundraisers, planners, and the research staff often know a good deal about the competition. Finally, outsiders can provide information; for example, the National Charities Information Bureau, former employees, suppliers, trade associations, newspaper and magazine articles, and even court records.

Like and Unlike

For the most part, marketers can confine themselves to dealing with like competitors. But they should recognize that there is another type of competition, less easy to identify, in which like competes with unlike. In the marketing texts, competition of like with like is usually called secondary competition. So most of our discussion has dealt with secondary competition. Competition of like with unlike is called primary competition. To the businessman, primary competition is competition between industries; to the nonprofit manager, it is competition between his sector of the nonprofit economy and other sectors, or competition between industries or between nonprofit sectors. This is competition, say, between travel and education, between volunteer work in the performing arts and volunteer work in politics, between giving blood to the Red Cross and giving money to the local Association for the Blind.

It is not so easy to identify primary competition because competitors are now defined by the specific situation in which the client finds himself. There are no similarities between products. It has been often noted that performing arts companies are loathe to raise ticket prices, and at least one of the reasons for this reluctance is the existence of a number of low-cost substitutes. Both Poggi and

Baumol and Bowen have concluded that if ticket prices drift out of line, people will substitute, say, movies or television for live theater and records for live music. And this tendency is heightened if we consider T costs, instead of the cost of tickets alone.[15]

Competitive Relations

Now, we deal with the strategic question: What should a nonprofit organization do about competition?

At the first, we must recognize that many nonprofit organizations do not enjoy much choice. In their daily transactions, their competition is more or less given, as it is with most businesses. Their short-run competitive strategy is simply to do as well as they can in accomplishing their goals. There is nothing one political candidate can do but run against whomever he faces. In fact, aside from studying the opponent's records, very little energy is devoted to activities of the opponent. Strategies are developed largely in response to opinion polls, and charges and countercharges arise as much from the media as from the campaign itself.[16] The Port of San Francisco competes with the Port of Oakland, and as Oakland has new facilities for handling containers and San Francisco does not, San Francisco is losing out. In this situation, San Francisco tries to keep alive and slow the loss of major importers to Oakland.

But even these organizations have more choices when contemplating longer-run decisions. For here, they can take themselves into areas where the competition is less severe, into areas where their own resources and capabilities afford them a competitive advantage of some sort. Take the programming decisions of the Public Broadcasting System as an example. The most important prize for both PBS and commercial television networks is audience. A larger audience means higher advertising sales to the commercial network and more members at local stations for affiliates of PBS. What kind of programming should PBS do? It could try to outdo its commercial rivals, say, by having better daily news programs. But here PBS would be at a competitive disadvantage, because television news is expensive to gather and to report. The commercial networks are already doing a good job with their news broadcasts (at least for viewers with short attention spans), and the commercial networks would doubtless fight to maintain their competitive lead. On the surface, this is not the kind of battle PBS should engage in.

What about live broadcasts? Commercial networks do less and less live programming as time passes. More and more it is recorded (or prerecorded, as they say)—all except sports. But many live programs are exciting and are capable of drawing sizeable audiences. This course, then, offers the potential of competing where the competition is weak and not interested in competing and where PBS presumably has the technical resources it needs.

This is not a full analysis, by any means, but it shows that a nonprofit organization that faces competition can include competitive factors in the formulation of its marketing strategy.

Beyond Competition

Although some nonprofit organizations take their competition as given, others can deal with it directly, by affecting the very nature of the competition itself. It can choose one of three courses: It can try to monopolize its market, it can attract more competition, or it can cooperate with its competitors.

Government bodies typically go for monopoly when formulating marketing strategy. Their managers see monopoly as serving well a variety of public interests and as shifting the burden of administration from locating buyers and stimulating demand to merely filling demand. But even "natural" monopolies—those seen as justified in the eye of the beholder—may find their market eroded if, over time, they fail to meet the changing interest of their clients.

- The laws governing the U.S. Postal Service do not permit any other organization to deliver first-class mail, the USPS's most profitable service.
- The public school establishment has long held that forcing the schools to compete with each other and with private schools will weaken them and result in poorer education for millions of students.
- The Federal Reserve System has been losing members since World War II, so that in 1977 about two out of every five banks holding about three-quarters of the nation's total deposits were members, thus weakening the Fed's control over the money supply.[17] The crux is that member banks must maintain reserves at the Fed that do not pay interest. Reserve requirements for nonmember banks, typically imposed by state government, are generally lower and often permit reserves to earn interest. One proposal, the natural one it would seem, is to pay interest on reserves held at the Fed. The Fed's response was predictable, however. It recommended legislation that would permit it to impose reserve requirements on nonmembers, in effect on all banks, members or not.

Monopoly also appeals to private NPOs. The United Way has long sought to control access to charitable donations by business employees. United Way serves as a single collection agency for many charities; by giving to the United Way, an employee contributes to them all with one donation (or a payroll deduction). But here, monopoly serves the interests of the businesses as well. Employers naturally want to control charitable solicitations that take place in their offices, and they want to avoid a new charity appeal every week. By the 1990s, however, United Way's grip on at-work solicitations had been broken. The Combined Federal Campaign for U.S. government workers had begun to allow non–United Way agencies to appeal for funds at the same time as United Way, with these agencies to receive their share of undesignated gifts. United Way, itself, had begun to permit and then encourage what it called donor choice. By 1992 some 70 percent of United Way affiliates were offering choices to their donors, and 12 percent of donors, one in eight, chose to give to non–United Way agencies.[18]

The outcome has been less money for United Way agencies and more for non–United Way agencies like the United Negro College Fund and Earth Share.[19]

In discussions of this solution to the competitive problem, we seem to leave the realm of marketing. There is no marketing if there is no choice, and at the very least, monopoly means no choice and it often means compulsion, but monopolization merely simplifies the marketing chores; it does not eliminate them. By serving as a single collection agency, United Way removes the need for the individual agencies that it represents to seek funds on their own from the general public. They still can seek other funds, however, and they must compete with other United Way agencies for their share of the monies raised. United Way itself is saved the effort of finding new businesses each year to run its campaigns, and therefore it can concentrate on more effective ways of raising funds.

One end of the competitive line is avoiding competition by doing away with competition. Blue Cross prefers to be sole supplier; it used to punish a company that signed with a health maintenance organization by taking away its Blue Cross option. At the other end, the organization seeks competition by trying to increase the number of competitors. Businesses prefer to sell in non-competitive markets and buy in competitive ones; and they conduct their businesses to make the markets in which they sell less competitive and to encourage competition among their suppliers. A nonprofit organization can, as a strategy, try to encourage competition in the markets where it sells. It would do this primarily to ensure a wider set of choices for its clients. Health maintenance organizations require that their members have choices between two or more alternative health programs. And they often require that members be allowed to rethink their choice from time to time, thus permitting them to change from one plan to another.[20]

Increasing competition to increase the satisfactions of clients is admittedly rare. Most organizations that are not forced to accept their competition as given try to ease the struggle among potential rivals by cooperation. The potential advantages are substantial: lower marketing costs, higher productivity of marketing expenditures, and the possibility of better service for clients. The United Way is of much greater worth to small, relatively unknown organizations, who would otherwise have to struggle with the better-known organizations to raise funds. The American Red Cross, the Salvation Army, the Boy Scouts, and the Girl Scouts all benefit substantially from United Way fund drives, but presumably they could do reasonably well on their own. The small fry, however, would be lost if every organization were on its own. Cooperation has the potential of lowering other marketing costs as well. The Texas Association of Developing Colleges, an affiliate of the United Negro College Fund, ran a cooperative advertising campaign in 1980 to increase public awareness of the colleges, recruit students, and raise funds. Institutional ads promoted all member colleges, while each individual college used additional materials geared to its own markets.[21]

Cooperation, moreover, may be required by law. Before a new hospital can be built, state laws and PL 93-641 require a certificate of need. A hospital with a wait-ing list will usually not be permitted to expand if there are enough hospital beds in total in the area. Public controls and restrictions on capital spending encourage hospitals to cooperate in the purchase of expensive medical technology.

Cooperation is indicated as well when competition is too frenzied and when cooperation serves clients' interests (at least in part). Goldin discusses compe-tition between Jewish fundraising organizations during the mid-1930s, when the JDC, the ZOA, the American Jewish Committee, B'nai B'rith, and some 300 other organizations were all soliciting donations:

Local agencies complained to the Council of Jewish Federations and Welfare Funds that the competition for dollars was unmanageable. Suppliants were specifically warned not to solicit funds in competition with local agencies . . . JDC and Zionists accepted a coun-cil formula in 1937, with allocations based on percentages of funds raised.[22]

NPOs often take other steps to moderate competition between them. Here are two examples.

Two youth groups in Santa Cruz, California were offering much the same services. Fearing that the Board of Supervisors would cut its grants to both, the two divided the market, one group helping children under twelve, the other helping adolescents from twelve to seventeen. They were able to say, success-fully, to the Board of Supervisors, "You need both of us."[23]

In a complicated deal, Barbra Streisand made an agreement that allowed char-ities to scalp tickets to her concert tour. She sold tickets to selected charities for $350 apiece, usually the best seats in the house, and granted the charities the right to resell the tickets for $1,000. Streisand gets her $350; the charity gets a Gross Marketing Contribution of $650 before programmed marketing costs.

The programmed costs were the rub. In Los Angeles six charities got tickets and thus competed to sell them. What would keep them from offering buyers limousines, champagne, and other costly gewgaws? How could they avoid driv-ing up their programmed marketing costs? By making a pact not to engage in such an arms race. Done by commercial firms such a pact would be a flagrant violation of antitrust laws, but such anticompetitive behavior is permitted (under certain conditions) in the nonprofit sector.[24]

SEGMENTATION

At some point in his career every marketer apprehends that his clients differ and that he can fashion a better marketing program by adapting himself and his program to these differences. This apprehension is what bottoms the idea of segmentation: that men differ and that the astute marketer must bend to the differences. Of course, there is nothing original or profound here, but one does not expect much originality or profundity in marketing.

Marketers find that it makes sense to recognize and adapt to differences among (and between) groups in the population. These groups may differ in race, sex, nationality, social class, marital status, age, religion, education, and income. They live in different ways and work in areas that differ by size, terrain, climate, and degree of urbanization.

But none of these ways in which clients and backers differ are of the essence. They are merely ways of *describing* segments. What is most important to a marketer is that people differ in the way they behave, in their responses to marketing stimuli—lower prices, advertising, an explanation by a volunteer, or the introduction of a new service. Audiences at pops concerts given by symphony orchestras rarely cross over to become subscribers to traditional concert series, which tells us that the two segments are cleanly separated.[25] Some donors—of blood, money, or time—have given before, others have given infrequently or only a little. Clients differ in their views of the world; they differ in what they are aware of, what they understand, what they like and what they prefer, what they believe, and what they intend to do. Clients differ in their sensitivity to total costs and in their expectations. Riders of mass transit differ in the purposes of their trips, where they are going, and their attitudes toward various modes of travel. Clients in a birth control clinic differ in whether they already use birth control methods, whether the methods used are modern or "folk" methods, whether those who do not use contraceptives want to, and whether those who want to are suited for them.[26]

Nonprofit businesses follow the same general approach, but they segment on different characteristics from other NPOs. Perhaps the most useful, and hence most common, is size. United Way chapters do not treat all businesses alike in planning their annual fund drives. Businesses with more employees will donate more than businesses with few employees. Through most of its history, the U.S. Postal Service ignored differences in the sizes of its business users. It treated them all alike. It did not send its sales force to learn the needs of its biggest users and thus serve them better; instead it put its sales force on such matters as fixing postage meters and distributing customer satisfaction surveys in post office lobbies. In spite of growing competition from overnight carriers, package delivery companies, faxes, and e-mail; in spite of the fact that its largest users ran up postage bills of a million dollars a month and a few spent two million dollars a day, the Postal Service made little effort to treat them any differently from any other users. The appointment of an experienced business executive as Postmaster General changed that. Now the USPS classifies business users into three groups:

	Number	Postal Revenues (billions)	Average Expenditures on Postal Services (thousands)
National accounts	165	$12.5	$76,000
Premier accounts	20,000	$14.0	$700
Business accounts	8,000,000	$17.5	$2

Source: William Keenan, Jr., "Can We Deliver?" *Sales and Marketing Management* (February 1994), p. 65.

Each has a different sales force, in an effort to focus the postal system's energies where they belong.

The groups of clients into which the marketer divides the market are naturally called segments. The opening paragraphs of this section illustrated the five criteria commonly used in segmenting markets:

1. Geography—region of the country, size of the county, climate, and population.
2. Demography—age, sex, income, education, family life cycle, occupation, social class.
3. Behavior—who makes the decision, how often they buy, how much they use, and whether they buy once or again and again.
4. Psychography—personality, lifestyle, needs, values.
5. Buying process—information needs, sources of information, benefits sought, degree of brand loyalty, awareness, intention to buy, price, and T costs.

Any of these, or all of them, can serve to define and describe segments.

An example of behavioral segmentation. One good example is giving clubs, which are groups of donors organized by the amount they give. To stimulate donors to give more, a business school might create a hierarchy of clubs: managers, executives, presidents, chairmen. (See Figure 7.1)

In direct mail, access to detailed records on behavior allows nonprofits to segment to a fair-thee-well. The Disabled Veterans of America, with a house list of 6.5 million donors, divides its donors into over one hundred segments. It needs thirty-six alone to classify donors whose last gift was between ten and twenty dollars. Which tells us that these donors are an important source of revenue to the DVA.[27]

An example of psychographic segmentation. Segments constructed on four of these five criteria should be easy to imagine, but perhaps psychographic segments are not so easy. Here there is an example of a psychographical segmentation done for United Way of America. The basic question was: How should United Way segment its donors to understand them better and ultimately increase their donations? *The Social/Civic Minded* are demographically more affluent, with more formal education, and more likely to be in professional and managerial positions. In

Figure 7.1
A Former Fundraiser Takes to Driving a Cab, Applies What He Knows about Segmentation

psychographic terms they are more active in community affairs, more concerned about the quality of life for others in the community, more likely to say they are frequently asked to give to charities, less suspicious of requests for charitable contributions, more likely to feel that they give a reasonable proportion of their income to charities, and much more likely to have a favorite charity that they support year after year.

The Pressured Exchangers have lower incomes, less formal education, and lower occupational status than the Social/Civic Minded. (Part of the fun of creating psychographic segments is that you get to name the segments.) In psychographic terms they are more likely to feel pressured when asked to give, either in the workplace or at home, more likely to prefer giving to small charities, more likely to prefer giving to a charity that will be helpful either to them or to someone they know, more likely to be uncertain about how to help others, more likely to say that people have to help themselves, and tend to see giving as a form of exchange from which they or people they know may benefit.

The Disconnected, like the Pressured Exchangers, have lower incomes, less formal education, and lower occupational status than the Social/Civic Minded. In psychographic terms they are less active in community affairs, less likely to attend church, less concerned about the quality of life for others in the community; they place more importance on the charity which they support, making sure their contribution is well-spent; and they are more likely to stress the importance of trusting a charity before they donate.[28]

When asked to contribute to United Way, Pressured Exchangers were most likely to contribute, followed by the Social/Civic Minded, and then by the Disconnected. The average donation of the Social/Civic Minded was the highest ($114), followed by Pressured Exchangers ($77), and by the Disconnected ($69). This means that although the Social/Civic Minded constitute 28 percent of the population, they account for 42 percent of United Way's donations.

A second example of psychographic segmentation. One study of giving by the rich segments donors into seven personality groups.[29] (The "rich" in the study had at least one million dollars of liquid assets.) The seven are (1) communitarians, business executives who want to give something back to their communities; (2) the devout, who give mostly to religious groups out of religious faith; (3) investors, owners of businesses who give not from a sense of obligation but to enjoy the tax deductions; (4) socialities, who combine fun with charitable activities; (5) repayers, who give to discharge an obligation to an NPO like a hospital or university that has helped them in the past; (6) altruists, who give, usually anonymously, because giving fulfills them; and (7) dynasts, the old rich who give because it is family tradition to give.

One does not want to make too much of segments based on personality. Most marketers spend very little time trying to measure personality or predict how personality influences behavior, mostly because personality doesn't seem to work very well. It does not work well, in brief, because personality is but one of many influences on behavior and because there is no simple, recognized method for accurately gauging personality. Moreover, this particular segmentation scheme is intended to apply broadly. Its suitability to a specific nonprofit is questionable.

What Segmentation Studies Tell Us about Nonvoters

Although turnout in presidential elections over the period from 1956 to 1972 averaged 61 percent, the turnout in recent years has been low. For example, only 54 percent of Americans eligible to vote did so in 1976, which means that 46 percent, or 65 million people, did not vote. In elections to the House of Representatives and the Senate, turnout runs a good deal lower. The average turnout in gubernatorial and senatorial elections runs still lower in nonpresidential years—45 percent in the nonpresidential elections between 1950 and 1960. (The figures range from Idaho with a turnout of 65 percent to Mississippi with a turnout of 4 percent.) Turnout for local offices is even lower, with 10 percent in an off year considered heavy.[30]

Why don't people vote? Or rather, why do they not vote? One researcher who has looked into this question found that nonvoters fell into six categories or, in our terms, segments.[31] The questions to engage the reader during the next few lines are (1) which segments are most obdurate in their nonvoting and which are likely to be capable of being attracted back to the polls, and (2) how might they be attracted?

The six segments are:

1. Positive apathetics, 35 percent of nonvoters, do not vote because they are so well off. Their life is going so well that voting is an empty gesture. Educated and contented, they do not need to vote.

2. The bypassed, 13 percent of nonvoters, are the stereotypic nonvoters. They have little schooling and therefore earn little. Many of them have never voted, or have voted only once (often for George Wallace, in the 1960s). They are poorly informed about politics and do not follow politics. Their political hero is now Jimmy Carter.

3. The politically impotent, 22 percent of nonvoters, feel they have no say; that nothing they can say or do will reach the government. Their feelings of helplessness often extend to their private lives as well; but they are not hostile to politics, earn average incomes, and belong to the middle class. Their hero is Ted Kennedy.

4. The physically disenfranchised, 18 percent of nonvoters, do not vote for legal or physical reasons. They may be unable to vote because they could not meet residency requirements after a recent move. They may find registering to vote too difficult. Or they may be in poor health and thus be unable to go to the polls on election day. They may be out of town on the day of the election and may have failed to get an absentee ballot.

5. The naysayers, 6 percent of nonvoters, do not fail to vote by accident. They do not vote by design, by plan, by philosophy. They know why they do not vote and they are willing to defend their choice. Usually, they know a good deal about politics but have decided that voting makes no sense.

6. The cross-pressured, 5 percent of nonvoters, are unable to make up their minds between the two candidates. They know a good deal about politics and they want to vote, but they cannot come to a decision. An Italian-American boy from Rochester, where Italian-Americans vote Democratic, marries an Italian-American girl from Cambridge, where they vote Republican; or a conservative unhappily finds that in many respects the Republican candidate is more liberal than the Democratic candidate. In both cases, a higher proportion of nonvoting can be expected.

This discussion makes one realize how bleak are the prospects of significantly improving voter turnout.

Most marketing texts point out that segments should be measurable, accessible, and substantial.[32] This means that there is no point in going after a segment if you cannot gauge it, if you cannot reach it, or if it is too small to bother with. No reader of this book needs to be told this.

Businessmen are supposed to have been rather tardy in recognizing the importance of segmentation, for, as marketers apprehend history, the period before World War II was dominated by the business belief that there was only one market for each product. Businesses did not cater to the whims of each small market segment. But nonprofit organizations were not so slack. In fact, it may be that segmentation was invented by the politicians. They do not use the word, to be sure, but when politicians gather to talk, the idea is there without question. They do not, in their serious moments, talk about the voter, or even the average voter; they talk instead about the vote—the Polish vote, the Irish vote, the Black vote, and the Italian vote; the aged vote and the youth vote; the farm vote, the right-wing vote, the labor vote, and the green vote; the Catholic vote and the Jewish vote. They study voting patterns and divide areas into three segments: safe for the other party, safe for their party, and safe for neither. Then they slight the first, contrive to persuade voters to turn out on election day in the second, and concentrate most of their time and money and sound bites on the third, where there are swing voters not yet committed to either party.

Most Marketing Decisions Require Segmented Thinking

This point is most easily made with an example. A public health organization is concerned about the sharp increase in smoking among women, particularly pregnant women and teenage girls. It plans to develop some public service announcements for radio, television, and print. It is tempting to aim such a campaign at all women, and perhaps at men as well.

But women differ in their media exposure and in their interests in smoking. Here are five obvious segments among women.

Segments	Possible Copy Focus	Best Media for This Segment
Nonsmokers	Don't start	Mass media like TV
Teenage nonsmokers	Smoking's not cool It smells bad Guys don't like it Girls don't like it	Radio TV Teen magazines
Young adults	Smoking's not healthy	Women's magazines?
Pregnant women	Smoking is bad for your baby (and for you)	Magazines for expectant mothers
Married women at home	Smoking's not healthy for you or your family	Soaps, other daytime television

Teenage girls read magazines for teenage girls and listen to a lot of radio. There are no mass circulation equivalents to *Seventeen* or *YM* to reach teenage boys. (Why is that?) Pregnant girls may continue to read *Seventeen* or *YM* but not pregnant women. They read magazines written for pregnant women, or perhaps general interest women's magazines. There is an additional copy point as well. Some, like pregnant women, will respond to more reasoned argument; others, perhaps teenagers, respond better to mere assertion.

There is no way around it. Until the segments are chosen the advertising agency can not proceed to write copy or select media. Once the segments are chosen, copywriters can write the messages that focus on the interests of that particular segment and media planners can choose media that will deliver the message efficiently.

Some decisions simply cannot be made without deciding which segments are most important. A public television station wants to measure its image among . . . among which groups in its viewing area? Until it has settled this issue it can go no further. You can not do marketing research until you decide which segments you want to study. In the same way, advertising programs begin with a statement of whom the ads are to reach, with decisions made on segments.

TWO CHOICES

These differences among clients and backers raise problems for any organization, and it is the modest claim of marketing that it has a solution. The problem is straightforward—as clients differ, what pleases one will not please another, and what stimulates one fails to stimulate another. Under these circumstances, no one marketing program will reach everyone, nor will it arouse all whom it does reach.

There are two solutions: (1) ignore the differences, or (2) adapt to the differences.

Treat All Alike

In this approach, clients are offered a meager choice—take it or leave it. This approach can be seen as denying the existence of segments in the market or, what is the same thing, as saying there is only one segment and that it contains all clients. There are benefits in such a course and, naturally, there are costs. This strategy means low expenditures on marketing; it requires no marketing know-how to execute and little marketing research to ascertain what clients want. It certainly suits the organization well. But in overlooking special interests of different segments, the organization may fail to produce the desired behavior, and clients will be less satisfied with their contacts with the organization. Moreover, if clients can do better elsewhere they will, and the client base will diminish.

This marketing strategy is most commonly seen in government agencies, who feel that it is more equitable, or easier, to bring about the behavior they desire by limiting choice or by compulsion. And such a strategy works reasonably well when the service offered on a take-it-or-leave-it basis appeals to most clients, or at least satisfies them, and when it is easy for the clients to accept their lack of choice. This latter condition holds when the service has no particular importance to the client and deals only with minor aspects of his life. (Is this why voters accept just two major political parties?)

It might be argued that government agencies have little opportunity to segment, in as much as they must treat all members of society alike. For their AIDS education campaigns, for example, most state public health officials choose the general public as their primary target.[33] And surely everyone must adopt the metric system at the same time. But it is still possible, and more efficient, to work harder with some groups than with others and to work on some segments earlier than others. Age might well be a factor, in that the young will adopt metrification in a trice, while many of the elderly, those over forty, will lack the will to change. Certain manufacturers and certain industries may be willing, and interested, in beginning metrification of their products now, while others will not change before they have to, and the cooperation of tool makers should be enlisted early. And because reading and viewing habits of citizens differ, it will prove (virtually) impossible to put together a communications effort that reaches all citizens equally well.

There is a lesson here about this strategy of treating all clients alike. It is impossible to do. There will always be some groups for whom the government's program is better suited or more apt, and there will always be some groups able to avail themselves of the government's program at lower T costs than other groups. Formally, a government agency may treat all its clients alike, but in its day-to-day operations it cannot avoid favoring some groups over others.

Adapt to Differences

In segmenting its clients or backers, an organization does two things: It selects groups of clients who are to receive the organization's marketing efforts, and it designs a separate marketing program for each segment.

Selection of segments can be done in a number of ways. Often it is merely tradition or indolence that decides. Many organizations make this important decision on ethical grounds. Still others, especially those dealing with customers or with backers, decide on economic or marketing grounds. A charity would deem it foolish to try to raise money from a segment that fails to return enough to pay the cost of reaching it. Perhaps the best course of action in picking segments is to do research on clients first, and then pick segments based on the research findings and on common sense, which may protect you when the research is wrong or misleading.

The second thing organizations do in adapting to differences is to design a separate marketing program for each segment. On occasion, this could mean designing from scratch a marketing plan tailored to each segment; but usually it means taking one basic marketing plan, changing bits of it here and there, and targeting the changed programs at separate segments. As an example of this basic-plus approach, take the Metropolitan Museum of Art. The Met could have just one class of members, but instead it has five: student, individual, family, sustaining, and supporting, which is itself divided into contributing, donor, sponsor, and patron. All of them receive much the same benefits, but more expensive memberships bag richer ones. In addition, there are special interest groups like the Friends of the Islamic Department and the Friends of the American Wing, which serve as the focus of special fundraising efforts.

Notice what this second step means. To prepare a marketing program, first it is necessary to analyze the behavior of the organization's clients, as we shall see in the next section. Since a segmented approach means many marketing programs, a segmented approach means many analyses of client behavior. Under the basic-plus scheme, it is assumed that clients (or backers) are pretty much the same, and therefore the model of client behavior will also be a basic-plus model, one basic model with changes here and there to reflect differences in client interests. But if the basic-plus model is inappropriate, models of client behavior will have to be built from scratch, one for each segment.

In recent years, culturally specific programs in drug and alcohol treatment have begun to emerge. There are treatment programs for American Indians, Hispanics, pregnant women, even night-shift workers (as opposed to day-shift). One program focuses specifically on blacks. It involves therapy sessions that explore the extent to which experience as a black person influences addition and recovery, and it places strong emphasis on involving the addict's family in treatment, on the premise that a clean drug patient who returns to a drug-infested neighborhood or family has little chance of staying clean.[34]

In Sum

What does segmentation mean, then? It means two important things—no one program will reach and move all clients (or backers), and no organization can hope to reach everyone. The marketer must work within these fundamentals.

TARGETING

Simply identifying segments is not an end in itself. You segment to help you choose which segments you will serve. This process is called targeting or target marketing—another bit of jargon—and it serves primarily to focus the NPO's marketing efforts.

It sometimes happens that when you have come up with a sensible way to segment your markets, the target markets emerge without further effort. Too often, however, segments do not easily or automatically translate into targets. The NPO may be forced to make hard choices, which means giving up some aims to pursue others. For example, the segments most in need of the NPO's services may be the hardest to reach using marketing tools.

THE MARKETING LOGIC FOR TARGET MARKETING

Why do marketers select targets, instead of going after the entire population?

Targeting Leads to Higher Satisfaction

Target marketing is the one beloved of most marketers; certainly not, however, because it requires higher marketing budgets. Marketers prefer clients who want to do what is good for them, or for the nonprofit organization, rather than clients who are forced to do this. Marketers in businesses select those target markets that will be the most profitable. Marketers in nonprofit organizations select target markets because such a step better suits their clients (and their backers). This is of value in and of itself. It means that clients are happier, or at least more satisfied. More satisfied clients are more likely to follow instructions, to return for additional services, and to talk to their friends about their experiences. Satisfied backers are more likely to give again and to give more.

Targeting Is More Efficient

An NPO can only do so much with the resources it has. It makes good sense to focus on certain targets and ignore others. Symphonic music appeals to only a small percentage of the population. An orchestra that tried to bring serious music to the masses would waste a lot of time and money and talent before it gave up. A neighborhood church that tries to be all things to all people—singles and marrieds, those who have little interest in traditional ritual and those who prefer the comfort of the ritual, those with children and those without, the rich and the poor, the educated and the uneducated, the believers and the skeptics—will find much of its efforts go for naught, and sooner or later the congregation will split into more homogeneous groups.

Targeting Can Provide a Focus

Target markets help make clear where the marketing program is aimed and where it is not. This helps not only the marketers but everyone to understand better what the NPO's overall mission is.

The idea has been widely used in this century by public health officials to contain contagious diseases (except AIDS). They try to locate carriers of the disease and those who may have been exposed to it, to whom they offer counseling to prevent further transmission (except AIDS). They also take steps to ensure that those who have been infected stop activities that might spread the disease (except AIDS). That is, they focus their counseling—read ''marketing''—only on those groups who have the disease or who are likely to have it. It is, as a result, a program with little wasted motion in it.

Targeting provides a clear focus for the NPO and for those who work in it. A state industrial development office has a much clearer idea of what it is and is trying to accomplish when it knows which types of industries it wants to attract. The manager of an organization for those born blind is in a better position to see opportunities for new programs than the manager of an NPO that deals with all forms of visual impairment, or that deals more broadly with (say) any sensory impairment.

Targets Allow the NPO to Tailor Its Marketing Efforts

Focusing on a target market means that marketing programs are more likely to meet the needs of that market, thus producing more satisfied clients. The closer match of program and client can occur in any of the general areas of marketing:

Function	Likely Benefits from Targeting
Pricing	Clients are more able and more willing to pay.
Advertising	Backers identify with the cause and feel they want to support it.
	Clients see the advertising message as directed to them.
Distribution	Clients have an easier time getting to the NPO's site. They come more often or regularly.
Product or service	Clients think the service is good. They want to continue or they want to repeat. It is so satisfying that they want to talk about it to their friends.

WHY YOU SHOULDN'T TARGET

Targeting Means You Can't Serve Everyone

We might as well look at the arguments against, even though targeting is too important a tool to be dismissed.

Targeting means that some segments will be poorly served by the organization. Heavy smokers, although the intended target for the messages linking smoking and cancer, will tend to ignore those very messages. Those most likely to give blood during a special blood drive are those who have donated before, not those who have never donated.

Businessmen can ignore such a problem. If a group of customers does not want to buy them and their product, they can ignore it. It is much easier, even in the face of competition, to sell toothpaste to those who already brush their teeth than to persuade those who do not brush to start, even though in the latter case there will be no competition. (Anyone who does not believe this does not have young children.) Some nonprofit organizations can ignore refractory segments too. A symphony orchestra should not try to appeal to mass audiences, because only one or two or three percent of the population is even interested in fine music. Certainly, a historic site should not try to attract visitors who are unlikely to be interested, and a coach will raise few funds from alumni who are bored by football.

Other nonprofit organizations, however, may not enjoy the freedom to cold-shoulder unresponsive segments. One of the hardest tasks is to convince peasants in Uttar Pradesh to adopt and use birth control techniques, and yet this is the task put to a government agency. Is it any wonder that the marketing efforts of government and other commonwealth agencies, required to work with just those market segments least likely to respond to their efforts, so often fail?

What are the implications of this? For nonprofit businesses, the implication is to pick as target markets the segments that are predisposed to the marketing programs of the business. Any nonprofit organization seeking donations from backers should target its efforts to the most responsive segments. For nonprofit organizations with no choice of their target markets, the implications are to set more realistic goals: Recognize that the target markets are harder to move and set objectives accordingly.

The Targets Chosen May Be Criticized

Singling out this target or that target offends some people on political or moral or aesthetic grounds. Haitian immigrants in America have rates of HIV infection much higher than the average in the population, but the idea of designing a special program aimed at Haitians was criticized by some as offensive. Homosexual men continue to have very high rates of HIV infection; the disease first appeared among them in the early 1980s and was for a time called the "gay plague." In those early years, a program of public health education designed for homosexuals was dismissed by gay activists as homophobia and gay-bashing; and the closing of the bath houses in San Francisco, which were Disease Central for several years, was delayed again because of vocal opposition.

Of course, if you can't stand the heat get out of the kitchen. But it is valuable to recall that marketing decisions can have political or moral or aesthetic dimensions, or rather that political, moral, or aesthetic considerations will influence marketing decisions. A higher percentage of black men smoke than white men. Is is too fanciful to imagine an antismoking campaign aimed at men in general being labeled as racist?

Targeting May Mean Picking Those Most Likely to Respond

There is a third reason why an NPO might not choose to target. The people who respond most easily to a marketing program may be the wrong people, that is, they may not be in the target the organization is trying to reach. In fact, this phenomenon occurs whenever people can choose whether they will expose themselves to a promotional message, allow themselves to receive information, or be subjected to the service provided by the nonprofit organization. Let us suppose a bond drive, held during World War II, during which a movie, replete with patriotic fervor and appeals to buy bonds, is shown at a local movie house. Suppose also that a substantial effort is made to fill the movie house for the showing of the film. Who is it that is most likely to attend? From a naive view, the intended targets for the bond drive are those who have not bought a bond at all, and those who have bought only a few bonds, the shirkers and the slackers. But only a few of them will attend; instead the house will be filled with people already committed to buying bonds, or who have already bought a number of bonds.

Whenever there is self-selection by the intended audience, those who respond are likely to differ from those in the target audience. Examples abound: Those most likely to watch the Republican telethon are diehard Republicans, not Democrats. Readers of *Consumer Reports* are well educated and well off, whereas the consumers who most need accurate consumer information are (presumably) those with less income and education. Those most likely to read and heed the warning that smoking causes cancer are nonsmokers, because they are not threatened by the information; and smokers who have recently quit, because they welcome any information that confirms their decision to stop. Those least likely to attend to the warnings are heavy smokers.

POSITIONING

Positioning deals with how an NPO wants to be seen by others, chiefly its clients and backers. Positioning means finding out what the NPO stands for and how others currently see it. It also means putting a program in place to influence its position.

Positioning is related to both the NPO's competition and target markets. It has already taken its measure of the competition, and it knows roughly where it and they stand, what its strengths and weaknesses are, what theirs are. Except that it has neglected to consider its clients (and backers). "*We* know our competition and where they stand; but do our clients know? And what is it they know?"

Once we shift our focus from the NPO's point of view to the client's we are considering the question of *positioning*. To a marketer, positioning means influencing how clients (and backers) see us, see our NPO, compared to the competition. It means that the NPO can and should take an active role to affect client perceptions of the playing field where the competitors meet.

"Position" as it is commonly used means a stand or opinion that one holds. "My position on death and taxes is that I'm against them," or "the AMA's position on national health has changed over the past decade." Marketers do not use "position" and "positioning" this way. To a marketer, positioning means an active attempt to influence how clients view the NPO.

All this has been in the abstract.

Figure 7.2
A One-dimensional Map of Political Issues

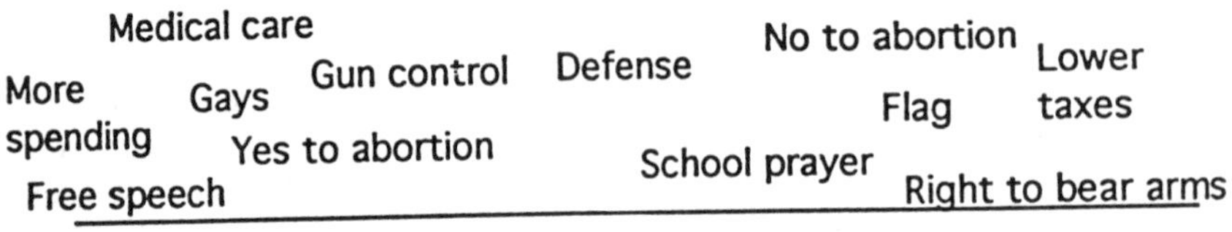

Medical care   No to abortion   Lower
More   Gun control   Defense   taxes
        Gays   Flag
spending   Yes to abortion   School prayer
Free speech   Right to bear arms

Figure 7.3
A One-dimensional Map of Leisure Activities

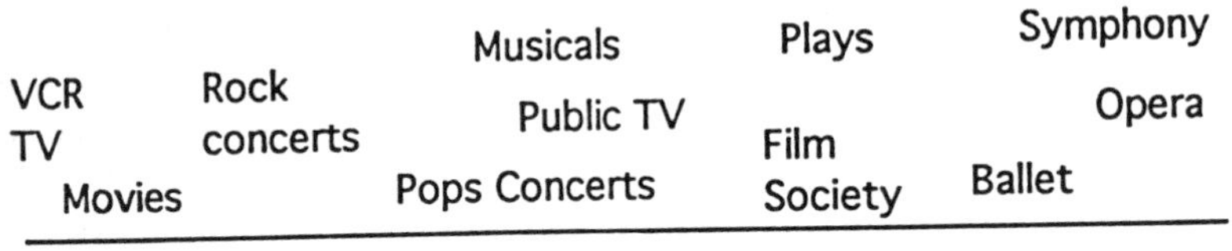

                        Musicals   Plays   Symphony
VCR   Rock   Opera
TV   concerts   Public TV   Film
      Movies   Pops Concerts   Society   Ballet

The basic idea is to imagine products or NPO located in a space, typically a two-dimensional plane. Then in this space it is possible, by using standard marketing research techniques, to place products (or NPOs) on the plane. The resulting diagram is usually called a *positioning map.*

It is most easily seen in terms of stands that a politician might take. Almost without thinking we tend to place the arguments we read in the daily newspapers along a single dimension, conservative versus liberal or the right versus the left. Take the following issues—desecration of the flag, higher taxes on the rich, support for gay rights, support for spending for defense, increased spending for medical care for the poor, and school prayer. Few people would have trouble locating these along a line (although naturally there would be disagreements). Most would get something like this (see Figure 7.2). This is an example of a one-dimensional positioning map. It not only gives us a picture. It also suggests that issues that are close on the page are related to one another. That is, they are similar in some abstract political space.

In politics one can be reasonably sure of the underlying dimension. But what is one to make of the following one-dimensional positioning map of a variety of leisure activities (Figure 7.3) in a medium-sized Southern city? As we move from left to right the activities pass from light to heavy, undemanding to challenging, mass audience to limited audience. Now consider a two-dimensional map of the same activities (Figure 7.4). This map was based on a survey of young adults who were potential symphony goers.

As with the one-dimensional map, activities that the young adults saw as similar are close together, and those that differ are far apart. But what is the second dimension? It was not apparent until the question was put to some young adults in focus groups. They said that the vertical axis dealt with formality, with the

Figure 7.4
A Two-dimensional Map of Leisure Activities

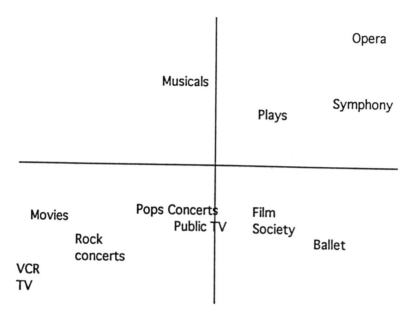

need to dress up, to go somewhere for an occasion, and that staying home to watch the tube or the Public Broadcasting System was so much more comfortable than going to a play or the opera.

QUESTIONS

1. Many government programs list as their target the general public. Sometimes it is one of several targets.

   "Target," however, suggests discrimination and a focus. Does it make sense to "target" the general public? Is this merely an evasion? An impossibility? Is it merely word play?

2. Audiences at pops concerts rarely subscribe to traditional concert series, the chapter says. Because they don't, some symphony orchestras see pops concerts as failures.

   Comment on the implied meaning of "failure." On the evidence given, do you think that pops concerts are failures?

NOTES

1. Robert Pruger and Leonard Miller, "Competition and the Public Social Services." *Public Welfare* (Fall 1973): 16.

2. J. Garrott Allen, "Commercial Blood in our National Blood Program." *Archives of Surgery* (February 1971): 124–125.

3. Vince Stehle, "Competition for Board Members." *Chronicle of Philanthropy,* April 17, 1990, p. 1.

4. Wilbert E. Moore, *The Conduct of the Corporation* (New York: Vintage, 1962), p. 255.

5. William J. Ferguson, *Greek Imperialism* (Boston: Houghton Mifflin, 1913), pp. 58–59. Also, A. E. Haigh, *The Attic Theater* (Oxford: Oxford University Press, 1907), p. 3.

6. Robert Frank, "The Conference Should Consider Establishing an Inhospitality Suite." *The Wall Street Journal,* May 23, 1994, p. B1.

7. Maria Newman, "California Schools Compete for Pupils in an Open Market." *The New York Times,* May 25, 1994, p. A1.

8. Tim Jeal, *Baden-Powell* (London: Hutchinson, 1989), p. 378.

9. Bruce Millar, "Too Many Charities." *Chronicle of Philanthropy,* July 10, 1990, p. 1.

10. Jane Louise Johnson, "Setting Tuition Levels at Public Institutions." *Journal of Higher Education* 47, no. 2 (March–April 1976): 125–126.

11.

$$\frac{1{,}000 \text{ numbers}}{6 \text{ numbers per week}} \times \frac{1}{52 \text{ weeks per year}} = 3.2 \text{ years}$$

12. All this material on the numbers game comes from my article, "The Numbers Game: An Economic and Competitive Analysis." *Quarterly Review of Economics and Business* 16 (Summer 1976): 19–36.

13. Irving Kenneth Zola, "Observations on Gambling in a Lower-Class Setting." *Social Problems* 10 (Spring 1963): 353–361.

14. John A. Howard, *Consumer Behavior: Applications of Theory* (New York: Mc-Graw-Hill, 1977), p. 33.

15. Jack Poggi, *Theatre in America: The Impact of Economic Forces, 1870–1967* (Ithaca, N.Y.: Cornell University Press, 1968), p. 94; and William Baumol and G. Bowen, *Performing Arts—The Economic Dilemma* (New York: Twentieth Century Fund, 1966), p. 174.

16. Xandar Kayden, "The Political Campaign as an Organization." *Public Policy* 21 (Spring 1973): 268.

17. Others argue that the Fed's most important way of controlling the money supply is through its open market operations, which makes the question of membership irrelevant.

18. See "Designations and Donor Choice in United Way Campaigns—1992" (Alexandria, Virginia: United Way of America, February 1994).

19. To see the proposal read the *Federal Register,* April 15, 1991, pp. 15, and 158–160.

20. This seems to echo the reasons for frequent elections in a republic.

21. *Fund Raising Management* (November–December 1979): 24.

22. Milton Goldin, *Why They Give: American Jews and Their Philanthropies* (New York: Macmillan, 1976), p. 149.

23. Millar, "Too Many Charities," p. 18.

24. David Johnston, "Barbra Streisand Turns Charities Into Ticket Scalpers." *Chronicle of Philanthropy,* June 14, 1994, pp. 48–49.

25. *Americanizing the American Orchestra.* Report of the National Task Force for the American Orchestra (Washington, D.C.: American Symphony Orchestra League, 1993), p. 29.

26. Julian L. Simon, "Market Segmentation in Promoting Contraception." *Studies in Family Planning* (March 1974): 90–97.

27. Holly Hall, "Dividing Up Donors Can Lead to Benefits in Fund Raising." *Chronicle of Philanthropy,* January 25, 1994, p. 30.

28. *Competitive Marketing, A Guide for United Way and Other Nonprofits* (Alexandria, Virginia: United Way of America, 1988), pp. 18–19.

29. Russ A. Prince and Karen Maru File, *The Seven Faces of Philanthropy* (San Francisco: Jossey-Bass, 1994).

30. Kevin V. Mulcahy and Richard S. Katz, *America Votes* (Englewood Cliffs, N.J.: Prentice-Hall, 1976), pp. 21–22. This book is short, clear, fascinating, and alas, out-of-date.

31. Arthur T. Hadley, *The Empty Polling Booth* (Englewood Cliffs, N.J.: Prentice-Hall, 1978), pp. 67–104.

32. Philip Kotler, *Marketing Management* (Englewood Cliffs, N.J.: Prentice-Hall, 1980), pp. 205–206.

33. Alan J. Bush and Victoria Davies, "State Governments' Response to the AIDS Crisis: An Advertising Perspective." *Journal of Public Policy & Marketing* 8 (1989): 57.

34. "Tailoring Treatment for Black Addicts." *The Wall Street Journal,* April 10, 1990, p. B3.

Chapter 8

Marketing Strategy— The Preliminaries

These next two chapters will look at the process of developing a marketing strategy. A clear, coherent marketing strategy underlies all of the NPO's marketing efforts and its annual plan, or at least it should; and in those NPOs where marketing plays an important role in the success of the NPO, it underpins its entire planning effort.

WHY EVEN BOTHER WITH STRATEGIC PLANNING?

Let us start at the beginning. Most NPOs already know what they stand for, what their aims are, who they are. They do not need anything more formal than a general agreement on such important matters before they can get back to the business at hand. And as long as matters stay as they are, there is little need for much more. They get by just as you and I get by every day, by muddling through.

Matters do not always remain stable, though. Clients' needs change, or the public's interest shifts from this cause to that and donations tumble. A group that is growing fast can predict with flinty assurance that the day will come when the fashion will shift from its cause to some other, sending donations down. There may be internal changes. The NPO may find itself running a deficit, for example; or perhaps the organization is considering a major capital campaign or the members of the board cannot agree on the organization's future. All of these are reason to pause and take stock, to do a bit of planning.

Corporations have used strategic planning for decades, and all large companies have full-time planners on the payroll. They do strategic planning to help them anticipate change and take advantage of it. Few NPOs, except for the very largest, have full-time planners on staff, but since the mid-1980s strategic planning has begun to infiltrate the nonprofit sector.

Before an organization can set its marketing strategy it must undertake some preliminary steps. It must find out how well it is meeting its goals; it must identify potential threats and possible opportunities; and it must have a clear idea of what it is and where it is going.

Broadly speaking, these preliminary activities, to which this chapter is devoted, fall into two phases: (1) Analysis of the NPO itself and its environment, which goes by the elegant name, SWOT analysis. Strategic planners call this first phase a situation analysis; (2) Strategy development, which includes a statement of the NPO's mission; consideration of alternative strategies, both long and short run; objectives; and, finally, action plans.

In what follows I will refer several times to the strategic planning undertaken by DIFFA, the Design Industries Foundation for AIDS. DIFFA was created in 1984 by designers from a variety of industries, from architecture to retailing, from fashion to industry, to raise and distribute funds to organizations that deal with AIDS patients.[1]

All was not well at DIFFA. It raised too much of its operating budget, 90 percent, through special events, the best known of which was the Love Ball, a dance contest in which contestants wore haute couture. It had eleven steering committees in different cities that organized special events in their areas to raise money, but they had little say about their own finances and depended on the New York staff, which was overburdened, for accounting help and audits. Finally, board members often doubled as special events managers; and board members were heavily involved in DIFFA's day-to-day operations. (This last is usually a bad sign, but not always.)

SITUATION ANALYSIS

In a situation analysis, the NPO takes a good look at itself and the world in which it operates, and it tries to identify its strengths, weaknesses, opportunities, and threats. First, however, we must consider the nonprofit's mission.

Mission

The mission statement outlines the NPO's strategic direction and states its business. At a minimum, it says what the organization is, what it does, why it exists, and whom it serves. Most NPOs have a formal mission. The strategic planning process is a good time to revise it, if it needs revision.

But does a nonprofit really need a mission? I am fortunate to have studied and taught at several of the best graduate schools of business. Only one had a clear statement, of what it was and what it stood for, that counted for anything. The rest, well, they used all the right words—excellence, excellence in research, excellence in teaching, managerial, future, rigor, good management practice, dynamic, global, excellence (again)—but the words didn't really mean anything. The mission statements were too general, and faculty could agree politely on what it was doing only because the mission didn't count for anything. Generalities and vague assurances served in lieu of a mission. I am not at all sure that this state of affairs weakened these schools. Perhaps the dean knew what we were or what we stood for, but I doubt it. In these schools, lack of mission was papered over by mere words, and then the faculty could get back to research, writing, and teaching.

Does a nonprofit really need a mission? Doesn't everyone involved already know what it is? Of course everyone doesn't know. There are always newcomers, always new staff, new volunteers, new backers. And even if they do know the mission, they may not know what the mission means. The meaning emerges over time from debates and discussions as to decisions. For example:

- I have rarely sat in on a discussion of programs—what marketers call "product policy"—without hearing someone say, "That's not the kind of organization we are," or "We don't do things like that." He is arguing from his understanding of the mission.

- Discussions as to whether to accept certain gifts or raise money in certain ways often give rise to a discussion of mission. Through a tie-in with some mortgage companies the Arizona State University Alumni Association offers its members discounts on (say) loan origination fees and the costs of appraisal (but not on interest rates). Deals on home mortgages clearly have nothing to do with ASU's mission, but do they have something to do with the Association's mission? Of course they raise money for the Association, but we may be sure that raising money is not part of the Association's mission. Perhaps the mortgage deals bind alumni more tightly to the university, but that rationale looks weak. To an outsider, mortgages don't seem to fit with any reasonable understanding of the alumni association's mission or the university's. The Yale alumni association won't touch mortgages; but it has a deal with a company that sells videotapes of Yale's great teachers. That seems like a good fit between the university's mission and what its alumni association is doing.[2]

- Mission often comes up in crises. When the president of American University was caught making dirty phone calls from his presidential office, many at the university were left wondering where their allegiance lay, with the man or the university. The mission of the university helped most of them decide that it was with the university.

- The Sacred Heart League of Wallis, Mississippi raises around twenty million dollars a year for Catholic missionary work and social services in Mississippi. That is all it does, raise funds. For many years its mission was a simple one: to produce direct mail. In the 1980s, as part of an organizational overhaul, it began to think not about the 1990s but the twenty-first century, 2050 in fact. Would mail be important then? The League couldn't be sure. So in preparation it redefined its mission to be "religious communication."[3] To an outsider the League has made two mistakes. It is hard enough to plan three or five years ahead. Sixty years moves beyond foolishness to decadence. The second is the statement of the mission. It has gone from plain English—to produce direct mail—to a cottony imprecision that edges close to vacuity. Particularly when the publications manager explains the change this way: "We realized that our purpose was *not* designing envelopes. It was to produce religious communications. . . . Then the question becomes, How do we use an envelope to do that?''[4] In other words, ''Thanks for the new mission statement, but we in the print shop have to get back to work now.''

In clarifying its mission, then, the NPO should consider two questions: What business are we in, and what business do we want to be in? The answer to the first should be obvious after an initial review and, if needed, after an update of the mission statement. But the answer to the second is not so obvious. A situation analysis, to be discussed next, will give the planners a fair idea of the business it should be in, but there are many possibilities. DIFFA had good cause to examine its mission for, as indicated above, all was not well. At its planning retreat DIFFA began with a brainstorming session. Each of the twenty participants, staff and board members, was asked to look five years into the future and state his vision of what DIFFA would ideally become. This, inevitably, led to a discussion of DIFFA's mission. Should it go beyond raising money and become involved in political advocacy? Should it endorse legislation that helps AIDS victims?

The outcome was twofold. First, the participants decided the mission should remain unchanged. Second, the mere process of debating the mission helped participants to reaffirm DIFFA's basic principles.

As a second example, let us consider the mission of the Advertising Council. As the reader surely knows the Ad Council designs advertising campaigns for significant public issues and asks the mass media to donate time and space to run the ads.

[Our mission is] to identify a select number of significant public issues and focus public attention on those issues through advertising and communications programs that mobilize the public will to deal with the issues; and help promote the necessary citizen actions to address the issues effectively.

In that process, we marshall volunteer talent from the advertising and communications community, the facilities of the media, and the resources of the business and nonprofit communities to create awareness, understanding, and generate appropriate public response.

We bring to our mission a fundamental belief that effective communications programs can make a measurable difference in our society.[5]

This tells us what we already knew, that the Ad Council does ads; but it also shows that the Ad Council understands the role of advertising in public issues, namely, that advertising does not do anything more than focus public attention, which, if other conditions are right, will ''help promote'' action. This is a vague, guarded statement, not likely to rally the troops to try one last time, but it avoids promising too much, which is the most common venial sin on Madison Avenue. The statement also addresses means—we use volunteers and donations—but it does not say who the Ad Council's clients and backers are. It should. The Ad

Council's clients are the nonprofits for whom it does ads. Its backers are the media who donate time and space for Ad Council ads and the volunteers from Madison Avenue who put together the campaigns. Finally, the last sentence: Is the Ad Council whistling in the dark here? Would the sentence differ if "fundamental," "effective," and "measurable" were dropped? Not by much. Too many adjectives make for weak prose and suggest the writer doesn't believe his own words.

One of the most striking developments in politics in the past few decades—many say it is one of the most ominous developments—is the emergence of single-interest groups, groups that concentrate on but one issue—abortion, gun control, nuclear power, or prayer in public schools. They draw their power in part because they are nonpartisan and have little to do with politics in the traditional sense; and in part because they choose the easier course of opposing rather than doing. But they also draw much of their force and cohesion from their single-minded concentration on a single issue, an issue that stands alone, not linked to any other. As such they illustrate the power and organizational effectiveness that can derive from a clear focus on mission.

Internal Analysis

An internal analysis tries to look with a clear eye at what the NPO can do and can't do, its history, successes, and failures. It often includes an assessment of the capabilities of the NPO's internal publics, such as its staff, members of the board, volunteers, and backers. It goes without saying that no strategy can succeed without their support. (Even if it could succeed without them, why would an NPO want to leave them out?) Typical questions asked in an internal analysis include:

- What is our current strategy? What do we stand for?
- How did we get where we are now? What can our own history tell us about where we are today?
- What is unique about our NPO?
- Who are our clients? Our backers?
- What are our principal services?

External Analysis

An NPO must track changes in the external environment and adapt to them, lest it lose touch with its clients and backers.

The Woman's Christian Temperance Union was founded in 1874 to improve public morals, primarily by urging the public to abstain from spirituous liquors. Its glory days came in the early decades of the twentieth century when the demands of World War I to conserve grain permitted Congress to pass the 18th

Amendment. Prohibition was a failure, however, as every schoolchild knows, and was repealed in 1933. Since the founding of Alcoholics Anonymous in 1935, attention has shifted from abstinence to treatment. In recent decades, responding to changes in addictions, the WCTU now also urges abstinence from narcotics. By and large, though, the WCTU now plays only a marginal role in American society. Contrast it with Mothers Against Drunk Driving (MADD), for example. The WCTU failed to change with the times.[6]

The trouble with this example is that it benefits from hindsight. It is far too easy to look back fifty years and see things that weren't at all obvious at the time. Let us pick an example of environmental changes where it is not clear what the organization should do.

The Ad Council once had the dominant share of public service advertising, but by 1992 its share had fallen to about 30 percent. What is happening in the world to complicate the Ad Council's life?

- The television networks, its chief medium, once had over 90 percent of prime time audiences. Cable, VCRs, and video tapes had cut that to around 60 percent in the early 1990s. This has nothing to do with its falling share, but it does mean that Ad Council public service announcements (PSAs) that appear on network television reach a smaller audience than before.

- There was less room available for PSAs, partly because the national media had adopted causes of their own, leaving less time and space available for other campaigns, and partly because there was more competition, more PSAs from all sources, for available time.

- Some national coalitions had arisen that were able to attract huge amounts of the available PSA time, leaving less time for the Ad Council. Two examples were the fund-raising drive for the Statue of Liberty in the mid-1980s and the Partnership for a Drug-Free America in the early 1990s.

- Some NPOs and public service groups were more willing than in the past to pay for their advertising. The government as well was spending a good deal more on advertising. As a result, the media had reduced the amount of time and space they gave away.[7]

This brief summary makes clear that the Ad Council's world has changed and continues to change. It is part of a situation analysis, but it says nothing about what the Ad Council might do.

NPOs shouldn't adapt willy-nilly. Most feel they stand for something that endures. The Boy Scouts has come under some strident criticism in recent years because it would not allow a homosexual to lead a troop, because it refused to allow a boy to join who was an atheist and hence could not take the Boy Scout oath, and because it would not allow girls to become boy scouts. It has also been accused of being out of touch, of pursuing nineteenth-century values at the end of the twentieth century. The Boy Scouts' counterargument, put in its simplest terms, is ''That's not the kind of organization we are or want to be. These 'old-fashioned, nineteenth century values' include duty, loyalty, com-

munity service, selflessness, and altruism that aren't so old-fashioned after all.''
All NPOs that are worth anything should stand for something, but they must
show enough flexibility to avoid going the way of the WCTU.

SWOT

The SWOT analysis is a way of taking inventory of the NPO's strengths,
weaknesses, opportunities, and threats. *Strengths* are the things the NPO does
well and can build upon: experienced staff, for example, financial solvency, or
a good reputation. *Weaknesses* include problems inherent in both the NPO or
its environment. Strengths may suggest directions the NPO can take. They help
the NPO stay focused and point up new opportunities for service. An experienced staff has the capability to manage more complex programs. A financially
sound NPO is able to undertake riskier programs than one that can barely pay
its bills. A positive reputation makes it easier to raise funds for new programs.

Perhaps the most basic of all guidelines governing marketing strategy is:
Operate from strength. Take the Food Bank of Hatfield, Massachusetts. It received donations of food from manufacturers, distributors, and supermarkets,
and through food drives. Its executive director was considering setting up a
nonprofit business as a way of generating more income. What were the Food
Bank's strengths?

The Food Bank had its own farm so it knew farming. It knew nutrition and
about feeding the hungry; it knew about food manufacturing and processing,
about surplus commodities, and about food distribution; it knew the profitability
of foods and it knew where the money was made; and it knew senior managers
in supermarket chains and their suppliers. In brief, it knew food. Naturally it
decided to consider a food product to be distributed through normal retail grocery channels.[8]

The most common weakness NPOs face is limited funds and all that implies
for staffing and other expenditures. It is indeed so common that most NPOs
correctly look past it to other, more manageable travails. Weaknesses can help
to identify strategies that the NPO should avoid or weaknesses can warn of
potholes on the road ahead. To sell a food product through normal retail channels, the Food Bank needed someone it did not have, someone experienced in
selling grocery products to call on retailers, wholesalers, and food brokers. It
could proceed without such a person, but it would expect a harder time getting
distribution and a longer time to breakeven. One of DIFFA's key weaknesses
was that it relied too heavily on one source of funds, special events. Special
events have been called the black holes of fundraising because they take so
much time and effort for, all too often, scant results. Special events must shift
with mercurial public taste. One year walk-a-thons are all the rage, the next
telephons or Volunteer Days, the year after that charity concert tours. A poor
call on the fashion of the moment could badly depress income.

This discussion of strengths and weaknesses may give a false impression.

Strengths do not exist in the absolute, nor do weaknesses. Something is a strength only in relation to a plan or an objective. Know-how, connections, fundraisers who know the local territory help a NPO prosper in its home town, but would do little for it in a regional or national program. The staff at a summer camp for disadvantaged children is well trained and dedicated to the camp and its mission. The camp director, trying to reduce turnover by giving the staff more work and thus more income, proposes expanding the length of the season by running leadership programs for corporations. The same staff that is a strength in working with poor children is cool to training what it calls "fat cats" from corporate America. The same staff is a strength for one plan, a weakness for another.

Opportunities represent openings, and *threats* dangers or constraints that the NPO must consider when developing strategies. The environment presents a wide array of both opportunities and threats. Does the NPO have the resources and skills to respond and achieve its mission? Few NPOs systematically work to identify the opportunities they might pursue, which is no surprise, given that the list of opportunities, or needs, seems endless but the means are few. Digging such opportunities up can point the way to effective strategies, which can form the basis of future success:

- Grant money that is available for certain programs provides an opportunity for expansion without excessive risk.
- Weak competitors allow an NPO easier entry into a market with unsatisfied clients.
- A potential partner shares resources, allows programmatic expansion, and capitalizes on the strengths of both organizations.

Nearly all NPOs face an environment that contains some thorns. They may threaten an individual program or occasionally the entire NPO. Identifying such threats provides the basis for finding a way to avoid them or some way around them. Threats can take many forms:

- Another NPO with much the same mission as yours seems to have begun targeting your current donors.
- New postal regulations will make the use of flats more expensive. (Flats are mail pieces larger than business-size envelopes.)
- Museums fear that the movement for American Indian burial rights might force them to inventory their collections of skeletal remains and funerary objects and give them up.

In an ideal world, the NPO would turn weaknesses into strengths and threats into opportunities. This is rarely feasible, but it is possible to step back after completing the SWOT analysis and try to determine what actions it implies. These possible actions then feed into the next step, strategy development.

Identifying opportunities, indeed discriminating between opportunities and threats, is easy only when looking backward. Looking to the future is far more difficult. As this is being written, there has been a great splash in the press about the information superhighway, or as some put it, the Information Superhighway. There have even been articles urging nonprofits to act now, before it is too late, to begin the process of adapting to this new world.

Is this an opportunity? Not for most nonprofits, I suspect, who live too close to the line to take a flyer on what may well prove faddish and about which almost nothing is settled, technologically, economically, or politically. Should any NPO commit itself to a plan that relies heavily on federal spending that is prone to stopping and starting? The safest course for most nonprofits is to wait and see, not to lead the march but to join it later, if a march it proves to be.

Threats can, of course, crop up without warning. The fall of the Berlin Wall and the rapid collapse of communism in Eastern Europe spelled bad news for human-rights groups, because the public thought that the scouting of the socialist dictators was some sort of final victory for human rights. But human-rights activists were claiming, in mid-1990, that nothing had changed and that the demand for their services remained steady. Facing a shift in public mood, many of these groups took steps to increase their donations, lest their income decline.

I do not mean to suggest that bad news is always a threat. Fundraisers often see bad news as an opportunity for a special appeal and for a call to rally the troops. In the summer of 1992, the U.S. Supreme Court issued an opinion on abortion, an opinion much feared in advance by both sides of the debate as likely to be a winner-take-all, loser-lose-all opinion. It was neither. The Court found a middle road, upholding the legality of abortion and *Roe v. Wade,* but sanctioning modest state restrictions on the practice of abortion. Both sides were sickened by such temperate moderation, and both used the only word used today in America to express political pique: They said they were outraged by the decision. Within a day or two both were running newspaper ads and using direct mail to raise money to undo the damage done by the opinion. Both had found an opportunity in a ruling that did not give them everything they wanted.

STRATEGY DEVELOPMENT

The NPO has done its situation analysis and has identified some potential courses of action. The next step is to choose among those options.

Three Basic Approaches to Developing Strategy

The following three basic methods are in common use in formulating strategy. There is, of course, nothing sacred about them. An NPO can use one or a combination of all three, or it can pick and choose from each what it finds useful.

Scenario approach. This was what DIFFA did in its retreat. It tried to develop alternative pictures of what DIFFA might look like over the next three to five years by asking participants to imagine what they would like DIFFA to become in the future. Then it picked the best scenario, which turned out to be "Steady As She Goes," and refined it.

The scenario approach is quick and dirty, it usually holds people's interest, and it is very useful for thinking through the Big Picture, that is, major shifts in mission, emphasis, or direction.

Critical issues approach. The planning team creates a list of critical issues and puts them into some kind of logical order. It then attempts to resolve each of the issues in turn, lists the proposed solutions, and chooses the best. Since decisions on one issue may well affect other issues, it is necessary to review prior decisions to make sure they still stand. At the very end, after resolving all the critical issues, the team reviews the NPO's overall strategy to ensure that it is sound.

DIFFA found it easy to create a list of critical issues. That is, it knew what was wrong: fund-raising, communications, board development, steering committees, and staffing. In each of these areas, DIFFA's planning team considered alternatives. Let us look at one of them which is related to marketing, namely, fundraising. The special events were a particular problem, partly because there was nothing else, so when an event didn't meet expectations, there was nothing to fall back on; but mostly because most of the special events money came not from corporate foundations or corporate giving programs but from advertising and sales promotion budgets. Foundation money tends to endure, to be stable; ad money doesn't. DIFFA decided that it needed to broaden the base of its support, one that would give it more stable income. To do this it drew up a new development strategy that called for:

- membership clubs for individual donors and for small businesses, with dues ranging from $2,500 to $50,000 a year;
- training of board members and directors of the steering committees in how to solicit major gifts; and
- giving board members would take more responsibility for fundraising. Each must donate or raise $5,000 a year.

Goals approach. This is often used by for-profit corporations. They usually focus on one or a few major goals that drive the corporation, like return on investment, cash flow, and market share. In each area goals are set, strategies developed to meet each goal, and detailed plans are worked up to accomplish the goals. Larger NPOs seem to have the best experience using a goals approach. The executive director or the board sets overall emphasis and directions for the NPO. Divisions and subunits then incorporate those goals into their own strategic plans. Finally, they work out detailed plans to accomplish their strategic ends.

It is worthwhile repeating the point made earlier about muddling through. Strategy aims to be planned, to be thought-out. But much strategy just grows.

You watch what happens and then go in that direction. Builders and real estate developers learn a kind of wisdom when they first start. They don't put in drains where they want them to go. They watch where the water wants to go and put drains and berms to guide it along its way. Henry Mintzberg likens the process to what a potter does. The potter "applies skill, experience to a shapeless lump of clay—using more a sense of what is right than anything else."[9]

James Brian Quinn pursues the same point in more cumbrous verbiage:

The processes used to arrive at the total strategy are typically fragments, evolutionary, and largely intuitive. Although one can frequently find embedded in these fragments some very refined pieces of formal strategic analysis, the real strategy tends to *evolve* as internal decisions and external events flow together to create a new, widely shared consensus for action.[10]

Muddling through—it's the way much of the world runs and things get done.

Identification of Strategic Alternatives

We have seen that the situation analysis should identify several possible courses of action for the NPO. In my experience, coming up with a list of things to do is child's play. Few marketing directors or executive directors are short on programs and services they would like to introduce, if they had the money. The problem is picking those programs that will best advance the NPO's mission and that meet financial criteria. Alternatives must be judged by three criteria.

Mission. The first as always is the mission. How well does the alternative support or advance the nonprofit's mission? It is all too easy to lose sight of this, particularly in large nonprofits.

Numbers. How much will the alternatives cost, what are the offsetting revenues and grant money, what is the net cash flow? It is common sense as well to explore other resource needs like staff, volunteers, and space.

Risk. Alternatives must be evaluated in terms of how risky they are. The typical small nonprofit cannot afford a serious financial mistake, and so it prefers to be safe rather than sorry. Larger NPOs or those in a hurry can, if they wish, choose higher-risk strategies. The University of Tennessee has a graduate business school at its main campus in Knoxville that runs an enormously successful executive education program, but its MBA program is small and weak, the school not being rated nationally. The dean proposed a revision of the curriculum to emphasize the quality movement pioneered by W. Edwards Deming. In addition, he proposed eliminating much of what passes for research in today's business school, focusing not on theoretical and abstruse research but research with short-term promise; in other words, research that can be used immediately instead of research that can be used at some indefinite time in the future, if at all.

This is clearly a high-risk strategy. The quality movement has all the marks of a fad, which when it is over will have a distinct but modest influence on corporate practice, just like so many other ideas of the moment. Changing the nature of research is even more risky for the faculty. Faculty members who buy the dean's idea and do nothing but applications research are stuck at UT. Because no other business school thinks of research in the same way, no other business school would consider hiring them.[11]

Who Does the Planning?

The simple answer is senior staff, senior management, selected board members, perhaps some volunteers, perhaps some clients, perhaps some backers. That said, many NPOs use planning committees or task forces to help in the process. Such task forces allow for the exploration of several alternatives or issues simultaneously, with each group issuing a recommendation on the area it has studied to a central planning committee composed of key board and staff members. This type of organization ensures detailed scrutiny of specific issues, and it also helps to ensure "buy in" to the planning process. And alternatives can be evaluated easily before proceeding further.

The essence of strategic planning, then, is to identify strategic alternatives and test them against the NPO's mission and its resources. In the case of a consumer protection organization, for example, its managers might face a number of issues: Should we try to attempt to address all consumer needs, or should we focus on specific issues? Should we focus on local and regional issues or work on a national level? Should we specialize by type of product—say, toys or drugs—or should we cover all consumer products? Should we function largely as an inside-the-beltway group that lobbies for legislation and aims for high public visibility, or should we do things like research and grass-roots activity? Should we merely criticize others or should we show the way by designing and manufacturing safe products?

These represent only a few of the alternatives the agency might face. All may be legitimate courses, but who would be able to afford to pursue all programs simultaneously? The planning process for this group would include a detailed study of these programs with an aim to setting priorities and allocating resources to serve the clients and still fit well with the organization's strengths. Such an NPO would also explore other possibilities, including networking or cooperating with other organizations that provide educational, legal, and economic assistance to avoid duplicating services.

Obviously, the planning process is more an art than a science. The relationship to the marketing function, however, is clear: The NPO's planning efforts must identify the needs of existing clients, determine how its offerings can be brought to potential clients, and work to assure that they will satisfy them.

Objectives

We come at last to the question of objectives. In preparing a marketing strategy, objectives come early, not last. But in discussing them, it is best to have a clear notion of the role of marketing before attempting to set down objectives. In fact, with a good understanding of what can be expected of a marketing program, the marketer is well on his way toward a good set of objectives. Moreover, good objectives are not just another pretty face. They are the sine qua non, the without-which-not, of effective control over marketing. And they also serve nicely in explaining marketing programs to others.

NPOs have two fundamental goals. The first is financial survival; or to put it in simple words, they strive to pay their bills. The discussion in Chapter 3 should have prepared the reader to recognize that even the term "breakeven" can mean different things to different organizations. To some (to repeat), breaking even means zero Gross Marketing Contribution; to others it means zero Net Marketing Contribution; to others it means that cash be available to pay current bills and to replace capital when the need arises; to still others it means adjusting the books after the fact by means of interfund transfers.

Economists and others imagine that survival is an absolute goal for businesses; but survival is not why a nonprofit organization exists, anymore than staying alive until the weekend is why you exist. An NPO survives to carry out its mission. Nonprofit organizations have tasks to perform, a mission to carry out. So the fundamental objective of the NPO is survival subject to carrying out the task. It can be put the other way around: The NPO tries to provide services and accomplish its mission subject to the requirement that it survive.[12]

Thus, we see (a) that there are two overall objectives—financial survival and the performance of mission—and (b) that assessing performance against the second objective can be difficult.

Marketing can help accomplish either of these objectives, as we have seen in Chapter 2 in the discussion of what marketing is. In fact, it is an understanding of the role of marketing that leads to the establishment of marketing program objectives. By program objectives I mean the objectives of the marketing program taken as a whole. Program objectives in nonprofit businesses look very much like those in commercial firms. They include sales, market share, Gross Marketing Contribution, Net Marketing Contribution, and client satisfaction.

Note the mention of market share. The Ad Council, mentioned a few pages ago, once had the dominant share of public service advertising, but by 1992 its share had fallen to about 30 percent. Now consider this. Should the Ad Council even care about its share of nonprofit advertising? First, an elementary point. Just because share is down doesn't mean that total number of ads (or advertising impressions) are down. It could be that the Ad Council is doing more advertising than it used to but that others are doing a great deal more. That brings up the second point. The Ad Council's mission is to focus public attention, mobilize the public, and help promote action. If others are doing proportionately more advertising and the Ad Council is doing proportionately less, who cares? They are both seeking the same end. Yes, there may be egos involved; yes, no one likes to see others come in and do one's job better. It would seem, however, that market share is the wrong objective for the Ad Council because it strikes too competitive a note where competition makes little sense. A better intermediate objective would be the number of advertising impressions its ads produce.[13]

The elements of the marketing mix contribute to reaching program objectives. The Irish Tourist Board has as its mission to make Ireland attractive to tourists.[14] Its marketing program objectives are: (1) to develop Ireland's resources—encouraging festivals, subsidizing the improvement of tourist accommodations and the like; and (2) to promote Ireland as a tourist attraction. What is a reasonable goal for one element of the tourist board's marketing mix, its advertising? Note that travel overseas (say from the United States to Ireland) is little affected by advertising. It is an expensive purchase, typically made after months of collecting information, and it is strongly income elastic. That is, as one's income increases one of the first things one thinks about is taking a trip, and as one's income falls foreign travel is one of the first things to go. Moreover, most tourists do not go to Ireland; they go through Ireland on their way to or from England, or France, or some other destination. Advertising cannot accomplish the program goal of promoting Ireland, but it can accomplish some things that lead to ultimate accomplishment of the program objective. For example, it can make tourists more aware of Ireland, and within limits it can alter their image and knowledge of Ireland. It may be able to arouse some interest among travel agents, and it may persuade some travelers to discuss Ireland with their travel agents. It will, of course, lead some who "have always wanted to visit Ireland" finally to decide to make the trip. This last group, alas for the Irish Tourist Board, will be small.

The next question is the question of subobjectives, objectives for the elements of the marketing program. More words will be devoted to this topic in the next chapter.

Setting short-term strategies and priorities is a relatively easy undertaking; most managers are accustomed to deciding what will be accomplished within the next month or quarter or year. Setting long-term goals is more difficult and in many ways, more important.

For example, a regional dance company with a vision of developing a major regional dance festival must make haste slowly as it woos dancers, audiences, backers, and individuals influential in the regional arts. This organization, then, would have a clear long-term strategy, supported by a number of short-term strategies.

Long-term goal:

Build a major regional dance festival.

Short-term goals:

Start a small, local festival;

attract prominent dancers.

Each year:

increase funding;

increase attendance;

expand advertising and public relations;

attract audiences from a wider area.

Just as a morning's walk is made up of many small steps and some general idea as to direction, pace, and length, a long-term goal must be supported by short-range goals if it is to be accomplished. The NPO must set its ultimate destination and then develop a course of action that builds to it over time. Ideally, each of these goals will be accompanied by one or more objectives that will outline the mechanisms for achieving those goals.

IMPLEMENTATION: GETTING THE JOB DONE

Strategy answers the question: What do we do? Implementation answers the question: How do we do it? What kinds of marketing resources are needed to do the job? How should they be organized? Should paid staff do the bulk of the fundraising or volunteers? How should marketing programs be done in face-to-face contact with clients or backers?

It is easy to believe that strategy comes first and implementation second, or as it has often been put, that strategy drives implementation. Anyone with experience in organizations, either profit or nonprofit, will wonder. For one thing, the overall strategy may call for marketing resources the NPO doesn't have, in which case the strategy will have to change. Implementation can drive strategy. For another, the people who implement strategy may be either employees or volunteers. If they do not buy into the strategy, it will not succeed.

Development of Action Plans

Action plans set down what is to be done, when, and by whom:

- What is to be done—tells exactly what is to be done, including hiring staff, beginning a new project, acquiring a facility, or ordering office equipment for a new venture.
- Who is responsible—indicates, by position or name, who will take responsibility for the completion of the action.
- Initiation and completion dates—specify when the activity is to be started and a target date for completion of the project.

At this level the nuts and bolts of planning are carried out to support the grand schemes and strategies that have been developed. In large corporations, action plans are developed by the managers who are responsible for carrying them out.

Monitoring of Plan Implementation

Management consultant Peter Drucker has written that, "Sooner or later, even good ideas must degenerate into work." Implementation of a strategic plan is the point at which the lofty, visionary work of planning comes to rolling up one's sleeves and placing emphasis on action.

Many NPOs dismantle planning groups when their work is done, ignoring that in many ways the most important part is to follow. At its best, the planning effort is ongoing. Planning is a process, not a destination. The development of action plans provides a natural framework for implementation and monitoring. The planning group will need only to pull out well-documented plans and discuss whether the action plans have been carried out and what the results have been.

Plans are less likely to become attractive shelf ornaments if those involved know that they will be called upon to discuss their role in implementation; public humiliation can be a powerful spur, knowing that a loss in esteem, merit, and possibly unemployment can result from a failure to work with the plan. Meetings should be held at least quarterly to monitor and discuss progress toward goals and objectives set during the planning process.

Revising Plans

It should be painfully obvious to all those attempting to plan for the NPO's future that both internal and external circumstances change continually. Developing and rigidly adhering to plans is by no means the goal; as a matter of fact, it is a mark of poor management. There is a need from time to time to update and revise plans that may have been ideal at the time they were developed but will not stay in tune with a changing reality.

It's a good idea to allow for the revision of plans by taking into account likely changes in the environment and in new ideas and developments. Again, this repeats the need for ongoing evaluation. The planning approach described here should become a part of standard operating procedure, with all major decisions vetted from the standpoints of strategy and their viability in the marketplace. New information that might affect the plans should be reviewed as well on a regular basis, say, quarterly.

NOTES

1. The source of my information on DIFFA is Holly Hall, "Making a 'Strategic' Plan." *Chronicle of Philanthropy,* September 18, 1990, pp. 23–26. The single quotes

change the meaning of the title from making a strategic plan to making a so-called strategic plan; just as *fresh fish* means fresh fish but *"fresh"* fish means so-called fresh and therefore not really fresh at all. So why the quotes around *strategic?* Is the editor trying to tell us something? Perhaps she just slipped up.

2. Goldie Blumenstyk, "Deals for Alumni." *Chronicle of Higher Education,* April 20, 1994, pp. A42 and A45.

3. Holly Hall, "A Non-Profit Look Ahead to 2050." *Chronicle of Philanthropy,* December 3, 1991, p. 31.

4. Ibid.

5. The Advertising Council, *Report to the American People,* pp. 89–90. This grandiose title signifies what most NPOs would call their annual report.

6. The WCTU is still active, though, with some 50,000 members; but its annual budget is less than $400,000, which, after paying the salaries of its nineteen staff members doesn't leave much left over for good works. See the entry on the WCTU in Peggy Kneffel Daniels and Carol A. Schwartz (eds.), *Encyclopedia of Associations* (Detroit: Gale Research, 1993), volume 1, p. 1394.

7. The example is based on "The Advertising Council: Corporate Strategy," a case study published in 1992 by the Harvard Business School.

8. Cynthia Massarsky, "Food for Thought—And Profit." *Nonprofit Times* (March 1994): 48–49.

9. Henry Mintzberg, "Crafting Strategy." *Harvard Business Review* (July–August 1987): 106.

10. James Brian Quinn, *Strategies for Change: Logical Incrementalism* (Homewood, Ill.: Dow Jones-Irwin, 1980), p. 15.

11. Walecia Konrad, "Can Tennessee Put Its B-School on the Map?" *Business Week* (March 11, 1991), p. 74.

12. But it is one thing to define objectives. It is another to measure progress toward meeting them. The business has many standard measures of how well it is doing (though none are ideal)—earnings per share, stock price, credit ratings, measures of return on invested capital, or funds available. No such convenient measures exist for the nonprofit organization. It is easy to get agreement on what breaking even means, of course, but it can be difficult to determine how well the organization is accomplishing its mission.

13. "Advertising impressions" is loose language for gross rating points. GRPs are briefly discussed in Chapter 14.

14. See the case study entitled "Irish Tourist Board," in Stephen A. Greyser, *Cases in Advertising and Communications Management* (Englewood Cliffs, N.J.: Prentice-Hall, 1972), pp. 514–583.

Chapter 9

Developing a Marketing Strategy

Alfred Chandler has defined strategy as "the determination of the basic long-term goals and objectives of an enterprise, and the adoption of courses of action and the allocation of resources necessary for carrying out these goals."[1] While Chandler was thinking of business, the same definition fits nonprofit organizations. Strategy for a nonprofit organization is a statement of what the organization as a whole stands for, what it aims to accomplish, and how.

At a very broad level, the strategic issues facing a nonprofit manager are much the same as those facing a businessman. Like the businessman, the nonprofit manager must acquire resources and decide how the organization is to be financed. He must decide what kind of an organization it will be and how large; recruit and hire people, motivate and control them; decide who his customers are to be, how he will communicate with them and distribute his products to them; and how he will price his output.

Marketing strategy is a *general* solution to the problems that all organizations face in (1) defining their target markets and (2) designing programs to serve them effectively. That is, a marketing strategy answers the following questions:

Target Markets

Who should our clients (or backers) be?

Marketing Programs

What services and products should we offer them?

How will we reach them with our services and products?

What price will we charge?

How will we communicate with them?

How will we organize and control the marketing effort?

A nonprofit organization is not free to take on any marketing strategy it chooses. Its marketing strategy should be subordinated to its overall organizational strategy, and it should reflect this strategy. This means that marketing should serve the interests of the organization, as well as adapt itself to the interests of backers, clients, volunteer workers, and employees. These last two groups are important because marketing is seen by many in our society as repugnant, and many of the people associated with nonprofit organizations base their interest and dedication on the fact that the organization does not foul itself with the shabby morals they associate with mercantile endeavor. Because this attitude is widespread, those nonprofit organizations that market products and services often find they must paper over their marketing with words, calling their advertising educational activities; their fundraising development; and their salesmen counselors, field representatives, advisors, docents, volunteers, or editors. Needless to say, marketing strategy is also influenced by financial considerations. Marketing programs consume resources, and they (usually) produce them; and the state of the reckoning of income and outgo commands every marketer's attention.

But before considering marketing strategy further, it is necessary to treat some preliminaries. The first section of this chapter develops several issues that inevitably seem to arise during the formulation of marketing strategy, and then it discusses marketing strategy itself.

THE FIVE INFLUENCES ON MARKETING STRATEGY IN A NONPROFIT ORGANIZATION

Competition can powerfully influence an organization's marketing strategy, as we saw in Chapter 7. There are five other influences as well that must be discussed as preliminaries to taking up marketing strategy itself.

Influence 1—Marketing Style

To many, marketing means the brassy hard sell, a black art practiced by the likes of Bernie Cornfeld, Joe Isuzu, and Professor Harold Hill. In fact, such humbug does disfigure marketing. To pick with even hand from both the profit sector and the nonprofit sector, we need only note the dishonesty we automatically ascribe to the used car salesman and the candidate for high public office.

Not all marketing is this way. In fact, not most. Organizations nevertheless can choose the degree of aggressiveness they want, from hard sell to soft sell to no sell. All of these marketing styles are seen in the nonprofit sector. We see the hard sell by college coaches recruiting young athletes who, they hope, will bring their college a national championship. Some charities solicit funds aggressively, spending more than half of what they raise on the solicitation itself, and few politicians and revivalists suffer from diffidence. We see the soft sell in organizations that provide information but then leave the client in peace to make up his own mind. Most public health campaigns employ a soft sell, as do most charities in raising funds.

Still other nonprofit organizations adopt a no-sell style, in which clients are not sought out. Instead, if they are lucky, they are permitted to find out about the organization and what it offers. The organization that adopts this style simply handles whatever clients come its way. This is the style adopted so successfully by Alcoholics Anonymous and copied by other anonymous organizations.[2] It is also assumed by many government agencies, which see no need for marketing and lack the necessary skills or money or inclination.

The question of style is the question of how active an organization is to be in marketing—in finding clients, helping them define their needs, and providing solutions. There are five factors that influence the choice of marketing style.

The first is the desires and interests of those associated with the organization—clients, volunteers, employees, and backers. Employees, in particular, often have convictions about what they see as hucksterism. The staff of a natural history museum is likely to support only a low-key approach in recruiting museum members, and in fact it would be capable of ensuring the failure of a policy that is too aggressive.

Second is the nature of the clients. Some respond better to an aggressive approach, others to a restrained approach. The revival preacher knows that diffident sermons win few souls among the congregation, and so in the higher interest he goads them with fiery exhortations. Given the task of discouraging twelve-year-olds from starting to smoke, we would probably design a campaign with strong, simple messages. Would we, in the interests of truth, tell them that even if they did smoke, they still probably would not get cancer? Would we tell them that if cancer were to come, it would not come for decades? We would not. The messages would present one side only. We would tell them it was not smart to smoke (which they might not believe), that smokers stand a much higher chance of getting cancer than nonsmokers, and that the stench of the smoke bothers everyone whose nose is in working order.

Suppose, on the other hand, we work for the Department of Transportation (DOT). We are to lobby Congress on behalf of the DOT to set high fees for users of inland waterways. The Assistant Transportation Secretary for Congressional and Intergovernmental Affairs said he treated the experienced politicians in Congress "the way you'd treat a grass-roots campaign for mayor." His methods included direct mail, telephone canvassing, and the publication of statistics, fact sheets, and reports. "Within a period of hours," he said, "congressmen will get a letter from [Transportation] Secretary Brock Adams, their staffs will get phone calls from us, and we'll send any information they ask for." This, clearly, is a high-speed, hard-sell approach.[3]

Sometimes cultural factors indicate a particular style, as for example in fund-raising, where Jews supposedly raise funds much more aggressively than gentiles.[4]

The third factor is the degree to which the organization is meeting its goals. An organization already fulfilling its objectives, an organization that is well-heeled, naturally tends to rest. It can afford a certain measure of aloofness if it wishes. One that is failing to meet its objectives—say facing too few clients, too many of the wrong kind, or financial deficits—may adopt a more aggressive style.

The fourth factor affecting an organization's choice of a marketing style is the nature of the competition and the organization's "need to win." Competition often, but not always, tends to breed at the lowest common moral level—at least, in America it does; an organization for whom winning is the only thing finds itself under great pressure to do or be done, to scrunch or be scrunched. Perhaps this explains much of the frenzy that surrounds the recruiting of athletes by institutions of higher learning. It is a measure of the American character that the competition for scholars is much more sedate—no press gangs there.

Finally, there is the question of how the organization wishes to try to influence the behavior of its clients and others it wishes to reach. Nonprofit businesses and for-profit businesses rarely consider this issue because the use of standard marketing techniques is taken for granted. Most nonprofit organizations have much wider choices. In fact they can, and they do, choose from among all the methods of changing behavior in the second chapter—violence, negotiation, legislation, satyagraha, brainwashing, gentle persuasion, and even marketing. Marketing is best suited to producing relatively superficial changes in clients already favorably predisposed to the aims of the marketing program. This means that marketing is usually only one of the methods of influencing behavior an organization will adopt.

Take the campaign mounted by the International Ladies' Garment Workers' Union and the Amalgamated Clothing and Textile Workers Union to curb imports of clothing and textiles.[5] In addition to advertising that urged consumers to look for the union label, the campaign included:

- A rally in Herald Square, New York, in the heart of the garment district, addressed by Senator Patrick Moynihan and the mayor of New York.
- Rallies in 150 other cities and towns.
- Two meetings between top labor leaders, including George Meany, and the president at the White House.
- Intensive pressure exerted by lobbyists on members of Congress.

This campaign makes use of a number of techniques to get across its message, and presumably others might follow, such as demonstrations, boycotts, or threats to deny political support; but the only standard marketing technique is the union label advertising.

The two unions were most certainly correct in pursuing this traditional line of attack. Politically sensitive issues are rarely resolved through the use of marketing techniques because the stakes and issues are too important. Power, not persuasion, is needed. Or rather, power persuades.

Influence 2—The Environment

We shall see that an organization's marketing strategy must adapt itself to influences within the organization. It must also reflect pressures and realities outside the organization, which, for want of a better word, we call the environment. The marketing program undertaken by an organization must conform to changes in economic and social forces, technology, and politics. And not only to change. It must also adapt to the current forces and attitudes in its society.

Between 1966 and 2005, while the number of Roman Catholics in America is expected to increase by one-third, the number of priests is expected to decrease by some 40 percent.[6] Although the primary causes of such a decline in fervor are unfathomable, a religious order is still permitted, though with becoming submission, to ask after the secondary causes. Among these causes should perhaps be included the increasing attractiveness of secular careers, the assumption of much charity by the state, the requirement that priests be celibate, and the public skepticism about religious questions that is a characteristic of a mature civilization. Whatever the causes are, they are not of such weak stuff that a little publicity or an energetic program of pastoral visits by recruiting fathers will have much of an impact. There will be some impact from such activities, to be sure. But not much, because the decline in fervor is beyond the reach of such a weak tool as marketing. A well-conceived and executed marketing program might increase the number of entrants from 7,000 to 7,500, perhaps 8,000, perhaps more; but there is no hope it could raise the number to 23,000. Such increases must come from elsewhere, and all the religious communities can do is wait, and pray, for changed conditions.[7]

Not only must an organization strive to mold itself to environmental changes, it must develop a good nose for how people stand before it can develop effective marketing programs. As we have seen, few Americans trouble to vote, and even in presidential elections only five or six in ten eligible voters go to the polls. To a marketer, this is a given. It is unlikely to change, and it certainly will not change as a result of a marketing program. If a marketer were given the job of getting out the vote, he would first despair of doing much. Next, he would try to learn enough about those who do not vote to build a program likely to work. Then, with impeccable marketing logic, he would aim his campaign only at those segments of nonvoters most likely to respond. If this is a large segment, he might make substantial impact; but if it is small, his program will accomplish little outside of the small segment. When faced with intractable social problems, marketing replaces economics as the dismal science.

Influence 3—The Effect of Organizational Form on Strategy

Even the organizational form of the nonprofit organization affects its marketing strategy. "The plain fact is that to this day economics has failed to develop a theory of the effect of ownership form on the operation of enterprises."[8] This is of little importance in business because the corporate form dominates.

Nonprofit organizations are more diverse. Let us return to the classification scheme described in Chapter 1 to see the influence of form on marketing strategy. Nonprofit businesses are much like any business, and their marketing strategy and plans center on customers and distributors, like those of any business. Common benefit organizations have members, not clients or backers. These organizations have two related problems, to enlist members and retain them. The American Medical Association, for example, claims to represent all U.S. doctors, but less than half of them are members, and in recent decades the proportion of U.S. doctors enrolled in the AMA has steadily fallen. Its problem presumably is both retaining current members and attracting young doctors.

Many common benefit organizations solve this problem with artless unconcern: Those who wish to become members stay and those who do not leave. This take-us-as-we-are attitude is rarely found in business. But common benefit organizations can have quite different objectives. Alcoholics Anonymous (AA), for example, does not care whether an alcoholic comes to an AA meeting; and it does not care whether, once having started to come, he continues to come. AA does not care partly because it is indifferent to whether it grows or shrinks. More important, however, is AA's philosophy of putting responsibility on the alcoholic: The alcoholic is put off from potential recovery by well-meaning friends who protect him from the consequences of his drinking. So as part of the process of accepting the consequences of his own behavior, the alcoholic is allowed to sink or swim in AA. There is a great deal of support, of course, from other alcoholics, but AA and its members never proselyte.

Service organizations also face two rather different marketing problems—one in dealing with customers, the other in dealing with backers. Dealing with customers involves familiar marketing efforts—identifying target markets, formulating a theory of how consumers behave, planning the marketing effort, doing it, and checking on its performance. Dealing with backers moves the marketing executive into fundraising with all its special rules of thumb and gobbets of conventional wisdom. But at root the process is still the same—finding potential donors, assessing their motives, planning the fund-raising campaign, and doing it.

It should come as no surprise to anyone with some experience in the world that some service organizations are good in dealing with clients and inept in raising funds, and that others are the other way around. Perhaps the classic example of the latter is Boy's Town, which was so successful in raising funds and so frugal in spending them that by 1972 it had amassed an endowment of $209 million, making it one of the richest communities in the United States. Little had changed in 1994 when by most measures it still had far more endowment than it needed.

Commonwealth organizations typically enjoy poor communications with their clients, and their services are often provided on a take-it-or-leave-it basis, which wonderfully simplifies the formulation of marketing strategy. In fact, the most serious marketing problem commonwealth organizations face is arousing an interest in focusing the organization's efforts on serving clients. The absence of any significant feedback from clients raises the other important marketing issue in commonwealth organizations, namely, deciding how well the organization is doing. Without sales to tell how it is doing, a commonwealth organization must undertake formal research to measure the degree to which its services are ineffective and its clients dissatisfied.

Influence 4—The Role of Professionalism

The role of professionalism that arises in strategy formulation is the question of the importance of professionals in defining marketing strategy.

According to Greenwood, a profession has five characteristics:

1. It is based on a systematic body of theory that requires lengthy training to acquire; based, that is, not merely on knowledge but on knowledge built on theory.

2. It is sanctioned by society, which allows the profession to control its schools, admit or reject newcomers, license its members, and hold confidential dealings with clients.

3. It has a code of ethics, based partly on tradition and partly on theory.

4. It has its own professional culture—associations, values, norms of behavior—and the concept of a career as a calling. One is called to the cloth but not to TV repair.

5. Finally, and central to our concern, the professional has authority over what passes between the professional and the client. The professional controls the interaction, not the client.[9]

What, after all, is the difference between a professional occupation and one that is not, say, a business? There is a matter of language. Professions have clients, firms have customers. Customers have the capacity to judge for themselves (a premise incidentally that some consumer activists consider quaint), to appraise their own needs and judge for themselves which product will serve them best. Customers can demand, and sometimes get, a refund. As was said once upon a time, the customer is always right. But when customers become clients, they cannot judge for themselves. They cannot diagnose their own illness, nor can they evaluate the quality of the professional's service. It is the professional who controls the situation: It is the professional who tells clients what their problem is and what the solution is. Clients can only take it or leave it.

In an organization dominated by professionals and professional thinking, marketing inevitably takes a back seat in the formation of much of the organization's overall strategy. The influence of professionals is particularly important in the selection of target markets and in specifying the goods and services the organization distributes to its clients, what marketers call the "product/market scope." Professionals often have a great deal to say about quality, as well. Dickens caught the professional's attitude toward quality in describing the new chief butler of the newly rich Mr. Merdle, who "would not allow a dinner to be given, unless it was up to his mark. He set forth the table for his own dignity. If the guests chose to partake of what was served, he saw no objection; but it was served for the maintenance of his rank."[10] Professionals also are found in business, but their influence on marketing strategy is very much weaker.

The secondary role of marketing in an organization controlled by professionals was put clearly, if unintentionally, in an article by Stephen L. Tucker advocating the introduction of marketing as a planning technique for hospital administrators.[11] Virtually all of the primary functions of a hospital are carried out by professionals, either doctors or nurses, leaving to marketing such weighty concerns as the patient's desire to have a choice of entrees at mealtime, the need for the gates in the doctor's parking lot to work correctly, and the need for a good system for paging doctors.

We see also the importance of professional standards and habits of mind in the use of marketing research. Professionals may feel they do not need research to tell them what clients need or how best to reach them. Moreover, research may be seen as information that does not meet the canons of the profession. Lawyers who work for the Federal Trade Commission must worry whether research based on consumer surveys will pass muster in the courtroom. Without training in the behavioral sciences, suspicious of surveys paid for by businesses, needing information that fits the legal definitions of evidence, these professionals naturally place little reliance on marketing research.[12]

Influence 5—The Role of Marketing

What role does marketing play in the organization? How important is marketing to the success of the organization? How much can marketing contribute to meeting the organization's objectives? Marketing is useful in dealing with the three general types of objectives.

Marketing generates resources. The first deals with generation of resources. Every organization needs resources to work on and to work with. The nonprofit organization needs people, it needs money, it needs clients and raw materials and facilities, and it needs skills. By way of illustration, a consumer retail cooperative needs managers who know retailing; the American Society for the

Prevention of Cruelty to Animals needs money to support its work; an advisory service on abortion whose services go unused needs clients; a museum needs access to private collections or else it cannot hope to acquire new items and build its holdings; and a legal aid society faced with legal issues in a new, complex area of the law needs new skills to defend its clients effectively.

Marketing can sometimes contribute to the generation of resources like these, and when it can it assumes a role of some importance to the organization. But "some" and "sometimes" need to be stressed. Just because a college, say, embarks on an active recruiting program for more students (or better students) does not mean that marketing drives the university. All marketing does is contribute *some* help in fulfilling *one* of the university's goals. Certainly, we do not expect the teaching and research of a university to be touched by marketing. Because Consumers Union (CU) spends almost 30 percent of its revenue on direct mail advertising to build circulation of its publication, *Consumer Reports,* does not mean that CU is infected by marketing. Yet here the goal is paramount, because aside from occasional noncommercial research grants, CU has no sources of revenue other than the sale of its publications. Still, the major purpose of CU is "to provide consumers with information and counsel on consumer goods and services." Generating funds is necessary, but it is not why CU exists nor does it provide a focus for the energies of CU staff members.

Marketing influences behavior. The second general objective to which marketing can contribute is to influence behavior, by persuasion and by adaptation. To nonprofit businesses marketing is *the* major tool for influencing the behavior of its customers and distributors. Most other nonprofit organizations use a variety of ways of influencing behavior, of which marketing can be one. A politician faces two fundamental problems: winning office the first time and winning office forever after. His success at the polls depends in part on environmental factors like the strength of his local party and the draw of the major party candidates running at the same time. It also depends on the politician's skill in getting out the vote of his party and in presenting himself to the electorate through meetings, advertising, and so on. When it comes to running for reelection, marketing again can contribute, but it is likely that more substantial accomplishments, such as jobs and legislative programs, have more impact on the electorate. Marketing does have a role in elections, but most of the time it is secondary. (We have made this point before.)

Marketing satisfies clients. Contributing to the satisfaction of clients' needs is the third general objective to which marketing can contribute. An organization that adopts a marketing posture is more responsive to its clients' needs. It is willing to expend time and money to learn what its clients want, and it is more willing to adapt itself to meet these wants. As a result of contact with an organization to whom marketing is important, clients should feel more satisfied than they might in dealing with another organization.

In a few years, the United States may have some type of national health service.[13] Hospitals and clinics are organizations in which the only important role of marketing concerns fundraising. Given that the contributions of marketing are otherwise nil, what differences would we see between a national health service that adopts a marketing point of view and one that does not? Perhaps the only significant difference would be in the handling of patient complaints against doctors and nurses, and against hospitals. If it shuns marketing, the national health service will set up no complaint procedures at all, or it will set up procedures that make it difficult to complain and impossible to win. If it adopts marketing, its procedures will provide reasonable and perhaps even quick redress for legitimate complaints.[14] And what will happen to all those fundraisers when universal coverage takes hold? My guess is, nothing. They will continue to raise funds just as if nothing has changed. Of course, their appeals will change from helping fund charity care to some other. I would be surprised if, after the adoption of national health, hospitals did not claim that they needed funds more than ever, so alluring is the billions of dollars that donors give to hospitals each year, and so pressing the hospitals' needs.

In trying to understand the role of marketing, then, the manager should not be content to say merely that marketing is or is not important. Our discussion so far has shown that in most nonprofit organizations marketing is critically important for a few objectives and of limited or no importance for the rest. It is a good idea to be specific: To *which* objectives does marketing contribute? In which parts of the organization is it important that marketing be competently executed? This is the point that Tucker's article, mentioned earlier, should have dealt with. Marketing has a place in hospitals and in health care, but its role is circumscribed and relatively minor.[15]

Yet another way of putting the point is to ask this question: "If the marketing job in this organization is done competently, professionally, how far along will the organization be toward meeting its mission?" Consumers' Union faces a number of marketing-like issues. It must decide which products to test and which products to review—some reviews are based on surveys of its members, not on tests; it produces and sells publications; it routinely queries its members on their experiences in buying, using, and repairing products; and it must find new subscribers and keep old ones.

It should be clear that only the last issue is central to CU's purposes. If the rest of the issues were resolved relatively ineptly from a marketing point of view, CU would not be injured and might not even be inconvenienced. The reader is welcome to disagree with this analysis; but my point still stands, which is that only one of the goals of CU, finding new subscribers, requires effective marketing; for the rest, it needs little in the way of marketing. This conclusion gives us a clear understanding of the role of marketing at CU.

The reader can get some experience with the concept of the role of marketing by exploring questions like these as he works through situations he faces. Thus, the role of marketing can serve to describe an organization's needs and situation. It can also be used to prescribe. It is lax to say that one nonprofit organization needs marketing, or that another has little use for marketing. One should be specific: In this organization, marketing has these specific responsibilities and no others. This is a first important step in setting marketing strategy and in establishing control over the marketing operation. For example, just what *is* the role of marketing in the typical hospital?

THE TWO ELEMENTS OF MARKETING STRATEGY

Targets

With these preliminaries under our belt, let us return to the issue of determining marketing strategy. Marketing strategy takes in two basic elements, the target market and the marketing mix.

Every marketing program aims above all else to meet the interests of a market segment or segments. This is true of programs dealing with both clients and backers. Since the marketing program builds all of its details and activities with the aim of reaching the target markets, the job of evaluating and selecting these markets is of first importance. It is a responsibility that properly falls on senior members of the organization's management.

The appraisal of target markets is based on a market analysis, as we saw in Chapter 7. One example of market analysis is the research required in a fundraising campaign to describe major prospects, who are usually the most important target of the campaign. The fundraiser must know bare bones, of course: who the prospects are, where they live, where they work, their telephone numbers, and their business titles. In addition, the fund-raiser must be able to rate the prospects, that is, to estimate what they are capable of giving.

Note first of all that the rating is the other side of the backers' interest in knowing how much they are expected to give. Since most backers are interested in such information, a good marketer tries to give it to them. Rating also helps in forecasting the amount the campaign can produce and hence helps in setting goals.

The process starts naturally enough with those backers who have shown interest in the organization or who have given before. But a good fundraiser tries to locate and rate new prospects as well. Let us imagine that a wealthy woman is being rated.[16] In addition to the bare bones, the rater collects a good deal of personal information: Where was the prospect educated, what are her political interests, what committees has she served on, what clubs does she belong to, what are her family connections, what honors has she received, even when is her birthday? It cannot hurt a fundraiser to know that the woman's first job during the depression was as a newspaper reporter, and it may help. Of course, the rater collects financial information: What is the prospect's net worth, her annual income, her holdings of securities? Is there a family foundation? What are her favorite charities? How much has she given in the past, and how often? There are many sources for such information like newspaper and magazine stories, proxy statements, wills on file in probate court, registry of deeds where tax stamps are found, and county plat books. Finally, the rater collects information directly bearing on the appeal: What is the prospect most interested in, is she close to anyone on the fundraising committee, and how familiar is she with the project that is being funded?

All this is background for the preparation of the rating itself. Normally, this is done by volunteers who are themselves prospective givers, because the person best able to estimate what the woman might give is a friend or business associate who has known her for years. This is not a job for a researcher; it is simply too important.

Marketers also try to see markets not in terms of products but in terms of the clients' interests. It is convenient to think of markets in terms of what the organization produces. A transit company thinks in terms of routes, schedules, and equipment. This view of a market, of what "business" the nonprofit organization is in, is called by marketers a production orientation. It is the view of the business or nonprofit organization as seen from the factory floor: "We are what we make."

But clients are not interested in products or services. They want experiences; they want to do things, to accomplish tasks, to overcome difficulties. Bus riders are not interested in routes, schedules, and equipment. In fact, they are not even interested in riding the bus. What they want is to go from point A to point B. They want to save time, or save money, or be on time. Taking this point of view is called by marketers a consumer orientation, or in our terms, a client orientation. It is the view of the business or nonprofit organization as seen by customers and clients, who care nothing for the service center or its machinery. "We are what our clients make of us. We are what they want." Marketers frown on the production orientation and smile on the client orientation.

There is one problem with taking the client orientation in defining markets, but there are three benefits. The problem is that it is easy to count passengers and collect information on routes, schedules, and equipment. They measure behavior and states of being. There are abundant comparative figures available as well. But taking the client orientation means measuring states of mind, which is expensive in both dollars and time, and requires some experience and skill on the part of management. Moreover, when such information is at hand, it is usually impossible to compare with the information collected by other transit companies. Typically, they will not have even tried to define their markets this way; but even where they have tried, their definition of states of mind and their methods of measurement will differ, and the results will not be comparable.

The Benefits of a Client Orientation

The first benefit is that a client orientation often throws a great deal of light on the client and his behavior. There can be nothing more valuable for a marketer. I first learned the importance of taking the client's side while reading a book by Paul Goodman. Goodman was discussing the problem of school dropouts, which trouble those who run the public schools. They assumed a production orientation toward the problem. They thought about what was taught, not what students learned; about what the schools provided, not what students experienced. Goodman straightened all this out in one line when he asked, "What are they dropouts from?"[17] The school administrators had a production orientation. "If students won't come to school, there must be something wrong with the students. Let's fix them." Goodman's approach said, "If students won't come to school, there must be something wrong with the school. Let's fix the school."

It is always tempting to take a production orientation. "If people won't vote, there must be something wrong with the people. Let's fix them." But the marketer must learn to take the voters' side. "If people won't vote, there must be something wrong with politics. Let's fix that." And if politics cannot be fixed, as indeed seems likely, then not much should be expected of efforts to turn out the vote. Here we see a second benefit of taking the client's side. It can help set more realistic objectives for a marketing program.

The third benefit of taking a client orientation is that it helps in identifying potential competition, "unlike" competition. As long as the Postal Service takes a production orientation, it has no competition because no one else can legally move first-class mail. But without question people are not interested in sending letters. When they send a letter they solve a communications problem—to send (1) a short message (2) that has the formality of a permanent record (3) where the sender and receiver need not attend simultaneously to the communication.[18] They will be happy to consider any other way of solving this problem: fax, E-mail, carrier pigeon, what-have-you. Such a view should help the Postal Service see more clearly where potential competition might arise.

The Marketing Mix

The second element of marketing strategy is the marketing mix.[19] This is a combination of a number of marketing elements—product and service offerings, channels of distribution, advertising, personal selling, publicity, and price—that the marketer manipulates to influence the behavior of his target markets. An effective statement of the marketing mix integrates all these elements into one consistent program, in which each element contributes toward meeting overall program objectives.

Just what this contribution can be requires experience and judgment to decide. Perhaps the most serious weakness of nonprofit managers who lack training in marketing is their credulous certitude about the power of advertising. Without a just appreciation of what advertising can and cannot do for an organization, a manager cannot hope to mount an effective communications program. Without a just appreciation of what marketing can do, a manager cannot prepare a sound marketing strategy. We have already begun to discuss this under the heading, "The Role of Marketing." We shall return to it again and again.

AN OVERVIEW OF MARKETING STRATEGY

Let us now look briefly at the two components of a marketing strategy: target markets and putting together marketing programs.[20]

Target Markets

We have already made the point in Chapter 7 that focus brings coherence and efficiency to marketing efforts. We have also made the point that it is easy to build what seems to be persuasive arguments against the idea of focusing on specific target markets.

Thinking long and hard about target markets is a recommendation of ideals. When a lot is at stake, most NPOs will take formal, deliberate steps to define these target markets. But most NPOs cannot, or will not, do this. They muddle ahead, learning as they go and adjusting to what they learn.

For example, the AIDS Committee of the Friends Meeting of Washington, a Quaker congregation, runs a Saturday night coffee house each week for those with AIDS. The Committee apparently was surprised to discover that the patrons were mostly gay men; but once it did discover this fact, it began advertising mostly in the *Washington Blade,* a weekly that covers the gay scene. What happened here happens often in the nonprofit sector. A program is begun, perhaps with little thought given to whom the clients are likely to be. After the fact, potential clients sort themselves out and the NPO can at last clearly define its target market and begin effective communications.[21]

In NPOs the selection of target markets is not the result of cool, rational marketing analysis. There will typically be debate among staffers and volunteers as to proposed targets measured against the two central criteria, mission and cash flow. Take a symphony orchestra that wants to broaden its educational role.[22] It is considering an expansion of its programs for preschoolers to high school students. The debate would be vigorous. I use pluses and minuses to show pro and con arguments:

- Youngsters are the audiences of the future too far in the future, since the average age of the audience is mid-thirties.

+ Focusing on youngsters is the right thing to do.

- We have many competing uses for our limited resources. In the area of education alone we could expand our efforts on community-based education for audiences of all ages, or we could focus more on professional training for our musicians.

+ If we don't do it, no one else will.

- Symphony audiences have been around for nearly two centuries. During most of that time no orchestra ever did this type of education. Yet symphony music thrived during this period.

+ The schools are cutting back on their music programs, or dropping them altogether. Where will tomorrow's audiences come from?

− The same place they have always come from. Our audiences have education well above average, and the higher incomes that implies. Audiences learn to love good music in college and afterwards, not in grammar school or even high school.

+ I learned to love good music in high school.

− One swallow does not a summer make.

+ Well we must do. We're an orchestra. That's what we're here for. [Argument from the mission.]

− We are an orchestra. But we must spend our scarce resources—the musicians' time and energy—where it will do the most good. We need ticket revenues now, not ten or twenty years from now. [Argument from the financial objective.]

In brief then, selection of target markets is central to all marketing efforts, but in a nonprofit organization it is not always easy to come to a decision.

In the next section of the book, "The Elements of the Marketing Program," we turn to, well, it's obvious from the title.

NOTES

1. Alfred D. Chandler, Jr., *Strategy and Structure: Chapters in the History of the Industrial Enterprise* (Cambridge, Mass.: MIT Press, 1962), p. 13.

2. In his book *Odd Man In* (Chicago: Quadrangle, 1969), pp. 76–77, Edward Sagarin lists: Addicts Anonymous, Adults Anonymous (for convicts), Alcoholics Anonymous, Business Failures Anonymous, Checks Anonymous (for forgers), Divorcees Anonymous, Ex-Convicts Anonymous, Fatties Anonymous, Gamblers Anonymous, Illegitimates Anonymous, Narcotics Anonymous, Neurotics Anonymous, Overeaters Anonymous, Recidivists Anonymous, Schizophrenics Anonymous, Smokers Anonymous, Suicides Anonymous, and Teenagers Anonymous (for delinquents).

3. "User Fees Move Closer to Inland Waterways." Business Week (February 20, 1978), p. 27.

4. See Milton Goldin, *Why They Give, American Jews and Their Philanthropies* (New York: Macmillan, 1976). But also see Irving Warner, "Here's the Secret of Jewish Fund Raising." *Chronicle of Philanthropy,* March 8, 1994, pp. 53–54.

5. *The New York Times,* April 14, 1977, p. D1.

6. See Richard A. Schoenherr and Lawrence A. Young, *Full Pews & Empty Altars: Demographics of the Priest Shortage in United States Catholic Dioceses* (Madison: University of Wisconsin Press, 1993), pp. 333–334 and passim.

7. This assumes the religious communities do not themselves wish to change, to become more "competitive."

8. Sam Peltzman, "Pricing in Public and Private Enterprise." *Journal of Law and Economics* 14 (April 1971): 110.

9. Ernest Greenwood, "Attributes of a Profession." *Social Work* 2 (July 1957): 44–45.

10. Charles Dickens, *Little Dorrit* (New York: Heritage, 1956), p. 539.

11. Stephen L. Tucker, "Introducing Marketing as a Planning and Management Tool." *Hospital and Health Services Administration* (Winter 1977): 37–44.

12. See William L. Wilkie and David M. Gardiner, "The Role of Marketing Research in Public Policy Decision Making." *Journal of Marketing* 38 (January 1974): 38–47.

13. This sentence was first written in 1979. So far, I am only off by sixteen years, not bad for a professor.

14. The interested reader may wish to consult R. Klein, *Complaints Against Doctors: A Study in Professional Accountability* (London: Charles Knight, 1973): and Scottish Home and Health Department, *Suggestions and Complaints in Hospitals, Report of the Working Party* (Edinburgh: HMSO, 1969).

15. For further corroboration, see Robin E. MacStravic, *Marketing Health Care* (Germantown, Md.: Aspen Systems Corporation, 1977), and any issue of the *Journal of Health Care Marketing.*

16. The process is pretty much the same with institutional backers like foundations and corporations.

17. Paul Goodman, *Compulsory Mis-education and The Community of Scholars* (New York: Vintage, 1966), p. 15.

18. The reader is invited to disagree with this analysis. What is it that letter writers *really* want?

19. For some background on this term, see Neil H. Borden, "The Concept of the Marketing Mix." *Journal of Advertising Research* 4 (June 1964): 2–7. It has been reprinted widely.

20. A particularly clear, simple treatment of marketing strategy is Gary J. Stern, *Marketing Workbook for Nonprofit Organizations* (St. Paul: Amherst H. Wilder Foundation, 1990). It is a user-friendly, how-to manual.

21. Elizabeth Greene, "A Meeting Place for People with AIDS." *Chronicle of Philanthropy,* February 9, 1993, pp. 5–8.

22. For more on this issue, see *Americanizing the American Orchestra, Report of the National Task Force for the American Orchestra: An Initiative for Change* (Washington, D.C.: American Symphony Orchestra League, June 1993), pp. 107–140.

Part IV

THE ELEMENTS OF THE MARKETING PROGRAM

Chapter 10

Product and Service Strategy

Products and services are the most conspicuous and public of the marketing activities of a nonprofit organization. In this chapter, we look at what products and services are and how marketers manage them.

SERVICES AND PRODUCTS

Services are valuable actions (or in public life merely the promise of an action). They float in a sea of impermanence: They are intangible, often incapable of being seen, heard, tasted, or sniffed; and they are often "manu-factured," literally made by hand, a human hand directed by a human mind.

Because they are intangible, services cannot be stored; there are no inventories of services; and because they are (often) handmade in the presence of the client, the client must go to where they are made. For the same reason they tend to be heterogeneous, not of uniform quality, reflecting their human makers. Finally, because they cannot be stored and because demand fluctuates, slow periods with excess capacity and busy periods with lines cannot be avoided.

Nonprofit organizations for the most part produce services, not products, intangibles, not tangibles. Since services must be made by hand, this means that most nonprofit organizations are labor intensive. Without much plant and equipment, relying largely on human hands to do the job, they find it difficult to contain rising labor costs by substituting capital for labor. In business it is the other way around—increasing capital increases production efficiency, which in turn permits and supports rising (real) wages. Nonprofit organizations suffer unusually during times of high inflation because there is so little they can do other than passing on their higher costs or running higher deficits. The standard examples of this pernicious process are found in cultural institutions. No machine can replace a curator, a cellist, or a coryphée, and few can enable them to perform their work more efficiently.

Many NPOs produce products as well as services. We know what a product is: It is a thing denoted; a thing weighty, visible, palpable. But it is standard marketing thinking that a product is more than its tangible parts. In this it resembles capital investments. Most of us see capital investments in their visible aspect, as a machine or a bridge. But an economist sees it as a pool of services frozen into the machine (or bridge) when it was produced and that can be drawn upon during its life. Thus, we should imagine a word processor not as a mess of wires and circuit boards, but as a reservoir of processed words that the users draw down as they type. Capital is valuable precisely because it makes available a stream of services in the future.

It is useful to see a product in the same way. Products congeal services into tangible form. They have their tangible aspects, to be sure, but these are not of the essence. Just as a business does not buy machines merely to have machines, consumers do not buy products merely to have products. Products are bought for the services they will yield, services built-in at the factory, as it were, and like capital, a product is a reservoir of services that can be drawn upon during the life of the product.

For this reason it is easy to overemphasize the difference between products and services. Here we will adopt the conventional viewpoint that the two differ. But marketers must train themselves to look beneath the surface. They must see a product as of value only for the services it delivers. They must do this for the most elemental of all reasons, at least to marketers. They must do this because it is the way their clients do things. It is the way they behave.

There are some other problems with the notion as well. Some nonprofit organizations do not admit to having products. At least not under that name. While preparing the first edition of this book I happened to look into two books on the arts, and naturally I turned to the index of each. Neither had a listing for ''product,'' nor did they list anything that appeared to be a substitute for product. The same is true of most books and journals dealing with public administration and with hospital administration. It seems that managers of arts organizations, public officials, and hospital administrators do not worry much about the issues to be discussed here.[1] The reader may wish to consider reasons for this.

The notion of product sits poorly in other contexts as well. Carol Kovach discusses the problems of defining what the product might mean in a zoo.[2] Animals and the settings in which they live *are* a zoo. Without them a zoo is merely a park. Are they the zoo's product? Not if exchange is part of being a product; because the animals are not sold, nor are they exchanged for anything, nor are they consumed in ''use.'' Rather they are more like ideas (and causes). They are ''on view,'' much as we might imagine ideas are on view. So although animals and settings are the zoo, although zoo administrators think of animals and exhibits as the zoo, they are not the zoo's product.

What is the zoo's product then? Kovach says that people go to zoos to enjoy themselves and to learn about animals. (In the process they also learn about themselves.) Thus, she sees the animals and settings as "generators" of the experiences that zoo visitors seek. It is these experiences, she argues, that are the zoo's product. Animals are the zoo's main selling point, they are why people visit the zoo, and without them there is no zoo; but they are not the zoo's product.

The student of marketing must train himself to look beyond the surface of the nonprofit organization's offering. A product is more than a thing. It is more than its tangible parts. Rather than a thing denoted, it is better thought of as a thing connoted, for accompanying it are services and associations that make up much of its meaning.

Some products, in fact, are little more than these associations. Lipstick is nothing but aromatic, tinted grease, but no one would argue that that is what lipstick is or that its function is to protect the lips. Charles Revson of Revlon caught the idea neatly when he supposedly said, "In the factory we make cosmetics. In the store we sell hope."

The distinction between products and services weakens for yet another reason. Most products are sold accompanied by services (although it is not the case that most services are sold accompanied by products). A retailer or producer may assemble the product, install it, maintain it, repair it, and dispose of it; he may provide training; he may deliver it, he may finance it, and he may warrant it. All these services form part of the product. In fact, along with its physical form, they *are* the product. Services often accompany a service as well, as for example, the guarantee furnished along with its medical services by the Blanchard Valley Hospital (see Figure 10.1).

Ideas and Causes

Ideas and causes are neither services nor products. They are conceptions, thoughts, notions. But nonprofit marketers sometimes sell ideas, as when the Water Department urges citizens in Northern California to conserve water, or the Police Department urges citizens to save the 911 emergency number for emergencies.

It is possible to say that an idea (or a cause) is a product just like another. To do so we must force the meaning of the word, however. Nonprofit businesses have products that group together to form product lines, and they work to develop new products. Other nonprofit organizations have services that group together to form lines of related services, and they may develop new services. But one's ear instantly takes offense to learn of a public interest group whose ideas group together to form an idea line or that they engage in new idea development. Why is this?

Because products and services are not merely products and services. They do not have an existence separate from that of the client. Products and services exist, as it were, to be traded with the client for money or other valuables. They

Figure 10.1
Blanchard Valley Hospital's and Blanchard Valley Extended Care Facility's Guarantee to Our Patients

Although we can't guarantee the results of your medical care, we do guarantee:

1. That the services you receive will be performed to your satisfaction. This includes your nursing care, your food, the cleanliness of your room, services of all our ancillary departments and our Emergency Department. In fact, any and all services you receive at Blanchard Valley Hospital or in the Blanchard Valley Extended Care Facility.

2. If you are not satisfied, the service(s) which do not meet your expectations will not be charged to you, subject to the simple requirements listed in 3A through E below.

3. If you are not satisfied with the service(s) you are receiving at Blanchard Valley Hospital or the Blanchard Valley Extended Care Facility, charges for such service(s) will not be billed to you or your insurance company IF:

   A. You advise us within twenty-four hours of the time service(s) is not rendered to your satisfaction and if, upon investigation, your complaint is found to be justified, the "no charge" guarantee will be in effect and your account will be credited with an appropriate amount which represents the cost of such service(s).

   B. The guarantee stated above does not cover waiting for services in those departments where the more seriously ill patient is treated first.

   C. To be eligible for the "Guaranteed Services" program, all of your past accounts with the Blanchard Valley Hospital Association and any past accounts for a person for whom you or your guarantor has financial responsibility must be paid in full.

   D. Because of the nature of human illness, we cannot guarantee the results of your medical care nor can we guarantee the services provided by your physician(s) or dentist(s).

   E. Patients wishing to discuss and/or take advantage of the "Guaranteed Services" program should call Ext. 251. If your phone is not activated, ask your nurse to make the call for you. A member of the Administrative Staff is on call twenty-four hours per day and will contact you immediately upon receiving your call.

4. The "Guaranteed Services" program is approved by the Board of Trustees of the Blanchard Valley Hospital Association on an annual basis and will be reviewed and considered for renewal annually.

5. The concept of the "Guaranteed Services" program is to credit your account for those services as outlined above, which you find unacceptable. Cost liability incurred in this program will be funded from the Association's investment income so that the program's cost will not be charged to any other patient.

6. The term *Blanchard Valley Hospital Association* refers to the corporate entity and includes the Blanchard Valley Hospital and the Blanchard Valley Extended Care Facility.

Crediting a patient's account under the "Guaranteed Services" program is not an admission of liability, either expressed or implied, in relation to hospital or extended care facility services rendered.

Source: Blanchard Valley Hospital, Findlay, Ohio.

can be seen only as enticements to correct behavior, as a *quid* that does not exist in the absence of a *quo.* Products and services are half of the bargain between the nonprofit organization and the client: "You do that for me, and I'll do this for you."

Ideas (and causes) are different. They are not exchanged, but transmitted, one way, from organization to target audience. Most of the time the objective of the communication is to draw out correct behavior, as in the water conservation campaign. The deal between the nonprofit organization that is promoting ideas and the client is: "Do this. It's for your own good." But sometimes the aim is no more than influencing knowledge or opinion, in which case we are no longer considering marketing, at least as it was defined in Chapter 1. Thus, groups opposed to abortion try, among other things, to communicate to the general public the percentage of pregnancies that end in abortion, which in the early 1990s ran about 30 percent; and those in the other camp use coat hangers to remind us of the costs to pregnant women of making abortion illegal again. Neither group wants immediate action. Each is trying to educate the public and form a climate of opinion in which it can pursue its goals.

In such cases as this, where the organization is promoting an idea (or a cause), it is best to say merely that there is no product or service, not in the sense in which most people use the words.

PRODUCT STRATEGY

Product strategy is a statement of the general criteria that are to govern any changes in products offered by the nonprofit organization. Flame of Hope, Inc., coordinates the efforts of sheltered workshops—organizations that aim to re-habilitate the mentally retarded by teaching them useful skills—that turn out products developed by Flame of Hope. What kind of products should these be? The first was a candle, and it seemed ideal:

this project is ideally suited for the retarded because of the creative aspect of the candle operation. Each participant realizes an immediate and positive sense of achievement, because he actually see [sic] what he has produced by his own labors; in addition, the packaging and shipping needs and demand for quality control and inspection provide an acceptable challenge and satisfy the retardate's need to achieve.[3]

Here is the beginning of a statement of product strategy for Flame of Hope: "All products must be simple enough so they can be produced by a retarded worker and yet challenge him to achieve at higher levels." This part of its product strategy deals with questions of manufacture. The complete product strategy would also set down some marketing criteria, for example, that the product have a low retail price, that it be large enough to carry an informative label about the mentally retarded workers who made the item, and that it be capable of being distributed through the same channels of distribution as all the other products of the sheltered workshop.

Four factors influence the general criteria that make up product strategy, all of them old friends. The first is *the organization's mission*—its purpose, the legal constraints on its activities, and what it has come to stand for. How is a small museum, for example, one rarely able to buy new objects, to decide whether to accept a gift or a bequest? The answer is contained in the statement of the museum's purpose, which is what makes a museum different from an attic. In drawing up this statement "the museum should first of all consider its purposes and define them succinctly but clearly. What is it to collect? How to preserve, authenticate, and research its collections? How exhibit and interpret them? Art museums must decide what period to cover, what geographic area to encompass and what kinds of material to gather."[4]

The items carried by a museum's retail shop are influenced by the museum's mission. Legal considerations also intrude. The IRS has ruled that profits from a museum's retail shop are free of tax only if the goods sold are artistic or educational. But even without this ruling most museum shops would want to sell items related to their collections, items that would broaden or extend the visitor's experience. "The museum sales desk and merchandising program is more than a source of revenue. It is an extension of the museum collection outside its walls, a type of interpretation . . . a kind of taste-making, with strict canons of authenticity and appropriateness."[5]

Related to these overall strategic issues is the second factor, the desire and *interests of people in the organization.* Top executives always exert their influence in setting product strategy, but in nonprofit organizations one can expect to find professionals and even volunteers influential in such questions.

The third factor influencing product strategy is *finances.* The financial constraints on product planners are the most difficult to describe briefly, because of the diversity of financial requirements of the nonprofit organizations themselves. But the basic charge is that the product planner develop products that fit with the overall financial responsibilities of the organization.

Let us see what this might mean. The product planner knows, or guesses, a price that clients will pay. Then he designs a product attractive enough to command that price but whose cost is low enough to produce a positive Gross Marketing Contribution. As the market price determines the maximum cost, the product planner must come up with a product that can be produced at that cost and still be attractive enough to command the needed price.

For products that must break even, the process is much the same. The product planner may start with a guess as to what the market will bear and then design a product whose cost absorbs the price. More typically, he will start with some basic product of given cost and try to find a price that will just cover the cost.

Finally, the product planner may be fated to have some or all of his products run at a loss, either negative Gross Marketing Contribution or negative Net Marketing Contribution. But organizations with such products still set financial constraints. They take the form of limits on the size of the losses: Gross marketing losses on new products shall not exceed thirty percent of incremental revenues, but no new product can run larger incremental net marketing losses than $10,000. Now it is the product planner's chore to develop products that fit these constraints.

The fourth factor bearing on product strategy is nonfinancial: *barriers to en-*

try, competitive, market, and organizational factors that inhibit chances for success.

THE PRODUCT PORTFOLIO

Two of these four criteria are so important that it is worth looking at another tool that focuses exclusively on them. The two are mission and cash flow. A nonprofit will normally have a mix of products and programs: Some will contribute to its mission and produce surplus cash, others will contribute but run at a loss, and so on.

The product portfolio is a way for looking at all of a nonprofit's major products and programs on one sheet of paper, plotted against the two key criteria of mission and cash flow. Reduced to its bones a product portfolio looks like this:

| | Cash Flow | |
	Negative	Positive
Supports Mission	II	I
Doesn't Support Mission	IV	III

The cells are numbered in terms of decreasing attractiveness. In I we find products that contribute to the mission and run at a surplus, the best of all possible worlds. In II products advance the mission but run at a loss. In III are products that the NPO wishes it could drop because they detract from its mission. It doesn't, however, because they run at a surplus. Products in IV carry both negatives, they don't contribute to the mission and they run at a loss.

Each of the cells also implies a general product strategy:

I. build and strengthen these products

II. try to reduce losses and earn surpluses

III. try to make more relevant to mission

IV. drop

These are only general strategies, however, because no important decisions are ever made on the basis of these two criteria, important though they may be.

As an example, let us look at XYZ University. Table 10.1 shows fourteen major programs at the university, their financials, and the ratio of their contribution to revenue. They are also grouped into three classes by their importance to XYZ's mission. Working from these figures and a consideration of impor-

Table 10.1

Fourteen Major Programs at XYZ University (All dollar figures in millions)

	Revenue a	Direct Costs b	Net Marketing Contribution c=a-b	Ratio of Contribution to Revenue c/a
Core activities				
Graduate school	$8	$14	$(6)	(0.8)
Law school	19	9	10	0.5
Undergraduate	76	91	(15)	(0.2)
Business school	13	7	6	0.5
Engineering	7	9	(2)	(0.3)
Libraries	6	12	(6)	(1.0)
Research Institute	7	7	0	0.0
Related activities				
Dorms	21	15	6	0.3
Food	10	10	0	0.0
Bookstore	6	5	1	0.2
Other				
Athletics	14	17	(3)	(0.2)
Stadium	3	6	(3)	(1.0)
University press	7	6	1	0.1
Executive training	8	2	6	0.8

tance to mission, one can construct the product portfolio in Figure 10.2. It shows the core activities in the upper half of the chart, because they all support the university's mission. Executive training is where it belongs, in the southeast corner. It contributes six million dollars but it has little to do with the mission. The stadium loses money and it has nothing to do with the mission, but XYZ is stuck with it. It is part of every American campus. (One last comment. The size of the circles in Figure 10.2 is proportional to the revenues each program generates. That's why the undergrad circle is so large and the stadium circle so small.)

The product portfolio, then, (1) gives management a perspective on the entire organization and (2) suggests some general strategies for the products located in the four cells.

FOUR PRODUCT DIMENSIONS

A manager with responsibility for product planning in a business—a product planner—has four principal variables to juggle, and a product planner in a non-profit organization encounters the same four.

Identifying Names

Called "brand names" by marketers and either "trademarks" for products or "service marks" for services by lawyers, identifying names serve four func-

Figure 10.2
Product Portfolio for XYZ University

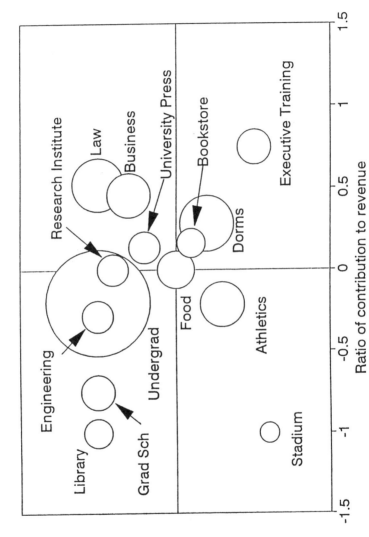

tions. First, they can provide *a basis for differentiating products* that are otherwise difficult for the client to tell apart, much as the numbers on football
uniforms enable football fans to tell one player from another. Second, they serve
as *a focus for promotional activities,* that is, they give the marketer something
to talk *about.* A bus company that wishes to promote low weekend fares will
have an easier time if it gives the weekend service an identifying name, so that
it can promote the service by name. Party labels, Democrat and Republican,
which once indicated differences in political beliefs and philosophy, still serve
as the focus for electoral campaigns, political organization, and fund-raising.

Third, brand serves as *a source of information.* Merely identifying a political
message as coming from a Republican source changes the meaning of the message. And we might well imagine a situation in which the fact that a product is
made in a sheltered workshop would tell some clients that the product was
poorly made.

What's in a name? To someone who does not know the nonprofit, there's a
good deal in a name. Some charities in San Antonio, Texas faced up to the fact
that their names didn't mean much to backers who knew little or nothing about
them.[6] (Marketers would say such backers are low-involvement backers, and
they would guess that most backers for most NPOs are low involvement.) Which
would you donate to, the Children's Service Bureau, which is probably some
government agency—it says "bureau," right?—or to the Emergency Shelter for
Abused and Homeless Children, at a time when homeless children and child
abuse is a national concern?

For the purpose of being listed in the Combined Federal Campaign the San
Antonio charities changed their names to something more descriptive. Actually,
they didn't give up their old names. They filed requests for DBAs at the country
courthouse, "doing business as." These permitted them to adopt an alias for
the Combined Federal Campaign without surrendering the name for which they
were best known in the community. When the Federal Campaign was over, the
Children's Service Bureau found its federal campaign contributors had increased
41 percent over the previous year, a whopping increase.

Fifteen NPOs adopted a DBA alias. One need not know much marketing to
see that the alias is better than the original name:

Original Name	Name Used in the Combined Federal Campaign
Southwest Neuropsychiatric Institute	San Antonio Children's Center
Brighton School	Brighton School for Children with Down's Syndrome and Similar Development Disabilities
Family Focus	Advocates for Child Abuse Prevention
Downtown Drop-In Center	Children in Crisis and Rescue Center

Names, to repeat, provide information. The fourth function of an identifying use name is to serve as *a source of reassurance*. Most American travelers face substantial perceived risk in making decisions about where to eat on the road. They are not so much interested in dining as in refueling, safely, in clean surroundings, above all predictably. They are not so much interested in the level of quality (whether the food tastes good) as in how uniform the quality is (whether it is predictable). Howard Johnson's shrewdly seized on this need for reassurance by serving up comestibles whose quality never, ever varies. Uniform quality is in fact a prerequisite for a successful brand. In order for the trademark of the nonprofit International Wool Secretariat, "Woolmark," to have any meaning, the secretariat must control who uses the trademark and how. "To use the Woolmark, a manufacturer has to sign a licensing agreement to satisfy our standards [and] accept our quality inspectorate in his factory."[7]

Package

Expected to protect a product during transport and storage, the package also provides a surface on which messages can be printed. For some businesses the package is both an important part of the product and a major selling device.

The importance of package to nonprofits is not so great, however. Services do not (usually) come in packages, and nonprofit products that do use them are of minor importance. There are exceptions, however. The most dramatic is the dial package used to dispense contraceptive pills. These need to be taken according to a strict regimen—once a day without fail for twenty-one days, then the woman stops and begins again seven days later. With the dial package the woman turns the dial until the day for her first pill shows through a little window, then she opens the package and takes the first pill. The package automatically tells her if she has taken her pill, and as it turns in only one direction it is hard to make an error. Here the package forces conformity to the required regimen simply, clearly, cheaply. Here the package is very much a part of the product.

Package is a part of the product when it also makes the product harder to use. Child-resistant containers protect children from injuring themselves by accidentally ingesting household poisons and drugs; but for elderly or handicapped patients, child-resistant containers pose problems. The American Pharmaceutical Association surveyed pharmacists on how their patients ("customers" actually) did with the containers. Eighty-five percent indicated that patients (often or very often) had trouble opening the containers; 61 percent (often or very often) left the containers open; 63 percent (often or very often) transferred the medication to another container; 37 percent (often or very often) spilled the medication while opening the container; and 58 percent (often or very often) either accidentally or purposely broke the cap while opening the container. In addition, the survey found "a disturbing number" of cases in which the patients took no medication at all because they could not open the container.[8] All these infelicities are no less a part of the associations and experiences that make up a drug than its chemical action or its action through the workings of the placebo effect.

Product Quality

The third dimension is product quality. Many nonprofits have little choice in the quality they offer. They may lack the money to produce a higher level of quality, they may lack the will, or they may lack clients who appreciate, or demand, quality. A legal aid society may wish to give a high level of legal representation to its indigent clients, but usually it must be satisfied with something more modest. Here marketing considerations play little role. The legal aid society simply does as well as it can.

A second consideration limiting the marketer's choice of quality levels is professional standards. Organizations in which professionals play important roles will try to set quality levels in terms of "what is right," of "what should be." In business the professional, expected to contribute to profits through his services, trims his standards to the marketplace. In a nonprofit organization the professional has more leeway and more organizational support to see that the organization serves, as it did for Mr. Merdle's chief butler, "for the maintenance of his rank."[9]

But there are limits to professional influence even in a nonprofit organization. The insistence of Pierre Boulez, the former music director of the New York Philharmonic, on giving frequent performances of avant-garde and new music was one factor that led to his resignation. (Members of the orchestra referred to him as "Twentieth Century Limited.") Even the most lofty of professional standards must live in a world too often indifferent to conspicuous eminence. And a governmental telecommunications company may wish to install the very finest equipment but find its price too high. (Would such a minor concern stop any government agency? I doubt it.)

Within these constraints, the marketer must find a level of quality suitable to his clients, or levels suitable to different segments. Publishers regularly sell the same book in cloth and paper to appeal to two different markets. Hospitals regularly provide three levels of accommodation, ward, semiprivate, and private; but the ethical imperatives, or economics, of medicine do not permit different quality levels of care in one institution. (Different levels of medical care are provided instead by different health care institutions.)

Quality levels can have a strong impact on an organization's clients and backers. Alumni like a winning football team and will back it and its school. (Although whether winning and quality are the same is for the reader to consider.) Inroads, Inc., is a nonprofit that selects bright, minority high school students who wish to study engineering or business and supports them through their college education. Inroads does not take everyone, however. In Pittsburgh it started with 500 black students:

Number

500	Were screened. Half are rejected.
250	Were interviewed by Inroads staff. Two-thirds are rejected.
85	Were invited to a two-day seminar for indoctrination and training in interviewing. Half are rejected.
45	Receive Inroads summer internships to begin preparing for college. Roughly half drop out during college.
20 to 25	Complete four years of college.

Such a program, which starts with 500 to produce twenty-five, is strongly committed to high quality; and those who survive are well prepared to enter business. While the program produces only a handful of educated minority persons, their quality is so high that the program has won substantial support from corporations who back Inroads.[10]

Service Quality

In reading a section like this on product quality, the words have the unfortunate effect of suggesting that we are talking about products and not services. To counteract this let us explicitly discuss service quality for a moment.

For many nonprofit organizations the one feature of their product that is flexible and that can make the difference between acceptance and rejection by clients is service. A state-run airline has the greatest difficulty in changing its aircraft, and at least some difficulty in altering its routes and schedules. The most flexible part of the airline's product is its service—flight information, passenger information, passenger reservations, meals, beverages, amenities on board, airport reception, and baggage handling. In the same way, a postal service is bound in most product areas by its plant and equipment, but it can alter its service standards relatively easily.

A report written for the Australian Post Office, which ran both postal and telecommunications services, recommended that the APO work to raise its standards of customer service.[11] To those on the inside, the APO consisted of facilities for moving the post, large amounts of telecommunications equipment, and the people who run them. But to the customer the APO was the postal clerk or the sales officer in telecommunications. The contacts between customer and sales officer, of which there were three million a year, were complex and relatively unstructured, covering such areas as credit, accounts, billing, and installation. In brief, the report recommended that the APO take the following steps:

Develop training materials in giving modern, pleasing, and effective customer service. The training should be given to all employees who come in contact with customers. Sales Officers should receive service training along with training in product knowledge.

Performance standards should be set for each job classification. The creation of standards can be modeled after techniques used by air lines, large retailers, and telephone companies in North America.

Develop a simple but effective way of measuring actual service performance. The simplest way of doing this is for the manager in the area to oversee the actual performance of the service.

The report concluded by saying:

Outstanding customer contact service, no less than outstanding technical service, is the product of good planning, training, setting of standards, measurement of performance and the taking of corrective action on the basis of observed results, and despite some thinking to the contrary, it is not the product alone of selecting personnel "who naturally like people," "who have a flair for public relations," "who are good at handling the public," etc., although these attributes, for whatever they may mean and be worth, are probably helpful in the training and development of a good customer contact employee.

Product Line

Most nonprofit organizations offer a variety of related products, which marketers call a product line, the fourth product dimension. Offering a variety of products to clients is the most elemental reflection of the existence of client segments. Just imagine the popularity of an ice cream chain that offered only one flavor. The NPO must offer variety to backers too, because their differing charitable goals and their different tax and legal situations will dictate that no one way of giving will satisfy all. (See Figure 10.3 for an example of different ways to donate to the United Jewish Appeal.)

The Oxford University Press (OUP) publishes dictionaries. It began in the early 1900s with *the* dictionary, the Oxford English Dictionary, which over seventy years and a supplement grew to a twelve-volume behemoth containing over a quarter of a million headwords and almost two million illustrative quotations, all done without computers or word processors, in the early days without even typewriters.[12]

From this gargantuan venture flowed a torrent of dictionaries: the Concise Oxford, the Shorter Oxford, the Little Oxford (with only 44,000 entries and 688 pages), the Oxford Paperback, and the Pocket Oxford. (Defining words is one thing. Writing titles is another: The Concise is shorter than the Shorter and longer than the Little. In-house, the Concise is known as the Cramped Oxford Dictionary.)

The OUP also publishes dictionaries on history, biography, literature, science, nature, music, ballet, art, theater, medicine, mythology, religion, law, computing, nursery rhymes, saints, sailing, and geography. It has published dictionaries of

Figure 10.3
Some of the Ways Donors Can Contribute to the United Jewish Appeal–Federation of Jewish Philanthropies of New York, Inc. (All of these ways are forms of what is called planned giving. Donors are able to give to the charity and in return receive financial and tax planning benefits, such as annual income payments during their lifetimes.)

How to choose a charity to invest with.

Investing with a charity could give you a greater return on your money than investing yourself. But choosing the right charity to invest with is an important financial decision. You want smart investors who are experienced in the field of financial and retirement planning. You want a variety of financial products to choose from. And you want a stable organization with a history of putting money aside, keeping it and making it grow for people like you and the community whose needs it serves.

UJA-Federation of New York.
$370 Million in assets. And an unbeatable expert staff to help everyone from small investors to major philanthropists.

If it's financial security you're looking for, you can rest assured with UJA-Federation of New York. We've been providing charitable services to Israel and the Jewish community for 75 years. And we keep on going.

Whether you're simply looking to get a better return on a $10,000 investment or you're looking to hand-tailor a complex charitable program, we've got some of the best people to work with you and your own professional advisors. We develop strategy and plan and execute a wide variety of financial programs. Over 50 estate and financial professionals, both on staff and volunteer, including lawyers, accountants, tax specialists and financial planners help us maintain an unmatched pooled resource of counselling, up-to-date information and accounting and legal advice. Some of our staff are recognized experts in the field. And our advice is free.

What we always look for is a stable, reasonable, better than conservative return that often beats the current yield on your assets. If you invest with us, we're always aware that ultimately you're leaving us something in the future. We therefore owe you something today. And that's a solid return, a lot of security and a minimum of risk.

Life Income Plans.
How we help you while you help us.

If your personal financial goal is significant tax reduction or increased income, one of our life income plans could be right for you.

Our Charitable Remainder Trust pays you either an annuity (a set amount each year based on the initial principal you give us) or a fixed percentage of the principal re-valued each year. We keep paying you for your entire lifetime or up to 20 years, whichever you choose. After that, the remaining principal goes to UJA-Federation of New York to be used for the things that are important to you.

Our Charitable Gift Annuity offers added tax benefits. By purchasing a fixed annuity from us outright you are making partially tax deductible contributions. You therefore receive both income benefits and tax deductible benefits. This makes it a financial plan perfect for both retirees and for people planning their retirement. And we receive your contributions and put them to work for charity.

You pick the financial product. You pick the charity.

We've got lots of ways for you to invest and all let you meet your personal financial goals while really making a difference in the world. Our programs include life income plans like Charitable Remainder Trusts and Gift Annuities, tax-wise gifts of real estate and business interests, creative uses of personal property like art and collectibles, unique alternatives to private foundations and more. We also have special plans for protecting your IRA or other retirement plans from tax reduction. And you can designate your philanthropy to UJA-Federation of New York or to any of our 130 human and social service agencies in the Greater New York area or in Israel.

You can choose to let your money help needy children, the aged, disabled individuals. You can provide scholarships or resettle Soviet Jews. Or you can earmark your money for programs in Israel. Whatever you choose, you can rest assured that at UJA-Federation of New York we can find the right financial program for you. And the right cause.

Financial Stability and Philanthropy.
Nobody puts the two together better than we do.

You demand some financial stability. And you recognize that you've reached a time in your life when you want to give something back. The Department of Planned Giving and Endowments of UJA-Federation of New York lets you do both efficiently, profitably and with a minimum of risk.

To find out how you can meet your financial goals and help support a wide variety of charities, make an appointment to see one of our experts today. It could make a big difference in your future. And in ours.

Department of Planned Giving   NYTMS94
and Endowments
UJA-Federation of New York
130 East 59th Street, New York, NY 10022

For more information or to arrange a free confidential consultation with no obligation, clip this coupon or call Neal Myerberg at 212-836-1811 today.

☐ Please call me. I'd like to set up an appointment to meet one of your planned giving experts.
☐ Please send me more information about:
☐ Charitable Gift Annuities ☐ Current Payments ☐ Deferred Payments
☐ Charitable Remainder Trusts ☐ Gifts of Real Estate ☐ Private Foundation Alternatives
☐ Gifts of Personal Property ☐ Protecting Private or Company Retirement Plans
☐ Other_____
Name_____
Address_____
City_____ State_____ Zip_____
Age (optional)_____ Tel._____ Best time to call_____

Charitable Gift Annuity of $10,000.

AGE	RATE	EQUIVALENT* ANNUAL RATE
65	7.3%	8.4% ($ 840)
70	7.8%	9.1% ($ 910)
75	8.5%	10.0% ($1,000)
80	9.6%	11.6% ($1,160)
85	10.9%	13.4% ($1,340)
90	12.0%	15.1% ($1,510)

*Net rate after tax savings from charitable deduction (assumes combined federal and state income tax rate of 35%)
For people under the age of 65, the Charitable Gift Annuity can be used for retirement planning as well. The annual annuity payments begin at age 65.

🔷 UJA-FEDERATION OF NEW YORK
We help 4.5 million people a year. One at a time.

foreign languages as well, everything from Latin to Iban. It publishes picture dictionaries in fifty-four languages. Its best selling dictionary is the Oxford Advanced Learner's Dictionary of Current English, for nonnative speakers of English.[13]

We see here the product line defined in its three dimensions—length (how many separate product lines), width (how many products in each line), and depth (how many varieties of each product).

		← — — — — — — — — Length — — — — — — — — →			
		English Language	Foreign Language	Scientific Medical	Arts	Children's

Product Line Width	↑	Scholarly Popular Other	Latin Greek etc.	Computing Medicine Biology Mathematics	Ballet Art Theater	Poetry Stories Picture books

Depth is not shown because I do not have the numbers. But we can imagine that the OUP might offer four scholarly English-language dictionaries, six popular dictionaries, and a dozen others on (say) slang, usage, ethnology, Shakespearean sexual terms, and Victorian criminal argot. Then a marketer would say the English-language offerings had the greatest depth.

In the early 1970s, after the Supreme Court ruling that established women's right to an abortion, many abortion clinics were established that provided one basic service, first-trimester abortions. By 1980, however, most of them offered a wide range of services, related to gynecology, sex, and pregnancy.[14]

Museums too offer a line of services: guided tours, special lectures and demonstrations for schoolchildren; guided tours and gallery talks for the general public; lectures, classes, clubs, and study groups for adults; classes, clubs, and study groups for children not in school groups; presentations at schools; loans of specialized materials and collections to schools; films; TV and radio programs; and performing arts presentations prepared by the museum. Many also have joint programs with colleges and universities, do research, and publish everything from an annual report to books, periodicals, catalogs, scholarly papers, and catalogs of their collections.[15] Some have even gotten into the business of sponsoring foreign tours.

Charity auctions. An unusual example of product line is a charity auction. It must offer a variety of ways to gamble because different bettors have different interests, and the nonprofit needs enough variety to keep people busy and bidding for several hours. To do this it must offer several games and other activities. (I will use ''player'' to describe the bettors and bidders at the auction.)

The setting is black tie optional with first-class decor, an open bar, and good food. The aim is to put the players in the mood to spend big, not fifteen dollars but five hundred or a thousand. To encourage players to bet, part of the ticket price is returned to them in play money. It cannot be transferred or given to other players, and it can only be used to gamble.

The *duck pond* contains donated items with a value less than twenty-five dollars, say. There might be three duck ponds for ten, fifteen, and twenty-five dollars. The player pays fifteen dollars to pick from the fifteen-dollar pond, but he is assured he will get a prize with more than a fifteen-dollar value. The player pays his money, picks a duck from the pond, reads the number on the bottom, and collects a bag containing his prize. In addition, there is a mystery prize. Spread among the three ponds are five ducks that give the player a new compact disk player worth three hundred dollars (donated, of course). Volunteers circulate to encourage people to play.

A *silent auction* is held at several booths—art, liquor, kitchen, garden, and the like. In a silent auction, players enter their bids on bid cards found in the booths. Thus, players can see what has already been bid and what they must bid to win. They also know when the auction will close. (There is more to it than that, however. Players sometimes may hide an item, or remove the bid card, or remove the number from the item to keep anyone else from bidding. All of these need policing.) The booths are for donated items that are too expensive for the duck ponds; or rather, the duck ponds are for items too cheap for the booths. For example, cheap donated liquor goes to a duck pond or the open bar; expensive donated liquor goes to the booth.

A *raffle* is held for a valuable prize, such as a boat or a new Toyota. A group of players buy chances in advance of the auction. For a car worth $15,000, there would be 150 tickets sold at $150, thus raising $22,500 for a $15,000 car. On the night of the charity auction, one of the 150 tickets is drawn and the winner drives home in a new car. (This example is explained in more detail in Chapter 16.)

The *key club* is yet another raffle. Volunteers are assigned to sell 600 keys for ten dollars a piece, each key offering a chance on a $2,200 large screen TV. Thus, the key club raises $6,000. The players cannot try their keys until 10:30 P.M., which keeps them there, bidding on other items. It may happen that all the keys may not sell during the evening. If not, sometime after 10:30 it becomes obvious that the winning key has not yet been sold.

The *live auction* is just what it says. An auctioneer gets up and auctions off some one hundred donated items, including in one batch the unsold keys from the key club. This auction takes up most of the evening after dinner.

WHY HAVE NEW PRODUCTS?

A nonprofit business develops new products for the same reason business do, to increase profits and market share. Ocean Spray, the cranberry cooperative, has been very aggressive in all phases of its marketing operations, but in particular it has developed so many new products over the years—jellied cranberry sauce, whole berry cranberry sauce, jellied cranberry-raspberry sauce, cranberry-

Figure 10.4
Four Strategies for Expansion

	Existing Markets	New Markets
Existing Products	Market Penetration	Market Expansion
New Products	Product Development	Diversification

orange relish, cranberry juice cocktail, low-calorie cranberry juice cocktail, cranberry apple drink, low-calorie cranberry apple juice drink, grape cranberry drink, cranberry prune juice drink, and cranberry apricot juice drink—that fresh cranberries now account for less than 5 percent of its total sales.[16] Its problem is straightforward, of course—to get rid of all those cranberries without permitting prices to be buffeted by natural supply and demand forces.

But an organization need not develop new products to expand. Marketers generally look at four strategies for expansion: market penetration, market expansion, product development, and diversification (see Figure 10.4).[17] As we might expect, they deal with both product and market simultaneously. Market penetration means pushing harder to sell present products to present markets, wooing clients to buy more, or more often. Market expansion means trying to sell present products in new markets. (Inroads, the organization that works with bright black students, operated in only nine cities in 1980. Its plan was to expand to fifteen or twenty new cities in the next ten years, by simply taking the current program into new markets.) Product development means developing new products but selling them to the present market. (Most of Ocean Spray's expansion probably fits here.) Diversification means developing new products for sale to new markets.

Take as an example a symphony orchestra that is looking for more revenue. Under market penetration, it might work harder to persuade its traditional audience to buy tickets. This might involve a telephone campaign by symphony volunteers, extra promotions, two-for-the-price-of-one ticket sales, or some kind of contest for new ticket buyers. Market expansion would mean taking the symphony's current program into other markets—performing, say, at a location in the southern suburbs on Sunday afternoon in an attempt to reach persons afraid to travel downtown at night, or for a national convention visiting the city. Product development might mean pops concerts, concerts on the waterfront, or special concerts at the large state university near the city. Diversification might carry the orchestra into a new area like opera performances and, based on what most arts research seems to suggest, a different audience from the one that comes to the symphony; or perhaps a chamber orchestra might be developed to perform for yet another, specialized audience.

The normal expectation in business is that a business will develop new products. If a business does not develop them, the argument runs, its competitors will and the company will find itself losing market share with products that no longer appeal. Nonprofit organizations have more flexibility. They may, if they wish, develop new products and new services. Indeed some are like businesses in that they must change merely to remain healthy and competitive. The Educational Testing Service faces a rapidly changing environment. It is safe to say that in 1970 educational testing was a reasonably stable industry. But since then doubts about the fairness of tests have arisen; the Federal Trade Commission has found that test preparation centers that coach students do in fact raise their scores; and there has been a back-to-basics movement by parents and others who are possessed by the quaint belief that high school graduates should be able to read and write, to add and take away. By 1978 more than half the states had passed or were considering laws that mandated minimum competency testing as a prerequisite to promotion for graduation; and at the same time, state education departments in Michigan, New York, and California had begun to develop their own tests. In 1979, New York put into effect a truth-in-testing law that requires that test questions along with the answers be made available for public inspection. The ETS has no choice but to adapt to this changing environment.

But there are many nonprofits for whom the development of new products is uncalled for. There might be several reasons for this. Perhaps the most important is that the long-run survival of the organization is not threatened by some outside factor that can be overcome by the development of new products. There are good reasons for developing new products and new services, but certainly no organization should develop them without such reasons. An opera company may, if it wishes, stage premieres, as the Seattle Opera has done with world premieres of Thomas Pasatieri's "Black Widow," Carlisle Floyd's "Of Mice and Men," and the West Coast premiere of Pasatieri's "The Seagull"; but it may just as well confine itself to the safer course and stage only the existing repertoire.

A second reason for avoiding new product development is that it is risky financially, organizationally, and sometimes professionally. Just how much product development costs depends in part on how much money is available. One reason PBS imports so much British television is that it is cheap, about $30,000 an hour (in 1977) compared to about $360,000 an hour for domestically produced shows.[18] Or take brand, in this case, an identifying symbol. NBC spent three quarters of a million dollars on consulting fees and fourteen months developing a new logo to replace its familiar peacock. It soon found that the very same logo, an abstract N composed of a red trapezoid and a blue trapezoid, was already in use by an educational television network in Nebraska. But in Nebraska the logo had been developed by the network's art director for less than

$100.[19] Not only can new product development be expensive, it can also be risky. The poorest reason for an opera company to stage premieres is to develop permanent additions to the operatic repertoire, because the opera-going public is generally cool to new works and passionate about the standard repertoire. The New York Opera has, over many seasons, staged some sixty contemporary operas, but only four, "The Turn of the Screw," "Susannah," "Ballad of Baby Doe," and "Lizzie Borden" return with any degree of regularity.[20] Note the risk here. If "return regularly" means the opera was a success, only four in sixty succeeded, or about 7 percent. This is low, even by commercial standards.

Most of these problems are illustrated by an exhibition put on some years ago by the Cleveland Art Museum of the paintings of John Liss, an obscure German painter who died in about 1630. As Liss was not a popular painter then or now, the exhibition presumably had as its target audience scholars, experts, and connoisseurs. The general public could not be expected to come, and as a result paid admissions would make only a scant contribution to the costs, which were substantial. This much could reasonably have been foreseen, and hence there was little financial uncertainty. The exhibit was sure to lose money.

In mounting such an exhibition, moreover, there was a substantial professional risk for the curator. There was no way to tell before the money had been spent to organize the exhibit whether the assembled paintings, drawings, and etchings would form a collection, albeit only a temporary one, or whether they would merely conglomerate and gain nothing from being available for comparison and study.

The exhibition posed other problems, as well. It naturally used up money, exhibition space, and curatorial time that could have been put to other, perhaps better, uses with broader appeal. Current sentiment in the art world seems to run strongly to avoiding the elitism implicit in such an exhibition, preferring instead to exhibit easier, or more popular, fare.[21] Finally, the significance of such an exhibition, of a painter of whom little is known and many of whose attributions are doubtful, is difficult to communicate; it is hard to explain to the general public why they should come, and it is hard to instruct the connoisseur who visits the exhibition in the significance of Liss's work.

None of this says that the Cleveland should not have assembled the exhibition. No museum looks at such important questions from only one side. The analysis does tell us what to expect—losses, small audiences, difficulties in communicating, and the risk of an artistic failure. That the museum went ahead was, well, "courageous" is the word one would most certainly expect to find in the art critics' reviews.

Even if an organization wants new products, it need not develop them itself. It can let other organizations bear the expense and the risks and simply buy them, or act as a distributor or sales agent for the product. PBS relies heavily on British imports for its dramatic programs like the popular Masterpiece Theater. Most domestic stations do little programming themselves; instead they buy from the small number of stations that actively produce programs, like WGBH Boston, WNET New York, and WETA Washington. Even then, most of what is carried on the network is not new at all. In 1977 three out of every four network programs were repeats.[22]

Why, then, should an organization develop new products? For internal purposes, to counter the competition, and to meet the interests of clients (and backers). A symphony does not vary its programs because it fears competition; it varies its programs because audiences want variety and the musicians crave the stimulation of new works. Internal reasons may include the interests of employees, volunteers, and others associated with it; and they certainly also include such crass reasons as improving Net Marketing Contribution or increasing market share.

An interesting example of product development that beats the competition and serves the interests of clients is the effort by some public schools to woo students back into school cafeterias. The competition, of course, is provided by the fast food outlets near the schools, and by that most awesome of competitors, doing without; in this case skipping lunch. One way to compete would be to serve food as it should be served, fresh, prepared on the spot by someone with training and taste. This would cost too much, however, even if cooks and fresh food could be found; more important, many students would reject such unfamiliar fare. There is perhaps no area of human endeavor in which the differences between a marketer and others become so clear: Marketers provide clients what they will eat; others, like nutritionists, provide them with what is wholesome and nutritionally correct. In Las Vegas, before the fast food program was introduced, only about 10 percent of the students ate in the high school cafeteria. After the program was introduced, featuring tacos, pizzas, hotdogs, and french fries, all enriched to meet USDA standards, the participation rate rose to 90 percent (and incidentally, the school system turned an annual deficit of $200,000 to a cash profit of $1,250,000).[23]

FIT

Fit is a rough measure of the marketing barriers that the new product must overcome. The better the fit, the easier it is to develop and introduce the product, and the more likely it is to succeed.

Fit analysis enables one to evaluate these barriers and gives an indication of the extent to which they affect the chances of success for the new product. In other words, fit helps assess the organization's strengths and weaknesses in pursuing a given course of action. It is important to note that strengths and weaknesses do not exist in the absolute. They only have meaning as they aid or hinder the achievement of an organizational goal.

This last statement means that the fit analysis proceeds in two major stages. The first determines the requirements of the proposed new product. This means having a reasonably clear understanding of the overall objectives sought and the basic structure of the new product process. The second major stage determines whether the firm can meet the entry requirements, whether it can overcome likely obstacles and use its competencies and particular strengths to best advantage. This second point is the core of the fit analysis.

Product-Organization Fit

A question that must be dealt with is how close the proposed new product is to the organization's existing products. Can it be priced using current pricing procedures? Can it carry the organization's usual trademark or service mark? Can it be advertised in advertising media the organization is experienced at using? Can it be distributed through the organization's normal channels of distribution? If the answers to all these are "Yes"—and getting the answers may be an exacting chore—the fit is good and we can expect the introduction of the new product to go smoothly. But if the proposed product requires a *new* marketing strategy, it will be more difficult to introduce and there will be more risk.

The nonprofit organization must look at its other resources and skills as well with an eye to spotting potential trouble spots. The standard business approach, called a "resource audit," examines the following:

1. *Finances.* A nonprofit organization that is pinched financially must shape its product planning to conform, just as one that is flush with funds is influenced by its wellbeing. For many nonprofit organizations, the key is not how much money the organization has, but how much it can raise. Theater companies headed by good fundraisers can do things denied to lesser beings.

2. *Raw materials.* Access to the raw materials used in manufacturing is also important. To a university press, raw materials means manuscripts, where they are, and whether it can attract them.

3. *Location.* Sometimes location is strong in that it provides access to certain publics or backers. A nonprofit organization in New York City is closer to foundations and individuals interested in the arts than, say, a nonprofit organization in Dubuque. Innovative arts programs make more sense for a New York organization than for one in Dubuque. (But location is only one of many influences.)

4. *Public acceptance.* The degree of public acceptance for a nonprofit organization also influences product planning. The Centers for Disease Control paid heavily for its involvement in the swine flu program in 1976 and 1977:

   CDC was almost the last Federal agency widely regarded by reporters and producers as a good thing, responsible, respectable, scientific, above suspicion. This gave [the CDC's director] Sencer terrific clout. The Presidency after Watergate, the military after Vietnam, physicists, universities, to say nothing of HEW or Congress for God's sake—none of them remotely in the same league! Even a hint that any one of them was blocking Sencer's urgent memo would have been a big story . . . human interest . . . good guys (the best) against bad . . . Now CDC's lost its innocence.[24]

   It may be years before the public is willing to go along with the CDC again.

5. *Plant.* Plant can also be a resource—or handicap—in that what it can do influences

product planning. Some theaters are capable of scenic and lighting effects that others are not capable of, and this will influence the repertoires of both. Zoos are tightly constrained by their present facilities for housing and exhibiting animals. No chance of putting wildebeest in the area normally used by the hippos.

6. *Personnel.* The skills and interests of both management and staff are important. A museum with little experience in mounting elaborate exhibitions must take this into consideration in planning its new exhibits.

Product-Client Fit

Dealing with the behavioral dimension of new product success is referred to as "product–client fit." The success of the proposed new product rests on a small set of critical assumptions as to the behavior of clients. To the extent that these assumptions are correct, the proposed new product is more likely to succeed. These buyers may, of course, be any targeted group, but because most new products have a low degree of newness, and because nonprofit organizations usually target their new products at existing clients, the fit analysis usually deals with the organization's existing clients.

Fortunately, selling to these customers is the easiest of all possible sales jobs. These clients know the organization and its products, and the organization knows the clients' needs and interests. When you play in your own front yard and use your own ball, you play at an advantage.

It is best to focus on a small number of critical dimensions. They can be uncovered by focusing on the question: What behavioral and attitudinal changes *must* occur for the new product to succeed? A simple classification usually suffices. For example, a marketer might break the purchase/consumption cycle into three phases:

1. *Purchase*—the set of activities that precede and accompany the purchase.
2. *Consumption/support*—the activities that support consumption but that are not directly related to use (installation, repair, maintenance, and the like).
3. *Consumption/use*—the consumption and use of the product.

In each of these three phases we might ask a number of questions, based naturally on our model of client behavior:

- How are decisions made in this area?
- What information does the client need?
- What sources of information are used?
- With whom is the activity carried on?
- Where is the decision made?

This approach serves as a descriptive device that enables the marketer systematically to consider and record behavior of the targeted market for the new services. Note that if the marketer has a great deal of trouble answering questions like these, it is itself a cue that his knowledge about the market he hopes to sell to is limited. This is in itself a barrier to entry.

Product-Competition Fit

One must look to the differences between the organization's proposed new product and competitive offerings. Of course, nonprofit organizations that face little competition will skip this step. There are two central questions that must be explored.

The first deals with what might be called "competitive edge"—the degree to which the new product differs from the competition and the degree to which clients value the differences.

The second deals with competitive resources. An organization may have a good product–organization fit and a good product–client fit and still fail because the competition is stronger, bigger, or better. Hence, it is prudent to focus on competitors. What are their stakes in this competition? If the product or service is important to their financial well-being, they may try to respond if attacked. This first point deals with their interest in competing, in other words. How capable are they of responding? And what are their likely responses?

All this sounds remote if we confine our attention only to competition between nonprofit organizations. But a fair amount of competition goes on between nonprofit organizations and businesses. Some examples: The Postal Service and other government agencies, nonprofit hospitals, nonprofit blood banks, nonprofit research institutes, and nonprofit test developers and publishers (such as the Educational Testing Service) all compete with profit-making counterparts. Such competition presents problems for the nonprofit organization, because profit competitors are much more likely to serve only those parts of the market that are profitable. Should a nonprofit hospital find itself in competition with a profit-making hospital, the latter will have mostly patients who can pay their way, thus forcing a larger number of indigent patients onto the nonprofit hospital than it might otherwise have to deal with. If a profit-making opera company were formed, it would perform only on Friday and Saturday nights, and only the most popular operas, leaving to the nonprofit company the operas with less audience draw and the less attractive nights.[25]

There is little theory to guide the analysis of competitive behavior, and hence the nonprofit organization must do the best it can.

DEVELOPING NEW PRODUCTS

Let us assume that we want to develop new products (and services). How do we do it? The process by which new products are developed is short in explanation but long in doing.

First, set overall strategy, for both the organization and marketing program. New products are not an end in themselves, but rather merely contribute to overall goals. Here a preliminary fit analysis would also be performed.

No matter how well one has thought out the basic questions raised earlier on the overall role of marketing in the nonprofit organization, the question is sure to arise again with new force in dealing with new product questions. It is, in fact, by the very process of deciding day-to-day product issues that most non-profit organizations set their overall strategy. Few work out such questions in advance, although they should; and when they do, exceptions and queries soon arise as to the meaning of the general statement of policy and its application to the case at hand. No sooner has a museum decided what its collections are to be than some beautiful, or valuable, or important gift that does not fit in the collection is offered, and the debate starts anew. One must expect, therefore, to find constant discussion on this point.

Second, generate ideas. This stage implies the organization is committed to new products, any new products, but is short on ideas. This is true of many businesses, but not of most nonprofits. Hence, the techniques of generating ideas are best left undiscussed.[26]

Third, design the new product.

Fourth, evaluate feasibility. There are two different questions to be answered in this stage, which is often lengthy. The first is whether the new product can be made and the second is whether it can be sold. It is at this stage that the organization tries to satisfy itself that the problems pointed up by the fit analysis can be overcome.

The second feasibility question deals with marketing. New products at this stage begin to go through a series of marketing research studies to determine their acceptability to clients. Five such tests are:

- Concept test. This tests the concept, the *idea* of the product. Perhaps the client sees a picture, perhaps a mock-up. Often all he knows is what he is told about the product.

- Use test. The client is *given* the new product and asked to use it. Then the client is interviewed to find out such things as whether the product worked, how the client used it, whether he liked it, whether he would like to buy more, and why he stopped using it, if he did.

- Extended use test. Now the client is asked to *pay* at least something for continuing to use the product. This begins to add a note of economic reality to the test and thus allows the first estimates of how much can be sold at what price.

- Limited sale test. The product is now put on sale, typically in a store or other limited environment. But this stage might well be a test mailing. Clients do not know it is a test, which makes it a realistic test of the marketing programs; although *after* they have bought, more marketing research it may be visited on them. Such limited tests usually escape the notice of the competition.

- Full-scale sales test. This is the final marketing test, and as it can be expected to draw a competitive reaction, it should provide the most useful information of all on the viability of the new product under normal competitive conditions.

At the same time these marketing tests are going on the production questions are being considered. Does the organization have the technical skills to produce the new product? The necessary plant and equipment? What will it cost to make the new product? For all these questions a pilot plant often provides much information, as well as providing a product for the marketing tests.

Taken together, all these tests can be very expensive. But not all products merit such expense. And it is possible to gain such information in other ways. One standard way is to start small, selling in only one or two cities, or in only one region, rather than trying to leap into national distribution all at one time. This is called a "roll-out," and it is how Ocean Spray typically introduces its new products. Recall that this is Inroads' strategy as well: now in only nine cities, with plans to expand to fifteen or twenty more. Sometimes noncompeting organizations that have introduced a similar product will be willing to furnish information about their introduction.

Finally, introduce the new product. A complex, time-consuming, expensive process in and of itself. At the end of the introduction, the product is perhaps well launched, but even now it may fail.

Three Examples of New Product Development

Let us consider three examples, the first the hypothetical development of a new academic journal, the second the start-up of a new congregation, the third a new program for the Baltimore Symphony.

A new academic journal. An academic association is considering starting a new academic journal to deal with research and applications of research in the field of nonprofit marketing.

Step 1 would require considering whether the journal fits with the association's overall purposes, and whether the articles proposed for the journal are suitable to the association's image and what it wants to accomplish.

If the association is already producing an academic journal or two, the product–organization fit is probably good. It knows how to deal with printers, how to set up an editorial staff, how to promote a new journal, how to control subscription revenues, and so on. If it has never produced such a journal, the fit is poor and it will probably have to hire someone experienced in publishing. It can be assumed there are few other nonprofit marketing journals, so there is little concern from like competition. But there are many, many, many, many academic journals, and the competition for good manuscripts is intense. The interest of scholars is clear; they want to publish in the best journals they can. So it may be difficult for the new journal to compete effectively for good manuscripts. The product–client fit will also probably cause some problems, because identifying and describing potential subscribers will be difficult. It might be that the association would not expect that most of its members would be interested in the new journal.

As is often the case with an analysis of fit, the conclusions are iffy. But it does provide us with some warning of two potential trouble spots.

Step 2 can be skipped, as the idea is already clearly formed. Just possibly some members of the association might consider alternative forms that the journal might take, or alternative editorial approaches; but most likely those backing the journal would have pretty clearly in mind what it is they want.

Step 3 would also be abbreviated, because aside from such trivial questions as to the size of the journal, the number of pages it will contain, whether it will contain advertising, the quality of the paper, and the use of four-color printing, the only questions of substance deal with editorial matter; and they will for the most part be decided by the editor, although he may make a show of working within guidelines set down by the association for its new journal.

In Step 4 there would be no prototype issues (although commercial magazines run up sample issues to show potential advertisers what they will be buying). The methods by which magazines are produced are known to people with experience in publishing, and the uncertainties are low, except for one—whether there is enough editorial matter of the right quality. No association wants to put out a new journal that is below its standards, no matter how low the standards are. This would involve some careful research. The association would probably commission a study group to find out how many articles on nonprofit marketing were appearing and in what journals, at what rate the number of articles was increasing, and how many seem to meet the quality standards of the proposed journal. There would be relatively little exploration of circulation, primarily because estimating circulation for what is admittedly a poorly defined market is difficult, ''poorly defined'' meaning that many potential subscribers will not realize that the journal is for them, which will make it hard to communicate the qualities of the new journal.

Let us look at the five types of marketing testing that might be done under Step 4.

- Concept—already done when the idea was conceived. The study group may try the idea out on influential members of the association, however. A mail questionnaire may be sent to members of the association, or an editorial, ''From the President,'' may appear in a current journal to solicit comment.
- Use test—there will be none.
- Extended use test—ditto.
- Limited sales test—probably none, but it is possible to try a test mailing as a rough estimate of potential circulation (and hence potential losses).
- Full-scale sales test—none.

In Step 5 the new journal is launched, which means all the panoply of modern academic publishing—finding an editor, assistant editors, referees and reviewers;

putting together a production and editorial staff, soliciting manuscripts, negotiating contracts with printers, settling accounts with the Postal Service, signing up an advertising sales agent; planning and executing the print advertising, publicity, and direct mail; writing the solemn, first editorial, making sure the assistant editors, referees, and reviewers are doing their jobs, and watching the losses pile up faster than anticipated.

Developing a program for a new church. A look at the development and introduction of a program for a new Baptist church will illustrate some fundamentals of the process.

The Mecklenburg Community Church (MCC) was founded late in 1992 in Charlotte, North Carolina.[27] Few new churches do as MCC did, simply open their doors and wait for parishioners. They either split from another church, bringing members with them, or they engage in telemarketing and direct mail to announce the new church and invite attendance. The average Protestant church in the United States has about one hundred members; the MCC had none, of course.

MCC's pastor concluded that he had no hope of attracting those who were already happy at their current churches, a conclusion no marketer would dispute. So he decided to concentrate on those who were young and didn't go to church. He thought of them as "unchurched Baby Boomers," a phrase not likely to pass into general use. How should the pastor approach this segment of his market? Why weren't they going to church? What could a church do to help them with their needs? What kind of service would they like the most?

To answer these questions the pastor commissioned a research study of the three most promising areas in the counties surrounding Charlotte. (As is common in marketing research, the areas were defined by their ZIP codes.) The study showed that many of the respondents avoided church because they felt either that church services were wearisome or that churches always had their hands out asking for money. It also showed that one of the most important concerns for respondents was their family, particularly raising children. Finally, it showed that respondents were more likely to respond to marketing built around special events than marketing that made heavy use of advertising or telemarketing.

The pastor now made a leap of faith, if you will pardon the expression, and judged that the results made sense and that he would commit his church to them. His decision here is worth a brief note only because it is all too common for NPOs to commission research and then never use it. As a corrective to this tendency, marketers usually suggest that research focus tightly on action and on results that translate into action. Perhaps the pastor did not make a leap of faith. He had spent some $9,000 on research, a move that might be seen as dangerously eccentric, and he may have felt that he had to go forward to get his church underway.

First, he decided to announce his presence in a direct mail piece mailed to 23,000 households. The headline read, "Give up on church? We don't blame you,'' and the copy built on this theme. Second, he decided to position his church—sermons and church programs, for example—on raising children. To communicate this position in a professional way, he put together a special event held at the University of North Carolina at which child-rearing experts discussed how to be more effective in raising children.

Here we see in capsule the entire new product development process, although ''development'' is probably not the right word. The pastor already had developed; he had his theological and liturgical convictions. Given those, however, he was willing to consider any of several possible colorings to make his efforts more attractive, provided it did not compromise his theological beliefs.

The pastor succeeded in his efforts. He rapidly built his membership to 300, of whom 80 percent were local residents who had indeed given up on church. Note that I did not say that the marketing effort succeeded. We cannot know that. What we do know, almost certainly, was that the marketing program attracted visitors to services. To use marketing jargon, the program induced trial. Trial is one thing: based on a superficial decision, easy to bring about, too often failing to lead to permanent change; conversion is quite another thing: far harder to bring about but much more likely to stick because it is based on experience with the product. Here the marketing program—research, direct mail, the special event—all contributed to bringing people to the church; but they decide to stay and become members for reasons that have nothing to do with marketing, because they like the sermons and the church programs, because they make friends, and perhaps because they begin to sense a change for the better in their lives.

New orchestra programs to improve cultural diversity. The Baltimore Symphony Orchestra (BSO), committed to broadening its audience, began a consultative process in 1988 by inviting 140 community leaders, mostly black, to two meetings, one during the day, and one in the evening.[28] The leaders were asked to share their views of the BSO and how they thought the BSO could address their interests. Orchestra leaders listened and took careful notes without engaging in extended discussion. From the meetings, four areas of concern emerged: (a) education, (b) marketing and public relations, (c) BSO linkages with organizations in the black community, and (d) inclusiveness in the organization at all levels. The group set up a community outreach committee with four subcommittees to address each of those concerns, and a staff member with experience as a community organizer was hired to coordinate the outreach project. This grass-roots participation resulted in a number of specific programs and projects, some more successful than others. One such project was a program entitled *Live, Gifted, and Black,* a joint project of the BSO and the American Symphony Orchestra League, consisting of readings of unpublished works by four black composers. Two thousand people, mostly black, attended this well-received event. ''If we had put on a concert of four unpublished white composers, we would have attracted about two hundred people,'' said the BSO's executive director, ''if we were lucky.'' The BSO's Associates (the orchestra's volunteer association) have also become involved, working to bring in people from diverse backgrounds.

In addition, the American Composers Orchestra (ACO) and the BSO commissioned Hannibal Peterson's *African Portraits,* premiered by the ACO in 1990 at Carnegie Hall, and given its second performance by the BSO in 1991. According to the BSO program notes, "Multicultural and multilingual, *African Portraits* is divided into two acts. It features the orchestra, the Hannibal Peterson Quintet, a blues singer, a gospel singer, a griot, African percussionists, narration, and a chorus."

Here is an example where the new product, black music, opened up a new market, black audiences. Thus, it is a form of diversification. Unfortunately, we do not know what happened next. What we see at the BSO is what we saw at the Mecklenburg Community Church—a trial, one that attracted over 2,000 people. But will they convert from trial to adoption?

NOTES

1. The two books were Tom Horwitz, *How to Set Up and Run Successful Nonprofit Arts Organizations* (Chicago: Chicago Review Press, 1978); and Alvin H. Reiss, *The Arts Management Handbook,* rev. 2d ed. (New York: Law-Arts Publishers, 1974).

2. Carol Kovach, "A Hungry Problem for Zoos: In Search of New Prey," in *Research Frontiers in Marketing: Dialogues and Directions,* edited by Subhash C. Jain (Chicago: American Marketing Association, 1978), p. 351.

3. "Flame of Hope, Inc." (Boston: Harvard Business School, 1970).

4. Edward P. Alexander, *Museums in Motion* (Nashville, Tenn.: American Association of State and Local History, 1979), p. 122.

5. Ibid., p. 207.

6. Bruce Millar, "What's in a Name? Increased Donations for Texas Charities That Changed Theirs." *Chronicle of Philanthropy,* May 29, 1990, p. 14. Also see Jennifer Fisch, "What's in a Name? More Than You Think." *NonProfit Times* (January 1992), p. 1+.

7. Nicholas Staveley and Chris Hawes, "Old Product Development: Warming Up with Woolmark." *Advertising* (Winter 1979–1980): 18.

8. "Child-Resistant Containers—Effects on Patient Care." *Journal of the American Pharmaceutical Association* NS15, no. 9 (September 1975): 502–505. It is odd that the APA surveyed pharmacists and not their customers.

9. Charles Dickens, *Little Dorrit* (New York: Heritage, 1956) p. 539.

10. *Business Week* (June 2, 1980), p. 54.

11. Dwight D. Phelps, *Marketing Strategy for the Australian Post Office* (Melbourne: Australian Post Office Headquarters, 1971), pp. 68–77.

12. For the fascinating story of the OED and its first editor, read K. M. Elisabeth Murray, *Caught in the Web of Words: James A. H. Murray and the Oxford English Dictionary* (New Haven: Yale University Press, 1977).

13. Israel Shenker, "The Dictionary Factory." *The New Yorker* (April 3, 1989), pp. 86–100.

14. *Business Week* (December 10, 1979), pp. 68, 73.

15. *Museums USA* (Washington, D.C.: National Endowment for the Arts, 1974), pp. 38, 39, 44, 45.

16. Personal communication, June 2, 1980.

17. H. Igor Ansoff, *Corporate Strategy* (New York: McGraw-Hill, 1965), p. 109.

18. Benjamin M. Compaine, *Who Owns the Media?* (White Plains, N.Y.: Knowledge Industry Press, 1980), p. 119.

19. "Peacock vs. the Pea." *Time* (January 19, 1976). One might argue NBC's side by taking the position that NBC had a great deal to lose if the logo were not right. But it is hard to imagine that the logo has much of an effect on anything at all—few viewers will tune out because they do not like the logo, and no advertisers will be driven away because of the logo. Three-quarters of a million is too much.

20. *New York Times,* April 3, 1977, p. 19.

21. It should be pointed out, however, that the director of the Cleveland Museum, Sherman Lee, was an unashamed elitist who hated to stoop. See, for example, his article, "The Art Museum as Wilderness Area." *Museum News* (October 1972): 11–12.

22. Compaine, *Who Owns the Media?*, p. 119.

23. *New York Times,* January 19, 1978, p. 31.

24. Richard E. Neustadt and Harvey V. Fineberg quoting an unnamed television reporter in *The Swine Flu Affair* (Washington, D.C.: Department of Health, Education and Welfare, 1978), pp. 97–98.

25. This would probably be true today, but in the early years of this century, in New York City, there were two highly competitive opera companies, one profit making, and both thrived. See John F. Cone, *Oscar Hammerstein's Manhattan Opera Company* (Norman: University of Oklahoma Press, 1964).

26. For some discussion of idea-generating techniques, however, see Part III A, "Concept Generation and Evaluation," in *Corporate Strategy and Product Innovation,* edited by Robert R. Rothberg (New York: Free Press, 1976), pp. 221–267.

27. "Building a Church Through Research." *NonProfit Times* (March 1993), p. 39.

28. *Americanizing the American Orchestra, Report of the National Task Force for the American Orchestra: An Initiative for Change* (Washington, D.C.: American Symphony Orchestra League, 1993), pp. 33, 45.

Chapter 11

Delivering the Goods (and Services) by Means of Channels of Distribution

The problem facing a manufacturer of almost anything is the straightforward problem of getting products from his shipping dock to his customers, who typically are scattered wide and far. He cannot go to them. They will not come to him. Car companies, office supply companies, cookware makers, publishers, and furniture makers cannot expect customers to come to the factory. They distribute their goods through distributors so that customers can find what they want in a local store or take delivery at their homes.

But not every company manufactures things. In fact, most do not make just goods, they make services as well. Perhaps that is all they make. Some three-quarters of the American economy is now services; and in the nonprofit sector almost everything is services. Bakeries, restaurants, resorts, barbers, to say nothing of colleges, zoos, theater companies, subways, and hospitals all expect clients to come to the factory where the service is produced.

Both of these solutions raise marketing problems for nonprofit organizations. If an NPO expects clients to come to it, it must find out where clients want to come and try to locate there. Clients bear T costs in coming to the "factory." If the T costs are too high, they will not come; if they are just high, clients will come but they will come less often than they might. If, on the other hand, an NPO uses normal channels of distribution, then it must persuade these channels to give it a fair shake: to stock its products or display them or perhaps even to be able to answer questions about them.

Using normal retail channels means that the success of a marketing program depends on individuals and organizations over which the marketer has no control. Without control he must entice them into cooperating with him, which means that he has a marketing problem. Here are five examples:

- A center that counsels adults with sexual disfunctions must rely on others for referrals—hospitals, clinical psychologists, the courts, clergy, and state and local welfare agencies.
- Amtrak must rely on travel agents to display its schedules and promotional materials, and the International Association for Medical Assistance to Travelers hopes they will display the association's name and perhaps distribute its booklet.
- A citizens' group wants to make it easy to recycle aluminum beer cans produced by a local brewery. It must rely on the brewery for cooperation, and on the beverage wholesalers who will have to handle the empty cans on their way back to the brewery and the can producer.
- A local theater group requires the cooperation of merchants who permit the group to place posters in their windows.
- A federal agency that wants to encourage people to protect themselves against burglars must enlist the support of local police forces to distribute its materials.

Most public television stations accept what anyone else would call advertisements but that the stations call corporate messages or announcements or participations. To the advertiser public TV is an attractive advertising medium—viewers are well educated, have good incomes, and are interested in the shows; and the amount of advertising is light, typically no more than two spots per break and two breaks per hour. In spite of what PBS implies—that there is a public broadcasting system—PBS is no such thing. There is no network. Each station stands on its own.

So while it is easy for an advertiser to buy time on Fox or CBS, it is cumbersome to buy a national audience on PBS. The advertising agency must buy from each station, one at a time. It is rather like drinking a glass of wine one spoonful at a time, and having to negotiate over the price of each.

Enter a middleman, filling a classic distribution need, performing a classic distribution role. Instead of contacting each station individually, the advertising agency, the (for-profit) Public Television Representatives and Public Broadcasting Marketing make it easy for the advertiser. For example, with one buy through Public Broadcasting Marketing the advertiser can place messages on fifty-two stations representing some 60 percent of U.S. television viewers.[1]

THE ROLE OF THE MIDDLEMAN

It is a commonplace of marketing that you can do away with the distributor but not with his job. Regardless of who performs the functions of distribution, they must be done. Just what is it that the middleman does? What is his role? To a marketer he has five functions:

1. *Physical distribution.* Transporting goods and storing them.
2. *Contact.* Searching out prospective clients. Communicating with them by means of advertising, selling, sales promotion, and display.

3. *Financing and bearing risk.* Providing credit. Financing inventories. Bearing the risks associated with taking title and extending credit.

4. *Negotiation.* Setting terms. Pricing.

5. *Sorting.* Concentrating goods from many suppliers. Breaking bulk and reassembling into new concentrations. Dispersing to consumers or other middlemen.

A second answer to the question of what the middleman does comes from microeconomics. The economist talks of utilities of possession and form and of time and place. It is, that is, a good thing to have goods and services as you want them, when you want them, and where you want them. Middlemen deal with utilities of time and place (although exceptions abound). Take a nonprofit business run by a trade union, say, a drugstore. While the pharmacist may compound and mix prescription drugs and thus be a manufacturer, most of the time all the pharmacist does is move pills from big bottles to little bottles. Both compounding drugs and moving pills illustrate the creation of form utility by a middleman. But most of the value added by middlemen arises from their creating place and time utilities. Said in clearer words, the drugstore maintains stocks that are accessible to union members where they want them and when they want them.

In terms of the functions of distribution, this nonprofit drugstore does the following:

1. *Physical distribution.* Stocks a wide variety of drugs. Transportation is probably nil; most customers go to the store. Some nonprofit drugstores may deliver or mail drugs to their customers.

2. *Contact.* Continuous but small effort through union publications, posters, and so on. Each order might also contain information about the drugstore and its products.

3. *Financing and bearing risk.* Finances inventories. May extend credit. Union's backing probably means less risk than a retail drugstore would have to bear.

4. *Negotiating.* Negotiate with (1) the union to set acceptable gross margins and other terms and (2) pharmaceutical companies to obtain volume discounts. No negotiation with union members.

5. *Sorting.* Receives goods from many suppliers and disperses them to customers. Primary function is breaking bulk and reassembling (from big bottles to little bottles).

WHAT ARE MIDDLEMEN PAID?

Middlemen are paid for delivering the where and the when that customers value. How much they are paid depends in part on how much they do. A state lottery ticket is a simple product. It sells at a single fixed price, most sales are made to repeat buyers, display plays a minor role in the sale, advertising assumes importance only when there is something new like a special drawing or a new type of ticket, and the percentage paid in prizes and the frequency of drawings are given. What is the middleman's role? Not much. He has to order enough tickets to keep from running out, sell them on request, handle the cash, return unsold tickets, keep records. For such a modest role he needs little training or experience, and for such a modest role he receives little compensation, on the order of 5 percent of the ticket price. It is so simple, in fact, that state lotteries can use vending machines, which leaves the retailer to face the glum fact that he has been replaced by a machine.

Federal crime insurance, sold by the Federal Insurance Administration to city residents and businessmen, is not so simple. To sell crime insurance, insurance brokers or agents must at least trouble to mention the insurance to their existing customers, who already buy homeowner's insurance or fire insurance for their businesses. They must also see to it that businesses who want the insurance are inspected for the adequacy of their security devices—locks, bars, grills, and other utensils of modern retailing. They must help fill out the application and look up the premium in a table, and they may be involved if claims arise. For all this they need a modicum of knowledge and must expend some slight effort; because of these requirements, among other reasons, they are paid around 15 percent of the initial premium.[2]

Nonprofit businesses expect of middlemen roughly the same things that regular businesses expect: That they display products, advertise, set prices, handle returns and repairs, and so on. But the first of these is display, because it ensures the product is available and ready for sale. University presses work hard to woo bookstores to stock and display those few of their books that sell well,[3] and government tourist boards try to see that travel agents have brochures on their country and that they display them.

The interests of middlemen can affect any part of the marketing mix. They may feel that the NPO's advertising or sales promotion are ineffective and, as a result, not cooperate as they might. They may feel the recommended price or gross margin is too low and refuse to stock the product; or they may stock it but not push it because they feel the price is too high. They may even influence whether an NPO adopts a new product. Here is an example of where they influenced the nature of the product; in fact, whether there even was a product.

A museum in a large urban area was considering a fifty-minute laser light show in its planetarium dealing with cowboy and western music. The museum had a large and important collection of Indian and cowboy artifacts, and felt the laser show, while rather unusual, was related to its collections. The planetarium stood unused most of the week, and the museum director was looking for a way to increase revenues. The city received about thirteen million visitors a year, of whom seven million were tourists. Much of the tourist market could be reached by promotion in the local newspapers, billboards, and "tourist" media. But 60 percent of the tourists, about 4.2 million, took a tour operated by one of the sixteen tour companies. The economics of the laser show were such that the museum had to attract tour business or the venture would fail.

But there were problems. Tours, which were usually three hours long, included two or three stops, twenty or thirty minutes in length, where tourists got off the bus to go through an attraction, like the Indian village on the edge of town or the wax museum. If the attraction charged a general admission fee, the tour operator received a discount. For example, the Western Music Hall of Fame charged $6.00 for general admission, but tour companies paid only $4.50. The result was that tour operators tried to get their tourists in and out of an attraction as quickly as possible.

It is now easy to guess what happened. Tour operators approached about the planetarium show said it was far too long, and what with loading, unloading, watching the show, and a quick tour of part of the museum the stop at the museum would run ninety minutes. One company suggested the show be boiled down to run no more than six minutes. The idea was dropped.

Nontraditional Channels

While most of the chapter deals with distribution through traditional channels, the reader will encounter some unusual middlemen in nonprofit marketing. One curious example is the use of vouchers, whereby clients act as middlemen to distribute funds provided by a backer. In one scheme funded by the U.S. Department of Health, Education, and Welfare, cultural vouchers were distributed to ten community groups, which used them to purchase cultural and educational services from eight cultural institutions in New York City.[4] The cultural institutions then took the vouchers to a voucher agency, which paid them a certain amount for each voucher.

A voucher scheme like this enables a backer like HEW to give money to NPOs without having to decide exactly how much to give to each one. Instead, the backer merely decides which community groups (or individuals) are to receive the vouchers and which institutions are eligible to accept the vouchers, and it redeems the vouchers when they are presented for payment. The backer provides the money, but the clients decide which organizations receive how much. Thus, vouchers measure client demand in much the same way as sales measure demand; and it is to be expected that if the amounts represented by the vouchers are large, the nonprofit organizations will become more responsive to client interests and more willing to change, which is an important outcome to a marketer.[5]

THE CLIENTS' INTERESTS IN DISTRIBUTION

Middlemen exist because most manufacturers could not exist without them. But they also serve the interests of clients (and industrial buyers), otherwise they would not patronize them. What are these interests that clients have in distribution? There are three—convenience, variety, and information.

Convenience

Clients as well as backers value convenience, and as we have seen, the notion of making things more convenient, of adapting more closely to how people behave and how they want to behave, is a major consideration in making marketing what it is. Convenience comes in many forms—a product can be made easier to repair, a package easier to use, or a price easier to pay. In distribution, convenience means three things.

The first is convenience in terms of travel time. Stores have always tried to locate near their markets, which may mean where people live, where they work, or the routes they follow traveling to and from work. In America today, perhaps the straightforward measure of this convenience is driving time. In most large cities, emergency rooms and outpatient clinics are few and far between, which means they are hard to reach. One of the major components of the demand for improved health care facilities has been the demand for decentralization. Decentralized health care facilities are, above all, convenient.[6]

The second component of convenience is the speed with which a transaction can be completed, and the certainty of that speed. When a blood bank keeps potential donors long past their appointment, it reduces their willingness to give again. When a venereal disease clinic takes twenty minutes to process a patient one time and two hours the next time, it discourages that patient from returning. Note that both of these dimensions of convenience, driving time and transaction time, are components of the client's T costs.

The third component of convenience involves the ease of shopping. Instead of physical nearness or driving time, many consumers think of convenience in terms of how much they can accomplish in a single buying trip. One way that colleges disseminate information to prospective students is the fair. At the fair, students from local high schools find 100, 200, or even 300 college admissions officers, each manning a booth or table, each available to answer questions and give the prospective applicants application forms, catalogs, and other materials. For the colleges the fairs produce leads, plus some exposure to students who otherwise might not know of them; for the students and their parents, who often accompany them, they serve as inexpensive sources of information because the fair provides one-stop shopping—in one two-hour trip students contact dozens of schools, receive a great deal of material (free shopping bags are provided), and get answers to their specific questions from the admissions representatives. (Questions for the reader: Why is the fair more convenient than simply writing letters to the colleges? Which segment is most likely to be attracted to such a fair?)

Variety

This third convenience factor is closely related to another client interest in distribution, an interest in variety. Clients usually like to have choices, and for many products the wider the choice made available by the middlemen, the better. Imagine buying fabric to make a dress at a store that prided itself on having only one kind of fabric and in only three colors; or imagine buying furniture at a store that carried only a few styles. The army once enjoyed the luxury of treating all of its recruits the same, since it did not have to trouble about pleasing them. It paid no heed to the interests of its recruits in having a choice as to occupational specialty. But with the coming of the volunteer army, the army has moved to meet these interests, at least in part, by offering volunteers choices as to what they will do, and where they will be stationed.

Information

Finally, middlemen serve clients' interests for information. Consumers often ask retail sales clerks for information about the products or services they buy. A nonprofit abortion referral agency, one that does no abortions itself, will naturally provide a good deal of information to women seeking its services. Retailers often put up point-of-sale materials that provide information, and retail displays can be most informative.

Costs of Distribution

Someone, somewhere, somehow must perform the distribution job—and bear the costs of distribution. In commercial transactions a manufacturer ships to a wholesaler, say, and the wholesaler pays the freight. The wholesaler, in turn, delivers to the retailer. He may choose not to charge for delivery, in which case he considers such charges in setting his overall margins, or he may charge, in which case the retailer also pays freight. Finally, some retailers charge for some deliveries to the consumer. When the manufacturer ships to another manufacturer it is usually F.O.B. Again it is the customer who pays the freight.

Ultimately, then, the final consumer bears (most or all of) the cost of distribution, as well as all other costs—production, finance, personnel, and so on. A commercial firm rarely considers paying these costs itself. A nonprofit organization has more flexibility—it can absorb a little or most of the costs of distribution to reduce the total cost of the transaction to the consumer. There are examples all around us. A library has branch libraries to lower the costs in time and effort to reach the library. In California, voting precincts are curiously designed so that most voters can walk to the polls. The traditional way to distribute food stamps is to set up shop, hang out a sign saying "County Welfare Office," and wait for business, which puts most of the cost on the poor recipient. But it is also possible to take the office to likely applicants by using a mobile office built into a truck. This method offers maximum flexibility to visit housing projects and shopping centers and to change routes and schedules as needed. Mobile units have been used as part of community improvement projects, to bring library books and museum exhibits to urban ghettos, to register voters, flog college admissions, collect blood, distribute contraceptives, and provide medical care.

Some nonprofits have this problem coming and going, or picking up and delivering. The U.S. Postal Service has mailboxes almost everywhere, in cities always only a few blocks from where you are standing at any given moment (or perhaps across the street). But for any other transaction you must go to the post office itself. Most citizens can expect to receive their mail, when they do, outside their door, a fine system for the citizen but not for the Postal Service, which would prefer to shift more of the delivery costs to the citizen. How? By requiring mail to be picked up at some central point—at a campus post office, boxes on the ground floor of an apartment house, or a cluster of mailboxes at the entrance to a new housing development—anywhere except at your door.

There is wide latitude for such shifts in cost. One spectacular example is the supermarket, which shifts to the shopper the not inconsiderable costs of finding the groceries and waiting in line, and the trivial costs of taking them off the shelf and wheeling them to the checkout counter. This system replaces one in which a store clerk does all this labor, busily going to and fro while the customer stands.

Now, shifting some costs does not mean shifting all the costs. It is quite conceivable to charge more for extra convenience.

MIDDLEMEN'S INTERESTS

Just as you must adapt your marketing to clients' interests, so too must you adapt to the interests of the middlemen who sell or handle your products. the marketer must be able to take the middleman's side, to see the world as he sees it. For some years, Consumers Union, Physicians for Automobile Safety, and Action for Child Transportation Safety have been trying to push the Department of Transportation (DOT) into setting a new standard for children's car seats. Until the DOT acts, unsafe seats costing about $15 or $20 sit on store shelves alongside safe seats for $30 or $40. Many parents, not well informed and apparently uninterested, choose the unsafe but cheaper seats. But the retail stores are part of the problem too. The sales clerks have little interest in selling the more expensive, safer seats because they are harder to sell. Nor are they trained to explain the complicated details of crash protection. The attitudes and beliefs of these clerks have a strong influence on the objectives sought by the safety groups. Any successful marketing program must adapt to these interests. It is because such a marketing program, one that would reach sales clerks and change their interests and selling behavior, is likely to fail that the safety groups have sought a nonmarketing solution, namely, mandatory safety standards. (There is another factor as well. Turnover among retail sales clerks is so high that a great deal of the resources put into training them in crash protection would go for naught.)

Middlemen have two broad classes of interests. They are interested in being paid, and they are interested in other things that indirectly affect monetary matters. Let us look briefly at some of these other things, which—to repeat—are interests to which an astute marketer tries to cater.

Middlemen value products and services for which there is a proven demand.

Given a figurative choice between opening a box and standing back while the customers buy or going out to collar customers, the middleman naturally prefers the easier course. If the products or services put out by the nonprofit are hard to sell, the middleman will not do anything about it. A ticket agent selling theater tickets loves a hit. He neither can nor will do anything to save a flop.

Middlemen value protection from competition. Competition is valued only in the abstract; everywhere else middlemen contemn competition. Distributing theater tickets through all ticket agents available serves the interests of the theater, and perhaps of the audience; but it does not serve the interests of commercial ticket agents.

Middlemen value financing and access to inventories. Middlemen are normally expected to carry inventories so that when a customer or client comes in, a sale can be made; but inventories are expensive to acquire, stock, insure, and maintain. So when an organization ships its merchandise on consignment, when it helps finance inventories, or when it places its own inventories so that the middleman may order and receive his shipment quickly, the organization is adapting itself to the middleman's concerns. Financing inventories may seem of little value to a middleman, but it is not so. About 60 percent of U.S. savings bonds are sold through payroll savings plans. Why would an employer trouble to serve as a middleman between the U.S. Treasury and their employees? (Technically, they are underwriters.) Because they are patriotic, of course—and because they are paid. They receive a flat fee for each bond sold, usually ten cents, and the money they receive from the sale of a bond does not have to be turned over to the Treasury until the second working day of the month following the one in which the bond is issued. This means that they have the use of the funds withheld from their employees' paychecks for as long as a month, courtesy of the Treasury's financing of their inventory of bonds.

Finally, middlemen value information—on what to stock, how to price, how to reduce pilferage, how to return unsold merchandise, how other middlemen are doing, and so on.

All these "other factors" take second place to the main interests of middlemen: gross margin and turnover. They are, after all, in business, often with their own money sunk in the firm, or in larger firms with goals to meet for profits and sales. They look with a keen eye on the gross margin offered by the seller. And when it is inadequate, the unsurprising conclusion is that they will be inadequate and their efforts meager.

Retailing Arithmetic

Retailing arithmetic deals with the simple computations that retailers use to plan and control their businesses. The nonprofit marketer needs to know two terms: gross margin and turnover. *Gross margin* is the difference between a product's cost and its price. Most retailers and wholesalers determine prices by a cost-plus method in which a certain percentage of the product's cost—invoice cost minus discounts for prompt payment plus freight charges—is added to the cost to give a final price. But while retailers set prices based on costs, gross margin is almost universally quoted as *a percentage of selling price.* Thus, a product costing a retailer eight cents and selling for a dime is said to carry a margin of 20 percent, not 25 percent. The difference between a product's cost and its price is called variously: margin, gross margin, markup, markon. The reader can expect to hear all these and more.

Suppose a university bookstore buys a statistics text for $36.80 and sells it for $46.00. The gross margin is $46 − 36.80 = $9.20, and in percentages the gross margin is $9.20/$46.00 = 20 percent, which just happens to be the usual gross margin on textbooks. Suppose the bookstore has a policy of granting faculty members a 10 percent discount. When a faculty member buys he pays $46.00 − 4.60 = $41.40, and the gross margin is $41.40 − 36.80 = $4.60, or $4.60/46.00 = 10 percent. A 10 percent discount has cut the bookstore's gross margin in half.

Note that gross margin is not profit. A store can have a gross margin of 20 or 30 or 40 or 50 percent and still lose money. Gross margin is not profit. It is what is left after the retailer pays for his stock-in-trade. He still has many other costs to pay for—personnel, rent, legal fees, advertising, utilities, insurance— before he obtains a profit, if he does.

The second term that needs definition is *turnover.* Turnover is the number of times the average inventory in an item is sold during the year; it is the number of times the inventory turns. A product that carries a 50 percent gross margin but turns slowly may be less profitable than an item that turns rapidly but carries only a 10 percent gross margin.

There are three methods for calculating turnover (or stockturn, as it is some- times called), all usually giving about the same result:

1.
$$\frac{\text{Cost of goods sold}}{\text{Average inventory at cost}}$$

2.
$$\frac{\text{Net sales}}{\text{Average inventory at selling price}}$$

3.
$$\frac{\text{Sales in units}}{\text{Average inventory in units}}$$

Suppose a university bookstore carries an average inventory of calculators of 35 units during the year, and that during the year the bookstore sells 187 cal- culators. Then, using the third of the formulas just above, the turnover is 187/ 35 = 5.3. A jeweler might experience a turnover of one or two, while the fresh produce department of a grocery store must turn its produce fifty times a year, otherwise it is only a produce department. Along with gross margin, turnover is an important control figure to retailers and wholesalers. Why? Inventory is the principal form of capital for a retailer, and turnover measures how effectively he uses that capital.

It is in the matter of gross margins and turnover that the conflict between ethical values and business practice intrudes. Some social critics condemn the costs of distribution as too high. They argue that middlemen do not perform a useful service and their gross margins are therefore too high. Needless to say, such reasoning does not nourish the middleman. For one, in the United States, at least, where distribution is intensively competitive, one may be sure that all the fat has been sweated off. Even the most voluble social critic could not run an American wholesaler, say, at a lower cost than the wholesaler himself. In addition, middlemen perform functions for which they want fair compensation. Unless an NPO gives them adequate gross margins they will not support the nonprofit organization, although they may tolerate it. Unless a government printing office grants margins comparable to the margins on trade and reference books, it can expect that its books will be poorly distributed and that it will have to handle many small orders from bookstores and by mail. In Australia the Australian Government Printing Office grants booksellers a gross margin of 33 percent, only a little below what bookstores try to get, 35 or 40 percent. Because the prices of many government publications are printed on the cover, or known by the public, bookstores cannot charge more. The 33 percent is enough to enlist their tolerance but not their support.

As a second example, a state-owned airline might well try to reduce the commission given travel agents; and it may be that in its own country it can get away with the reduction. But in overseas markets, it must either pay competitive commissions or lose the agent's attention and with it market share.

The need for gross margins to be ''right'' is not the whole story, however. The Boy Scouts of America sells scouting equipment through retailers. Most of the equipment turns relatively slowly, and the BSA, as a result, grants retail gross margins similar to the gross margins the retailers expect to receive on those items. But the Boy Scout uniform—pants, shirt, cap, socks, belt, and so on—is an item that requires the retailer to do little selling. The demand is developed by the number of scouts in the area. Because the demand is proven, the retailer is willing to take smaller gross margins, about 25 percent instead of the normal 40 percent that most retailers would want.

This point can be put more broadly. Middlemen receive compensation in return for the roles they perform. The more valuable the role, the higher the compensation. Publishers have long maintained a double price structure for books. A university bookstore buys a textbook at a discount designed to give it a 20 percent gross margin, but the same book purchased as a trade book would carry a 40 percent gross margin. In either case, the retail price is the same. Why is the gross margin higher for trade books? Because the textbook is ordered against a proven demand, and the bookstore need do little to sell it—open up the carton, stamp on a price, and collect the money.[7] But with trade books, they must order and hope they will be bought, or promote them. If they do not sell, they must mark them down and get rid of them. As such books are not ordered against a proven demand, the risks are higher, and the bookstore receives more compensation.

Push versus Pull Strategies

Marketers divide marketing strategies into two broad categories, one called a push strategy, the other a pull strategy. (See Figure 11.1.)

Suppose there are four parties—a producer, a wholesaler, a retailer, and the consumer. In a push strategy the producer sells to the wholesaler, who then sells to the retailer, who in turn sells to the consumer. Once the producer has sold the product to the wholesaler, the wholesaler is expected to take responsibility for selling to the retailer; and in the same fashion the retailer takes responsibility for selling to the client. In the pull strategy, the producer takes the prime responsibility for selling to the client, in that he directs his advertising and promotion primarily at the client. The retailer's role is reduced to filling the demand that has been generated by the producer, and the wholesaler's role to filling the demand from the retailers. The producer reaches around the levels in the distribution system, sells directly to the client, and *pulls* the product through the distribution system. In the other system, the producer *pushes* the product onto and through the channels of distribution, leaving all the selling to the middleman.

Since in our society selling adds more value to a business than filling orders, the gross margins granted under a push strategy are higher than margins granted under a pull strategy. This is yet another illustration of the basic principle that gross margin is compensation for services provided. A middleman who does more is paid more.

The Importance of Recognizing the Middleman's Interests

Let us look at an example of how important it is to bend to the middleman's interests. One aim of most family planning programs is increasing the use of contraceptives by both men and women. Some who need contraceptives will visit a clinic, undergo a medical examination, receive instruction in birth control technique, and perhaps even receive the contraceptives themselves. This, one would guess, is the course preferred by the family planners. Another course is to do without contraception, still a major response to the problem, perhaps the major response. Some rely on friends for advice, and others prescribe for themselves. All of these ways, with the exception of doing without, require the cooperation, or at least tolerance, of pharmacists. They can, if they wish, provide birth control information to those who ask, and they decide whether to display contraceptives or keep them under the counter.

Figure 11.1
Push and Pull Strategies

Push Strategy

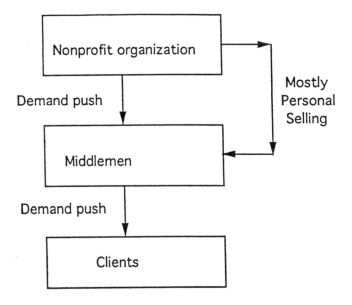

Pull Strategy

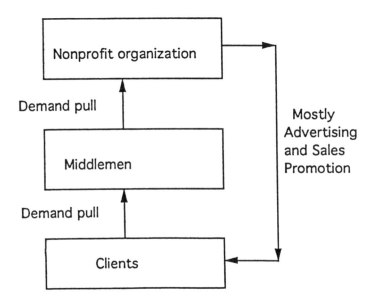

At first glance, enrolling the pharmacists in birth control programs is an appealing idea. There are many more drugstores than family planning centers (or public health offices) and they are everywhere—there are some 50,000 in the United States. Even more important, most people expect to find contraceptives in drugstores.

Let us look at some research. Ninety-two pharmacists in Hawaii returned a mail questionnaire in which they answered questions on their practices and beliefs concerning contraceptives.[8] They reported they had learned nothing about contraception in school. From their knowing nothing it follows immediately that most felt their knowledge of condoms, foams, creams, jellies, and the pill was adequate, much as any layman might feel. But less than half felt adequately informed about the more up-to-date IUD or sterilization or abortion. Most approved the use of contraceptives by married couples, and two-thirds approved their use by those who were not married and under twenty.

Their role in providing information was modest—4 percent were asked for advice fifteen times a week or more. (By way of comparison, for nonprescription items such as aspirin and fungicides, 53 percent were asked fifteen times a week or more.) Twice as many women asked for information as men.

These pharmacists routinely displayed contraceptives for women but not for men. Only one pharmacist displayed condoms in self-service counters; 13 percent did not carry them at all, and 85 percent sold them only on request. One pharmacist went so far as to require a prescription for this nonprescription item. With contraceptives used by women, foams, jellies, and so on, the proportions were different: Almost 60 percent displayed them on self-service counters, 20 percent sold them only on request, 9 percent only on prescription, and 7 percent did not even carry them.

One reason for keeping male contraceptives under the counter was that displaying them was illegal. At least that is what one-quarter of the respondents believed, although it was not true. One in seven said they did not display contraceptives because the public "would not like it"; one in nine said that they did not like it, that displaying contraceptives ran counter to their personal feelings.

In a roundabout fashion the authors of this study propose enlisting pharmacists in the cause of family planning.

Only eight percent of the pharmacists reported that they dispensed literature on birth control obtained from family planning organizations; thirty-one percent dispensed such literature provided by pharmaceutical manufacturers. One wonders whether any voluntary organizations have designed and made available family planning information and instructional materials designed specifically for distribution by the pharmacists.[9]

Yes, the marketer thinks, but is it in the pharmacists' interest to do more than merely distribute such material? Could they be expected to do more than passively display such material when it was provided? A first guess would be no, but the proposal could be researched and even tested. As it stands, this proposal is guilty of failing to take into account the pharmacists' interests and concerns. For the family planner there can be no more fundamental mistake.

The Importance of Recognizing Clients' Interests

How can one reduce smoking and drinking among teenagers? By passing a law that says no one may sell to those under a certain age? We can all guess the results. Young people have often viewed such restrictions with indifference. As have retailers, who run few risks of selling to those underage.

Why not attempt to restrict distribution then? Several states have begun experiments to restrict vending machines. Utah, for example, prohibits cigarette vending machines in public places. Pittsburgh has approved a requirement that the machines accept only tokens whose sale can be controlled.[10]

What can one expect of such efforts? Casual smokers will find it a bit harder to buy cigarettes. Heavy smokers will not be inconvenienced, once they adjust to the new scheme. There will be an effect, but it will be a small one.

The point is that convenience is not all that important an interest to young smokers. Make cigarettes less convenient to buy and most young smokers will adapt. (The way to discourage young smokers is with a stiff tax on cigarettes; but America being America a good deal of the tax would be undone by smuggling.)

FOUR MANAGEMENT ISSUES

By way of continuing our discussion of distribution, we consider four important issues that arise: first, whether to use distributors at all; second, how many distributors are needed; third, how to set objectives; and fourth, how to manage decor.

The First Issue: Should an NPO Sell Direct to Its Clients?

That is, should it even use distributors? This is a classic problem in business. The issue is: Should the firm use middlemen, or should it go direct and sell to its customers without using them. The decision rests on the complex interplay of market, product, middlemen, company, and financial factors. If, for example, the number of customers is small and concentrated in a few cities or regions, if the product has a high bulk-to-weight ratio, if good middlemen are hard to find because the company is relatively new, distributing direct is what might be expected. One would expect to find middlemen used where, say, order sizes tend to be small, customers are widely dispersed, the product is standardized and needs little technical support, and management lacks both experience in running a sales force and the financial resources to build one.

Most nonprofit organizations value their backers highly and do not relish letting others deal with them. They go after backers directly—important ones in person, small fry by mail or other advertising. There are a few exceptions. The United Way and the United Negro College Fund are examples of cooperative organizations of citizens and social welfare agencies (or Negro colleges) who, in the interest of lower costs and reduced competition, serve as fundraising middlemen for their member agencies. What functions does United Way perform?

Physical distribution: None, other than distributing pledge cards, posters, and the like.

Contact: Communicates the purposes of fundraising middleman and of member agencies. Some general advertising. Attempts to stimulate volunteers to ask for funds.

Financing, risk bearing: Bears risk that donors will not fulfill their pledges.

Negotiating: Establishes and maintains relations with employers who sponsor United Way campaigns.

Sorting: Collects, then disperses money to client agencies.

There is another intermediary as well. Most United Way campaigns first enlist the cooperation of employers and then raise funds from their employees. So:

Member agencies band together to form a
Fund-raising middleman that enlists the cooperation of
Employers to permit solicitation of their
Employees, the source of funds.

In dealing with clients, nonprofits are much like businesses, in that some distribute through middlemen, some go direct, and some do both. As one example of doing both, take the Boy Scouts, which owns two retail outlets itself but distributes most of its equipment through some 3,000 retailers. Another example is that of the large museum that distributes some of its own publications locally through its own staff, but uses a commercial publisher to distribute general publications and a university press to distribute more scholarly books. A third example is a blood bank. A blood bank needs donors. Typically, it has one central location to which donors are expected to come. The inconvenience of the trip and the wait and any monetary costs are borne by the donor. This may not generate enough blood, simply because the system is too inconvenient for many donors. So the blood bank goes to them in mobile units. Now it is the blood bank that bears most of the costs, and they are substantial. Now it is both reaching out through intermediaries—churches, universities, and businesses that serve as hosts—and going direct through its central blood bank.

The decision about whether or not to go direct does not arise very often. Typically, it arises only when a nonprofit organization comes into being, or when it substantially alters its marketing programs, say, by adding different services or seeking new target markets. For example, when a state first sets up a state lottery it must decide whether to license sales agents, set up its own outlets, or to do both. Once the lottery is in operation this particular decision is unlikely to arise again, since all marketing logic dictates that new games be distributed through existing channels.

Early in its life, Population Services International of Chapel Hill, North Carolina, which puts out information on birth control and sells contraceptives, became the exclusive U.S. agent for two "remarkable and highly popular British condoms."[11] How should they be distributed? There are normal distribution channels for condoms—drugstores and vending machines—where a man would expect to buy them, but he would have to ask for them because, at the time, they were (usually) kept under the counter, not put on display. Because one of the reasons for founding Population Services was to distribute birth control devices more widely, it made little sense to use the very channels its founders felt were inadequate.

So they gave up the possibility of widespread but under-the-counter distribution, rather than try to encourage pharmacists to display condoms. As a result, they were forced into selling direct. They considered opening retail shops displaying and selling condoms, modeled after Swedish "Birds and Bees" shops where such items are sold along with mod clothes and soda fountain items, but they rejected the idea. The only way they could reach a mass audience without using existing channels seemed to be by using the mails, which was the distribution channel they chose. This decision to go direct came about largely as a result of beliefs of PSI's founders as to what PSI was and what it should stand for, in other words, its mission. It would be hard to find such examples among business firms where the mission of the company determined its distribution channels, because profitability usually dominates.

Going Direct with Your Own Service Outlets

Most nonprofits provide services, not products. Since they must be made (mostly) by hand, since they cannot be stored, most services must be distributed direct. That does not mean the nonprofit organization cannot take its service producers on the road and make its services more accessible. It merely means that ultimately the client must come to the point of manufacture—the theater, the exhibition, the historic site, the bus stop, the health maintenance organization, the park, the classroom.

The two basic issues in site location are the where and the when.

The where. Marketers would like to site service outlets so that clients would incur only modest T costs to find and use the facility. The easier the outlet is to find and use, the more likely it is clients will come and the more likely they will return. This is the basic rationale underlying the location of city parks, athletic facilities, and street clinics.

The when. This is just as important. When should the outlet open for the day and when should it close? Hospitals never close but street clinics could do so. Services must be produced when clients want them because, as we have seen, services cannot be stored. Clients will not be shy about turning down attractive services offered at the wrong time, like say a bracing sail in November at Hurricane Island, an Outward Bound school in Maine. Campers want to go to camp in the summer when it is warm and when they are not in school.

Where and when clients want services are not completely set by fate. By changing other elements of the marketing mix an NPO can encourage clients to come or to stay away. Theaters charge more on weekends when demand is strong, because theatergoers are willing to pay more; and they charge less on weeknights, because theatergoers won't pay as much. In this way they discourage demand on weekends and stimulate it on weekdays. A reservation system can help shift the when. Mamouth Cave National Park in Kentucky does not take visitors as they come. There is a limit on the number of daily tours in the caves and a limit on the size of the parties. So the park requires a reservation. Without it, no tour.

The Operations Viewpoint

The operations people are powerfully interested in these questions as well. The costs of maintaining and operating a group of service outlets depends mostly on the capacity of the service outlets. That is, it does not so much depend on the number of clients but on the maximum number of clients for which the system was designed. Once a system—say, a 3,000-student college—is up and running, costs won't differ much whether the college has 3,200 students or 2,900. Another way of saying this is that many NPOs are high fixed-cost operations: Once in operation, costs don't vary much as the number of clients changes.

While the marketer argues for low T costs in the form of convenient location and easy opening hours, the operations people dream of their own form of a rational world, one in which costs of operation are kept down. That is, while marketing talks serving clients, operations talks efficiency, often the efficiency of a single service outlet.

So the director of the NPO has to weigh the two: To lower T costs the NPO usually (or often) has to bear higher costs of operations; to lower operations costs clients have to bear higher T costs.

The Second Issue: How Intense Should the NPO's Distribution Be?

Whether an organization goes direct or not, it must also decide how intense its distribution is to be. The more coverage given a market, the more intense the distribution.

The intensity of distribution varies across product types. Military recruiting offices are found in every city of any size, but government-run bookstores are not, there being five in Washington and only nineteen in the rest of the country.[12]

Table 11.1
One Measure of Intensity of Distribution for Eight State Lotteries

	Population (in millions)	Number of Agents	Population per agent
Connecticut	3.1	3,500	900
Massachusetts	5.7	3,500	1,600
Maryland	3.9	3,000	1,300
Michigan	9.0	8,000	1,100
New Hampshire	.7	900	800
New Jersey	7.3	5,000	1,500
New York	13.3	8,300	2,200
Pennsylvania	11.8	11,000	1,100

Source: David Weinstein and Lillian Deitch, *The Impact of Legalized Gambling* (New York: Praeger, 1974), pp. 26, 54.

The intensity of distribution even varies within the same product type. The figures in Table 11.1 show the intensity of distribution for eight state lotteries as measured by the population per retail sales agent. The median figure is 1,200 people per sales agent, but there is considerable variation. New York's figure is particularly high, which means that the intensity of distribution in New York is much lower than in the other states, and New Yorkers have a harder time finding a sales agent.

Clients' interests in convenience are better served by many outlets, but the interests of middlemen are better served by fewer outlets. Remember ticket agents, before computerized ticket services? To the consumer, the most convenient way would be to have a ticket agent on every corner. But too many outlets would not serve the agents' interests, because the sales volume would be so small that few agents would want to enter the business. (And in fact it would not serve theatergoers' interests in variety either, because the selection of tickets held by any one ticket agent would be too scanty.) Now think of the TKTS scheme discussed in Chapter 4. TKTS has one box office, in Times Square, which is convenient only to theatergoers already in Times Square, which, of course, just happens to be where all the theaters are; but the selection of shows and ticket prices is exceptional, and anyone who shows up at the box office is likely to get a ticket. Of course, having only one box office makes it easy for the TKTS people, and for the shows that must send over their tickets.

Marketers in business divide intensity of distribution roughly into three levels: *Intensive distribution* means that the product is widely available, and that any outlet that wants to carry the product can carry it. *Exclusive distribution* means only one outlet per geographic area can carry the product, and the geographic area can be very large indeed—only one importer may have the right to distribute a French cognac in all of Australia. *Selective distribution* is an in-between situation, in which only some of the available outlets can distribute a product.

As the word "selective" suggests, outlets are picked over: Many are called but few are chosen. Let us look at exclusive distribution first.

Exclusive distribution. As a way of illustrating what exclusive distribution means and also to show that I am willing to take my own medicine, let me follow my own advice from Chapter 4 and try to explain how it is that in most cities, all but the largest, there is only one animal shelter. This is what we observe. What does it tell us about the process by which people adopt pets? Let us build the analysis on the model of client decision making.

First, problem recognition: How do people decide that they are going to adopt a pet? Right at the start, the notion that "people" adopt is inept. What segments are we talking about? My guess is that those most likely to adopt a pet have young children and are themselves young, say, under thirty-five. Let us say this is the target market. Now, how does the target market decide? I do not know. For most people, that is, for most members of the target market, the process probably takes several months. It is without question a decision that can be postponed, if need be, and it is made infrequently, perhaps only once or twice in a lifetime.

Note that just because problem recognition is the first stage in the process, it does not mean that it counts for very much as far as the nonprofit organization is concerned. Here is such a case. Although it might be nice to know how adopters come to decide that they are going to adopt a pet, it is probably irrelevant to the marketing strategy of most animal shelters. Instead they define their mission as filling a demand, not stimulating it. Animals not adopted are destroyed. There are in this country a dozen or so shelters, however, who by policy never destroy animals. For them it is quite important to understand this first stage of the process.[13] The lesson here is that analysis of client behavior should not be done without good cause.

Second, search for information: What pet should I get? What does it cost to buy and to keep? Where do I get one? How do I take care of it? And, most important for the animal shelter, Should I buy one or try to get one free? If free, from whom, a neighbor or the pound? Potential adopters have several sources of information: books about pets, talking to the owner of the local pet store, looking in the window of the pet store. More likely, they will talk to other pet owners and draw on their own experience with pets, either their own or pets of others. As to which animal to adopt, the most important source of information is seeing and inspecting the animal in the shelter. Probably little money will be spent searching for information, and the adopter is probably in no rush, except where the animal is to be given as a present (say) for a child's birthday. There is little perceived social or financial risk involved, but there may be some concern on the part of the adopter as to the health of the pet, because it is not always easy to tell whether an animal is healthy or not; that is, some adopters will perceive some functional risk. Reassurance on this functional risk probably comes from the adopter's trusting the shelter.

Evaluation and decision are the third and fourth steps and will almost certainly take place in the pet store or the animal shelter. Presumably, the adopter goes to the animal shelter because he does not want to pay much for his pet, but the important consideration is not OOP costs for the pet but T costs. Most probably go to the animal shelter expecting to pick up a pet, rather than going merely to look; and most do not have a clear idea of what they want. Instead they look until they find something they like (much the way a man buys a tie). Because the adopters do not have a good idea of what they want, they want a shelter that has many animals, thus catering to their interest in variety.

Finally, postpurchase evaluation. The adopter takes the pet home and sees how the animal works out. In marketing jargon, the adopter is sampling the animal, and if he does not like the sample, he may well return the animal to the shelter. Most adopters are probably satisfied with their new pets, and they serve as a source of information to other potential adopters for many years. There is very little repeat buying.

Although much of this is conjecture, it seems to make some sense, and it does explain the fact that the animal shelter needs to have only one place of operation. Because the decision is made infrequently and the decision to adopt probably takes several months to resolve, travel time to the shelter is of little importance to the adopter. Travel time forms a small portion of the T costs of adoption. A single place of operation also serves adopters' interests in variety. In any city at any time, there are only so many animals available for adoption. If there is only one shelter, all the animals must be there, giving clients more choice. With more than one shelter, clients would have less choice, but more convenience. My guess, and it is only a guess, is that most adopters would be willing to take a longer drive to the shelter if the shelter had a wider selection.

Like all such armchair analysis, this one may be wrong. The animal shelter can do some cheap marketing research by asking its existing clients to stick a pin in a map to show where they live. In short order the size of the shelter's trading area will form on the map. Along with some simple questions on demographics, such a simple study should give the shelter much useful information on its clients. (What such a study misses is clients who do not patronize the shelter.)

What do we learn from this about exclusive distribution? It works best for products that are purchased infrequently, are consumed over a long time period, and require information (in this case, in the form of wide selection) or service to fit the clients' interests. In addition, exclusive distribution often serves the middleman's interests as well, giving him protection from competition, perhaps an assured market, and thus the incentive to invest the time and resources needed to develop that market. A ticket agent with exclusive rights to tickets will work to develop all the performing arts; but if there is a ticket agent on every corner, none of them will do anything more than handle what demand comes their way.

Intensive distribution. Now let us look at the other extreme, intensive distribution.[14] Whereas exclusive distribution means only one outlet, intensive distribution means many outlets. At its most extreme it means that the marketer distributes through any outlet that is willing to carry the product. This is the

Table 11.2

Estimated Ratio of Population to Number of Retail Outlets Needed to Distribute Condoms in India, by Size of the Market

Size	Number of Persons per Outlet
1 million and over	650
100,000 to 1 million	600
50,000 to 100,000	500
20,500 to 50,000	622
Towns under 20,000	700
Large villages with urban characteristics	725
Other villages	2400

Source: Indian Institute of Management Study, cited in Timothy R. L. Black and Philip D. Harvey, "The Commercial Distribution of Contraceptives," in *New Concepts in Contraception,* edited by Malcolm Potts and Clive Woods (Baltimore: University Park Press, 1972), p.82.

way the IRS distributes its tax forms—through any organization that wants to carry them (and of course through the mails). Perhaps the most intensely distributed product in the United States is soft drinks. They are on sale almost everywhere.[15]

Intensive distribution makes behaving correctly (or buying) easy, or easier, and hence it aims mainly at the satisfaction of client interests in convenience. Other consumer interests, such as an interest in variety or in information, are not well filled by this type of distribution. Since the retailer sees the product he carries carried by many other retailers, his interest in protection from competition is poorly served and he will do little to sell the product beyond stocking it.

Contraceptives in poor countries are commonly distributed through medical channels such as health centers, clinics, and hospitals, but hundreds of millions, perhaps billions, of people never see a doctor in their fugitive lives; and as the amount of medical care supplied in a country is influenced strongly by national income, the poorest countries, which most need access to contraceptives, are least likely to have access. Contraceptives in rich countries are commonly distributed through commercial middlemen, and the distribution is intensive; in the United States drugstores carry contraceptives, and since drugstores are practically everywhere, so are contraceptives.

Much the same thing can be said of poor countries, but in them it is not drugstores that are everywhere but rather petty retailers, that is, retail shops in general. Unlike the use of medical channels to distribute contraceptives, the use of petty retailers requires little extra capital or human resources, and hence, except for the programmed costs of establishing and maintaining distribution through such middlemen as well as the gross margin paid them, the extra costs are small.

This is the proposal put forward by Black and Harvey, and as an example they estimate the number of retail outlets required to distribute condoms in different size markets in India (see Table 11.2).[16]

It is not to be expected that petty retailers will welcome contraceptives, because typically they will be conservative businessmen, little inclined to run risks and short of capital. The marketing program must surmount these likely obstacles by offering the retailer attractive gross margins, credit, display materials, perhaps free samples and incentives to display and promote contraceptives. In addition, the marketing program must also reach the middlemen, who are typically wholesalers and who sell to the petty retailers. The wholesalers' salesmen must find their interests attended to in the marketing program, lest they simply ignore it.

The Third Issue: What Objectives Should an NPO Set for Its Distributors?

Objectives for the distribution portion of the overall marketing program follow from the role of the middlemen in that strategy. If middlemen are to train clients in the use of a product, then training becomes an objective for the marketing program.

Without question the single most important objective is availability. Above all, middlemen have the job of making the products and services available to target segments. This means selecting the right middlemen to handle the product, and it means ensuring that once within the middlemen's place of business the product or service continues to be accessible. Availability by itself is vague, but it can be translated into objectives that can be measured, and hence are useful. Middlemen should:

1. Maintain inventories. This is normally measured in terms of the percentage of orders lost because middlemen were out of the item. (The marketing term is "out-of-stock.") Normally, middlemen would be expected to weed out of inventory overage stock.

2. Display. It is not enough to have inventory on hand. It must also be available within the store, or place of business. This is precisely the problem discussed earlier about the pharmacists who sell condoms only on request. Marketers in business measure display in terms of amount of shelf space devoted to their product (in both absolute amounts and as a proportion of all space devoted to that product).

3. Cover assigned markets. A public health agency that wishes to display health information for travelers in the offices of travel agents is not so much interested in the proportion of travel agents it reaches as in the proportion of travelers exposed to its brochures. It might well reach 60 percent of the travelers by being in only 20 percent of the travel agents. And if the agency had the resources only for doing a good job with the 20 percent, its objective would become maintaining effective distribution to reach 60 percent of the traveler market.

4. Sell and inform. Many middlemen carry part of the nonprofit organization's responsibility to sell or to communicate with target audiences. For one organization this may mean nothing more than that the middleman display a poster or other point-of-sale materials. But for another, the middleman might be expected to involve himself

substantially in the client's affairs and furnish him with a product or service close to what he needs; or to use mass media to reach the intended audience. For example, in running the MBA Admission Forum, which is a college fair for prospective MBA students, the two coordinating agencies, the Graduate Management Admission Council and the Association of MBA Executives, undertake to promote the forum. In Chicago, in 1979, this meant press releases to local news media, dissemination of a radio public service announcement, display ads in the Sunday Arts and Fun School Section of the Chicago *Tribune* and the Sunday Chicago *Sun-Times,* two daily run-of-the-paper ads in the *Tribune,* two run-of-the-paper ads in the daily *Sun-Times,* ads in *Chicago Magazine,* the Chicago edition of *Time* and *Reader,* and ads in a number of campus newspapers in the Chicago area.

The Fourth Issue: Site Decor

Those marketers with their own service facilities must attend to one final aspect of distribution—the physical characteristics of the facility, the site decor. The cleanliness of the facility, its general appearance, the state of repair of the furniture in the public rooms (waiting rooms, classrooms, theaters, railroad cars), the degree of privacy and comfort for clients, the demeanor and appearance of the staff—all can contribute in some measure to the staff's motivation and efficiency, and even more important, to clients' satisfaction.

You already know this. A handful of the top universities deliberately court master architects to enliven their campuses. A library should look and feel like a library; its appearance should make patrons want to lower their voices. At summer camps campers do not want to live in cinder block huts or dormitories. They want to live in tents and log cabins.

It would be easy to make too much of this issue of decor. We are talking, after all, about a superficial aspect of service quality. Certainly, the quality of the core services delivered by the NPO is far more important. But decor may count heavily when clients and backers have little else to go on or when they lack the capacity to independently evaluate a service. Then surface appearances do count.

A Final Word

This chapter has laid heavy emphasis on the traditional middlemen who, as independent businesses, do things for pay. When a nonprofit organization distributes its products or services through such middlemen, the organization must cater to the interests of the middlemen. Above all this means financial interests.

But throughout the chapter there have been examples of middlemen who distribute things not for pay: pharmacists displaying birth control information, policemen handing out information on avoiding burglaries, and so on. The organization that uses such channels as these must still put together a marketing program that caters to the needs of its middlemen, even though these interests no longer include financial interests. This resembles the discussion of T costs in Chapter 2. When there are prices, one analyzes behavior using T costs, which (naturally) include OOP costs. When there are no prices, one analyzes behavior using T costs. When distributors receive compensation for distributing products and services, the marketer must adapt to the distributors' interests, which (naturally) include financial interests. When middlemen receive no compensation, the marketer must adapt to the distributors' interests. Moral: Know thy middleman.

QUESTIONS

1. Assume that a state is rethinking its entire procedure for conducting elections and that one of the issues to be analyzed is how many polling booths there should be and where they should be located. As best you can, analyze this issue, using the concepts developed in this chapter and in previous chapters.

2. Why is it that private and public universities have such different distribution strategies? Private universities rarely have multiple campuses, and when they do the multiples are usually specialized educational units—like a center of oceanographic studies or a museum. Public universities often have many campuses.

3. Many government services are distributed through nongovernmental agencies. But except for postage stamps, postal services are available only at the post office. Why is this the case? Would it be a good idea for the Postal Service to try to enlist middlemen to distribute its services?

4. The chapter says that soft drinks are probably the most intensively distributed of all products in the United States. What do you think is the most intensively distributed product of a nonprofit organization? The correct answer is probably a public good, like the protection afforded the citizenry by our military forces. The citizen has this service wherever he goes, whether he wants it or not, without lifting a finger. But what about products and services that are not public goods but are distributed through middlemen (profit or nonprofit)?

5. One would hypothesize that states with larger populations will have more lottery sales agents. Examine this hypothesis using the data given earlier in the chapter and describe the relationship by fitting a line to the data. What do you conclude?

NOTES

1. Joe Mandese, "Going Public." *Marketing & Media Decisions* (September 1990): 34–35.
2. What might be some of the "other reasons?"
3. The average sale of a university press book is below 1,500, a sales volume that makes a book as interesting to a bookseller as a winter thaw.
4. Gary Bridge, "Cultural Vouchers." *Museum News* (March–April 1976): 21–26. The eight institutions were the American Museum of Natural History, El Musco del Barrio, the Museum of Modern Art, the New York Zoological Society, the New Museum,

the Brooklyn Museum, the New York Botanical Garden, and the Museum of Contemporary Crafts.

5. A longer discussion is found in Gary Bridge, "Citizen Choice in Public Services: Voucher Systems," in *Alternatives for Delivering Public Services,* edited by E.S. Savas (Boulder, Colo.: Westview Press, 1977), pp. 51–109. Also see William J. Baumol, "On Two Experiments in the Pricing of Theater Tickets," in *Economics and Human Welfare,* edited by Michael J. Boskin (New York: Academic Press, 1979), pp. 44–51.

6. In addition, they are smaller, less forbidding, and more familiar, which are important features to some of their clients, and because they are in closer touch with their neighborhoods, they may be more responsive to their needs.

7. This is overstated. The bookstore also has to decide how many books to order, return unsold books, trace lost orders, untangle errors, prevent shoplifting, stay open all year round while doing 60 percent of its business in a week or two, deal with professors who order textbooks and then tell their students they need not buy them, handle special orders, and run a number of other businesses—magazines, records, beer mugs, clothing, and stationery as well as trade books. I would not want to run a college bookstore.

8. M. Joyce Rumel, Laurence Reich, Lorraine Stringfellow, and Ronald J. Pion, "The Pharmacist's Neglected Role." *Family Planning Prospectives* 3 (October 1971): 80–82.

9. Rumel et al., "The Pharmacist's Neglected Role," p. 82.

10. "Youths Mock Ban on Cigarette Vending Machines." *New York Times,* November 23, 1990.

11. Population Services International, Harvard Business School case (4-572-064). PSI has since changed its name to Population Planning Associates.

12. In Atlanta, Birmingham, Boston, Canton, Chicago, Cleveland, Dallas, Denver, Houston, Detroit, Jacksonville, Kansas City, Los Angeles, Milwaukee, New York, Philadelphia, Pueblo, San Francisco, and Seattle. Besides all-important political considerations, what other factors would have led to the selection of these nineteen cities?

13. Willima Mathewson, "With Right Tactics, It's Easy to Market a Three-Legged Cat." *Wall Street Journal,* March 6, 1975, p. 1 ff. According to the article, 85 percent of the cats and dogs that pass through animal shelters or animal control agencies each year are destroyed.

14. A better term would be "extensive distribution," but it is too late to expect the familiar term to be displaced.

15. The reader with some idle time may enjoy doing a small study. Note how many businesses and offices in your area sell soft drinks or have vending machines that sell them. Estimate the time to walk to each. Plot locations and times on a small map. Now you have a picture of intensive distribution.

16. Timothy R. L. Black and Philip D. Harvey, "The Commercial Distribution of Contraceptives," in *New Concepts in Contraception,* edited by Malcolm Potts and Clive Wood (Baltimore: University Park Press, 1972), pp. 69–96.

Chapter 12

Prices and Other Costs Borne by Clients

This chapter deals with price. At least it appears to deal with price. In fact, nonprofit marketers cannot confine their analysis solely to price. Price is an important part of out-of-pocket costs, and OOP costs are in turn one of the three elements that make up T costs. T costs influence clients' behavior, not just price. To take a simple example, NPOs sometimes set a zero price to encourage their clients by reducing the barriers, that is, the costs, that inhibit their behavior. However, to repeat an earlier chapter, a zero price does not mean that there is no cost borne by the client.

There will be situations, nevertheless, where T costs are mostly price. In such situations it does little harm to ignore the other two components of T costs and pretend that there is only price.

INTRODUCTION

Price goes by many names—fee, tuition, charge, donation, duty, contribution, offering, gift, rate, fare, toll, tariff, consideration, and dues. One could argue for taxes, tribute, and confiscation, saying that they are the price one pays for governmental services; but this strains the meaning of the word, and such questions are not addressed by marketers anyway.

All nonprofit organizations face pricing problems. Nonprofit businesses, of course, face pricing problems similar to those encountered by business firms. Many nonprofit organizations sell some of their output and must price it. A city is one example. As a commonwealth organization it provides many services free; for example, police, firemen, schools, and roads. It also sells many services, and each requires a price. There will be parking fees and fines, and perhaps charges for extra police protection at stadiums or theaters. There may be fees for garbage collection or industrial waste disposal, and the schools may charge for books or levy special lab fees. There may be permits required to use the tennis courts, greens fees, tickets sold for the stadium, and fees charged concessionaires.

The city hospital will certainly have to set a number of prices for rooms, drugs, and medical treatments. There may be fees for landing at the airport, renting a hangar, or using a bridge. The city may sell maps and tax real estate transactions, and inevitably there will be licenses for, to name a few, pawnbrokers, sound trucks, barbers, taxis, rooming houses and pushcarts, bowling alleys and bars, marriages and dogs.

All nonprofit organizations face pricing problems, but not all nonprofit organizations charge prices. By tradition, design, or the requirements of their charters, these organizations set prices at zero. This is a phenomenon almost unknown in business, the only important exception being the prices set by broadcast media. The television audience does not pay a price to watch TV, and the choice of programs is made without consideration of monetary costs. (This is because until cable and pay-per-view there was no way of excluding people who refused to pay.)

To a marketer price is not an objective fact, but a perception. What counts, therefore, is how clients and backers perceive prices. Of course, presumably there is some link between perceived price and true price. In those cases where the marketer knows, or surmises on the basis of his model of client behavior, that perceived price and true price are roughly the same, he can proceed to work with the true price. But where clients show that they do not know the true price, or that they seriously misjudge it, the marketer will have to base his recommendations on their perceptions. University tuition provides a vivid example. A student who goes four years to a state college pays, let us say, $4,000 a year for his tuition, or $16,000 in all. Yet in the same four nine-month periods, working without a college degree at say five dollars an hour, he could earn $32,000 before taxes, and, let us say, $26,000 after taxes. It appears that his education has cost him $16,000 when in fact it has cost him $26,000 in addition to the $16,000 for tuition.[1] Note as well that tuition is visible, an OOP cost, while the foregone wages are invisible, an opportunity cost; and thus the real issue here is not price at all, but the T costs of education. Yet when do the students protest? When the tuition is raised. What should command their attention instead is an increase in the average wage.[2]

Marketers must train themselves to use perceived prices and T costs, and they must count themselves lucky when the perceptions are close enough to true prices (and T costs) so that they can avoid the slight trouble of measuring clients' perceptions.

TWO IDEAS FROM ECONOMICS

In this section, the relation between costs and prices is discussed in an effort, probably misplaced and unlikely to succeed, to undo the reader's certitude that in the beginning there were costs and that prices were created later. Then we turn to the issue of consumer surplus.

The First Idea: The Primary Influences on Price Are Demand and Competition

Why is it bad form to work from costs to price? It is not bad form. What is bad form is thinking that costs *cause* prices, or rather that an increase in costs forces an increase in prices.

To be sure, there are situations when costs do have a strong influence on prices, or they appear to. The U.S. Postal Service raises its rates when its costs go up, as do regulated industries like AT&T and monopolies like my local electrical utility, a nonprofit cooperative with the singular name, Middle Tennessee Electric Membership Cooperative. When a gift shop in a hospital buys a gross of trinkets, it will set its price by simply marking up the landed store cost.

One often encounters stories in the press that show cost increases leading to price increases:

The highest annual tuition ever charged by an institution of higher education will be the $12,500 that entering students will have to pay at the medical school of Georgetown University in Washington.

Another medical school in Washington, the one affiliated with George Washington University, will charge incoming students $9,000 a year tuition.

Both institutions were forced to adopt steep tuition increases because of the expiration this year of the District of Columbia Medical and Dental Manpower Act under which Congress had provided assistance.[3]

Here the simple relationship between costs and price becomes less simple. Can it really be that the costs of medical education at George Washington are so much lower than at Georgetown as to permit George Washington's tuition to be 28 percent below Georgetown's? Dare we entertain the possibility that Georgetown is wasteful? There is another oddity here. How is it that these tuition increases were not made earlier? Medical schools usually need money, and if Georgetown can still enroll the quality students it wants at $12,500, it could have enrolled them at that price a year earlier. (I am neglecting inflation here, but without any damage to the argument.) Why didn't it raise its tuition earlier?

A gift shop in the hospital also raises difficulties, as does my electric utility. In the gift shop, we will find some items priced to give a gross margin of 35 percent, with others priced to give a gross margin of 50 percent. If costs cause price, do they also cause gross margins? If not, why do the gross margins differ? Finally, the Middle Tennessee Electric Membership Cooperative pays TVA one price for all its power, but the rate it charges homeowners is higher than the rate it charges businesses and industrial plants.

There are so many obvious examples where cost has nothing to do with price that one wonders how anyone could continue to believe otherwise. Think first of important matters, those dealing with your own financial life. Take a house. Suppose the time has come to sell the house that you bought for $80,000. Will you use a calculator to figure your costs and then set a price? Why not? Because if you did, it would have no meaning. Suppose it turns out that your house is now worth $135,000 but that the price you computed on the basis of your costs is $107,000. Your price will be $135,000, and the cost-based price will be forgotten. Suppose, on the other hand, the market value of the house has only risen to $87,000. Do you hope a prospective buyer will be comforted when you say, "It's true the market value is only $87,000, but I can show you the figures here that make it clear that my costs have been high and I have taken only a small extra for profit. Therefore, you must pay me $107,000." The only time a cost-based price turns out to be the right price is when there is a buyer at that price.

Labor markets operate in much the same way. Is your salary determined by the costs of your education and training and by any other costs you happen to feel are relevant? For example, what you need to earn to live as you wish to live? Nurses have long grumbled about the fact that they receive a lot of training but little money. Why do they not simply base their wages on costs?

At the same time, situations are often found where costs must differ and yet prices are roughly the same. Columbia University has to pay New York prices for the goods and services it buys, and we would be surprised to find that Brown University, in Providence, Rhode Island, has to pay more. Yet Brown's tuition was $15,871 in 1991 while Columbia's was $14,802. Brown's costs are lower, it appears, yet its price is higher.

Universities and performing arts organizations are good examples of these problems. Universities do not start with the cost of educating a student and then mark up the cost to reach a tuition. Performing arts organizations do not start with the costs of a performance and split it up among the tickets so that all costs are covered. Why not? For the same reason costs are ignored when pricing a house. Tickets must be sold for what they will bring, not for what it costs the performing arts organization to produce a performance. If a university (or a theater) set its prices on its costs without thinking, it would find itself priced out of the market and would end up with *less* revenue, not more.

The first rule of pricing, then, is that prices must adapt to what the market will pay, in a word, to demand. That is why universities do not set tuition at, say, $38,000, to cover what they consider their full costs. There is little demand for university education at that level, particularly when you add to the tuition the opportunity costs of an education. A symphony that derives only one-third of its income from ticket sales does not triple the cost of its tickets to cover its "full cost," because if it did, no one would come. It would go broke.

Imaginary costs. We can see the importance of demand by considering the Case of the Imaginary Costs. Given the many types of costs and given the errors that creep into forecasts of costs, it is not impossible that an organization will do its sums wrong and find a cost figure that is too high. What if it does not catch the error, however, and in ignorance figures a price and finds clients willing to pay? Now it discovers its error. Should it reduce its price? Suppose the organization includes as one of its costs an imaginary cost, but finds that the price based on the imaginary cost is a price clients are willing to pay.

What might such an imaginary cost be? A sunk cost is an imaginary cost. A nice example comes from the Oxford University Press, maker par excellence of dictionaries. The greatest, without question, is the OED, the Oxford English Dictionary, begun in 1888 to be finished within ten years, not finished for over fifty years, upon which the effort to update it began. It goes without saying that a dictionary is out of date as soon as it is published, but the last volume of the OED was published forty years after the first.

Now what about all the costs of preparing the dictionary, collecting cites, writing definitions, proofreading, and the like, now stretching back for a century? They are long since paid; they are unquestionably sunk, but they still worry about them at the Press. I interviewed the Marketing Director at the Press.[4] We were discussing how the Press had chosen a price for its compact disk version of the OED (plus the Supplement). He explained how he had muddled about trying one price, finding it way too high, and settling on a second that buyers seemed willing to pay. "Of course," he said, with a distinct note of regret in his voice, "no price can ever recover the development costs. They go back a century."

I was stunned. What he was saying was that the Press had a special kind of off-the-books accounting, a place in its memory where it stored a century's worth of development costs, keeping them ever fresh, against a better day when finally, decisively, someone would somehow pay them off. At least he knew that they had no relevance to the pricing of compact disks.

Here is yet another example of an imaginary cost. New York University works hard to make sure that continuing education programs pay their own way ("really pay" is the way the *New York Times* put it). As an example of this art, for a certain period each year it monitors which students check out books from the library, and how many they check out, so that it can include in its reckoning of costs a portion of the library's costs.[5] It then calls up from the vast deeps what it calls a full cost. But it is a conjuring trick. Full cost is an imaginary cost. We have been over this ground before, in Chapter 3. Students do not care about NYU's costs. They judge what they get for what they pay. If NYU wants to charge a certain price for continuing education it may justify the price in any way it wishes. If students will not pay, the justification is specious; if they do pay, the justification is unnecessary.

Competition. Demand is one force that destroys any simple relationship between cost and price. The second is competition. No matter what an organization's costs are, no matter what the best price is, if competitors are important in its markets, it must price with an eye to the competition.

Melissa D. Gerrity, a financial aid official at Harvard, said that a tuition target figure was set, usually with an eye to what competitors would probably be charging, and then room and board estimates were added to arrive at a total figure.

She said that the three amounts were "floated around" to faculty members and administrators and gradually refined with consideration of what "the politics of an eight percent increase or ten percent or whatever would be."[6]

If an organization's services are better than those of its competitors, it may be able to charge a premium. Perhaps that is why Georgetown charged $3,500 more than George Washington. Or perhaps the assumption that they compete with each other is false.

This fact of competition adds a pleasantry to NYU's laborious efforts to figure its costs. Since the only thing that counts is whether the price sticks, what NYU has done is tell its competitors what the market will bear. They can now go ahead and set their fees without the need for such imaginative accounting.

Objectives and mission. There is a third consideration as well, and that is what the organization is trying to accomplish. Businesses use price along with the other elements of the marketing mix to help them accomplish their overall goals. Nonprofits do the same, but with the added flexibility that they may, if they choose, break any supposed link between costs and price. Many nonprofits do not even pretend to cover their full costs with their prices. Certainly, this is the case with the universities, which incidentally makes the explanation of the increase in Georgetown's tuition all the more unsound. Since Georgetown's tuition does not cover its costs anyway, how compelling is the explanation that it has raised tuition because its costs went up? Presumably a more honest explanation would have been that Georgetown had lost one source of revenue, and, unable to make it up anywhere else, it decided to raise tuition by enough to make up for the lost revenue, and that given its competition and the nature of its students, Georgetown expected the increase to stick. This is not the same thing as saying that rising costs have driven up tuition.

Why is it, then, given all the obvious evidence to the contrary, that the belief that costs cause prices is almost ineradicable? For one thing, there are situations in which costs do in fact cause prices, provided that competition, organizational objectives, and clients permit. This is important enough to be said again: Contrary to what has been argued in the past several pages, cost does cause price *provided* the competition allows it, the clients pay it, and the organization's goals permit it. That these are not otiose qualifications will not have escaped the reader's attention.

Another reason why it is so easy to think that price increases are caused by cost increases is that price increases are often announced *as if* they were caused by cost increases. When is the best time for the general manager of the Bay Area Rapid Transit System to raise fares? Immediately after a new labor contract is signed. He could have raised fares six months before—he has little competition to worry about, demand is highly inelastic, and it would have served some of his organizational goals by generating more operating revenues, but no one raises fares before labor negotiations lest the union be driven to a frenzy of greed, and the politics of the fare increases dictate that the manager appear to be forced to raise fares. To conclude that because a price increase follows a cost increase, prices are caused by costs is the *post hoc propter hoc* fallacy from logic. We might as well argue that the savages who beat on upturned tubs during an eclipse of the moon do in fact drive away the devil who has tried to swallow it.

That costs cause prices seems to make sense for yet a third reason. When businesses, and nonprofit organizations, work up a price they usually start with cost and work toward price. But the sequence is not

It is more like this:

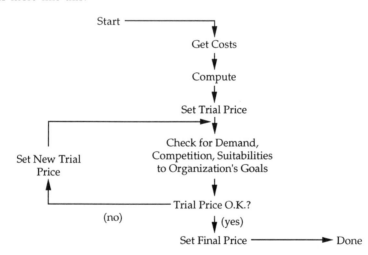

Finally, there are circumstances in which prices are flat out based on costs. A nonprofit druggist might have hundreds or thousands of items in stock. He cannot hope to set prices unless he uses a set of simple rules for translating

invoice costs into retail prices; but he can get away with this only so long as the prices at which he arrives are right in terms of his customers, his competition, and his own objectives.

In spite of all this, costs are important and one should not be in the activity of setting prices if he does not know his costs. But which costs? Relevant costs, which for most pricing decisions mean variable costs and incremental programmed costs; but they come after, not before. It is possible, and sometimes valuable, to use costs as a guide to a trial price. The best way to use costs is to ignore them at first, work out a trial price without even knowing costs, and then use costs to work out the implications of the proposed price.

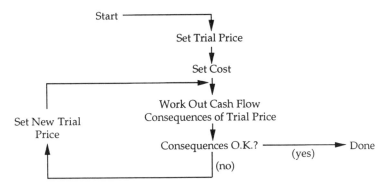

Say that a symphony is invited to play a pops concert for the annual dinner of the country club. The first step is for the general manager of the symphony to estimate what fee he thinks he can charge for the service. *Then* he should look to his costs, to see if the fee is large enough to cover the costs. Since this is a short-run decision, the only relevant costs are those that are variable or programmed. Nonvariable costs can be ignored. If, for example, the symphony must find an activity for its musicians because the contract calls for them to be paid, musicians' fees are irrelevant. If it must hire the musicians for an extra service not already covered by the contract, the extra musicians' fees must be considered. Even with a good estimate of the cash consequences of the concert in hand, the manager still may have other considerations to weigh, like whether it will help the symphony raise money by appearing at the country club and how the price quoted to the country club will affect prices they can charge other such groups.

The Second Idea: Consumer Surplus or There's Always Someone Who Will Pay More

As is the case with most fundamental economic concepts, the idea behind consumer surplus is rooted in common experience. Everyone has found himself buying something and getting a sweet deal, that is, paying a price lower than he was prepared to pay. I went once into Panglois, a bookstore in Harvard Square, looking for nothing in particular, and found a twelve-volume edition of Gibbon's *Decline and Fall of the Roman Empire* that had been published in London in 1837. The pages were in perfect condition, the margins were wide, the type was attractive; the maps were wonderful and had been hand-colored; but the once beautiful leather covers were decrepit and hanging loose. Still, I had always wanted to read Gibbon and I had never been able to bring myself to buy one of the ugly, cramped modern versions. Except for the covers, it was just what I wanted. I looked inside the cover of the first volume and found the price, three dollars, which meant all twelve volumes would be thirty-six dollars. It was a close thing—everything I love in a book, a book I wanted for my library, but those tattered covers—and at the time, on a student's budget, thirty-six dollars was a lot of money. I went to the bookseller and innocently asked how much the Gibbon cost. "Three dollars," she said.

I was willing to pay thirty-six dollars, but I got the set for three dollars. This difference between what a client (or consumer) is willing to pay and the price he does pay is called his consumer surplus. In this case, mine was thirty-three dollars.

The idea is easily seen by looking at a hypothetical demand schedule for an imaginary product (which is only sold one to a customer).

At a price of a	We expect to sell b	...and therefore earn a × b
$5	1	$5
4	3	12
3	5	15
2	10	20
1	18	18

The revenue to be realized at any of the five prices is in the last column. If we ignore the issue of costs, we would attract ten buyers with a $2 price and gross $20. Note that a $2 price excludes eight buyers (each buying one unit each) who would have bought at $1. Some of the ten who bought at $2 have gotten a good deal, just as I did when I bought my Gibbon. One buyer of the ten would have paid $5 for his purchase, but he had to pay only $2. Two more of the ten who bought at $2 would have paid $4, and another two would have paid $3 each. The total consumer surplus is the sum of the individual consumer surpluses: $3 + (2 × $2) + (2 × $1) = $9. Had the seller known better, had he been able to identify who was willing to pay more and somehow charge them more, he would have grossed $9 more. That is to say, he would have contrived to do the following:

Charge 1 buyer $5 and gross $5,

Charge 2 buyers $4 and gross $8,

Charge 2 buyers $3 and gross $6,

Charge 5 buyers $2 and gross $10,

which yields ten buyers paying $29, compared with the same ten buyers paying $20.

The implications of this have not escaped the businessmen, and over the years businesses with a substantial amount of monopoly power derived from patents or from other, less savory means have come up with a number of schemes for extracting some of the consumer surplus. But most cannot do this, and naturally, the buyers stay mum. Even I, with a Ph.D., knew better than to tell the bookseller that I was willing to pay thirty-six dollars.

Some ways to extract consumer surplus. A nonprofit organization has more flexibility, however, and it should work at uncovering those clients who are willing to bear higher OOP costs and then try to extract higher prices from them. As a simple example, the Metropolitan Opera has always added a suggested donation of 20 percent to the bills it sends its subscribers. Thus, the bill looks like this:

Season tickets	$2,900
Suggested donation	380
Total	$3,280

Not every subscriber donates, of course, but those who do are those who are willing to pay more for their tickets, and the Met has managed to extract some of their consumer surplus.

As another example, consider a prep school that holds a fundraising fair each year, at which it sells items donated by parents and friends. This year it receives from the mother of one student a stereo that lists for $400. The OOP cost to the school is clearly zero. What price should it set? One way would be to select a single price and hope that the stereo would sell at that price, but for a certainty someone would be willing to pay more, maybe even more than $400. But there are two pricing schemes that can extract some of the consumer surplus. One is an *ordinary auction,* which, if run by a skilled auctioneer, can uncover the highest price that some one person in the audience is willing to pay. A second scheme is the so-called *Dutch auction,* in which the price of the stereo is originally set at a very high level and then reduced bit by bit until someone buys. The price might be set at $600 at 7 P.M. and reduced twenty-five dollars every fifteen minutes, or $100 an hour, until it is sold. To buy the set, a buyer places a bid in writing and the stereo is sold as soon as the falling price reaches the highest bid. A buyer might submit a bid of $390. If there are no higher bids, the price will reach $400 at 8 P.M., and it will reach his bid when the price is next reduced at 8:15. With volunteers circulating to promote the stereo and solicit bids, the Dutch auction, like the regular auction, will come close to finding the highest single price that a person in the audience is willing to pay.

There is another situation where the notion of consumer surplus applies, and that is when prices are reduced. The problem is that in reducing prices the organization gives up some consumer surplus if it must charge the same price to everyone. The Boston Museum had this problem some years ago when it stayed open free on Tuesday evenings so that the poor could come. Free meant free to everyone, and everyone came in great numbers. The museum knew it, for the guards who worked in the coatroom described Tuesday evenings as "wall-to-wall minks."[7]

If the organization can figure out a way to charge different prices to different clients, it is on its way toward increasing its revenue. There is a standard way of pulling off this trick. It is to set a single price to everyone and then give discounts to those segments you wish to favor with lower prices. The way to reduce university tuition to impecunious students is not to reduce tuition to all, but to give scholarships to those deserving the lower tuition and let everyone else pay the full fare. Performing arts organizations hate empty seats because they represent lost revenues without any offsetting reduction in costs. How to fill them? Not by reducing the price of all tickets. That would give away some of the consumer surplus currently being extracted by the people who have already bought their tickets (or who would have bought at the original price). It is better to reduce ticket prices in such a way that the lower prices do not spoil the market for full-price tickets. There are so many examples at hand, some of them discussed elsewhere in this book, that the reader cannot fail to find them. Since it is good practice, and will sharpen the reader's skills at analysis—do it.

The moral of this discussion on consumer surplus is that *there are always some clients who are willing to pay more than the current price. There are always some backers who are willing to give more.* The nonprofit organization should work to find these segments.

WHY HAVE PRICES AT ALL?

Prices inform and prices allocate. A high price beckons suppliers to the market and frightens buyers away. A low price drives out the suppliers but brings a horde of buyers. Somewhere the willingness of the buyers to pay matches the willingness of the suppliers to produce, and supply equals demand. Prices have communicated to both buyer and seller in this situation, talking of profits and costs to one, and satisfaction of needs and T costs to the other.

Sometimes it happens that price cannot affect the supply in the short run. Fresh mushrooms last only a few days, although most merchants worth their salt will keep on trying to sell them. While they are on the market, they fetch what they can. If many mushrooms come to market, the price will fall; if only a few come, the price will rise. These price changes have nothing to do with calling for more supply. They simply ration what is already on the market. In like fashion a theater or an opera company has a fixed supply of performances and seats. It, too, must sell its seats for whatever it can get.

Many nonprofit organizations operate in nonprice markets, which means that they function without the clear and simple message of prices telling suppliers whether they should expand or contract their production, telling clients whether they should consume more or less. Most of the U.S. blood supply and all of the blood donated in the United Kingdom and Australia come from donors who receive nothing for their donation. These donors supply the blood that hospitals and surgeons demand on behalf of their patients.

What balances the demand for blood and the supply? How do we know there is not already an oversupply? Can we conclude that there is too much supply because 20 percent of the fresh blood donated each year is thrown away because it is overage?[8] When there is a shortage the price does not rise, because there is no price. If there were too much blood, how would donors know? The blood banks would turn them away, saying in essence that they should come back next month. Blood banks would have shorter hours, raising T costs of a donation by increasing the inconvenience of giving and the time it takes to give. And we might expect the medical definition of length of time a donor should wait before donating again to increase, reducing the safe number of donations from (say) five a year to three.[9]

When there is a shortage, blood banks try to lower the T costs of giving. They will put blood banks on wheels and take them to the donors. They will appeal for blood and concoct various ways of paying donors that do not involve money (give blood now and protect your family against blood needs for a year). Physicians will decide that the safe period is shorter than before, enabling frequent donors to give more frequently. In addition, physicians will try to use less blood, perhaps by doing less elective surgery, or by requesting less blood for an operation than they once did, and manufacturers and scientists will try to find ways of making a single unit of blood go farther.

The market for blood, then, will clear. Not as efficiently as if there were prices, but given time, organizations and donors will adjust, and supply will (roughly) equal demand. The most important of all these adjustments is the medical need for blood, however. If we had twice as much blood available in this country as we do now, physicians would probably manage to use it. If we had half as much, they would make do with that amount too. The absolute minimum required for medical needs is probably well below the present amount being donated. If so, the blood market illustrates a situation in which the demand for blood adapts and adjusts to its supply.

Reasons for Not Having Prices

There are four arguments, in fact, for not pricing, that is, for giving goods and services away. One is a standard economic argument that it is foolish, or at least uneconomic, to spend more to collect a fee than it is worth. It was this type of thinking that led the National Park Service to abolish the ten-cent fee to ride the elevator in the Washington Monument. It cost more than ten cents to collect. Second, there may be no prices as a matter of public policy or because prices are politically unthinkable, which is much the same thing. Imagine a policeman charging for answering a call or a congressman for helping a constituent solve a problem. (Forget about the congressman. Just imagine the policeman.) Third, some nonprofits are so well endowed that they need not charge: foundations, for example, that provide journals and other services at no charge; and museums that furnish free music and refreshments to their visitors. Finally, prices are not called for when there is no intent to influence the client's behavior.

The Role of Price in a Nonprofit Organization

The argument so far has been that nonprofit organizations differ from businesses in that they are more likely to be operating in markets without prices. This argument cannot be pushed too far, however. While businesses operate in price markets, they themselves do not operate this way internally. Prices guide and coordinate markets, but internally, within the corporation, guidance and coordination are achieved by rules, procedures, persuasion, and executive fiat. One economist, in fact, has defined the business firm as an organization within which there are no market exchanges, in which management monitors and directs production.[10]

There are two major reasons why a nonprofit organization would want to price its goods and services rather than give them away, and a number of minor reasons.

The first major reason is to generate resources, that is, cash. Since the mid-1960s many nonprofit organizations have begun to charge for what were formerly free services. Museums have begun charging admission, bridge authorities have begun collecting tolls, and historic sites once free now collect admission. And I believe it to be the case, although I have no evidence, that NPOs now rely more on cash from selling things than they did in the past.

The second major reason for pricing is to influence the client's behavior. A public library charges no admission because it wishes to place no barriers on readers, but it has fines for overdue books to encourage readers to return them. The fines are typically so small as to be a nuisance rather than a hardship, but they do serve as inducements. Organizations sometimes set prices to limit the use of its services, in a sense to prevent a run on the bank. There are charges for duplicates—say, college transcripts, licenses, and birth certificates; and parking meters are intended to prevent a few drivers from hogging the same space all day long. (They raise some revenue too.)

Price can also affect a client's attitudes, beliefs, and opinions. A price forces a client to decide whether he actually needs the service or not. Prices in and of themselves also increase a client's appreciation of the value of what he is buying. More than anything else, theater managers love to be able to say "sold out," because they feel that audiences who must work to obtain a ticket, who have higher T costs, value the performance more. Conversely, nonprofit services that are too easy to come by are sometimes put down as not worth the effort.

There are a number of lesser reasons for establishing prices as well. Why does the U.S. government charge for crop insurance, or for safety inspections of aircraft? Not primarily to generate resources or affect the aircraft industry, but because such charges are required by law.[11] Why does a computer center in a university require each user to have an account, so that each time the computer is used the account is charged with the cost? When the account runs out, the user gets no more time until he goes to the slight trouble of renewing his account. This is an example of pricing that serves no other purpose than to count the output of the computer center, although it is not that simple. A computer center also measures such things as:

Items	Units
Number of jobs	Number of jobs
CPU time used	Seconds
Core used	Page-hours
Number of disc reads	Number
Pages printed	Number
Plotter use	Seconds

One of the simplest ways of measuring the total output of the computer, of combining all these things into one number, is to price each function and charge each user accordingly. In a university setting, computer accounts have no other meaning. They certainly do not influence the behavior of students or other users, nor do they generate resources. They exist simply to count the output. Sometimes, however, a researcher may receive a grant that includes funds for computer time. Then the price takes its usual meaning, and the computer center sells time to the researcher for real money.

PRICING OBJECTIVES

There are three types of objectives that can be set for a price, or for a pricing scheme. The first, organizational objectives, deals essentially with miscellanea. The other two deal with the impact of price on behavior and on cash flows, and hence they merit more discussion. Note that these last two objectives mirror the two reasons for having prices in the first place.

Organizational Goals

Encourage growth of the NPO. Government agencies often price below market-clearing prices, perhaps setting prices equal to marginal costs. Any price that is below the market price shields the client from the full cost of the agency's service. Not only does the client consume more than he would if he had to bear his share of the costs, but he is less aware of what the agency's costs are. Both of these lead to higher budgets, which are the objective of every government agency.

Be simple enough for employees to understand. It can be argued that most clients need not understand the price structures they encounter, but most organizations would want their own employees (and volunteers) to understand them. First-class postage within the United States is the same everywhere, and some mass transit companies charge the same fare, or none at all, over wide areas. Nothing could be simpler than price structures like these. The telephone company, on the other hand, has different long distance rates between every two points, and the rates differ by time of day and day of the week. No wonder consumers' perceptions of long distance rates are so much in error.

Clear the shelves. Nonprofit organizations sometimes price to clear the shelves. The flea market at a private school is expected to net several thousand dollars, but above all the aim is to sell out. Nothing is more dreary for the volunteers than having to come back and arrange for the disposal of unsold merchandise. Auctions perforce do the same thing. Every item moves.

Motivate managers. An organization might want other things from its prices, such as providing incentives for its employees to behave correctly toward clients or motivating its managers to be more efficient. An example of the latter arises when one department in an organization receives products or services from another and is charged for them, a charge that is called a transfer price. What the transfer price should be depends primarily on what behavior the organization wants of its managers. A museum can encourage curators to use its print shop by setting the transfer price below the market price for printing jobs, and it can discourage them by setting prices that are higher than market. Normally, an organization wants its managers to make the best possible use of the resources that are sold by one department to another. Sometimes management is also concerned with facilitating decisions about prices to outsiders like clients or middlemen.[12]

Influencing Behavior and Attitudes

The second broad pricing objective is the use of price to encourage (or discourage) use of a service (or purchase of a product). In the Las Vegas school lunch program a student can buy a cheeseburger combo, including fries or a salad, and milk or a low-fat, low-sugar shake for eighty cents. To discourage the student from drinking a soda, substituting a soda for the milk or shake pushes the items into the a la carte category and jacks the price to $1.10. The assumption underlying pricing for these uses must be that the price itself, which is only part of OOP costs, is a large portion of T costs.

Expanding demand has always been assumed, and defended, as the only sensible pricing objective for public utilities and publicly owned businesses. This has led economists to advocate setting prices equal to the marginal costs of production. Were this scheme to generate positive cash flows, it would doubtless be in widespread use. But characteristically, in a monopoly, marginal cost pricing cannot produce enough revenue to pay the bills, hence the need for a subsidy, hence controversy and public debate, hence relatively little marginal-cost pricing in the United States.

Price used in this way should, naturally, be used with specific target segments in mind. Otherwise the segments will be selected by accident, as we have seen earlier. Reduced mass transit fares for the elderly will benefit them, but exactly who benefits from such fares when they are available to all cannot be determined without research (although one can make some good guesses).

Stimulate trial or earlier purchase. Perhaps the most familiar use of prices is a sales promotional device. (See also Chapter 16.) Price reductions are a standard technique to introduce a new service. They are particularly attractive to middlemen (but only if they feel the product will sell anyway). A reduced price along with service innovations can also help attract trial users. It is one thing to consider taking a university extension course at a cost of hundreds of dollars, plus nights tied up, plus lost time studying. It is another to be able to sample lectures in the first weeks of the semester for, say, one dollar each. (See Figure 12.1.) Unions sometimes waive initiation fees and give away turkeys to lure new members. Opera and ballet companies, dance troupes, and symphony orchestras can all experiment with short subscription series as a means of attracting those audiences unlikely to attend otherwise, perhaps for financial reasons or perhaps to avoid a commitment to buy a full series.

Encourage repeat purchases. It is also possible to aim price appeals and special prices at loyal clients and thus encourage them to buy again. Museum shops give discounts to museum members for this reason (as well as to make membership in the museum more attractive). Some years ago Fairleigh Dickinson University, in Rutherford, New Jersey, put in a plan whereby brothers, sisters, husbands, or wives of full-time students could attend the university at half tuition. (The plan also allowed their parents or grandparents to take courses at no charge, if space was available.) Under the plan, only one student in a family would pay full tuition.

Price to stem demand. Price is also used to retard demand. Examples would include sin taxes on alcohol and cigarettes and proposals to top up current gasoline prices with an additional tax. (Is it merely a coincidence that these three items are highly price inelastic?)

A more difficult problem arises in situations where trade-offs are involved. In pricing on-line computer information retrieval services, the marketer hopes to find a price that will encourage legitimate uses of the system but discourage frivolous ones.[13] This is a common problem that also arises in the design of complaint systems, systems designed to allow clients to have their complaints heard, perhaps even judged. The T costs of filing a complaint should discourage

Figure 12.1
A Price Reduction Buried in the Body Copy, Intended to Stimulate Trial

Get the Spirit

Test your wings like Minnesota's soaring eagle. That spirit to learn, to extend yourself, can move you to explore a special interest, start or finish college, improve job skills, or examine new careers. These opportunities are open to everyone through Extension evening and weekend classes at the University of Minnesota.

Learning options include one-evening $1 Sampler lectures on popular topics, short-term Informal Courses for no credit, and hundreds of courses that you can take for credit and apply toward a degree or certificate. Test your wings. Call for the 1979-80 Extension Classes Bulletin that describes courses, degree programs, and student services.

376-3000

- simple mail and telephone registration
- free professional program advising and counseling — day or evening
- bachelor's degrees available in architecture, accounting, business, computer science, English, electrical engineering, food science, geography, political science, social welfare, speech-communication, and 15 other majors; certificates and graduate degrees also

Registration for fall classes is August 20 to September 13
Classes begin September 24

Open House

Stop by the Extension open house, September 5, at Nolte Center on the Minneapolis campus. Meet with program advisers and Extension staff who can explain evening programs. Hours are 5 to 8 p.m. Park free in Nolte Center Garage.

Extension Classes
Continuing Education and Extension
University of Minnesota

The University of Minnesota is an equal opportunity educator and employer.

most irresponsible complaints without discouraging too many justified ones. The United States will face this problem when national health insurance is introduced, and countries with ombudsmen already face it. The basic approach is to work not so much with price alone but with T costs, and to recognize that there is no way to exclude every irresponsible complaint without excluding some justified ones. It means, in brief, that no matter what the decision is, it will be wrong. In New Zealand, the ombudsman requires that petitions be written and signed, and that the complainant pay a small fee. Most complaints presented to ombudsmen will be current, but it is common for ombudsmen to refuse petitions where the cause for the complaint occurred, say, more than a year before the petition is filed.[14]

Influence how clients judge quality. In addition to influencing behavior, prices also can influence attitudes. One example of some interest to marketers is the relation between price and quality. Clients want to know the quality of the product or service they are buying, and as a result the marketer's model of client behavior must (sometimes) deal with the question of how clients judge quality. For many goods and services, judging quality presents little challenge; clients judge it on the basis of inspection, reputation, what others tell them, or their own past use. There will be other cases where the quality is hard to judge, however, perhaps because the client cannot see the product before he buys it— as in judging the performance in office of a presidential candidate—or because other factors make it difficult to judge quality. How does a consumer judge the quality of vodka? All vodkas taste the same, which is to say that they do not taste at all. Yet Heublein has always managed to exact a higher price for "Smirnoff" vodka than for "Relska." When he was asked what the difference could be, the president of Heublein replied, "A very embarrassing question. Shall we say it's a difference in pricing policy?"[15] In other words, Smirnoff's prices were higher because—because Smirnoff's prices were higher. A similar situation arises in the judging of the quality of condoms. Because they are sealed in a package, first-time and infrequent buyers cannot judge their quality. Quality is important to them, though, and in this case they would be expected to judge on the basis of price. A group of authors has reported that, for example, in India "many customers thought that price was a definite indicator of the quality of condoms."[16]

Prices also influence attitudes because clients, and backers as well, see ethical dimensions in a price. A price must be just, or at least equitable. Since the marginal costs of providing transit service are higher during rush hour, so the argument goes, rush hour fares should be higher. But "a proposal of this sort is likely to be considered inequitable by many if not most of the lay population on such grounds as that the rush-hour riding is less comfortable, is more of a necessity, is more heavily concentrated among low-income groups . . . or is according to some naive method of cost allocation . . . less costly."[17]

Financial Goals

The last board pricing objective deals with cash flows. Financial goals can be thought of in these terms: How much of the costs borne by the organization should to be passed on to the client by means of prices?

Financial goals raise problems. They often conflict with other organizational goals. One cannot expand service by reducing prices and expect to increase cash flows.[18] One may not be able to serve specific market segments without treating all segments alike and thus producing less revenue. In addition, financial goals often suffer from considerable ambiguity in practice. Let us see why.

What are some other reasonable pricing goals for a university to consider in pricing the use of its copiers? There are four that merit discussion. The first is that the university should just cover its costs. To which the reader should immediately say, *which* costs? Perhaps the university should cover its variable costs and run at zero Gross Marketing Contribution for paid copies.

A second possible objective is to cover full costs or some other imaginary cost.

The third possible objective is to generate as much cash as possible. This works from the obvious fact that the copier is already in place, in operation, and that the university might as well generate as much cash as it can toward the costs of its operation. This has a flaw as well: "As much as" is so vague that it cannot be used. (The textbooks would say the objective is nonoperational.) Can anyone know for sure that we are not already generating as much cash as possible? No. Alternatively, we can consider as a hypothetical case that this has been the objective for (say) a year. Now that the year is over, the dean wants to know whether he has met his objective. No one can tell him, however. Because no one can tell him this objective is worthless.

There is a final, fourth objective that has nothing whatever to do with cost recovery, and that is to price at a competitive parity. If all the other copiers on the edge of the university campus charge a dime a copy, the dean should too. If they charge eight cents, the dean should also.

There are three lessons here. The first is that there is *never* any simple relationship between costs and price (or almost never). In a business, competition and demand are of first importance in determining prices, along with the business's objectives. In nonprofit organizations there need not be *any* relation, simple or otherwise, between costs and price.

The second lesson merely repeats a lesson from Chapter 3. There is no such thing as *the* cost. There are many costs, and an effective marketer, indeed an effective manager, must decide which costs are relevant to his particular problem and learn to estimate them. A business tries to ensure that its products cover their variable costs and programmed costs and produce a positive net marketing contribution.

The third lesson is that a nonprofit organization may choose to put major or exclusive emphasis on any of the objectives discussed above—competition, demand, client interests, or the goals of the organization.

METHODS OF SETTING PRICES

Let us comment on three methods we observe in use by nonprofit organizations to set prices: cost-based pricing, demand pricing, and just price.

Cost-Based Pricing

Starting with cost, "cost-based pricing" builds in a mechanical way to a price. Sometimes it starts with cost and goes no further, as with charitable hospitals run by a government or by religious groups that sell medications to their patients at cost.

Most retailers, profit as well as nonprofit, base their prices on cost. They apply a standard markup to cost to arrive at a price. (In addition, most businesses use the same approach to start their pricing process, cost plus a percentage of cost to give a trial price.) We would expect to see such markup pricing in many nonprofit organizations: bookstores owned by universities, museum shops, birth control clinics that sold, say, condoms or pills, public utilities, student cooperatives, and hospital pharmacies.

For the nonprofit organization trying to cover costs, markup pricing has two advantages. Prices are simple to set and they appear to be fair. The simplicity should be obvious: All a clerk need do is read the invoice, apply a standard percentage, and arrive at a price. There can, however, be complications. Take a hospital pharmacy that buys its drugs at a price that is below the wholesale price paid by the neighborhood druggist. If the hospital is trying to hold down drug costs to its patients it should base its drug prices on the cost it pays; but if it expects the pharmacy to produce positive Net Marketing Contribution (as most hospitals do), it would choose the higher price. One textbook does not even trouble to draw a distinction.

A percentage mark-up, if this method is used, should be based on standard wholesale costs since some manufacturers have a special hospital price which is less than wholesale. The cost should also be considered as the cost of the smallest original container . . . regardless of the size . . . purchased.[19]

That is, use the highest cost that can be found.

In our society it is generally believed that prices should be related to costs. As such, markup prices, which are based on costs and are the same to all buyers, are generally seen as fair. A public utility or hospital or university that argues its prices should cover its costs finds general support in the American culture, even though those who support the statement usually have no idea what "cost" means.

Nonprofit organizations that engage in projects of long duration whose cost is uncertain use another type of cost-based pricing called cost-plus pricing. A nonprofit research institute may propose an ambitious R&D project to the Air Force. As the project proceeds the institute bills the Air Force for costs incurred plus a fee, usually less than 10 percent of the costs. The total price is based on cost, but the cost is not determined until after it has been incurred.

Demand Pricing

It is not always possible to set a price that is based mechanically on costs, as we have seen. For one thing, costs do not always come neatly labeled as they do on an invoice. A ballet company faces problems in sorting out the mixture of variable, semivariable, nonvariable, and programmed costs, and hence it cannot easily answer the question: "What will an extra performance in the park cost?" There simply is no invoice cost to be marked up. Moreover, we may guess that nonprofit organizations would prefer to cover their costs—opera companies, scholarly journals, mass transit companies, universities—but that they cannot because the public will not pay the full cost (whatever that means). This means we are talking about demand.

Pricing that considers demand first and cost second is called, naturally, demand pricing. A demand price is attuned to what clients will pay. Which seems simple enough until we encounter situations in which costs are higher than price and clients are willing to pay more. In such a case, do we have cost pricing or demand pricing?

Perhaps an example of pure demand pricing is pricing tickets to a charity ball, or a gala at the opera. Here costs play little role, prices merely being set as high as backers will bear. Demand pricing is obviously followed by performing arts organizations and other nonprofits who do not cover even operating costs from ticket revenues. They would like to generate more revenues but do not increase their ticket prices. Why not? Clients simply will not pay any more.

There is a second consideration that affects demand pricing: the competition. Most museum gift shops sell at least some products, typically reproductions of the museum's holdings, that are not available elsewhere. For these items there is no like competition, but there are close substitutes in the form of other gifts. We would expect that a museum exclusive would bear higher gross margins than is normal for museum shops—in part because people are willing to pay more but also because there is little competition for such exclusive items.

A museum certainly does not wish to price its memberships by working from an imaginary cost to a membership price. Rather, it might well set its fees roughly equal to those of the competition. Table 12.1, for example, compares membership fees at two museums, "ours" and our "dominant competitor's." In the highest two classes of membership, ours is much underpriced, and it appears there is considerable room for raising fees. For the rest, ours is mostly priced under the competition by relatively small amounts. An increase in indi-

Table 12.1

Comparative Annual Membership Fees, by Type of Membership, at Two Competing Museums

Type of Membership	Competitor's Fees	Our Fees	
Patron	$2,000	$1,500	
Friend	1,500	1,000	
Sponsor	600	500	
Supporter	300	250	
Contributing	150	150	
Sustaining	75	80	Class 1
		60	Class 2
Family	50	40	
Individual	30	20	
Special	15	10	

vidual and family memberships seems called for, as well as increases for sponsors and supporters. Whether one would want to increase special membership fees, intended for students, depends on how our museum views its responsibilities toward students. It goes without saying that such a comparison should match membership benefits against membership benefits, as was done in Chapter 11 in comparing the numbers game with a state-run game.

Competitive factors can sometimes assume first importance, for example, when an organization sells a product in a market with several competitors. Then it may simply set its price at "market," at what competitors are getting. (Exactly what this means is not completely clear, because usually each competitor offers a somewhat different product and price.) This appears fair to some people, and it nicely solves the problem of setting prices.

One must look past the surface of the pricing procedure to its substance, however. Above is the quote that advises a pharmacist in a hospital not to mark up his invoice cost, but to look about for some other, higher cost, the "standard wholesale cost," and mark that up. The quote also tells us the pharmacist to use as his cost the cost associated with the smallest container, regardless of the size he actually buys. Since unit costs increase as container sizes decrease, the unit cost associated with the smallest container will be the highest of all. "Standard wholesale cost" and "smallest container cost regardless" are two more examples of imaginary costs. What the quote is really saying to the pharmacist is that he should find some price the market (or third-party insurer) will pay and then botch together some costs to make the price look fair. Basing prices on relevant costs is cost-based pricing. Basing prices on imaginary costs is demand pricing.

Another variant of demand pricing is *price discrimination*. Discriminatory pricing means charging different prices to different customers for the same product: one price to the general public, a lower one to museum members; one price for front row seats, a lower one for last row seats; one bridge toll for those without monthly toll coupons, a lower one for those with them; one price for the hardcover book, a lower one for the paperback.

Why would one want to discriminate? The businessman discriminates because price discrimination increases profit. A nonprofit marketer may wish to increase his revenue, but usually nonprofit marketers discriminate for other reasons—to adjust prices more closely to ability to pay, to elicit different behavior from different market segments, or for reasons of equity. State universities discriminate against out-of-state students because (1) they can get away with it—demand as always rules; (2) one price to all is not seen as fair: Out-of-state students "should" pay their fair share (whatever that means); (3) places at state universities should go first to residents; and (4) state taxes "should" not support higher education in states that do not reciprocate.[20]

To discriminate one must be able to single out the segments that are to receive the special prices; and clients who receive the lower prices should not be able to resell what they have received to other clients who are willing to pay more. It is not so much of a problem for nonprofits as it is for businesses, because most nonprofits produce services, which cannot be resold. The scholarship student cannot resell his right to attend class, the museum member cannot resell his right to receive a discount, and a welfare client at legal aid cannot resell the legal advice he receives. Still, some policing mechanism is often needed. Performing arts organizations do not need ushers to help people find their seats; clear labels are all that are needed for that. Ushers are used mostly to enforce discriminatory prices, to make sure that the groundlings do not sit in the stalls.

There are two other conditions required for price discrimination, but they are obvious. One is that the competition should not be able to undersell the organization, which is a way of saying that organizations best able to discriminate hold considerable market power, their competition being weak or nonexistent. The other is the standard exhortation to spend no more on the discriminatory scheme than it yields in extra revenue.

Just Price

- One researcher found that in states where the state monopolized the liquor trade the prices of advertised liquor brands tended to be lower than advertised prices in states where liquor retailing was in private hands. How could this be? The researcher conjectured that

  Monopoly states . . . apparently set the prices (or margins) largely with reference to other monopoly states. As a group, they apparently believe (judging by the trade literature) that their present revenues are "fair" and "what is necessary."[21]

- The department of Water, Sewage, and Gas in Palo Alto, California, has a lifeline rate for water. It is a low rate to ensure that no family is denied water.

These are examples of *just price*, an ethical concept of pricing that arose during the Middle Ages. Medieval theorists were less concerned with what does happen than with what should happen, a charge that is sometimes laid in modern times to economists. Thomas Aquinas saw the just price as being equal to the sellers' cost, where cost could include, for example, the loss one suffers in parting with a cherished item and the cost of moving and storing goods. Other theologians considered that the market price, the price set by common estimation, was the just price. The merchant was exhorted to avoid the sin of greed, meaning that he should not buy merchandise to sell it unchanged at a higher price or charge more than he needed to maintain himself and his family in a style suitable to his station; to charge more to someone in dire need was to commit the sin of avarice.

It has been argued by some that businesses engage in a modern form of the just price when they base their prices on full cost. A full-cost price does not go up during periods of high demand, periods of shortages, and it does not go down when demand weakens. By not raising prices in times of high demand, the argument goes, businesses act responsibly by not exploiting the consumer when they might. (But when demand falls . . .)

Ethical concepts like just price assume particular importance in nonprofit organizations, most particularly in organizations that receive a major portion of their funds other than from their fees and prices, that is, other than from things they sell, and in which professionals are involved in administrative decisions. We observe three methods of just pricing in nonprofit organizations: the flat fee, the voluntary price, and the price adjusted to means.

The *flat fee* is a price that is the same to all comers, regardless of the true cost of serving them. Sometimes the flat fee is below costs, often well below it. Fees set by governments are often of this type. Some transit authorities have only one fare (or none at all) over large portions of the system.

Probably the most common method hospital pharmacies use in setting drug prices is some form of markup pricing. Assuming a pharmacist applies a constant percentage markup to all drugs, cheaper drugs will carry a smaller dollar gross margin than expensive drugs. Since some of the costs of running a pharmacy do not vary with the invoice cost of the drugs it dispenses, such a system is (incorrectly) criticized by some as inequitable or unjust. Therefore, many pharmacies use other schemes. One is a dispensing fee, a fee that reflects the overall cost of running the pharmacy but is not tied to the cost of the medication. A recently proposed variant is a per diem charge for medications that is determined by the type of medical treatment provided the patient and the length of his stay, but that does not reflect the cost of the medications he receives (except for drugs of exorbitant cost). In plain English, the patient is charged for drugs whether he uses them or not. Such a system eliminates the need to price individual drugs and may provide an opportunity to generate more revenue as well, since the per diem fee need not merely cover the pharmacy's costs.[22]

The flat fee is exceptionally simple and therefore easy to administer; it may also appear fair to most clients. It seems most useful in situations where the fee is small in relation to the client's income or to the amount the client normally spends for the good or service. The ease of administration, for example, only comes about where the nonprofit organization handles hundreds or thousands of transactions a day.

Voluntary pricing is a system whereby no price is set, although one may be suggested. Instead, the client selects the amount he wishes to pay. Such prices are usually called by a name other than price, and they are often tax deductible. One example is a donation. The client decides whether to give and how much. Here are three examples:

- In the past this system of pricing was widely used only in churches (if pricing is the correct word). It has also been used by other nonprofits like amateur theatricals, musical concerts, charity bazaars, and the like. Recently, however, there has been new interest in voluntary pricing because of its adoption by the Metropolitan Museum of Art as a means of pricing admissions. A number of museums, and other organizations, I do not know how many, have also adopted such a system. The Met's scheme requires that every visitor pay something, but the visitor decides the amount.

- It is common among theater companies, symphonies, opera companies, and the like, to request donations from their subscribers when they are asked to renew. Subscribers who choose to donate in effect volunteer to pay a higher price.

- There are more than one thousand business improvement districts in the country. They are groups of businesses each of whom agrees to pay a special, continuing surcharge on its real estate taxes. The city collects the taxes but turns them over to the group to finance local improvements. These typically include better lighting, extra (private) police, extra street cleaners, perhaps even renovations of certain eyesores in the neighborhood. (Such voluntary taxpaying groups first must bargain hard with their cities to keep the city from reducing the level of services it provides as the improvement district increases its efforts.)

The major advantage of voluntary pricing is that the price is adapted to the individual's pocketbook and to his perceptions of value. In marketing terms, it segments people on the basis of ability to pay. This means that it extracts some of the consumer surplus. Voluntary pricing also presumably generates a higher level of client satisfaction and frees the nonprofit organization from the chore of setting a price (but not necessarily of setting a suggested price).

The disadvantage is that voluntary pricing is not suitable for most nonprofit organizations. Certainly, one would never encounter voluntary pricing in a hospital. The patient could not be expected to come close to an estimate of a correct price. Rather, it is used where the average amounts donated are pin money, a few dollars, say, and where the result of a client's failure to find a "correct" price is not serious, as with a donation above the regular price. As the amounts at stake are small, most clients are willing to go along with the scheme, and they have little incentive to cheat. But once the suggested donation rises too high—ten dollars per head might be such a point in 1995 dollars—it is to be expected that the client's cooperation will deteriorate.

Price adjusted to means refers to prices that are higher for the well-to-do and

Table 12.2
Annual Membership Dues, Better Business Bureau of Greater East Tennessee

Number of Employees	Amount
1 - 4	$135
5 - 10	$175
11 - 19	$225
20 - 49	$300
50 - 99	$400
100 - 249	$550
250 - 499	$650
500 - 749	$800
750 - 999	$950
1,000 plus	$1,250

Source: Mary Siler and Walter Schultz, "The Better Business Bureau of Greater East Tennessee."
     April 1989, unpublished.

lower for the poor or higher for the large and lower for the small. Voluntary pricing is one such scheme, but it is the client who decides. With prices adjusted to means it is the organization that decides. Universities exact tuition from all their students but reduce the price to students with few financial resources by granting them scholarships. Financial need is the most important factor in determining the price charged these students. The practice of increasing prices on the opening night of the opera is a traditional way of raising extra revenue from the Best in Society, or at least the Richest. (This is also an example of demand pricing.) And courts in some states have experimented with setting fines based on the defendants' income. The more the criminal earns, the more he pays in fines.[23] And finally, the Better Business Bureau charges larger member firms more. (See Table 12.2.)

Prices adjusted to means are also common in government pricing. In 1976 food stamps could be purchased by families receiving public assistance—say, because of a retarded child—or by families hit by unemployment, or by low-income families. A family of four with no income paid nothing for its stamps. As its income rose it would come closer and closer to paying the face value of the stamps, and above a certain income—$553 a month for a family of four—it became ineligible for food stamps. The price became infinite, one might say.

OTHER PRICING ISSUES

This chapter has focused mostly on broad strategic issues of pricing. Once having settled the strategic, there still remain tactical issues. Let us look at three of these.

How Much to Charge

As one would expect, nonprofit businesses generally adopt the pricing rules and attitudes that their competitors adopt. Thus, they focus heavily on how much clients are willing to pay and what competitors are asking.

Other NPOs have more flexibility. If it is important to subsidize the client, then some form of below-cost pricing may make sense. Prices may break even to give a zero Gross Marketing Contribution, or to give a zero Net Marketing Contribution, or to give a zero after some interfund or after-the-fact adjustment.

When Should Clients Pay?

NPOs try to get their money in advance, well in advance if they can. Many NPOs contrive to do this. One buys stamps, cash cards, season tickets, and commuter passes and pays tuition in advance, sometimes months in advance.

Clients may not be able or willing to pay in advance. In that case, the NPO may ask that they pay at the time they receive the service. Examples include parcel post, stamps (again), single tickets (as opposed to season tickets or commuter passes). You pay at the time in the museum gift shop, at the state lottery agent or the lottery vending machine, at the animal shelter. Perhaps one might even consider withholding taxes as a form of paying as you go, although the government sees it primarily as a way to reduce tax evasion.

Finally, when the client has a strong desire or need to pay later, the NPO may grant credit or simply allow the client to pay later when a bill is presented. Most colleges and universities offer payment plans for tuition, and nonprofit employment agencies do not typically collect their fees until their jobseeker finds a job.

If the payments are delayed a week or a month, the NPO must finance the receivables, as any organization must. If the payments are delayed for years (say), a gift of $200,000 a year for five years, then one must recognize that the value of the gift has to be discounted using a standard discounted cash flow analysis.

Who Pays?

We have assumed that it is the client who pays. But the NPO must recognize that others are involved as well. Teenagers attend Outward Bound schools but their parents pay the bills. When you go into the hospital, you pay part of the bill but third parties, such as private insurers and the government, will pay most of it. You use an employment agency but the fee is typically paid by the employer.

QUESTIONS

1. Five or ten seconds after I suggest that a voluntary pricing scheme be used to price university education, I notice a sly smile steal over the faces of some of my students. Why? What does this say about the applicability of voluntary pricing schemes?

2. Fines for parking violations are a type of price. Which type? What marketing considerations should enter into the setting of parking fines? What are reasonable objectives for such fines? How would you measure performance against objectives?

3. Some nonprofit organizations (and many for a profit organizations) have a double-price system, whereby the client pays one price to enter and a second price to attend a particular event or function within. For example, a natural history museum charges for admission to the museum and again to the planetarium. What are the marketing consequences of pricing in this fashion? Must the two prices be related in any way, or can each be set without considering the other?

4. What marketing considerations affect determination of a ''lifeline'' rate for essential utility services (light, water, gas, or phone)?

5. Throughout the chapter price was spoken of in terms of the client. What about the backer? He bears a price in terms of foregone consumption, . . . and what else?

6. Assume you are in charge of setting prices at a charity fair for a local, private school. The owner of a three-store chain of record outlets, the mother of one of the students, donates twenty-five compact discs of popular favorites by the Boston Pops. This CD carries a manufacturer's suggested retail price of $14.99, but it is available from time to time on sale for as little as $12.99. You wish to gain the most revenue possible from these CDs.

   What will you do?

7. Colleges typically charge one tuition to all undergraduates—those studying studio arts, engineering, biology, history, economics.

   What are the pros and cons of one tuition? What are the pros and cons of tuitions varying by discipline? Why not, for example charge a higher tuition for engineering when the demand for engineering is strong, and cut tuition when demand slackens?

NOTES

1. One study in the mid-1960s estimated tuition for Canadian MBA students at only 10 percent of the T costs of the degree. See David A. Dodge and David A. A. Stager, ''Economic Returns to Graduate Study in Science, Engineering and Business.'' *Canadian Journal of Economics* 5 (1972): 182–189.

2. This example is overly simplified, leaving out as it does the possibility of part-time and summer earnings, and a number of other financial inflows and outflows. Still, the basic point remains valid. Note that part-time work is always rather poorly paid— another form of opportunity cost borne by the student.

3. *New York Times,* March 3, 1977, p. 20. 1977 by the New York Times Company.

4. Interview with Simon Ratten, Marketing Director, Oxford University Press, May 17, 1988. For background on pricing of compact disks see Francis X. Clines, ''O. E. D.'s Gegabyte Task: Transferring to Disks.'' *New York Times,* October 17, 1987, p. A13.

5. *New York Times,* September 9, 1979, Education Section, p. 12.

6. *New York Times,* March 3, 1977, p. 20.

7. Michael O'Hare, "Why Do People Go to Museums? The Effect of Prices and Hours on Museum Utilization." *Museum* 27, no. 3 (1975), footnote 4 on p. 137. O'Hare must have smiled as he wrote the phrase about the poor: The museum was open on Tuesdays so that "poor people, especially those who work, could come."

8. Richard K. Titmuss, *The Gift Relationship* (New York: Viking, 1971), pp. 55–58.

9. Blood plasma, the fluid part of blood, which is in fact mostly water, is replaced by the body within a few hours of a donation. The red blood cells are not replaced for several weeks. Donors cannot donate too often lest the insufficiency of red cells cause anemia. But the frequency with which donors safely donate varies from country to country. In Britain donors can give twice a year, in Australia four times a year, and in parts of the United States five times a year.

10. R. H. Coase, "The Nature of the Firm." *Economica,* New Series, 4 (1937): 386–405, reprinted in *Readings in Price Theory,* edited by George J. Stigler and Kenneth E. Boulding (Homewood, Ill.: Irwin, 1952), pp. 331–351. Also see a more recent discussion, Armem A. Alchian and Harold Demsetz, "Production, Information Costs, and Economic Organization." *American Economic Review* 42, no. 5 (1972): 777–795.

11. "User Charges." Circular No. A-25 (Washington, D.C.: Executive Office of the President, Bureau of the Budget, September 23, 1959).

12. Transfer pricing is a formidably technical field. But for elementary expositions of transfer pricing, see Joel Dean, "Decentralization and Intracompany Pricing." *Harvard Business Review* 33 (July-August 1955); and William R. Henry and W. W. Haynes, *Managerial Economics* (Dallas: Business Publications, 1978), pp. 481–491.

13. See Douglas Ferguson, "Marketing Online Services in the University." *Online* (July 1977): 15–22, reprinted in *Readings in Public and Nonprofit Marketing,* edited by Christopher H. Lovelock and Charles B. Weinberg (Palo Alto: Scientific Press, 1978), pp. 199–204.

14. See Walter Gellhorn, *Ombudsmen and Others, Citizen's Protectors in Nine Countries* (Cambridge, Mass.: Harvard University Press, 1966); and Larry B. Hill, *The Model Ombudsman: Institutionalizing New Zealand's Democratic Experiment* (Princeton, N.J.: Princeton University Press, 1976).

15. *Forbes* (January 15, 1960), p. 17.

16. R. A. Miller, J. S. Haider, J. S. Croley, and H. C. Gustafson, "Survey of the Sale of Contraceptives by Pharmacies in Dacca, East Pakistan." *U.S. Public Health Reports* 83, 1 (1968).

17. William Vickrey, "Some Implications of Marginal Cost Pricing for Public Utilities." *American Economic Review* 45 (May 1955): 605–620. Quote on p. 606.

18. But there is an important qualification to this sentence. What is it?

19. Clifton F. Lord, *A Guide for Pharmacists, The Smaller Hospitals* (Atlanta: Georgia Pharmaceutical Association, 1966), p. 31.

20. One good discussion of price discrimination is found in Armen A. Alchian and William R. Allen, *University Economics* (Belmont, Calif.: Wadsworth, 1969), pp. 113–117, where it is called "multipart pricing." Another, more theoretical discussion, but still short, is A. Asimakopulos, *Microeconomics* (Toronto: Oxford University Press, 1978), pp. 301–304.

21. Julian L. Simon, "The Economic Effects of State Monopoly of Packaged-Liquor Retailing." *Journal of Political Economy* 74 (1966): 194.

22. R. M. Bower and C. D. Hepler, "A Statistical Approach to Per Diem Pharmacy." *American Journal of Hospital Pharmacy* 31 (December 1974): 1179.

23. Wade Lambert, "Three States, Seeking Alternatives to Jail, Will Test Fines Tied to Criminals' Income." *Wall Street Journal,* December 30, 1991, p. B1.

Chapter 13

Communications

Nonprofit organizations communicate with various publics in an effort to influence their knowledge, attitudes, and behavior. Some nonprofit organizations put very large portions of their total revenues into communications. Consumers Union, for example, spends around 30 percent of its annual revenues for advertising,[1] and in raising funds some charities spend more than 30 percent, with a few like Richard Viguerie, fundraiser nonpareil for conservative causes, spending more than 50 percent. Percentages this large are rare in business. The American Statistical Association, on the other hand, spent .5 of one percent of its gross income in 1976 on promotional activities, and in (fiscal year) 1974 the Veterans Administration spent on advertising $1 million of its $13.3 billion budget, or .008 of one percent.[2]

THE FORMS COMMUNICATION TAKES

Any organization has four complementary ways of communicating with those it wants to reach:

Advertising—an impersonal presentation, paid by an identified sponsor, usually in mass media.

Personal selling—a presentation in person (sometimes over the telephone) made to potential purchasers or those who influence the purchase.

Sales promotion—temporary incentives to spur sales or other desired behavior.

Public relations—any of several programs designed to influence an NPO's image.

An Abstract Model of Communications

This model is shown in Figure 13.1. Part A illustrates two ideas. The first is that communications is an iffy process. Noise distorts the message so that the recipient does not understand the message as it was sent. For example, the recipient might not realize a message is for him until it is almost over, or he may not understand one of the words in the message. The second idea is that there is typically some sort of feedback from recipient to sender. This is easy to see if sender and recipient are face-to-face. With mass communications the feedback takes other forms—how recipients behave after they receive the message or what they know and are aware of afterwards, for which research is needed. With feedback the noise can be quite substantial, making it hard for the sender to figure out just what the recipient is trying to say. Recall the discussion of the meaning of a vote at the beginning of Chapter 6.

Part B shows the model in a bit more detail and in the process suggests all of the places where communications can go wrong. The sender must decide what to say and how to say it, two of the most enduring and difficult tasks throughout human history. An additional difficulty arises because of who does what: The person who decides what to say is usually not the person who decides how to say it, mixing still more noise into the process.

Selecting media appears to come after the message has been completed, but it doesn't. Certain types of messages go best in certain media and will not work in others. Telephoning, for example, cannot transmit pictures, and television works poorly for messages that are long or complex. (Is this why politicians make such heavy use of TV in their election campaigns?) Media selection is also influenced by who the recipients are. To reach teenagers one uses radio, in spite of the fact that it has no pictures and is limited to simple messages. A complex message that has to adapt to what the recipient says would be delivered in person, face-to-face.

The message is transmitted and received by the recipient. That is, the recipient may receive it if he happens to attend to that particular magazine issue or that part of the talk given by his parole officer. Just as it is difficult for the sender to decide how to say what he wants to say, so there is no sure way to ensure the recipient does in fact understand the message. Three well-documented psychological processes muddy the waters at this point. They are called selective processes: selective exposure, selective attention, and selective retention. Recipients pick and choose what they want to hear. Try to tell them something they don't want to hear and they will often tune the message out, either figuratively by not listening (say) or literally by switching channels or turning to another page. Recipients can decide what they give their attention to, and they are prone to pay attention to comfortable messages, not ones that might do them some good. Finally, recipients selectively remember and selectively forget.

At this point the recipient does something. Or rather he does no such thing. Or rather, well, one can't be sure what will happen at this point. Most will

Figure 13.1
An Abstract Model of Communications

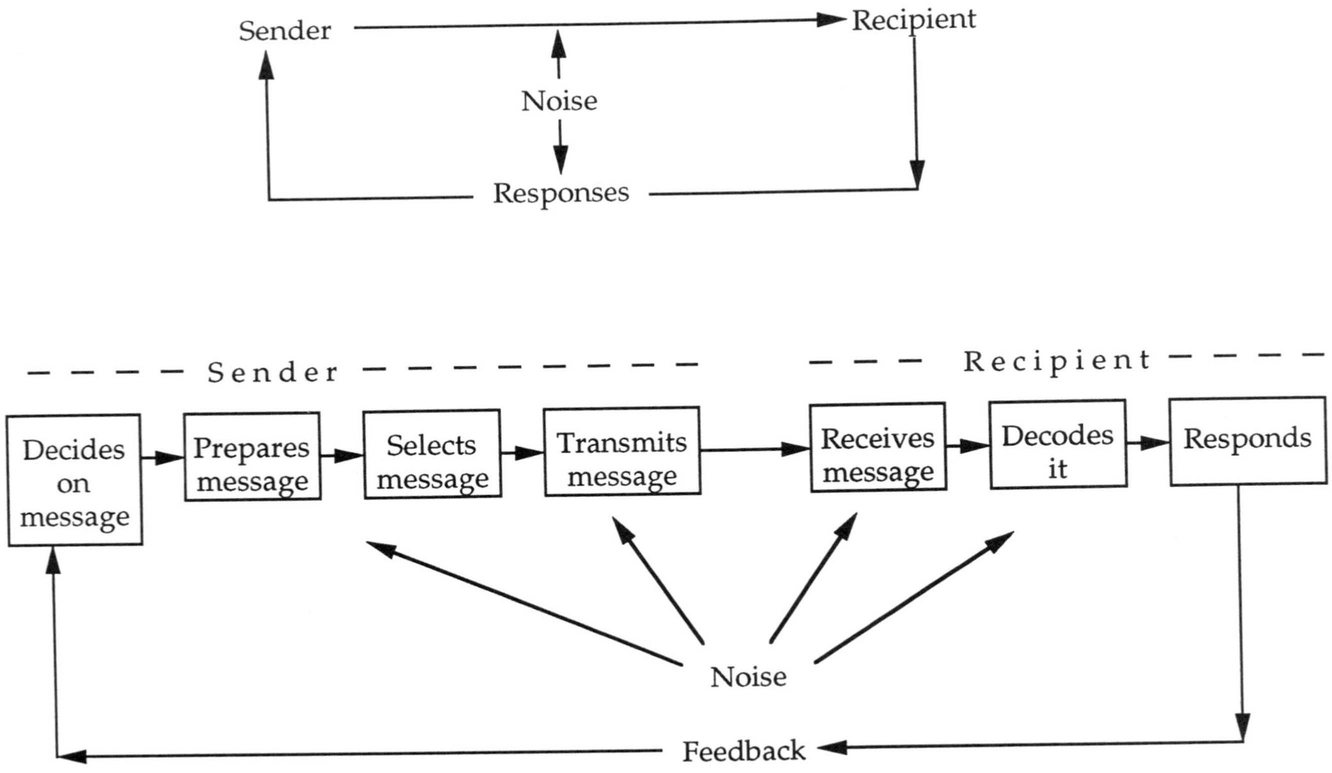

correctly judge the message is not for them and forget it, totally. Some may absorb the message and make it theirs. Others, perhaps most, will yawn, not always even politely, and go about their business; but a seed may have been planted that may grow at some time in the future; or the recipient may strongly disagree with the message, may actively argue against it, and may emerge feeling stronger in his opinions than before. The alert reader will have noticed how often the word "may" is used in this paragraph. Just another reminder that communications is an iffy process.

THE MESSAGE

What is said by an organization's advertising or employees is an important dimension in designing a communications program.

Many nonprofit organizations offer a variety of services and products to their clients. They stand for many things. A women's referral service in northern New Jersey helps direct women to governmental or private agencies that can help them, provides counseling services for women, runs peer support groups for separated or divorced women, and maintains a telephone hot line. Such an agency is hard put to describe itself in plain English. What, after all, is a "referral service" and what are "peer support" groups? They are admittedly difficult words, coming as they do from the engines of modern social science. Most words, surely, would be easy to understand. Take "inflation." No doubt everyone understands what inflation means. In a study done in England, more than one in three of the respondents had no idea at all what inflation meant: "something to do with politics" or "blowing up a bicycle tyre." Another 19 percent understood it, but only in general terms as having to do with the economy. And at the height of the countrywide debate on whether to have a referendum about Britain's entry into the Common Market, about two-thirds of the British public were unable to suggest even vaguely what the word "referendum" might mean.[3]

In planning a communications program, a nonprofit must find a clear, direct way of describing what it is and what it does. Here is how one referral service—for careers for women—in Providence, Rhode Island, struggled with this problem:

To convince someone to use your service, you must first define exactly what that service is. This is not an easy task especially if you have already spent a great deal of time designing your program and working with others in the same field. Jargon has a way of seeping so deeply into the unconscious that you can soon find yourself communicating only with the initiated. To test your ability to communicate, you might find it helpful to try to explain your service to an overly critical friend who knows little or nothing about what you've been doing.

Clarifying what your service does offer can also help you to focus on what it does not offer. Working from these facts you can then isolate the points that make your service special and therefore "salable." These, in turn, influence the way you plan your advertising.

In our case, "career education" was a term few people understood when we began. Even now there are debates about its meaning. We chose, therefore, to create a separate identity for the service portion of our Project, calling it "Career Counseling" and using the mass media to create an awareness of the name. Gradually the public came to understand that it meant information, guidance and referrals related to careers, but not job placement. We also had to run some long, factual advertisements to establish our service in people's minds before we could be clever or humorous in our approach. We learned the hard way that people must know exactly what is being offered before they will respond to "clever" offerings.[4]

The message, therefore, must *say* something. For most NPOs this something will be information, for as we have seen at great length in Chapter 4, clients (and backers) have interests in information, and an NPO's communications aim to fill these interests, at least in part. Contrary to the reader's experience with lectures, however, mere transmission of information need not be dull. Experienced advertisers and salesmen work to cast the messages in terms that are important to the client; they stress not just the information itself but the *benefits* that clients will enjoy from behaving properly.

The informational content of communications depends on other factors as well. The more complex the information, the longer the copy needed to get the point across. A newspaper ad announcing new museum hours can be short and to the point: "The Cross Museum, now open six days a week, 10–5," with an address. This brevity reaches an extreme in reminder advertising, which serves only to remind: "Don't wait. Get your pap smear now," and "File early." But an ad in the same newspaper for a five-week summer music festival may take up an entire page of fine print because there are so many activities scheduled for different days, and because the audience needs so much information about tickets, accommodations, parking, performances, and performers.

In addition, advertising and personal selling work along with other communications, such as communications mounted by middlemen; and if they can be depended upon to carry some of the communications burden, there will be less for the organization's ads and salesmen to do. A university press will do some advertising of its new books, but it also expects the firm that distributes its books to work to sell them. On the other hand, when important "others" are known to do a poor job, the organization's own communications must bear more of the burden. In political campaigns, one would expect to be able to rely on TV news to project a least part of the candidate's position. But this is not the case. TV news stories are brief and concentrate not on these aspects of the campaign that a voter should hear or think about, but on those aspects that make good pictures. As they say, a talking head is bad television. Hence, conclude Patterson and McClure, television news provides voters who have little exposure to other sources of news with relatively little information about positions and issues. In such a situation, television advertising (and other forms of communication) *must* provide them with this information.[5] Finally, how much the client already knows has an impact. Because most people recognize Billy Graham's face, leaflets and billboards advertising his crusades can afford to show little more than his face, plus the particulars of the crusade. As one of his advisors has said: "When you see an advertisement for a Cadillac, it just says Cadillac and shows you a picture. Billy is like a Cadillac. We don't have to explain."[6]

Of course, the nonprofit organization must concern itself with how it tells its story as well as what it says. The standard recommendations rest on the fact that viewing (or reading) time is very short, only a few seconds. As a result the text must attract the viewer's attention, convey its message concisely, and by arousing the viewer's curiosity motivate him to continue. A straightforward prose style should be used, with an emphasis on clarity. The greatest fault is wordiness. Good visuals can make words redundant or carry most of the message themselves. One rule of thumb says never use more than seventy-five words (this paragraph already runs more than one hundred), using visual materials to get complicated points across. Of course, the type should be attractive and large enough to be easily read, and the appearance of the communication should be attractive.

These recommendations merit two comments. The first is that they are vague, and thus provide little help for the manager trying to judge whether copy is acceptable. What is "straightforward" prose? How can one be sure to attract the viewer's attention? As Walter Sickert has written, "We all know how difficult it is, in drawing up the simplest communication, not to say the contrary of what we mean." At the very least, a professional should write the copy, or pass on its suitability. If the stakes are large, the copy should be tested (or pretested, as the wordsmiths say) before it is used. The second comment is that the principles in the previous paragraph apply to all communications, not just advertising. In fact, all its recommendations come from a book on museum management and deal not with advertising but with the labels on museum exhibits.[7]

The basic issue is deciding what is to be said. A new service, like the referral service in Rhode Island discussed above, must expect to spend time and effort (and even money) informing potential clients what it will and will not do. Because such a service is used infrequently by most women and because it never knows when or where its advertising will reach a prospective client, the referral service must maintain a continuous presence in the community with its communications. An established service, on the other hand, like a city-owned bus line, will find that most of its passengers already know what they need to know. Its communications will be aimed primarily at new users, or infrequent users, who want to know schedules, routes, and fares; the first two are conveyed in timetables or schedules at the bus stops, the second by the bus driver.

The issue of what to say becomes much more complex when the message moves beyond being primarily informational. Political campaigns and speeches provide little information about a candidate's real views, and they are a notoriously inaccurate guide as to what he will do once elected. Instead of trying to provide information they try to persuade and develop an image for the candidate. However, this is a topic well covered in the advertising texts, so there is no need to discuss it here.

A BRIEF LOOK AT MEDIA

Media refers to the methods by which the message is transmitted to the audience. We will look at standard advertising media—print, broadcast, mail, and the like—in the next chapter, and still other media in the two chapters after that. Here, then, we will look at media that don't fit anywhere else.

• Displays	• Electronic billboards
• Booths	• Tear-off sheets
• Brochures and flyers	• Bookmarks and book jackets
• Take-ones	• Mobile vans
• Talk shows	• Trade fairs
• Catalogs	• Reply postcards
• Annual reports	• Slide shows
• Posters	• Videos
• Newsletters	

Even this list would not make much sense to a college admissions officer, because his list of media would include "college night" programs, college fairs, off-campus receptions and dinners for potential students and their high school counselors, as well as visits to homes, churches, high schools, and two-year colleges.

In February 1992 the news broke about William Aramony's lavish salary, questionable expenditures, and nepotism involving United Way spin-offs. United Way had to deal with the general public, of course, since it gave the money. It also had to communicate with its 2,300 affiliated organizations throughout the country. To do this it held a teleconference at which it reviewed what it had found and what it planned to do. Aramony also announced that he was resigning but that he would stay on until his successor was chosen. This went down so poorly with the affiliates that United Way held a second teleconference a week later to announce that an interim president had already been chosen to replace Aramony until a permanent replacement was found.[8]

The point is that the marketer has many communications devices. All of these devices can be used to supplement a basic communications program, and in fact their major marketing advantage is their very flexibility. As an example, a manual for army recruiters discusses media relations (making free use of the media), advertising, displays, exhibits, posters, community relations (speaker's bureau and the like), special events and promotions, banks, demonstration teams, exhibits, and sports clinics.[9] Family planning efforts in underdeveloped countries often can make use of folk media, which are popular forms of entertainment like puppet shows, street opera, and popular drama that can serve as communications channels. In addition, of course, folk entertainment can provide programming for more familiar mass media like radio and television.[10]

As a final example, campaigns of all sorts can make use of promotional "one-off" materials. Campaigns to enlist and attract applicants to local colleges have used such educational materials as skywriting, tee-shirts, and balloons; and political campaigns have long quickened American political dialogue with banners, emery boards, calendars, paper dresses, buttons, bumper stickers, ash trays, and funny hats.

The nonprofit marketer must also be alert to the existence of nontraditional media because they may provide good access to target markets that are otherwise difficult to reach. Electronic bulletin boards, the Internet, and video cassettes have all begun to play a role in marketing communications in recent years. In interviewing a number of teenage intravenous (IV) drug users, researchers discovered that heavy metal rock had features that made it a possible medium. For one thing, teenagers liked heavy metal—it was fast paced and loud, dramatically displayed good and evil, and snubbed its nose at adult culture. Even talking to these teenagers about heavy metal was a good sign. Few adults could do that. Finally, heavy metal was memorable, something a marketer generally likes in a medium; but among IV drug users it was of even more importance. IV drug users often appear incoherent, living in another, stuporous world. Reaching one whose mind has been dulled by heavy use of drugs is more than a challenge; it is a near impossibility, but users who could not remember where they slept last night could often recall, word for word, the lyrics of their favorite heavy metal album. The conclusion is that AIDS educators should consider using heavy metal lyrics.[11]

In fact, almost everything a nonprofit organization does, even if formally outside the area of communications, says something about that organization. Suppose the music director of an opera company wants to expose children to the joys of opera. The obvious way to communicate this message is to say nothing at all. Instead, he should hold special performances of short operas with strong, simple plots, in English, and let those who will learn for themselves.[12]

But there is still more, because as we have seen, distributors and other parties also can serve as communications channels. Under its original plan for Federal Crime Insurance, the Federal Insurance Administration planned very little direct communication with potential buyers. The burden of the task of communicating with buyers fell to the insurance brokers and agents. And in most tourist areas, hotels, restaurants, gas stations, and the like often serve as a distribution points for tourist literature and advice.

Videos

Before we go on, let us consider in a bit more detail two new media. Videos[13] can present a combination of voice and picture and they are strong in showing demonstrations. Because they are still fairly new, the arrival of a video in the mail comes as a surprise, and because of that they are likely to be watched. And of course, a whole generation, perhaps the last two, have been raised on television.

Not everyone approves of videos, like board members, particularly conservative board members, particularly old, conservative board members who remember when people read and who themselves are used to getting their information from the written word. And like television, videos are without question a poor way to deliver complex or detailed information.

How do NPOs use them?

- The Environmental Defense Fund sends its members a video newsletter on their first anniversary with the Fund, as part of its effort to persuade them to renew their membership.
- St. Joseph Home for severely retarded children, in Cincinnati, used a video in soliciting funds from corporations and foundations.
- Virginia Military Institute showed a twelve-minute video at special fundraising events, and sent a revised version of the tape to some thirteen thousand alumni and friends to soften them up for telephone calls asking for contributions.

Videos are not cheap. Merely copying a fifteen-minute tape costs a couple of dollars, which means that VMI spent some $25,000 to copy its video message. They are expensive to produce too, often between $10,000 and $30,000, at least $1,000 a minute but as much as $5,000 a minute. Add production, duplication, and mailing of the tapes, and cost can easily climb over $100,000. All this assumes the nonprofit pays, which it often does not, enjoying donated services and supplies that reduce costs substantially.

Videos are not cheap for another reason. Viewers are used to watching network quality production. They will not abide a video filmed in a church basement with a hand-held camera in poor light. Poor quality can damage an NPO's reputation and make it look unprofessional.

Computer Networks

These have already begun to be a medium of communications between nonprofits. The National Council of Nonprofit Associations has set up an electronic bulletin board, HandsNet, to allow community-based NPOs to communicate with each other;[14] antismoking activists use SCARCnet to digest the daily news and plan responses, and alcoholic control groups have their own ALCNet.

(Reader: Note the fashionable use of capitalization after the first letter. Take a stab at how long it will be before such capitalization will be overdone and no longer fashionable.) It is a safe prediction to say that networks and bulletin boards will become an important medium for reaching clients and backers in the near future.

Finally, let me say that I never fail to marvel at the ingenuity people put into finding new ways to send (and receive) messages. We write on the sides of buildings and on sidewalks; we write on the sky but not on water, yet; and there have been proposals to project images on the moon. Advertising has begun to show up on Internet, on children's schoolbooks, and in museum exhibits. My rough and ready hypothesis is that any blank surface or empty air is a possible medium, and I suspect darkly that as you read this someone is scheming to use that space or air. Why not messages on tax returns, or in church on Sunday, or at the bottoms of yogurt containers? A lovely example of all this is WFYI in Indianapolis, which has found a blank surface on which to promote its TV shows, namely, cover sheets that go out with a fax. (See Figure 13.2.)

BUDGETING

How much should be spent for all communications? How much of the total budget should go to advertising, to personal selling, and to sales promotion? How much of management's time should be spent on public relations and begging for public service announcements? To these important questions there are few adequate answers.

This is not unique to the nonprofit sector. Businesses also suffer from the absence of good rules to make such decisions, although advice as to what to do abounds.

Budgeting in Nonprofit Businesses

In addition to all the methods available to any nonprofit organization, which are discussed below, nonprofit businesses can also judge the size of their budgets by old-fashioned economic criteria. This is most clearly seen in nonprofit businesses that do most of their business by mail. For them, deciding how much to spend on advertising becomes primarily a question of deciding which budget promises to yield the highest Net Marketing Contribution. Fundraisers will certainly make their decisions in the same way, on the same criteria. For example, a subscriber to *Consumer Reports* let his subscription lapse while he was overseas. When he returned he found ten renewal notices, all mailed about a month apart. Consumers Union is sure to use economic criteria in deciding how much to spend in chasing after lapsed subscribers.

Figure 13.2
Fax Cover Sheet as a Medium of Communication

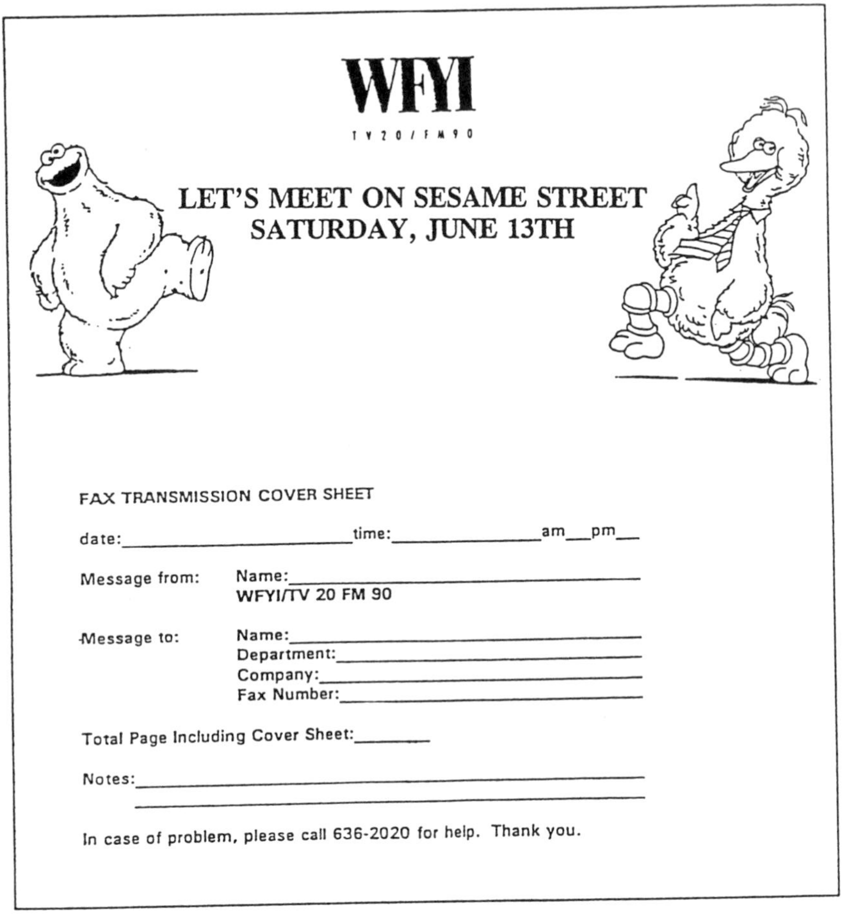

WFYI
TV 20 / FM 90

LET'S MEET ON SESAME STREET
SATURDAY, JUNE 13TH

FAX TRANSMISSION COVER SHEET

date:_____ time:_____ am___pm___

Message from: Name:_____
                WFYI/TV 20 FM 90

Message to: Name:_____
                Department:_____
                Company:_____
                Fax Number:_____

Total Page Including Cover Sheet:_____

Notes:_____
      _____

In case of problem, please call 636-2020 for help. Thank you.

Budgeting in Other Nonprofit Organizations

There are four basic approaches to selecting a communications budget, and to selecting an advertising budget: (1) seek special funds, (2) spend whatever is available, (3) use the task method, and (4) follow what others do.

Seeking special funds. In this approach to budgeting, the organization tries to raise special funds for specific communications programs. Whatever it can raise, it spends, and nothing else. Sometimes backers will provide funds for communications as part of an overall gift, as for instance when a corporate sponsor of a program on the Public Broadcasting System includes in its gift some money for publicizing the program.

Spending what is available. From time to time, the organization looks in the till and what it finds it spends on communications. This is the method commonly used by nonprofit organizations that are strapped for funds. It can hardly be called planning, but it does yield a budget. Political candidates sometimes find their campaigns in severe financial straits, and since the media demand cash in advance from political candidates—for there is no deadbeat deader than a defeated candidate—they are forced to spend only what they have on hand, which, however, may well include borrowed money. (There is another reason why the media demand cash in advance. Those who regulate gifts to politicians can see no difference between a bad debt of $10,000 and a gift of $10,000. Since giving too much violates federal law, the media take pains to be paid up front.)

The task method. Here a method is developed for meeting each of the objectives for the communications campaign. With a clear statement of the campaign's objectives in hand, the advertiser defines the specific communications tasks that must be accomplished to reach each of the objectives. For example, to reach 80 percent of the electorate an average of two times before the election, the campaign will need forty thirty-second TV spots, 200 ten-second radio spots, and number 100 showing in outdoor. To reach the labor vote will take fifteen ads in union publications, plus speeches by the candidate at four major conventions during the summer and early fall. With estimates like these in hand, the advertiser can then figure out what it will all cost, and he has a budget.

Of course, it is not all that easy. An organization that wants to reach working women who could use career counseling may have trouble deciding how to get in touch with them. And the task method requires choosing sensible objectives from the beginning.

Still, it is a useful way to begin any determination of a budget. Even though by itself it rarely does the whole job, in combination with the other methods, it adds a good deal of order and rationality to the budgeting process. For example, it is all too common for an organization trying the task method for the first time to arrive at a budget many times larger than it can possibly afford. But common sense comes to the rescue. One university extension division, for example, that was offering noncredit courses to adults set as its overall objective reaching all adults in its community with a high school education who were under thirty, but at the same time the extension division limited the overall communications budget to 4 percent of expected tuition revenues.

Following what others do. This means basing your budget on what other comparable organizations are doing—either your competition or other organizations that are like yours. In order to do this, a common yardstick is needed, and it is provided by budgeting advertising as a percentage of sales. In using an advertising-to-sales ratio, the manager says to himself, "We expect sales next year to be about ten million dollars. Since we have usually put about 5 percent of our sales into advertising, our budget next year should be around $500,000." Employing such a rule of thumb clearly implies that the manager cannot predict what his advertising will do for him, because he is not working forward from advertising to sales, but rather backward from sales to advertising. Give him the sales first, and he will then tell you how much advertising is needed. I first encountered this situation in writing a case study on the New York State Lottery. I asked the account executive for Fuller & Smith & Ross, the advertising agency, how he had decided on an advertising budget for the first year of the lottery. He said that he worked from the lottery's own estimate of sales and applied a set percentage. "I treated it just like an industrial account," he said, and he concluded in one sesquipedalian word, "Setitatthestandardfigureoneandahalfpercentofsales."[15] Now it turns out that oneandahalfpercentofsales is a common advertising-to-sales ratio in industrial marketing. What was puzzling then, and is still puzzling now, was how this account executive contrived to place the marketing of lottery tickets in the same category as the marketing of dollies, conveyor systems, wiping rags, and grinding wheels. Here was an advertising executive so ill at ease with the budgeting problem thrown up by the lottery that he grasped the first straw to float by and solved his problem. (But not the lottery's.)

Academic marketers sniff at setting budgets as a percentage of sales (or of budget). Such a procedure cannot reach a best solution to the problem. The logic is backward, as we have seen; the procedure ignores competition and it ignores profits. The academy has developed many elegant mathematical solutions to the budgeting problem as well, and in addition, marketing research techniques and market experiments are available that will aid in finding better budgets.

But marketers continue to use advertising-to-sales ratios in spite of this. Why? Businessmen use it because they are typically forced to make decisions with little time for deliberation, and in the face of substantial uncertainties about what competitors are planning to do. The better marketers use advertising-to-sales ratios intelligently, as a check on the correctness of budgets perhaps reached by other methods. Nonprofit marketers use such figures for much the same reasons, but for other reasons as well. Many nonprofits assign the marketing function to people without the proper experience. For them, such rules make life easier, if not better. It reaches an extreme when an organization makes heavy use of volunteer marketers, who need guidance about the proper levels of expenditure. Many organizations have trained people in their headquarters, but not in their field organizations. For them, a simple rule of thumb makes a great deal of sense. As one example, the Boy Scouts advises local councils as follows: "As a rule of thumb when developing a public relations plan for an event, about three percent of the event budget should be allocated to the public relations."[16] Of course, even the best rules are no substitute for a competent marketer.

Since advertising-to-sales ratios are so important, let us look at a few figures. Some are traditional advertising-to-sales ratios. In (fiscal year) 1976 the Postal Service spent about $3.1 million on philatelic advertising, and it expected the total revenue for all philatelic products to run about $74 million. Hence, its A/S ratio for this product line was $3.1/$74 = .042 or 4.2 percent.[17] Nonprofit organizations that have no sales would work in terms of the advertising-to-budget (A/B) ratio. A study of twenty-one independent, baccalaureate, liberal arts colleges compared their admissions and recruiting costs with their total educational and general budget and found the ratio of the two items was about 3 percent. Since about 6 percent of all admissions and recruiting costs goes for advertising (for mailing lists, postage, posters, and display advertising), the A/B ratio for these schools was about .2 of one percent of total budget (6 percent of the recruiting budget).[18]

There are two problems with figures like these. One is that there are few of them. Figures like these are not readily available, and the figures here are given merely as examples.[19] The other is that of definition: What is included in the numerator of the ratio and in the denominator? Are the costs of "college nights" used to attract potential students part of advertising costs? What about the costs of the catalog? The catalog would be needed even if there were no recruiting; therefore, its cost is not advertising, unless the catalog has been tricked out at an extra cost to sell the school as well as serve its traditional function. What about the costs of production, such as printing 800 posters and 40,000 mailers, paying the photographer, the model, and the layout artist, or reproducing videotape cassettes for public service ads? Are these to be included as well? Until the reader knows the answers to such questions as these, he cannot know what the figures stand for. The same applies to the denominator. When one symphony compares its advertising to all revenues, a second to revenues from ticket sales only, and a third to all earned revenue from tickets and other sources, the resulting figures are not comparable. Hence, the reader must be cautious and see the following figures only as indications of magnitude.

Two sets of figures deal with government agencies, Table 13.1 and Figure 13.3. The first shows composite A/S ratios for a group of English nationalized industries and government public bodies;[20] the second shows A/B ratios for twenty U.S. government agencies. The average A/S ratio over ten years for the English organizations was .31 of one percent; but this conceals a drop in the A/S ratio from a median of .36 of one percent in the first five years to a median of .22 of one percent in the second five, cause unknown. Most of the U.S. government agencies had A/B ratios below .3 of one percent, the median for all being .2 of one percent. The four agencies with the largest A/B ratios were the Bureau of the Mint at 4.6 percent; the Consumer Product Safety Commission, 7.4 percent; the American Revolution Bicentennial Administration, 23.9 percent; and the U.S. Travel Service, 29.9 percent. The reasons for the last two agencies having such large A/B ratios are apparent, but the reader may wish to mull over the communications needs of Bureau of the Mint.

Figure 13.4 contains A/S ratios for forty-one mass transit companies. The median here is .1 of 1 percent. Of the twenty companies below the median, fifteen did no advertising at all. This again reminds us of the problems raised by the definition of advertising, for every mass transit company must make a certain minimum of information available to its riders. The question is whether such expenditures are classified the same by all companies.

Finally, Table 13.2 shows that A/S ratio for the Houston Grand Opera has

Table 13.1
Ratios of Estimated Media Expenditures to Sales for English Nationalized
Industries and Government Bodies, 1969–1978

Year	Ratio[a]
1969	.36
1970	.34
1971	.36
1972	.35
1973	.37
1974	.28
1975	.21
1976	.21
1977	.22
1978	.26
Ten-year median	.31

Source: Advertising 62 (Winter 1979–1980): 40.
[a] In 1969, the A/S ratio was .36 of one percent.

run 3 or 4 percent in most years; when the total communications budget for both advertising and public relations is divided by sales, the ratio has run 5 or 6 percent in most years.

Sales Force Budgets

The discussion above has ignored budgeting for the sales force, but it only merits a short discussion. It is not because the sales force is unimportant, but because it is generally easier to arrive at something close to a "best" size for a sales force than it is for the advertising budget.

There are two methods of budgeting the sales force, that is, of deciding how big the sales force should be.

Work load. In this method, the number of salesmen is determined by the amount of work they have to do. And since the readiest measure of the amount of work is the number of sales calls, this method (usually) works from the number of sales calls to the number of salesmen.

Let us see how a nonprofit business would use the work-load method. A state lottery has 1,000 accounts. Fifty are so important that they must be called on by a salesman every week. These are the A accounts. There are 150 B accounts that merit a call every month and 800 accounts that merit a call only once a quarter. So the total work load for the sales force is 7,600 calls a year. The salesmen manage to spend, let us say, 190 days a year in the field and average

Figure 13.3

Stem-and-Leaf Diagram of Advertising-to-Budget Ratios for Twenty Federal Agencies, 1974

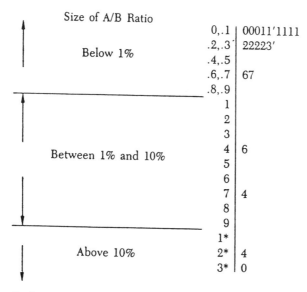

Explanation: Most agencies had an A/B ratio less than 1%, the median A/B ratio being 2/10 of 1%. The smallest figures, shown 0,.1|0, are less than 1/10 of 1%, and the next smallest shown 0,.1|1 equal 1/10 of 1%. Read other lines as:

$$.6,.7|7 \quad = \quad 7/10 \text{ of } 1\%$$
$$4|6 \quad = \quad 4.6\%$$
$$2*|4 \quad = \quad 24\%$$

Source: Kenneth W. Clarkson and Robert Tollison, "Toward a Theory of Government Advertising," in Richard O. Zerbe, Jr. (ed.), *Research in Law and Economics*, vol. 1 (Greenwich, Conn.: JAI Press, 1979), p. 141.

4.2 calls a day. So a salesman produces 190 × 4.2 = 798 calls a year. Hence, the organization needs ten salesmen (7,600/798 = 9.6).

Type	Number	Needed Calls per Year	Total Calls on Account per Year
(1)	(2)	(3)	(2) x (3)
A	50	52	2,600
B	150	12	1,800
C	800	4	3,200
	1,000		7,600

Figure 13.4
Stem-and-Leaf Diagram of Advertising-to-Sales Ratios of 41 Mass Transit Companies in 1972

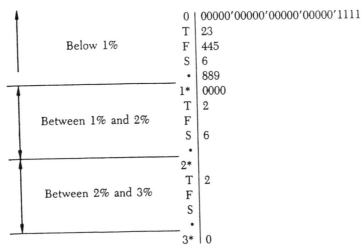

Explanation: From the top $0|0$ = 0%, $0|1$ = 1/10 of 1%, $T|2$ = 2/10 of 1%, $T|3$ = 3/10 of 1%, $1*|0$ = 1%, $3*0$ = 3%. Note the T stands for *two* or *three*, F for *four* or *five*, S for *six* or *seven*, and • for *eight* or *nine*.

Source: Ray A. Mundy, David W. Cravens, and Robert B. Woodruff, "Potential for Marketing Management Applications in Public Transportation Planning," in Robert C. Curhan (ed.), *1974 Combined Proceedings of the American Marketing Association* (Chicago: AMA, 1975), p. 277.

This method fits a number of nonprofit situations. A private school uses volunteers to raise money and decides, more or less arbitrarily, that each volunteer should telephone six parents. It is now a simple matter to decide how many volunteers are needed. A university plans a phonathon to raise funds, and from past experience knows that a volunteer can complete six calls an hour and work effectively during an evening for 2.2 hours. Hence, one volunteer produces 2.2 × 6 = 13 calls, and the university needs 270 volunteer evenings to reach the 3,500 alumni for whom it has current phone numbers.

In the example above, we are assuming that a salesman is assigned an important role in the overall marketing program and if he has more to do, he makes fewer calls. A member of a committee soliciting large corporate donations for a prep school has a good deal of material to present and may have to answer a number of questions. As a result, this member may be able to make only one call a day. On the other hand, people distributing religious materials door-to-door do little more than hand out the material, say a word or two, and move on. Because their task is modest, they will make dozens of calls a day.

Market potential. The other method of determining the size of the sales force

Table 13.2
Advertising to Sales Ratios for the Houston Grand Opera Association, Inc., 1965–1972

Sales and Expenses (in thousands)	1965	1966	1967	1968	1969	1970	1971	1972
Ticket sales and Student Matinees	$111	$148	$224	$234	$226	$233	$266	$303
Advertising	4	5	6	6	8	15	19	12
Public Relations	3	3	5	5	3	5	6	6
Total Communications	7	8	11	11	11	20	25	18
Ratios (%)								
Advertising/Sales	4	3	3	3	4	6	7	4
Total/Sales	6	5	5	5	5	9	9	6

SOURCE: Financial Statements, Houston Grand Opera.

bases the decision on the size of the market, not size in geographic terms, which would be reflected in the work-load approach (how?), but size in terms of sales potential, in dollars and cents. The rule is simple, an example of marginal thinking. As long as there is enough business so that an additional salesman can pay for himself, he should be added. As an example, the Denver Veterans Administration Hospital hired a woman to recruit blood donors. At the time, the hospital did not have its own blood, nor was a patient required to replace the blood used. As the hospital needed blood, it drew on the local blood banks, paying $12.50 a unit. After the fact, the hospital discovered that the recruiter paid for herself. The number of donations increased by almost 1,600 units, while a comparable hospital nearby showed no such increase. Since the VA Hospital received a $12.50 credit from the Denver blood bank for each unit it replaced in the local blood bank, the value of the recruiter was approximately $12.50 × 1,600 = $20,000, which far exceeded her salary. On this analysis, a marketer would start to think about adding a second recruiter.[21]

Most sales force decisions in nonprofit businesses probably combine the work-load and market-potential approaches, since it is to be expected that the two will give somewhat different answers. The Health Service Plan of Pennsylvania, a health maintenance organization, set up a seven-man sales force to enroll members; two were to call exclusively on large employers and five were assigned to geographic territories (in and around Philadelphia) to sell to both smaller customers and individuals. Presumably, both work load and market potential influenced the decision to hire seven salesmen.[22]

SETTING COMMUNICATIONS GOALS

An important part of an overall marketing plan is a statement of what the plan intends, that is, what is to be accomplished. This is of particular importance in communications because of the widespread confusion between marketing objectives and communications objectives, and because of the inherent difficulties in measuring the effect of a communications effort.

The first step in setting communications goals is to do nothing at all about communications goals. Rather, the first step is to think through goals for the overall marketing program. In an ideal world these goals would form a hierarchy, with subsidiary goals reflecting and supporting overall program goals, which themselves would be clear, easy to measure, and free from internal contradiction. In practice many, perhaps most, nonprofit organizations do not trouble to set goals,[23] and those that do tend to set simple goal structures, with one goal becoming paramount.

For a nonprofit business, overall marketing program goals look much like the goals of any business—sales, share of market, and profits. For nonprofit organizations that are not businesses, marketing program goals deal with serving clients and influencing behavior. All this has been discussed in Chapter 8 on marketing strategy.

Where does communications now fit in? Its role is to contribute to overall program goals. In some cases most of the burden of the marketing effort falls on communications. Getting new subscribers for a nonprofit literary magazine is done exclusively by advertising, some of it print advertising but most of it direct mail. Some charities put major efforts into door-to-door fundraising each year, and again communications, this time personal selling, plays a large role in meeting total program goals. In other cases the role of communications may be limited to generating inquiries, say, about the suitability of locating a plant in a certain state. Finally, communications may be unable to do little more than get the word out, to create awareness of a new program or changes in the existing program, or to generate interest in clients to find out more about a program.

Awareness

Among communications intended to change mental states we find those that aim to increase awareness, disseminate information or generate interest, impress employees and volunteers with the importance of their work, boost the morale of distributors and provide them with sales information, or change the image of the organization. In all of this the target audiences are ultimately expected to do something, of course. But the aim of the communications is to set the stage, so to speak, so that the desired behavior will be forthcoming at some future time. A change in behavior is not the immediate object.

Some religious sects, for example, attempt to proselytize by visiting homes and distributing tracts. They hope to find converts, but their primary role seems to be creating awareness of their God and spreading the Word. Another example of using communications to create awareness was the strategy of AIDS groups in the early 1980s. AIDS was still new at that point, which in communications jargon means there was little awareness of AIDS. The first job that the AIDS groups faced was generating awareness. To do that they relied heavily on special events, ranging from simple walkathons to posh, black-tie galas that featured Big Name Celebrities.

Special events aren't the best way to raise money. They do indeed raise money, but the cost of the events typically takes at least a third of the amount raised and sometimes a good deal more. Because a special event is by definition one-off, it is hard to know ahead of time whether it will be a big success or a little success or a bomb. Unpredictable cash flows are no fun for any nonprofit manager. A third weakness of special events is the nature of the donors. They tend to be the wrong ones, not donors who are interested in the cause but in the entertainment or the event. Thus, special events don't attract good quality donors. Finally, special events require a great deal of elbow grease and legwork. Anyone can do one or two, but after that the NPO begins to see its staff burn out.

Then why did AIDS groups rely so heavily on special events in the earlier years? Because they raised money and because they raised awareness better than any other fundraising strategy. Raising awareness was just what these groups were after and just what the special events produced.

Knowledge

Most of the communications generated by governmental agencies aim to provide knowledge. The U.S. Census Bureau collects enormous amounts of data each year and produces hundreds of weekly, monthly, quarterly, and annual reports, as well as large numbers of occasional reports and, of course, the census itself. It wants potential users of this information to know exactly what is available, in what forms and at what cost. The simplest way of conveying this type of detailed, complicated information is through a catalog; but the Census Bureau has also organized a nonprofit Data Users Service to help explain what is available and to service customers. In both these activities conveying information, not bringing about a certain behavior, is the paramount concern.

Behavior

Communications can also try to change behavior or to bring about desired behavior: stop smoking, take the cloth, join the navy and see the world, play football for Ohio State, register to vote, get a pap smear, vote the straight ticket, buy an illustrated book on arachnids or an authentic reproduction of an Attic kylix, stay on the wagon, use less fuel, shower with a friend.

The natural realm for communications, however, is affecting mental states, and it has a chance of doing this. But communications is much weaker when it comes to getting anyone to do anything. The reason is one on which marketers more or less agree: The causes of behavior are many, and only under special conditions do communications cause people to behave differently. Let us look at an example.

The New Jersey Department of Labor and Industry has on occasion placed ads in *The Economist,* the British weekly dealing with business, economics, and politics. One ad (Figure 13.5) listed British companies already operating in New Jersey under a headline that said, THESE 72 COMPANIES WITH BRITISH INVESTMENTS HAVE FACILITIES IN NEW JERSEY. HERE'S WHY. The goal of such a program is clear: to induce more "companies with British investments" to locate in New Jersey.

Many things affect the accomplishment of this goal, most of them factors over which the Department of Labor and Industry has little control. The decision about whether or not to locate in the United States at all will be affected by the firm's own goals, its expectations for the future, its financial condition, the labor it needs, and where its principal markets are. After deciding to locate in the United States, the firm must then choose a site, a process that may take many

Figure 13.5
New Jersey Ad

additional months and involve collecting information on such things as state financial aid; access to raw materials; educational, community, and social environment; taxes and other business costs; and labor legislation.

Given the large number of other considerations that affect the decision, it is not realistic for the marketing program to be given the objective of "making the sale." A more manageable objective would be that the marketing program interest good prospects in visiting the state to receive a full presentation of the state's story. If the marketing program accomplishes this objective, *and if* all other considerations are right, the state will win some of the companies it woos.

In working toward this overall objective, the Department of Labor and Industry will probably do three things. One is to identify prospects. It is not enough to treat as the target market "companies with British investments." The target market needs sharper definition. Since companies thinking about locating in the United States have substantial informational needs, the second goal for the marketing program would naturally be to fill some of those needs—by answering questions, putting prospects in touch with other state and local agencies, helping to analyze markets, and conducting tours of potential sites. Finally, there will be a communications effort. It will have two objectives: (1) get the word out to prospects and (2) make good sales presentations to those who visit the state.

Now we can consider the department's advertising goals. What can one expect of such advertisements? What contribution to the Department of Labor and Industry's overall marketing goal can be expected of the advertising? The answer is, not much. No manager is going to throw down his copy of *The Economist* and say, "That's it. We locate in New Jersey." As time passes, the manager will talk to many people and receive calls from industrial development representatives in many states, not only New Jersey.

There are two realistic objectives for ads such as these: (1) advertising can be expected to create awareness, to add New Jersey to the list of possible sites to be considered; and (2) it can be expected to generate inquiries. Then, if a large number of other factors are right, a plant may be located in New Jersey. Awareness and inquiries are necessary for such a decision to be made, but by themselves they are hardly sufficient. Both of these objectives, by the way, can be defined precisely enough so that they can be measured (awareness in England, inquires in Trenton), but the effect of such ads would doubtless be weak and therefore hard to detect.

MEASURING THE IMPACT OF COMMUNICATIONS

All of the discussion so far has dealt with *what* to measure in order to evaluate communications. There is a second, related question, and that is *how* to measure? There are four general approaches: observe behavior, observe physical phenomena, survey clients, and experiment.

In the first, the researcher or a mechanical device observes and records what the client does. While this research can only observe what can be observed, it can be particularly useful because it produces a detailed record of what clients actually do. It does not depend on the client's ability to interpret a questionnaire or remember what he did or thought last week. Perhaps most important is that it is honest, with no waffling or rationalizations.[24] Certainly, one step in developing a full understanding of how borrowers use the credit information that is provided to them by law would be to observe what they do when they receive it.

Observing phenomena means counting things like pledge cards, sales, attendance, and renewals. All this is familiar territory. Here we observe behavior as well but not directly; rather, we observe the leavings of behavior. This enables the researcher to deal with behavior that is difficult or impossible to observe directly. There is no way a researcher can detect the impact of anticigarette advertising by merely observing smokers. Instead, the researcher must look to records on the per capita consumption of cigarettes (and other things.)[25]

Surveying can measure states of mind as well as behavior, but it is usually used to measure the effectiveness of communications campaigns where there is only a weak link between the communications and behavior. New Jersey's efforts to attract British industry is a good example. Survey measures are probably the most common way to evaluate communications, because they are relatively inexpensive and because most researchers have a great deal of familiarity with surveying.

Experimentation involves control, above all. An experiment that merely measures an effect before and after a communication and reports the change as the result of the communication is hardly an experiment. Why? Because the differences between before and after need not be caused by the communication. The effects of a two-week advertising campaign to urge British subjects to vote in the European parliamentary elections were reported as follows:

	Before the Advertising	After the Advertising
Awareness of European Parliament	61%	76%
Awareness of elections	45	71
Awareness of the election date	14	56
Will probably vote	26	28
Will certainly vote	28	32

Source: Mike Churchman and Douglas Smith, "The UK Campaign for the European Parliamentary Elections." *Advertising* 61 (Autumn 1979): 35.

At the same time the advertising was running, however, there was a good deal of public relations activity like press briefings, trips to Luxembourg to see the Parliament in action, and a nationwide essay competition for schoolchildren that gained "excellent" newspaper and radio coverage both before and after the winners visited Luxembourg. The election generated a good deal of legitimate news as well, inasmuch as a substantial number of left-wing members of Parliament were against Britain's membership in the European Economic Community, and hence against the election. There is no hope that one can determine advertising's distinct contribution from the results in the table above. Note, however, that the headings in the table beg the question by implying that the advertising is all that counts. Instead of ''after the advertising,'' a more candid heading would have been ''after advertising, public relations activities, discussions in the press and in Parliament, and other happenings that are unknown but that occurred during the period between the two surveys.''

It is probably the case most of the time that experimental controls are used informally, except in the case of direct mail. One might identify a population similar to the target audience for a communication but which is not receiving the communication. Then it is possible to compare or calibrate the effect of the communication by observing what happened in the population that did not receive the communication. If a series of posters designed to increase awareness of a water shortage produce a 10 percent increase, what does it mean? If we know that another similar town with no posters also recorded a 10 percent increase in awareness, we have the clue we need. This type of informal control is often called a quasi-experimental approach.

One example of a quasi experiment involved a community health program that aimed at reducing the incidence of cardiovascular disease.[26] Three northern California towns were involved. One isolated town served as a control and received no communications at all. The other two shared the same radio stations and TV channels but had different newspapers. Over the two-year course of the study, both received similar mass media campaigns in the prevention of cardiovascular disease: about fifty TV spots, three hours of television programming, one hundred radio spots, several hours of radio programming, newspaper columns, newspaper ads, newspaper stories, billboards, posters, and materials mailed to participants. There was a campaign in Spanish for Spanish-speaking residents. In one of the towns, eighty high-risk residents and their spouses received intensive person-to-person instruction, including three interviews and physical examinations, a letter informing the person that he was a high risk, ten weeks of group classes and home counseling sessions in the first year, and additional special counseling in the second year. Before the campaign began, a year later and then two years later randomly selected residents in each community were interviewed and given physicals. The results showed that the mass media campaigns had reduced the incidence of disease compared to the control, but that the face-to-face counseling, while initially more successful, had lost most of its effect by the end of the second year.

The controlled experiment is more rigorous. The researcher sets up a formal procedure for randomly assigning individuals within the population being studied to ''treatments''; that is, some are randomly assigned to receive the communication, others not to receive it. Where the researcher knows that certain variables affect the outcome he controls for those variables. Randomization in essence allows him to control for variables of whose presence he is unaware, or that he cannot control. Experimentation tends to be expensive, and, of course, one must have a population on whom one can experiment. Only experimentation, however, enables a researcher to establish a causal link between this and that, allowing the researcher to say, "This causes that." Such a causal link is of small moment to most practicing marketers, however, and experimentation is probably the least used of the four techniques.

A MASS MEDIA CAMPAIGN AGAINST SUBSTANCE ABUSE FOR PRETEENS AND ADOLESCENTS

Two researchers have drawn up a set of recommendations for a mass media campaign dealing with substance abuse by preteens and adolescents.[27] Their recommendations nicely illustrate what is involved in a major use of mass media. These are not general, all-purpose recommendations. They deal only with drugs and drinking by youngsters.

Planning Issues

- Develop a long-term plan with realistic, measurable objectives. "Long-term" means that one should not expect much results in six months or even eighteen months. Measurable objectives always provide a focus and a clear-eyed way to judge results. But one should never forget the difference between things that count and things that can be counted.

- Use qualitative research like focus groups and projective techniques. Such research is not projectable but it can provide rich insight into what the target audience knows and how it behaves.

- Focus on children in elementary school, in fifth and sixth grade. That is, catch the children just as they prepare to move to junior high, seventh, eighth, and ninth grades, where there is a good deal of drugs and a good deal of drinking. The campaign should focus on trial substances like beer and marijuana, reinforce existing intentions not to use, and teach skills for coping. Then as the students move into high school, reinforce the earlier lessons through shorter programs.

  This is not what most people would think of as use of mass media or marketing. Instead it is mostly good, old-fashioned education. The idea of starting young is sound, but not for all abuse problems. It is far too early, for example, to discuss drunk driving with a fifth grader, who will not drive for several more years.

- Try to engage the public, increase its awareness of the setting in which substance abuse takes place and promote debate on public policy options. In other words, think big. Substance abuse doesn't occur only at the corner of 136th Street and Amsterdam Avenue. It is part of a much larger social context. But anyone with a grain of marketing sense should sniff at that "public." All marketing logic says, focus on clear targets. That dictum would certainly apply here. The "public" is only a little interested in substance abuse among preteens and adolescents; but some members of the public, opinion leaders, parents, some school teachers, are very interested. Focus on them. Don't broad-cast, that is: narrow-cast.

- Parents are clearly part of the overall setting and should be heavily involved. In fact, many of them, most of them, all of them—check one—will want to be involved. Both the "Just Say No" campaign and Partnership for a Drug Free America used public service announcements (PSAs) aimed at parents.

The messages to parents should be straightforward: Talk to your children, learn to recognize the signs, enforce rules and discipline. The reader can probably recall seeing PSAs that dealt with just such copy points.

Message Issues

- The campaign should anticipate resistance and address it. This is nothing new. Greek teachers of rhetoric four hundred years before Christ knew that one had to deal with weak arguments, stubborn facts, and skeptical listeners right up front. It is never good form to build only on the strengths of one's argument without addressing its weaknesses. The weaknesses will not go away, and if the speaker doesn't mention them, then someone else will: "I see that my opponent has conveniently overlooked. . . ." The solution is simple: Admit the weak points and then go on.

We all know that drug addicts are responsible for a great deal of crime in our city. In spite of that I think we should legalize drugs. Here's why. First, . . .

- Stress universal benefits. Don't focus on ones that deal too much with health. Adolescents think they are immortal, anyway. More important benefits are love, status, security, and acceptance.

- Stress the short-run costs of substance abuse. On basic marketing analysis one shouldn't expect awareness of long-run costs to do much. Most children, for example, know by age twelve that smoking is dangerous; but they can easily ignore the dangers. But:

—they are too remote.

—they don't apply to me anyway. I'm different.

—I can see for myself that a joint on Friday night doesn't lead to addiction by Sunday.

—I only do drugs from time to time, with the other girls.

What are the short-run costs, then? The violence in the drug scene, discolored truth, subpar athletic performance, and the stench of smoker's breath.

- Avoid fear campaigns. They are hard to do and they rarely succeed. If they produce fear that is too weak and too remote, they make no impact; if they produce fear that is too strong, they lose credibility and the audience tunes it out. Perhaps the classic example of the latter was the Victorian conviction that masturbation caused blindness.

- Focus on the big themes in preteens' lives. They want to be independent and grown-up, to be part of the group, and to snub authority and convention. Much of a teen's life takes place in his peer group, and a great deal of substance abuse starts there. So try to deal with these. Train the preteens to resist peer pressures dealing with trial substances like beer and marijuana. Train teenagers on the role of social pressures, the ways advertisements try to persuade, and alternative ways of refusing.

- Role models should be peers, older teenagers who are popular or more mature who manage without doing drugs. Such role models will be more trustworthy and therefore more credible.

- Celebrities can play a role but one must be cautious. Too often the viewer remembers the celebrity but not the message. Celebrities can go out of fashion quickly: In the future "everyone will be famous for fifteen minutes," said Andy Warhol, who was famous for longer than fifteen.[28] Celebrities often get themselves into trouble and in the process undermine their credibility and with it the entire campaign. Finally, many teenagers think celebrities don't do anything except for pay and if they are being paid, then obviously . . .

- Build lifestyle messages into the campaign and try innovative techniques like stories, themes, vignettes, and characters that tap into cultural belief systems. A nice example of a lifestyle message is Virginia Slims' for the liberated woman: You can compete with men without losing your femininity.

- Tie the campaign to word of mouth (WOM). WOM is far more credible, and therefore persuasive, than a PSA or a brochure.

Doing the Campaign

- Pretest the messages and the media. A campaign has many options and no one approach will work best in all situations. Besides, teenage culture changes quickly; today's verity is tomorrow's embarrassment. The campaign must be tested not only with target groups but with important gatekeepers like newspaper editors and public service directors (who control time given to public service announcements).

- Select media that offer the best way to reach preteens and adolescents. Which means, in brief, more radio, less of other mass media.

- Consider other ways of getting on the air besides PSAs. The campaign might buy time instead of beg for it; it might try to place infomercials on cable; or it might try to work directly with broadcasters to develop a full campaign.

- Include PR in the campaign. Try to get legitimate news coverage of the campaign. This won't reach many preteens, but it will reach opinion leaders and parents.

- Look for tie-ins between the campaign and businesses. The American Heart Association has led the way here by persuading restaurants to offer Good Heart meals. Booklets on substance abuse could be distributed in many retail outlets.

- Plan to do a formal evaluation, both to follow the progress of the campaign and demonstrate its impact after it is over. This is the lowest form of common sense and does not need further explanation.

QUESTIONS

1. Computer networks are likely to become an effective medium for reaching clients in the near future. But no medium reaches everyone, and each medium reaches only some segments efficiently. From what you know and have read about computer networks, they will best reach which segments of the population?

2. The quasi experiment on heart disease in Northern California, discussed at the end of the chapter, found that the mass media campaigns were more effective in the long run than face-to-face training. This flies in the face of a universal belief in marketing that personal selling is far more effective than mass media communications. What likely explains the odd results in this study?

3. St. Joseph's, the institution for severely retarded children, used videos to solicit funds from corporations and foundations. The videos were "particularly effective." But that cannot be. Surely, no corporation or foundation looks at a video and sends off a check for five or ten thousand dollars. Corporations and foundations want written proposals, financial statements, mission statements, and the like, and then after some time, at least weeks but maybe months, they decide to give or not to give.

   How then could a video have been "particularly effective?" Effective at what?

4. The British nationalized industries discussed in the section on budgeting spent very little on advertising, roughly .3 of one percent of overall revenues. Why do you think they spend so little?

NOTES

1. *Consumer Reports,* October 1976, p. 601.

2. *AMSTAT News,* April 1977, p. 11; and U.S. General Accounting Office, Survey of Public Information Expenditures (Washington, D.C.: Office of Management and Budget, 1975).

3. Hilde Behrend et al., "What Does the Word 'Inflation' Mean to You? and What is the Connection Between Wage Claims and Prices?" *Industrial Relations Journal* (September 1971), cited in Frank Teer and James D. Spence, *Political Opinion Polls* (London: Hutchinson, 1973), pp. 102–103.

4. "Attracting Clients to Service-oriented Programs," part of the Career Education Project (Newton, Mass.: Education Development Center, Inc., 1975), p. 6.

5. Thomas E. Patterson and Robert D. McClure, *Political Advertising: Voter Reaction to Televised Political Commercials* (Princeton, N.J.: Citizens' Research Foundation, 1973).

6. Quoted by Marshall Frady in *Billy Graham* (Boston: Little, Brown, 1979), p. 296. The reader may wish to note the next few Cadillac ads carefully, to see if this description is correct.

7. Edward P. Alexander, *Museums in Motion* (Nashville, Tenn.: American Association for State and Local History, 1979), p. 184.

8. John S. Glaser, *The United Way Scandal* (New York: Wiley, 1994), pp. 13–23.

9. *Publicizing Army Recruiting in the Community* (1974). It was probably produced by the USA Recruiting Command (USAREC) or its Advertising and Sales Promotion Directorate.

10. Frances J. Berrigan, *A Manual on Mass Media in Population and Development* (Paris: UNESCO, 1977), pp. 33–34.

11. Joseph A. Korbata, Mark L. Williams, and Jay Johnson, "Rock Music as a Medium for AIDS Intervention." *AIDS Education and Prevention* 3, no. 1 (1991): 47–49.

12. The music director will have to do a few other things as well. See A. Holmes, "Hottest Ticket Around, Houston's Opera Program for Students." *Opera News* (March 2, 1974), pp. 8–9.

13. Vince Stehle, "Fund Raising's Video Revolution." *Chronicle of Philanthropy,* July 16, 1991, pp. 1, 20–23.

14. See Elizabeth Greene, "Public-Policy Center Helps Create Statewide Non-Profit Coalitions." *Chronicle of Philanthropy,* May 1990, p. 26; and Eben Shapiro, "Tobacco Firm Seeks Antismoking Network's Records." *Wall Street Journal,* March 30, 1994, p. A7.

15. And oneandahalfpercentofsales is the figure still used by the Connecticut lottery too. See "The Daily Gamble." *Media Decisions* (August 1978): 61.

16. Public Relations Division, Boy Scouts of America, *Year-Round Public Relations Planning* (North Brunswick, N.J.: Boy Scouts of America, April 1977).

17. Ralph M. Gaedeke, ed., *Marketing in Private and Public Nonprofit Organizations* (Santa Monica: Goodyear, 1977), p. 263.

18. Academy for Educational Development, Inc., *Admissions/Recruitment: A Study of Costs and Practices in Independent Higher Education Institutions* (September 1978), pp. IV–12 to IV–16.

19. One problem is that the Form 990 that nonprofit organizations file with the IRS does not have a separate line for advertising expenses. A second problem is that figures like these are of much less significance to nonprofit marketers; hence, since they do not demand them, there is no one trying to supply them.

20. Some public bodies were classified as nationalized industries: the Eggs Authority, the Cheese Information Service, the Milk Marketing Board, and the Dairy Council.

21. R.G. Chapman and A. Blevins, "The Value of a Salaried Hospital Recruiter for Blood Donors." *Transfusion* 12 (1972): 330–332.

22. "Health Service Plan of Pennsylvania." Case 9-574-074, from the Intercollegiate Case Clearing House, Boston, Mass.

23. Regina Herzlinger discusses some reasons for this in "Why Data Systems in Non-Profit Organizations Fail." *Harvard Business Review* 55 (January–February 1977).

24. William Wells and Leonard Lo Scuito, "Direct Observation of Purchasing Behavior." *Journal of Marketing Research* 3 (August 1966): 227–228.

25. On this topic see the interesting report by Richard A. Ippolito et al., "Staff Report on Consumer Responses to Cigarette Health Information" (Washington, D.C.: Bureau of Economics, Federal Trade Commission, August 1979).

26. J.W. Farquhar et al., "Community Education for Cardiovascular Health." *Lancet,* volume 1 for 1977, no. 8023 (June 4, 1977): 1192–1195.

27. William De Jong and Jay A. Winsten, *Recommendations for Future Mass Media Campaigns to Prevent Preteen and Adolescent Substance Abuse* (Cambridge: Center for Health Communication, Harvard School of Public Health, November 1989).

28. *Bloomsbury Dictionary of Quotations* (London: Bloomsbury, 1991), p. 404.

Chapter 14

Advertising

Although Edward Gibbon, the historian, was referring to preaching, his phrase cryptically but nicely describes advertising; it is "the rapid communication of the prevailing impulse."[1] That is, advertising works best when it stays on the well-traveled lane. We see lots of ads for shampoo and soap because we think that having clean hair and a clean body is a good thing. Such a prevailing impulse is unknown among young children, which explains why ads for soaps and shampoos do not run on Saturday morning. To put it another way, advertising cannot bring back men's hats, but the return of hats will bring back hat advertising. That is the reason why ads from bygone days tell us so much about the (minor) concerns of those days, and why such ads seem so dated. Modern advertising stays in the middle of the road, but it follows every turn and dip.

ADVERTISING'S CHARACTERISTICS

The textbooks, however, tell us that advertising is an *impersonal* form of communication, *identified* as the sponsor or source and *paid*. This describes much nonprofit advertising but not all of it. Some nonprofit advertising is public service advertising, which is not paid. Some, a small amount, is paid for by an outside party, as when a corporation pays for a newspaper listing of an educational television program or a government agency agrees to fund advertising for a family planning clinic. "Paid" also means that traditional advertising media are used, such as print or broadcast media, direct mail, or outdoor displays.

Advertising is standardized. Every reader or viewer is exposed to the same message. It is inherently less flexible than face-to-face communication and far less powerful. But standardization also brings lower costs, and therefore the cost of advertising per audience member is cheap. It is the size of the audiences, mass audiences, that makes it seem so expensive, for advertising can reach large numbers of geographically scattered persons more or less simultaneously. Finally, standardization ensures uniformity in communication, which makes advertising particularly suited for image building.

Advertising typically has three uses in nonprofit organizations.

1. Advertising can stimulate dormant impulses. This means that advertising works best when the client is already predisposed toward the cause or the message. Advertising can work when clients are not already predisposed but it works less well. Advertising is rather like sailing. When the wind is blowing in the right direction, the sailboat can run before the wind or reach with ease and efficiency. But sailing against the wind, although possible, is tough and slow.

2. Advertising can generate awareness and knowledge. A classic instance is advertising by performing arts groups. Their ads make people aware that a new play is coming, and they deliver the knowledge needed for playgoers to make a decision—who, when, where, how much, and how to order. Such ads are, of course, aimed at people who already like the theater.

3. Advertising can induce trial, which is marketing jargon for stimulating a client to try a product. In marketing practice there is a big difference between trial and adoption. A client may try a product on various slender pretenses—just to see what it's like, ad was cute, why not?, had nothing better to do. The client sees the trial as involving little cost and no commitment. Hence, even a slight nudge as given by advertising might do the trick. Adoption means commitment, of a sort, and advertising is not likely to do the job. What convinces a client to adopt is his satisfaction with the sample. I went to the theater, he thinks, it wasn't bad and I saw some of my friends there, yeah I think I'll go again, maybe sign up for their starter kit, three plays and a reception after one of them.

THE POWER OF ADVERTISING

It is in the area of communications that the natural limits of marketing to which we have several times referred are most easily explored, for it is here that one encounters superficial and naive theories of the power of advertising. We often read in the popular press of the sinister presence of advertising in electoral campaigns. The stories usually say that candidate X advertised and won, but for obvious reasons they say nothing about his opponent who also advertised. Every marketing teacher faces the problem: Students already know all about advertising, believe it to be powerful, almost irresistible, and believe that given enough time and money, advertising can do anything. As the philosopher says, "Nothing is so firmly believed as what we least know." The teacher's problem is to counter such views by training his students to analyze the conditions under which advertising is likely to be profitable and those under which it is not. This means teaching them to understand how advertising works and because "works" is vague, teaching them how to set reasonable advertising objectives.

There is further evidence of this naiveté in the wistful postmortem that often follows a mass media failure. When a nonprofit organization sponsors a mass media campaign designed to encourage responsible drinking, the marketer is not surprised when the campaign fails. The very idea of responsible drinking is difficult to put into words—it has something to do with not drinking too much, so that the drinker or those close to him will not be harmed—and as a result it is difficult for the campaign to be clear about what is expected of the drinker. "Don't drink and drive" is clear; "Drink responsibly" is not. Moreover, the circumstances surrounding drinking—the friends who are also drinking, the role drinking plays in growing up, the general social approval of drinking, the merriment the drunkard causes, the ease with which an alcoholic or one on the way to alcoholism can deceive himself, the easy availability of alcohol—all suggest that mass media efforts will produce very little effect. In fact, we can be more specific; a campaign urging responsible drinking can be expected to (1) generate increased awareness of responsible drinking principally among those who do not drink or who already drink responsibly, (2) generate little awareness among problem drinkers, and (3) bring about no changes at all in behavior.

When the campaign fails, then, the postmortem should run along the lines that the failure was to be expected. Instead, it is common to see the failure explained either as defective evaluation or poor execution; either that the evaluation measured the wrong things at the wrong time, or that the campaign ran for too short a time in the wrong media at the wrong times with the wrong theme. Such efforts to deal with what, on correct analysis, is convincingly understood again show mistaken beliefs about how advertising works.[2]

All too often it is difficult to do much better than this, typically because it is so hard to set down clear, measurable aims for a communications effort. When this happens, the communications program is simply out of control. This is unfortunate, of course, and it is inefficient, but such things do happen. But done with common sense, an evaluation after the fact can still provide useful information to management, even in the absence of clear objectives.

Even when there are objectives, clearly put and capable of being measured, it is easy to slip. There are many, many instances. P.J. Watson describes a campaign held in Portsmouth City to collect unused medicines from people's homes.[3] The prime objective was "concerned with the return of medicaments," but this was not the sole objective. There were three others: (1) to persuade people to return surplus and outdated medicines and potentially dangerous horticultural preparations, (2) to dissuade people from using medicines prescribed for others, and (3) to encourage people to be more responsible in the use and care of medicines.

Note right off that "concerned with the return of medicaments" is vague. The canonical approach is to be specific: The object is to collect—what?, at least a ton of medicines?, at least 5,000 containers? A marketer would insist on knowing the target market—from whom are the medicines to be collected? The general public? If so, which parts of the general public? It is simply less efficient to try to reach an undefined group than a specific target market, he would argue.

The orthodox approach also calls for more detail on the other three communications objectives, those that aim to persuade, dissuade, and encourage. How are we to know that people have been encouraged to be more responsible? How are we to measure the amount of dissuasion? Settling such issues in advance makes things much easier after the campaign is over.

In fact, without such detail, there is nothing that can be said about the success of the campaign, one way or the other. Watson simply ducks the issue. He gives his results in terms of what could be measured: "The total weight of substances destroyed was 1 ton 2 cwt. 39lb (1,138 kg)." And in his conclusion he says, "The campaign was certainly successful. . . . It generated public interest and awareness."[4] But he presents no evidence for his other three objectives, nor does he refer to them again.

I have compared the communications objective of this campaign against an unfair standard. The return medicine campaign had a budget of £300 and relied heavily on volunteers. It is probably fairer to say that the objectives set down for the campaign were not the true objectives, but rather that the intent was to do *something* about the large amounts of unused and outdated medicines. And a meager budget allows no careful measures. This campaign, then, shows a campaign muddling through in the best British tradition. Communications campaigns involving larger amounts of money and volunteer time must do better.

THINKING THROUGH ADVERTISING OBJECTIVES

How, then, should one set reasonable advertising objectives? It is best to think of objectives as occurring on three levels, as discussed in Chapter 8. *Organizational objectives* deal with objectives for the organization as a whole. Marketing objectives rarely show up at this level. Instead, typical organizational objectives deal with the NPO's mission, its financial condition, perhaps its size or whom it hires. *Program objectives* deal with programs, no surprise there. Such programs contribute to organizational objectives. Typical marketing objectives that one encounters at this level deal with revenues or contributions, increases in use of services, competitive objectives such as share of market, and program financial objectives like breaking even or holding losses (net marketing contribution) to a certain figure. Finally, there are *mix objectives.* These deal with objectives for elements of the marketing mix. Four examples follow:

Element of the Marketing Mix	Sample Mix Objective
Product	Improve handling of complaints
Price	Adjust price of a new service to ability to pay

Distribution   Test a new channel of distribution

Communications   Generate awareness of the new fall program

It is hardly necessary to point out that these objectives—like handling complaints better—are far from the NPO's mission, but they do contribute to that mission, in an indirect fashion.

Let us talk about mix objectives. In preparing for an advertising campaign for the British Section of Amnesty International, the fundraising department said it had three objectives. The question for the reader is: Are these program objectives or are they advertising objectives? The three were to (1) develop a large, active membership, (2) increase public support for Amnesty International, and (3) generate funds for AI's activities.[5]

There isn't much advertising can do for the first objective. AI can use mail to seek new members, and some will in fact join. But it cannot find active members, because members become active after they join and find out more about AI. Advertising can't turn members into active members. Experience with AI and other members does that.

Increasing public support is not the type of task advertising is good at. The NPO must be worthy of public support to start with. The most advertising can do is spread the word about what good work the NPO is already doing. Most NPOs would leave this job to word of mouth and to public relations.

Finally, generating funds. AI is a heavy direct mailer which means that advertising does play a major role. But many other things must be right. AI lives in the hurly-burly of politics, revolutions, and hangings. It must keep a careful ear to what is in and what isn't. Human rights abuse in Turkey or El Salvador may move the public one year and leave them unmoved, and unwilling to give, the next.

I conclude that none of these three are advertising objectives. Rather, they are higher-level program objectives. (It goes without saying that they have nothing to do with why Amnesty exists.) They are not advertising objectives, to repeat, but advertising can play a role in their accomplishment. If the advertising is well done and if other things also support the program objectives, then they may be accomplished.

What about sales, or funds raised? Are they reasonable advertising objectives? Usually not. They are best thought of as program objectives. But having said that, one must admit that there are some situations where sales is a good objective, situations in which advertising takes the full credit, or blame, for the sale. The simplest situation is a direct mail campaign, for instance, one to raise funds. Here the behavior is easily defined, the effects of the advertising can be unmistakably traced to the advertising, and the response occurs shortly after the mailing is dropped. These are ideal conditions. Although fundraising is a program objective, advertising plays a major role in achieving the program objective.

That is why I said that in Amnesty International's third objective, advertising does play "a major role."

Few situations are this tidy, however. Few organizations want to raise funds once and then stop. They must therefore be concerned with giving over time. Because today's donor will give next year, and at a lower cost, objectives for the main campaign are harder to set. No organization wants to wait until next year to decide how well it has done. So a simple, easily defined behavior may not be enough.

Another untidy issue concerning objectives arises when the effects of the advertising are not easy to trace. An ad is run today. A client in the target market behaves "correctly" at some time in the future. What is the connection between the two? If the client's decision has taken several months, during which time he has collected information from a number of sources, how can we hope to disentangle the unique influence of advertising? The simple answer is that we can't. The effects of advertising carry over into future time periods, as well. Thus, as we have seen before, the financial evaluation of a direct mail campaign to raise funds must take into account future donations that have not yet been realized. All this assumes, however, that the nonprofit has something to sell and thus receives a clear message as to the effectiveness of its communications. Many nonprofits do not sell anything, so it is particularly hard for them to think in the terms urged by the economist, which involve setting off added communication costs against added revenues.

Of course, for some nonprofits the preceding paragraphs overstate the case. Organizations that make heavy use of the mails have a relatively easy time of it. The response to the ad comes within a few weeks, and using coded reply cards and colored envelopes makes it child's play to figure out which ad, which list, or which headline produced which response. Such organizations also find themselves in a different competitive situation. We have seen that one useful way to define competition is in terms of the decision: If we know from among what the client is choosing, we know who competes with whom. But in direct mail, decisions are made when the mail piece comes. Few clients put all appeals for funds aside and then at the end of the month make up their mind. In other words, the decisions are made one at a time, and no one group of competing alternatives is *ever* considered.

To sum up this discussion of objectives, the most useful way to approach the matter of objectives is on three levels,

- objectives for the entire organization—fulfilling the mission, staying afloat financially, surviving

- program objectives—enlisting volunteers, increasing sales, raising more money, reducing turnover among current members

- marketing mix objectives—increasing the number of calls per volunteer by two, generating name recognition among potential corporate sponsors, using prices to discriminate between those who can pay and those who can't.

ADVERTISING MEDIA

The media are the means by which messages, or copy, are transmitted from the nonprofit organization to the client (or backer). Selecting media is one of the important decisions that must be made in the process of putting together an advertising campaign. (Note: *Medium* is singular and *media* plural. Marketers still keep this distinction. No one ever says *mediums*.)

The basic issues are two: identifying who is to be reached, and identifying which media reach them best. Once again we see the fundamental importance of having a clear notion as to target markets. If the NPO does not know which clients it wants to reach, it cannot hope to choose advertising media well. However, getting the information is not always easy. There are many different bases for defining market segments, but the media generally provide only demographic information about their audiences. As a simple example, take a university extension course that wishes to reach adults over thirty who have at least a high school diploma. The university will probably find the local newspapers cannot say how many readers it has with those characteristics. Instead, it will only be able to report that (say) 45 percent of its readers are over twenty-five years of age and that 65 percent have a high school education or better. Moreover, since newspapers in most markets enjoy little competition, readership studies are done infrequently, and the most recent figures might well be several years old. Radio stations are even worse, many having never done any audience research at all. This forces the media planner to guess. And, in fact, the poor quality of audience research can influence how an NPO that advertises heavily defines its market segments. If the NPO defines its targets in terms of simple demographics, the process of media selection is simpler.

The process of selecting media is complex, depending on the size of the budget, the activities of competitors, the objectives of the advertising, the impact of the advertising on distributors and "others," and the desired combination of frequency (the average number of times an ad reaches the same person) and reach (the cumulative total number of people reached by at least one ad). Nor should the media planner mechanically match the characteristics of the audience with the characteristics of the target market. This is most easily seen in direct mail campaigns, where it is obvious that the mailing lists should be chosen in order of their return, the list with the best return being used first, then the list with the next best return, and so on. (Which lists are best is normally determined with a test mailing.) This idea is called the high-assay principle, after the gold miner's saw to dig first in the mine with the highest assay. The high-assay principle applies to all media selection as well, and says: "Advertise first in the target market that is richest in clients (or backers)."

Let us look briefly at the characteristics of the six major types of advertising media:

Broadcast Media

1. *Television* combines sight and sound, and combined with people's beliefs that TV is a "big" medium it produces a powerful impact on many viewers. Its cost per viewer is small, but as the audiences tend to be large, so is the cost. Production costs are high, too. Professionally produced thirty-second TV spots can cost over $100,000, which reminds us that it is a thirty-second medium. That's not much time to get across a message of any complexity. TV offers some selectivity in geographic and demographic segments, and it reaches almost everyone with some frequency. That in turn means there is usually a good deal of wasted coverage with TV ads, because so many are exposed to ads who are not in the target market, and the message is perishable. Finally, the quality of the color transmission is often poor.

While most TV is expensive, not all of it is. Most city ordinances require cable stations to make time available, even an entire channel, to community groups like NPOs. In large cities some cable franchises have set up NPOs to facilitate access to cable channels; for example, in Chicago, local cable operators were forced to set up the Chicago Access Corporation to oversee programming on an all-nonprofit channel.[6]

2. *Radio* is relatively cheap and reaches focused audiences, like teenagers, commuters, and foreign-language speakers. It is cheap to prepare commercials and to change them, but radio does not have the prestige that TV has, and like TV its message evaporates as soon as it is broadcast. It appeals to the ear only, of course, and there is always a good deal of wasted coverage. Unlike TV, for which there is a great deal of detailed audience research by day-part, there is little research on radio audiences.

Print Media

3. *Newspapers* have to be purchased and they have to be read, indicating a higher degree of involvement on the part of the reader. Print allows for longer copy. Because there are so many newspapers, they offer much flexibility in adjusting messages to various geographic areas. They are published frequently, ads can be run without much advance scheduling, and the cost is relatively low. Reproduction is poor and color reproduction execrable. Readers don't really read the paper, they read their favorite sections, and yesterday's newspaper is only good for wrapping fish. That is, no one keeps old newspapers around to reread them.

4. *Magazines* offer good reproduction, socioeconomic selectivity, and, for those magazines available in regional editions, geographic selectivity. They are kept around, not thrown away immediately. Costs tend to be high, and long lead times are necessary.

5. *Direct mail* is expensive and is considered junk mail by most.[7] It is easier to measure the effectiveness of direct mail than of any other medium. There are no

Table 14.1
Sample Direct Mail Rental Fees

Who	Number of Names	CPM
Buyers of sports products	600	$80
Senior managers in business	62	$125
Buyers of food and wine cookbooks	99	$90
Donors to liberal or humanitarian causes	276	$55
Buyers of remote control airplanes or boat kits	77	$80
Professionals who specialize in personal injury law	61	$110
Subscribers to *The Anchor,* a religious magazine	29	$55
Hispanic credit card users	78	$100
Buyers of travel accessories	6	$95
Entrants to a 1993 lottery	16	$65
Buyers of mail order apparel	187	$70
Buyers of kosher nuts and chocolates	3	$75
Republican donor master file	723	$55
Entrants to a contest run by *New York Times* radio station	30	$60
Mail order buyers of lawn and garden products	21	$70
Subscribers to Canada's leading church newsmagazine	12	$125

Source: January, February, and March 1994 issues of *Fund Raising Management.* CPM means cost per thousand names.

competing ads, and the availability of lists allows for highly selective mailings with little waste circulation. (See Table 14.1 for a sample of mailing lists available and their costs.) Direct mail offers an NPO several opportunities: It can build its own house list; it can combine educational materials with fundraising appeals; it can personalize mail and thus make it appear less impersonal; it enjoys tight control over the sequence and timing of its messages; and it enjoys substantial government postage subsidies. But maintaining current lists and dealing with the Postal Service can be vexing, and many people loathe junk mail.

Display Media

6. Billboards and transit advertising can carry only very short messages. They have little demographic selectivity, and they rarely attract the reader's full attention. But they are cheap, allow for much repetition, run twenty-four hours a day, and can be focused on specific geographic locales. Color reproduction is good, too. No one clips a billboard for reference, but transit ads can provide tear-off response coupons. (See Figures 14.1 and 14.2.)

Many NPOs use posters, which they place in retail stores or on utility poles. Produced cheaply and placed in stores by volunteers, posters are about as cheap a medium as one can find. Although they enjoy limited readership, they are specific to both time and situation, and like transit ads they can include tear-offs for interested parties.

Figure 14.1
Part of the Hogle Zoo's Outdoor Campaign

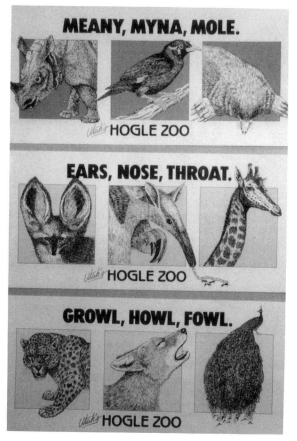

All this is too general, however. The National Indian Youth Council raises funds through the mails, and it is interested only in the problems of making effective use of the mails. A political candidate sees direct mail as enabling him to reach informed, selected voters with specific information, as well as serving as a fundraising vehicle. But the candidate will look to other media as well. He sees television as reaching a large audience that is basically uninterested in politics, and uninformed as well, but that provides him with a medium for building recognition. He also sees television as a channel for news, and much of his campaign is built on getting news coverage. Newspapers reach readers— it is difficult to describe them more precisely—who tend to be more interested in politics and know more about it. They are also the most complete source of news about a political campaign, and in campaigns where the budget is too small to allow for television, they assume particular importance. Radio is cheap and tends to catch the audience missed by other media, although like television,

Figure 14.2
An Attention-Getting Ad from a Lutheran Church

radio involves little effort on the part of the listener. In 1968 and 1972, Richard Nixon made considerable use of radio because (1) radio suited Nixon's style and voice better than television, (2) radio required little preparation other than a quick run-through just before the broadcast, (3) radio meant less risk of overexposure, which is a problem with TV, and (4) the audiences were quite big, as high as ten million, compared, say, to 8,000 at a rally or 1,000 at a dinner.[8]

PUBLIC SERVICE ANNOUNCEMENTS

What is particularly important for nonprofit organizations is the fundamental difference between broadcast media and all other media. A newspaper publisher can distribute his wares however he wishes, but a radio station uses the air; and the airwaves are owned by the public in much the same way that the roads and waterways are. To use the airwaves a broadcaster must receive a license from the Federal Communications Commission. This allows the licensee to broadcast material ''if public convenience, interest, or necessity will be served.''[9] Exactly what is meant by ''public convenience, interest, or necessity'' no one knows, for Congress did not say, leaving it to the courts to guess, a process called judicial interpretation.

In his license application, the broadcaster states what percentage of air time he will devote to commercial uses and what percentage to noncommercial uses. The application also sets out what percentages he will devote to news, entertainment, religious, educational, and agricultural programs, and how much of his time will be devoted to local programming and how much to network. When the license expires, usually after three years, the broadcaster returns to the FCC to renew it. The FCC notifies the public, holds public hearings, looks carefully at the station's record, compares what the broadcaster promised to do three years earlier with what he actually did, studies public comment on the station's performance, and in the name of ''public convenience, interest, or necessity'' renews the license.[10]

Part of a station's noncommercial time is devoted to public service announcements:

A public service announcement is an announcement for which no charge is made and which promotes programs, activities, or services of Federal, State or local governments (e.g., recruiting, sales of bonds, etc.) or the programs, activities, or services of nonprofit organizations (e.g., UGF, Red Cross Blood Donations, etc.) and other announcements regarded as serving community interest, excluding time signals, routine weather announcements, and promotional announcements.[11]

While the station must run some PSAs, it decides which PSAs to run and which to reject; it decides in its license application what percentage of its time it will devote to PSAs, and it decides frequency and scheduling. If it chooses, it may count as PSAs spots only five or ten seconds in length, or even two-second IDs; if it chooses, it may run some PSAs after 11:00 P.M. or before 7:00 A.M.; if it chooses, it may work off its obligation by running a large number of PSAs during the summer when business is slack and none during the Christmas season when it can sell every second; if it chooses it may arbitrarily refuse all PSAs of a certain type, say, those dealing with controversial issues like abortion or those that seek to raise funds; if it chooses it can cold shoulder local organizations and concentrate on running canned materials from national organizations like the Ad Council; if it chooses it can write scripts for PSAs, film talking heads in the studio, or take a film crew into the field, but it can also refuse to do any of these things.

What do public service directors look for in selecting PSAs for broadcast? They seem to consider four things:

1. The PSA must be technically right. It must be the right length, for example; it must be of broadcast quality, arrive neither too soon nor too late, and be from a bona fide NPO.

2. The PSA must avoid controversy for the station, the owner, the manager, and the public service director.

3. The PSA must be of interest to the station's audience. This is important because the station's profits come from selling advertising time, and the value of that time depends on the size and quality of the station's audience. A PSA that does not appeal to a station's audience is a poor PSA. This third consideration also explains the frequent stress that public service directors place on local appeal. A PSA with local appeal is superior to one without it. And since most of the PSAs prepared by the Ad Council are prepared with a national audience in mind, it is not surprising to find that material from the Ad Council is frequently rejected.

4. PSAs should not compete with commercial clients or reduce sales. Public service directors are cool to running PSAs for an NPO that also buys media. For example, according to a survey of 1,400 radio and television stations, broadcasters were less willing to run

PSAs for the army than they were before the army spent ten million dollars for recruiting ads.[12]

In addition to these four factors, there is no question that many public service directors find the work they do with nonprofit organizations personally satisfying, although this is difficult for a nonprofit manager to engage and of little value in explaining how public service directors make their choices.

Broadcast media *must* find time for public service advertising. Print media, billboards, and the like may run such advertising free if they wish. Many, perhaps most, carry at least some public service advertising.

Print media usually regard PSAs as fillers, items to fill empty spaces that appear at the time the publication is made up. This means that they rarely know that a PSA will run until the publication is made up. If a newspaper, for example, finds it has twenty-five lines to fill, the makeup editor goes to a box containing approved PSAs, and he hunts until he finds one that fills the space. Occasionally, a PSA is part of a campaign that engages the attention of senior management. When that happens, the PSA gets much better treatment—larger space and space that is set aside for it. Few nonprofit organizations, however, can count on such good fortune.

Getting More PSAs

Once we understand what public service directors (PSDs) want, we can lay down three brief guidelines for getting more PSAs.[13]

The first guideline is that the NPO must do its homework. If an NPO shows up with audio cassettes and no script at a radio station that reads all its PSAs over the air, it can't expect its PSAs to run. Doing one's homework means visiting the station, talking to the PSD, and adapting one's advertising materials to what the PSD wants. For a normal size city this means staying in touch with a couple of dozen PSDs and tailoring the nonprofit's PSAs to each station and each newspaper. One of the fundamental tenets of marketing is to make it easy for clients and backers to do what the NPO wants. Here is yet another example.

Second, the NPO must provide feedback to the PSD. Have you ever given someone some advice and then never heard from them again, leaving you wondering just what happened? You didn't like that, did you? You would have liked to have known what happened. PSDs are like you. They would like to know that the ads they ran had an impact of some type. Telling them what happened serves four objectives: (1) it satisfies their curiosity and thus marks yours as one nonprofit in a hundred, (2) it demonstrates that your NPO has professional standards; the station's support won't be wasted, (3) it provides yet another opportunity to say Thank You, and (4) it provides yet another opportunity to stay in touch with the PSD.

Third, the NPO must say thanks. Can you imagine raising money and not thanking the donor? Well yes, you can imagine it; but most NPOs, most grown-ups, know better than to ask, receive, and then not say thanks. Yet NPOs fail to say thanks all the time when the donation is free air time or free space. So one of the simplest and most effective ways to stand out in the crowd of PSA seekers is to say thanks. Really, that's all. Just say thanks. More astute NPOs will find ways to say thanks in special ways. Joseph Papp, the New York theater director, used to give fabulous parties to which his backers were invited. It was his memorable way to say thanks.

EVALUATING ADVERTISING

It is simple to evaluate a nonprofit organization's advertising if there are no clear advertising objectives. Study the results until you find some you like, set yourself the aim of reaching those very results, and conclude the advertising was effective. This method of evaluation—first find the results and then set objectives—is most useful in justifying advertising campaigns involving expenditure of public monies and in criticizing such campaigns. For example, to ridicule the army's advertising do three things:

1. Draw Conclusions. There is something bad about the army's recruiting advertising.
2. Research. Find that recruiting costs traceable to print advertising run "high."[14]

Magazine	Cost per recruit traceable to magazine advertising
Newsweek	$84,000
Redbook	14,200
U.S. News & World Report	12,000
Time	7,500
Cosmopolitan	6,700
Esquire	3,200
Playboy	3,000
Reader's Digest	1,700

3. Define objectives. The objective of the army's advertising is to produce recruits.

Anyone who has read this far can easily see that producing recruits is a program objective, not an advertising objective. Why do recruits join up? There will be some factors pushing them like the inability to get a decent job, and there will be benefits like learning a trade and foreign travel pulling them. No one in his right mind reads an ad and signs up. The role of advertising is almost purely communications—to make potential recruits aware of what the army offers and to let them know a few of the benefits they would have. These are sensible advertising objectives. If the advertising does its job in generating awareness and knowledge, and if the rest of the army's offer is competitive— pay, benefits, job satisfaction, and the like—then recruits will be tempted to take the next steps of collecting more information on the army and perhaps even contacting an army recruiter. The recruiter is the one who has the best chance, face-to-face with the potential recruit, of signing him up. If the recruiter does sign him up, he will have helped meet the program objective.

There is a lesson here. If you do not know the objectives of an advertising campaign, you cannot evaluate it. Since outsiders rarely know objectives, outsiders can rarely evaluate an advertising campaign.[15]

Models of Advertising Effect

Since most organizations cannot expect to have an easy time linking their advertising and their clients' behavior, they are forced to use other objectives. Since advertising is preeminently a medium for changing a person's mind, let us consider some models of how advertising might work, which will allow the development of more specific advertising objectives.

Advertising can be seen as bringing about three types of responses: cognitive, affective, and behavioral. Cognition refers to what the late Victorians called "the higher mental faculties," perceiving, recognizing, judging, learning, reasoning. Affect refers to feelings, emotions, and moods (from which we get the word *affection*). Behavior, of course, is acting—doing or intending to do.

The oldest model of the communications effect is the AIDA model. The client first becomes Aware, then has his Interest roused, Desires, and Acts. Note that awareness is cognition, interest and desire affect, and action behavior (see Figure 14.3).

Note two points. One is that an ad's effects are assumed to follow a sequence: Awareness comes *before* interest, which comes *before* desire. The other is that all of these states of mind can be set as advertising objectives. A performing arts group may work to make potential audiences more aware of its offerings, more interested in its offerings, more desirous of attending, or more likely to buy. All of these can be measured using standard marketing research techniques.

A second model is the "hierarchy of effects" model. It has the client passing through six stages shown in Figure 14.3. Again we see an orderly view of advertising effects: First awareness, followed by knowledge (but no feelings one way or the other); then affect develops, from mere liking to a preference for a particular choice; then conviction or intention, followed finally by action.

It turns out that such models miss by a wide margin explaining certain types of behavior, and that the order

$$\text{Cognition} \rightarrow \text{Affect} \rightarrow \text{Behavior}$$

seems to apply best only to high-involvement decisions where, in addition, the client believes there are substantial differences between his choices.[16] This would apply to a student considering which college to attend, a teenager choosing between a secular or religious life, or a client choosing between a health maintenance organization or a more traditional fee-for-service medical service. In such situations, the argument goes, the client will actively seek out infor-

Figure 14.3
Two Models of Advertising Effect

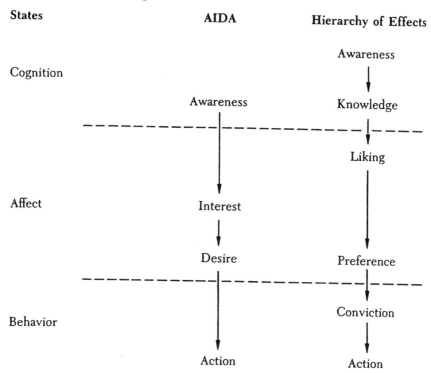

| States | AIDA | Hierarchy of Effects |

Cognition — Awareness — Knowledge

Affect — Interest — Desire — Liking — Preference

Behavior — Action — Conviction — Action

mation, including information contained in advertising; develop some knowledge based on the information; develop a preference, and then finally, make up his mind. With these types of decisions, the function of advertising is to build awareness, create knowledge and liking among those aware, and finally, entice those who like the product to buy it.

Suppose, instead, that the client is highly involved in the decision but that the alternatives appear to be much alike—perhaps because they are in fact the same, or perhaps merely because the alternatives are so complex that their differences are hard to detect. Then presumably the only way the client can learn about a particular alternative, or develop a preference for it, is by using it. Here, then, the assumed course is

$$\text{Behavior} \rightarrow \text{Affect} \rightarrow \text{Cognition.}[17]$$

First, the client acts, perhaps on the advice of a friend. Second, he decides on the basis of his experience that he likes the alternative he has chosen. Finally, he begins to learn about his choice. The learning comes partly from his experience, but also from the client's paying attention to advertising messages that support his choice. This may well be the way most people react to serious mental health problems, like those encountered in dealing with an alcoholic or a disturbed child. The involvement level of someone close to a disturbed child is high, without question, and there is a great deal of uncertainty surrounding various courses of action. It is even hard for parents to recognize that a child is disturbed rather than merely passing through a phase.

Most parents probably see only small differences among the various mental health alternatives that are available to them, for it is not easy for the average parent, untrained in mental illness, to pick up the differences.[18] Only by trying, which they would probably do on the basis of a doctor's recommendation or a friend's, will they begin to develop some liking for the therapy they have chosen and then some knowledge of it (not, however, from ads, but from books, other mental health publications, and other parents with the same problems).

Again we see the implications for setting advertising objectives. The marketer's main job is to encourage prospects to sample the service. Thus, sales promotion is the key marketing technique, not advertising, and advertising's role is to provide information after the sale.

The final model is of substantial importance to nonprofit markets, as it deals with low-involvement decisions, those that are of little importance to the client. This model was developed by Herbert Krugman, who was interested in explaining why TV advertising was so effective in use but has so little effect in the laboratory.[19] He decided that most TV viewers are not involved in the products advertised (or with television itself), and since they were not involved they did not trouble to defend themselves against the ads. The theory here is that people resist changing beliefs and attitudes they hold dear by using three "selective processes" already discussed in Chapter 13: selective exposure, selective recall, and selective interpretation. The heavy smoker avoids exposing himself to antismoking ads, tends to forget them when he is exposed, and distorts what he does remember—all to resist their ominous message. But in low-involvement decisions, where beliefs and attitudes are not strongly held, these selective processes do not come into play.

With some low-involvement activities, advertising is assumed to work quietly, producing awareness first and then perhaps some knowledge, but not much. In the polling booth the voter recognizes the politician's name and chooses it for no more substantial reason than his recognition. Then as a result of voting, he changes his attitude toward the politician. The sequence is as follows:

$$\text{Cognition} \rightarrow \text{Behavior} \rightarrow \text{Affect.}$$

The role of advertising here is, above all, to build awareness of the choice and some knowledge about it.

Now recall the argument from Chapter 2, to the effect that many nonprofit marketers were burdened with the chore of trying to market in very low-involvement situations (while others had to deal with very high-involvement situations). The Susan B. Anthony coin and the two-dollar bill, Keep Oregon Green, and Support the Meat Boycott are low-involvement activities for most clients. (But not for all clients. Think segments!)

The low-involvement model has proven to be illuminating in understanding how political advertising works. As with the ads that intrigued Krugman, political ads presented a puzzle—they did not seem to have much effect. This was discovered first by Lazarsfeld in 1948, and it has been confirmed many times since.[20] Furthermore, voters' attitudes changed little during the campaign; and in particular, those persons with a great interest in the election decided how they would vote earlier than persons with less interest.[21] This would be no surprise in Australia or England where campaigns run three or four weeks, but it was a puzzle in America.

Part of the explanation seems to lie in the degree of involvement. Lazarsfeld studied a presidential election, one in which presumably most voters are highly involved. Because they are, they are not much affected by advertising. They screen out the effects of advertising, and most other political communication as well, by using various selective processes. This means simply that in high-involvement political races advertising does not count for much in affecting how people vote.

But in low-involvement races, like those for county coroner or state treasurer, advertising does produce an effect, at least it has an opportunity to produce an effect. The low-involvement voter is exposed to ads on TV, but he does not evaluate them or develop a stand. The ads have cognitive results, not affective results. At the polls a flicker of awareness—recognition of a name, say—is sufficient to trigger a vote. Only after the election, if then, does the voter learn what he hath wrought with his vote.

In high-involvement situations, then, the marketer tries to get people to expose themselves to information, and to use it: "Shop and compare" might be a typical message. In a low-involvement situation, he tries to get people to behave. "Come in and get a free sample, no obligation, no salesman will call." If you can get enough people to try it, presumably some will repeat. Thus, instead of working the birth control message exhaustively, try to get people merely to take some action—write in for a pamphlet, come to a talk on contraceptives, or come into the clinic for a five-minute paper-and-pencil diagnostic test, anything to get some behavioral response.

Another example of low-involvement behavior is giving to United Way. The ideal in such drives is to get people to commit to giving by means of a payroll deduction, rather than a single gift once a year. Why is this type of giving low involvement? As the amounts at stake are small and giving is socially acceptable, there are no perceived risks. There is very little deliberation or search for information. In fact, talking about the gift may even suggest that the backer is a cheapskate. Finally, the amount of the gift is not made public, although the boss may know. There are no risks for giving, and probably only minor risks from giving too little or not giving at all.

What is the aim of the United Way's promotional activities in this case? Not to develop attitudes about United Way or build preferences for giving to the United Way, but to make backers aware of the campaign, aware of the United Way, and give them enough information so that they can give.

If this is correct, what is the function of the public service announcements on United Way run during National Football League games? They are clearly designed to influence people's feelings about United Way. From the low-involvement view of giving, these ads work their effects on backers who have already given, not on those who have not given before. The ads support the development of favorable attitudes, but chiefly among existing givers.

The following four lessons can be derived from this discussion:

1. Develop objectives only after thorough analysis of the behavior of clients (or backers). This means that it is not easy to set objectives, nor is it proper entertainment for a clerk.

2. Make sure the objectives can be measured. To set specific objectives, an organization usually needs to find out where it is. To set "increasing awareness from 15 to 30 percent" as an objective, for example, the organization must already know that the current awareness level is 15 percent.

3. Spend money for marketing research. It is impossible to maintain control over an advertising program without research.

4. Expect the first three steps only to reduce the uncertainty surrounding the advertising program. They will not eliminate it, because of the difficulties of setting good objectives and measuring progress against the objectives, and because objectives that can be counted are too often not the objectives that count.

QUESTIONS

1. The chapter says that most NPOs don't bother to thank those who give them free time and free space. On its face this seems odd, particularly since all nonprofits thank contributors of money and services. How might you explain this oddity? That is, propose a rough theory that might explain it.

2. Note the following one-half column ad that ran in *The New Yorker* magazine (Figure 14.4). Use the three levels of objectives to formulate some reasonable advertising objectives for this ad. Be sure to analyze how travelers make decisions to go to this country or that.

NOTES

1. Edward Gibbon, *The Decline and Fall of the Roman Empire,* Chapter XX (London: John Murray, 1838), III, p. 292.

2. For a description of the effects of a ban on advertising see Reginald G. Smart and Ronald E. Cutler, "The Alcohol Advertising Ban in British Columbia: Problems and Effects on Beverage Consumption." *British Journal of Addiction* 71 (1976): 13–21.

Figure 14.4
The Wales Ad Illustration to Accompany Question 2

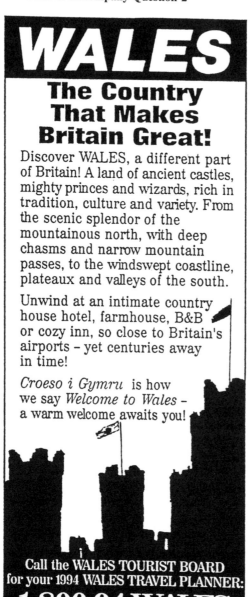

3. P. J. Watson, "A Medicine Return Campaign." *British Journal of Addiction* 72 (1977): 83–89.

4. Ibid., pp. 88, 89.

5. See "Value For Money in Charity Advertising," in Paul Feldwick (ed.), *Advertising Works* 6 (Henley-on-Thames: NTC Publications Ltd., 1991), pp. 264–284.

6. Sean Mehegan, "Nonprofits Put Cable TV to Use." *Nonprofit Times* (August 1993), p. 18.

7. I do not know why it is called "direct" mail, instead of simply "mail." I have never heard of indirect mail.

8. *Washington Post,* February 12, 1973, Section A, p. 16.

9. Communications Act of 1934, Section 307.

10. Historically, being granted a license renewal has been only slightly less certain than death and taxes.

11. Code of Federal Regulations, Title 47-Telecommunication, Subchapter C, Part 73.112, Note 4 (Washington, D.C.: U.S. Government Printing Office, 1976).

12. "Army Recruiters Find Broadcasters Reluctant to Take Free Ad Campaign." *Broadcasting* (September 11, 1972), p. 26.

13. I draw here as well on Holly Hall, "How Charities Can Get Public-Service Ads in Print and on the Air." *Chronicle of Philanthropy* V, no. 19, July 13, 1993, pp. 31, 32.

14. The figures are from *Changing Times* (March 1975): 38.

15. If this discussion seems too fanciful, the reader has much to learn. Start by reading Steuart Henderson Britt, "Are So-Called Successful Advertising Campaigns Really Successful?" *Journal of Advertising Research* 9 (June 1969): 3–10.

16. Here I am following Michael L. Ray, *Marketing Communications and the Hierarchy-of-Effects* (Cambridge, Mass.: Marketing Science Institute, November 1973).

17. Ray calls this the Dissonance-Attribution Hierarchy, for reasons we need not go into.

18. Discussed by Thomas L. Woods, "The Family as a Consumer of Mental Health Services," edited by Gerald Zaltman and Brian Sternthal in *Broadening the Concept of Consumer Behavior* (Chicago: Association for Consumer Research, 1975), pp. 35–44.

19. Herbert E. Krugman, "The Impact of Television Advertising: Learning Without Involvement." *Public Opinion Quarterly* 29 (Fall 1965): 349–356.

20. Paul Lazarsfeld, B. Berelson, and H. Gaudet, *The People's Choice* (New York: Columbia University Press, 1948).

21. Ibid., p. 54.

Chapter 15

Personal Selling

WFYI, the public television station in Indianapolis, wanted to raise more money not so much by increasing the number of donors but by increasing the number of major gifts, which to most TV stations means $1,000 and up. It planned to do this by making its appeals more personal. It identified prospective donors by comparing the station's own list of donors with donors giving to other nonprofits such as local arts and educational bodies, who often publish names of those who gave big gifts in their newsletters and annual reports.

In the process WFYI discovered Claudette Prospère, as we may call her, the elderly widow of a local businessman, who had been making large gifts for various arts groups in Indianapolis, but not to WFYI. The station chose not to call on Mrs. Prospère. It sent her instead a videotape of one of her favorite operas and a basket of fruit. (And how, one may ask, did WFYI know what her favorite operas were and that she preferred fruit to flowers or a lace doily? The source doesn't say, but most likely the answer can be summed up in two words, database marketing.)

Not long afterward, she increased her annual contribution to the station to $3,000. The following year she gave $5,000 and the year after that $10,000. And still at this point, according to the station's chief fundraising officer, "No one at the station has ever met her, but simple tokens of appreciation have really paid off."[1]

Indeed they have paid off. It is a pretty tale, boys and girls, full of innocence and warmth and clean living winning through in the end. Do not be fooled, though. The story, published in a trade publication for nonprofit organizations, was newsworthy precisely because Mrs. Prospère gave big without anyone calling on her. It is news, that is, for the same reason that man bites dog is news.

It doesn't happen very often. The way to raise big money or to get people to make major commitments of any kind is face-to-face, that is, by personal selling.

INTRODUCTION

Few nonprofit organizations can rely on advertising alone for their marketing communications, because standardized, impersonal messages are not suitable for all purposes. Instead, they support their advertising with personal selling (as well as public relations and sales promotion).

Businesses already have a vocabulary to talk about this area of communications. They talk about sales, salesmen (or salespeople), sales quotas, a sales force. No such terms exist in nonprofit organizations. "Personal communications" is awkward and a little pompous but it will do. However, its derivatives—personal communicator, personal communications quota, and personal communications force—are indigestible even to a professor. Thus, while this section is about personal communications, the familiar words of business will be used. This is arbitrary, but it is not likely to confuse the reader. Note as well that I use "salesman" instead of "salesperson," although I know that both men and women sell. Some of my former students who sell tell me they are comfortable with the term, and to my ear it reads better.

It would not seem at first glance that personal selling has much role in nonprofit organizations. At least that is what I thought when I first began studying nonprofit marketing. It is not the case. Nonprofit businesses can be expected to have full-time paid sales forces—university presses, health insurance groups like Blue Cross–Blue Shield, health maintenance organizations, the Conference Board, state lotteries, the College Board. Many more nonprofit organizations have part-time or volunteer sales forces. No electoral campaign is complete without a door-to-door canvass to get out the vote, and many charities solicit funds door-to-door or in the streets. Educational television stations use volunteers during fund drives to man phones and plead for funds on air. The most effective university alumni funds use telephone volunteers (and direct mail) to reach small donors and those who do not give; but larger donors are touched in person, again by volunteers. How do you persuade a truant to return to public school, particularly these days when they are skipping school not as a lark but because they are on drugs, or can't read, or are afraid of being mugged in the halls? You might try postcards or telephone calls; but the old way is still best: Only the truant officer can find the truant who is trying to avoid him, fossick out the cause of the truancy, and perhaps convince him to return to school.

The religious recruiter is a central figure in efforts to attract young men to the priesthood, but as vocations come from a Higher Source, the role of marketing communications is distinctly secondary. Still, it does have a role. Advertising can arouse some interest, generate inquiries, perhaps, and keep a religious order's name before young men; but it is the recruiter who can answer the questions and objections that parents have and the youngster himself, and who can encourage, perhaps press, a youngster having trouble making up his mind. Finally, William A. Nolen has written of the efforts of interns on the surgical service at Bellevue Hospital to recruit blood donors. Without blood surgical interns perform no elective surgery, a dreary fate for future surgeons. The difficulty was to get the patient or his family to donate blood before the operation, that is, before it was too late. The proceedings were conducted with the brazen mendacity of a medicine man pitching snake oil: Uninspired interns would tell family members that blood was needed for operations that in fact did not need blood, or that four units of blood were needed for operations that normally needed only one. Others were more inventive:

"Your father must have blood immediately," one of my co-interns once said to a big family. "If you don't all donate, we'll just have to give him dog blood, and that doesn't always work well." ... A more subtle approach was to simply stand at the foot of the bed, shaking one's head in dismay, watching the clear sugar-water infusion running into the patient's veins and muttering, "If only it were blood" ... just loud enough for the family to hear ... this approach was good for at least a pint.[2]

Selling Versus Mass Communications

When it comes to getting people to do things, personal selling is generally much more effective than communications by mass media. (Mass media are generally better in generating awareness and knowledge.) Why not use salesmen all the time, then?

The first reason is that they are expensive. We can get a rough idea of how expensive by looking at some numbers. Suppose the membership director of a trade association wants to increase membership. He plans to do this by calling on prospective members in field trips. Over the next year or so he expects to spend half his time in the field calling on prospects and half at the national office, attending to other matters and preparing for his next trip. He expects to average three calls a day on his trips; and given vacations, holidays, and sick leave, he expects to be in the field twenty-two weeks in the next year.

Membership director's annual salary	$35,000
Portion allocated to field trips, 22/52	$14,800
Weekly field expenses x number of weeks	
$360 x 22	7,900
Transportation (mostly by car)	8,000
Total field costs of 22 weeks in the field	$30,700
Number of calls in 22 weeks	
= 22 weeks x 5 days/week x 3 calls/day	330
Average cost per call = $30,700/330 =	$93

The average cost per call is very high. Of course this $93 figure depends on the assumptions I made, but they are all reasonable. There is nothing wild about them. Estimates of the average cost of a sales call in business run a good deal higher, from $100 to $300.

My point, however, does not deal with numbers. Don't think that a typical sales call in the nonprofit sector costs $93. Think instead that a typical sales call is expensive. This means that an NPO should not send a salesman out unless he is tracking big game, like prospective members to a trade association, who are worth such an expensive way of delivering a message.

There is a second reason why nonprofits don't use salesmen all the time. When clients or backers come by the tens or hundreds or even thousands, one instinctively thinks of salesmen. Some few clients can be identified and if they are big enough, the sales force can track them to their lairs. When clients come in the tens of thousands or millions, most of them will be small and in an economic sense not worth much as individuals. Then the only sensible approach is to use mass communications.

NPOs have one advantage over businesses, though. They can employ volunteer salesmen. Then the numbers shift strongly in favor of the personal touch. So when the costs of direct mail fundraising began to rise, as they did in the late 1980s and early 1990s, some NPOs began to look for a cheaper substitute and found it in telephone solicitations by volunteer solicitors.

The Power of Personal Selling

The two characteristics that make personal selling so effective oppose those that make advertising effective—personal selling is not standardized and it is not impersonal. The salesman can adapt his message to the specific needs of the client he is trying to influence; he can answer objections and questions; and he can ask the prospect to commit himself, to make a decision and act on it. Let us look at fundraising for a moment. To Soroker, rating is the process by which a fundraiser communicates to a prospective backer what he is expected to give.[3] For example, when a contributor is invited to a $1,000-a-plate dinner, he is being told that he is expected to give $1,000. Similarly, a church giving plan built on the tithe tells the backer what is expected of him. Soroker discusses rating in face-to-face solicitation.

> Rating in conjunction with face to face solicitation can be most effective. In face to face solicitation, the worker notifies the prospect of the rating and utilizes the face to face solicitation to move the person to this figure. At some fund raising meetings the ratings are placed on the individual's pledge card. One system utilizes ratings on pledge cards. Individuals are asked to merely raise their hands if they accept the rating. This has the advantage of no one else in the room knowing what the rating is. It has the disadvantage of individuals [sic] not knowing what their peers are donating.[4]

In addition to telling a contributor what he is expected to contribute, a salesman can help a client who does not know what he wants or what he needs. A salesman can help him define his problem, search for alternative solutions, and evaluate them. In all of these methods we see an adaptive, two-way flow of communication that characterizes personal selling but that is absent in advertising.

Personal selling involves contact between two human beings. It is not a remote, impersonal encounter, but one in which the salesman and the client each affect the other. As an example of this mutual influence consider a volunteer worker in a fundraising campaign. One of the most important steps in raising funds face-to-face is the assignment of workers to prospects. The general belief among fundraisers is that workers should not solicit gifts that are larger than their own gift, which, as a matter of form, they give before they begin soliciting. Why is this so? Because otherwise the prospect affects the worker and lowers his expectations. That's right. The prospect lowers the solicitor's goals.

In ninety-nine out of a hundred cases an individual who gives less than the prospect he is soliciting is at a real disadvantage psychologically. The fact that he gives less than the prospect he is soliciting cannot but weigh heavily on the worker's mind. As a result he is apt to be satisfied with a much smaller contribution than would an individual who gives in the same range or even larger. Accordingly, one should avoid giving any worker the card of a prospect who gives substantially more than the worker himself.[5]

But correctly assigned, a worker generates pressure on the prospect to give as much as the worker has given. Soroker gives this human interaction prominence when he says, "People give to people, not to causes."[6]

The interaction itself of client and salesman can come to be valuable, and for the client, compliance with the salesman's entreaties produces an immediate reward in the form of approval from the salesman.

The Role of the Salesman

Just what is it a salesman does? We can consider four interrelated parts of the salesman's role.[7]

1. Salesmen persuade clients or backers to undertake a course of action, in plain words, to do what the salesman suggests. Sometimes this can mean that the salesman must collect information about the client's problems and help the client weigh various solutions. Thus, someone advising battered wives to leave their husbands and make a new start has a complex set of problems to deal with and a great deal of information to collect, as does a fundraiser who is trying to help a large donor negotiate tax and legal mazes that lie in the way of the donation. More often salesmen simply persuade someone to do something, perhaps to do something without giving it a lot of thought. "Come on. Give a hundred bucks. Everyone else on the floor has. We want to get one hundred percent participation so we can beat the accounting department." The salesman may simply persuade the client to try something. A powerful way to sign up

new volunteers is not to sign them up at all, but to have a current volunteer ask a friend who is interested in volunteering to come in and give (say) three hours on a project. If things work right, if the prospective volunteer likes what he sees and does, he will be eager to do more.

2. Salesmen provide services, take orders, deal with fulfillment. ''Fulfillment'' is marketing jargon for what has to be done after the sale is made, to complete the sale. In a nonprofit business invoices have to be prepared, the order has to be picked, packed, and shipped, and someone has to deal with it if it fails to arrive on time or isn't what the customer ordered. In a fundraising campaign, information must be entered into a database; thank-yous must be sent; a promised premium must be picked, packed, and sent; perhaps reminders, if the contributor is slow to meet his pledge.

To order Christmas cards from the Art Institute in Chicago, one consults the catalog, decides, and picks up the telephone. At the other end will be a salesman whose job is to take your order, to provide some service, and most likely to sell you on buying more than Christmas cards.

3. Salesmen collect information on clients and backers. Face-to-face can provide an enormous amount of information that cannot be gotten in any other way. The Mary Babcock Reynolds Foundation tries to meet with all of its grant seekers to learn directly from the applicants about their idea, how they intend to proceed, and, most important, who they are as individuals.[8] A graduate business school I know of asks all applicants to submit to a personal interview. (Those who can, come to the school; the school goes to those who can't.) The purpose is twofold. It gives the admissions staff an opportunity to sell the school in a way that would otherwise be impossible. More important, it allows the school to screen out those students likely to have a hard time finding a job at the end of the program. Schools boast about the jobs their graduates get and how many get jobs. No business school wants to admit a student who is so picky or bizarre that he will be unemployable.

4. Salesmen provide support for clients, educate them, and build good will. Providing support and building good will serve to support the important educational function that so many NPOs have as part of their missions.

A Second Look at the Salesman's Role

Salesmen can also be classified by the types of jobs they do. There are five of them: active selling, passive selling, client service, client contact, and education and advice.

Active selling means seeking out prospective clients and persuading them to buy (or to behave correctly). These salesmen, sometimes called order makers, play a key role in raising funds and moving the NPO forward against obstacles. *Passive selling* means not seeking out but being sought. When the local public TV station conducts its annual fund drive, one often gets a glimpse of the phone banks. They are staffed by passive sellers or order takers. In economic terms their value is much lower than that of order makers. *Client service* means a variety of chores, installing or repairing a product, handling complaints, giving out information, or responding to routine requests. Most NPOs have people on staff or volunteers who do little else than service clients and backers. *Client contact* means any contact outside of selling or client service. In other words, it is all other face-to-faces with clients or backers. It thus includes everything from a hello by a cafeteria worker on the steam table to a lengthy discussion with a case worker.

Finally, *education and advice:* Personal selling, to repeat, involves contact between two human beings. When the salesman is only passing on information or advising the client, the human contact can become particularly important. Listen to this mother describe her attempts to get help, for herself and for her sexually abused child.

The first thing that happens when you try to get help is you call somewhere and you get brochures. And they all say the same thing: "What do you do if you suspect your child is being abused?"

There is a need for that kind of brochure. There is a need for a lot of education on the subject, [but] what I felt I needed most back then was some human contact, some support, some guidance, somebody telling me I wasn't this terrible, horrible person, someone just to be there if I just needed to talk to somebody.

As Homer says in *The Iliad,* "A friend's persuasion is an excellent thing."

I describe this last role as a type of selling, but it is here that the traditional meaning of the "selling" and "salesman" is stretched beyond the breaking point. I include education and advice here for only one reason. Those who educate and advise often exhort and try to persuade, meaning they often wear a salesman's hat.

A nice example of this blend of sales and the human touch is found in the fundraisers employed by the American Friends Service Committee (AFSC), a Quaker organization devoted to relief, community service, and education for peace. The AFSC's fundraisers call on prospects and current donors to solicit gifts. This personal cultivation is a major part of the AFSC's fundraising strategy. But the fundraisers do not confine their activities to fundraising. In the words of one staff member:

They give the donors what can best be called "nurturing attention." It is *personally* nurturing, in addition to nurturing the gift. A good many of these contributors tend to be older. Their gift is their vicarious way of being involved with the program and the AFSC.

Many of them give in an open-handed way. They believe in the Service Committee and what we are doing. They support us in a general way.

Of course, there are lots of them who care about Central America too, or the Middle East or whatever.

The fundraisers cultivate or nurture these relationships with phone calls, with letters, with Christmas cards, with visits. On a visit it is not a matter of going in and saying, ''Let's see, you gave $500 last year. How about upping that to a thousand this year?'' Many times, money isn't even mentioned. Rather, the visit is a time when the contributor as a person receives a personal report.

In making a call, the fundraiser would bone up on what the donor is focused on. If the donor focuses on the Middle East, the fundraiser will bone up on that. If it's a major donor, sometimes field staff will go along on that visit to talk to the donor and make the report.

Part of the nurturing had an educational aspect to it.

Some people call the Service Committee spirit-led. Some call it conscience-based. Whatever the reason, we do do controversial things, not just controversial in terms of the general public but things that we ourselves in the Service Committee find controversial. Not all 75,000 [AFSC] donors can be close enough to understand how we Quakers work, our consultative process, how we came to a decision to do something controversial.

So another of the fundraisers' jobs is interpreting the AFSC to people who may be very unhappy about something we have done.

One example of this is the work we've done on affirmative action. On the surface this has been uncomfortable for people, even those close to us philosophically. I mean, people who relate affirmative action to quotas and to segmenting and separating people. Many of our contributors try to look at people without noticing their color, or what-have-you. So having the fundraisers able to interpret and explain our work lends a great deal to us and supports the AFSC tradition.

Fundraisers have to be an ear. They have to listen for people who are upset with the AFSC but not upset enough to take away their contribution. Sometimes of course they do stop contributing. But what they often want is just someone to listen to them.

Most fundraisers say that they get a great deal of joy from their contacts with donors.

They find that they're out there dealing with really wonderful people who support us and are enthusiastic about our work. I know some fundraisers who say it is a privilege to be constantly thrown into contact with the kind of concerned contributors they meet.[9]

VOLUNTEER SALESMEN

Volunteer salesmen are used in two different ways. One is to contact clients and deal with them in a nonprofessional, nonbureaucratic way. In other words, to provide a human touch. A Candy Striper in hospitals, for example, is not a paid employee but someone ''who really cares about patients,'' as one writer put it, without thinking what he had written. Since Candy Stripers have no medical training they spend most of their time in contact with patients, talking to them in the outpatient clinic, and dealing with preoperative patients; but they help in other ways like assisting wives of foreign interns and representing patients on boards and committees.[10]

The other way volunteers are used is to persuade people to change their behavior. They might try to persuade people to buy something (Girl Scout cookies), to give something (newspapers to the Salvation Army), or to change their behavior in some way (run for office or use a condom).

Volunteer salesmen are of considerable importance in American elections. Before an election they visit their neighbors and deliver a pamphlet for their candidate. The pitch is appropriately low key: "Good evening, Dave. I'm working for United States Senator Orrin Knox. He's a good man and I think we need him in the Senate. I hope you and Peggy will vote for him. Please read this pamphlet and show it to Peggy too."[11] This effort can be mounted throughout the entire electoral region. Volunteers are also used on election day, but the locale and the pitch now change. The volunteers no longer try to educate the voter or even suggest a ticket. Their sole chore is to winkle the voters from their homes and get them to the polls. This is not a nonpartisan effort, however. They limit themselves to getting out the vote only in areas that have heavily favored their party in the past, because a voter from a Democratic ward can safely be assumed to vote Democratic.

Perhaps the heaviest use of volunteer salesmen is in fundraising. Volunteers in hospitals, for example, help raise funds by getting involved in a variety of projects—gift shops, snack shops, secondhand thrift shops, television rentals, baby photos, memorial funds, benefits, and Christmas card sales.[12] But such efforts are nickel-and-dime stuff. Volunteers also man telephones in fundraising campaigns conducted by many organizations like charities, universities, and public television stations, and here the returns can be more substantial, although only small donors are approached by phone.

The highest use of volunteers is in calling on prospects expected to give, or capable of giving, large amounts. These individuals, corporations, and foundations are relatively few, but they contribute much. Hospital fund drives, as an example, expect to receive 75 to 80 percent of the money raised from only 12 to 15 percent of the prospects, and these few prospects will receive calls in person from the chairman of the fundraising drive.[13]

Peer Pressures

As we have seen, the special nature of the interaction between salesman and client is what makes personal selling different, and so much more effective. But there is another factor that often comes into play. Just as salesman and client affect each other, when clients meet face-to-face in a group, each client affects the others. This effect presumably arises from the pressures toward conformity that normally arise in small groups and the difficulty each client has in concealing his behavior from the others.

It is sometimes worthwhile trying to create support groups even when the groups do not meet face-to-face. All political candidates struggle to consolidate their supporters, because their vote is assured (provided they vote at all) and because they are likely to try to convince other voters. Hence, the time-honored "citizens committees" like Teachers for Knox and Lawyers for Atreides. Less formal groups of supporters can be assembled, as well, by asking the candidate to list his family, friends, acquaintances, and associates and using this list as a base, asking each person on the list to add his friends and associates.

The most elaborate way of doing this is the "social precinct" idea of Stephen Shadegg, an experienced political campaign consultant.[14] Shadegg tries to identify energetic, informed supporters who would not otherwise be picked up as a party member or a supporter of the candidate, and then to enter into the inner, social lives of these people. The process starts with the candidate and his campaign workers listing potential social precinct workers (SPWs). Campaign researchers then prepare background summaries of the SPWs, such as their occupations; where they bank, go to church, work, and relax; their net worth and their family connections. SPWs are first contacted by letter, not a letter asking them to work for the candidate, but one asking for their opinion on a forthcoming piece of legislation.[15]

Dear Jim:

The Banking and Insurance Committee of the Senate is considering HB-146. The sponsors of this bill claim it will give more protection to a bank's depositors. If you could take time to read the enclosed copy of this proposed legislation and let me have the benefit of your thinking, I would be most grateful.

Some of our staff members will work up information on the proposal but I feel the need of your knowledge and your understanding. A long time ago, Jim, I learned that the people back here don't always think the same way as the people in Arizona.

Gratefully yours,

Orrin

If the SPW answers the letter, he has been recruited. The second contact is another letter, one that assumes the senator and the SPW have a continuing relationship. Then successive mailings turn to bulk mail.

Some SPWs, flattered by the attention, ask what they can do to help, while others are asked to do several things:

- Provide an index of public sentiment toward the candidate, either by telephoning or in another way.
- Keep the campaign staff advised about what the opposition is doing, by recording media usage, for example.
- Counteract statements of the opposition, such as help to quell a rumor.
- "Prepare a climate of disbelief" by suggesting in their everyday conversations that the opponent will probably follow such-and-such course or make so-and-so declaration.
- Most important, mention the candidate's name favorably to persons they meet.

This last is interesting. Because the SPW is not known to be with the candidate or with the party, his views are taken as expressions of his own convictions, which of course they are, or else he would not cooperate; and hence they are more likely to be accepted by his friends and acquaintances. Shadegg stresses the importance of keeping the SPWs motivated by providing them with valid reasons for injecting the candidate's name into conversations—typically by feeding them inside information that becomes a natural platform for discussing the candidate and his opposition. Shadegg's plan is elaborate and expensive, but it nicely illustrates one way in which peer support and pressures are mobilized.

Outside of auctions and the like, creating group pressures is not a situation of much importance in business, but it does arise in nonprofit contexts. One way, for instance, we might try to influence behavior—say, to increase attendance at church or to help smokers stop—is to ask people to take a pledge whereby they promise publicly to behave in a certain way. It is the public nature of the commitment as well as the feeling among those taking the pledge, that we're-all-in-this-together, that makes pledges work.[16]

Creation of group pressures is also important in some fundraising campaigns. When I was a boy, my church had a fund drive each year, at the end of which it published a list of who gave how much. This stimulated some of my friends to give an odd amount, like $1.37, in order to have a listing all to themselves. But larger donors were presumably shamed into giving more than they otherwise would have given. Some universities raise money from classes at their twenty-fifth reunions by bringing the members of the class together for a fine dinner, an address on the needs of the university by the president, and finally, an appeal for funds. This is answered by several well-to-do alumni who have agreed in advance to stand up and donate large gifts. Then fundraisers at each table try to extract sizeable pledges from those sitting at the table, and they announce large pledges as they are made. Such a face-to-face situation brings strong pressures to bear on donors—but all in a good cause.

THE ELEMENTS OF SALES MANAGEMENT

Let us look briefly at each of the principal elements of sales management: recruiting, selection, and training; compensation; and sales supervision.

Recruiting, Selection, and Training

These three are all part of one process. Recruiting means generating bodies, getting people to apply for a job, no questions asked (or at most only a few); selection means sifting those likely to succeed from those not likely—"many are called but few are chosen"; training means teaching those selected what they need to know to do the job.

We consider these three in the context of a safe sex campaign aimed at gay men, not all gay men but gay men cruising in "public sex environments" (PSEs) that I will call simply "public settings"—remote parking lots; public restrooms with parking lots nearby, especially at dusk or at night; beaches that tolerate nudity; adult bookstores; highway rest stops and truck stops; and all-night convenience stores where youngsters and street people congregate.[17] These are settings where gay men often go for casual sex.[18]

The focus, to repeat, is not *all* gay men but only those in public settings. How can an AIDS group reach these men with its safe sex message? It should be clear that mass media will not do the job. There are media for gay men but none for gay men in public settings. Even if there were, mass media couldn't do the job. The job of seeking these men out and persuading them to consider safe sex or practice it and the job of answering their questions and handling their objectives must be carried out face-to-face. The marketer calls a person who does this a salesman, but the term doesn't quite fit. "Educator" or "teacher" or "trainer" falls better on the ear; "peer educator," the term chosen by the AIDS group, does not. I will call him simply a "trainer." Finally, note that these trainers are not paid for what they do. They are volunteers.

Recruiting. Why "him"? Shouldn't that be "him or her" or even worse, the phrase that reads "him slash her"? (A hint there of male violence toward women?) No. One of the most elementary rules of thumb is that selling works best when like calls on like. To explore the drug behavior of young, unmarried women, send interviewers who themselves are young and unmarried and, best of all, who have done drugs themselves; otherwise you face higher refusals and less complete interviews. Thus, our volunteers need to know the world of male sexuality, speak its language, and have experienced the emotional adjustment brought about by fifteen years of AIDS. Such peers narrow the psychological gap between the trainer and the man in need of help. A good deal of the trust trainers will enjoy in this job is the prospects' knowledge that the trainers themselves are at risk and are giving their time out of personal concern.[19]

We have already enunciated the basic principle—like deals with like. Now we can see where we must focus our recruiting. Our volunteers must be part of the gay or bisexual community. They must also be recruited from subcommunities that match the target populations selected by the AIDS group for safe sex education, such as Latinos, or Asians, or gays who have come out of the closet, or gays or bisexuals who are college age.

Selection. This is straightforward. The project administrator writes a job description and then selects those who are closest to it and who can commit the time necessary to train and devote to the job. (See Figure 15.1.) The administrator will also try to asses whether the prospective trainer seems to have the skills necessary to do the job, such as making contact with gay men in order to exchange information, listening, and building trust.

Training. The trainers must themselves be trained to do their job. But for a change of pace, let us turn to sales training in two quite different situations, preparing priests to deal with parents of boys considering the priesthood and training board members to raise funds.

Sales training programs must deal with the realities that the NPO faces, its competition, its resources, its overall mission. For example, large NPOs will be able to have formal training sessions, will be able to train salesmen at several

Figure 15.1
Job Description for a Safe Sex Trainer

MINIMUM QUALIFICATIONS: Successful candidates will have:

1. A knowledge of gay/bisexual male sexual activity with some personal experience with this population and comfort working with gay men.
2. Assertive social and communication skills in order to make effective connections with strangers in public settings.
3. A willingness to follow commonly agreed-upon ethics and policies of the agency and to represent themselves and the program accordingly.
4. A basic knowledge of AIDS transmission and prevention and a willingness to increase knowledge through training and personal study.
5. A commitment and resolve to practice safer sex methods in personal life.

PREFERRED: Individuals with diverse cultural experience including a knowledge of: ethnic minorities, bilingual communication skills, substance abuse, married bisexual cultures, adolescents' subculture, and/or street wisdom.

DUTIES:

1. Working in teams of two, volunteers will provide two to four hours a week of outreach education, discussing safer sex information in public meeting places or PSEs.
2. Volunteers will attend a regular support meeting to review their efforts and enhance outreach skills. Volunteers agree to accept the group decisions regarding outreach standards of quality.

SALARY: The satisfaction of making a difference in the epidemic.

Source: David Loren Beckstein, *AIDS Prevention in Public Sex Environments* (Santa Cruz: Santa Cruz AIDS Project, 1990), p. 32.

stages of their careers, and may be able to use full-time staff trainers. A smaller NPO will catch as catch can, perhaps doing most of its training in the field, on the job. The objectives of such training are clear. By making its salesman more assured and knowledgeable, the NPO will enjoy better morale, higher productivity, lower turnover, and happier clients.

What kind of training does a recruiting priest need? In his ineffable chapter, "Winning the Home Front," Poage gives the following advice for dealing with parents of a teenager considering becoming a priest.

As soon as a boy or girl evidences interest in the seminary or convent, therefore, it is a good idea to have the youngster mention it to the parents. If mother and dad have plenty of time to think the matter over, they are not likely to be startled into opposition.

It is also very important to visit the home as soon as you are convinced the youth has become serious about entering your seminary or community. At least show the parents the courtesy of calling upon them.

When making arrangements for this visit, it is always prudent to ask the youngster: "When would be the best time for me to come?" Generally, it will be some evening or a weekend, for you want to have both mother and father present. Once you have set a date and hour, you can be confident they will be ready. For your part, be punctual. It is never polite to keep them waiting.

When you meet the parents, for heaven's sake don't say: "I just happened to be passing by and thought I'd drop in to see you." That is a lie and they know it. Nor should you apologize for the visit: "Please forgive my intrusion. I don't want to take up much of your time."

It is pathetic to listen to the way some recruiters handle themselves. Your visit is not being made by chance or accident, so let the parents know it. Mention how pleased you are to meet them . . . how interested you are in the family. You might say: "I have become so interested in your son (or daughter) that I just had to meet you." That lets the parents know your visit was planned and has a definite purpose behind it.

Many recruiters, especially beginners, can sense a tension or reserve on the "first" visit. They can almost feel the wall of resistance that the parents instinctively throw up against any attempt to separate them from their child. It is important to recognize this tension and to take measures to remove it. This can be done in several ways:

1. You might start out with a reference to some achievement of the youngster in studies or athletics. This convinced you of the child's potentialities.

2. Or you might introduce the matter of the youngster's vocation as a hypothetical case— not as the specific problem of their son or daughter.

3. It is sometimes good to mention that you did not come to "sign up" the boy or girl, but merely to find out more about the family.

4. You might ask the parents' opinion about your vocation program, asking advice on how you can improve it to the greater advantage of youngsters like their own.

Just as it is essential to remove initial tension and resistance, so it is equally necessary to avoid early dismissal. You don't want to leave until you have presented your case in full. This can best be done by making a planned approach and having attractive literature or some colored slides to show. When you have an interesting presentation lined up, few parents can resist hearing you out.

When the visit is not the first one but a repeat visit, the approach will, of course, be different. Presuming that the parent either refused permission to let the child sign up, or was hesitant about the whole idea, try to approach this new call from a different angle. Don't say, "I have come back to see if you have changed your mind." This implicitly says: "You were wrong, but maybe you have reconsidered." Most parents are then more adamant than ever.

Instead, say something like this: "Since my last visit, I've been studying this matter, and I've come up with a couple of ideas that are so good I wish I'd thought about when I first talked to you." The point to express on the parents is that you have been thinking about their side of the problem and that you have some new angles or ideas that they will find worthwhile to consider.[20]

Poage's training is avuncular, easy, just what an inexperienced priest might like to hear from one with experience.

The Basis of a Training Program

The three basics in a sales training program are product, selling, and motivation and control. Salesmen need to know what the NPO and its services are, what it does for whom and what it doesn't do. Salesmen need training in selling; for example how does one find good prospects, how does one handle objections, how does one ask for the order and close the sale? Finally, salesmen need to learn how they are rewarded for what they do, and they need to understand the mechanical aspects of selling, how to write up an order, for example, or how to trace a late shipment.

Let us say that a nonprofit wants to bring its board members up to speed in fundraising.[21] It is not a minor issue. Board members often dislike fundraising because, like the rest of us, they fear rejection, and not knowing that other board members may feel the same way, they are reluctant to speak up and ask for help. Because there will be few board members needing training at any one time, the program will be informal. It will still cover the three basics, though.

Product knowledge. To raise funds the board member needs to know the NPO. (This is true whether the board member raises funds or not.) The natural way to impart such information is to have the board member visit the NPO's offices and service centers; talk to volunteers, clients, and backers; perhaps go through the same training that all new volunteers go through. Board members should, of course, read what is available—financial statements, the NPO's strategic plan, evaluations of effectiveness, research on clients, and the like.

To graduate from this product phase of training, the board member might be asked to speak to groups interested in the NPO's work. Such talks ensure that the board member knows the NPO well and begins to develop the conviction that comes purely from having to convince others of a point of view. (Every teacher understands the principle: The best way to learn is to teach.) At these talks the board member does not ask for money. It is too early. He is still in training.

Sales skills. The standard outline for training in selling includes six steps.

1. *Prospecting and qualifying the prospects.* In simple words this means finding sales prospects and screening out those who are unlikely to buy; or finding likely donors and screening out those who are unlikely to give.

2. *The approach* is comprised of two stages: what happens in preparing to meet the prospect and meeting him. The first involves preparation for the call, reviewing the history of the account and the objective of the call, deciding how best to make the call (telephone, mail, or face-to-face), and when best to call. The second involves the sales call itself—the opening lines, the follow-up, the transition from small talk to the purpose of the call.

3. *Sales presentation.* Here the salesman might follow the AIDA approach, mentioned in Chapter 14. He tries to get the prospect's attention, stimulate his interest, arouse his desire, and lead on to action. If the product can be demonstrated or even given a fake demonstration by means of a video tape, this is the time for it.

4. *Handling objections.* One of the simplest techniques for helping a salesman be more productive is to teach him how to handle objections. A salesman can benefit from learning to do this because this knowledge puts the salesman more

at ease and gives him more control over the exchange. Poage tells us that recruiters for religious orders encounter five common objections from parents of adolescents who want to take the cloth: "The child is immature or too young, undue influence has been brought to bear, the child has an obligation to his parents, objections due to the experience of parents and others, and arguments from the nature of life."[22]

Although he tells us that some of these arguments could "easily be answered by a first-year seminarian," just knowing what the common objections are helps in meeting them. It would be even better, however, for experienced recruiters to train inexperienced recruiters in the successful techniques they have developed for overcoming objections. Certainly, one of the most basic things to do with volunteer fundraisers is to give them a little practice in countering common objections.

Slightly off the point, training in handling messages can also be directed at clients, so that they will follow directions better, understand more of what they hear, or resist the sales pitch. For example, a program that trains the poor to read credit agreements carefully and to ignore a salesman's pitch would help them buy the products they need more cheaply. Certainly, the most ancient of all such encounters is the seduction of girl by boy. Would it help the girl if she had heard the boy's lines before and knew how to answer them? Indeed it would, and a Syracuse University professor has been collecting these lines for just such a purpose. They range from "Want to see my etchings?", a venerable line that must be incomprehensible to most modern boys and girls, to "If you say no I'll become mentally ill." Other worn lines included "If you love me you'll have sex with me," "You have beautiful eyes," "Don't worry, you won't get pregnant," "If you get pregnant I'll marry you," "I love you," "If you really loved me," "It's late. Why don't you stay overnight, I promise I won't touch you," "I can't stop now," and "Everybody else is doing it." This commonsense, simple technique was so effective that after a number of sex education sessions in a summer program to prepare disadvantaged youth for college, the boys complained the sessions were ruining their sex lives.[23]

5. *Close.* The salesman who cannot ask for the order is a poor salesman, indeed. Salesmen need help, though, in knowing how and when to close, and how to lead up to it.

6. *Follow-up.* This is usually a second sales call done to pick up any dissatisfaction, handle complaints, and assure the prospect of the salesman's interest in the account.

Now let us return to training the board member. His will be a mixture of on-the-job training and what we might call "elsewhere" training. The new board member will benefit from talking to experienced fundraisers, listening to how they overcame their fear of failure, discussing the best way to frame the task, and learning how to handle objections. But on-the-job training is even better. The board member goes with another board member and watches him make a pitch, then does it himself, accompanied by another board member for moral support.

Outside training. The assumption so far has been that the training is do-it-yourself; but there is an endless number of outsiders eager to train the board members for pay; many nonprofit associations run workshops in fundraising, and there are hundreds of books and pamphlets on the subject. Some NPOs have had good luck using their own fundraising consultant to train board members. Since their time is so tight, one-on-one training suits them well.

Motivation and control. Board members are typically busy people whose time is valuable. How can they be motivated to do a good job raising funds, and what kind of controls should they be subject to? Peer pressure and competition both provide effective means of motivation. At quarterly board meetings, for example, progress toward annual fundraising goals might be discussed, along with which board members are on track to make their annual goals. And friendly competition is always able to spur some extra effort.

Control is based on written plans and written goals: "All board members are expected to generate at least $15,000 a year in contributions, either by soliciting other donors or by giving themselves." Some NPOs use a subcommittee of the board to oversee fundraising; others have had good results having a single board member responsible for the board's efforts.

Sales Compensation

There are three ways to pay a sales force: salary, commission, and some combination of the two, which may well include a bonus. The most important determinants of which plan to choose are (1) what the salesman is expected to do and (2) what competing organizations do.

NPOs pay a salary when the salesman's role is something other than closing a sale. It might be cultivation of a client, or opening the door to a later solicitation, or educating the client. These are concrete objectives, but because they are not easily measured and may involve effort over a considerable length of time, they are not suitable for the automatic incentives in a commission plan. The salary allows the NPO to tell the salesman what he is to do and how.

If the salesman's role is straightforward and if it generates revenue—close sales—then it is possible to pay on a straight commission. Girl Scout troops selling cookies don't cultivate customers nor do they educate the customer about Girl Scouting, nutrition, or anything else. They (and their parents) simply sell cookies, for which the Girl Scout organization rewards troops, not the girls, with a commission, about fifteen or twenty cents per box that retails for about two dollars. (The girls earn cookie badges, tee shirts, and other goodies.)

Salesmen at the Better Business Bureau of Greater East Tennessee (BBB) earn 50 percent of the first year's revenue from a new BBB member, 7.5 percent of the first renewal, and nothing after that. There are two things worth mentioning here. It seems odd to pay only for the first year's renewal, but the BBB has found that when a new member has renewed once, he is likely to remain a member for years. What makes sense to the administrators, however, is surely received coolly by the sales force. In fact, some of the salesmen will be moved to try to get around the system. Which leads to the second point: Salesmen get a 50 percent commission for a new member, but what is a new member? Is it one that is late in paying and is technically no longer a member? Is it a "drop," a member last year but not this year, or is it an account that has not been a member for some years. One can see the temptation for the salesmen: "Wait. You're already late. Tell you what. We're good friends and here's a favor you can do for me. I'll tell them you want to drop your membership. Then next month when I come by, I'll sign you up again but as a new member. That way I get a higher commission."

The final point dealing with straight commission relates to control. Paying a salary, the NPO in essence tells its salesmen what to do. Paying a straight commission, the NPO loses control of its salesmen. They decide for themselves how to allocate their time and who the best prospects are; and they may refuse any substantial chores, like educating a client, that do not lead directly to a sale.

Many NPOs define the role of their sales forces as a mixture of these two. They are supposed to close sales, but they do other things as well, perhaps providing after-sale service or engaging in educational efforts with clients. In such cases it is common to pay a combination of some salary and some commission.

One must not assume that the compensation plan is an all-purpose motivator. A commission will not motivate salesmen to sell if, for example, they don't understand their products or lack adequate sales training or don't know how to plan their sales calls. Compensation is part of an overall motivation and incentive plan.

Sales Supervision

Since all workers need supervision, what's so different about sales supervision? The difference is that the salesman usually doesn't work under the eye of the boss, and that the salesman experiences a good deal of rejection but without any support from his peers or his boss. So an NPO should put special care in supervision—that is, in directing its sales force and motivating it.

The most useful supervisory tool is the sales plan. The salesman is asked to put down whom he plans to call on, what he plans to achieve on the calls, even when he plans to make the calls. Such a plan is approved by the salesman's supervisor, who now has a basis for comparing aim and accomplishment. Of course, the sales supervisor is not a shy flower. He will make suggestions to the salesman, urging him to put more emphasis on these kinds of clients or those kinds of call objectives, and the sales supervisor will continue the sales training by making calls with the salesman in the field where he can see for himself problems the salesman faces and show him how to solve them. He will also keep an eye on how the salesman divides his time between calling on existing accounts and prospecting. For most, prospecting is much harder work than calling on existing clients, and few salesmen will do enough of it on their own.

The motivational tools are much the same as used elsewhere in the nonprofit organization. Certainly, the most common is the quota. Thus, the recruiter for the U.S. Army is given a quota of four recruits a week. Given the resources he needs and sufficient training the recruiter should be able to do the job. If he does not meet quota, he knows questions will be asked.

In nonprofits, salesmen generally get satisfaction and motivation from the nature of the organization. What motivates the board member raising funds? A sense of accomplishment when he persuades a friend to donate $2,000 and, even more important, the sense that he is helping the NPO carry out its mission. Certainly, that is the basic motivation for the safe sex trainer, the conviction that one by one he is spreading the message to play it safe.

Finally, sales managers use incentives. Peer pressures, for example, can goad salesmen to excel. Some NPOs post a list of top performers; others point out the top performers at sales meetings. Sales contests are another common motivating tool.

A Sales Call

With all this as background, let us return to the trainer and his safe sex message, and observe him on a sales call.

He is on a path behind a public rest room, leaning against a picnic table. A second man in his late thirties has been eyeing the trainer for several minutes. The trainer decides to talk to him.

Trainer: Hi, how you doing tonight?

Man: Hi, pretty good. How are you?

Trainer: Fine. Sure is a warm night. I like this time of the evening just after sunset.

Man: Yeah, it's a pretty sky tonight. You're a pretty sight yourself.

Trainer: Thanks. You know, one of the things I do when I visit here is chat with people. I'm not really into playing around but I like to talk.

Man: Hmm. What do you talk about?

Trainer: Well, you know this is quite a busy playground . . . guys sure get it on here a lot and I wonder sometimes if they're aware of how to be safe with sex.

Man: (Silence)

Trainer: I see a lot of condoms left on the ground over there by the large bushes and I guess some guys are thinking about protection from the AIDS virus. What do you think about it?

Man: You've got to be careful these days. You never know who might have it.

Trainer: Sounds like you've given this some thought. Do you bring condoms with you when you come here?

Man: Sometimes. I usually have one with me but tonight I came straight from work.

Trainer: You're smart to have a condom with you. Rubbers are the best protection from getting AIDS. Here I have some condoms (hands him a packet).

Man: Good, now there's nothing stopping us from having some fun?

Trainer: No. As I said, I don't play when I come here. You know, nobody should be getting AIDS these days. We now know exactly how to prevent it. As long as you don't have blood contact with someone else's blood or cum, you can remove any risk of getting it. And that means condoms with anything anal.

Man: What about giving head? I never swallow the cum, I spit it out.

Trainer: I think it's smart not to let somebody cum in your mouth whether you swallow it or not. If a person is carrying the virus, there will be lot of it in his cum. There are ways cum in the mouth can enter the bloodstream. If you like it that you or your partner can shoot cum into the mouth, the safest thing is to wear a condom during sucking and cumming.

Man: What's the good of getting sucked off if we have to suck on rubber?

Trainer: I know it takes a little getting used to. You know, I have some mint flavored condoms that you can try. Here it is and also here's a gold coin condom which doesn't have such a rubber taste.

Man: Yeah, well I usually only jack off with guys here anyway.

Trainer: Well, that's certainly safe. In that packet I gave you is a lubricant that's water-based and is good to use with condoms. You probably know that you don't want to use an oil-based lube like Crisco or Vaseline. Oil will cause the condom to break. This lube is made with a water base and it has an ingredient that will help to kill the virus as well.

Man: Thanks.

Trainer: So, what decisions are you making when you have sex here that will keep you safe?

Man: Well, I know I need to use a condom. . . . Maybe I'll give it a try when I go down on somebody. It's something to think about.

Trainer: Yeah, with sex these days, you can never be too careful. I know there are some times when it is especially difficult to play safe. After a few drinks or after getting stoned, it is very hard to use protection. Or the excitement of the moment can cause guys not to bother with condoms.

Man: Yeah, I know what you mean about that.

Trainer: But, the risks of getting AIDS are just too high to ever take a chance. Especially here, where you can't know very much about your partners. If you have sex without using condoms with just one man here, it's like having contact with all the other guys he's been with.

Man: I never thought about it like that. Well, thanks for the condoms.

Trainer: Nice talking to you. Take it easy and play safe.[24]

Here we see the trainer employing many of the standard selling skills. He has already qualified the prospect because they are both in a public setting. The preparation for this "call" has been done well in advance, so the trainer can move directly to the opening lines and the initial small talk, which, given the setting, quickly turns to talk of sex. When the man says, "You've got to be careful these days," the trainer begins to make the transition to his sales presentation. He devotes a fair amount of time to handling the man's objections and questions, as befits his dual role as salesman and educator. Finally, he asks for the order, "Take it easy and play safe." In all, it is low-key, focused, and likely to succeed in its intent—getting one more gay man to think harder about safe sex and perhaps change his behavior.

Finally, note what is missing from the dialogue. There is no supervisor looking over the trainer's shoulder, evaluating his performance, and making suggestions. Like most salesmen out on a call, the trainer is isolated from the organization he works for. If he succeeds, there is no one to share his success. If he fails, there is no one to cheer him up and urge him on. His performance depends heavily on whether he is the right man for the job (recruiting and selection), whether he has been well trained (training), whether he has the self-discipline and energy to do the job without direct supervision (motivation), and whether he is rewarded for doing his job (compensation).

QUESTION

1. Soroker is quoted as saying, "People give to people, not causes." Can that possibly be right? Surely, the cause is more important than that. Or is it? Comment.

NOTES

1. Vince Stehle, "A Broadcast Call for Major Gifts." *Chronicle of Philanthropy,* October 19, 1993, pp. 23–24.

2. William A. Nolen, *The Making of a Surgeon* (New York: Random House, 1970), p. 122.

3. This differs from the definition of rating in Chapter 5, where it meant estimating how much the prospect was capable of giving. But sometimes the two—communicating and estimating—go hand in hand and are done at the same time. See Gerald S. Soroker, *Fund Raising for Philanthropy* (Pittsburgh: Pittsburgh Jewish Publication and Education Foundation, 1974), pp. 99–101.

4. Ibid., p. 100.

5. Ibid., p. 90.

6. Ibid., p. 21.

7. I am following, at a distance, ideas developed by Robert N. McMurray, "The Mystique of Super-Salesmanship." *Harvard Business Review* 39 (March–April 1961) pp: 113–122; and Derek A. Newton, "Get the Most Out of Your Sales Force." *Harvard Business Review* 47 (September–October 1969): 16–29.

8. Holly Hall, "Inside a Foundation: How Grants are Made." *Chronicle of Philanthropy,* December 11, 1990, p. 7.

9. David L. Rados, "The American Friends Service Committee" (1990, unpublished).

10. See American Hospital Association, *The Volunteer Services Department in a Health Care Institution* (Chicago: AHA, 1973). Also see AHA, *Guidelines Concerning Volunteers in the Social Work Department of the Health Care Institution* (Chicago: AHA, 1973).

11. Stephen C. Shadegg, *The New How to Win an Election* (New York: Taplinger, 1972), pp. 120–130. Shadegg says such a modest plea works because voting for someone your neighbor is voting for is as good a reason as any for a voter not firmly committed to either candidate.

12. See Harold P. Kuntz and Margaret Burrows, *Effective Use of Volunteers in Hospitals, Homes and Agencies* (Springfield, Ill.: Thomas, 1971), pp. 100–105.

13. See *Hospitals,* the journal of the American Hospital Association 46 (March 1, 1972), an issue devoted to fundraising.

14. Shadegg, *The New How to Win an Election.* Chapter 9 deals with the social precinct, pp. 103–119.

15. Ibid., p. 108.

16. See, for example, J. H. Hallaq, "The Pledge as an Instrument of Behavioral Change." *Journal of Social Psychology* 98 (February 1976): 147–148.

17. This material on safe sex is drawn from David Loren Beckstein, *AIDS Prevention in Public Sex Environments* (Santa Cruz, Calif.: Santa Cruz AIDS Project, 1990).

18. I confess that I do not fully understand what goes on in these encounters; and although I have a keen curiosity about almost all aspects of life, this is one of the few areas where knowing nothing sates it.

19. Ibid., p. 33.

20. Godfrey R. Poage, *Secrets of Successful Recruiting* (Westminster, Md.: Newman, 1961), pp. 88–90.

21. The inspiration for this section was Holly Hall, "How to Help Trustees Overcome Their Fear of Fund Raising." *Chronicle of Philanthropy,* April 20, 1993, pp. 28, 32.

22. Ibid., p. 94. I do not know what "objections due to the experience of parents and others" or "arguments from the nature of life" are, and Poage does not say.

23. *The New York Times,* March 3, 1977, p. 37.

24. Beckstein, *AIDS Prevention,* pp. 21–22.

Chapter 16

Public Relations and Sales Promotion

In this chapter we deal with the last two of the four methods of communication: public relations and sales promotion.

PUBLIC RELATIONS

Public relations cannot easily be described, because it covers so many different activities. That's why I used such vague language in Chapter 13 when I defined it as "any of several programs designed to influence an NPO's image." Somewhere, each of the following has been considered public relations: training of volunteers and staff, combating rumors, running a speakers' bureau, writing newsletters and brochures, writing advertising copy, making films, managing a crisis, handling complaints, preparing annual reports, writing letters, ghosting books and speeches, working with editors, answering reporters' questions, lobbying, appearing before government commissions; and handling "special events" like anniversaries, awards dinners, tours, exhibits, picnics, bowling leagues, fundraising events, contests, and open houses. At the University of Michigan, the vice president of university relations, who is responsible for internal communications, publishes: (1) the *University Record,* which goes to 23,000 academics (faculty and students) with items of interest to them; (2) the *UM News,* which goes to 14,000 nonacademic staff members with items about general university activities; (3) the *Report to the University Community,* a crisis publication for all members of the university community that is produced only when needed; (4) *News Briefs* phone lines, which provide callers with current facts and developments; (5) *At The Table,* which deals with collective bargaining issues and goes to between 5,000 and 8,000 staff members every other week;

and (6) *Management Intercom,* which provides information for supervisors and managers on university policies and procedures.[1]

In essence, public relations tries to tell the NPO's story to its publics. As part of this process, PR people often use research to find what its publics know and what they believe, before they try to guide these publics into understanding the NPO and accepting it.[2]

From this we can immediately see three of the problems that public relations faces. First, PR simply bears the message, it does not prepare it. By this I mean the most important influence on a public's perceptions of an NPO is what it does, not what it says, particularly not what it says about itself. Lizzie Borden gave her father forty-one whacks. No PR could hope to guide the public to understanding and accepting Lizzie's means of self-expression, nor can a vigorous PR campaign do much to convince the American public that its senators and representatives are clean. Second, in the absence of research it is impossible to assess the PR effort, and even with research it isn't easy. The best one can hope for is to measure communications effects and pray that they in some way contribute to program objectives and organizational objectives.

An NPO's Publics

The third problem that public relations faces deals with that "public." It is public relations, but it should be "publics relations," a more descriptive term but, as one can easily determine, nearly unpronounceable. It should be publics relations because public relations deals with more than one public. One simple breakdown is to think in terms of those with whom the NPO normally deals in its day-to-day affairs, and those with whom it does not have regular or close ties. The first is *internal* publics, mostly employees, volunteers, clients, and some of its backers; but it can also include suppliers, members of the NPO's channels of distribution, and perhaps its neighbors. The second is the NPO's *external* publics, which includes members of the press, most of its small backers and some of its large backers, government officials, regulators, and its competitors, and other NPOs working broadly toward the same end.

Different publics see nonprofits differently, which should be no surprise. Clients do not so much see the NPO itself as its services and how well it serves them. Someone attending the theater focuses on the performance, not whether the troupe is for-profit or nonprofit. Backers and volunteers judge the NPO on how well it serves those it seeks to help. Volunteers see the organization from behind the scenes as do the many backers who serve as volunteers; those backers who do not volunteer form their impressions more superficially, usually from communications put out by the NPO itself. How else can the average graduate of a law school tell whether his school is moving ahead than to rely on what the dean says? Board members tend to see an NPO as a political organization set in a web of competing interests. They often are most concerned that the NPO play a respected role in the community. Employees and, to a lesser extent, suppliers see the NPO as their livelihood, the place where they earn a living.[3] The third problem, then, is that no NPO can be all things to all men. Inevitably, in satisfying some of its publics it dissatisfies others.

The Tools of PR

Let us look at the tools PR uses to work its ends. *Publicity* is customarily defined as impersonal communication run free of charge by the press without the source of the story identified.

This last is, in fact, its major advantage because of the effect the source of a message has on its credibility: People place greater confidence in communication from a trustworthy source. An ad protesting a new tax sponsored by Mobil Oil will be seen by most readers as different from the same ad sponsored by the Sierra Club. A news story predicting environmental damage from the new tax, whose placement is effected by either Mobil or the Sierra Club, will be seen by most as straight news and be the more effective because of it.

Because publicity must have some news value, otherwise it cannot masquerade as news; because it is run when an editor says so and not when the sponsoring organization wants it to run; because it cannot be repeated as ads can or directed easily at specific target audiences, publicity cannot be as effective as advertising or personal communications. It has a role in a total communications program, but usually it is only a minor one. Nor is it correct to say the publicity is free. Done as it should be done, it will absorb resources—money, time, energy, supplies—that could be devoted to other ends, which is the definition of an opportunity cost.

Publicity is usually disseminated in the form of a *press release,* which is a story prepared in the format used by the media for which it is intended. Since a PR department relies so heavily on gifts from the media, that is, free time and space, it must be sure that its press releases conform to what the media want, that they are indeed news so far as the media are concerned, that the story is timely and accurate, and that the press release is easy to use. This means, for example, that the press release sent to a newspaper should conform closely to that newspaper's style. We have gone over this same ground in discussing public service announcements.

Often an NPO will invite the press to hear an announcement or interview a VIP or announce the results of a study. *Press conferences* are a dime a dozen in most major markets, which means it is not easy to get reporters and editors to attend. The usual rule, compounded in equal parts of experience and common sense, is: Don't call a press conference if the publicity can be disseminated in other ways, say, by a press release or a video.

In addition, press conferences pose a substantial danger. Reporters who attend expect to ask questions. Because reporters find it no easier to stay on the point than anyone else, once the questions have begun, there is little an NPO can do to direct them or control them. A press conference designed to announce the successful completion of a capital campaign may find reporters wanting to ask about high turnover among volunteers or poor service at one of the NPO's facilities, or even the salaries of its executives, whatever their editors feel is most newsworthy.

This raises the problem of *handling bad news* or *crisis management.* The prime responsibility for dealing with bad news is the NPO's senior managers and the board, assuming that they are not part of the bad news. The role of PR falls into two broad categories: One is anticipating bad news, the other is dealing with bad news that pops up without warning. Such occurrences have become common enough in America that there is a small group of specialists who make a living dealing with crisis management.

Perhaps the foremost rule for dealing with a crisis is: Don't make things worse than they are. A lovely example of how to make things worse was given by William Aramony, under fire for his lavish lifestyle and other corrupt practices at United Way of America. Asked to justify his use of a limousine, he was quoted as saying, "I can't afford to be waiting for taxicabs," a comment that made him appear arrogant and out of touch.[4] Not making things worse can be difficult for one used to what passes for public discourse in this country because it means not lying to the press, and not insulting the press by stonewalling, covering up, or pretending nothing is wrong.[5]

An NPO can also take steps to prepare to handle crises when they arise. What might one possibly do in advance? One begins by assembling a crisis management team, typically the president, a lawyer, the public relations director, and perhaps a member of the board or a key staffer. American University did not have a crisis management team. Its president was responsible for handling most aspects of any crisis that might arise. Then the president himself was found to be making obscene phone calls from his office. American University now has a crisis management team.

The team imagines five or ten worst possibles, and considers how it might respond to each. A theater knows it will have accidents and fires from time to time, just as a municipal utility knows it will have blackouts, a youth development group knows its major contributor will die, and a nationally ranked collegiate football power knows that sooner or later, probably sooner, it will be caught violating NCAA rules governing the game and some of its players will be found incapable of reading simple English. From such an exercise and from a look at what other NPOs have done comes a general communications plan, flexible enough to deal with different types of crises. This is the point at which the spokesman is chosen, the one person in the organization who will deal with the press and the general public. It is routine practice, as well, to compile a crisis phone directory, with phone and fax numbers of key personnel, each of whom receives a copy. The biggest nonprofits have found it useful to have a dry run from time to time, rather like lifeboat drills on ocean liners.

A crisis nicely illustrates one type of pressure on senior managers. Something big and bad has happened, but they have no reading on its impact or even who knows about it. In Gotham City one might call Batman, but in what passes for the real world the crisis management team commissions a quick marketing research study. "Quick" means a telephone survey, perhaps of the general public, perhaps of major contributors, members, or executives in the NPO's affiliates. One of the first things United Way of America should have done when the news broke about its president's lavish lifestyle and other corrupt practices was do a survey. But the news traveled so fast and so hard that William Aramony was gone within a few weeks. The first survey of the public feelings toward United Way was done more than a month after the news broke, with a second study in July, five months after the crisis erupted.[6]

Sponsorships of events such as AIDS walks and athletic tournaments can generate a great deal of secondary press coverage, as well as raise money, which is usually their prime purpose. As such they are a useful arrow in the PR department's quiver.

The Media

"Know the enemy" is an old rule for good warfare. At times the media can seem like a hostile force, trying to provoke the NPO. It makes good sense for PR people to know reporters and to meet them away from the job. An NPO with a large enough budget might want to join a trade association like the Public Relations Society of America.

A well-managed PR department builds a strong list of media contacts. The list might be as small as a few people on the local weekly and daily papers or one that ranges wide over several types of media and many countries. Such lists contain material that doesn't change, like a radio station's call letters and location on the dial or newspaper deadlines, and things that might change at any time, such as the names and titles of editors, news directors, reporters, public service directors, and columnists. A marketer should have a keen nose for things that nettle his backers, in this case, the press. One need do no research to know that members of the media expect accuracy in what they receive, and that accuracy begins with the names, titles, and departments. Misspelling the name of a TV news reader, say, is bush league; but how can one possibly be up-to-date when names, titles, and departments change so frequently? Simply by calling, once a quarter say, to verify all the information on the list.

It is a standard piece of advice to appoint media people to your board. How easy it is to say, how difficult it is to do. Not only are there dozens of possible slots for everyone in the media worth cultivating, not all media people are eager to join boards, which only further increases the excess of demand over supply. In such a situation the prudent NPO keeps at it. It also can use a fallback position and ask a media representative to serve in an advisory position in lieu of serving on the board.

The media live on news. "Man bites dog" is news, "dog bites man" isn't. The NPO that hopes to get media coverage must take reasonable steps to ensure that its press releases are indeed news. This means, among other things, not sending out press releases when there is no news; not, for example, sending out a press release every week, regardless. If the media were short on news releases, this would be poor advice, but the media are awash in requests for space and time, most of them, as the media know all too well, driven by self-interest. Newsworthy means different things to different media. TV needs news that makes good pictures, or perhaps pictures that can pass as news. Print likes pictures too, but it is interested in the detailed facts underlying the story.

The astute NPO tries to teach the media that it can be relied upon when the media need it. From time to time the media need background information or information that they can trust. Providing background raises the position of the spokesman in the eyes of the public and, of course, strengthens the spokesman's position with the media.

Becoming an organization the media can rely on also means being responsive. This means a quick response to requests for information, even on items that are only of slight importance to the NPO. Given enough time, the media come to feel that the NPO can be relied upon and trusted; and that when bad news comes, the NPO doesn't retreat behind a screen of "Don't Knows" and "No Comments."

Finally, it is a wise move to thank reporters. One can always find something to commend after a story has run. It is not necessary to read a book like this one to know that reporters like to be thanked just like anyone else. The problem is not knowing what to do, but doing it.

SALES PROMOTION

The old saw in marketing is that advertising provides a reason to act but sales promotion provides an incentive to act. Like most neat sayings this one contains only a partial truth. We have already seen that advertising does far more than provide reasons to act, but there can be no doubt that sales promotion spurs clients or backers to do something, perhaps to do something now instead of later, perhaps to do more than they might otherwise have done.

- As part of a fundraising drive, Consumers Union ran what it called a raffle. With a grand prize of $25,000, and over a thousand other prizes, it was intended to stir donors to give more and sooner than they otherwise might. Entries had to be received by a certain date. Entries that arrived before the date qualified for an Early Bird Bonus worth $5,000.

  The raffle provided an incentive to give, and clearly it went beyond the satisfaction that one might get simply from giving to a worthy cause.

- Commonwealth organizations often run amnesties. The tax authority announces that for a period it will accept overdue taxes from taxpayers without penalty. The public library says that overdue books may be returned during the month of March without any late fees. The police urge citizens to turn in illegal, or unwanted, guns, for which they will pay ten dollars each, no questions asked. All stimulate action now by providing a temporary benefit.

• The local PTA holds a phonathon to raise funds for the school, enlisting students to make the calls. In addition to providing pizzas, cookies, and soft drinks for the students, the PTA also runs a contest with prizes for the three students who raise the most money, get the most gifts, and complete the most calls and lesser prizes for those who place second.

Finally, let us see how sales promotion works by eavesdropping on a telephone solicitor (TS) talking to a prospect on the telephone. The prospect has already said no to gifts of $500 and $300, but the telephone solicitor doesn't give up. Following his call sheet on his computer screen, he next asks for $200.

TS: That will help the children a lot and we can arrange for you to pay only fifty dollars a quarter, if you like.

Prospect: I like that. But tell you what, instead of fifty a quarter I'll just give you fifty bucks. Yeah, that's about what I can afford.

TS: Thanks, Robert, for your offer. It will certainly help the Center improve life for our abused children. But I wonder if you could possibly make that $200. You're a father, and you know how special children are and how desperately our children need help.

Prospect: Oh, I understand all right. I love kids. But wanting to help the children and being able to do something is two different things. I think I'll stick to the fifty bucks. I need a new washing machine, and I don't see how I can swing more than that.

TS: Let me ask you this. Are you a Celtics fan?

Prospect: Is the Pope Catholic?

TS: Then you'd probably like the premium the Center is giving to all Challenge Donors. For a $200 donation, you get two tickets to a Celtics game.

Prospect: I didn't know that.

TS: It's good for you and good for us here at the Center. You help the children, you help them a lot, and you and a friend will have a great evening out.

Prospect: I don't know. That's a lot of money. You say I can pay in four installments?

TS: Not and get the tickets. When we receive your check for the full amount, we'll send you the tickets.

Prospect: Well, I shouldn't be doing this but . . . okay, it's a deal. But I'd rather put it on my MasterCard.

TS: Robert, that's wonderful. You have just made some children very happy. And your credit card is fine. Just let me get the details. Your tickets will be in the mail in a few days.

From these examples we see that sales promotion has two characteristics. It is temporary and it provides an incentive to act.

1. Temporary. A sales promotion—or simply a promotion—may run for an

hour or a month, but it is never intended to be permanent. Indeed, part of the explanation for why sales promotion works so well is that its clients are moved to act for fear that if they wait, they'll miss out. "Act now" means "before it's too late." If the incentive were not temporary, there wouldn't be much incentive to act. The cartoon makes the same point. It showed a counter card in the Post Office that said "First-class Stamps. Now 29¢!" (This at a time when first-class stamps cost twenty-nine cents.)

2. Incentive to act. Promotions offer something extra as a spur to act. It may be a reduced price or a free gift or even the good feeling that comes from doing something good for the salesman.

In 1993 fundraisers at the State University of Stony Brook, New York had a problem. Only half of the parents who pledged to give actually gave. Stony Brook decided to ask donors not to pledge but to use a credit card instead, which does away with the pledge. Now, what could Stony Brook do to encourage donors to use their credit cards? In 1994 student callers told parents that those who used a credit card and gave before a certain date would have their names printed in the commencement program.[7]

The incentive here was having one's name in the program.

The types of sales promotion programs and their execution must, of course, reflect the NPO's vision of itself. When Consumers Union holds a raffle as part of a subscription appeal for its magazine *Consumer Reports,* we may be certain that CU, long critical of excesses and dishonesty in marketing practices, will be scrupulous in running its own raffle. Of course, no one is perfect. The Environmental Defense Fund had a mailing to enlist members that the Fund probably referred to as a membership solicitation, but that you or I would simply have called junk mail. As a promotion, new members received a premium, a copy of *50 Simple Things You Can Do to Save the Earth.* The first simple thing was to stop junk mail.[8]

SALES PROMOTION OBJECTIVES

These are the three most common objectives.

1. Induce trial. This is marketing jargon for encouraging clients to try the product, more or less as a test. This is what sampling is all about, and trial sizes, and packages. Sometimes price reductions also induce trial.

2. Encourage repeat behavior. The YWCA may have good success in enrolling new members but tepid success in persuading them to continue their memberships. Working from first principles, the first thing one would want to know is why aren't members re-upping? If the locker rooms aren't clean or the parking lot is too dark, there's not much any sales promotion can do. Assuming such problems are minor, though, then premiums or price reductions or even a contest with prizes for those who sign up the most return members may help solve the problem.

3. Encourage clients to consume more and backers to give more. Most NPOs already have ways of encouraging their backers, say, to give more. They might set up an advisory council composed of large donors, or offer different levels of membership depending on the size of the donation, or appoint large donors to the board. None of these are temporary measures and hence none are forms of sales promotion.

What might it use as sales promotion techniques? We have already seen Celtics tickets used this way. It might sell tickets to a raffle to raise yet more money. It might offer prizes for donors who gave substantial increases over a previous year's gift.

CLIENT PROMOTIONS

Promotions fall into two broad classes: client promotions and trade promotions; the first aimed at clients and backers, the second aimed at channels of distribution (and perhaps the NPO's volunteers). One expects to find the heaviest use of client promotions among nonprofit businesses and the least use among commonwealth organizations.

Premiums—merchandise offered free (or cheap) along with a regular purchase (or donation)—include posters, bumper stickers, tee shirts, greeting cards, bookmarks, and calendars. Back-end premiums are those that kick in some time in the future. ''Donate now and get a discount on your tickets next year.'' Front-end premiums are delivered on the spot. ''Donate now and receive a free map [in the next few weeks].'' (See Figure 16.1.)

An animal shelter might give away a collar with each pet adopted during a given period, or a public TV station a tote bag with a $50 donation. Note that the premium usually costs little; but in any event its cost is low in proportion to the main purchase. The TV station may have a basic membership for $40, but with a gift of $75 the viewer receives a $12 tote bag, and with a gift of $125 the viewer receives a $30 book. (I give retail values here. The $12 tote probably costs less than $6 and may even have been donated to the station. The $30 book would probably cost around $16 or $17 dollars through normal book wholesale channels.)

Probably the best premiums stimulate action and convey something of the NPO's mission. Earth Share gives EcoWriters, its name for pencils made from old newspapers, as premiums to encourage small donations. They exemplify Earth Share's basic message, which is to help save the earth. EcoWriters make a good deal more sense for Earth Share than (say) plastic key chains or even ordinary wooden pencils.

Premiums are surely one of the oldest forms of sales promotion, having been around at least since 1907, when what was to become the American Lung Association began using Christmas Seals to generate donor support. They made the nonprofit stand out, and donors liked to stick them on their Christmas card envelopes.

Figure 16.1
The Audubon Society Offers a Premium, a Free Backpack, to New Members

RECEIVE A
FREE
BACKPACK
WHEN YOU
JOIN NOW

PEEL OFF TOKEN AND PLACE IT INSIDE
TO ACCEPT YOUR FREE GIFT

National Audubon Society
Americans Committed to Conservation

NON-TRANSFERABLE

Peter A. A. Berle

YOUR SIGNATURE
950 THIRD AVENUE, NEW YORK, NY 10022

Premiums not only interest clients and backers, they interest the IRS. If I give $200 to my favorite charity, and it gives me a premium worth $45, can I deduct the full $200 or only $155? Here is the current rule:

A contribution of $25 or more can be deducted in full if the premium bears the name or logo of the charity and cost the charity less than $5. A contribution can also be deducted in full if the premium has a fair market value not more than 2 percent of the donation or $50, whichever is less. These limits are adjusted for inflation each year.[9]

I can only deduct $155.

Coupons entitle the client to save money on the purchase of a specific product. (See Figure 16.2.) Commercial firms distribute coupons through the newspaper, through the mails, and by putting them in (or on) the package containing the product. NPOs distribute them through newspapers and direct mail, as well, and they may also ask their volunteers or staffers to distribute them. The University of Minnesota night school wanted more students. So it ran ads in the *Star-Tribune* containing one-dollar coupons. With the coupon and one dollar a prospective student could attend the first class meeting of a night school course, to see for himself whether the course was what he wanted.

Samples promise a cheap trial or a free trial. Product samples can be distributed in many ways: doorknob delivery, through the mails, in stores, in a product, or on another product. Services are harder to sample, because the client must come to the service site, incurring T costs in the process.

In New York City, good seats for ten operas for two at the Metropolitan Opera run over three thousand dollars. How might a youngster, interested perhaps, but not sure and definitely not wanting to spend three thousand find out whether the opera is for him? He buys tickets one at a time, in the cheap seats; he may even stand (cheaper still); or he may buy the Met's ticket sampler, which gives him tickets to three popular operas at a special low price.

Many hospitals in recent years have taken to offering free programs in areas such as healthy eating, stopping smoking, and techniques for reducing high blood pressure. The hospital provides these samples in part to build its database. Moreover, some of the participants, when they need medical help, will call the hospital and ask it to suggest a physician, who, of course, will be affiliated with the hospital. Note in this example that it is possible to track responses to the free seminars and determine whether they pay for themselves, although making this determination may take many months or longer.

Both of these examples point up the power of samples. They give the client a detailed, vivid idea of what the NPO offers. There can be no better way to communicate such information. Once the client has sampled the product, though, marketing communications lose a good deal of their force. A young woman who has been to three operas and decides she doesn't like opera is probably lost forever as a potential subscriber. She knows for herself that she doesn't like

Figure 16.2
An Off-price Coupon Used by the Natural History Museum of Los Angeles to Encourage Recycling and Increase Attendance

See The
SNOOPY:
GOOD GRIEF! HE'S 40!
Exhibit

at the Natural History Museum of Los Angeles County, now through February 18, 1991. Bring in an empty soda can and save $1.00 off an adult admission at the museum box office. For more information and hours call the museum at (213) 744-6292.

(The A&W logo appeared here.)

$1.00
OFF
ADMISSION

PEANUTS © United Feature Syndicate, Inc.

opera and no communication can persuade her that she does. It goes without saying that samples won't work if the product or service being sampled is poor.

As a final word, note the use of "sample" as a transitive verb. To a marketer it is good English to say, "We plan to sample six hundred clients this weekend," meaning that we plan to give samples to six hundred clients. "Sample," of course, has a second meaning in marketing when it refers to drawing a sample for a survey. Any reader of this book who cannot tell from the context which is which needs professional help.

Sweepstakes, contests, and raffles. To understand these three let us start with an illegal game—chain letters. They pay cash based on luck. It depends on who breaks the chain. And to play you pay, in that to keep the chain alive you must send money to the name at the head of the list. Chain letters are illegal because there is a prize, winning depends on luck, and you pay to play. Any game that involves all three—prize, chance, and consideration—is simply illegal.

In a sweepstakes there can be no consideration. (See Figure 16.3.) The contestant need buy nothing, need donate nothing, need do nothing. All he need do is enter. Once entered, winners are determined by some chance mechanism. In a contest there can be no chance. A contest is a test of skill, as the name implies. A pie-baking contest to benefit the local Parent-Teacher's Association demands skill on the part of the cooks (as well as the judges). To put it another way, a judge decides the winner of a contest; a drawing decides the winner of a sweepstakes.

A charity raffle. In a raffle participants contribute to a pool, and the winner is determined by a drawing. Let us look at a raffle run as part of a fundraising evening for the city's shelter for pregnant girls. The shelter is going to raffle a car, worth $22,000 at retail. Several months before the event it contacts the local Acura dealer to ask him if he will donate $1,000 to the cause and sell the shelter a $22,000 Acura at cost, which is around $18,000, to be paid for after the raffle. He agrees, and the car is parked on the lawn so everyone entering the event sees it.

There will be five bidders, all of whom are able to buy such a car and are prepared to bid. One, for example, is Dr. Jane Doe, who agreed a few months ago that she did need a new car, that she liked Acuras, and that she would be pleased to support the shelter by bidding and buying if she wins, indeed perhaps even paying more than the retail value. Three other individuals have made the same promise.

The fifth bidder is The Syndicate. It is headed by an aggressive bond salesman who has spent the last nine weeks on the phone and in person signing up fifty syndicate members, each of whom has already written the shelter a check for $500. That is, the Syndicate can bid as high as 50 × $500 or $25,000.

The bidding starts and rather quickly is over. Let us say the Syndicate wins with a bid of $24,000. It must now hold a simple drawing from a hat, the lucky winner, one of fifty, to take title to a $22,000 car that cost him but $500 (before

Figure 16.3

A Sweepstakes (here called a raffle) to Stimulate Contributors (The box and the statement, "I do not wish to contribute" make this a legal sweepstakes)

The Consumer Reports Raffle

EXCLUSIVE ENTRY NUMBER: 378728620 021204

☐ **YES,** I want to enter the Raffle and help Consumer Reports by making a tax-deductible contribution. I am enclosing my check, payable to Consumers Union for:

☐ $15 ☐ $25* ☐ $35 ☐ $50 ☐ $100 ☐ Other $ _____ (maximum $2,000)

* A gift of $25 or more enrolls you as an Associate Member of Consumer Union.
You'll receive our lively behind-the-scenes newsletter and discounts on CU's books and publications.

☐ I do not wish to contribute at this time, but please enter me in the Raffle.

```
                                      ⠄O⠄⠄ ⠄ ⠄⠄⠄⠄S
                                      ⟋40⠄⠄ ⠄ ⠄ ⠄ ⠄⠄⠄⠄
                                      N ⠄ ⠄ ⠄ l⠄e, TN   7⠄ ⠄3
```

| $5,000 "EARLY BIRD" BONUS
DEADLINE
MARCH 15, 1991 | ☒ | 378728620 021204 |

WFRUU

Detach and mail this portion

1st Prize - $25,000

THIS ENTRY NUMBER: 378728620 021204

HAS BEEN ISSUED EXCLUSIVELY TO:

You must return your entry to be eligible for a prize.

HOW TO ENTER

1. Simply return this entry form in the envelope provided along with your tax-deductible contribution. You needn't contribute to win a prize, but we hope you'll be as generous as you can. You'll be helping us to protect your interests as a consumer.
2. If you contribute $25 or more, you will become an Associate of Consumers Union.

CONSUMERS UNION OF U.S., INC. is a not-for-profit, tax-exempt organization, contributions to which are tax-deductible in accordance with law. Contributions are not accepted from any commerical interest. A copy of our latest financial report may be obtained by writing: Office of Charities Registration, Department of State, Albany, NY 12231, or from CU.

The Consumer Reports Raffle

KEEP THIS PORTION FOR YOUR RECORDS.

taxes and related exactions). The remaining $1,000 in the Syndicate's hands is also subject to a drawing, one of forty-nine to take all.

Let us say that Dr. Doe gets carried away and bids $26,000, thus beating the Syndicate and winning the car. As before, the Syndicate must hold a drawing, the lucky winner this time to go home with a check for $15,000 with the shelter getting the remaining $10,000.

How much does the shelter get? If the Syndicate wins, the shelter gets $24,000 less the cost of the car or $6,000. If Dr. Doe wins, it gets her $26,000 plus $10,000 from the Syndicate less the cost of the car, or $18,000.

Refunds and rebates are reductions in price (or in T costs) that come after the purchase. The client, for example, might send in a proof of purchase and receive a check in the mail.

TRADE PROMOTIONS

Let us now look briefly at three important forms of trade promotion, all intended to motivate retailers to give the NPO a better deal.

Free goods offer extra merchandise to buyers who order a specific product. Thus, a sheltered workshop might offer, for a limited time, one free wooden carving for every ten the retailer buys. The retailer reasons like this: "I normally buy eight at a time. I buy 'em for $2.50 and sell 'em for $5, so I make eight times $2.50 or $20. If I buy two more, then I buy ten and I get another one free, all of which I can sell for $5." Let's see:

Revenue from 10 carvings	$50	
Cost of 10 carvings	25	$25
Revenue from the free carving	5	
Cost of the free carving	–	5
Total gross margin		$30

"If I order only three more, I can increase my gross margin by 50 percent, from $20 to $30."

Price-off (or an off-invoice allowance) is a price reduction given under certain terms. A social welfare agency sells hand-made Christmas cards each year door-to-door. In recent years it has found that several major bookstores and a couple of department stores are willing to carry the cards, but the stores tend to order late in the season, when the agency is hard pressed to fill the orders. So it offers retailers a deal: "Order by September 1st for delivery no later than November 1st, and we'll cut the wholesale price of the cards by 5 percent on the first five dozen you order, and 15 percent on any over five dozen." The Woolly Mammoth Theater Company in Washington, D.C., used a slightly different form of price-off promotion. To reach people who couldn't afford its usual ticket price, $17 to $22, the theater offered tickets to its preview performances on a pay-what-you-can basis, accepting as little as twenty-five cents. The promotion had two objectives, to increase preview audiences and to encourage people who had never seen live theater to attend.

Allowances are incentives, either in the form of price cuts or cash payments, to retailers to feature in some way the NPO's products. An NPO might offer an advertising allowance, which the retailer would earn if he advertised the product (subject to certain conditions). A nonprofit publisher might offer a display allowance to booksellers in an effort to get better displays for what it hopes will be its big seller in the coming selling season.

MANAGEMENT ISSUES CONCERNING SALES PROMOTIONS

Let us imagine a repertory theater that puts on some twelve plays over a thirty-six-week season. Attendance is not as high as it should be, although ticket prices are competitive, the plays are well reviewed, and the theater's advertising and location do not seem to be cause for concern. The theater would naturally think of several possibilities, from trying to raise more funds to staging easier plays, easier on the audience, in a phrase, "more popular." We, however, will look at sales promotion issues. The theater is considering some kind of sample, on the assumption that once potential audiences see how good the plays are they will want to come back for more. A reduction in ticket prices is also a possibility. As it considers what to do it has decisions to make in four broad areas.

Product. Which products should an NPO promote, which sizes, which varieties, which models? Should it promote products that it already produces, or should it make up special, only-for-this-promotion products? The theater must decide which plays to sample. At first glance one would use the most popular plays because they would do the best job of convincing potential audiences to come back for more, but the popular plays are already nearly sold out because they are, well, popular. Sampling popular plays means the promotion would reach fewer prospects. Perhaps the theater could make up a special play just for a sample? It wouldn't be too hard to come up with a review or an evening with scenes from several current and past productions. Perhaps, in addition, the theater could run its samples on nights when it is normally closed.

Timing. The theater's slowest seasons are in the month preceding Thanksgiving and the five weeks after New Year's Day. Should the theater promote its sample during these slow seasons when there are lots of empty seats, or should it promote when patrons prefer going to the theater? The slow season is when it needs the extra business most, but if people don't like to go to the theater before Thanksgiving for substantial reasons, a price reduction or a sample won't make them change their minds. Just imagine a special on Christmas tree ornaments in June. If the theater offers discounted tickets, should it offer them during

Tuesdays and Wednesdays, the slowest days of the week, or during the rest of the week, when attendance is higher?

Price cut versus added value. The theater might simply offer temporary reductions in its ticket prices to all new subscribers; but as it believes its prices are competitive, it might add value instead of cutting price. It might do this by including a voucher to pay for parking or dinner, or it might offer patrons discounted copies of their choice of one of the plays, or it might give out a freebie such as a mug, a tote bag, or an umbrella.

Value now versus value later. The final issue for the theater deals with when it might choose to add value, if it does choose such a course. It might add value immediately, as with a dinner voucher, or it might add value to be collected in the future by, say, offering to all who sample the theater's wares a special discount on next year's tickets or inclusion in a drawing to be conducted on opening night, seven months hence.

Evaluating Sales Promotions

Advertising usually deals with communications like increasing awareness and knowledge. The natural measure of its effectiveness is, therefore, changes in states of mind. Are clients more aware? Do backers understand us better? Sales promotion usually deals with behavior, and its natural measure is changes in behavior. Are students trying the new pub in the basement? Are more mothers who live in the projects coming in to have their children vaccinated under the back-to-school vaccination program?

It's not quite so simple, however. Suppose we run a raffle to encourage donors to give before the end of the year. Those who do give are eligible for the prize drawing. We can't simply say that the promotion was a success because the number of donations increased 10 percent before the end of the year. Why not? Because some of those donations would have come in later, after the end of the year. We haven't so much increased donations as shifted them in time. Without the sales promotion we might have some donations today, some others tomorrow. With the sales promotion we might have more today, less tomorrow but in aggregate no more than before. Note that vague and irritating "might," there *might* be no more than before. Normally, without some careful record keeping and even more careful analysis, figuring out just how many donations are merely stolen from the future and how many are new is a tough task.

CAUSE MARKETING

Cause marketing, or cause-related marketing, is a type of incentive marketing, and hence it fits loosely under this section on sales promotion. Normally, when someone buys a Liz Claiborne tee shirt, the transaction is a straightforward commercial one. The buyer looks at the tee shirt, judges its style, fit, and quality, ponders for a moment whether she needs yet another tee shirt, judges whether the shirt is worth the price, and decides. Under cause marketing there is an additional incentive to motivate the buyer. She sees that some of the tee shirts contain this message, "Don't Die for Love—Stop Domestic Violence," and she learns that a portion of her purchase price goes to NPOs trying to stop domestic violence.

So cause marketing straddles both the commercial and noncommercial: Businesses use it to increase sales and support nonprofits, and NPOs use it to raise revenue.[10]

Let us look at two examples:

- Avon Products, Inc., which sells beauty products, has a program dedicated to fighting breast cancer, the most commonly diagnosed cancer in women, the "Breast Cancer Awareness Crusade."[11]

  Although most corporations fund broad-scale education and research, Avon decided to promote early detection services. Through its sales force, the largest direct sales force in the world, Avon can reach women with limited education, tell them about its crusade, inform them about early detection services, and distribute fliers with information about breast cancer and how to find local centers that offer mammograms.

  Avon also sells a Breast Cancer Awareness Pin for two dollars. A goldtone pin with the pink ribbon, it represents the international symbol of support for those with breast cancer. Profits from sales of the pin fund the crusade.

  Avon has also created partnerships with government agencies and nonprofit organizations to add further credibility and support to the program, and provide additional outlets for distributing information.

  Avon will also try to reach women typically missed by the medical system. In alliance with the National Alliance of Breast Cancer Organizations (NABCO), it has created the Avon Breast Health Access Fund. Using funds from the sale of the Breast Cancer Awareness Pin, NABCO will create toll free phone numbers to help such underserved populations as women in prison, mentally ill women, recent immigrants, and the elderly.

- Ralston Purina's cause-related marketing for the past seven years has revolved around pets. Its Big Cat Survival Fund (Fund) and Purina Pets For People (PFP) Program both encourage existing customers to purchase the Purina brand, but PFP also encourages people to own a pet.

  The Fund supports the preservation of big cats such as cheetahs, tigers, pumas, and leopards. The program aims to increase public awareness about the preservation of big cats and raise funds for zoos to conduct scientific research and artificial and in-vitro fertilization for big cats. The Fund is supported by national publicity that includes free-standing inserts, a colorful zoo poster, and a public relations campaign. Purina also encourages zoos to promote its Fund.

  Each year, during August and September, a percentage of every purchase of Purina cat food goes to fund the Fund. The Fund also accepts contributions. In its first four years the Fund raised more than $2 million.

  PFP is Purina's largest pet food promotion. It was created as a solution for two seemingly unrelated problems: loneliness among the elderly and pet overpopulation. (On average, more than ten million dogs and cats are taken in by animal shelters each year, but only 1.5 million are adopted. The rest are destroyed.) Under the PFP, senior citizens are matched with homeless dogs and cats in humane shelters across the nation, who help them to select a compatible pet.

Seniors may adopt these animals free of charge. With every adoption, Purina donates $100 to the participating shelter to cover the pet's adoption fees, initial shots, and spaying or neutering. Purina also provides the seniors with a collar, leash, food, water bowl, and starter supply of Purina pet food.

Purina developed this cause-related program after research revealed that pets (a) provide a sense of security and protection and (b) often give seniors a reason to keep busy and plan a daily routine.

Purina supports PFP by donating a portion of Purina pet food sales (up to $1 million annually). Although the promotion is seasonal, running only in September and October each year, humane shelters run it year round.

One immediately sees three points from these examples. Corporations expect cause marketing programs to line their own pockets. Second, corporations use cause marketing programs to improve their images and give the appearance of corporate responsibility. Third, the amounts, from the corporation's side, look small. Between 1987 and 1993, Ralston Purina donated on average $1 million a year to its cause, a pittance in terms of its sales or its marketing budgets or its profits or even the salary of its president.

I referred above to another term for cause marketing. "Cause-related marketing" is not just another glib marketing phrase; it is a glib marketing phrase for which American Express holds a service mark. More and more one sees "cause marketing," perhaps because it is not service marked.[12] American Express got into the cause biz in 1984 when, during a nationwide campaign to restore the Statue of Liberty, it agreed to donate to the restoration a penny for each use of its credit card and a dollar for most new cards. The campaign was a success for both parties. The Statue of Liberty got over two million dollars, and use of the American Express card increased sharply.[13] American Express contributed in other ways, as well. During the eight-year fund drive the Statue of Liberty-Ellis Island Foundation mailed solicitations to some twenty-one million people. American Express donated the use of a list of names it owned, and it paid the postage on two mailings sent to its clients. Other corporations got involved in Statue of Liberty cause marketing as well, although American Express seems to have gotten most of the public acclaim. These corporations were asked to pay $5 million each for the right to use the Foundation logo in their marketing efforts. Some $65 million was raised through such sponsorships.[14]

Affinity Cards

Closely associated with cause marketing are affinity cards. A bank, let us say, forms an alliance with an NPO to promote its MasterCard to members and friends of the NPO. Among the affinity cards that have been issued are such groups as Future Astronauts of Idaho, California Bar Association, U.S. Historical

Society, and one with the ineffable name, the Elvis Mastercard. MBNA, a huge issuer of credit cards, had over 400 affinity cards in 1991.

Fleet Bank of New York has an agreement with the Nature Conservancy, a conservation organization. We know what the Nature Conservancy gets from the deal—money: six dollars of the annual fee for each card and 20 percent of the bank's fees. What does Fleet Bank get? It gets an inexpensive way to penetrate a quality market, because in its agreement with Fleet Bank the Nature Conservancy promises to work to convince its members to apply for the Fleet card, and once they have the card, the Conservancy will encourage its members to use it. Fleet gets more credit cards issued and in use, both of which generate income for the bank. Perhaps most important of all, it enhances its corporate image with a highly visible form of corporate philanthropy. Banks certainly look for economic benefits from affinity cards, but my suspicion is that affinity cards are peripheral to their overall marketing strategies.[15]

Affinity cards grew rapidly in the 1980s but, as is the way with all markets that grow rapidly, the growth eventually slowed and then, in the 1990s, stopped. There are three reasons for this, the first a pure marketing explanation. Tie-ins with NPOs are weak benefits to most card users. Second are economic reasons. In the 1990s low interest rates on credit became more important to card users than tie-ins with charities. (It doesn't help that the IRS frowns on affinity cards. A check to a charity is a gift, and a deduction. Use of an affinity card is neither.) Finally, it is a kind of law of nature that rapid growth of anything is followed by falling growth and eventually stagnation.

The size of the group has a major effect on the success of a card. Sierra Club has some 25,000 that generate up to $400,000 a year. But smaller groups will see little benefit in affinity cards because the income produced is so small.[16]

As with premiums and sweepstakes, legal issues arise here as well. Most states regulate for-profit fundraisers and paid solicitors. Are firms that raise funds by means of cause marketing fundraisers or simply one-half of a charity–business joint venture? Suppose Liz Claiborne is not specific but simply offers to donate to nonprofit organizations through the purchase of a product. It might well be held a paid solicitor. But if it offered to contribute so much per product purchased, it might not. Suppose ABC Corporation says it will donate twenty-five cents per product but during the promotion raises the price twenty-five cents? Just who is donating the money, ABC or the buyer? Many states would judge that it is the buyer who is giving the money, not ABC, and they would therefore see ABC as a paid solicitor.[17]

QUESTIONS

1. What is the difference between publicity and public relations?
2. The chapter discussed Fleet Bank's deal with the Nature Conservancy. Yet the deal doesn't look all that good to Fleet Bank. It pays six dollars of the annual fee and 20

percent of its charge to the Nature Conservancy. Clearly, these affinity cards are not as profitable as the Bank's regular cards. Then why is Fleet Bank doing it? (Hint: It's not because Fleet wants to support the Nature Conservancy.)

3. The U.S. Postal Service sells stamps to collectors. It advertises that stamps are fun, beautiful, historic, perhaps even (in the long run) profitable. But it rarely uses promotions to sell its stamps and never uses price promotions. Can you see why?

NOTES

1. Michael Radock, "Public Relations for Educational Institutions," in *Lesley's Public Relations Handbook,* edited by Philip Lesley (Englewood Cliffs, N.J.: Prentice-Hall, 1978), p. 294.

2. A competent, general-purpose guide to this area is Robert H. Ruffner, *Handbook of Publicity and Public Relations in the Nonprofit Organization* (Englewood Cliffs, N.J.: Prentice-Hall, 1984).

3. Jon Van Til, "Riding the Nonprofit Elephant." *Nonprofit Times* (August 1993), p. 12.

4. John S. Glaser, *The United Way Scandal* (New York: John Wiley & Son, 1994), p. 27, a fascinating book.

5. See Dieudonnée ten Berge, *The First 24 Hours* (Oxford: Basil Blackwell, 1990), pp. 35–76; Ian I. Mitroff and Christine M. Pearson, *Crisis Management* (San Francisco: Jassey-Bass, 1993); and *Media Resource Guide,* 5th ed. (Los Angeles: Foundation for American Communications, 1987), p. 21.

6. See Glaser, *The United Way Scandal.*

7. Holly Hall, "Softer, Simpler Appeals Win More Annual Donors." *Chronicle of Philanthropy* (Feburary 8, 1994), p. 40.

8. *Time* (November 26, 1990), p. 64.

9. See Revenue Procedure 92–102, *Internal Revenue Bulletin,* 1992–52.

10. The first good article on cause marketing was P. Rajan Varadarajan and Anil Menon, "Cause-Related Marketing: A Coalignment of Marketing Strategy and Corporate Philanthropy." *Journal of Marketing* (July 1988): 58–74.

11. Both this discussion of Avon and the following one on Ralston Purina come from *Cause Marketing Update* (December 1993/January 1994), pp. 4–6.

12. Is there such a word? If "trademark" can be a verb, why not "service mark"?

13. Fritz Jellinghaus, "Business Forum: Doubts About 'Cause-Related' Marketing; Profits Have a Place in Philanthropy." *New York Times,* March 29, 1989, Section 3, p. 2.

14. Jennifer Moore, "As Ellis Island Museum Opens, Fund Drive Prepares to Close." *Chronicle of Philanthropy,* September 4, 1990, p. 4. The $2 million that American Express is credited with is a lot of money; but the total raised to renovate both the Statue of Liberty and Ellis Island was $342.5 million. Compared to that figure, American Express's $2 million was not even a drop in the bucket, although it was perhaps half a drop.

15. For a piece on affinity cards in the United Kingdom, see Suzanne Horne and Steve Worthington, "Affinity Cards: How to Ensure a Beneficial Relationship," in *Researching the Voluntary Sector,* edited Susan K.E. Saxon-Harrold and Jeremy Kendall (Tonbridge, Kent: Charities Aid Foundation, 1993), pp. 51–58.

16. ''Affinity Cards Lose Some Allure.'' *Wall Street Journal,* November 14, 1991, p. A1.

17. For a brief discussion of these issues, see Betsy Hills Bush, ''More States Regulate Cause Marketing.'' *Nonprofit Times* (February 1994), p. 10.

Chapter 17

Control and Organization

So far this book has dealt with the analysis of marketing problems and development of solutions. In a word, it has dealt with planning. But eventually, the manager must turn from planning to doing (or as the best texts say, from planning to implementation).

In this chapter we treat briefly the two central problems that arise in getting things done. The first is how to control the marketing program. We have referred to this problem before and briefly mentioned the solution, namely, setting appropriate objectives, then measuring performance against these objectives, finally acting to bring the two closer. We shall also look at the difference between control in the short run and control in the long run. The second problem deals with organization: How can we bring the organization's resources to bear on the marketing problems that have to be solved? Who reports to whom? Who is responsible for what? Finally, relating directly to this issue, we shall look briefly at the problems of introducing marketing into a nonprofit organization for the first time.

MARKETING CONTROL

Marketing control takes simple ideas of control and applies them to marketing. The process is straightforward: As part of the marketing plan, the marketer sets objectives and decides on his strategies for dealing with product, channels, communications, and price. He then sets performance standards, which are measurable achievement levels for the marketing objectives. The membership director at a historical park has an objective to increase the number of members, but his performance standards are much more specific: Increase the number of members from 10,000 to 11,000 (1) by recruiting 400 new members and (2) by gaining

600 others by reducing the proportion of current members who fail to renew their memberships (from, say, 30 percent who do not renew to 24 percent).

The marketing plan is then put into effect, its results are compared with the performance standard, and the marketer takes steps to bring the two—performance standards and results—closer together.

Sound marketing performance standards are based on sound marketing objectives; and as the reader has surely noted, setting sound objectives requires thorough marketing analysis. Many nonprofits do not have the skill to do this well, nor do they take the time. As a result, I have seen nonprofit organizations where the correct response to a large difference between performance standards and results is to change the objectives and the performance standards, not the marketing plan. It makes little sense to pursue objectives that cannot be attained. Once the NPO has realistic objectives and written performance standards based on them, then when performance standards and results differ, the marketer changes the program to do better the next time around.

As with most such straightforward views of any human activity, there are problems. One is that objectives are often contradictory. An abortion clinic may want its fundraiser to raise 10 percent more money than last year and also wants him to increase the rolls of current donors by 15 percent as an investment for the future. But finding new donors usually reduces cash flow in the first year. Not all objectives are typically set down either. The board of a theater expects the marketer to fill the seats but not at the expense of the artistic quality of the performance or of the image of the theater.

The other major problem with objectives has been discussed before. That is the difficulty of counting what counts. Surely, you agree that what counts in a symphony orchestra is artistic development, musical growth, and the quality of the music. If you agree, alas, you cannot be saved, for this view of a symphony is the production orientation, scouted in Chapter 9. Marketers train themselves to take a client orientation. For them what counts is the satisfaction of the audience. That is not what general managers measure; they measure outputs: ticket sales, cash flow, deficits, performance against budget.[1] In general this will be a problem with any service organization, because there are so many potential ways of measuring output, none of which can be reduced to the common denominator of dollars.

Control, then, means setting objectives, translating them into performance standards, comparing results against the performance standards, and taking steps to correct problems. None of these chores is fit for a clerk. Marketing control is closely related to the entire process of marketing planning. It is not something pasted onto the end of the planning process or cobbled up as an afterthought. At the same time the marketer is making marketing decisions, he must also decide how he will control the marketing programs.

The control issues dealt with so far have concerned the short run: This quarter's plans call for the introduction of a new service, or this year's plans for a new program to enlist better support from distributors. There is a larger control issue that transcends the typical time period; that is, does management have the information it needs to make decisions? Not data—most nonprofits have plenty of data, more in fact than they can use—but information, relevant to their decisions and in a form they can use.

One of my earliest experiences in the Land of The Nonprofits was a tour put in as informal advisor to the board of directors of a small museum, which meant less grandly that the president of the board and I had lunch every month, for which she paid. The first problem was that no one on the board knew what the deficit was. The museum closed its books nearly seven months after the end of the fiscal year (just as Columbia University did when I was there). This meant that it could be seven months before the board found out whether a curator had overspent his budget, or how much had been lost on a special exhibit. The museum still kept its financial records on a cash basis instead of an accrual basis—a cash basis is really checkbook accounting, which is just how you keep your records—and what financial records there were could not be reconciled with monthly bank statements. That is to say, the members of the board could not reconcile them, although the bookkeeper could.

In addition, there was no system or order in the data needed to make marketing decisions or evaluate past decisions. Of course, admissions records were not kept in such a way that it was possible to determine how many visitors to the museum had paid the voluntary admission fee, although the total cash raised in this way was known. (There is nothing particularly remarkable about this. A survey done in the early 1970s showed that only 30 percent of American museums even bothered to count how many visitors they had.)[2] Of course, the expenses of the membership department were not separated from general and administrative expenses. Of course, there were no day cards listing the donations received each day along with the donor's name and address, which made it impossible to write six months later asking for another donation: "Dear donor. It's been almost six months since you sent your last gift. I thought you would be interested to learn what the museum has been doing, and how your last gift has been put to work." Of course, the museum gift shop, which should have been producing a Net Marketing Contribution of around $15,000 a year, was running in the red, and some of the stock on its shelves was four years old.

The first things the board president and I did had nothing to do with marketing. We introduced a new system of accounts, changed reporting relationships, and introduced a modest degree of planning.[3] (We had a good deal of help from others on the board. I am not the Compleat Manager.) After that we began to analyze what we identified as the key marketing problems—membership, admissions, fundraising, and the gift shop. We looked at the *types* of decisions that arose in each area and asked ourselves what kinds of information we needed to resolve each problem. This in turn led in two directions, more tinkering with the accounting system and some first efforts toward marketing research.

At the time, we described what we were doing as making some changes so that the museum would run better. Today we would make the same improvements, but we would say that we were introducing a management information system, and as part of it a marketing information system. So far have we come in recent years.

Just as marketing is part of the entire organization and not an island unto itself, so is the system used to control the marketing program part of the control system for the entire organization. Marketing control may raise special problems involving the use of marketing research for feedback information, but it must rely for its cost and revenue figures on the organization's overall accounting system. At the very least, this system should provide something like a Marketing Control Statement on each distinct and significant marketing activity. At the museum, for example, the accounting system should have provided a Marketing Control Statement (as in Chapter 3) for each exhibit, for the membership department as a whole, for the gift shop, and for two significant fundraising activities (the special "endowment" drive held each year and the more or less continuous efforts to raise money in the local area).

Marketing control is part of a broader set of issues, then. At the very least, control systems should move toward providing marketers with information that helps them make better decisions. For example, many educational institutions do not break out separate budgets for their programs in continuing education. Until they do, until they provide their directors with something like a Marketing Control Statement, they are certain to run less efficiently.

Control without Numbers

But control is not merely numbers nor is it merely accounting. It is part of the overall process of planning, which means deciding what it is you are going to try to accomplish and then measuring your progress toward those ends. It is important to distinguish between *outcomes* and the *activities* that lead to outcomes, between the destination and the trip. Marketers, indeed all managers, are interested mostly in the destination, but often in nonprofit organizations it is possible only to observe the trip. Control means looking after both. No manager can wait until the end of a trip to find out whether he is going in the right direction, nor can he wait for months to find out whether he has pulled out of the station. So while outcomes, the behavior of clients and backers, are of first importance, it is also useful to collect information on activities.

A good example of this is public relations, which we showed in Chapter 16 was a frail reed. This means that it is difficult for a public relations director to detect the impact of his activities, much less show that they have affected the behavior of the organization's clients or backers and produced the desired outcomes. Instead, public relations evaluations rely on intermediate measures. For example, an organization can prepare simple forms for staff and volunteers to use to record telephone and in-person inquiries. Such a form would typically list all common types of inquiries, something about the inquirer, what led to the inquiry, where the inquirer heard about the service or organization, and (often) where the inquirer lives.[4]

Stories appearing in the local press can be clipped and analyzed.[5] Which press releases were used, which photographs, which story ideas? Which ones were not? Which publications seem most willing to run the organization's stories? Norton goes on:

At least once or twice a year you should make an analysis of your clippings. How much space are you getting? How does this compare with the previous year? What changes have occurred in quantity and placement? (Sample checks should be used, not a time-consuming measurement of all articles.) What messages would a person receive who only learned of your agency from the press? Are basic concerns reported or do the articles focus primarily on such news as staff appointments and peripheral services? What opinions does the reader get from signed columns, editorials or letters to the editor?

It is much harder to find out what messages about your agency are being communicated by radio and television than by the press. Stations are numerous and spot announcements may be scheduled almost around the clock. Some major cities offer radio and television monitoring services similar to press clipping services but the cost is high.[6]

This is a plausible, sensible approach, sure to produce useful information. But it is a plausible, sensible approach only the first time around. After this has been done once, the public relations director should thereafter set objectives against which such activities as these may be set. It means nothing that the public relations department got 60 column inches of press coverage this year, although 60 column inches can mean a great deal if the goal for the year was 120 or 20.

Needless to say, such objectives must be used with care, lest the organization stand on its head to meet its intermediary goals and forget its real purpose. The reader need only attend to his daily newspaper for a week or two to find a story of a government program whose administrators are working hard to produce things that can be counted, the activities, and neglecting the things that count, the outcomes.

One additional control technique, then, is to control activities instead of outcomes. A second useful control technique is to require a written marketing plan. Nonprofit organizations need marketing plans if they are to exercise effective control over their marketing activities. They need not be long, by the way. The best plan I have ever seen was three pages long, but the quality of its analysis and the suitability of its recommendations to the problems at hand made it stand out, not its brevity. An outline for such a written marketing plan is found in Figure 17.1, and since it largely deals with what the entire book has been about, it needs no further explanation.

The Marketing Audit

From time to time the marketing program as a whole should be subjected to searching examination. Such an examination is called a marketing audit. In

Figure 17.1
Outline for a Marketing Plan

A.   Last year's objectives and performance against those objectives.
      Review of past Marketing Control Statements.

B.   Situation Analysis
      1.   External environment (clients, backers, competition).
      2.   Anticipated external threats and opportunities.
      3.   Organization's strengths and weaknesses.

C.   Objectives
      1.   Objectives for the organization as a whole. Marketing's role in meeting overall
            objectives. General objectives for the marketing programs.
      2.   Financial objectives.

D.   Marketing Strategy for Clients.
      1.   Markets and segments. Assumptions as to how clients behave.
      2.   Marketing mix recommendations for (1) products and services, (2) distribution,
            (3) communications, and (4) prices and T costs for each segment.
      3.   Objectives for the elements of the marketing plan.
      4.   Current activity on long-run projects.
      5.   Degree of risk involved in adopting recommended strategy.

E.   Marketing Strategy for Backers (parallels strategy for clients)

F.   Marketing Budget
      1.   Resources needed (people, time, money).
      2.   Allocation of resources to elements of the marketing mix, by time.
      3.   Pro forma Marketing Control Statements.

G.   Control and Organization
      1.   Plan of action, with scheduled activities and deadlines.
      2.   How marketing program is to be controlled. Performance standards. Marketing
            research needs.
      3.   Organizational responsibilities. Who is responsible for what.

marketing control one asks, "Are we doing things right?" In the marketing audit, one asks "Are we doing the right things?"[7] Control, therefore, takes the short view; the marketing audit takes the long view. The word "audit" was unfortunately chosen, implying as it does that accounts are being verified for correctness. The marketing audit is, instead, a careful investigation of the organization's marketing programs to weigh their quality and effectiveness.

It most usefully starts with a review of objectives—the organization's overall objectives, the marketing program objectives, and the objectives of each element of the marketing mix. In all but the best-managed organizations, the auditor is sure to find substantial discrepancies between what the organization says it is doing and what it is actually doing, and between what it says its objectives are and what they actually are.

The marketing auditor also examines the marketing planning process that we treated in Chapters 8 and 9. He should determine whether the organization is pursuing the best target markets, and whether it is allocating too much, or too little, to each market segment. He would also try to identify potential market opportunities and threats that the organization might be overlooking. As part of the review of marketing planning, the auditor would also evaluate the marketing mix as a whole for its internal consistency and balance. He would, of course, look critically at the way in which the marketing program was controlled and at the use made of marketing research.

A marketing auditor also scrutinizes the organizational aspects of marketing: (1) How the marketing function is organized. Are the current reporting relationships and lines of authority suitable? When the full-time marketer is hired, will he have enough authority to do his job? How should he interact with professionals on the staff? (2) Are the marketing personnel competent to do the jobs expected of them? Does the organization's general manager have the skills he needs to manage the marketing function? Marketing requires a modest amount of specialized experience and training. Just how much training does the marketer's superior need? (3) Does the organization provide the marketer with relevant information? What kinds of records are kept? What kinds are used? What is used for which decision? Are records on clients organized so that communications can be tailored to different interests of the segments? What procedures are followed to evaluate marketing communications?[8]

The audit is normally done by someone outside the organization. Outsiders have broader experience in marketing than anyone in the organization, they are typically more objective, and they are available to devote full time to the audit; but when an NPO hires its first full-time marketer, it makes good sense to ask him to do an audit. Even if he does not do as well as a more experienced consultant, it teaches him a great deal about the organization and its marketing problems, and it can serve as the basis for the development of marketing strategy.

MARKETING ORGANIZATION

If a marketing organization is the answer, what is the question? In general, there are three: (1) How can the NPO stay in touch with its clients and its backers, (2) how can the NPO exercise control over its volunteers and paid staff who work in the field with clients and backers, and (3) how can the NPO bring its special skills and resources to different programs, regions, and market segments. To sum up, the question that organization answers is: How can the nonprofit ensure that the voice of key parties like clients and backers is heard? These parties are not important for ethical reasons. They are important because they determine whether the nonprofit successfully performs its mission. They are important, that is, for strategic reasons. So another way of posing the question to the answer is: How can the NPO best organize its marketing effort to carry out its mission, or, in other words, how should its structure follow from its strategy? That is the key thought of this section: Structure follows strategy.

It is worth looking briefly at an example of this general rule. The Ad Council's strategy for most of its life focused on national media—network TV, national magazines, and, once upon a time, network radio. (It did not deal with national newspapers because, until recently, there were none.) It paid almost no formal attention to regional or local media. Its organizational structure followed directly from this strategy. Everything was centralized in New York City, where all of the national media are located. It helped, of course, that almost all of the major advertising agencies had their headquarters in the City as well.

When network TV began to lose its predominant grip on the American household, losing share to cable and the VCR, and local media became more important, the Ad Council at length reacted. It changed its strategy and decided to place more of its advertising in local and regional media. This was hard to do from New York, so it made an organizational move. It opened an office in Chicago to explore whether having an Ad Council office in a major market outside New York could increase the amount of advertising that it placed in local print and broadcast media.

Specialization and Coordination

Let us look at organization from a different perspective. People who think about such things say that there are two basic reasons for organizing. The first is to separate one job from another so that the individuals can know their jobs and bring their special skills and special experience to bear on them. One organizes, then, to differentiate between jobs and allow for specialization. This raises a problem, however, because carried to an extreme, the organization becomes a number of disjointed cells, with every man for himself. The solution is to integrate the efforts of the specialists into a coordinated whole. Coordination becomes particularly difficult in nonprofit organizations that make substantial use either of volunteer marketers or of part-time, paid marketers, because the marketing efforts in such organizations tend to start and stop; and it is the job of the coordinator to provide continuity. Specialization and coordination, then, are two more reasons for organizing.

It is informative to take the organization chart of a nonprofit organization, even a small one drawn on the back of an envelope, and locate on the chart marketing responsibilities. Who recommends prices? And who makes the final decision? Who recommends that new products be developed? Who makes the final decision? There is great diversity in the answers for different organizations. Schneider discusses responsibilities for a large, rapid transit investment (''large'' meaning $25 million, but then Schneider's book was written in the early 1960s). His list is found in Table 17.1. It shows that no one manager is responsible for the entire project, and responsibility for many decisions is shared.

The Postal Service, on the other hand, gives responsibility for its products to individual managers. Postal money orders generate about $50 million a year in fees (twice the size of the rapid transit investment), and the service is run by a

Table 17.1
Responsibilities for a Large Mass Transit Investment

Marketing Decision	*Responsibility of*
Pricing	Finance
Promotion	Public relations
Market research	Public relations, engineering, finance, planning, and schedules
Product:	
Speed	Schedules, engineering, and the superintendent of transportation
Comfort	Schedules, engineering, and the superintendent of transportation
Parking lots	Engineering
Equipment	Engineering

Source: Lewis M. Schneider, *Marketing Urban Mass Transit* (Boston: Division of Research, Harvard Business School, 1965), p. 162.

product manager for money orders. His responsibility is to recommend prices, product changes, market research, and so on, for money orders, the final decisions being made by higher Postal Service officials. Here one manager is responsible for all the decisions.

These examples illustrate extreme solutions to the important problems of specialization and coordination, of bringing the organization's resources to bear on the marketing program: Spread marketing responsibility throughout the organization or concentrate it under one manager. Why do we expect that in a health maintenance organization the field sales force, the advertising and publicity group, the market researchers, and those negotiating contracts with large institutional buyers will all be working together, be collected at one spot on the organization chart, all reporting to one manager? Why, on the other hand, does a museum make no effort to bring under one senior manager its principal marketers, the fundraiser, the membership director, and the head of the museum shop? Because in the HMO, organizing so that the marketing specialists all pull together is crucial to the success of its strategy. In the museum, each can more or less go his own way and ignore the others.

It is easy to see why the transit company spread its net so wide. The development of a new transit service required cooperation from almost every major administrative area in the company. To put all these under one head would mean having everyone report to the marketing director, which is not what marketing is all about. What the transit company did is common in business as well. Large investments, large projects of any kind are often supervised by a special project group or working committee because there are no standard organizational units designed to handle them and because they draw widely on corporate resources. They fall outside the normal range of organizational activity, and they therefore have no regular position on the organization chart. The temporary nature of the project group (structure) reflects the temporary nature of the project (strategies).

For the same reason, we find fundraising special events and capital campaigns usually run by committee. Marketing effort is needed only periodically, and the organization adapts to this.

The other extreme solution, the product manager, allows one manager or small group of managers to become specialists in their product. The product manager achieves coordination of the marketing efforts by that most ancient of stratagems; he does it all himself. Well, not quite. He must draw on others in his organization to design a marketing research study, analyze sales data, sign up a new advertising agency, and so on; but he is responsible for coordinating the efforts of these other specialists.

Three other factors apply here: the size of the job, amount at stake, and the role of marketing in the NPO. In organizations where there is not much to the marketing job, all marketing tends to be swept into one corner and placed under the responsibility of one manager. Hospitals typically do this, giving their less important marketing functions to (say) a director of public relations.

But when the job is complex and requires specialized knowledge, where the amounts at stake are large, and where marketing's role is substantial, marketing responsibilities are usually assigned to one manager or organizational unit. Hospitals recruit doctors and nurses. Recruiting is a marketing activity. Why isn't recruiting assigned to the hospital's director of public relations or to personnel? Because hiring doctors and nurses is too important. Too much is at stake, particularly with doctors, who can generate hundreds of thousands of dollars a year in revenues for a hospital.[9] And because recruiting requires specialized skills and knowledge and takes a lot of time. All this does not mean that part of the responsibility for finding doctors is not shared with others in the hospital. It means merely that the job is important enough and complex enough to require the full-time attention of someone with special skills, like a director of physician recruiting, who coordinates the entire program.

Much the same thoughts apply to the recruiting of nurses. Hospitals must have a minimum number of nurses on their staff, although nowhere near so much is at stake because nurses do not produce revenues but merely care for patients; nor is the recruiting job quite so complex. Nurses, for example, do not enter into lengthy negotiations, as the doctors do, on such matters as income guarantees, free office space, patient referrals, and time off for research. Here the third factor, the role of marketing, again comes into play. An effective marketing program to recruit nurses can be expected to make a significant impact on hiring. Marketing counts. And where it does, we tend to find marketing responsibility concentrated in one spot. If nurses were assigned to hospitals (say) on the basis of some governmental ukase, no hospitals would have directors of nurse recruiting because the role of marketing in such a situation would be nil.

These three considerations—size of the job, amount at stake, and marketing's role—interact in complex ways, so that it is impossible to expect this discussion to settle all issues. For example, why is there a product manager for postal money orders? The amount at stake is large, to be sure, but money order fees amount to only .5 of 1 percent of the Postal Service's total revenues. Is there enough to the job of managing money orders? To forego a detailed analysis, let us assert that the answer is yes. What about the role of marketing? Here, clearly, there is not a great deal of leeway for the marketer. People want for some reason to send money from point A to point B. The Postal Service cannot affect those reasons. People then choose from among the many ways of sending money, the most important being personal checks. The Postal Service requires that its customers bear high T costs. The out-of-pocket price of a money order is as high as private money order prices. Opportunity costs are high because customers must come to the post office, wait in line, and fill out a form, and in dealing with postal clerks there will often be AO costs as well. Personal checks are many times more convenient; they have lower OOP costs and T costs, and they provide a more convenient receipt. We may conclude that marketing has a minor role to play in selling money orders. Why then is there a product manager for money orders?

As a final example, let us look at Figure 17.2, which contains the organization chart for a marketing corporation for New York City, whose aim is to attract new businesses to New York City and to retain those already there. The organization chart shows two types of specialization: one by the nature of the target market, the other by function. There are two organizational units that specialize by market, one for the international market and the other for the North American market. The vice president and director of marketing research and planning heads up the functional unit. The separate marketing programs like the ambassador program and the retention program report to him, as well as the general marketing functions of public relations, market research, and marketing programs and planning.

This discussion has stressed the importance of specialization and coordination in understanding organizations and in designing them. There is yet another reason why organizations exist, and it deals with assigning the blame. Organization helps to do this by defining jobs and assigning tasks; that is, it helps answer two key questions: Who reports to whom? Who is responsible for what? Note that a job description deals with just these questions, and therefore a job description can be seen as an organizational tool as well as a control tool. (There is a sample job description in a few pages.) In fact, as the reader has surely guessed, the two are closely related. A well-organized marketing effort is one that is under control.

Organizing the Sales Force

Having looked at the question of how marketing fits into the organization's overall structure, let us look briefly at the internal organization of the marketing group itself. We shall do this in the context of how to organize volunteers.

Let us consider the three standard approaches to organizing a business sales force and then see how they might relate to a sales force of volunteers. All three

Figure 17.2
Proposed Organization Chart for a Marketing Corporation for New York City

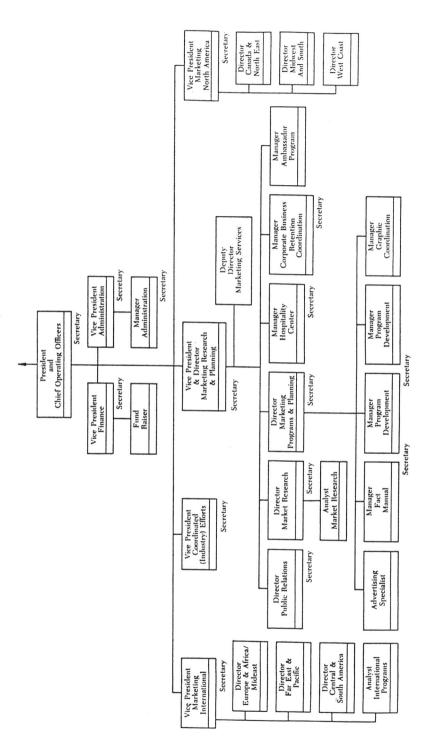

involve specialization of the selling effort. That is to say, each structure is designed to carry out a different marketing strategy.

1. Geography. Each salesman sells in a given geographic area, or territory, and he is responsible for all customers and all sales in the territory. Because he specializes by territory, the salesman comes to know the region and geographic peculiarities that affect his accounts. Along with salesmen in adjacent or nearby territories, he reports to a field sales manager, who himself reports to still more senior sales managers.

2. Customer. Each salesman sells to a given class of customers, perhaps a particular industry or perhaps a class of distributor. Because he specializes by customer, the salesman learns a great deal about his customers and their businesses, and is thus better able to match his company's products with the interests of his customers.

3. Product. Each salesman handles only one product line. This type of specialization leads to the salesman's having a great deal of detailed information about the product and how it can be used or adapted for use in many industries. Where the product is complex or technical, such an organization would be expected, because it would not be reasonable to expect that any one salesman could master the entire product line. For the same reason, product organization is also used when the company produces unrelated products.

These approaches have been presented as if they are distinct cases. In fact, sales forces can combine these alternative ways of organizing. A product specialist also has a territory in which he sells; or a product specialist may call on only one class of customer.

Now let us see how these approaches might apply in organizing a volunteer sales force. In the geographic organization, volunteers would call on all potential donors in their territory, but the territory would not be exclusive. Typically, they would share it with other volunteers. For example, there might be twenty solicitors in a given city, each assigned to call on, say, six potential donors. Any six. Some would be called on by more than one solicitor, others would be missed. In the customer organization, the volunteers would specialize by customer type—the most usual specialization being by size of gift. Donors expected to give large amounts would be called on in person, donors of gifts of moderate size would be reached by telephone, and pin-money donors would be contacted by mail. As we saw in discussing ratings of donors earlier in the book, it is worthwhile to learn the donor's special interests and concerns, so that the fundraiser does not discommode a football booster by asking him to support the cause of higher education. Yet another way of segmenting donors is by common interest, typically by school—law school graduates call on other law school graduates. Finally, in a product organization volunteers would specialize by product, that is, by the purpose for which they are raising the money. Several particularly interested in the graduate business school would raise money for that school only, more or less calling on whomever they wish. (I cannot imagine any university adopting either the first or the last organization, though.)

These have been presented as if they are distinct cases. In fact, most large university fundraising organizations would combine them. A volunteer from the business school will only work a certain geographic territory; there is no need for him to fly all over the country; or he will only work a certain industry in a certain territory, say, by calling on past graduates of the school who are bankers in midtown Manhattan, or who work on Market Street in San Francisco.

The most important organizational issues in marketing arise within the NPO; but organizational structures among other NPOs have began to play a role in marketing issues. We have already seen NPOs banding together in federations like United Way and Earth Share to raise funds. Computer networks have begun to meet some marketing needs as well. Antismoking groups use SCARCnet, the Smoking Control Advocacy Resource Network, to hold daily sessions on the latest tobacco news. To its 200 members it suggests sound bites for the media, provides copies of antismoking legislation for health officials to propose in their cities, and passes on the biographies and likely arguments of lobbyists for the tobacco industry.[10] Those fighting alcohol have their own ALCNet, gun control groups are considering a network, and a California foundation recently financed a project to reduce violence that included grants to buy computers and modems to set up a network for 300 users.

All of these help NPOs who would otherwise be only patchily coordinated at best to move as a group in the same direction and at the same time. Getting such coordination is a classic outcome of getting one's act together, in a word, of organizing.

INTRODUCING MARKETING INTO THE NONPROFIT ORGANIZATION

Any nonprofit that aims to influence the behavior of clients or backers over whom it has no control is already marketing. But it need not have a formal marketing program, nor anyone called a marketer. As the organization grows, however, eventually a formal marketing program will be required.[11]

A small organization makes no pretense. It performs marketing chores itself without much thought and with no planning. Sometimes, in fact, volunteers bear most of the responsibility for marketing. If marketing is important to the organization's success, though, the director will also involve himself.

As the organization begins to grow it identifies problems that call for marketing solutions but that it cannot solve itself. It may need help in putting out a mass mailing, in setting up a fundraising event, or in getting better press coverage. Still not ready for full-time marketing, it hires part-timers. There are many agencies and many consultants ready to provide such services. The organization might put a PR firm on a $10,000-a-year retainer (although this is such a small fee to most firms that the nonprofit group is likely to be assigned the least experienced person in the firm). Creative work—layout of brochures, copy writing of fundraising letters, or design of membership publications—is also commonly farmed out in this stage. A third function performed part-time is marketing research, but this function is likely to remain a part-time activity long after the nonprofit organization has grown to some size. The reason is that most nonprofits do not make constant use of marketing research; rather, they use it only from time to time, and thus do not have enough work for a full-time researcher.

Finally, when there is enough work for a marketer, one is hired full-time. There is no way of saying in general at what point a full-time marketer is called for. For what it is worth, one executive told me that she felt that a marketer was needed once the contribution or Gross Marketing Contribution from the marketing activities reached the range of $1 to $2 million a year. She based her estimate primarily on experience. But she also argued that at that level of sales, the costs of the marketer were relatively low. This was her line of argument:

When you have sales of $2.5 million, that is a sizeable amount of money. Now you want to hire a marketer. You want someone with some experience in the field and in marketing. So you go for someone around thirty years of age. Today, you can get a pretty good person like this for around $30,000. Not in Chicago, of course, and a few other large cities. But most everywhere else. Maybe you've got to pay $35,000. Add another 20 percent for fringe benefits, that gives you around $42,000. And a full-time marketing person will add to the secretarial load, might need another half a secretary, so that's another $7,000. Plus some travel, but not very much, another $2,000 a year. All told, the new marketer will increase costs by $51,000.

What do you get for that? You get close supervision of a business with sales of $2.5 million. So you are spending for control and supervision about 2 percent. That's not necessarily a bargain, but it is not expensive either.

Moreover, I have never seen it to fail. If you bring in someone brand new to a nonprofit institution that has never had a marketer before, the new marketer is always able to earn his or her keep by improving sales, by improving efficiency, by cutting out waste.

This last statement is a generalization that goes too far. A sounder analysis is based on marginal considerations. Thus, the argument would be that a full-time marketer should be able to increase Gross Marketing Contribution by enough to offset the addition to programmed marketing costs and at the very least leave Net Marketing Contribution at the same level. While the executive's generalization, then, needs a firmer base, it does indicate one of the arguments for hiring a full-time marketer, namely, that the marketer can pay for himself. The other line of argument is in terms of the requirements of the job. No organization should hire a full-time marketer unless there is enough for him to do. These two arguments—that the marketer should be able to pay for himself and that there should be enough to occupy a marketer full-time—echo the two bases for determining sales force size in Chapter 13.

Although the same questions must be asked at each stage of growth listed above, it is most convenient to focus on the questions that arise when a full-time marketer is added.

What Is the Marketer to Do?

The answer is embodied in the job description. It is not so much the job description itself as the thinking and analysis that precede it. Everything that has been discussed so far in this book bears on this very issue—what is the role of marketing in the organization? What objectives can reasonably be set for marketing? What specific jobs can the marketing function perform? What should the marketer do?

A sample job description for a symphony orchestra is found in Figure 17.3. Note that this is merely a sample, an *instance* of a job description, not a model.

Is There Enough for Him to Do?

This is relatively straightforward to answer, given that the organization has been using part-time marketers and consultants for some time. The organization merely looks at what it has taken in the past to perform the marketing tasks and uses this past experience to answer the question. For those organizations that show substantial seasonality or other fluctuations in marketing tasks, of course, the decision is not quite so simple. But most organizations that are in the process of adding a marketer are so short-handed anyway that they do not find much trouble keeping him occupied during slack periods. (Still, there are inefficiencies in such a course, and the nonprofit organization must not overlook them in estimating the increment to programmed costs that the marketer will cause.)

Even more common, perhaps, is giving the marketer two jobs: He is a marketer during the busy season and something else during the slow season. Admissions directors at summer camps, for example, have a work load that fluctuates widely during the year. To keep them busy during the slack periods, they are given other chores.

What Are the Financial Consequences of Adding a Marketer?

When marketing generates no revenues, the financial consequences are that the organization's total costs will go up. But in most cases the marketer is responsible for generating some revenues. Then the standard approach is to estimate whether or not he will be able to pay for himself.

As an example, consider the marketer discussed above, who represented an increase in the total costs of $51,000. And imagine for the moment that we are again discussing a symphony that has some unsold seats.

Figure 17.3
Job Description for the Marketing Director of a Symphony Orchestra

Position Title:	Director of Marketing
Reports to:	General Manager, Exeter Symphony Association
Scope:	Symphony-wide
Position Concept:	The Director of Marketing has responsibility for providing marketing direction and services for the Exeter Symphony Association

Functions:
The Director of Marketing will:
1. Provide a marketing perspective to the deliberations of Symphony management and the Executive Committee;
2. Prepare data on the Exeter Symphony Association's market size, segment trends, and behavioral dynamics as required by symphony management;
3. Conduct studies of the needs, preferences, and satisfactions of the symphony's market;
4. Assist in planning, promoting, and launching of the new symphony programs;
5. Develop communication and promotion campaigns for both new and established symphony programs;
6. Advise on music selection as it relates to marketing;
7. Analyze and recommend ticket prices;
8. Advise on the workability of new symphony programs from a marketing point of view;
9. Advise on new subscription sales and single ticket sales;
10. Advise on current subscriber satisfaction;
11. Advise on symphony fund raising;
12. Direct symphony public relations.

Responsibilities:
The Director of Marketing will:
1. Conduct a comprehensive marketing audit on the problems and opportunities facing the Exeter Symphony Association; such an audit should be conducted at least every three years;
2. Prepare each year, an in-depth marketing plan for the Association, which will serve as the basis for all marketing programs;
3. Prepare an annual budget to support the anticipated work projected by the marketing plan;
4. Prioritize the various requests for symphony services according to their long-run impact, earned income potential, time requirements, ease of accomplishment, cost, and urgency;
5. Select projects of high priority and set accomplishment goals for the year for ticket sales and fund raising;
6. Direct the public relations efforts of the Exeter Symphony Association;
7. Select, coordinate, and oversee any services provided by outside public relations, advertising, and graphics firms;
8. Prepare an annual report on the main accomplishments of the office of the marketing director.

Major Liaisons:
The Director of Marketing will:
1. Attend all meetings of the Executive Committee;
2. Be a member of the music advisory committee;
3. Be a member of the annual fund drive committee.

Source: General Manager, Exeter Symphony Association.

Concert Series	Maximum Capacity	Seats Currently Sold	Seats Unsold	Average Ticket Price	Maximum Additional Gross Marketing Contribution When Sold Out
Regular subscription	21,000	18,300	2,700	$6.00	$16,200
Pops	6,300	5,300	1,000	$5.50	5,500
Ballet	7,000	4,000	3,000	$5.00	15,000
Children's	4,000	3,000	1,000	$4.00	4,000
Young People's	9,400	9,000	400	$3.00	1,200
Festival	16,000	13,000	3,000	$6.00	18,000
					$59,900

But to sell more seats the marketing director wants $3,000 more for advertising, $2,000 for various promotion activities, and he wants to put $2,000 into ticket price reductions to special audiences (college students, the elderly, and musically gifted high school students). Based on these figures, the *changes* to the Marketing Control Statement given that every seat is sold will be:

Changes in Marketing Control Statement

Change in		
Revenues		$59,000
Variable costs		--
Gross marketing earnings		$59,000
Change in Programmed		
Marketing Expenses		
Advertising	$ 3,000	
Promotion	2,000	
Price reduction	2,000	
Added staff costs	$33,000	40,000
Net marketing contribution		$19,900

What we have here is a purely hypothetical argument. *If* all the seats are sold out, the marketer can more than cover his own costs. The analysis can also be turned the other way. As long as the marketer increases revenues by *at least* $40,000 he will leave the symphony no worse off in terms of Net Marketing Contribution than it is now. Whether such a sales performance can be attained is a matter of judgment.

What Are the Organizational Consequences of Adding a Marketer?

By the time an organization gets around to adding a full-time marketer it will already find several of its staff members actively involved in marketing and related activities. These will include fundraising, planning, and public relations as well as the standard marketing tasks—product, distribution, communication, pricing, and marketing research. The introduction of a full-time marketer will roil the organizational waters. At the very least, some employees will be reassigned to other duties. But the new marketer may well find that some of the people assigned to him are not up to their jobs, and he will itch to fire them. There are no easy solutions to these problems, but the organization that is adding a full-time marketer for the first time must not overlook their presence.

NOTES

1. Rosalie C. Hallbauer, "How Orchestras Measure Internal Performance." *Management Accounting* (February 1980): 54–57.

2. *Museums USA* (Washington, D.C.: National Endowment for the Arts, 1974), p. 47.

3. There was nothing particularly advanced in what we did. The level of difficulty was that represented in Mary M. Wehle, *Financial Practice for Performing Arts Companies* (Cambridge, Mass.: Arts Administration Research Institute, 1977); although Wehle's book deals more with financial accounting matters, and our concern at the museum was with managerial accounting, accounting for decision making and for control. Another book that would have been useful, but like Wehle's had not yet been published, is Robert N. Anthony and Regina E. Herzlinger, *Management Control in Nonprofit Organizations* (Homewood, Ill.: Irwin, 1975).

4. Alice Norton, *Measuring Potential and Evaluating Results,* part of a series called Managing Your Public Relations: Guidelines for Nonprofit Organizations (New York: Foundation for Public Relations Research and Education, 1977).

5. For stories likely to appear outside the local area, a clipping service will be needed.

6. Norton, *Measuring Potential,* p. 14.

7. David T. Kollat, Roger D. Blackwell, and James F. Robeson, *Strategic Marketing* (New York: Holt, Rinehart and Winston, 1972), p. 500.

8. This book is not written for the reader who feels that a checklist substitutes for analysis. Still, there are times when a checklist can help. For a checklist of what to ask when performing a marketing audit, see Chapter 14 in Douglas B. Herron's booklet, *Marketing Management for Social Service Agencies* (Columbus, Ohio: Association of Professional YMCA Directors, 1977), pp. 125–131. This is reprinted in *Readings in Public and Nonprofit Marketing,* edited by Christopher H. Lovelock and Charles B. Weinberg (Palo Alto: Scientific Press, 1978), pp. 267–271. Another checklist for a marketing audit is found in Rohit Deshpande, "Marketing Management," in *Management Principles for Nonprofit Agencies and Organizations,* edited by Gerald Zaltman (New York: AMACOM, 1979), pp. 397–399.

9. Donald E. Johnson, "Marketing Becomes a Key Factor in Hospitals' Physician Recruiting." *Modern Healthcare* (November 1979): 59–61.

10. Eben Shapiro, "Tobacco Firm Seeks Antismoking Network's Records." *Wall Street Journal,* March 30, 1994, p. A7.

11. For more on this topic, see Philip Kotler, "Strategies for Introducing Marketing into Nonprofit Organizations." *Journal of Marketing* 43, no. 1 (January 1979): 37–44.

Part V

OBTAINING RESOURCES

Chapter 18

Giving and Raising Funds

This chapter develops some more elementary economic tools applicable to non-profit marketing and describes some of what is known about givers and their behavior. The next chapter then looks at fundraising costs.

This is not a how-to chapter.[1] There is more than enough how-to ephemera already clogging the libraries and the mails: Plan! Get a Strong Leader! Do a Feasibility Study! Use Your Imagination! Don't be Shy! Ask for More! Besides, the basics of fundraising have been known for centuries, as for example in the *vade mecum,* found in a fourteenth-century Cistercian monastery, that advised the mendicant monks to write letters that began with the Salutation Honeyed; continued with the Exordium Tactful, the Narration Concise, and the Petition Humble, and concluded with the Peroration Graceful; and for good measure included twenty-two model letters, each urging a different reason for giving.[2] Finally, to a marketer there is nothing strange in fundraising. It requires the same habits of mind, the same models and methods, that any marketing program requires; and, tax and legal issues aside, it should be relatively easy for an experienced marketer to learn the vocabulary and technology needed.

GIVING IN THE LARGE

In aggregate, giving in the United States is large, the total in 1992 running $124 billion, or about $490 per capita.[3] By way of comparison this is almost the same amount that the American economy spent on advertising in the same year. Total giving is large, then, but when it is compared with the capacity to give, it does not seem so large. For example, in recent years total private giving has run a bit over 2 percent of the gross domestic product and individual giving has run about 2.1 percent of disposable personal income. The figure to keep in mind: Nationwide, backers give about two cents on the dollar.

There are four principal sources of gifts:

Four Principal Sources of Gifts in 1992

	(billions)	
Individuals	$101.8	82%
Bequests	8.2	7
Foundations	8.3	7
Corporations	6.0	5
	$124.3	100%

Source: Giving USA (New York: AAFRC Trust for Philanthropy, 1993), p. 10. The percentage figures do not add because of rounding.

Since bequests come from individuals, we can say that nine out of every ten dollars come from individuals.

Foundations are rich, as every schoolboy knows. The twenty-five largest together have assets of $52 billion, which is over one-third of the $142 billion of assets held by all foundations. But their giving accounts for only 7 percent of all giving (and 6 percent of their assets). Moreover, of all 32,000 foundations only 2,800 or one in eleven, have assets of over $5 million. The 30,000 foundations with assets of under $5 million are very small: more than half have assets of less than $250,000 and most pay out only a few thousand dollars a year in grants.[4]

Much the same is true of corporate giving; it is large in total, about $6 billion, but small as a percentage of a corporation's capacity to give. Corporate donations run between one and two percent of their pre-tax net income, which would be about .1 or .2 of one percent of their sales.[5] The Internal Revenue Code allows a corporation to deduct contributions to charitable organizations up to a maximum of 5 percent of its taxable income. Corporations may give more, but they cannot deduct anything over 5 percent. In 1973, 51,000 companies contributed the maximum, but they were all small, their average contribution being only $7,100. In the same year the twenty-five largest corporate donors gave an average of $6.2 million each, a total of $154 million, which was between 10 and 15 percent of all corporate contributions. The largest single donor in both 1991 and 1992 was IBM. In both years it lost money, a huge loss of $2.8 billion in 1991; but in 1991 it contributed $135 million and another $120 million the following year. In a survey of 428 corporations, the average contribution per employee was thirty-three dollars.[6]

Looking at the recipients, religious organizations receive almost half of all charitable giving, with human services, education, and health and educational institutions equally sharing another quarter:

Who Got The Money in 1992

	(billions)	
Religion	$57	46%
Human Services	12	10
Education	14	11
Health	10	8
Arts, Culture, Humanities	9	7
Public or Society Benefit	5	4
All Other	17	14
	$124	100%

Source: Giving USA (New York: AAFRC Trust for Philanthropy, 1993), p. 9.

These figures are a bit misleading because roughly half of the money donated to religious bodies is in turn given to other secular causes like welfare, international aid, health, arts, and education.[7]

How important was this giving to these nonprofit organizations? It depends on the nature of the organization. Common benefit organizations naturally obtain most of their financial support from membership dues and assessments, nonprofit businesses obtain most of their funds from sales and receipts, and governmental organizations depend on taxes. Organizations that do not fit in any of these categories tend to rely heavily on giving: religious groups, educational institutions, and cultural institutions.

The overall figures (for 1973) were as follows:

Source of Revenue	Religious	Educational	Health	Cultural	All Philanthropic	All Nonprofit
Sales	60%	65%	94%	46%	72%	23%
Dues and assessments	9%	21%	1%	5%	15%	66
Contributions	36%	14%	5%	49%	13%	11%
	100%	100%	100%	100%	100%	100%

Source: Research Papers, vol. 1, p. 345.[8]

Overall, giving provides 11 percent of the revenues of all nonprofit organizations and 13 percent of the revenues of all philanthropic organizations.

Figures like these must be viewed with caution. They are all based on estimates, often on estimates of estimates, and frequently the organizations chosen for study fail to represent all organizations. Naturally, then, different researchers will reach different conclusions. The figures above showed that giving provided

11 percent of the revenues of "all nonprofit organizations." "All" was based
on a sample of 432 nonprofit organizations, sufficiently large if the sample was
drawn with care. But even a slight shift in definition will change the conclusions.
Suppose we look at the same concept, gifts and contributions as a percentage
of total gross receipts, but instead, use figures from the IRS Form 990, which
nonprofit organizations are required to file each year. For the 90,125 organizations in this sample, gifts comprised 23 percent of their total gross receipts,
twice the figure mentioned above. And for the smaller organizations, gifts became very important indeed.

Givers give more than money. They also donate their time. In a survey by
Morgan and Associates, one in three donated time; in a second survey by the
Gallup Organization, four in ten donated time; in a third by the U.S. Bureau of
Labor Statistics, it was one in five. Women are a bit more likely to volunteer
than men; higher income earners more than lower income earners, and those
with jobs over those without.

All but 12 percent of American households contribute money to nonprofit
organizations in the typical year.

	Percent of Households with This Income	Percent of All Contributions by This Income Class
Lower income, below $10,000	48%	16%
Middle income, between $10,000 and $30,000	49%	55%
Upper income over $30,000	4%	29%
	101%	100%
Number of households	69 million	

Source: Morgan, "Results," p. 162.[9]

This table confirms what the reader already knows—that upper-income backers
are much more important than their mere numbers would indicate and that the
poor give little. It also says some things that the reader may not have known—
that middle-income backers give the bulk of the money, and that while the poor
give less in total, they give more of their limited means. That is, they are less
selfish than the rich.[10]

Giving is related to income in another way as well—except for the very
richest and the very poorest, as income rises the percentage of income devoted
to giving goes up as well.

Giving also increases with education, which is closely related to income and
age. College graduates give six times as much as people with only a grade school
education, and they still give three times as much after correcting for their higher
income. The old give more than the young, in part because they earn more, but
partly because they have more disposable income.

A recent study on giving by blacks and whites found that blacks and whites are equally likely to make charitable contributions, and figures given in the study show that whites give more, which is no surprise given their higher income.[11] There do not appear to be any studies on giving by occupational group, although entertainers—both those in show business and in athletics—are supposedly generous givers of both time and money. The most niggardly occupational groups are supposedly doctors and dentists. The doctors say that they make up for this by donating their services to voluntary health agencies and to hospitals. I do not know what the dentists say.

During the past decade aggregate giving has about kept up with the moderate pace of inflation. But in the background there is the federal government and changes in the tax code. During the 1970s, for example, the standard income tax deduction was increased six times, so that the number of taxpayers who itemize fell by a factor of two, from almost 50 percent in 1970 to about 25 percent in 1980. Increasing the standard deduction tends to decrease giving, because a taxpayer who uses the standard deduction is allowed no itemized deductions. When the tax code was changed in 1986, marginal tax rates went down, and owners of art who were covered by the alternative minimum tax found that they could deduct only the price they paid for works they might donate to a museum. The result was a sharp decline in the number of donations of art (from 2,100 in 1988 to 700 in 1990).[12]

Giving patterns differ by country, as one would expect. (See Table 18.1.) The British and the Spanish are prone to give but their donations run small, on average. The French seem the stingiest with few French giving and giving in small amounts. Both the Canadians and the Americans give large amounts. Where donations are made varies. The Canadians and Americans are most likely to give in church and their giving there accounts for over half of all giving. The Brits and French give to collectors in the street or those who go door-to-door.

A Look at Some Research

There are other ways of describing and understanding the nature of the influences on giving. Let us look at a fine pair of studies by Martin Feldstein and associates. Feldstein and Clotfelter developed a mathematical model that embodies some elementary economic theory concerning giving, which they then tested by using econometric techniques.[13] They were interested primarily in how giving varied with income, and with the costs of giving borne by the giver. They called the cost of giving the "price" of the gift. "The price of charitable giving is the amount of after-tax income or wealth that the individual foregoes to add one dollar to the receipts of a donee."[14] And the marginal tax rate needed to compute the price can be estimated from the backer's income, or from his income tax return, which is what Feldstein and Clotfelter used.

Income can be defined in a number of ways. But the income that influences giving is more than merely cash income in a given year. For charitable giving

Table 18.1
Comparisons of Charitable Behavior in Five Developed Countries

	Proportion giving in past month	Mean donation per month	Most used donating method	Highest proportionate yield[1]	Sector benefiting most
Britain	65%	£7.00	Door-to-door & street 27%	Charity event 23%	Medical 23%
Canada	62%	£22.00	Place of worship 26%	Place of worship 57%	Medical 29% Religious 29%
France	27%	£4.00	Door-to-door & street 7%	Advert or letter 18%	Medical 11%
Spain	71%	£7.50	Lottery 49%	Lottery 54%	Social welfare 39%
U.S.A.	55%	£19.50	Place of worship 33%	Place of worship 52%	Religious 33%

1. Read: In Britain charity events yield a higher proportion of donations than any other method.

Source: Peter Halfpenny, "The 1991 International Survey of Giving," in Susan K. E. Saxon-Harrold and Jeremy Kendall (eds.), *Researching the Voluntary Sector* (Tonbridge, Kent: Charities Aid Foundation, 1993), pp. 214. In 1991, £1.00 was worth about US $1.60.

depends not so much on income in any particular year, as on permanent income, which is a kind of average income over a number of years. The other thing wrong with cash as a measure is that cash ignores changes in value of other assets. My giving is likely to change if I discover the Kandinsky that I thought was worth $12,000 is not by Kandinsky and is only worth $200; and it is likely to change again if I receive a $430,000 bid to buy some land my father left me that I thought was worth $15,000, even if I have no intention of selling.

Since income and price can be defined in different ways, Feldstein and Clotfelter tried several different definitions. Their general approach was to fit a line to their data and use the fitted equation to estimate the responsiveness of giving to price and income. Because they used several definitions, they got several different estimates, but we may take as representative for our purposes the following estimates: Price elasticity of giving is −1.15 and the income elasticity is .8. That is, giving is price elastic and income inelastic. As income increases one percent, giving increases .8 of one percent: giving increases as income increases, but not as fast. As price goes up 1 percent—because Congress raises taxes (or reforms the tax code, as they prefer to say)—giving goes down 1.15 percent. Giving decreases as taxes increase, and it decreases faster.

These figures enable us to guess—Feldstein and Clotfelter would surely prefer "predict"—the effect of a proposed change in the deductibility of contributions. One such proposal is to eliminate such deductions, making all contributions come out of after-tax income. This has the effect of raising the price to one. As an example, in 1963 a family earning between $8,000 and $10,000 a year gave gifts averaging $165, and the average price was .84. With the elimination of the deduction, the price would increase from .84 to 1, and the average amount given would decrease 18 percent, or $30. Families earning between $25,000 and $50,000 per year gave an average of $2,125 in 1963, and they faced a price of .49. Eliminating the deduction for these families would in essence double the price, from .49 to 1, and lead these families to reduce their giving by 56 percent, or $935.[15] Here we see just what we would expect to see: Charitable deductions mean much more to the well-off than they do the middle-income groups.

When a business uses price elasticities, it is thinking in terms of changes in its quantity sold and changes in its price. Here, however, the changes in quantity deal with changes in contributions to NPOs, while the changes in price deal with tax revenues at the U.S. Treasury. A price elasticity smaller than -1 means that a (small) reduction in taxes produces an increase in contributions that is larger than the tax reduction, and that an increase in taxes produces a decrease in contributions that is larger than the tax increase.[16]

Feldstein goes on to examine other important questions. One is how price elasticity varies with income. The estimate of -1.15, after all, is an overall average, a single figure description of all income groups. Feldstein finds that the average elasticity is on the order of -1, and that there is "strong" evidence that the price elasticities for wealthy families, whose wealth is over $100,000, are smaller than -1.

All these results have been for givers who itemize their charitable deductions on their federal tax returns. What about givers who do not itemize? What about low-income givers who do not even file a tax return? In another study exploring this question, Boskin and Feldstein conclude that low- and middle-income households are sensitive to tax-induced variations in the cost of giving. They estimate the price elasticity of these households as generally being smaller than -2.[17]

GIVING IN THE SMALL

We have seen some of the research dealing with giving of groups of backers. Now let us turn to the individual donor and look briefly at his interests.

Let us first look at the question of taxes. There is no question that taxes count and count a lot. Or is there? Comparing average giving by taxpayers who itemize their deductions with those who do not provides one answer. In Morgan's survey, itemizers gave more (on average $775 versus nonitemizers' $140) at all income levels. Yet when people are asked about taxes, they appear to know very little; and they usually say taxes have little influence on their decision to give. In his survey, Morgan asked his respondents what their income was. Then he asked how much extra taxes they would have paid had their income gone up $100, and "If you contributed another $100 to charity, how much would it save you in taxes?" The results are astounding. So full of perplexities is the tax code that 72 percent of the respondents either did not know or gave answers that implied impossible marginal tax rates, rates below 13 or above 70 percent. (This was in 1973.) In fact, only one in five, or 21 percent, gave answers that could conceivably be correct. As one would expect, those with higher incomes were most likely to answer correctly, but the proportion giving a conceivably correct answer never rose above 59 percent (for those earning between $100,000 and $200,000 a year). Morgan constructed a six-point index to measure tax sensitivity, and by this index only 12 percent of his sample were sensitive to taxes; but, again, the proportion of correct answers and the sensitivity to taxes rose with income.[18] In general, then, most taxpayers understand little about the tax consequences of giving, presumably because it is not worth their while to consider different ways of giving and their tax implications.

There is a further consideration on taxation that should be mentioned. The usual assumption is that what determines whether taxpayers itemize is not charitable deductions but other items like property taxes, state and city income taxes, mortgage interest, and the like. Once taxpayers have piled up enough of these items to make itemizing worthwhile, they take all the other deductibles they can find as well. But still the evidence shows that itemizers give a good deal more than nonitemizers, which means that at least for itemizers taxes appear to count.

Morgan also found his respondents somewhat more willing to attribute tax reasons for giving to others than to themselves (we know what this means), and that few respondents volunteered tax reasons in explaining either their past giving or what they planned to give in the future. Morgan concluded his findings on taxes as follows:

We see much less sophistication and calculated consideration of tax effects than is often alleged to exist. This finding is similar to what we found a decade ago in interviewing upper-income people. . . . They were much less concerned with avoiding income taxes than with making money and getting things done.

There seem to be two points at which serious tax effects might be expected. One is the lower-middle-income groups where the opportunity to itemize at all is changing as the standard deduction is increased, raising the "price of charity" to 100 percent. The other is among the few very wealthy people who have foundations or are thinking of setting up foundations.[19]

Taxes count for some givers, then, but not for most. They give, presumably, to a cause, and, above all, they give because they are asked to give.[20] The reader knows well that he does not sit down once a month and, without being asked, send off checks to worthy causes. He must be asked to give, either by mail or in person. In terms of the decision-making model discussed in Chapter 4, being asked to give forces the backer to recognize that he has a problem that must be solved.

It is also possible to learn more about backers' motives in general by asking them. Morgan did this by asking backers a "why" question, a procedure fraught with research perils, as Morgan himself admits. Let us see why, as an aside. "Why" questions take the form, "Why did you do such and such?" The answers are usually unreliable in part for the reasons mentioned in Chapter 6: Respondents will answer although they do not really know why they behave as they do, they may very well know but not want to admit it, or they may know but not be able to put it into words. What all this means is that answers to "why" questions deal only with surface reasons and only those surface reasons that people are willing to acknowledge in public. The very nature of the question, in addition, implies a decision that has structure and rationale. But marketers believe that there is little thought given to repetitive decisions, which are after all usually low-involvement decisions. "When most people were asked directly why they gave money to a certain charity, they not only were unable to give an answer, but many also implied that they had never thought about their own charitable motives: 'Why do I give to the church? I really don't know. Why do I?' "[21]

Finally, "why" questions imply that there is a single most important reason for the respondent's behavior, but in many important decisions there are several interests and considerations warring with each other. A question that forces a respondent to choose between "price" or "quality" as most important in buying, say, insurance, when the respondent uses price as a measure of quality, is sure to produce a hash. The moral is to mistrust the answers to "why" questions unless they look right and are corroborated by other results less in question, such as inferences from people's behavior and evidence from other research.

Why, then, do backers say they give? The following table reports the sum of first and second mentions as a percentage of all reasons given for those who gave over $100.

Question: Why did you give to this organization?	
Approve, they need money, feel obligated	67%
Get some benefit	13%
Belong, we belong there	23%
Pressure, quota	5%
Other, don't know, no answer	13%
	121%
(n =)	4,539

Source: Morgan, "Results," p. 205.

"Clearly, we do not get very profound answers," writes Morgan.

In addition, answers that we know to be important are missing. For example, giving of money and giving of time tend to run together, as we mentioned earlier. Here is some evidence for this:

Question	Percent of those giving to the organization who answer Yes to question
Have you served on any committees or advisory groups for the organization in the past 5 years?	35%
Are you active in the organization now?	42%
Do you know personally anyone who is involved in running the organization?	74%

Source: Morgan, "Results," pp. 258-259.

Large gifts in particular go with gifts of time. For example, of those backers who gave over $5,000, 54 percent had served on a committee and 40 percent knew someone in the administration.

We have seen in the previous chapter that backers (and clients) have interests in information. Morgan asked his respondents questions dealing with one type of information presumably relevant to donors, namely, disclosure of how the charity works.[22] One-third of his respondents said that they would like more information on the charities they give to, and that the information they wanted was as follows:

Amount spent on fundraising	3%
Amount spent on administration	9%
Allocation of monies raised	9%
Amount of money going to people	7%
How the fund uses money	13%
Total wanting more information	41%

It is clear that most backers have little interest in such matters. He did not investigate, however, where donors get their information, those situations in which donors collect little information, or what other attributes of the charities donors want to know about besides how they are run.

There is another informational interest that most large donors have, which is: How much is the donor expected to give? Most successful fundraisers do not shilly-shally about this; at the appropriate moment they come right to the point. "Ladies, I'm here looking for money. We have a fundraising dinner next month at $1,000 a plate. Under the new election laws you can give only $1,000, and that is all your husband can give. But you can also give your help by calling a few of your friends in the next week or so and asking them to buy a ticket or two."

TWO TOOLS FOR THE FUNDRAISER

Who Gives How Much to Whom?

To understand better the nature of gifts, let us consider the question of what is involved in the giving of a gift.[23]

You spend, let us say, $100 a week on food. You are poor, I have a soft heart, and I want to help you out. So I decide to give you $50 a week. I might do this in three ways. I could (1) give you $50 cash and let you decide how to spend it; (2) give you $50 cash but require that you spend it only on food (I'd want to see receipts); or (3) buy $50 worth of groceries and give you those, no cash at all.

Do these three differ? Of course, if I buy you food, I may buy things you don't like to eat. I don't want to deal with this issue, however, because it gets in the way of my point. So let's pretend that when I buy groceries for you, I do a pretty good job and you have no complaints.

I ask again—do the three differ? The answer may surprise you. They are all the same. They do not differ. If I give you $50 cash, you can spend it any way you like, on food, or anything. I'll never know. If I tie the gift and make you spend the money on food, surely that will be different. It is not. Before I gave you the money you set aside $100 a week for food and nothing for "other things." With my gift you now set aside only $50 for food, which you combine with my gift to get you through the week. But only setting aside $50 for food when you used to set aside $100 means you now have $50 more pocket money than you did before. Tying funds to the purchase of food is the same as giving an out-and-out gift.

You should be able to see that the third way of making the gift has the same effect. If I buy the groceries, then you don't have to. If I buy $50 worth of groceries, then you will spend $50 less on groceries and have $50 more to spend on anything you wish.

We have seen that tying a gift in some way to a specific end can be the same as simply giving someone money and saying, "Spend it as you wish." There is a qualification, though. Let us now imagine a wealthy family that wants to endow the library at the school where the family's sons and daughters have gone for four generations, Prep School, let us call it. It is a tied gift. The earnings from the endowment can only be spent for library materials, nothing else.

Prep School spends about $300,000 a year for library materials. The family decides to give, say, $5 million, which Prep School expects will generate earnings of 5 percent a year, or $250,000. The school will use the money from the endowment to replace money it otherwise would have spent on the library. It will be as if the gift were pure cash.

Now suppose the gift is $10 million and generates $500,000 a year. Prep School still enjoys the fact that it no longer has to spend $300,000 a year out of its operating fund for materials. It still finds an extra $300,000 to spend on whatever it wishes. But not the last $200,000. The only way it can benefit from that is by buying more materials for the library than it has in the past, perhaps more than it wants to spend. In this case the tied gift of $500,000 has the effect of two gifts, one a simple cash gift of $300,000 to be spent any way Prep School wishes, the other a tied gift of $200,000 that can be spent only for the library.

Henry and Betty Rowan understand this. In 1992 they gave $100 million to an obscure state college in Glassboro, New Jersey. The Rowans had several suggestions for how the money might be spent, but the only real restriction on the gift was that it should not replace money the state allocated to the school.[24]

The only time a tied gift completely forces the hand of the recipient is when the recipient is not involved in the tied activity. Suppose I give you a $50 ticket to the opera each week and tell you that you must go or lose the ticket. You don't go to the opera now. My tickets won't save you anything, and you must go if you are to get anything from my gift at all. Or suppose a backer proposes to a law school a $3 million endowment for the purchase of materials on welfare law. No one on the faculty is interested in welfare law, nor is this type of public service law part of the law school's mission. If it accepts the gift, the law school's hands will be tied, and the gift will not be the same as a pure cash gift. (Of course, if they could still get at the donor, no headmaster or law school dean would give up so easily. They would work hard to alter the donor's intention, and make the gift less restrictive. No one likes large restricted gifts. Everyone likes small restricted gifts.)

This analysis, then, shows us that the effect of a gift may differ from its intention. This is most clearly seen when the government gives a business subsidy, or a welfare grant, or a foreign aid loan. Suppose a poor family spends $100 a week for food. The government cannot give this family a subsidy of $60 a week, because, being poor, the family will spend the money in ways deemed wicked by some taxpayers. Instead, the government ties its gift so that the $60 can be used only for food and for no other purpose. It is very strict about this, and every year one or two offenders are caught and publicly corrected. We know the true effect of the gift. The effect would be just the same if the government simply handed the family a check for $60. A family can pursue its wicked ways after all.

The Time Value of Money

The topic in elementary economics that is discussed here is the time value of money.[25] The idea is simple yet fundamental. It is that the sooner we receive money, the better off we are; for the sooner we receive it, the sooner the money can be put to work earning still more money, or buying "happiness." A dollar this year is worth more than a dollar next year, or as the saying goes, "A nearby penny is worth a distant dollar." This has nothing to do with the risk that if you wait to be paid your debtor may welsh on the debt; and it has nothing to do with inflation, which, of course, reduces the real value of money over time.

Table 18.2
Future Value of $80,000 at Three Interest Rates

	7%	14%	12%
Value at beginning of first year	$80,000	$80,000	$80,000
Interest earned in first year	5,600	11,200	9,600
Value at end of first year	85,600	91,200	89,600
Interest earned in second year	6,000	12,800	10,800
Value at end of second year	$91,600	$104,000	$100,400

For this section, you should pretend there is no inflation, and that the debt is sure to be paid.

To fix the idea, imagine a potential donor who approaches a university and says, "I can give you $80,000 cash now, or $100,000 in two years." Which should the university choose? It depends. It depends on what else the university can do with its money. It might be able to earn a certain return in the money market or renovate a laboratory without borrowing as much as it had originally planned. In either case, the value of the money would be determined by the interest rate. Suppose the university can earn a 7 percent return. It starts with $80,000 and in the first year adds 7 percent of $80,000, or $5,600, finishing the first year with $85,600. In the second year it earns, let us say, another 7 percent, this time of $85,600, or $6,000; thus, it finishes up with $91,600 at the end of two years. Clearly, it should have waited and taken the $100,000.

These computations, plus computations for two other interest rates, are found in Table 18.2. Earning 14 percent, $80,000 grows to $104,000 at the end of two years, and the university should prefer the $80,000 now to $100,000 later. At 12 percent, the two are worth virtually the same, and the choice between them would be made on a basis other than which was worth more.

The "sooner is better" principle only applies, of course, when the university is on the receiving end. When it is paying, the principle becomes: The longer paying can be put off, the better, because as long as the money is still in hand, it can be at work earning still more money. State lotteries have begun to offer huge grand prizes. Let us take a prize of $10 million. The lottery does in fact pay out $10 million, but typically it stretches the payments out over twenty years.[26] In the first year it pays out, say, $500,000, keeping the rest, $9.5 million in the state treasury for other purposes. In the second year it pays out another $500,000, but it still has $9 million that it can use. Depending on the value of these other things, the present value of the grand prize varies.

Market Interest Rate	**6%**	**8%**	**10%**	**12%**
Present value of $10	$5.73	$4.90	$4.26	$3.73

Note: all dollar figures in millions.

Whatever else that can be said about the $10 million grand prize, it does not cost the state $10 million—except in current dollars, which do not count for anything important. Between $4 and $5 million is more like it. And when you consider how sweet it is to be a debtor in inflationary times, which allows the debtor to pay each year in cheaper dollars, the real cost of the $10 million prize is smaller still.

These values of a twenty-year stream of payments are the present values of the stream; that is, at 6 percent, the present value of a stream of twenty annual payments of $50,000 each is $573,000. The simplest formula for computing present value is

$$PV = \frac{P_1}{1 + i} + \frac{P_2}{(1 + i)^2} + \ldots + \frac{P_n}{(1 + i)^n}$$

where
  PV = Present value of the stream of payments (or receipts)
  P_j = Payment (or receipt) in year j
   i = The value of money (say, the interest rate)
   n = The number of periods
For i = .06, we have the following

Year	$P_j/(1.06)^j$	Cumulative Sum
1	47,200	47,200
2	44,500	91,700
3	41,980	133,680
.	.	.
.	.	.
.	.	.
19	16,500	557,900
20	15,600	573,500

Let us think about a university again and apply this concept of time value of money. Annual alumni giving is usually cash, so the present value is equal to the amount of the gift. But only about 8 percent of the total support for education comes from alumni in this way. Much more important is giving for capital, which comprises about half of the total private support for education. Capital gifts are always large gifts, they are almost always securities, and they are normally given over a three- to five-year period. That is, capital gifts are usually pledges. Such money has a present value that is influenced by the interest rate, and, of course, the present value is less than the face amount of the pledge, just as the present value of a $10 million lottery prize is less than $10 million. But if you were a dean or a university president having just learned that a donor had pledged the university $50,000 a year for twenty years, which would you

Table 18.3
Estimating the Value of a New Donor

	Number (a)	Gift in Current $ (b)	Gift in Discounted $ (at 15%) (c)	Expected Average Gift (a x c)
New donors in year 1	1,000	$45	$45	$45,000
Still giving in year 2	500	$60	$51	25,500
Still giving in year 3	250	$60	$43	10,800
Still giving in year 4	125	$70	$37	4,600
Still giving in year 5	0	0	0	0
				$85,900

announce, a gift of $1 million, or one worth between $400,000 and $600,000, depending on interest rates over the twenty-year period? Robert Fulmer has written archly that the time value of money calls for "greater candor in reporting capital pledges."[27] Fulmer goes on to say that the Massachusetts Institute of Technology does not stop merely at the recognition of the time value of money. MIT asks donors to finance their pledges; that is, to give even more if the gift is paid over a number of years, in recognition of the smaller value of dollars paid in the future.

The Value of a Donor

Another question that the time value of money helps deal with is how much is a new donor worth? The difficulty lies in the fact that, having given once, some donors will give again in future years, and the value of a new donor must somehow take into account his future donations. Thus, a new donor is worth more than merely the first year's donation. But how much more? To answer the question, one must estimate (1) the rate at which donors drop away over time, (2) their average donations, and (3) a discount rate. Then computations like those in Table 18.3 will provide an estimate.

Given the assumptions in the table, these figures show that the present value of the donations of 1,000 new donors over a five-year period is $85,900. Hence the answer to the question is that a new donor is worth (has a present value of) about eighty-six dollars. This means, in plain English, that the NPO should not spend more than eighty-six dollars landing a new donor. Well—one should not get excited about that eighty-six dollar figure. It is based on assumptions as to (a) how fast donors turn over, (b) likely average gifts, and (c) the discount rate. Since all are projections, a sounder conclusion is to think of the value of a new donor as being "around eighty dollars" or "somewhere between seventy and a hundred" or "roughly twice the first gift." In like fashion most NPOs would not dream of spending eighty dollars to acquire a new donor worth ninety. They would feel it is ethically and morally wrong—although doing so would leave them with more cash than if they did not do so.

No one knows how long the average donor continues to respond to direct mail—and the number obviously differs for different kinds of nonprofits—but the most common guess is seven years, max. So my assumption of a four-year life is fair as an example.

This is an example of using numbers to reach a qualitative conclusion. All three of the estimates needed for this computation are estimates of the future. It would not be unkind to call them guesses. To repeat: Managers make the best use of numbers like these not by saying, ''The value of a new donor is $85.90,'' but by saying, ''The value of a new donor is about twice his first-year gift.'' Managers must not allow themselves to be fooled by their own calculations.

COSTS OF GIVING

In this section we look at the costs of giving: first, costs borne by backers and volunteers and, second, costs borne by nonprofit organizations. Then in the next chapter we look at the cost of raising funds.

Costs Borne by Backers

Backers give gifts in two forms: The first is the gift of self, when they volunteer their time, their talents, their blood, or their energies. The second is the gift of possessions, which is usually money but can be goods, services, or even rights of value. As we might expect, the cost of a gift of self is mostly an opportunity cost, while the cost of a gift of possessions is mostly an OOP cost if it is cash and an opportunity cost otherwise.[28]

Were it not for the fact that gifts of possessions are tax deductible, there would be little more to say. But they are, which makes it important to calculate OOP costs borne by backers after tax.

Let us do this by considering an asset—say, a fourteenth-century Tuscan pyx—originally bought for $3,000, now worth $10,000. The owner pays a federal marginal tax rate of 40 percent. (We ignore state and city taxes.) If the owner keeps the pyx, his wealth remains unchanged, at $10,000. He can do four other things, as well: sell the pyx and spend the proceeds, sell the pyx and give the proceeds away without taking a tax deduction, give the proceeds away and take a deduction, or give the pyx itself away.

If he sells, there is a capital gain of $10,000 − $3,000 = $7,000 of which (let us say) only one-half, $3,500, is reported as income. The marginal tax rate on this is 40 percent of $3,500 = $1,400, which leaves him with $8,400 net. If he donates the item to charity but takes no tax deduction, his net wealth is decreased by the full amount of the value of the pyx, $10,000. But if he takes a tax deduction, he is allowed (under certain conditions too complicated for a book on marketing) to deduct the full $10,000, thus lowering his total taxable income by $10,000 and his tax by 40 percent of $10,000, or $4,000.[29] The gross decrease in his wealth is offset by lower taxes, and his net wealth decreases only $6,000. Finally, he could sell the item and, in addition, donate $10,000 to a charity, taking a deduction. This is the same as the case discussed above, except that, in addition, the donor must come up with an additional $1,400 to make up the full $10,000. The table sums up this last transaction:

Net Wealth	Amount	Cumulative Amount	Source
Decreases by	$10,000	−10,000	Giving up an item worth $10,000
Increases by	$10,000	0	Proceeds from sale
Decreases by	1,400	−1,400	Capital gains tax
Decreases by	$10,000	−11,400	Cash donation
Offset by	4,000	7,400	Tax saved on other income

His net wealth decreases by $7,400. In summary:

Action	Net Wealth Decreased by
Keep asset	No change
Sell and pay tax	$1,400
Donate asset, no deduction	10,000
Donate asset, take deduction	6,000
Sell, donate $10,000	7,400

The last three items are what we are interested in, because they show the effects on net wealth of three ways of giving away $10,000. If the owner is determined to get rid of the asset, the best thing to do is sell and keep the after-tax proceeds. If he wishes not merely to rid himself of the pyx but also to contribute to a charity, the best thing to do is donate the pyx directly, not to sell it. The difference between the net decrease in wealth from selling and paying the tax, and donating the pyx and taking a deduction is $6,000 − 1,400 = $4,600. This measures the wealth dissipated, or consumption foregone, and it is the OOP cost of the contribution; or in simpler terms, it is the price of the contribution.

Costs Borne by the Volunteer

The volunteer who gives time or other gifts of self bears two costs: The first is OOP costs but, typically, these costs are small. "For wives doing volunteer work, out-of-pocket costs were common but not substantial in amount. . . . They amount[ed] to some $760 million for the survey year."[30] Since the number of hours volunteered was estimated at 2.7 billion, the average OOP cost per hour was $760 million divided by 2.7 billion = 28 cents an hour. But this is a very

Table 18.4
Percent of Heads of Household Who Volunteer, by Opportunities to Earn Money

	Not Working*	Working But Could Not Earn More	But Could Earn More
Percent time volunteering time	23%	30%	35%
(Total number)	564	1,261	956

Source: Research Papers, vol. 1, p. 209.
*Of those not working, 23 percent volunteer.

rough estimate dominated by a few cases extrapolated to population totals. It is rough, to be sure, and it is an average, which means there may be a great deal of variation in average OOP costs per hour concealed behind the mean; but it seems unlikely the figure could be off by a factor of ten; that is, it is unlikely that real OOP costs average more than $2.80 per hour. We are safe, then, in concluding OOP costs are probably "small." (See Table 18.4.)

The other major cost borne by the volunteer is opportunity costs. As we already know, opportunity costs are what is foregone. For those with nothing better to do, or whose decision to volunteer time is unchangeable, the opportunity cost is zero. But some volunteers—almost half of them, in fact—do have opportunities for other work. This does not dampen the eagerness of these volunteers to donate their time, as the figures in Table 18.4 show.

Those who give time are also more likely to give money: The giving of time and of money go together. This suggests that there is a giving group for which altruism takes more than one form.

QUESTIONS

1. Around 5 percent of Morgan's respondents reported they felt "pressure" to give. Would you expect the form that the pressure takes to vary by income? If not, why not? If so, give the forms by income.

2. Most state lotteries in the United States advertise that the profits from the operation of the lottery help to support public education. Profits means sales less (1) commissions to retail sales agents, (2) prizes, and (3) operating expenses. Profits typically run about 40 percent of sales. This means that the surpluses generated by the lotteries are paid to the state treasury but are earmarked for educational expenses only. (The actual amount spent on education by any given state is, of course, decided by the state legislature when it approves the state budget.)

   What exactly does this advertising claim mean? Make whatever assumption or assumptions you need to answer the question. Be clear about what these assumptions are.

3. Some years ago, the linguist Mario Pei wrote a letter to the *New York Times* complaining about all the fundraising appeals he received in the mail. He proposed a solution, namely, that all the worthy causes in a certain area, say, education or the blind, get together and issue a joint appeal in a single bulletin. Each organization would describe its purpose and activities. The donor could decide which to give money to, or even whether to give money to a certain bureau that would spread it around. This would (1) raise more money, (2) cut greatly the load on the post office, and (3) save a great deal of money, according to Pei.

Evaluate Pei's proposal. Which groups would come out best? Which groups would suffer the most? Why? Which donors would likely thrive under such a setup? What implicit assumptions is Pei making about why people donate? And so on.

4. According to a news story, fundraisers at Rhodes College in Memphis plan to use telephone solicitors ''to reach every living graduate of the college . . . and then [to] make the phone solicitations an annual event.''

There's something odd here. What is it?

5. Taking tainted money has been called the Robin Hood school of fundraising. For example, should Mothers Against Drunk Driving accept money from beer or liquor companies?

What are the pros and cons? What are the ethical issues? What is your personal opinion about an NPO's accepting tainted money?

NOTES

1. The reader who wants more information than is in this inestimable chapter and who can tolerate contrary opinions should (1) find suggestions for further reading in the footnotes; (2) read two monthlies, *Fund Raising Management* and *Philanthropy Monthly;* (3) go to his neighborhood public library where he will find books with titles like ''How to Raise Funds,'' or ''Three Hundred Fund-Raising Ideas''; (4) talk to other nonprofit managers to learn from them, and (5) get help from his national association. If he can afford it he can buy numerous how-to manuals of varying quality, go to seminars and workshops on fundraising, hire a fundraising consultant (or ''counsel'' as they prefer to be called—adds a touch of class), or set up a full-time development group.

2. E. Hereward Phillips, *Fundraising Techniques* (London: Business Books, 1969), p. 127.

3. By way of contrast, per capita giving in the United Kingdom is about $20 (U.S.), in Canada about $35.

4. The figures in the paragraph come from U.S. Bureau of the Census, *Statistical Abstract of the United States,* 113th ed. (Washington, D.C.: U.S. Government Printing Office, 1993), Table G18; and ''Financial Data and Rankings of Foundations.'' *Chronicle of Philanthropy,* March 9, 1993, p. 16. Both of these credit The Foundation Center as their source.

5. In England, the twenty most generous companies gave .4 of one percent of their profits in 1971. See the figures in J.P. Gallagher, *The Price of Charity* (London: Robert Hale, 1975), p. 27.

6. James F. Harris and Anne Klepper, ''Corporate Philanthropic Public Service Activities.'' *Research Papers,* vol. 3, pp. 1741–1788. Concerning the twenty-five largest

donors, the mean contribution was $6.2 million, the median $3.3 million. (See note no. 8.)

7. Brian O'Connell and Ann Brown O'Connell, *Volunteers in Action* (New York: Foundation Center, 1989).

8. The full citation for this table is as follows: Burton A. Weisbrod and Stephen H. Long, ''The Size of the Voluntary Nonprofit Sector: Concepts and Measures,'' in Commission on Private Philanthropy and Public Needs, *Research Papers Sponsored by the Commission on Private Philanthropy and Public Needs,* vol. 1, *History, Trends, and Current Magnitudes* (Washington, D.C.: Department of the Treasury, Commission on Private Philanthropy and Public Needs, 1977), p. 345. Surely, the reader will allow me to abbreviate. The *Research Papers* runs to 3,000 pages in six volumes and in spite of its age is crammed with good things.

9. This refers to James N. Morgan, Richard F. Dye, and Judith H. Hybels, ''Results from Two National Surveys of Philanthropic Activity,'' in *Research Papers,* vol. 1, pp. 157–323. Fat and fascinating. I refer to ''Morgan'' and ''his'' results for brevity.

10. It is more complicated than this. Paul Schervish and John Havens studied this question and drew the following conclusions: (1) measured in terms of *wealth* there is no evidence that the poor are less selfish than the rich, (2) measured in terms of *gross household income,* upper- and lower-income households are roughly equally as generous. See a summary in ''Do the Poor Pay More: Is the U-Shaped Curve Correct?'' *Chronicle of Philanthropy,* February 9, 1993, p. 32; and ''What Statistics Reveal About the Generosity of Rich and Poor: The Scholars Respond.'' *Chronicle of Philanthropy,* May 4, 1993, p. 41.

11. Emmett D. Carson, *The Charitable Appeals Fact Book: How Black and White Americans Respond to Different Types of Fund-Raising Efforts* (Washington, D.C.: Joint Center for Political Studies Press, 1989), pp. 3–5. Carson concludes that blacks and whites give substantially the same amounts, in spite of the fact that blacks earn a good deal less. I think Carson has misjudged his own evidence. Table B on p. 5 clearly shows that whites give more, on the order of $100 more.

12. *Annual Report* of the Art Advisory Panel of the Internal Revenue Service, 1989. Donations rose again in 1991 when the tax code was changed yet another time, just for the 1991 tax year.

13. Martin S. Feldstein and Charles Clotfelter, ''Tax Incentives and Charitable Contributions in the United States: A Microeconomic Analysis,'' *Research Papers,* vol. 3, pp. 1393–1417.

14. Ibid., p. 1396.

15. Feldstein used a log-log demand function, which calls for a formula for calculating elasticities slightly different from the one used earlier. Let C stand for contributions, P for price, ln for the natural logarithm, b for before the change, and a for after the change. Then the price elasticity, E, is

$$E = \frac{\ln C_a - \ln C_b}{\ln P_a - \ln P_b} = \frac{\ln(\text{Ratio of } C_a \text{ to } C_b)}{\ln(\text{Ratio of } P_a \text{ to } P_b)}$$

After a little manipulation, this becomes

(Ratio of prices) ^{E} = Ratio of contributions

With the figures above, this becomes

$$(1/.84)^{-1.15} = .82, \text{ or a decrease of } (1 - .82)100 = 18\%.$$

16. A temperature of forty degrees below zero is lower than a temperature of ten degrees below. That is, -40 degrees is smaller than -10 degrees. In the same way, an elasticity of -2 is smaller than an elasticity of -1, while an elasticity of $-\frac{1}{2}$ is larger than one of -1.

17. Michael J. Boskin and M.S. Feldstein, "Effects of the Charitable Deduction on Contributions by Low Income and Middle Income Households: Evidence from the *National Survey on Philanthropy*." *Review of Economics and Statistics* 59 (August 1977): 351–354.

18. Morgan, "Results," p. 178.

19. Ibid., p. 197.

20. I dismiss without comment such lists of reasons as to why people give as that proposed by Irving R. Warner, *The Act of Fund Raising* (New York: Harper and Row, 1975). Backers give, he tells us on page 61, for ten reasons—love, hate, fear, shame, guilt, friendship, loyalty, nostalgia, to impress others, and to impress the backer himself. Note that he does not include being asked to give. Why?

21. Morgan, "Results," p. 204.

22. Ibid., p. 202.

23. This section is based on Armen A. Alchian and William R. Allen, *University Economics* (Belmont, Calif.: Wadsworth, 1969), pp. 135–142.

24. Jennifer Moore, "Couple Gives $100-Million to N.J. College, Donation Is One of the Largest Ever Made." *Chronicle of Philanthropy,* July 14, 1992, p. 7. But can the state legislature ever bind itself so that such a restriction will stick? One should entertain some mistrust, it seems to me.

25. Readers who groan at reading yet another exposition of this simple point should skip ahead. For them this is an optional section.

26. Knowing how governments operate, I doubt any state would salt away $9.5 million just to be prudent or fiscally responsible. Much better to spend now, as much as can be spent, and leave it to legislators and taxpayers in future years to come up with the annual payments.

27. Robert A. Fulmer, "Cost/Benefit Analysis in Fund Raising." *Harvard Business Review* 51 (March–April 1973): 106.

28. Strictly speaking, even gifts of cash are opportunity costs, because money itself is valued only for what it will buy.

29. The labyrinth of the tax code is full of dark turnings and Byzantine complexities, and each year hundreds of new twists are added. Any discussion here simply illustrates the impact of taxes on giving. I do not pretend to understand the code. Even if I did understand it, it would have changed by the time you read this. Still, for more, read Allan J. Samansky, *Charitable Contributions and Federal Taxes* (Charlottesville, W. Va.: Michie, 1993). It has nearly 500 pages and should overwhelm a normal, healthy mind.

30. Morgan, "Results," pp. 168, 209.

Chapter 19

The Cost of Raising Funds

The information available on fundraising costs is poor, and there is not much of it. This section will cite a number of studies and give a number of cost-of-funds figures. But the reader must not be taken in.

THE PRESSURES TO HOLD DOWN REPORTED COSTS

There are substantial pressures to hold down fundraising costs, that is, to hold down reported fundraising costs.

Charity Watchdogs

Organizations like the Council of Better Business Bureaus and the National Charities Information Bureau recommend that NPOs spend no more than 35 to 40 percent of total revenues on fundraising. Such recommendations mean little to established NPOs with good brand names, like the American Cancer Society, which spent 16 percent of its budget on fundraising in fiscal 1989. But new NPOs, groups raising money for obscure or unpopular causes, groups that cannot easily enlist volunteer fundraisers, and groups that make heavy use of direct mail will find their fundraising costs near or over the 35 to 40 percent guideline.

Public Scrutiny on Nonprofits

A second source of the pressure to hold down costs lies in the temper of the age, which subjects the activities of nonprofit organizations to increasing scrutiny. Many nonprofit organizations find themselves facing hostile legislators or skeptical backers who do not approve of the amounts spent by these organizations to raise funds. In such a climate, given a choice as to classifying a cost as fundraising, or something else, the organization will choose the latter. This means that we expect reported fundraising costs to understate the true costs.

THE PROBLEMS OF OBTAINING ACCURATE COSTS

Why must one read reported fundraising costs with skepticism? Part of the reason is that not all fundraising costs are traceable. Instead of being directly and unambiguously associated with fundraising, they are costs incurred in common with other activities of the organization. A university president does not report part of his salary and the expenses of his office as fundraising costs, because many of these costs are not easily labeled "fundraising." Even if he did, the figures would mean very little, because the arbitrary division of costs that are in fact not divisible cannot produce anything that makes much sense.

Nonprofit organizations also enjoy flexibility in how they account for fundraising costs. A national charity, let us say, may receive some funds raised by its local chapters. The costs of these local fundraising efforts can be recorded only at the local chapter, however, and need never appear as fundraising costs on the financial statements of the national organization. A second wrinkle allows a charity to net the cost of a special event against its revenues and report only the net figure. For example, one Friends of the Zoo group holds a gifts dinner and reports spending $2,000 to raise $5,000, or a fundraising cost of 40 percent. A second Friends of the Zoo group holds a "special event" instead of a gifts dinner; and while it too spends $2,000 to raise $5,000, it merely reports that it raised $3,000 at an implied fundraising cost of zero. Finally, some nonprofits use for-profit firms to raise money. As we shall see later in the chapter, these firms are expensive in the sense that to raise a dollar they typically charge sixty or seventy or eighty cents. Such fees will not show up on the NPO's financial statements. That is, if a for-profit fundraiser raises $50,000 and takes $35,000 as its fee, the nonprofit will simply note that it raised $15,000, again at an implied fundraising cost of zero.

As an example of how bad the reported figures often are, Williams gives the median cost of capital campaigns by twenty-two institutions of higher education as 5 percent. Williams says only that her source is "studies" conducted by the American Association of Fundraising Councils; she does not trouble to say whether the costs are a percentage of funds raised or of total income, nor does she say if the figure is a median of a set of (twenty-two) percentages, or if it is, say, some median dollar cost as a percentage of some median dollar income. Finally, she has not read her own book. Two pages later she gives fundraising costs of twelve universities (as a percentage of total gifts income). The figures range from 7.2 to 29.9 percent, and the median of the percentages is 17 percent.[1] This process of underreporting can reach an extreme. In an analysis of 334 Illinois organizations that had raised at least $100,000 in total contributions, and whose financial statements had been filed in the State Attorney General's office,

Gross found that 127 reported no fundraising costs whatsoever. Gross concludes simply, "This is faulty reporting."[2] (And, it shows an incurious attorney general as well.)

Even if fundraising costs were soundly defined, accurately measured, and honestly reported, one would still need to look critically at the nature of the organization, examining how it raises funds and from where. It does not mean very much to learn that the United Way, which makes heavy use of volunteers, has lower fundraising costs than an organization that raises its funds only through direct mail, because mail is expensive and volunteers are not, and because mail gifts tend to be small. (United Way's costs aren't all that small anyway. It deducts roughly twenty cents on the dollar, eleven cents to pay for its overhead costs and nine cents to make up for pledges that it cannot collect.[3]) In addition, it is much less expensive to tap past backers than to find new ones, and an organization that is expanding its pool of donors is sure to be running higher fundraising costs than an organization that is not. Sources of funds, then, affect costs. Costs are also affected (a) by the age of the organization, with older organizations generally having lower costs; (b) by where the organization is located, with urban groups having higher costs; (c) by how well-known the group is, with well-known groups having lower costs; and (d) by the number of groups competing for funds from the same constituency.

There can be difficulties in counting the amount raised as well, which further befogs the comparison of costs with amounts raised. These difficulties always arise in capital campaigns, where many gifts are received over time. A capital campaign costing $600,000 raises $10 million; but only $5 million is received during the campaign, the rest being received over the succeeding six years. Here perhaps we could at least propose a common procedure, namely, comparing the cost with the discounted value of the funds raised. But with some gifts, this becomes very difficult. What is the value of a charitable remainder trust in which some intervening beneficiaries retain an interest? What is the value of a bequest whose value and time of receipt are both uncertain?

HOW TO READ FUNDRAISING COSTS

The reader presumably knows that averages can conceal a great deal. Table 19.1 gives costs by source of funds for a hypothetical nonprofit organization, where a single overall average, while of some use, hides more than it reveals. Even the average cost figures by source conceal important information. The table shows that funds from repeat donors cost 9 percent, on average. Some of the money raised from repeat donors comes easily, perhaps only costing one or two percent, because only one solicitation is needed. Where more solicitations are needed, funds may cost 5 or 10 percent; and finally, there will be some repeat donors who prove very costly to reach and who give only a small amount. For these donors, fundraising costs might be over 20 or 25 percent. In deciding whether to spend more to raise more, it is the cost of the most expensive money

Table 19.1
Hypothetical Summary of Funds Raised and Cost of Funds (dollar figures in thousands)

Source	Amount Raised	Fundraising Cost	Fundraising Costs as Percent of Amount Raised
Repeat donors	$2,470	$225	9%
New donors	330	335	102
Deferred gifts and bequests	171	27	16
Capital programs	22	1	5
Special events	36	19	53
Totals	$3,029	$607	20%

that is relevant. The average cost of 9 percent is of very little value for this decision, because the issue is not whether it is worth spending another nine cents to raise an extra dollar, but whether it is worth spending, say, another twenty-five or thirty cents to raise an extra dollar. It is the familiar dictum: average costs for understanding and describing the world; marginal costs for making decisions.[4]

As a final word, the reader should take care to note whether costs are reported as a percentage of funds raised or as a percentage of total income. Reporting costs as a percentage of funds raised makes good sense to a manager and is useful for internal control; but for public consumption most managers would prefer to report costs as a percentage of total income, because that is the way all other costs are reported and because reporting costs this way makes them look smaller.

TYPICAL FIGURES

With all these caveats in mind, let us look at some typical figures. Table 19.2 contains reported fundraising costs as a percentage of income for a number of organizations. The lowest percentage is 5 percent and the highest 40 percent, but the most representative figures lie between 10 and 20 percent. The diagrams also suggest how such figures are distributed. Another view of the distribution of fundraising costs is shown in Table 19.3. Large proportions of the organizations do not report any fundraising costs, or costs below .5 of 1 percent. These organizations presumably do not even try to raise funds. Of those remaining organizations who do raise funds, the median percentages lie between .5 and 10 percent in one case, and between 10 and 15 percent in the other three cases.

Two more examples are found in Tables 19.4 and 19.5. The first contains political fundraising costs, which in general are rather high. The second contains fundraising costs in various performing arts groups.

Another source of revenue for NPOs is gambling, which includes such

Table 19.2
Fundraising Expenses as a Percent of Income (Displayed on Side-by-Side Stem and Leaf Diagrams)

	Child Sponsorship	Conservation	Foreign Assistance	Individual Services[a]	Minority Groups	Religious Groups	Health
0	8		6		6	5	9
1	11	79	1	2	17	3	23334'56778'89
2	5		34	3	2		2468
3				4			
4					0		0

	Child Sponsorship	Conservation	Foreign Assistance	Individual Services	Minority Groups	Religious Groups	Health
Medians	11%	18%	19%	23%	17%	9%	17%
Number of Organizations	4	2	4	3	5	2	18

Source: *Forbes*, February 5, 1979, p. 50. *Forbes* used the figures from published sources such as financial statements.

Note: Read as follows: 0 | 8 = 8%, 1 | 11 = 2 groups at 11%, 2 | 5 = 25%.

[a] Planned Parenthood, American Red Cross, Disabled American Veterans.

games of chance as bingo, keno, punchboards, raffles, and tip boards. Some NPOs simply run, say, a bingo game twice a week; others have casino nights that feature regular casino games like craps, blackjack, and roulette. Like paid fund-raising solicitors and political fundraising, charity gambling is very expensive. The median cost of funds for charity gambling in twenty-two states runs about 84 percent, which means charities on average get sixteen cents of every dollar wagered (see Figure 19.1). State lotteries are an expensive way to raise funds too, about sixty-two cents on the dollar (see Figure 19.2). But lotteries are not in the business of raising funds. Judged as a nonprofit, their fundraising costs are high; judged as a nonprofit business their profit margins are high.

All these figures assume the NPO raises its own funds, perhaps with (paid) help from fundraising consultants. Some NPOs, typically commonwealth groups like public schools, are not allowed to have fundraisers on their staffs, and others choose not to do their own fundraising. Such groups, by necessity, hire outside fundraisers who design the campaign, conduct it, and give the NPO the proceeds net of their costs and profits. This is an expensive way to raise funds. Schools in Prince George's County, Maryland, grossed $2.3 million in a fundraising campaign and netted $1.1 million. The cost was 52 percent of the funds raised. In Connecticut some charitable and civic organizations, police unions and benevolent associations, and firefighter's unions use paid telephone solicitors to raise funds, at a cost of 74 percent,[5] and a similar study in Massachusetts found the cost of paid solicitors to run around 61 percent.

Table 19.3

Fundraising Costs as a Percent of Total Contributions, for 2,836 New York and 1,784 Illinois Nonprofit Organizations

Fundraising Cost	New York Organizations[a]		Illinois Organizations	
	Less than $100,000	*$100,000 and Over*	*Less than $100,000*	*$100,000 and Over*
Over 50%	6%	3%	4%	4%
41–50	3	2	1	1
36–40	2	2	1	2
31–35	2	2	1	3
26–30	2	3	2	5
21–25	3	5	[b]	6
16–20	5	6	2	7
11–15	5	10	2	10
1/2–10	19	36	11	24
Less than 1/2% or none reported	54	30	76	38
	100%	100%	100%	100%
Total contributions to all organizations (millions)	$47	$1,065	$22	$424
(*n* =)	1,458	1,368	1,450	334

Read: 6 percent of those 1,458 New York organizations that raised less than $100,000 had fundraising costs over 50 percent.

[a] Two columns do not add to 100 percent due to rounding.
[b] Less than one-half of one percent.

Source: Adapted from M. J. Gross, Jr., "Fund Raising and Program Cost Ratios." *Philanthropy Monthly* 8 (June 1975): 30.

THE HIGH COSTS OF DIRECT MAIL

We have seen that overall fundraising costs for operating funds run 10 to 20 percent of the funds raised and funds for capital campaigns run under 10 percent. Direct mail costs run very much higher. Amnesty International USA, which makes heavy use of direct mail, spent, in the mid-1980s, between 25 and 30 percent raising its money.

To see why direct mail is so expensive we must focus on three numbers, the cost (per thousand) of a mailing, the response rate, and the average gift. Here are some representative values for these three:

Cost per thousand	$226
Response rate	1% and .8 of 1%
Average gift	$20 and $25

These look about right for the early 1990s. Response rates for prospecting did run on the order of one percent and average gifts on the order of twenty to twenty-five dollars. The cost per thousand (CPM) includes everything:

Table 19.4
Costs of Political Fundraising, Mostly From the 1976 Presidential Campaign

Event	Amount Raised (millions)	At the Cost of Millions	At the Cost of % of $ Raised	Line
All fundraising by Republican National Committee	$20.53	$6.310	31%	1
"Salute to the President" Dinners	4.29	.790	18	2
Four Democratic National Telethons				
1972	3.80	1.900	50	3
1973	4.22	2.270	54	4
1974	5.40	2.560	47	5
1975	3.60	2.750	75	6
Four Rock Concerts for Jerry Brown	.32	.135	42	7
Committee for Jimmy Carter	7.94	1.230	15	8
Democratic National Committee Direct Mail	2.16	.930	43	9
Major Contributors and fundraising events	3.06	.574	19	10
Wallace Campaign (Direct Mail)	1.42	.380	27	11
McGovern Campaign in 1972	15.00	4.500	30	12

Source: Herbert E. Alexander, *Financing the 1976 Election* (Washington, D.C.: Congressional Quarterly Press, 1979), lines1 p. 404, 2 p. 405, 3–6 p. 395, 7 p. 22, 8 p. 239, 9–10 p. 705, 11 p. 718, 12 p. 722.

Postage	$ 78
List rental	46
Mail shop	13
Merge-purge	18
Printed materials	63
Miscellaneous	8
	——
Total CPM	$226

Now assume we mail 100,000 pieces, get a response of 1 percent and an average gift of twenty dollars. It's easy to figure the net marketing contribution:

Pieces mailed	100,000
Response rate	1%
Number of responses	1,000
Average gift	$20
Total gifts	$20,000
Less costs of 100,000 pieces @ $226 per 1,000	22,600
	——
Net Marketing Contribution	(2,600)

Table 19.5
Average Fundraising Costs for Five Types of Performing Arts Organizations, 1965 to 1971

	1965–1966	1966–1967	1967–1968	1968–1969	1969–1970	1970–1971
91 Symphonies						
Fundraising Costs						
1. As percent of Total Operating Expenses (TOE)	1.2	2.1	2.0	1.5	1.4	1.4
2. As percent of Local Nongovernmental Funds raised (LNF)	3.1	6.1	6.1	4.5	4.0	4.0
31 Operas						
. . . as % of TOE	.9	1.1	.8	.8	.8	1.0
. . . as % of LNF	9.9	9.6	6.8	8.5	5.9	7.7
27 Theatres						
. . . as % of TOE	.7	.8	.5	.4	.6	.5
. . . as % of LNF	5.4	5.4	3.4	2.2	2.9	2.6
9 Ballets						
. . . as % of TOE	1.2	.7	1.7	2.2	1.5	1.5
. . . as % of LNF	7.4	4.0	8.2	7.4	5.1	5.9
8 Modern-Dance Groups						
. . . as % of TOE	.3	.3	1.2	.5	.1	.2
. . . as % of LNF	6.0	2.8	12.9	8.5	1.6	3.7

Read: In 1995–1996, 91 symphonies devoted 1.2 percent of their total operating expenses to fundraising. This amount was 3.1 percent of all local, nongovernmental funds raised.

Source: Ford Foundation, *The Finances of the Performing Arts*, vol. 1 (New York: Ford Foundation, 1974). Figures are on various pages in Appendix C. Costs as a percent of TOE are on line 2280 in this Appendix, and costs as a percent of LNF are line 2280 costs divided by line 1220 income.

Figure 19.1
Stem-and-Leaf Diagram of the Cost of Charity Gambling as a Percent of Proceeds

6	44
6	
7	4
7	5677
8	0013444
8	677
9	2234
9	5

Read: The smallest cost, at the top, was 6 | 4 or 64 percent of the proceeds; the highest cost, at the bottom, was 95 percent. The median was 84 percent.

Source: "Charity Gambling State by State." *Chronicle of Philanthropy,* May 18, 1983, p. 28. The *Chronicle* got its figures from a nonprofit organization, the National Association of Fundraising Ticket Manufacturers.

This mailing loses money.

Now, let us look at the other three combinations and put them side by side (see Table 19.6).

The moral is that prospecting is a breakeven operation, but only when one looks only at the first year. Even on the most favorable assumptions, direct mail does not produce net marketing contributions of any size, compared to a nonprofit's needs. The answer to the question of why direct mail is so expensive lies in the fact that prospecting is basically a breakeven operation in the first year. It is breakeven because of the interplay of response rates, average initial gifts, and cost per thousand.

We normally think of direct mail as different from (say) radio or newspapers. The latter are mass media; direct mail is a targeted medium. But in prospecting, "targeted" doesn't mean the high efficiencies one might expect from the word. Typically, only eight to ten thousand reply for each million prospect pieces dropped. House lists, donors who have given before, don't respond in tenths of a percent. Responses can run 20 or 40 or 60 percent, and the average gift is higher as well. That's targeted audience, and that's when, in the second year, that direct mail begins to pay.

Pieces mailed	100,000
Response rate	20%
Number of responses	20,000
Average gift	$30
Revenue	$600,000

Figure 19.2
Stem-and-Leaf Diagram of Costs of Operating Thirty-One State Lotteries in 1991

8	0
7	8
7	134
6	56778889
6	0011234
5	578889999
5	2
4	
4	
3	3

Read: The lowest cost was 33 percent of lottery sales, and the highest 80 percent. The median
    was 62 percent.

Source: Compiled from "Gross Revenue of Selected States from Parimutuel and Amusement
    Taxes and Lotteries: 1981," Table 485 in U.S. Bureau of the Census, *Statistical
    Abstract of the United States, 1993* (Washington, D.C.: U.S. Government Printing
    Office, 1993), p. 307.

Cost @ $226 CPM	22,600
Net Marketing Contribution	$577,400

Now let us put the two together. The details are found in Table 19.7. The NPO
has a house list that generates a sizeable surplus from its three mailings each
year, but to replace losses from its house list and to increase the house list the
NPO's prospect mailings lose money. The net of the two produces a direct mail
cost of just under 29 percent, which proves the point that direct mail is expensive. Actually it doesn't prove anything. It merely illustrates the point, for the
conclusion rests completely on the assumptions that were made. But, to repeat,
the assumptions are reasonable, and without question the overall conclusion is
correct: Direct mail is expensive. So direct mail is expensive because of the
interplay of three factors:

1. the prospect response rate,
2. the prospect average gift,
3. the CPM of direct mail.

Put all three together in a nonprofit that is growing rapidly and that relies heavily
on prospect mailings and you get high fundraising costs, 30 percent or more.

Table 19.6
Net Marketing Contribution from Prospect Mailings under Four Sets of Assumptions

Basis: *100,000 pieces*

Response rate	1%	1%	.8 of 1%	.8 of 1%
Number of Responses	1,000	1,000	800	800
Average Gift	$25	$20	$25	$20
Revenue	$25,000	$20,000	$20,000	$16,000
Cost @ $226 CPM	22,600	22,600	22,600	22,600
Net Marketing Contribution	$2,400	(2,600)	(2,600)	(5,400)

SUMMARY

We ''presumed'' some pages ago that nonprofit organizations with low fundraising costs do not even try to raise funds. Although this is probably true of the organizations in Table 19.3, not all organizations are required to report to state authorities. Religious bodies, for example, raise more money than any other part of the nonprofit sector, yet they do not report their finances. Moreover, their fundraising relies largely on individuals, who give as an expression of their faith, or by habit, without the need for spending much to raise the gift. Even larger gifts, such as those brought by in a capital drive, will be solicited by a volunteer at low out-of-pocket costs, virtually none of which are borne by the religious body itself. So this chapter is but a survey and a quick one at that.

We can summarize this discussion by saying (1) most small nonprofits and many large nonprofits report no fundraising expenses at all, or report very small expenses; (2) of those that were examined above, reported fundraising costs typically ran on the order of 10 to 20 percent of the funds raised; (3) some organizations, perhaps 5, 10, 15, or 20 percent of them, spend more than 20 percent in raising funds; (4) reported figures probably understate the true costs of fundraising; and (5) some ways of raising money, starting with direct mail through charity gambling and the use of paid telephone solicitors, are much more expensive than the typical figures given here.

Table 19.7
Why Direct Mail Costs So Much

A. Basis

Size of house list	70,000
Turnover in house list	19.0%
Response to house list mailings	24.0%
Response to prospect mailings	0.8%
Cost of mail (per thousand)	$226
Average house list gift	$36
Average prospecting gift	$25
Number of house list mailings per year	3

B. Replacing Losses and Increasing the House List

I. Cost of prospect mailings

Lost house list people per year	13,300	
Mailing size needed to replace losses		1,662,500*
Planned increase in house list	9,000	
Mail size needed to increase house list		<u>1,125,000</u>
Size of both mailings		2,787,500
Cost of prospect mailings @ $226/1,000		$629,975

II. Income from prospect mailings

2.7 million x .8% x $25	$557,500
III. Net surplus from prospect mailings	($72,475)

*13,300/.008 = 1,662,500

C. Income from House List

# of mailings	x	Size of house list	x	Avg. gift	x	Response	
3	x	70,000	x	$36	x	24%	$1,814,400
Less: mail costs: 3 x 70,000 @ $226 CPM							$47,460
Net revenue							$1,766,940

D. Net Income from Both Prospecting and the House List

Income			
From prospecting	$557,500		
From house list	$1,814,400		
		$2,371,900	100.0%
Costs			
From prospecting	$629,975		
From house list	$47,460		
		$677,435	<u>28.6%</u>
Net direct mail revenue		$1,694,465	71.4%

QUESTIONS

1. Here are fundraising costs for the top ten United Way chapters and the national headquarters in 1988. What do the figures mean?

Where	1988 Income	Fund-raising Expenses	Fundraising as Percent of Total Income
New York	$151	$2	1.3%
Chicago	82	4	4.6
Los Angeles	79	7	9.3
Detroit	60	4	6.1
Washington	56	3	6.0
Philadelphia	55	2	3.9
Cleveland	47	2	3.8
Houston	47	3	6.6
Boston	41	3	6.7
Atlanta	38	2	5.6
Alexandria, Virginia*	29	0.23	0.6

* National United Way organization.

Note: Dollar figures are in millions.

Source: Annual reports.

2. This is a question for those who know a bit of statistics. A study of college and university fundraising, mentioned in this chapter, found that to raise a dollar the mean fundraising cost was sixteen cents and the median cost was eleven cents. What can you deduce about the underlying distribution of fundraising costs?

3. Nonprofits who use direct mail lie awake at night wondering when and by how much the Postal Service will raise third-class rates. Suppose postage goes up 10 percent. Using the figures in the chapter for CPM, response rates, and average gift, explore the implications of a postal increase. What might an NPO do when rates go up?

NOTES

1. Jane M. Williams, *Capital Ideas* (Ambler, Pa.: Fund Raising Institute, 1979), pp. 136 and 138.

2. Malvern J. Gross, "Costs of Fundraising." *Philanthropy Monthly* 8 (March 1975): 21.

3. Bruce Millar, "U. of Pennsylvania Workers Reject Fund Drive by United Way Alone." *Chronicle of Philanthropy,* April 23, 1991, p. 24.

4. For more on the use of marginal analysis, see David L. Rados, *Pushing the Numbers in Marketing* (Westport: Quorum, 1992), Chapters 2 and 5.

5. Public Charities Unit, *Paid Telephone Soliciting in Connecticut During 1989 for Charitable, Civic, Police, and Firefighter Organizations* (Hartford: Department of Consumer Protection and the Office of the Attorney General, April 9, 1990).

Chapter 20

Volunteers and Board Members

Traditional values in America have long included those of participation by citizens and personal service to the community. Americans believe—at least in the past they have believed—that they can influence the course of their society, individually sometimes, collectively more certainly. They believe that they can make a difference. (Naturally, they also believe just the opposite. That's why they say ''You can't fight city hall.'')

Just as they need backers, NPOs need volunteers. (To an economist they are just one more resource that NPOs need.) Nonprofit organizations of all kinds make heavy use of volunteers, so heavy in fact, that many organizations could not survive without them. Trustees and members of boards volunteer substantial amounts of time and donate money, expertise, and (often) the services of the firms they work for.

In marketing, we likewise encounter volunteers. Volunteers with extensive experience in marketing may audit an organization's marketing programs. They may merely provide advice to, say, a political candidate on issues and on advertising. And we have seen in Chapter 6 how volunteers may serve in marketing research.

Volunteers man the operating posts as well. In one study, 71 percent of nonprofit organizations surveyed (in Chicago in 1968) reported the number of volunteers exceeded the number of paid employees. After making an estimate of what the volunteers' time would have cost these organizations, the study found that in 20 percent of the organizations the payroll for volunteers would have exceeded the employees' payroll, and in 25 percent it would have fallen between 20 and 100 percent of the employees' payroll.[1] For the country as a whole the American Association of Fund-Raising Council estimates that in 1975, Americans put in nearly six billion hours of volunteer philanthropic work, time worth about $25 billion.[2]

As with all other aspects of the nonprofit sector, there is great diversity. Nonprofit businesses, universities, most art organizations, and most international charities make little use of volunteers, and the volunteers they do use tend to be board members. Others, like hospitals or election campaigns, need many volunteers but rarely place them in positions of importance. Still others like the Rainbow Foundation, Alcoholics Anonymous, the Girl Scouts, the Junior League, and the shops run by Oxfam have few paid staff and are mostly run and staffed by volunteers.

The American Red Cross (ARC) started with volunteers and added paid staff when there were not enough volunteers to do the job. In 1990 there were some seventy volunteers to each paid staff member. In years past, most Red Cross chapters were governed mostly by volunteers who were directly involved in providing disaster relief and other services. Other NPOs, who started with a paid staff, view volunteers as extensions of the paid staff, responsible to it and non-permanent, the first to go in a financial crisis. One simple way to uncover the organization's basic philosophy toward volunteers is to determine which jobs are considered inappropriate for volunteers. The more important the job that volunteers cannot touch, the less important the volunteers are. Think about hospitals or legal aid, where doctors and lawyers make all the decisions that count. Think about United Way, where volunteers do the two most important tasks, perhaps the only tasks: raising money and deciding who gets how much.

GIVING TIME AND GIVING MONEY

Giving time differs from giving money in five ways.

- Quite obviously, the T costs differ. When one gives money, the T costs are mostly out-of-pocket costs; when one volunteers the T costs are mostly time costs. This is true even recognizing that those who volunteer often give money as well. A gift of money gives rise to a tax deduction. A gift of time does not, although the IRS does allow volunteers to deduct mileage costs, meals, and a few other items.

- The NPO can spend a gift of money as soon as it arrives. Except in menial chores that require no training, volunteers cannot be used as soon as they arrive. Before they can start, they need explanations, training, perhaps some practice. Moreover, money can be used in any part of the NPO for any purpose. Volunteers cannot. They must be used in those areas where they are best suited and where the nonprofit's mission permits.

- Backers are often outsiders who give money but may know little or nothing about the NPO they give to. Because volunteers see the NPO from the inside, they know it in a vivid, personal way; because they know it so well, they are more likely to give money. When Michael Milken, the former junk bond promoter, was released from federal prison, hundreds of NPOs proposed that he serve his 1,800 hours of community service with them. Why? He has a keen financial mind and financial street smarts; he would bring visibility to whatever groups he chose to work with; and through his contacts he might help pull strings. But the most important of all was this: Because giving of time and giving of money go together, Milken on the scene today is likely to mean a fat donation tomorrow.

- Money is fungible. Churches that run bingo games all sing the same tune: A thousand dollars from a sinner buys just as much medicine as a thousand from a saint. Volunteers are not fungible; each is an individual, with all that implies for differences in motivation, intellect, energy, skills, and drive. A gift of money is a gift of money; a gift of time is something else. As Walt Whitman wrote, "I do not give lectures or a little charity. When I give I give myself." (*Song of Myself,* 39.)

- In recent years, there has been a good deal of scrutiny of fundraising costs, but none of the costs of attracting volunteers. And because the value of a volunteer's time does not appear in its financial statements, an NPO that makes extensive use of volunteer fundraisers will appear to have lower costs than one who does not use volunteers,[3] which may help it demonstrate its financial efficiency.

WHO VOLUNTEERS?

A sizeable proportion of the American public volunteers each year, but no one knows just what the proportion is. Perhaps it is one in five, perhaps it is one in two. The evidence is mixed.

According to one study, some forty-seven percent [of adults] volunteer each year; another found that twenty percent volunteered; a third that 226 million Americans volunteered in 1985[4], which given the population in 1985 was everyone no longer in diapers. Still another survey reported that only one-third of respondents had volunteered for any kind of NPO in the preceding thirty days.[5]

Why such differences? Researchers define volunteering in different ways. Some, in fact, ask the respondents to define it themselves. Questions differ too as well as procedures used for drawing the sample. We do not need high numerical precision, however, to reach a sound qualitative conclusion—Americans volunteer. Moreover, they tend to feel that volunteering is a good thing, that everyone should volunteer to help those who are less well off.

Americans are not the only ones who volunteer, as the following figures show:

	Britain	Canada	France	Spain	U.S.
Percent of respondents volunteering in the past month	15%	25%	10%	11%	20%
Average hours volunteering per month	1.8	5.2	1.6	1.6	2.2

Source: Peter Halfpenny, "The 1991 International Survey of Giving," in Susan K. E. Saxon-Harrold and Jeremy Kendall (eds.), *Researching the Voluntary Sector* (Tonbridge, Kent: Charities Aid Foundation, 1993), p. 215.

We have just pointed out why one should not place much faith in such numbers. This survey shows 20 percent of Americans volunteering in the last month versus one-third reported just a few lines above. Here at least the same research method was used in all five countries. We should mistrust the numbers, but the differences among the countries probably do mean something. Thus, for example, we are probably safe in saying that Canadians volunteer more than the other four, the French and the Spanish do the least, and the Brits and the Yanks come somewhere in between.

Let us return to the Land of the Free and the Brave. Americans typically spend a couple of hours a week at their volunteer chores. They are likely to be married, in their thirties or forties, have some college education and a good income, and be female. They are most likely to do their volunteering at church—serving as an usher or as a Sunday School teacher or helping to raise funds. Education and health organizations are the next most common NPOs where volunteers show up. Volunteering in the school mostly means volunteering in grammar school—PTA activities, serving as a homeroom parent, teaching, tutoring, serving on a school board. Health care volunteering typically means visiting the sick, caring for the elderly, fundraising, and the like.[6]

Community involvement and attendance at church influence volunteering and presumably are influenced by it: Volunteers are more likely to be actively involved in community affairs and are more likely to attend religious services frequently. And, to repeat a point already made, giving of self and giving of money go together.

| | Participates as a Volunteer | | |
	Less than 3 hours a week	More than 3 hours a year	No volunteering at all
All respondents			
Average Annual Contributions	$700	$1,020	$510
As a Percent of Income	2.3	3.6	2.0
Backers Only			
Average Annual Contributions	$720	$1,110	$600
As a Percent of Income	2.4	3.5	2.2

Source: American Volunteer 1981 (Washington, D.C.: Independent Sector, 1981), p. 26.

That is, both those who volunteer and those who don't give. Those who volunteer give a good deal more.

WHY PEOPLE SAY THEY VOLUNTEER

We saw in Chapters 6 and 19 that "why" questions can be misleading because clients and backers may not know why they behave as they do but they may still answer, or they may give a conventional, safe answer. But as long as we do not make too much of the answers we can learn something by asking two questions: "Why did you first volunteer," and "Why do you continue to volunteer?" Note yet again the preoccupation of marketers with trial and adoption, why did you *first* and why do you *continue*. No one who wants to think like a marketer can afford to confuse the two.

	Why I First Volunteered	Why I Continued to Volunteer
Do something useful	56%	56%
Enjoy the work	34	35
Benefits for family or friend	27	25
Religious concerns	22	24
Interest in the NPO's mission	10	30
Good experience	9	6
Had free time	9	6

Read: When asked why they first volunteered, 56 percent of respondents said that they wanted to do something useful.

Source: Giving and Volunteering in the United States (Washington D.C.: Independent Sector, 1988), pp. 29, 30.

There are three points here. The first is that with one exception, the reasons people first volunteer and continue to volunteer are pretty much the same; and the reasons would be on anyone's list—the work is useful, the work is fun, it benefits someone they know, religious motives guide them, and they are interested in what the NPO does. The second point deals with the one exception. Volunteering teaches volunteers a good deal about their NPO, and what they learn increases their interest in the nonprofit they are working with. Third, notice what is missing here. No one talks about selfish reasons—the approval society gives to those who volunteer, or the opportunities to network, learn new skills, and develop contacts. No one talks about getting time off from work or being bored and looking for something to do. Yet these reasons should be there as well, although for most they would be minor reasons. Just another reminder to be wary of the answers to questions that start with "why."

Canadians do mention selfish reasons. When asked, they said they volunteered to help other people, to help make the community a better place, to learn and practice new skills, to get out and meet new people. They also said that their employers seemed to like the idea that they were volunteers.[7]

What do volunteers do? Just about anything that paid employees do. There are some jobs that we naturally associate with volunteers—Scout leaders, the PTA, neighborhood fundraising, the election canvassers, Candy Stripers, and those who work with children and with the sick, the lame, and the blind. As one would expect in a developed and diverse economy, volunteers perform other jobs that are not so much in the public eye.

- Black bears in some parts of the country have become so habituated to humans that naturalists fear the bears might become sitting ducks during hunting season. The solution? Bear walkers, provided by Earthwatch, an NPO that organizes volunteers for scientific projects. Bear walkers walk with the bears during much of the six-week fall hunting season to scare off hunters.[8]

- One can spend one's vacation as a volunteer working with Habitat for Humanity International to build and rehabilitate housing for low-income people. (Volunteers are expected to pick up a good portion of the costs.) The Council on International Education Exchange organizes volunteer work camps to engage in community service like building playgrounds here or abroad.

- The Evangelical Council for Financial Accountability uses volunteer teams of accountants and lawyers to audit its members and prospective members.[9]

- The Phoenix Children's Hospital uses volunteers to make patients' visits less frightening and less lonely. Most of the volunteers do the predictable: They feed the children, change their diapers, play with them, and help them with their school work. But huggers have a special job—they simply hold infants, for hours at a time if need be, to provide the human contact felt to be so important to their healthy development.[10]

- Several thousand elementary, secondary, and high schools have volunteer mediators, usually students, who mediate disputes in an effort to find ways to moderate violence in the public schools.[11]

CHANGING CLIMATE FOR VOLUNTEERS

In recent years, it has become harder and harder to attract good volunteers. The prime reason is demographic change. Women, long the principal source of volunteers for many NPOs, are more likely to work. As more and more of them pursue careers, or at least hold full-time jobs, fewer volunteer and those who do volunteer have less time to give.

Also, the proportion of the population aged eighteen and older that volunteers in any capacity seems to have fallen from 52 percent in 1981 to 45 percent in 1988. (I say "seems to" because, as shown earlier in this chapter, the studies on the proportion of adults who volunteer show large differences in their results.) Particularly large drops occurred among women, from 56 to 47 percent and among those aged twenty-five to forty-four, from 59 to 49 percent. These are large changes in a seven-year period. Those who do volunteer often seem more picky, reluctant to do administrative chores or fundraising, more interested in how much time they will have to put in and what they will get out of it.

Volunteerism is yet another area of public life quickened by the legal profession. A group that counsels rape victims that has used volunteer counselors in the past and that wishes to continue using them will now have second thoughts. If the counseling provided by their volunteers is not up to professional standards, the dissatisfied clients may sue. As of 1990, most states exempted directors and officers of NPOs from lawsuits that charged them with personal responsibility for actions undertaken on behalf of their organizations. Only half of the states offered similar exemptions for volunteers. The two states with the largest populations, California and New York, offered exemptions only to volunteers who are board members.[12] But stay tuned. In Congress and other legislatures there is much talk and some action to protect volunteers as well.

NPOs competing for these volunteers have changed as well. As AIDS, homelessness, drug abuse, and abortion have become fashionable, or have come into the public eye, groups dealing with them have had less difficulties attracting volunteers, as have more business-like NPOs like the Girl Scouts or United Way. Smaller groups, those dealing with less visible issues, and those that have lost their hold on the public have been hit the worst.

ATTRACTING VOLUNTEERS

The first step is the obvious one of identifying the NPO's volunteer needs; and, since the needs change, they must be redefined and rethought from time to time.

Volunteers want to work at something that is interesting, that they feel is important and stimulating (but not too much). Finding the right match of volunteer with the right job can be difficult, but a poor match can cause dissatisfaction on both sides. The chief indicators of this dissatisfaction come when volunteers vote with their feet. Either they don't show up to do their tour, or there is high turnover among volunteers. A friend of mine went through two training sessions for volunteers at a nonprofit in Nashville. Two months later she was the only one in her class who was still an active volunteer. To a marketer such behavior speaks volumes, or at least a page or two.

It has become more and more difficult to recruit volunteers during the daytime. The women who were once the mainstay of such volunteering now work. At least most of them do, but not all. NPOs have adapted to changes in the labor force by seeking volunteers in nontraditional ways and from nontraditional sources.

- Many who work on the weekends have their days off during the week, when they could volunteer. For example, those who work for country clubs, parks, and recreational sites; for cultural attractions like zoos, aquariums, and museums; for churches and synagogues; and for retailers and shopping centers.

- Many work evenings. In New York City over a million people work at night. These include those who work at banks, hospitals, theaters, restaurants, and as police, security guards, and janitors. Many would have some time to volunteer during the day.

- Still others work shifts, either the swing shift or the graveyard shift. Such jobs as these are naturally found in businesses and other organizations that stay open twenty-four hours a day—police and fire departments, hospitals and hotels, the U.S. Postal Service and overnight delivery companies, and radio and television stations.

- Some work odd hours, or are underemployed, or work from time to time as a temp, or work only in the season. Substitute teachers, airline pilots and stewards, camp counsellors, university professors, part-time retail help, and painters are some examples, as well as those who are self-employed like lawyers or consultants.

- Some work full-time during the day but still can find some time to volunteer. Lower-level employees like secretaries or machine operators are sometimes available before or after work or during lunch, if the site where they are to volunteer is close enough. Upper-level employees have more flexibility and can adjust their hours to accommodate a quarterly board meeting or a monthly planning meeting.

- Most large corporations encourage their employees to volunteer, and many do more than simply encourage them. They recognize their efforts, urge executives to join non-profit boards, sponsor companywide projects, and give employees time off to volunteer.[13]

- Many high schools have begun to encourage or require—precipitating the inevitable lawsuits—their students to participate in community activities.

- Courts often order people to perform so many hours of community service. NPOs interested in such volunteers normally stay in touch with the courts and provide them with materials that explain what the nonprofit does and what its volunteers do on the job.

Following basic marketing logic, each of these is a different segment. Each merits a separate program because the NPO will have to reach them in different ways. We know how and where and when to catch hospital workers, but how do you pitch temps or people who work at summer camps and resorts when you want them in the winter?

Nonprofits have adapted in other ways to the shortage of volunteers. Friends for Youth in the Bay Area, California, matches children in trouble with a supportive adult in an effort to help the child avoid trouble, hence its name. It reduced its requirements for volunteers, thus making it easier to recruit them. The group had traditionally asked volunteers to commit themselves to a year's tour as a Friend. This proved too long for many potential volunteers, and the group had increasing difficulty attracting them. So it set up a second track for volunteers involving projects where the volunteer did not have to commit to a full year.[14]

Changes in the environment have made it harder to find volunteers, but this last example suggests that sometimes the fault lies not in our stars but in ourselves. Sometimes the nonprofit must bear the blame. One that I know of would only interview volunteers during bankers' hours, 10 A.M. to 3 P.M. Its director showed some surprise when I pointed out the obvious. Thus the nonprofit that is having difficulty attracting volunteers must look within, and, following impeccable marketing logic, it must ask its volunteers and former volunteers what its problems are. Still, it is possible to suggest some general areas that need to be explored:

- *Membership.* Some NPOs expect that volunteers join the organization or special groups like an auxiliary. The marketer would ask what the T costs are of such an expectation, and what's in it for the volunteer. Certainly, requiring membership of short-term volunteers makes little sense.

- *Assignments.* The jobs given to the volunteers should be within their competence, resources, and the time they have. If an organization asks a volunteer without a home computer to keep its books, it must expect that things won't work out. NPOs should also try to offer a variety of jobs to their volunteers. This makes it more likely that someone can do it and enjoy it. A take-it-or-leave-it choice is not a good idea when volunteers are in short supply and may very well leave it.

- *Schedules.* The NPO must make things easy for volunteers and prospective volunteers. Interviews and training sessions, for example, must be offered at times when volunteers can come, at night perhaps, or on weekends.

- *T costs.* The NPO must also estimate the T costs borne by its volunteers. Of course, volunteers expect to give of their time. But what about out-of-pocket costs? How much do volunteers have to spend for gas and parking each month? Does the job require volunteers to buy special clothes? Do they feel obligated to buy things for clients and, a quite different question, do they? How do all of these in total stand in proportion to the volunteers' income?

Just as one would expect, in response to the shortage of volunteers, new nonprofits have arisen that do nothing but deal with the shortage of volunteers. Many cities have clearing houses that compile lists of community groups looking for volunteers. Presumably, such lists make it easier for volunteers to find the right job for them. Still other nonprofits aim to increase the supply of volunteers. doingsomething enlists volunteers. (The name spoofs the popular TV show of the late 1980s, "thirtysomething.") Each month doingsomething sends its volunteers a mailing that describes upcoming projects on the first Sunday of the next month. The volunteers choose as many or as few as they like to participate in, thus giving them flexibility in how often and how intensively they volunteer. As few nonprofits bend this far to accommodate their volunteers, it is likely that doingsomething has tapped a segment who would not otherwise volunteer,[15] based on the rule of thumb that a new marketing mix usually attracts a new segment.

Finally, in seeking volunteers one cannot be a wallflower and expect the volunteers to somehow show up. The lesson here is the same as the lesson in raising funds. One must ask. Many of those over age fifty-five already volunteer, and they say that they would be willing to do more, if they were asked.[16] One must also ask the volunteers themselves to ask, say, by asking each one to give brochures to three friends or by asking them to write to newspaper editors, legislators, or funders about their experiences as a volunteer.

Selection and Training

Recruiting is only the first step. Those who are not suitable must be screened out in the selection process, and those who are selected must be persuaded to accept. This process is most usefully accomplished if the organization has written job descriptions for its volunteer positions. Many NPOs, perhaps most, use a coarse screen that lets virtually all who apply through. But where the task is more demanding or requires specialized skills, it may be that few are chosen.

Training varies, as does selection. For the simplest tasks the volunteer can simply pitch in and make himself useful, using his native abilities and learning on the job. More demanding tasks merit more thorough training. Volunteers who work with AIDS patients surely have one of the most difficult jobs any volunteer can have. At one New York AIDS agency they receive fifty to sixty hours of training in death and dying, AIDS, cancer, and the management of pain. But one training session is not enough. These volunteers work off-site, visiting patients in their homes, driving them to the doctor's office, and the like. Doing even the best job they can, they face loss, grief, and emotional pain. Without frequent additional support and training, such volunteers burn out quickly.

MANAGING VOLUNTEERS

The nonprofit manager must treat volunteer jobs much like other jobs. This means that the manager must

- invest in recruiting, selection, and training of volunteers, which we have already discussed.
- turn down those volunteers who won't do.
- set clear expectations about what's expected of the volunteer and what's not, and what the volunteer can expect.
- try to engage the interests of staff and professionals in volunteers.
- have a formal system for appraising volunteers and their work.
- stay alert to potential indications of trouble, like tardiness, absenteeism, turnover, and complaints. Volunteers are only part-timers, with plenty of other things they might do.
- be sensitive to the mindlessness of much that passes for work in our society. For most, one or two evenings of telephoning are interesting, perhaps even stimulating. Ten or fifteen evenings are not, even in a good cause.

We have looked briefly at the general approach that an NPO must take in enlisting and retaining volunteers. As a final look at this issue, let us look at the problems of evaluating and firing volunteers.

Evaluating Volunteers

Most nonprofits evaluate their paid employees, but many do not evaluate their volunteers. Yet if they want to keep them and keep them productive, they need to evaluate and monitor their performance. It is not too strong to say that people want to be evaluated. It tells them how they are performing and gives them a sense of accomplishment.[17] Evaluations help the NPO as well to produce more productive, more satisfied volunteers. They may even help protect the NPO from being sued for the acts of volunteers working on its behalf.

Evaluation is particularly important with volunteers who work off-site, where their performance is not easily observed. The basic solution is one known to every sales manager: The volunteer's supervisor travels with the volunteer as he goes about his chores. In Missoula, Montana, where volunteers at the Foster Grandparent Program work with children, staff members monitor their performance by visiting the volunteers each month, and by requiring volunteers to attend regular meetings with other volunteers and staff members.[18] Several approaches to evaluating volunteers have proved useful.

Self-evaluation needs little explanation. Volunteers rate their own performance, on a one-page form, say. Sometimes the supervisor may rate the volunteer as well, and then the two can discuss both ratings face-to-face. Self-evaluation works particularly well for those managers who feel uneasy about rating their volunteers. It also is a good first step to more formal ratings in later years.

Peer reviews by experienced volunteers of their less experienced counterparts also go down well because the reviews are friendly and not threatening. They also use very little staff time, which is always a blessing.

Tests and quizzes work particularly well with docents and tour guides who show visitors around. They are trained before they start, of course, but as everyone realizes, once learned is not always learned. Thus, each year guides at the Philadelphia Zoo take a six-page walking quiz that asks them questions about objects and animals throughout the zoo grounds.

Telephone monitoring is another review technique for off-site volunteers. New volunteers at Big Brothers/Big Sisters in Manhattan spend hours each week alone with their young charges. They are required to talk every week by phone with the social workers assigned to them, who also talks to the child's guardian or parent. After two months the calls drop to one a month. Then at the end of the first year the volunteer, the child, the social worker, and the parents meet to decide whether to continue the relationship for another year.

Group evaluations work well in debriefing a special event or a one-time function. Volunteers sit down to discuss what went right and what didn't and lay plans to correct mistakes the next time around.[19]

Firing Volunteers

Most NPOs that make good use of volunteers treat them like employees, which includes having a written policy on letting volunteers go. But before firing the volunteer, the nonprofit should take the normal steps—it should talk to the volunteer about performance problems, retrain him, reassign him to another position.

The solution starts earlier, though. The NPO should avoid the problem in the first place by doing a background check and by taking other precautions. For example, volunteers should be given a written description of what their duties are, and as discussed above, they should receive regular performance evaluations. Some NPOs have a probation period to help ensure the volunteer is right for the job, during which time he can be dropped without explanation.

What might be done when the volunteer's performance falls below the mark? Here are five possibilities:

- Induce the volunteers to see on their own that things aren't working out. Post performance scores for example, or have a workshop where normal performance standards are discussed.
- Assign a "buddy" to a volunteer who isn't working out. The buddy tries to guide the volunteer through various jobs, provides additional training, and catches errors.
- Help ex-volunteers maintain their ties to the NPO by having a club for former volunteers. Club members might be asked to help on occasional projects.
- Set up special work areas or special projects for volunteers who can't work up to the norm.
- Ask the volunteer to stop providing direct services but instead to provide indirect advisory services. That is, take them out of the loop.

The most important consideration for the nonprofit executive is how the firing will be seen by other volunteers. Is it seen to be fair, is it seen to be nonarbitrary, is it seen to be required by the circumstances? If the answers are No, the NPO may have a problem retaining its volunteers. It is hard enough to be treated shabbily at work, but where one is giving his time and energy, the NPO must tread with cat's paw.

THE BOARD

We have seen, back in Chapter 1, that NPOs usually do not have owners. They stand on their own, perpetuating themselves typically through their boards of directors. For all their similarity to other volunteers, board members are not the same. For one, they are far harder to fire when it turns out they are not fulfilling their obligations. It is here that written guidelines can help a great deal in (say) making it easy to let a member go who has missed three meetings in a year or who has failed to meet the fundraising requirement. Of course, the most important difference is their responsibility. They are legally and morally responsible for the governance of the organization.

The Role of the Board

Their responsibilities fall into three broad categories: governance, use of funds, and accountability to the public. That is, they must ensure that the nonprofit has a functioning management structure; that its costs, salaries, and the management of its assets conform to reasonable standards; and that it provides, on request, financial statements and annual reports.

A typical list of the board's responsibilities includes the following:

- define the mission and purpose of the organization
- select the senior executive, and review his performance
- ensure the organization has sound plans and adequate resources
- ensure that its assets are preserved and managed effectively
- monitor performance of the organization's programs
- improve its image
- serve as a final court of appeal for management differences
- assess its own performance and renewal

Being asked to serve as a trustee of a charitable or cultural institution has always been a mark of personal and social success. Here, as almost everywhere else, it helps to be rich. It is far more difficult to buy one's way onto a board today because being on a board isn't as much fun as it used to be. Being rich is important because board members are often expected to raise a certain amount, either by donating funds themselves or by raising it from friends and associates. Such a requirement seems to ensure a base of support and commitment from the board; but does it allow board members to give less than they otherwise might if there were no minimum contribution? The only research on this question suggests the answer is Yes: Requiring board members to make a minimum donation means they donate less than they would if there were no requirement.

The American Symphony Orchestra League studied the matter.[20] It compared orchestras of similar size with minimum contributions and without. For example, take medium-sized orchestras, those with budgets between $700,000 and $1.05 million. (An odd cut-off point, $50,000 over a round million.) Fifty-four percent of such orchestras required a minimum gift of their board members and received on average $35,000 from their board members. Those who did not require a gift received $45,000. One study alone in the social sciences never proves a point or demolishes one. The best conclusion here is that in some NPOs minimum giving requirements may not work as intended, with the emphasis on ''some'' and ''may.''

The diversity of NPOs is reflected in what boards do and in what it is thought they should do. Some argue that the board's primary role is setting overall strategy for the NPO and then delegating the execution of the strategy to the Chief Executive Officer (CEO) and through him to the staff and volunteers, much as corporate boards do their jobs. The board plays a role in major decisions like capital expenditures, management of assets, and hiring the CEO, but the

CEO does the rest. Wood has called this the corporate style for operating a board.[21]

A second type of board is one that participates in management. Board members may work with staff members and gather information through a variety of contacts, formal and informal. Every board has individuals who are experts in (say) labor negotiations or pension law or public relations. These individuals often find they participate by advising staff members in their areas of knowledge.

A third kind of board is the rubber stamp, a role so passive that a more proper title might be a Board of Nondirectors. This board simply lets the CEO have his head. The kindest way of viewing this type of board is that the board trusts the CEO to run the NPO. In many NPOs, perhaps most, governance takes second place to raising money. Board members are chosen with fat donations in mind; major donors are invited to join the board. Some NPOs have taken this even further and guarantee a seat on the board to anyone who donates over a certain amount. In the same fashion, fiduciaries who control trusts or foundations and executives who influence corporate giving may also be asked to join.

The result is no surprise. The board has thirty or forty or fifty members, far too many to deliberate strategy and examine the course of the NPO. Instead, the board merely ratifies decisions already made. In such cases, the board usually appoints a smaller group, perhaps with only a half dozen members to provide direction; or one or two members of the board with a strong interest in the organization end up making the major decisions.

The Covenant House in New York City had this kind of board.[22] In the early 1970s, a dispute arose between members of the board and Father Bruce Ritter, the president and founder. The board lost the dispute, some members of the board resigned, and Father Ritter had himself designated the ''sole member'' of the corporation with authority to appoint and dismiss board members. The board became, as a result, a rubber stamp. By 1989, when allegations of financial and sexual misconduct were made against Father Ritter, the board was out of touch with his activities. Its meetings were often poorly attended; it did not know that Father Ritter had loaned money to two of its own members, and it lacked a plan for the growth of Covenant House and an appreciation of its budgeting and personnel problems.[23]

Covenant House is but an extreme example of a general trend that boards aren't so much fun anymore. Board members in the 1990s have serious business to attend to. They must attend board meetings, typically four times a year, as well as more frequent committee meetings, and they must come prepared. In its attempt to turn itself around, Friends for Youth set new requirements for its board, asking each board member to participate in a thirty-hour training program. This had the intended effect—several board members resigned, and those who didn't renewed their commitment to serve.[24] Board members must give money and they must help raise it. Lar Lubovitch Dance Company expects each of its thirteen board members to give or help raise $5,000 a year. The Association for the Prevention of Cruelty to Animals in New York requires new trustees to pledge in writing to make a "substantial" donation, to "actively" engage in fundraising, and to devote at least two hours a month to the activities of the ASPCA.[25] Everyone except Scrooge knows how to give (and even he learned how in the end), but few know how to raise money. For many board members raising money is fraught with problems because they fear rejection.[26]

As the burden of being a board member has increased, it has become more difficult to attract board members. As corporations have downsized, those left with jobs tend to work longer hours and have less time for volunteering. Scandals like those involving Covenant House and United Way have made potential board members leery of accepting appointments. Attracting board members can be particularly difficult for small, struggling groups that need prestigious board members to help them raise funds. Programs to recruit and train board members exist, but they tend to emphasize finding minority members, not corporate executives. Board members must even worry about being sued. Most states now have statutes that protect board members from legal claims and many NPOs indemnify their directors; but directors of charitable organizations can still be held personally liable for some of the misdeeds committed by the NPO.

- When the Brooklyn Women's Hospital went bankrupt in the mid-1970s, having failed to withhold enough Social Security taxes, the U.S. Treasury tried to recoup the money from a former board member by assessing him $295,000.
- The executive director of another badly strapped NPO paid monthly bills with money withheld for federal income taxes. One director had to spend more than $5,000 in legal fees before the IRS dropped its claim that the members of the board should make good on the diverted funds.[27]

Most nonprofit groups indemnify their directors, so such stories are rare. Most nonprofits are honest, so such stories are rarer. Still, prospective board members who are smart read the audited financial statements and ask tough questions before they accept their new responsibilities.

The impression given above is that it is hard to attract corporate executives as board members. Only partially true. Some, like doctors, accountants, and lawyers, are eager to serve to make contacts and network. And for all its risks and uncertainties, being a board member of the cream—say, a major art museum like the Kimball in Fort Worth or the Toronto Philharmonic—is a plum for those who move in high society.

The drill for getting and keeping board members is much the same as the drill for getting and keeping volunteers. Volunteer board members are busy people. They need to be prodded and poked, motivated and enticed, reminded of the obligations and responsibilities they have assumed. Because they are busy it is well worth taking pains to ensure their time at board and committee meetings is productive. Just as public relations cannot tart up a poor performer, at least not for very long, an NPO cannot expect board members to attend meetings that are dull or lack direction. And it is the most elemental common sense that board members should be notified more than once of upcoming meetings. A typical procedure at well-run NPOs involves (a) an annual schedule of board meetings and committee meetings, (b) a reminder mailed a month before each meeting, followed soon after by (c) a telephone call or a visit from the board chairman, in which the chairman spends some productive time getting the board member up to speed for the meeting. This last is important because too many board members do not read the reports sent to them until they arrive at the meeting.

QUESTIONS

1. Corporations sometimes use executive search firms to help them locate qualified executives. For this service, they pay a fee that is based on the executive's compensation.

   Board members of NPOs traditionally have been recruited by the CEO and other board members. But some nonprofits are beginning to use search firms paying fees that run anywhere from $2,500 to $12,000.

   Should search firms charge for their aid or should they provide their services pro bono? Should an NPO make use of these services?

2. Just what is a volunteer (outside of the army, where one is ordered to volunteer)? Is a volunteer one who is encouraged to volunteer by his employer or his spouse or his commanding officer? Someone who is pressed to volunteer? Is a volunteer a high school student whom the school requires to perform (say) sixty hours of community service to graduate? Can one be paid, like Peace Corps, Vista, or ACTION volunteers, and still be a volunteer?

   Does motive count? Does one have to be pure in heart and want to do good? Or can one volunteer because it will lead to a job, or for the prestige, or to make connections, or to learn new skills?

3. We regularly read of some lucky criminal who, in lieu of time, is fined and sentenced to (say) 2,000 hours of community service. What do the other volunteers think to see someone forced as punishment to do the same work they are doing?

4. When asked why they volunteer people rarely give selfish reasons. What kind of research might one do to uncover such reasons?

5. The New/Fourth World Movement was founded in the mid-1950s. Today, an international organization, it has over 350 volunteers who live and work among the poor in eighteen countries. Sixteen of its volunteers work in the United States, living in places like Harlem and the poorer sections of Brooklyn. The volunteers received a stipend of $5,400 in 1993. Is "volunteer" the correct term? Why or why not?

NOTES

1. *Foundations, Private Giving, and Public Policy, Report and Recommendations of the Commission on Foundations and Private Philanthropy* (Chicago: University Chicago Press, 1970), pp. 231–232.

2. *Annual Report* (New York: American Association of Fund-Raising Council, 1976).

3. But there have been proposals to require NPOs to record as a donation on its books the value of volunteers' time. If any reader can figure out a use for such information, please write to me.

4. The three studies are: *The Charitable Behavior of Americans: A National Survey* (Washington, D.C.: Independent Sector, 1986); a press release by the Bureau of Labor Statistics cited in the *Wall Street Journal,* May 1, 1990, page 1; Virginia Hodgkinson and Murray S. Weitzman, *Dimensions of the Independent Sector: A Statistical Profile.* 2d ed. (Washington, D.C.: Independent Sector, 1986).

5. "Survey Finds Americans Less Interested in Volunteering." *Nonprofit Times* (February 1994), p. 6.

6. Source: *Americans Volunteer 1981* (Washington, D.C.: Independent Sector, 1981).

7. *Canada Gives, 1988* (Toronto: Canadian Centre for Philanthropy, 1988), p. 92.

8. David Stepp, "Few Bears Have a Human Following as Gerry's." *Wall Street Journal,* September 26, 1991, p. A12.

9. Betty S. Harper and Phil Harper, "Religious Reporting: Is It the Gospel Truth?" *Management Accounting* (February 1988): 37.

10. "Giving Sick Kids the Warm Shoulder." *Chronicle of Philanthropy,* July 16, 1991, p. 4.

11. Sharon Massey, "Schools Find Pupil Mediators Cut Violence." *Wall Street Journal,* February 24, 1994, p. B1.

12. *State Liability Laws for Charitable Organizations and Volunteers* (Washington, D.C.: Nonprofits' Risk Management & Insurance Institute, 1990).

13. Jennifer Moore, "92% of Big Companies Encourage Volunteer Efforts, Survey Finds." *Chronicle of Philanthropy,* June 30, 1992, p. 13.

14. Susan Wegryn, "Friends for Youth Turns Itself Around with Creative Fundraising and a Greater Commitment from Board." *Nonprofit Times* (January 1991), p. 3.

15. Susan Wegryn, "doingsomething Tops 'Yuppie' Volunteers for Short-term Volunteer Opportunities." *Nonprofit Times* (December 1990), pp. 3, 7.

16. Kristin A. Goss, "13 Million People Over Age 55 Volunteer, and Many More Would Do So If Asked." *Chronicle of Philanthropy,* June 30, 1992, p. 13.

17. Holly Hall, "Evaluating Volunteers: It May Be Tricky, but It Can Pay Off." *Chronicle of Philanthropy,* January 26, 1993, pp. 30, 32.

18. Ibid.

19. Ibid., p. 32.

20. *Policies and Procedures of Orchestra Governing Boards* (Washington, D.C.: American Symphony Orchestra League, 1991).

21. Miriam Wood, "What Role for College Trustees?" *Harvard Business Review* (May–June 1983): 52–62.

22. Covenant House provided shelter for homeless youths. In 1989, it had a budget of $87 million, and served some 25,000 youths a year in seventeen locations in the United States, Canada, and Central America.

23. *New York Times,* May 2, 1990, p. A12. Also see *A Report to the Board of Directors of Covenant House* (New York: Cravath, Swaine & Moore, Kroll Associates, 1990).

24. Susan Wegryn, "Friends for Youth."

25. Janice C. Simpson, "Prestigious Positions on Charitable Boards Now Require Much More Time and Effort." *Wall Street Journal,* January 7, 1988, p. B1.

26. Holly Hall, "How to Help Trustees Overcome Their Fear of Fund Raising." *Chronicle of Philanthropy,* April 20, 1993, p. 28.

27. Claudia H. Deutsch, "Giving Less Time to Good Causes." *New York Times,* July 15, 1990, Section 3, Part 2, p. 23.

Selected Bibliography

BOOKS AND OTHER PUBLICATIONS

Christian, Jack. *Marketing Designs for Nonprofit Organizations.* Rockville, Md.: Fund Raising Institute, 1992.
————. *Discover Total Resources: A Guide for Nonprofits.* Pittsburgh: Mellon Bank, 1991.
Kotler, Philip, and Alan R. Andreasen. *Strategic Marketing for Nonprofit Organizations.* Englewood Cliffs, N.J.: Prentice-Hall, 1991, 4th edition.
Lovelock, Christopher, and Charles B. Wienberg. *Public and Nonprofit Marketing.* Palo Alto, Calif.: Scientific Press, 1992, 3rd ed.
Newman, Danny. *Subscribe Now!* New York: Theatre Communications Group, 1977.
The Professional Performing Arts: Attendance, Preferences and Motives. Madison, Wis.: Association of College, University, and Community Arts Administrators, 1977.
Stern, Gary J. *Marketing Workbook for Nonprofit Organizations.* St. Paul, Minn.: Amherst Wilder Foundation, 1992.

JOURNALS

Trade

Chronicle of Philanthropy (Washington, D.C.: Chronicle of Philanthropy).
Fund Raising Management (Garden City, N.Y.: Hoke Communications: Hoke Publications).
NonProfit Times (Princeton, N.J.: Davis Information Group).

Academic Journals

Journal of Nonprofit and Public Sector Marketing (Binghamton, N.Y.: Haworth Press).

Nonprofit Management & Leadership (San Francisco, Calif.: Jossey-Bass).
Voluntas (Manchester, England: University of Manchester Press).

ARTICLES

Andreasen, Alan R, and Russell W. Belk. "Predictions of Attendance at the Performing Arts." *Journal of Consumer Research* (September 1980): 112–120.

"College Learns to Use the Fine Art of Marketing." *Wall Street Journal,* February 23, 1981.

Cox, Meg. "Orchestra Thrives by Playing the Music People Didn't Want." *Wall Street Journal,* July 19, 1984, pp. 1, 12.

Guy, Bonnie S., and Wesley E. Patton. "The Marketing of Altruistic Causes: Understanding Why People Help." *Journal of Services Marketing* 2 (1988): 5–15.

Rothschild, Michael L. "Marketing Communications in Nonbusiness Situations or Why It's So Hard to Sell Brotherhood Like Soap." *Journal of Marketing* 43 (Spring 1979): 11–20.

Smith, Craig. "The New Corporate Philanthropy." *Harvard Business Review* (May–June 1994): 105–116.

Varadarajan, R. Rajan, and Anil Menon. "Cause-Related Marketing: A Coalignment of Market Strategy and Corporate Philanthropy." *Journal of Marketing* 52 (July 1988): 79–90.

Index

Abortion, 168
Academic journal(s), development of, 220–222
Action for Child Transportation Safety, 233
Ad Council (*See* Advertising Council)
Adams, Brock, 179
Advertising, 312–331
  defined, 312–313
  evaluation of, 325–330
  fear campaigns, 308
  political, 286–287, 288–289, 329
  power of, 313–315
  uses, typical, 313
Advertising Council, 163–164, 165, 172–173, 384
Advertising effectiveness, measuring, 304–307
Advertising media, 318–322
Advertising objectives, 315–317
  mix, 315
  organizational, 315
  program, 315
Advertising-to-budget (A/B) ratio(s), 294–296
Advertising-to-sales ratio(s), 293–296
  for English nationalized industries, 295

for U.S. government agencies, 295
Agranoff, Robert, 118–119
AIDS, 301
  education, 31, 150, 289
  organizations, 190
ALCNet, 290
Alcoholics Anonymous (AA), 165, 179, 182
Alcoholism
  treatment of, 70
  treatment programs, 151
All other costs (AO), 84–98
Allen, J. Garratt, 130
Amalgamated Clothing and Textile Workers Union, 180
American Automobile Association, 136
American Composers Orchestra, 224
American Friends Service Committee (AFSC), 339
American Heart Association, 309
American Medical Association, 182
American Pharmaceutical Association, 205
American Red Cross, 39, 141, 434
American Revolution Bicentennial Administration, 295
American Society for the Prevention of Cruelty to Animals, 184–185

American Symphony Orchestra League, 223, 445

American University, 162, 358

Amnesty International, 71, 121, 316

Amtrak, 71, 85, 227

Animal shelter(s), 245, 372

Antismoking campaign(s), 148–149 (*See also* Smoking behavior)

Antismoking groups, 390

Aramony, William, 288, 358

Arizona State University Alumni Association, 162

Art Institute (Chicago), 338

Arts audience(s), 121

Association, 19

Association for the Prevention of Cruelty to Animals, 446

Association of MBA Executives, 249

Auction(s)
    Dutch, 261–262
    ordinary, 261

Auction, charity (*See* Charity auction)

Audience development, 67–69

Australian Post Office, 207

Avoidable cost(s), 53

Avon Products, 372

Backers, defined, 16, 18

Bagozzi, Richard, 29

Baltimore Symphony Orchestra (BSO), 223–224

Barzel, Yoram, 88–89

Baumol, William, 139

Bay Area Rapid Transit System, 258

Becke, Dorothy, 77

Beddington, John, 116–117

Better Business Bureau, 349

Bierce, Ambrose, 93

Birth control, 154

Blair, Ed, 30

Blanchard Valley Hospital, 197

Blood, supply and demand, 263

Blood donation(s), 325

Blood donors, 116–117
    recruiting, 300

Blue Cross, 141

Board of directors, 444–448
    role of, 444–445

Boston Museum, 262

Boulez, Pierre, 206

Bowen, G., 139

Boy Scouts of America, 132, 141, 165–166, 236, 241, 294

Boy's Town, 183

Breakeven analysis, 58–59

Breast disease, 87, 372

Brown University, 255

Budgeting, for communications, 291–300
    approaches to setting a budget, 292–295
    in nonprofit businesses, 291–292
    in other NPOs, 292–300
    in political campaigns, 293

Bureau of the Mint, 295

Burns, Ken, 119

Car seats, 233

Cardiovascular disease, 306

Carpooling, 70–71, 72, 74–75

Cartwright, Dorwin, 64

Cause marketing, 371–374
    affinity cards, 373

Cause-related marketing, 373

Census Bureau, 117

Centers for Disease Control, 216

Chain letters, 367

Chandler, Alfred, 177

Channels of distribution, 226–250
    intensity of distribution, 243–248
    nontraditional, 230
    selling direct, 240–243
    setting objectives for, 248–249
    site decor, 249

Charity auction, 210–211
    duck pond, 211
    key club, 211
    live auction, 211
    raffle, 211
    silent auction, 211

Charity watchdogs, 420

Child-resistant containers, 205

Children, mental illness in, 328

Choice, ways of dealing with, 25–26

Church(es), establishment of new, 222–223

Clark, John M., 53

Cleveland Art Museum, 214
Client behavior
    deciding, 75–76
    as decisions, 70–77
    evaluating decisions, 76–77
    general approach to, 67–69
    information collection, 70–72
    information evaluation, 74–75
    modeling, 122
    outside influences on, 69–70
    perceived risk(s), 72–73
    problem recognition, 70
Client orientation, 188, 189
Client satisfaction, 110–111
Clients, defined, 16, 18
Clients' interests in distribution
    convenience, 230–231
    information, 232
    variety, 231–232
Columbia University, 255
Combined Federal Campaign, 140, 204
Common benefit organizations, 17
Commonwealth organizations, 18
Communication
    abstract model of, 283–285
    message strategy, 285–288
Community improvement project(s), 232
Competition, 129–142, 180, 218
    arguments against, 132–133
    arguments for, 131–132
    as an influence on price, 257
    "for what?", 133–134
    identifying, 134–138
    information on, 138
    like and unlike, 138–139
    relations, 139–140
Competitive prizes, 133–134
Complaint systems, design of, 267–268
Condoms, 247, 269
Consumer behavior (See client behavior)
Consumer orientation (See Client orientation)
Consumer Product Safety Commission, 295
Consumer protection, 171
Consumer Reports, 155, 185, 291, 362
Consumer surplus, 259–262

Consumers Union (CU), 185, 186, 233, 360, 362
Contraceptive(s), 237, 247–248
Contribution (See Gross marketing contribution)
Control without numbers, 380–381
Coordination, 384
Cornfeld, Bernie, 178
Corporate giving, 400
Corporations, nonprofit, 11–13, 19
    privileges of, 12–14
Cost allocations, 59–60
Cost per thousand (CPM), direct mail, 425–426
Cost theory, elements of, 46–47
Cost(s), estimating, 99–101
Cost-based pricing, 271–272
Costs of giving
    costs borne by backers, 414–415
    costs borne by the volunteer, 415–416
Costs, estimating, 59–60, 99
Costs, fundraising, 420–430
    how to read, 422–423
    problems in obtaining, 421–422
Costs, imaginary, 256
Costs, types of
    avoidable (See Avoidable costs)
    fixed (See Nonvariable costs)
    marginal (See Marginal costs)
    nonvariable (See Nonvariable costs)
    opportunity (See Opportunity costs)
    programmed (See Programmed costs)
    relevant (See Relevant costs)
    sunk (See Sunk costs)
    traceable (See Traceable costs)
    variable (See Variable costs)
Council on International Education
    Exchange, 438
Covenant House, 446
Cullis, J. G., 92
Cultural diversity, 223
Culyer, A. J., 92

Dance audiences, 67–69
Dance festival(s), 173–174
Data Users Service, 302
Decisions, high-involvement, 326–330

Decisions, low-involvement, 328–329
Decline and Fall of the Roman Empire, 260
Demand, as an influence on price, 254–256
Demand pricing, 272–274
Deming, W. Edwards, 170
Denver Veterans Administration Hospital, 300
Department of Health, Education, and Welfare, 230
Department of Transportation, 179
Design Industries Foundation for AIDS (DIFFA), 161 passim
Dewees, Donald, 96–97
Dickens, Charles, 184
Direct mail, 319
    high costs of, 425–431
    objectives of, 316
    testing, 112–113
Disabled Veterans of America, 144
Distribution, costs of, 232–233
Distribution, intensity of
    exclusive, 245–246
    intensive, 246–248
Distribution channels (*See* Channels of distribution)
Doingsomething, 441
Donor choice, 140
Donor(s), value of, 413–414
Drucker, Peter, 175
Drug treatment programs, 151
Drugstores, 237–240
    nonprofit, 228

Earth Share, 141, 363, 390
Earthwatch, 438
Economic analysis of giving (*See* Giving)
EcoWriters, 363
Educational Testing Service, 213, 218
Ehrenberg, Andrew, 64
Elasticity, 94
    of mass transit trips with respect to fare, 94–95
    of trips to travel time, 95–97
Election campaigns, advertising in, 321
    (*See also* Political canvassing)

Election(s)
    meaning of a vote, 105
    voting in, 181–182
    why people don't vote, 146–147
Enterprise, individual, 19
Environmental Defense Fund, 290, 362
European parliamentary elections, 305–306
Evaluating advertising (*See* Advertising, evaluation of)
Evangelical Council for Financial Accountability, 438
Evoked set, 136–138
Experimentation, as a research technique, 112–113
Exploratory research, 107

Fairleigh Dickinson University, 267
Family planning, 237, 289
Fares, mass transit (*See* Mass transit)
Federal Communications Commission, 322–323
Federal crime insurance, 229, 289
Federal Insurance Administration, 229
Federal Reserve System, 140
Federal Trade Commission, 84, 123, 184, 213
Feldstein, Martin, 403
Financial aspects of marketing, 45–60
    reasons for concern, 46
Financial goals of an NPO, 270
Fit
    product-client, 217–218
    product-competition, 218
    product-organization, 216–217
Flame of Hope, 199
Flossing, 87–88
Floyd, Carlisle, 213
Focus group(s), 107
Folk media, 289
Food Bank (of Hatfield, Massachusetts), 166
Food stamps, 232
Foundation(s), 19, 400
Friends for Youth, 440, 446
Fulmer, Robert, 413
Fund accounting, 55–58

Fundraising
    by Jewish organizations, 142, 180
    rating prospective donors, 187–188
    records for, 115
Fundraising consultants, 424

Gallup poll, 117
Gambling (*See also* Lotteries; State lotteries)
    cost of operating, 423
Gardner, David, 77
George Washington University, 254, 257
Georgetown University, 254, 257
Gibbon, Edward, 260
Girl Scout(s), 349
Giving
    economic analysis of, 409–410
    effect of taxes on, 405–406
    elasticity of, 403–405
    in the large, 399–405
    motives for, 406–408
    in the small, 405–408
    of time and money, 434–435
Goldin, Milton, 142
Goodman, Paul, 188
Graduate Management Admission Council, 249
Graham, Billy, 287
Greenwood, Ernest, 183
Gross, Malvern, 422
Gross margin, 234–235
Gross marketing contribution, 54
Gun control, 390

Habitat for Humanity International, 14, 438
Haitian immigrants, 154
Hambury, Thomas, 61
HandsNet, 290
Harvard University, 257
Health maintenance organization(s)
    (HMO), 72, 300
Health Service Plan of Pennsylvania, 300
Hearings, payments for participation in, 84
Heavy metal, 289
High-involvement decision(s) (*See* Decisions, high-involvement)
Hill, Professor Harold, 178
HIV, 154

Homer, 30
Homosexual men, 154, 351–353
Hospital, 184
Hospital queues, 92–93
Housing, 110–111
Houston Grand Opera, 295
Howard, John, 136
Howard Johnson's, 205
Human rights, 168
Hurricane Island, 243

Iliad, The, 339
Implementation, 174–175
Inroads, 206–207, 220
Interfund transfers (*See* Fund accounting)
Internal Revenue Service (IRS), 85
International Association for Medical Assistance to Travelers, 227
International Ladies' Garment Workers' Union, 180
Internet, 289
Involvement, 33
Irish Tourist Board, 173

Jacobs, Bruce, 110–111
Jacoby, Jacob, 64
Job description, 392
Junk mail, 319
Jury duty, 97–98
    T costs of serving on, 98
Just price
    flat fee, 275–276
    price adjusted to means, 276–277
    voluntary pricing, 276
"Just Say No" campaign, 308

Kotler, Philip, 28
Kovach, Carol, 196
KQED, 109

Lar Lubovitch Dance Company, 446
Legal aid, 185
Library, 232
Liss, John, 214
Literary Digest, 118, 120
Lotteries, cost of operating, 424
Low-involvement decision(s) (*See* Decisions, low-involvement)

Macbeth, 49
Mail, as a research technique, 112
Mamouth Cave National Park, 243
Marginal costs, 48
Marketing
    definition, 24–27
    and education, 31–32
    as exchange, 28–30
    introducing into the nonprofit organi-
        zation, 390–395
    part-time, 390–391
    role of (*See* Marketing strategy, five
        influences on)
Marketing audit, 381–383
Marketing control, 377–383
    activities, 380
    outcomes, 380
Marketing control statement (MCS), 54–
    55
Marketing implementation (*See* Imple-
    mentation)
Marketing planning
    as a control tool, 381
    mission, 161–164
    situation analysis, 161–168
Marketing research, 104–124
    behavior, 113–115
    costs of, 124
    descriptive research, 108
    exploratory research, 107–108
    feedback research, 108–110
    four basic questions, 107
    lost letter technique, 113
    managerial issues in, 115–122
    need for, 104–105
    predictive research, 108
    problems with ''why'' questions,
        407
    states of being, 113
    states of mind, 113
    survey questionnaires (*See* Question-
        naires)
    tests for new products, 219–220
    typical project, 111–115
Marketing strategy, 160–175, 177–191
    (*See also* Strategy)
Marketing strategy, five influences on,
    177–191

environment, 181–182
    marketing 178–181
    organizational form, 182–183
    professionalism, 183–184
    role of marketing, 184–187
Marketing style (*See* Marketing strategy,
    five influences on)
Mary Babcock Reynolds Foundation, 338
Mass transit, 93, 258
    advertising, 295
    riders, 143
    T costs of using, 93–97
    time spent enroute, 95–97
Massachusetts Institute of Technology,
    413
MBA Admission Forum, 249
McClure, Robert, 286
Meany, George, 180
Mecklenburg Community Church, 222
Media
    advertising (*See* Advertising media)
    alternative, 288–290
    computer networks, 290–291
    video, 290
Medical care, 39
Metric system, adoption of, 150
Metropolitan Museum of Art, member-
    ships in, 150–151
Metropolitan Opera, 365
Middlemen
    payments to, 228–230
    role of, 227–228
    their interests, 233–234
Milken, Michael, 434
Mintzberg, Henry, 170
Mission, 199
    as an influence on price, 257–258
Models of Advertising Effect, 326–329
Morgan, James N., 405–406
Mothers Against Drunk Driving
    (MADD), 165
Moynihan, Daniel Patrick, 122
Ms Magazine, 70
Museum(s), 210
    competition among, 131
    gift stores, 272
    membership prices, 272–273
    new programs, 229–230

National Audubon Society, 71
National Blood Transfusion Service, 106
National Broadcasting System (NBC), 213–214
National Charities Information Bureau, 138
National Consumer Law Center, 84
National Council of Nonprofit Associations, 290
National Health Service, patient complaints, 186
National Indian Youth Council, 321
National Safety Council, 30
Nature Conservancy, 374
New Jersey Department of Labor and Industry, 302
New product development
  general approach, 218–220
  reasons for, 211–215
  three examples, 220–224
New York Opera, 214
New York Philharmonic, 206
New York Shakespeare Festival, 88
New York State Ballet, 85
New York State Lottery, 294
New York University, 256–257
1936 Presidential Straw Poll, 188
Nixon, Richard, 322
Nolen, William A., 335
Nonprofit, definition of, 8–10
Nonprofit business, 16
Nonprofit organization(s) (*See* Organization(s), nonprofit)
Nonvariable cost(s), 50–51
Norton, Alice, 381
Nuclear Regulatory Commission, 84
Numbers game, 134–136
Nutrition programs, 215

Objectives, for communications programs, 300–304
Objectives, marketing, 45, 184–187, 378
  generating resources, 184–185
  influencing behavior, 185
  satisfying clients, 185–187
Ocean Spray, 211, 220
Ombudsmen, 269
Opportunity cost(s), 47–48, 84–98

Organizations
  501(c)(3), 22
  501(c)(4), 22
Organization(s), nonprofit
  formal taxonomy, 20
  importance in the economy, 7–8
  numbers of, 7
  second classification, 16–18
  varieties of, 5–7
Orientation, freshman, 38
Out-of-pocket costs (OOP), 84–98
Outward Bound, 178, 243
Oxford University Press, 208, 256

Partnership, 19
Partnership for a Drug-Free America, 165, 308
Pasatieri, Thomas, 213
Patterson, Thomas, 286
Payroll savings plans, 234
Pei, Mario, 417
Perceived risk (*See* Client behavior)
Performing arts, 138
Personal interviews, as a research technique, 112
Personal selling, 333–353
  compared to mass communications, 335–336
  cost of, 335
  five selling jobs, 338–339
  peer pressures, 341–343
  power of, 336–337
Persuasion, 26
Peterson, Hannibal, 224
Pets, adoption of, 77, 245–246
Phoenix Children's Hospital, 438
Physicians for Automobile Safety, 233
Placebo effect, 206
Pledge(s), 343
Plutarch, 62
Poage, Godfrey, 345
Poggi, Jack, 138–139
Political advertising (*See* Advertising, political)
Political campaign(s), 286–289, 293
Political canvassing, 76
Pops concerts, 143
Population Services International, 242

Port of Oakland, 139
Port of San Francisco, 139
Positioning, 155–157
Positioning map, 156
Postal money orders, 386–387
Price(s), 252
    adjusted to means, 276–277
    ethical aspects, 269, 274–277
    flat fee, 275–276
    function of, 262–263
    in hospital pharmacies, 271, 273,
       275
    just (See Just price)
    objectives, 257
    perceptions of, 253
    primary influences on, 254–259
    reasons not to have, 263–264
    role of in an NPO, 264–265
    seasonal-time-of-day (STD), 124
    three methods of setting, 271–277
    voluntary, 276
    when clients should pay, 278
    who should pay, 278–279
    zero, 252, 253
Price discrimination, 273–274
Price-quality relationship, 269
Pricing objectives
    behavioral and attitudinal, 266–269
    financial, 270–271
    organizational, 265–266
Primary demand, 82 n.21
Product(s), defined, 195–196
Product dimensions
    brands and trademarks, 202–205
    package, 205–206
    quality, 206–207
Product line, dimensions of, 210
Product manager, 386
Product/market scope, 184
Product portfolio, 201–202
Product strategy, 199–201
Production orientation, 188, 189
Professionalism, as influence on market-
    ing strategy (See Marketing strategy,
    five influences on)
Programmed cost(s), 51–53
Programs, nonprofit, causes of failure,
    32–36

Promotion (See Sales promotion)
Public Broadcasting Marketing, 227
Public Broadcasting System (PBS), 139–
    140, 213, 214–215, 227
Public health campaigns (except AIDS),
    152
Public relations, 309, 355–360, 390
    dealing with the media, 359–360
    evaluation of, 380–381
Public relations tools
    crisis management, 358–359
    press conferences, 357
    press release(s), 357
    publicity, 357
    sponsorships, 359
Public Service Announcement(s) (PSAs),
    308, 309, 322–325
    defined, 323
    guidelines for getting, 324–325
    requirements for, 323
    station obligations toward, 323
Public service directors, 309
Public sex environments, 31, 343–344
Public television representatives, 227
Publics, 356–357
Pull strategies, 237
Push strategies, 237

Quasi experimentation, 306
Questionnaires, 115–122
    errors, nonsampling, 117–118
    errors, sampling, 119–120
    problems with interviewers, 118
    problems with respondents, 118–119
    problems with wording, 115–117
    sampling ratio, 120–121
Queues, 88–93
    causes of, 92
Quinn, James Brian, 170

Rabushka, Alvin, 110–111
Radio, renewal of license, 322–323
Ralston Purina, 372
Rating a potential donor, 336
Recruiting doctors and nurses, 386
Recruiting priest(s), 73, 345–346, 348
Recycling behavior, 78
Relevant cost(s), 47

Religious recruiter, 334
Repeat behavior, 110
Research, marketing (*See* Marketing research)
Responsible drinking, 314
Retailing arithmetic, 234–237
Revson, Charles, 197
Ridesharing (*See* Carpooling)
Ritter, Father Bruce, 446
Rockefeller, Nelson, 122
Roe v. Wade, 168
Role of marketing, 386 (*See also* Marketing strategy, five influences on)
Role of the salesman, 337–340
Roman Catholic priests, recruiting of, 181
Rossi, Peter, 123
Rothschild, Michael, 33
Rowan, Henry and Betty, 410

Sacred Heart League, 162
Safe sex, 31, 343–345, 351–353
Sales compensation, 349
Sales force, organization of, 387–390
Sales force budgets, 296–300
    market potential, 298–300
    work load, 296–298
Sales management, 343–353
    compensation, 349–350
    recruiting, 343–344
    selection, 344
    supervision, 350–351
    training, 344–349
Sales promotion, 360–371
    allowances, 370
    charity raffle, 367–369
    client promotions, 363–369
    common objectives, 362–363
    coupons, 364
    defined, 361–362
    evaluation of, 371
    free goods, 369
    management issues, 370–371
    premiums, 363–364
    price-off, 369
    refunds and rebates, 369
    samples, 364–366
    sweepstakes, contests, and raffles, 367

Sales supervision, 350–351
Salvation Army, 14, 141
Satisfaction
    of backers, 38
    of clients, 37–39, 76–77
    defined, 37
Savings bond drives, 64, 234
SCARCnet, 290
Schneider, Louis, 384
Seat belt(s), 86
Seattle Opera, 213
Secondary demand, 82 n.21
Segmentation, 142–151
    five criteria for, 144
    psychographic, 144–146
Selective processes, 328
    in psychology, 283
Semivariable costs, 51
Service organizations, 17
Service outlet(s)
    decor, 249
    location, 242–243
    operating, 243
Service(s), defined, 195–196
Shadegg, Stephen, 342
Sheltered workshop(s), 199
Sickert, Walter, 287
Simpson-Curtin formula, 100
Sin taxes, 267
Situation analysis
    external analysis, 164–166
    internal analysis, 164
    SWOT analysis, 166–168
Smirnoff vodka, 269
Smoking, 31
Smoking behavior, 63–67, 70
Smoking Control Advocacy Resource Network, 390
Social precinct (in election campaigns), 342–343
Software, computer, 72–73
Soroker, Gerald, 336
Special events, 301
Specialization, 384
St. Joseph Home, 290
State lottery, 228–229, 241
    intensity of distribution, 244

State University of New York at Stony
  Brook, 362
Statue of Liberty, 165
Strategic planning (*See* Marketing strat-
  egy)
Strategy, 168–174
    approaches to developing, 168–170
    critical issues, 169
    goals, 169–170
    objectives, 172–174
    scenario, 168–169
    who plans, 171
Streisand, Barbra, 142
Substance abuse, campaign against, 307–
  309
Suicide, 62
Sunk costs, 48–50
Susan B. Anthony coin, 107, 329
SWOT analysis (*See* Situation analysis)
Symphony orchestra(s), 212–213, 223–
  224

T costs, 83–98, 252–253, 263, 267
    defined, 85
    of volunteering, 434, 441
Targeting, 151–155
    marketing reasons for, 151–153
    reasons not to target, 153–155
Telephone, as a research technique, 112
Telethon(s), 155
Texas Association of Developing Col-
  leges, 141
Ticket pricing, 272
Tied gift(s), 409–410
Time, monetary value of, 96–97
Time costs
    subcategories of, 87
    waiting, 88–93
Time value of money, 410
Titmuss, Richard, 106
TKTS, 78–80, 244
TNT Express Worldwide, 132
Tolls, bridge, 49–50
Tourism, 173
    local, 229–230
Traceable cost(s), 53
Trade union organizing campaigns, 63
Trial, 313

Truant officer, 334
Tucker, Stephen L., 184
Turnover, 235–236

U.S. Census Bureau, 302
U.S. Department of Transportation
  (DOT), 233
U.S. Postal Service, 132, 140, 143, 218,
  232, 384
    facing competition, 189
U.S. Travel Service, 295
United Negro College Fund, 141, 241
United Way of America, 1, 39, 117, 140–
  141, 144–146, 241, 288, 329–330, 358,
  359, 390
Universities, measures of competition, 137
University bookstore, 236
University of Michigan, 355
University of Minnesota, 365
University of Tennessee (UT), 170–171
University tuition, 253
Unrelated business income tax (UBIT),
  15
Utilities, in channels of distribution, 228

Variable cost(s), 50
Venereal disease, 100
Videos, cost of, 290
Virginia Military Institute, 290
Virginia Slims, 309
Volunteer(s), 433–448
    attracting, 439–441
    evaluating, 442–443
    firing, 443–444
    in fundraising, 337
    managing, 442
    how to organize, 387–390
    as salesmen, 340–341
    selection and training, 441–442
Volunteer army, 232
Volunteering, reasons for, 437
Volunteers of America, 14
Voting, cost of, 84
Voucher(s), 230

Wanamaker, John, 52
Warhol, Andy, 309
Washington Blade, 190

Washington Monument, 264
Welfare, 85
WFYI, 333
Wilde, Oscar, 45
Wilkie, William, 77
Williams, Jane, 421
Woman's Christian Temperance Union
   (WCTU), 164–165

Woolly Mammoth Theater Company, 369
Woolmark, 205
Word of mouth, 309

Yanovsky, Basile, 101
Yeats, William Butler, 106

Zoos, nature of product, 196–197

About the Author

DAVID L. RADOS is Professor of Marketing at the Owen Graduate School of Management at Vanderbilt University. He has written three books, including *Pushing the Numbers in Marketing* (Quorum Books, 1992).